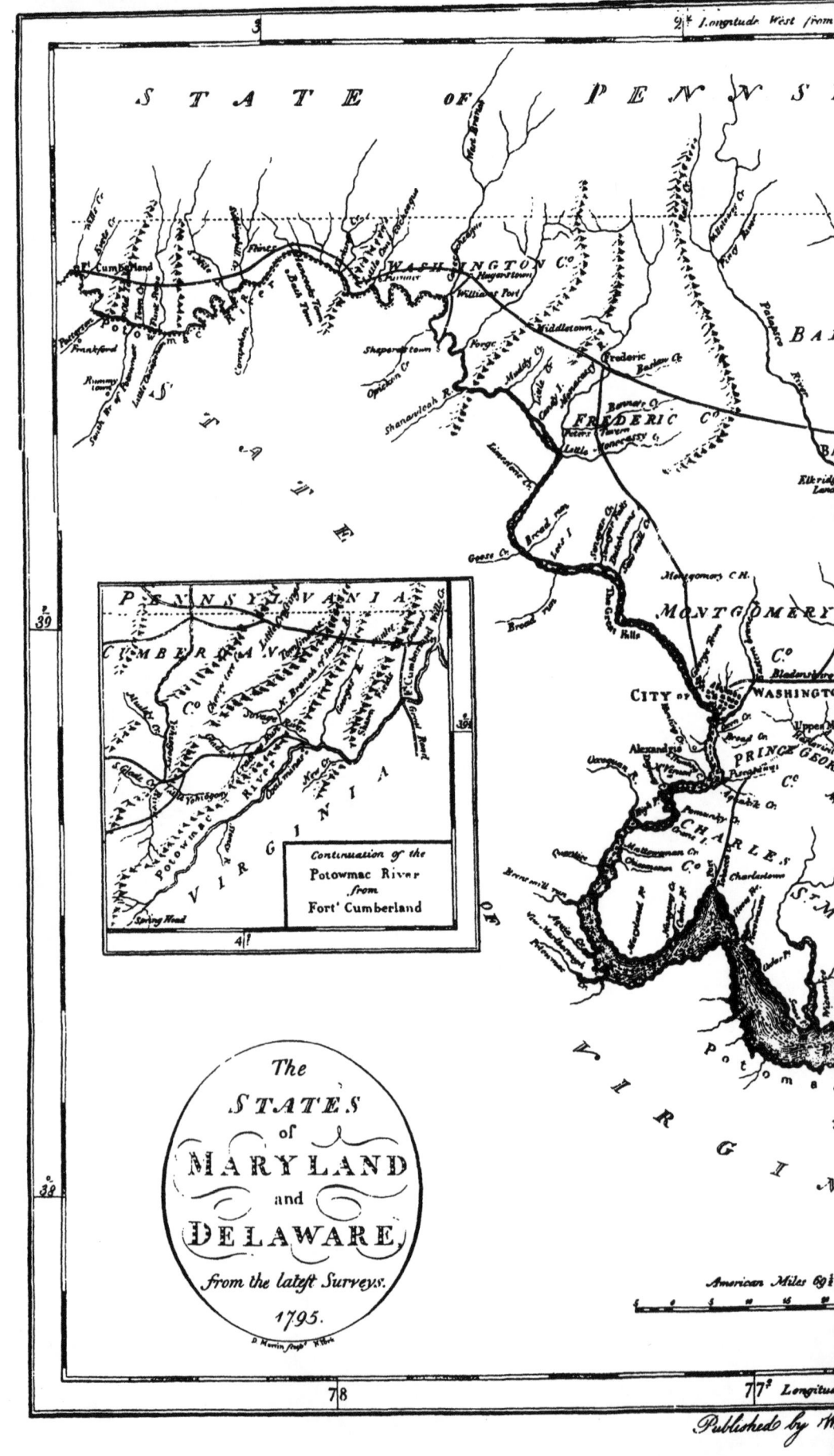

The
STATES
of
MARYLAND
and
DELAWARE,
from the latest Surveys.
1795.

Continuation of the
Potowmac River
from
Fort Cumberland

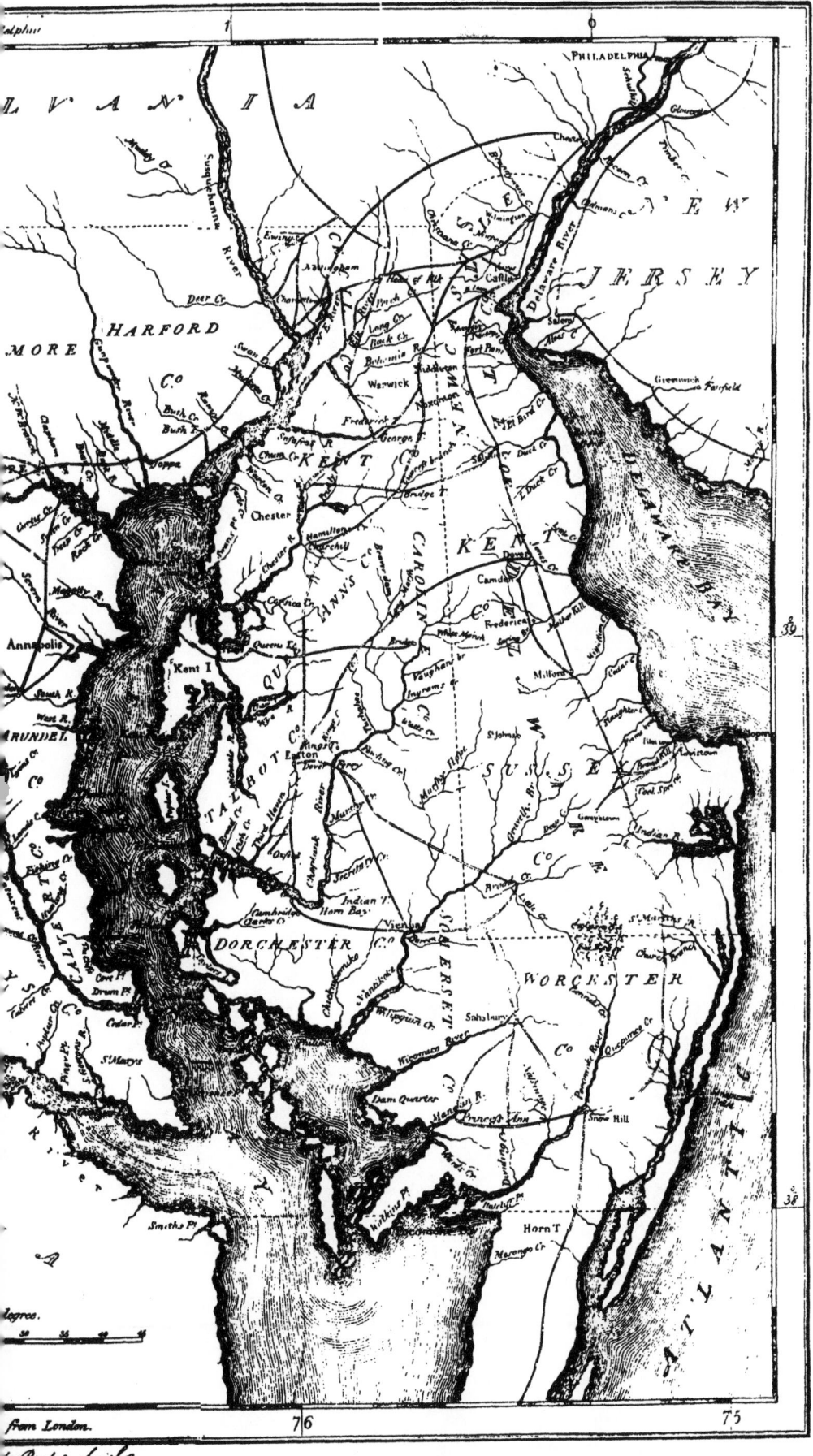

FIRST CENSUS
OF THE UNITED STATES
1790

MARYLAND

HEADS OF FAMILIES

AT THE FIRST CENSUS OF THE
UNITED STATES TAKEN
IN THE YEAR
1790

MARYLAND

CLEARFIELD

Reprinted for Clearfield Company, Inc.
by Genealogical Publishing Co., Inc.
Baltimore, Maryland
1998

Originally published: Government Printing Office
Washington, D.C., 1907
Reprinted: Genealogical Publishing Co., Inc.
Baltimore, 1965, 1972, 1977, 1992
Library of Congress Catalogue Card Number 73-186488
International Standard Book Number 0-8063-0491-X
Made in the United States of America

HEADS OF FAMILIES AT THE FIRST CENSUS
1790

INTRODUCTION.

The First Census of the United States (1790) comprised an enumeration of the inhabitants of the present states of Connecticut, Delaware, Georgia, Kentucky, Maine, Maryland, Massachusetts, New Hampshire, New Jersey, New York, North Carolina, Pennsylvania, Rhode Island, South Carolina, Tennessee, Vermont, and Virginia. The law which authorized this enumeration appears on page 6.

A complete set of the schedules for each state, with a summary for the counties, and in many cases for towns, was filed in the State Department, but unfortunately they are not now complete, the returns for the states of Delaware, Georgia, Kentucky, New Jersey, Tennessee, and Virginia having been destroyed when the British burned the Capitol at Washington during the War of 1812.

These schedules form a unique inheritance for the Nation, since they represent for each of the states concerned a complete list of the heads of families in the United States at the time of the adoption of the Constitution. The framers were the statesmen and leaders of thought, but those whose names appear upon the schedules of the First Census were in general the plain citizens who by their conduct in war and peace made the Constitution possible and by their intelligence and self-restraint put it into successful operation.

The total population of the United States in 1790, exclusive of slaves, as derived from the schedules, was 3,231,533. The only names appearing upon the schedules, however, were those of heads of families, and as at that period the families averaged 6 persons, the total number was approximately 540,000, or slightly more than half a million. The number of names which is now lacking because of the destruction of the schedules is approximately 140,000, thus leaving schedules containing about 400,000 names.

The information contained in the published report of the First Census of the United States, a small volume of 56 pages, was not uniform for the several states and territories. For New England and one or two of the other states the population was presented by counties and towns, that of New Jersey appeared partly by counties and towns and partly by counties only; in other cases the returns were given by counties only. Thus the complete transcript of the names of heads of families, with accompanying information, would present for the first time detailed information as to the number of inhabitants—males, females, etc.—for each minor civil division in all those states for which such information was not originally published.

In response to repeated requests from patriotic societies and persons interested in genealogy, or desirous of studying the early history of the United States, Congress added to the sundry civil appropriation bill for the fiscal year 1907 the following paragraph:

The Director of the Census is hereby authorized and directed to publish, in a permanent form, by counties and minor civil divisions, the names of the heads of families returned at the First Census of the United States in seventeen hundred and ninety; and the Director of the Census is authorized, in his discretion, to sell said publications, the proceeds thereof to be covered into the Treasury of the United States, to be deposited to the credit of miscellaneous receipts on account of "Proceeds of sales of Government property:"

Provided, That no expense shall be incurred hereunder additional to appropriations for the Census Office for printing therefor made for the fiscal year nineteen hundred and seven; and the Director of the Census is hereby directed to report to Congress at its next session the cost incurred hereunder and the price fixed for said publications and the total received therefor.

The amount of money appropriated by Congress for the Census printing for the fiscal year mentioned was unfortunately not sufficient to meet the current requirement of the Office and to publish the transcription of the First Census, and no provision was made in the sundry civil appropriation bill for 1908 for the continuance of authority to publish these important records beyond the present fiscal year. Resources, however, are available for publishing a small section of the work, and the schedules of New Hampshire, Vermont, and Maryland have been selected. In these states the names of heads of families in 1790 were limited in number, and the records are in a condition which makes transcription comparatively easy. In the following pages all the information is presented which appears upon these schedules, and the sequence of the names is that followed by the enumerator in making his report.

It is to be hoped that Congress will again grant authority and money for the publication of the remaining schedules, in order that the entire series, so far as it exists, may be complete. For several of the states for which schedules are lacking it is probable that the Director of the Census could obtain lists which would present the names of most of the heads of families at the date of the First Census. In Virginia, for example, a state enumeration was made in 1785, of which some of the original schedules are still in existence. These would be likely to prove a reasonably satisfactory substitute for the Federal list made five years later.

THE FIRST CENSUS.

The First Census act was passed at the second session of the First Congress, and was signed by President Washington on March 1, 1790. The task of making the first enumeration of inhabitants was placed upon the President. Under this law the marshals of the several judicial districts were required to ascertain the number of inhabitants within their respective districts, omitting Indians not taxed, and distinguishing free persons (including those bound to service for a term of years); the sex and color of free persons; and the number of free males 16 years of age and over.

The object of the inquiry last mentioned was, undoubtedly, to obtain definite knowledge as to the military and industrial strength of the country. This fact possesses special interest, because the Constitution directs merely an enumeration of inhabitants. Thus the demand for increasingly extensive information, which has been so marked a characteristic of census legislation, began with the First Congress that dealt with the subject.

The method followed by the President in putting into operation the First Census law, although the object of extended investigation, is not definitely known. It is supposed that the President or the Secretary of State dispatched copies of the law, and perhaps of instructions also, to the marshals. There is, however, some ground for disputing this conclusion. At least one of the reports in the census volume of 1790 was furnished by a governor. This, together with the fact that there is no record of correspondence with the marshals on the subject of the census, but that there is a record of such correspondence with the governors, makes very strong the inference that the marshals received their instructions through the governors of the states. This inference is strengthened by the fact that in 1790 the state of Massachusetts furnished the printed blanks, and also by the fact that the law relating to the Second Census specifically charged the Secretary of State to superintend the enumeration and to communicate directly with the marshals.

By the terms of the First Census law nine months were allowed in which to complete the enumeration.

The census taking was supervised by the marshals of the several judicial districts, who employed assistant marshals to act as enumerators. There were 17 marshals. The records showing the number of assistant marshals employed in 1790, 1800, and 1810 were destroyed by fire, but the number employed in 1790 has been estimated at 650.

The schedules which these officials prepared consist of lists of names of heads of families; each name appears in a stub, or first column, which is followed by five columns, giving details of the family. These columns are headed as follows:

Free white males, 16 years and upward, including heads of families.
Free white males under 16 years.
Free white females, including heads of families.
All other free persons.
Slaves.

The assistant marshals made two copies of the returns; in accordance with the law one copy was posted in the immediate neighborhood for the information of the public, and the other was transmitted to the marshal in charge, to be forwarded to the President. The schedules were turned over by the President to the Secretary of State. Little or no tabulation was required, and the report of the First Census, as also the reports of the Second, Third, and Fourth, was produced without the employment of any clerical force, the summaries being transmitted directly to the printer. The total population as returned in 1790 was 3,929,214, and the entire cost of the census was $44,377.

A summary of the results of the First Census, not including the returns for South Carolina, was transmitted to Congress by President Washington on October 27, 1791. The legal period for enumeration, nine months, had been extended, the longest time consumed being eighteen months in South Carolina. The report of October 27 was printed in full, and published in what is now a very rare little volume; afterwards the report for South Carolina was "tipped in." To contain the results of the Twelfth Census, ten large quarto volumes, comprising in all 10,400 pages, were required. No illustration of the expansion of census inquiry can be more striking.

The original schedules of the First Census are now contained in 26 bound volumes, preserved in the Census Office. For the most part the headings of the schedules were written in by hand. Indeed, up to and including 1820, the assistant marshals generally used for the schedules such paper as they happened to have, ruling it, writing in the headings, and binding the sheets together themselves. In some cases merchants' account paper was used, and now and then the schedules were bound in wall paper.

As a consequence of requiring marshals to supply their own blanks, the volumes containing the sched-

ules vary in size from about 7 inches long, 3 inches wide, and ½ inch thick to 21 inches long, 14 inches wide, and 6 inches thick. Some of the sheets in these volumes are only 4 inches long, but a few are 3 feet in length, necessitating several folds. In some cases leaves burned at the edges have been covered with transparent silk to preserve them.

THE UNITED STATES IN 1790.

In March, 1790, the Union consisted of twelve states—Rhode Island, the last of the original thirteen to enter the Union, being admitted May 29. Vermont, the first addition, was admitted in the following year, before the results of the First Census were announced. Maine was a part of Massachusetts, Kentucky was a part of Virginia, and the present states of Alabama and Mississippi were parts of Georgia. The present states of Ohio, Indiana, Illinois, Michigan, and Wisconsin, with part of Minnesota, were known as the Northwest Territory, and the present state of Tennessee, then a part of North Carolina, was soon to be organized as the Southwest Territory.

The United States was bounded on the west by the Mississippi river, beyond which stretched that vast and unexplored wilderness belonging to the Spanish King, which was afterwards ceded to the United States by France as the Louisiana Purchase, and now comprises the great and populous states of Louisiana, Arkansas, Indian Territory, Oklahoma, Missouri, Kansas, Iowa, Nebraska, South Dakota, North Dakota, and Montana, and most of Colorado, Wyoming, and Minnesota. The Louisiana Purchase was not completed for more than a decade after the First Census was taken. On the south was another Spanish colony known as the Floridas. Texas, then a part of the colony of Mexico, belonged to Spain; and California, Utah, Arizona, and New Mexico, also the property of Spain, although penetrated here and there by venturesome explorers and missionaries, were, for the most part, an undiscovered wilderness.

The gross area of the United States was 827,844 square miles, but the settled area was only 239,935 square miles, or about 29 per cent of the total. Though the area covered by the enumeration in 1790 seems very small when compared with the present area of the United States, the difficulties which confronted the census taker were vastly greater than in 1900. In many localities there were no roads, and where these did exist they were poor and frequently impassable; bridges were almost unknown. Transportation was entirely by horseback, stage, or private coach. A journey as long as that from New York to Washington was a serious undertaking, requiring eight days under the most favorable conditions. Western New York was a wilderness, Elmira and Binghamton being but detached hamlets. The territory west of the Allegheny mountains, with the exception of a portion of Kentucky, was unsettled and scarcely penetrated. Detroit and Vincennes were too small and isolated to merit consideration. Philadelphia was the capital of the United States. Washington was a mere Government project, not even named, but known as the Federal City. Indeed, by the spring of 1793, only one wall of the White House had been constructed, and the site for the Capitol had been merely surveyed. New York city in 1790 possessed a population of only 33,131, although it was the largest city in the United States; Philadelphia was second, with 28,522; and Boston third, with 18,320. Mails were transported in very irregular fashion, and correspondence was expensive and uncertain.

There were, moreover, other difficulties which were of serious moment in 1790, but which long ago ceased to be problems in census taking. The inhabitants, having no experience with census taking, imagined that some scheme for increasing taxation was involved, and were inclined to be cautious lest they should reveal too much of their own affairs. There was also opposition to enumeration on religious grounds, a count of inhabitants being regarded by many as a cause for divine displeasure. The boundaries of towns and other minor divisions, and even those of counties, were in many cases unknown or not defined at all. The hitherto semi-independent states had been under the control of the Federal Government for so short a time that the different sections had not yet been welded into an harmonious nationality in which the Federal authority should be unquestioned and instructions promptly and fully obeyed.

AN ACT PROVIDING FOR THE ENUMERATION OF THE INHABITANTS OF THE UNITED STATES

APPROVED MARCH 1, 1790

❧

SECTION 1. Be it enacted by the Senate and House of Representatives of the United States of America in Congress assembled, That the marshals of the several districts of the United States shall be, and they are hereby authorized and required to cause the number of the inhabitants within their respective districts to be taken; omitting in such enumeration Indians not taxed, and distinguishing free persons, including those bound to service for a term of years, from all others; distinguishing also the sexes and colours of free persons, and the free males of sixteen years and upwards from those under that age; for effecting which purpose the marshals shall have power to appoint as many assistants within their respective districts as to them shall appear necessary; assigning to each assistant a certain division of his district, which division shall consist of one or more counties, cities, towns, townships, hundreds or parishes, or of a territory plainly and distinctly bounded by water courses, mountains, or public roads. The marshals and their assistants shall respectively take an oath or affirmation, before some judge or justice of the peace, resident within their respective districts, previous to their entering on the discharge of the duties by this act required. The oath or affirmation of the marshal shall be, "I, A. B., Marshal of the district of ———, do solemnly swear (or affirm) that I will well and truly cause to be made a just and perfect enumeration and description of all persons resident within my district, and return the same to the President of the United States, agreeably to the directions of an act of Congress, intituled 'An act providing for the enumeration of the inhabitants of the United States,' according to the best of my ability." The oath or affirmation of an assistant shall be "I, A. B., do solemnly swear (or affirm) that I will make a just and perfect enumeration and description of all persons resident within the division assigned to me by the marshal of the district of ———, and make due return thereof to the said marshal, agreeably to the directions of an act of Congress, intituled 'An act providing for the enumeration of the inhabitants of the United States,' according to the best of my ability." The enumeration shall commence on the first Monday in August next, and shall close within nine calendar months thereafter. The several assistants shall, within the said nine months, transmit to the marshals by whom they shall be respectively appointed, accurate returns of all persons, except Indians not taxed, within their respective divisions, which returns shall be made in a schedule, distinguishing the several families by the names of their master, mistress, steward, overseer, or other principal person therein, in manner following, that is to say:

The number of persons within my division, consisting of ———, appears in a schedule hereto annexed, subscribed by me this ——— day of ———, 179-. A. B. *Assistant to the marshal of* ———.

Schedule of the whole number of persons within the division allotted to A. B.

Names of heads of families.	Free white males of 16 years and upwards, including heads of families.	Free white males under 16 years.	Free white females, including heads of families.	All other free persons.	Slaves.

SECTION 2. And be it further enacted, That every assistant failing to make return, or making a false return of the enumeration to the marshal, within the time by this act limited, shall forfeit the sum of two hundred dollars.

SECTION 3. And be it further enacted, That the marshals shall file the several returns aforesaid, with the clerks of their respective district courts, who are hereby directed to receive and carefully preserve the same: And the marshals respectively shall, on or before the first day of September, one thousand seven hundred and ninety-one, transmit to the President of the United States, the aggregate amount of each description of persons within their respective districts. And every marshal failing to file the returns of his assistants, or any of them, with the clerks of their respective district courts, or failing to return the aggregate amount of each description of persons in their respective districts, as the same shall appear from said returns, to the President of the United States within the time limited by this act, shall, for every such offense, forfeit the sum of eight hundred dollars; all which forfeitures shall be recoverable in the courts of the districts where the offenses shall be committed, or in the circuit courts to be held within the same, by action of debt, information or indictment; the one-half thereof to the use of the United States, and the other half to the informer; but where the prosecution shall be first instituted on the behalf of the United States, the whole shall accrue to their use. And for the more effectual discovery of offenses, the judges of the several district courts, at their next sessions, to be held after the expiration of the time allowed for making the returns of the enumeration hereby directed, to the President of the United States, shall give this act in charge to the grand juries, in their respective courts, and shall cause the returns of the several assistants to be laid before them for their inspection.

SECTION 4. And be it further enacted, That every assistant shall receive at the rate of one dollar for every one hundred and fifty persons by him returned, where such persons reside in the country; and where such persons reside in a city, or town, containing more than five thousand persons, such assistants shall receive at the rate of one dollar for every three hundred persons; but where, from the dispersed situation of the inhabitants in some divisions, one dollar for every one hundred and fifty persons shall be insufficient, the marshals, with the approbation of the judges of their respective districts, may make such further allowance to the assistants in such divisions as shall be deemed an adequate compensation, provided the same does not exceed one dollar for every fifty persons by them returned. The several marshals shall receive as follows: The marshal of the district of Maine, two hundred dollars; the marshal of the district of New Hampshire, two hundred dollars; the marshal of the district of Massachusetts, three hundred dollars; the marshal of the district of Connecticut, two hundred dollars; the marshal of the district of New York, three hundred dollars; the marshal of the district of New Jersey, two hundred dollars; the marshal of the district of Pennsylvania, three hundred dollars; the marshal of the district of Delaware, one hundred dollars; the marshal of the district of Maryland, three hundred dollars; the marshal of the district of Virginia, five hundred dollars; the marshal of the district of Kentucky, two hundred and fifty dollars; the marshal of the district of North Carolina, three hundred and fifty dollars; the marshal of the district of South Carolina, three hundred dollars; the marshal of the district of Georgia, two hundred and fifty dollars. And to

obviate all doubts which may arise respecting the persons to be returned, and the manner of making the returns.

SECTION 5. Be it enacted, That every person whose usual place of abode shall be in any family on the aforesaid first Monday in August next, shall be returned as of such family; the name of every person, who shall be an inhabitant of any district, but without a settled place of residence, shall be inserted in the column of the aforesaid schedule, which is allotted for the heads of families, in that division where he or she shall be on the said first Monday in August next, and every person occasionally absent at the time of the enumeration, as belonging to that place in which he usually resides in the United States.

SECTION 6. And be it further enacted, That each and every person more than 16 years of age, whether heads of families or not, belonging to any family within any division of a district made or established within the United States, shall be, and hereby is, obliged to render to such assistant of the division, a true account, if required, to the best of his or her knowledge, of all and every person belonging to such family, respectively, according to the several descriptions aforesaid, on pain of forfeiting twenty dollars, to be sued for and recovered by such assistant, the one-half for his own use, and the other half for the use of the United States.

SECTION 7. And be it further enacted, That each assistant shall, previous to making his return to the marshal, cause a correct copy, signed by himself, of the schedule containing the number of inhabitants within his division, to be set up at two of the most public places within the same, there to remain for the inspection of all concerned; for each of which copies the said assistant shall be entitled to receive two dollars, provided proof of a copy of the schedule having been so set up and suffered to remain, shall be transmitted to the marshal, with the return of the number of persons; and in case any assistant shall fail to make such proof to the marshal, he shall forfeit the compensation by this act allowed him.

Approved March 1, 1790.

Population of the United States as returned at the First Census, by states: 1790.

DISTRICT.	Free white males of 16 years and upward, including heads of families.	Free white males under 16 years.	Free white females, including heads of families.	All other free persons.	Slaves.	Total.
Vermont	22,435	22,328	40,505	255	[1] 16	[2] 85,539
New Hampshire	36,086	34,851	70,160	630	158	141,885
Maine	24,384	24,748	46,870	538	None.	96,540
Massachusetts	95,453	87,289	190,582	5,463	None.	378,787
Rhode Island	16,019	15,799	32,652	3,407	948	68,825
Connecticut	60,523	54,403	117,448	2,808	2,764	237,946
New York	83,700	78,122	152,320	4,654	21,324	340,120
New Jersey	45,251	41,416	83,287	2,762	11,423	184,139
Pennsylvania	110,788	106,948	206,363	6,537	3,737	434,373
Delaware	11,783	12,143	22,384	3,899	8,887	[3] 59,094
Maryland	55,915	51,339	101,395	8,043	103,036	319,728
Virginia	110,936	116,135	215,046	12,866	292,627	747,610
Kentucky	15,154	17,057	28,922	114	12,430	73,677
North Carolina	69,988	77,506	140,710	4,975	100,572	393,751
South Carolina	35,576	37,722	66,880	1,801	107,094	249,073
Georgia	13,103	14,044	25,739	398	29,264	82,548
Total number of inhabitants of the United States exclusive of S. Western and N. territory	807,094	791,850	,541,263	59,150	694,280	3,893,635

	Free white males of 21 years and upward.	Free males under 21 years of age.	Free white females.	All other persons.	Slaves.	Total.
S. W. territory	6,271	10,277	15,365	361	3,417	35,691
N. "						

[1] The census of 1790, published in 1791, reports 16 slaves in Vermont. Subsequently, and up to 1860, the number is given as 17. An examination of the original manuscript returns shows that there never were any slaves in Vermont. The original error occurred in preparing the results for publication, when 16 persons, returned as "Free colored," were classified as "Slave."

[2] Corrected figures are 85,425, or 114 less than figures published in 1790, due to an error of addition in the returns for each of the towns of Fairfield, Milton, Shelburne, and Williston, in the county of Chittenden; Brookfield, Newbury, Randolph, and Strafford, in the county of Orange; Castleton, Clarendon, Hubbardton, Poultney, Rutland, Shrewsbury, and Wallingford, in the county of Rutland; Dummerston, Guilford, Halifax, and Westminster, in the county of Windham; and Woodstock, in the county of Windsor.

[3] Corrected figures are 59,096, or 2 more than figures published in 1790, due to error in addition.

Summary of population, by counties: 1790.

COUNTY.	Number of heads of families.	Free white males of 16 years and upward, including heads of families.	Free white males under 16 years.	Free white females, including heads of families.	All other free persons.	Slaves.	Total.	COUNTY.	Number of heads of families.	Free white males of 16 years and upward, including heads of families.	Free white males under 16 years.	Free white females, including heads of families.	All other free persons.	Slaves.	Total.
Western shore:								**Eastern shore:**							
Allegany county.....	(1)	1,068	1,283	2,188	12	258	4,809	Caroline county......	1,355	1,812	1,727	3,489	421	2,057	9,506
Ann-Arundel county..	2,288	3,142	2,850	5,672	804	10,130	22,598	Cecil county........	1,899	2,847	2,377	4,831	163	3,407	13,625
Baltimore county.....	3,503	5,184	4,668	9,101	604	5,877	25,434	Dorchester county...	652	2,541	2,430	5,039	528	5,337	15,875
Baltimore town and precincts........	1,736	3,866	2,556	5,503	323	1,255	13,503	Kent county........	1,305	1,876	1,547	3,325	655	5,433	12,836
Calvert county.......	(1)	1,091	1,109	2,011	136	4,305	8,652	Queen Anns county..	1,589	2,158	1,974	4,039	618	6,674	15,610
Charles county.......	2,043	2,565	2,399	5,160	404	10,085	20,613	Somersett county....	(1)	2,185	1,908	4,179	268	7,070	15,610
Frederick county.....	4,379	7,010	7,016	12,911	213	3,641	30,791	Talbot county.......	1,434	1,938	1,712	3,581	1,076	4,777	13,084
Harford county......	2,044	2,872	2,812	5,100	775	3,417	14,976	Worcester county....	1,420	1,985	1,916	3,725	178	3,836	11,640
Montgomery county..	2,088	3,284	2,746	5,649	294	6,030	18,003								
Prince Georges county.	1,837	2,653	2,503	4,848	164	11,176	21,344	Total	17,342	15,591	32,208	3,907	38,591	107,639	
St. Marys county.....	1,530	2,100	1,943	4,173	343	6,985	15,544								
Washington county...	2,452	3,738	3,863	6,871	64	1,286	15,822	Grand total	55,915	51,339	101,395	8,043	103,036	319,728	
Total...............		38,573	35,748	69,187	4,136	64,445	212,089								

[1] Schedules destroyed.

ALLEGANY COUNTY.
[Schedules destroyed.]

ANN-ARUNDEL COUNTY.[1]

NAME OF HEAD OF FAMILY.	Free white males of 16 years and upward, including heads of families.	Free white males under 16 years.	Free white females, including heads of families.	All other free persons.	Slaves.	NAME OF HEAD OF FAMILY.	Free white males of 16 years and upward, including heads of families.	Free white males under 16 years.	Free white females, including heads of families.	All other free persons.	Slaves.	NAME OF HEAD OF FAMILY.	Free white males of 16 years and upward, including heads of families.	Free white males under 16 years.	Free white females, including heads of families.	All other free persons.	Slaves.
Ashm——,* Ann.......	(*)	(*)	(*)	(*)	(*)	Couden, Robert.....	(*)	(*)	(*)	(*)	(*)	Williams, ——*......			1		74
Wilson, Thomas......	(*)	(*)	(*)	(*)	(*)	Ghiselin, Mary......	(*)	(*)	(*)	(*)	(*)	Thomas, John........	1		4		40
Ritch——,* Adam.....	(*)	(*)	(*)	(*)	(*)	Harison, Alexander..	(*)	(*)	(*)	(*)	(*)	Chew, Sarah........	2	1	2		
M——,* Patrick......	(*)	(*)	(*)	(*)	(*)	Steuad, Charles.....	(*)	(*)	(*)	(*)	(*)	Lockey, Isabella.....		1	1		
——,* Thomas.......	(*)	(*)	(*)	(*)	(*)	Gather, Ann........	(*)	(*)	(*)	(*)	(*)	Carroll, Lizy........			2		
Ulud, Oliver........	(*)	(*)	(*)	(*)	(*)	West, James........	(*)	(*)	(*)	(*)	(*)	Douls, Samuel.......	1		1		5
But——,* John.......	(*)	(*)	(*)	(*)	(*)	Randal, John........	(*)	(*)	(*)	(*)	(*)	Gossaway, Elizabeth..		1	2		4
Wag——,* John......	(*)	(*)	(*)	(*)	(*)	Williams, Joseph....	(*)	(*)	(*)	(*)	(*)	Colten, Daniel.......	2		5		4
Shuca——,* Philip....	(*)	(*)	(*)	(*)	(*)	Davidson, John......	(*)	(*)	(*)	(*)	(*)	Hancock, Jane.......			1		
Ross, John..........	(*)	(*)	(*)	(*)	(*)	Kelly, Hugh........	(*)	(*)	(*)	(*)	(*)	Wills, Daniel........	1	5	5	(*)	(*)
Gaston, Ann........	1	(*)	(*)	(*)	(*)	Egan, Patrick.......	(*)	(*)	(*)	(*)	(*)	Wills, John.........	3	2	1	(*)	(*)
Burniston, Joseph....	1	(*)	(*)	(*)	(*)	Ham——,* James....	(*)	(*)	(*)	(*)	(*)	Ramon, Sarah.......			1	1	(*)
Herbit, Edward......	1	(*)	(*)	(*)	(*)	Welch, John........	(*)	(*)	(*)	(*)	(*)	Cony, Robert.......	1		3	5	(*)
Jones, Charles.......	1	(*)	(*)	(*)	(*)	Ha——,* Nicholas...	(*)	(*)	(*)	(*)	7	Smith, Gilbert Hamilton......	1	5	4	(*)	(*)
Hewit, Thomas......	1	(*)	(*)	(*)	(*)	Bruer, *——sanah...	1		3			Oliver, Daniel.......		5	1	(*)	(*)
Madcap, William.....	3	(*)	(*)	(*)	(*)	*——gar, ——......			3			Hughes, Edward.....	1		3	(*)	(*)
Baker, Charles.......	(*)	(*)	(*)	(*)	(*)	Carson, ——.......	1		1			Taman, Nisa........	1		4	(*)	(*)
Taylor, James.......	1	(*)	(*)	(*)	(*)	Redmon, ——*.....	1	3	1		(*)	Gary, Leonard......	2	4		(*)	(*)
Welman, John.......	1	(*)	(*)	(*)	(*)	Starplke, Godloop....	1		4			Tucker, Isaac.......	2		5	(*)	(*)
Neth, Lewis........	1	(*)	(*)	(*)	(*)	Orrick, Thomas.....	2	1	4	1		Griffis, John........	1		5	(*)	(*)
Peacock, Samuel.....	1	(*)	(*)	(*)	(*)	Chambers, James....	1	2	5	1		Tucker, Seaborn.....	1		5	(*)	(*)
Faeburn, Benjamin...	(*)	(*)	(*)	(*)	(*)	Tuck, William......	1		2			Hughes, Samuel.....	1	2	6	(*)	(*)
Maccubbin, James....	(*)	(*)	(*)	(*)	(*)	Isabel, Robert......	1		2			Marshel, Thomas....			3	(*)	(*)
Williams, James.....	(*)	(*)	(*)	(*)	(*)	Thomson, Alexander..	1		2			Tucker, Betty.......	(*)		1	(*)	(*)
Middlet——,* Gilbert.	(*)	(*)	(*)	(*)	(*)	Tennins, Thomas....	3	5	5	(*)		Wood, James.......	1		1	(*)	(*)
Hallowl——,* David...	(*)	(*)	(*)	(*)	(*)	Duvall, Gabriel.....	1		1	(*)		Sullvan, Thomas.....	1		4	(*)	(*)
Ridgiy, Charles......	(*)	(*)	(*)	(*)	(*)	Worfield, Charles....		5	4	(*)		Spicknall, Leonard...	1		1	(*)	(*)
Piper, Thomas.......	(*)	(*)	(*)	(*)	(*)	Rummels, Lucy.....		3		(*)		Robinson, Elisnor...	1		1	2	5
Rauli——,* Mary.....	(*)	(*)	(*)	(*)	(*)	Richards, Clement...	1		3			Griffis, Liddington...	1		7	2	
M——,* Elizabeth....	(*)	(*)	(*)	(*)	(*)	Higgs, Henry.......			3	(*)		Wood, Morgan......	1	1	8		2
Thay——,* Sarah....	(*)	(*)	(*)	(*)	(*)	Williams, Jane......		(*)	3			Wood, ——,* 8nr....	1	2	2	2	30
Faeburn, Ann.......	(*)	(*)	(*)	(*)	(*)	Mayo, John........	1	(*)	3			Maynard, ——*.....	2	1	3	2	1
Fitn——,* Richard....	(*)	(*)	(*)	(*)	(*)	Purdy, John........	1	(*)	3	(*)		Trott, ——*........	2		4	2	1
Guim——,* John.....	(*)	(*)	(*)	(*)	(*)	Triga, Charles......	1	(*)	1			Welch, ——*........	1		2	2	1
Hig——,* Relph......	(*)	(*)	(*)	(*)	(*)	Sands, William.....	1	(*)	1	(*)		Wilkins, ——*......	3		1	9	3
Sand, John.........	(*)	(*)	(*)	(*)	(*)	Urrel, Thomas......	1		2	(*)		Johnson, ——,* Jnr...	5		8	2	
Lilly, William.......	(*)	(*)	(*)	(*)	(*)	Umphries, John.....		1		(*)		Martin, ——*.......			2		
Middle——,* Elizabeth.	(*)	(*)	(*)	(*)	(*)	Dickson, M——.....			5	(*)		Salmon, ——*.......			7		
Richard, ——*.......	1		2	1	1	Smith, Henry.......	3		3	(*)		Cook, ——*.........	3	2	8	3	8
Ray, John..........	1		2			Brice, John........			3	(*)		Thomas, Jane.......			2		
Rough, William......	1	1	4	2		Dunn, Patrick......		(*)	1	(*)		Mitchel, Thomas....	3	1	3	1	
Ross, Sarah.........	1		4			Ridgley, Harry.....	(*)	(*)	(*)	(*)		Roberts, Edward....	3	1	4	1	
Clarke, Joseph......	2	1	3			Key, Philip........			2		5	Hogskins, Nanny....			1		
Smith, John.........	1	3	2			Petty, John........	2		1			Worthington, John...					2
Wallace, Charles.....	1		2			Stift, Elizabeth.....			1	1	1	Coe, William.......	4	3	2		5
Beard, Mathew......	1		2			Fouler, ——*.......	1	2	2			Simmons, Joseph....	2	1	1	1	(*)
Green, Frederick.....	1	5	2			Fouler, ——*.......	1	2	3	1		Truman, Thomas....	1	4	3		(*)
Brucer, Nicholas.....	1		3			Thompson, ——*....	1		2	1		Chooney, Thomas....	1		4		(*)
Boyl, Mary.........	(*)	(*)	(*)	(*)	(*)	Chatlin, ——*......	1		3			Slaughter, Thomas...	1	2	4		(*)
Ross, Frederick......	(*)	(*)	(*)	(*)	(*)	Wilshaw, ——*.....	1		2			Bush, Mary........	4		3		(*)
Long, Sam..........	(*)	(*)	(*)	(*)	(*)	Parson, ——*.......	1		2			Borter, Elizabeth....			3		(*)
Richards, Paul......	(*)	(*)	(*)	(*)	(*)	Daniels, ——*......	1	2	2								
Murry, William......	(*)	(*)	(*)	(*)	(*)	White, ——*........	1		2		3						

[1] No attempt has been made in this publication to correct mistakes in spelling made by the deputy marshals, but the names have been reproduced as they appear upon the census schedules.

* Illegible.

ANN-ARUNDEL COUNTY—Continued.

NAME OF HEAD OF FAMILY.	Free white males of 16 years and upward, including heads of families.	Free white males under 16 years.	Free white females, including heads of families.	All other free persons.	Slaves.
Williamson, Mary				(*)	(*)
Lattimore, Randolph B.	1			(*)	(*)
Ogle, Ann	1	1	2	(*)	(*)
Small, Charlotte	1		2	(*)	(*)
Syball, Henry	4	2	3	(*)	(*)
Harrison, Samuel, Sn^r	2	2		4	1
Raulings, Samuel	2			(*)	(*)
Boyer, Adam	3	2		(*)	(*)
Hammond, William	4			(*)	(*)
Tootle, Elizabeth	3	(*)	(*)	(*)	(*)
Bots, John	1	(*)	(*)	(*)	(*)
Woolford, John	1		4		
Smith, James			4		
Wood, William	1	3	2		9
Ward, Elizabeth	3	1	2	2	10
Gist, Thomas	3	2	4		
Randel, —*	1	1	2		
Armsucathor, —*	1	1	1		
Surls, —*	1	4	4		
Brown, —ge*				7	
Birchhead, —lah*	2	1	4		19
Taylor, —*	2	3	4		
Clarke, —*	1	1	3		
Chew, —*	3				22
Oliver, —*	1	1	2		
Brown, —*				8	
Brown, —*				5	
Oliver, —*	2	1	3		
Birckhead, —*	1	2	3		
Scrivenor, Francis	3	3	5		3
Wood, John	1		3		7
Wood, James, Sn^r	1		2		1
Woodard, Bazel				5	
Neal, Mathew				3	
Ward, Robert	2	3	4		
Whittington, James	2	2	4		
Cobreth, Aaron	1				
Lane, Harrison	2		2		
West, John	2	2	2		
Lane, Thomas, Sn^r	2		2		
Scrivenor, Lewis	1	2	2		
Luppin, James				(*)	
World, John	1		1	(*)	
Mumford, Joseph	1	1	3	(*)	
Johns, George	1		2	(*)	
Woodfield, Thomas	1	4	2	(*)	
Hinton, Jane	1		2	(*)	
Parrott, William	1	1	(*)	(*)	
Stallings, Thomas	2	3	3	(*)	
Stallings, Jane	1			(*)	
Parrott, Thomas	1	(*)	(*)	(*)	
Whittington, Thomas	1	(*)	(*)	(*)	
Weems, William	2	(*)	(*)	(*)	
Hogsway, —*				(*)	
Smith, Joseph	2	4	2		10
Whittington, —*	1	3	3		6
Brown, —*	2	2	3		
Trott, —*	2	3	2		
Brown, —*	1		4		
Turner, —*	2	6	2		
Roberts, —*	2	3	2		
Stone, —shal*	5	3	4		
Scrivenor, —*	1	1	2		
Birckhead, —*	1		3		2
Batson, —*	1		2		7
Chew, —*	1	3	3		11
House, —*	2	4	4		1
Whittington, —*	1	4	2		
Trott, —*	2	1	2		
Burgess, —*	1	6	5		2
Nowell, —*	3	2	2		16
Burgess, —*	1		1		
Joseph, —*		2	2		9
Clagett, Thomas John	1	4	4		8
Harrison, Walter	1			1	9
Simmons, Priscilla	1	2	1		7
Wyval, Marmaduke	1	3	8	1	14
Tillard, Thomas	1	3	4		(*)
Deal, Joseph	1	1	4		17
Tongue, Thomas	2	3	2		
Phillips, John				2	
Dupan, Kate					1
Couman, Joseph, Sn^r	2	4	2		(*)
Scrivenor, William	2	1	2		(*)
Russel, Kizzy	1		5		(*)
Camdin, Sarah	2		5		(*)
Griffis, David	1	3			(*)
Crandel, Joseph	3		3		(*)
Gardener, John	2	1	3		(*)
Allein, Adam	1	3	3		(*)
Freeman, Alexander	1		3		
Hinton, Thomas	1		3		
Pearson, Thomas			(*)	3	
Conner, Richard	1	1	3		
Martinon, Thomas	1	(*)	(*)	(*)	(*)
Duvall, Robert	2	(*)	(*)	(*)	(*)

NAME OF HEAD OF FAMILY.	Free white males of 16 years and upward, including heads of families.	Free white males under 16 years.	Free white females, including heads of families.	All other free persons.	Slaves.
Flours, Ann	1	(*)	(*)	(*)	(*)
Simmons, Isaac	1	(*)	(*)	(*)	(*)
Gardener, Peter		(*)	(*)	(*)	2
Randel, David				2	
Nowell, Gilbert	1	2	6	4	1
Simmons, Elizabeth	2	1	3		6
Simmons, Richard	2	1	2		10
Simmons, William	1		3		
Simmons, Abraham	1		4		3
Fisher, William	1	1	4	12	
Pattison, —*	3				26
Childs, —*	2	3	4		9
Carr, —*	1		5		
Armiger, —*	5		2		2
Powell, —*	1	1	2		1
Carr, —*	1	2	3		1
Miles, —*	2		2		
Lambeth, —*	1		3		
Lambeth, Henry	2	1	2		
Lambeth, John (ship carpenter)	1	1	2		
Lambeth, John (Son of W^m)	3				
Lambeth, John, 3^d	2	2	6		7
Ratlief, Rachel			3		
Lambeth, William	2	3	5		
Roberts, William	1	3	1		
Carr, John, Sn^r	1	3	3		(*)
Busey, Samuel	1	3	1		
Lambeth, Benjamin	1	1	2		(*)
Brown, Richard	2	2	4		(*)
Gatwood, John	2	3	4		4
Hill, Abel	2		2	3	(*)
Weems, David	1	6	3		(*)
Wood, Ann			3		(*)
Anderson, John	1		4		(*)
Mussy, Charles	1	1	4		(*)
Lane, Nathaniel	1	1	1		(*)
Armiger, William, Sn^r	1	2	2		(*)
Parmore, Edin	1		4		(*)
Drury, Samuel	1	2	4		(*)
Parker, Rachel			2		(*)
Drury, William	2		1		(*)
Williams, John	1	2	(*)	(*)	(*)
Hutton, Joseph	3	1	(*)	(*)	(*)
Urquhart, William	2	2	(*)	(*)	(*)
Ellexson, Charles	2	3	5		(*)
Smith, Samuel L.	2				2
Marciney, Jacob	4				5
Tillard, William	1	2	2		13
Hardiesty, —*	1	4	2		(*)
Sheckels, —*	1		4		4
Drury, —*	1		1		6
Sollars, —*	2	2	1		
Cooley, —*	2		2		6
Lane, —* jur	1	4	2		9
Griffin, —*	1		2		
Allein, —*	3	1	2		32
Gardiner, —*	2	3	2		6
Dove, —*	2		2		3
Henwood, —*	2		3		
Cooley, —*	1	1	4		3
Hutton, —*	2	1	2		12
Donell, —*	1		2		
—*, Senior	1		2		14
Griffin, —*	2	1	2		2
Blunt, —*	1	2	4		
Harrison, Benjamin	1				
Stallings, John	1	1	4		
Childs, Joseph	2	2	1		6
Childs, Siphus	2				1
Darnall, Richard	1				153
Darnall, Bennit	1				157
Darnall, Nicholas	2		1		13
Got, Ezekel	1	1	2	4	17
Owins, Isaac, jn^r	1	1	2		(*)
Owins, Jane			3		(*)
Owins, James			3		(*)
Drury, Charles	1	4	3		(*)
Parrott, John	1	5	2		(*)
Childs, John	1	2	2		4
Sherbit, George	1	2	2		(*)
Sherbert, Thomas	2	2	4		(*)
Sherbert, Benjamin	1	2	5		(*)
Joice, Abel		2	2		(*)
Joice, Betty			5		(*)
Knighton, William	1	2	2		(*)
Winterson, Joseph	1		5		(*)
Ashley, Johnathan	1		1		(*)
Ward, Samuel	1		1		(*)
Hill, Joseph			2		(*)
Ned, Free					(*)
Baily, John	1	2	2		(*)
Hill, Susanah			2		12
Arnold, Liddy	3		2		
Disney, James	3	2	2		20

NAME OF HEAD OF FAMILY.	Free white males of 16 years and upward, including heads of families.	Free white males under 16 years.	Free white females, including heads of families.	All other free persons.	Slaves.
Watkins, Benjamin	3		5		21
Gantt, Dr Robt	1				4
Weems, Col. Jno.	2	3	3		114
Griffin, Frederick	1	1			
Conner, Richard	2	2	2		
Ball, —*	1	2	4		
Mills, —*	8		3	1	23
Leach, —*	1		1		15
Franklin, —*	1	3	2		10
Atwell, —* (Son of Jno.)					
Crandel, —*	1	2	1		
Crandel, —*	1	1	3		2
Owins, —*			2		
Purgason, —*		1	4		1
Gott, Elizabeth	1	1	4		7
Deal, —*	1	2	3	4	2
Fouler, —*	1	2	2		
Norman, —*	1	2	2		
Williams, —*	1		3		
Joice, —*	1	2	4		
Randel, Augustus	1	2	4		1
Wason, John	1	6	2		
Howard, Hannah	1		1		
Wason, Richard	1		3		
Woodfield, Elizabeth		1	4		
Wells, Benjam	1	1	2		1
Simon				5	1
Barker, John	1	2	4		
Wells, Samuel	1	1	3		
Atwell, John	1	2	1		
Furrer, Zeital				2	
Crandel, William					(*)
Deal, John	1	3	1		(*)
Alley			6		
Madcap, Sarah			2		(*)
Norman, Benjamin			1		
Norman, Thomas	4	5	4		(*)
Randel, Christopher	1		2		
Norman, Nicholas	1		2		(*)
Flatt, Ruth	3		2		(*)
Howard, Hannah	1		3		(*)
Watson, William	1	2	3		(*)
Phips, John	1		6		
Spencer, Philip	1	1			(*)
Gillam, Jacob	1				(*)
Crandel, George	2				(*)
Atwell, Benjamin	2	3			
Cutler, Jacob			2		
Foster, Nathaniel	3	1	2		2
Gardener, George	2		2		
Mace, Joseph	2		1		
Parish, Aaron	3		3		
Parish, Peter	1		2		
Smith, Philip	2	1	5		15
Harrison, Richard, jn^r	2		1		
Osburn, —*			2		1
Barker, William	1	2	4		1
Cowan, —*	3		4		3
Mace, —*	2		2		
Tucker, —*	3	2	3		
Tucker, —*	3	1	6		4
Chew, Daniel	3		4		8
Norris, Thomas			2		4
Norris, —*	2	1	2	1	4
Phips, —*	1		2		3
Sims, —*	1		7		
Popham, Benjamin	1		1		
Franklin, William	1	4	10	9	26
Franklin, —*	1		2		1
Busey, —*	1	3	2		
Cave, —*	3	4	1		1
Hewit, —*	2		2		
Franklin, Jacob	2	4	4	1	33
Harrison, Benjamin, Sn^r	2		5		31
Johns, Susanah			2		21
Johns, John	1	1	3		9
Tidings, Caleb	1				
Galloway, Joseph	2	1	1	8	41
Broun, Nanny				7	
Deal, James			3		
Atwell, Daniel	1	3	2		6
Langton, Ann	1	2	3		(*)
Cole, John	4	1	1		(*)
Joice, Elizabeth	1	1	2		(*)
Smith, Anthoney	1	1	2		(*)
Hall, William	1		3		34
Butler, James	1	1	3		(*)
Welch, Robert	1	5	3		(*)
Welch, John	2	1	1	1	(*)
Stewart, David			2		(*)
Lee, Stephin	1	2	3		3
Welch, Aaron	1		3		1
Askew, Lyles	1	2	4		
Plummer, Henry	2		4	(*)	(*)
Bufford, Benjamin	3	1	3	(*)	(*)

* Illegible.

ANN-ARUNDEL COUNTY—Continued.

NAME OF HEAD OF FAMILY.	Free white males of 16 years and upward, including heads of families.	Free white males under 16 years.	Free white females, including heads of families.	All other free persons.	Slaves.
Chancy, Benjamin	1	1	1	(*)	(*)
Hardiesty, John	1	1	2		
Caw, Benjamin	1		2		
Smith, John	4	2	(*)	(*)	(*)
Simmons, Isaac	1	2	(*)	(*)	(*)
Carr, Robert	1	1	4	3	
Boyd, Thomas	1		3		
Pindel, Gasanay	1	2	4	3	
Chancy, Abraham	1	1	1		23
Pindel, Philip	1		1		1
Dove, ——*			2		12
Sheckels, ——*	1	1	4		
Sheckels, ——*	1	1			5
Simmons, William	4	2	3		5
Macclney, ——*	1	1	3		
Brashers, ——*	1	3	3		10
Parmore, ——*	1	4	1		
Hopkins, ——*	3	4	2		
Green, ——*	1	1	4		52
Wills, ——*	3	6	3		4
Sheckels, ——*	2	1	3		
Elisha, ——*	1	2	5		
Brashers, ——*	1	1	2		2
Brashers, ——*	1	2	2		3
Ward, ——*	3	4			30
Owins, Isaac	3	3	2		15
Childs, Zacariah	1	1	5		6
Parrott, ——*	2	2	3		
Mackall, ——*	2	3	5	2	32
Shepperd, ——*	1	7	3		3
Chancy, ——*	2		3		
Hopkins, ——*	3	4	2		
Boyd, Thomas	1	1	1		3
Armiger, John	1	1	3	2	
Brashers, Elizabeth			3	4	
Kirby, William	2	6	4		
Young, John	2	1	6	3	
Orrion, John	2		6	2	
Smith, John, jnr	2	1	3	2 1	29
Lane, Thomas	2	1	5		
Lane, Ann	1	2	7		24
Tidings, Richard	2	2	2		
Owins, Benjamin	1	2	5		
Ward, Henry	1	2	3		
Plumoner, Johanna	2	4	3		20
Roberts, Richard	1	3	1	1	
Pattison, Daniel				10	
Nettles, Eleus	1	2	4		2
Holliday, Richard	1	4			8
Duvall, Marsh Marine	3	5	4		8
Brogden, Richard	1				12
Crabb, Elizabeth	2				15
Chagett, John (of Edwd)	1	2			26
Watkins, Nicholas	4	1			28
Welch, Jacob	1	2	1	1	
Ritchardson, William	2	2	1	(*)	(*)
Tayler, John	2	1	3	(*)	(*)
Davidson, James	3		4	(*)	(*)
Nichols, John, jnr	2	1	3	(*)	(*)
Nicholson, Stephin	2	1	1	(*)	(*)
Jacobs, John	1	2	1	(*)	
Raulings, Aaron	2		6	1	13
Knighton, Gasaway	1	4	1		3
Iiams, Rebecca	2		3		16
Iiams, Plummer	2		3		16
Cowman, Joseph	2	2	1		11
Selman, William	1	1	2		
Rachel, Free				4	
MacColloch, James	3	1	7	1	15
Steuart, John	2		2		
Brogden, William	2		2		45
Beard, Richard	1	1	1		
Gibbs, Thomas	1		5		19
Holliday, John	2	2			6
Wilson, Rebecca	1	2	3		
Atwell, William	3	3	3		
McKinsey, John	2	2	3		
Stewart, Ann			1		33
Headin, Barnit	1	2			18
Danielson, Richard	2	1			
Williams, William	1	1	3		
Beard, ——	1		6		
Beard, ——	2				8
Watts, Richard	2	2	4		
Beard, ——	1	1	2		15
Carter, ——	1	1	3	1	
Lee, Stephin	1	1	2		
Lee, Edward	1		2	2	
Ward, William	3		5		
Davidson, Richard	1	2			
Lusbey, Deborah			3		
Mayo, James	2	1	5		
Thomas, Elizabeth	1		2		
Lee, John	2	2			
Watkins, Richard	1	2	4		10

NAME OF HEAD OF FAMILY.	Free white males of 16 years and upward, including heads of families.	Free white males under 16 years.	Free white females, including heads of families.	All other free persons.	Slaves.
Watkins, Ann	2		3		4
Watkins, Joseph	2	1	2		4
Stockett, Ann	6		1		8
Stockett, Noble	2	5	1		26
Raulings, Gasaway	1	1	4	1	27
Chapman, William	1	1	2		9
Stewart, James	1	1	2		2
Harwood, Ann	1		2		28
Harwood, Richard, jur	2	5	2		35
Watkins, John	1		2		6
Brewer, John	1	1	1		
Watkins, Ann (Widow of Joseph)		4	3		14
Daniel, Free				9	
Jack & Robin				2	
Norris, Martin	1	1	1		2
Galloway, Benjamin	1	1	1	(*)	(*)
Ceaser & Cupid				(*)	(*)
Gasaway, Henry	1	2	1		2
Dorcey, Joshua	1	4			4
Jones, Sarah	1	2	1		7
Sprigg, Richard	1	1	4		82
Witrick, Philip	1	1			
Norman, William	1	2	3		
Cheston, James	2		3		53
Batty, Ferdinando	1	3	3		
Waters, Wilson	1	2	3		
Hally, Patrick	1	2			9
Stockett, Joseph	2	1	2		
Johnston, William	2	2	1		41
Faro, Stevin	1	1	2		12
Hall, Benjamin	1		2		
Waters, Nathan	1		2		8
Lee, Edward	1		2		2
Mayo, Henry	1	3	6		15
Wayman, Francis	1	2	2		
Lynthecum, Thomas	2	2	5		
Lynthecum, Francis	1	2	1		1
Lynthecum, Joseph	1	2	2		5
Purden, William, Snr	2	2			
Purden, ——*		2	5		
Alkin, Ann		1	2		
Phips, ——		1	2		
Sanders, ——*	1		2		39
Davidson, ——*	1	2	4		
Davidson, Sarah			3		
Brewer, William	2	1	3		23
Mayo, Isaac	1		2		
Nicholson, Elizabeth		2	2		18
Gasaway, Nicholas	1	1	2		25
Pearson, Mary	1	1	3		
Polly, Free				9	
Raulings, Rarah	1	2	3		12
Pearson, John	1		3	3	
Harwood, Thomas & Richard	3		4	2	49
Richardson, Richard	1		4		43
Chew, Samuel Lloyd	1	2	3		55
Harrison, Samuel, jur	1	3	4	4	50
Stewart, William	5		7		47
Sifton, John	4		1		6
Sifton, Edward	1		2		14
Iiams, Samuel	1	1	4		
Broun, William	1		2		2
Craggs, John	1	3	1		2
Alkin, Richard	1		3		
Furgison, Elizabeth			3		
Lukins, Mathias	1		4		
Stewart, Charles of Charles	1	1	4		
Stewart, Mordiaca	2	3	6		8
Jenifer, Daniel of Saint Thos	1				8
Chapman, Thomas	1	2	3	(*)	(*)
Survoy, Richard				(*)	(*)
Danielson, Thomas	1	1	6		
Welch, Ben	2	1	5		
Maccubbin, Samuel	1		5		29
Watts, Richard	4	1	2		
Day, Elizabeth	1		4		
Glover, Elizabeth		1	4		
Kirkland, Edward	1		1		
Pearce, Mary	1	2	6		
Barry, Mordiaca	3	2	3		
Guinn, Francis	2	2	7		5
French, William	2	1	2		
Pearce, Johanna	1		5		
Ward, William, Snr	3		9		
Nicholson, John	1	1	1		
Nicholson, John, jur	3	3	3		
Jacobs, John	3	1	3		
Richardson, Philip	4		3		5
Grover, John	2		5		
Icleheart, James	1	2	2		7

NAME OF HEAD OF FAMILY.	Free white males of 16 years and upward, including heads of families.	Free white males under 16 years.	Free white females, including heads of families.	All other free persons.	Slaves.
Nancy, Elijah					2
Selman, Leonard	2	2	4		14
Sanders, ——*	2		3		4
Sanders, Robert	2	1	3		4
Grover, Solomon	2		5		6
Selby, William	2		5		7
Selby, Joseph	1	2	7	1	9
King, Thomas	1	2	3		15
Butler, Joseph Noble	1	1	3	1	9
Raulings, Richard	1	1	1		5
Howard, Joseph	1	5	8		26
Ryan, John	1		2		
Grovel, Benjamin	1		2	1	
Hamlin, Elenor	1	3	1		
Howard, Benjamin, Esqr	2	1	1	1	17
Rodes, John	2			(*)	(*)
Phelps, Zacariah	2	2	2		
Phelps, Bazel	2		1		
Davis, William	1	5	3		4
Everheart, John	1	1	1		
Welch, Henry Oneal	1	1	1		17
Bleak, Philip	1		4		
Stewart, William, 3d	2	2	2		
Williams, Joseph	2	3	2		2
Williams, Thomas	2	3	4		
Harwood, William	1	5	5		17
Bazel, John	1	4	1		
Stewart, David	7	2	2		10
Davis, Mary	2		3		5
Sanders, Robert	1	2	3		7
Bird, William	1	2	3	(*)	(*)
Eliott, Robert	2	1	2	(*)	(*)
Sanders, James	2	1	2		
Stewart, Edward	2	2	1		2
Knighton, Nicholas	2		6		
Bosford, John	3	2	4		
Fouler, Thomas	3		3		
Nichols, Isaac	1		3		
Sansbury, Richard	1		1		
Jacobs, Samuel	1	2	4		19
Hall, Henry	1		3		28
Watkins, John	1	2	4		8
Maguire, Samuel	2		3		
Selby, Joseph	1		7		9
Doyle, Peter	1		6		
Howell, John	1		6		
Evins, Elizabeth	2		2		
Patrick, Dorothy	2		2		8
Merikin, William	1		3		
Davis, George	2	3		1	8
Eliott, Samuel	1	3	4		
McCauley, Ann	1	1			7
Corraway, Margaret		2	2		
Eliott, William	1	2	3		14
Hopkins, Philip Hammond					16
Cowman, John	2	3	6	1	7
Hall, Mathew	2	1	5		25
Hall, Richard	2		5	1	4
Hall, William	1	4	4	1	16
Selby, Jymima	1		1		
Prout, Sarah	1				24
Rutlin, Ann		1	1		
Selby, Joseph	1		7		9
Gary, Elizabith	1	2	4		
Eliott, William	1	2	2		
McDonald, Michael	1		2		
Madcap, George	1		2		
Green, Sarah	1		2		
Talbert, Thomas	1		2		8
Gather, Edward	3		4		10
McCauly, Thomas	2		4	1	
Tucker, Zacariah	1		3		
Cadle, James	1		3		
Cadle, Zacariah	1		3		
Cann, Ingrum	4	2	4		
Robinson, Charles	2		2		
Cadle, Sami, Snr	2	6	4		4
Cadle, Samuel, jnr	2		6		
Roberts, John	4		3		
McCauly, Francis	1		3		
Will, Free				3	
Tucker, Richard	1		2		
Tucker, Thomas	1	6	2		7
Talbert, Thomas	1		2		
Bignall, Thomas	4	2	3		21
Hood, Ann			5		42
Higgans, Richard	4	1	5		26
Carroll, William	1		5		
Sappington, John	2	1	5		
Hopkins, Joseph	2	5	8	7	5
Smith, Robert Jne	1		2		12
Williams, Osburn	1	1	2		
Edwards, William	1	1	1		12
Edwards, Cadwalader	1	3	2	1	4

*Illegible.

ANN-ARUNDEL COUNTY—Continued.

NAME OF HEAD OF FAMILY.	Free white males of 16 years and upward, including heads of families.	Free white males under 16 years.	Free white females, including heads of families.	All other free persons.	Slaves.
Lynthecum, Thomas	3	1	3		
Lynthecum, John, jr	3	4	4		1
Andrews, William	1		4		
White, Francis	2	4	4		
Jones, Philip	1		3		
Jones, Cornelious	3		2		
Hopkins, Richard	4	3	6	2	10
Cager, George				18	
Badger, Nan				8	
Anderson, York				3	
Anderson, Ceaser				3	
Tanner, Philip Hopkins	2	1	3	1	3
Wheeler, Richard	3	1	3		5
Marriott, Silvanus	3		3		6
Hopkins, Elizabeth	3	1	4	1	10
Johnson, William	1		2		
Hopkins, Elisha	2	1	4	1	10
Hall, William			2		
Worfield, ——*	2	1	2		20
Gather, ——*	1	4	3		
Gather, Seth	1	2	2		
Hall, Joshua	1		3		5
Marriott, John	1		3		
Rummels, Cassandria	1		5		
Worfield, Caleb	1	3	2		
Allein, William	1		2		8
Worfield, Joshua	2	1	4		
Gather, Vachel	2	2	4		24
Phelps, William	4		3		
Fouler, Priscilla	1	3	3		
McCocklin, Peter	2	1	2		1
Badger, Charles				7	
Calvert, Philip				7	1
Anderson, Andrew	2	2	2	1	1
Anderson, William	2	2	2		
Anderson, James	2	3	4		3
Anderson, Ann	1		2		
Taylor, Samuel	2	1	4		2
Thomson, John	1	2	1		
Woodard, Henry	1				
Stewart, Edward	2		1		9
Belmear, John	1	1	2		
Anderson, James	1	1	1		8
Melone, John	1		1		
Basford, Stephin	4		5		4
Lynthecum, Thomas	1	2	1		
Oliver, Elizabith			4		7
Stansbury, Elisha	2	1	4		
Donalson, Moses	1	1	3		
Anderson, James, Sn'	1	1	2		3
Chaney, Samuel	1	2	2		
Chaney, Joseph	1	2	7		
Chaney, Benjamin	1	3	3		
Cooper, John	1		2		
Mullikin, Belt	2	2	6		21
Mullikin, Thomas	3	2	6		16
Gather, Joshua	3	1	2		
Danderson, Thomas	1	2	6		
Danderson, Moses	1	4	3		
Danerson, Joseph	1		3		
Smith, Edward	1	1	2		
Worfield, John	2		5		
Millar, Nehemiah	1	1	3		
Millar, John	2		1		
Burgess, Thomas	2	2	2		
Boughcock, John	1		3		
Marriott, Thomas	2	4	4		9
Donaldson, Elija	1		3		
Mitchel, Hugh	1	2	3		
Jones, Tenmiah	2	2	5		28
Marriott, Joshua	2	1	3		2
Couman, Joseph	1		2		
Silance, John	1		3		
Cupid, Free				5	
Fell (family free negroes)				7	
Nick				8	
Hamton, Thomas Gill	1	2	7		
Danielson, Richard	1		2		
Pen, Mary			5		
Pen, William	1		5		
Iiams, Charity			3		
Waters, Josephus	3	3	4	1	4
Elder, John	1	3	1		
Iiams, Thomas	2		3		
Iiams, Penelopes			2		
Croghogan, Robert	1	3	1	7	19
Rice, Nathaniel	2	2	5		
Scott, Joseph	2	1	2		
Roderick, James	2	3	6		11
Tennins, Edmond	3	7	6		
Pen, Joseph	2	1	2		
Chaney, James	1	2	2		
Noles, Clement	2	2	2		
Iiams, John	2	3	1		
Macklefish, Thomas	1	3	1		

NAME OF HEAD OF FAMILY.	Free white males of 16 years and upward, including heads of families.	Free white males under 16 years.	Free white females, including heads of families.	All other free persons.	Slaves.
Deaver, Richard	1		1		
Snoden, John	2	3	4		66
Hening, Michael	2	2	4		
Hardiesty, John	2	1	3		
Hardiesty, Henry	2	4	3		
Hardiesty, Joshua	1		1		
Preston, Francis	1	4	1		
Shaffer, Lewis	1		1		48
Thomas, John Chew	1	1	1	2	20
Sappington, Francis			2		5
Griffith, Henry, jnr	2	2	1	2	15
Lansdel, Isaac	2	1	2		
Primus				2	
Conaway, Siman	2	1	3		
Worthington, John	1	1	3		17
Simpson, Francis	1		5		16
Gatheril, Stephin	1		6		1
White, Griffith	3	4	1		1
White, Charles	1	4	3		9
Selman, William	1	2	5		10
Worfield, Joshua	1		2		16
Worfield, James	2		3		13
Worfield, Seth	2		3		
Worfield, ——*	1	4	2		
Moxley, Nahimiah	4	2	6		3
Moxley, Thomas	2	3	3		1
Watkins, William	1		5		
Cross, Martin	1		1		
Nicholes, Benjamin	1	1	3		
Nichols, Thomas	1	1	3		
Jane, Thomas	3		1		
Henning, Dr James	1	1	3	1	1
Lansdel, Isaac, jnr	2		5		5
Mobley, Reason	2	1	4		4
Maccauly, Thomas	1	3	4		
Cooper, George	3	1	2		
Leak, Joseph	3	1	2		
Rogers, Nicholas	2		3		5
Page, Tiffery	1	2	4		
Waters, John	1	1	2		
Mabbit, Anthoney	1		3		
Cambel, Samuel	1	1	6		
Alderidge, Zacariah	1	2	7		
Icleheart, Edward	1		3		
Icleheart, Zacariah	1	3	5		
Stewart, Stephen	1	2	3		2
Cross, George	2		2		
Ridgley, Henry	1		4		24
Sappington, Polly			2		8
Sipe, John	3	3	2		
Herring, Sabret	1	3	3		
Turner, Thomas	1		2		
Gasaway, Brice	1	4	5		
Iiams, Sarah			3		
Worfield, Rachal			3		22
Worfield, Joseph	1	1	3		2
Worfield, Azil	1	2	3		5
Worfield, Davage	2	2	4		16
Waters, Thomas	1	2	2		2
Macklefish, Eli	1		1		
Brougton, Thomas	2	2	3		
Dickerson, John	2	2	1		10
Burgiss, Sanda	1		1		7
Wheeler, Henry	1		4		
Deaver, Steven	1	4	4		4
Lewis, Thomas	1	1	4		
Loney, Lott			2		9
Worfield, Susanah			2		
Worfield, Caleb	1	1	3		
Jane, Thomas	3	1	3		4
Waters, John	1	2	2		
Macklefish, David	1		1		14
Waters, Mary			1		
Pen, Joshua	2		4	1	
Gather, Agness	2	1	5	9	9
Purdy, Henry	1	3	4		
Gather, Zacariah	1		2		3
Ray, John	4		7		
Carr, Walter	2		1	5	
Holland, Henry	3	2	2		14
Ray, Joseph	1		5		
Welch, Edward	1		2		3
Beard, Joseph	1		1		
Whitefoot, Thomas	1		6		3
Whips, John	1	5	2		
Shields, William	1	2	3		10
Howard, Thomas, Sn'	1		2		5
Howard, Thomas, Jn'	1	4	5		
Grunniss, Samuel	1	1	5		2
Ray, John Sheckels	1		1		40
Ridgley, Lucy			5		1
Grahame, James	2		5		10
Simpson, William	3		3		
Calwight, Leonard	3		3		
Thompson, Henry	1		2		

NAME OF HEAD OF FAMILY.	Free white males of 16 years and upward, including heads of families.	Free white males under 16 years.	Free white females, including heads of families.	All other free persons.	Slaves.
Thompson, Zacariah	1	1	3		6
Banks, Mury	2	2	3		8
Wellen, William	2	1	6	4	13
Ridgley, William	5		3		3
Howard, Joseph	1		3		13
Baker, John	1		2		
Waters, Henry	2		2		
Kendel, John	1	1	2		
Hening, Elizabeth		3	4		
Ryan, John	2		5		
Worthington, Walter	3	1	1	1	5
Conner, Laurance	1		1		
Holland, Joseph	1		5		
Mayo, John	1	2	5		
Hazard, John	1	1	1		
Forsythes, John	1		1		
Isral, Bazel	1		2		5
Isral, Robert	4	1	2		9
Carr, Isaac	1		2		
Burgess, Vachel	1	2	3	1	2
Dorsey, Thomas	1		3		9
Ridgley, William, of W⁼	1	3	3		
Spurrior, Thomas	3	2	2		1
Dells, John	3		1		
Dells, James	1		6		
Spurrior, Joseph	1		7		
Hood, Edward	1		4		
Ridgley, Margaret	1		1		
Macklefish, Henny	1		4		
Gather, Rezin	1		4		
Ridgley, Bazel	1	4	1		
Bann, Philip	1		2		
Burgess, Bazel	1	2	2		5
Dorsey, Ann		1	5		14
Watkins, Nicholus	2		4		
Calvert, William	1		2		
Butcher, John	3	1	2		2
Wilson, John	3	3	6		
Hughes, John	3		2		
Deaver, William	1		2		12
Watkins, Gasaway			2		
Deaver, William	3	3	2		3
Hobbs, William	1		5		
Dorsey, Patt		3	2		7
Ridgley, Hannah			7		1
Worfield, Ann	4		2		10
Treakle, Christopher	1		2		
Treakle, Greenberry	3	1	5		5
Mills, Thomas	2	2	5		
Burgess, Colo' Jne	1		2		15
Green, John, of Richd	1		6		6
Dorsey, Lancelot	3		4		4
Ridgley, Nicholas	1	5	6		1
Barns, Phill	3		2		
Worfield, Vachel	3	6	2		11
Gassaway, Eli	1	2	5		4
Gasaway, Thomas	2		2		9
Worthington, Nicholas	1				
Matheus, Nicholas				9	
Meriah					2
Ridgley, Charles	1	2	2		
Craton, John	1	1	1		
Riley, Mark	1	1	1		1
Mannico, Philip	1	1	2		
Mannico, Philip, Sn'	2	1	5		
Bond, Thomas	2		2		
Wilson, Edward	2		2		
Mackeifish, Abriel	1		3		
Burgess, Joseph	2	2	6		9
Holland, Anthoney	2	1	3		52
Scrivenor, Rebecca	1		2		
Broun, James	2		1		14
Gue, Henry	2		2		
Broun, Frederick	1		2		1
Dorsey, Phelemon	2	1	6		11
Skerritt, William	2		4		9
Dorsey, Joshua	1		2		
Gallant, James	1		2		
Mayo, James	1		2		
Barthelo, Thomas	1	3	3		
Grimes, Greenberry	1		3		
Macdonnald, Francis	1		2		23
Dorsey, John, of Jn°	2	3	6		6
Mockbee, Stephin	2		2		
Mason, Thomas Deaver	2	1	3		5
Howard, Rebeca			2		
Crockett, Henry	4	1	5		
Hobbs, Joseph	1		3		16
Dorsey, Richard	1		3		
Pool, William	1		2		
Pool, James	1		7		1
Worfield, Seth, Jn'	1		2		2
Worfield, Beal	1	2	2		4
Worfield, Benoni	1	3	1		

*Illegible.

ANN-ARUNDEL COUNTY—Continued.

NAME OF HEAD OF FAMILY.	Free white males of 16 years and upward, including heads of families.	Free white males under 16 years.	Free white females, including heads of families.	All other free persons.	Slaves.
Hall, Elijah	5	2	4		
Shepley, Duncan	1	1	4		
Barthelo, Thomas	2	3			
Grimes, George	2	3	1		
Worfield, Eli	2	2	2		
Sanders, Alexander	1	1	1		2
Mcgore, Henry	1		3		
Musgrove, Anthoney	2	1	5		
Musgrove, Samuel, Snr	1	2	2		13
Musgrove, Samuel, Jnr	1	3	3		
Musgrove, Anthoney	2	2	5		
Forrist, James	3		1	1	
Allein, Johnathan	2	1	3		6
Fisher, John	1	3	4		
Worfield, Charles, of Jno	1	3	4		8
Spurrior, Aaron	3	2	6	1	
Bishop, Joshua	3	2	4		
Lightfoot, John	2	4	1		
Dorsey, Vachel, of Jno	2		1	1	
Worfield, Benjamin	2	1			10
Welch, Samuel	1	2	6		
Welch, Charles	4	5	6		
Welch, Philip	3	5	2		2
Ridgley, Eli	1	3	1		2
Poole, William, Snr	1	3	2	2	1 6
Guthriel, Francis Raulings	3	2	5		
Pool, James, Snr	2	2	5		
Beho, Moses	2	4	4		
Welch, John	2	4	1		
Blackburn, William	2	1	7		6
Artison, John	1	4	7		
Worfield, Robert	2	1			
Worfield, Ephram	1		3		
Schogal, Christopher	1	4	5		3
Mulielicks, Thomas	1	2	5		
Moles, Joseph	4	3	6		
Selman, John	3	1			
Bisset, Thomas	2	1	4		6
Clarke, Thomas	1	4	5		
Horris, Scythe	1	3	4		
Wilson, Thomas	1	4	4		
Todd, Sanders	1	1	3		
Todd, Samuel	1	1	3		
Hittle, William	1		3		
Foreman, John	1	1	3		
Allein, John	1	3	3		
Johnson, William	3	1	3		
Hammond, Philip, jnr	4	1	3		10
Hardin, George	1	3	1		5
Hood, William	1	4	5		
Burgess, Joshua	2	1	5		12
Macdonald, John	1	1	5		5
Mackelfish, Richard	1	1	2		
Parker, Gilbert	1		2		
Ellis, Obidiah	4	4	2		
Wayman, John	2		7		12
Dorsey, Lucey B	2	4	8		
Smith, Jno	1		2		
Smith, Mathius	1		2		
Armstrong, James	2	1	2		
Wood, William, 3d	2	2	6		
Fisher, William	1	1	4		
Fisher, Bazel	2		4		
Fisher, John	2	2	4		8
Lett, Obidiah			3		
Collins, Timothy	1		3		
Griffin, James	1		2		
Westuards, John	2		1	1	
Poole, Samuel	1		7	1	
Smith, George	3	1	4		
Monkieth, Robert	1	1	4		
Loar, John	2		4		
Mercer, Welding	1		2		
Deaver, Jonas	1	1	1		
Hipsley, Charles	2		2		
Shipley, Talbert	3		8		
Cook, Thomas	4	1	2		
Goodlin, John	1	1	5		
Worfield, Dr Charles Alexr	3	2	4	3	16
Peddicoat, Tosper	2	2	2		
Hobbs, Thomas	2	1	5	2	
Cramblick, Jacob	3	2	2		3
Cramblick, Henry	3	1	4		
Cramblick, Michael	1	4	3		
Orrions, Charles	3		4		
Gary, John G	1	2	3		1
Barns, Michael	4	6	3		
Hobbs, Henry	4	5	2		
Howard, Joshua	1	2	2		
Traplin, William	3		3		
Hobbs, Noah	2	4	1		
Hobbs, Joseph	3	2	1		
Leatoh, John	1	1			
Higgans, Joseph	1	1	4		
Lyntheoum, Nathan	2		4		
Merryweather, Rubin	2	2	5		38
Gary, William	2	2	1		
Barns, James, of Adam	2	3	7		13
Barns, John	1	1	2		
Laurance, Levin	1	1	3		4
Nelson, Harvey	1	2			10
Bond, Thomas	1	1	2		14
Davis, Henry	1	3	2		
Broun, Frederick	4	2	5		11
Beachgood, Rebecca	1	4	3		
Powers, Stephin	2	3	1		
Lyntch, James	1	2	4		
Bedford, John	1	1	2		
Gather, Thomas	3		2		
Phenton, Thomas	1		2		
Pool, Charles	2		4		
Hood, John	2	1	4		26
Wagers, James	1	6	1		7
Shipley, Adam	2	1			
Hinks, Mary	1	3	1		
Hood, Benjamin	2		4		
Hood, Elizabeth	1				12
Ilams, John	1				
Goldsborough, John	1	2			6
Whips, George	2	4			
Whips, Benjamin	1	5	4		
Frost, William	3	2	4		1
Pool, Richard	2		4		
Hickey, Edmond	4		3		
Fouler, Thomas	2		4		
Pattin, Thomas	1		4		
Barns, Nathan	1		4		
Porter, James	2	4	3		
Mercer, Andrew	2	2	1		2
Butler, William	1		3		
Parlet, Joshua	2		3		
Crosland, George	2		2		
Chancy, Nathan	1		2		
Selby, Eli	4	1	3		
Smith, James	1		5		
Shipley, William, Snr	3	2	3		9
Shipley, Robert	2	4	6		
Shipley, William, jnr	4	5	3		
Long, James	1	1	5		
Mason, Edward	1		4		
Barns, Nathan	1	1			
Thomas, Edward	1	2	5		
Kennesly, Samuel	2	4	3		
Word, William	1	1			
Wuannick, John	1	1			
Dorsey, Edward, of Vachel	1				12
Charles', Free family				7	
Dorsey, Vachel	3	2			19
Tibble, Samuel	1		2		
Limes, Armond	1	3	2		
Wason, Edmond	2		1		1
Millar, John	1		2		
Dorsey, Charles	3	4	6		3
Barns, James	3		3		
Anchor, Edward	3		3		
Barns, Peter	4		3		
Butcher, John	1		3		
Bishop, Sarah	1	2	5		
Hipsley, Benjamin	1		1		
Day, Thomas	2		3		
Barns, John, Snr	3	1	3		
Barns, John, jnr	2		3		
Coll, Michael	2		6		
Bishop, Greenberry	2		4		
Manley, Joseph	1		3		
Jones, John	2		1		
Norwood, John	2	2			12
Jones, Thomas	2	1	5		
Norwood, Belt	2	7	5		5
Pattern, Richard	2		4		
Burgess, Michael	1	2	5		5
Black, Kit	1		2		
Hobbs, Len	1		2		
Booker, Bendigo	2				1
Norwood, Samuel	2	2	3		
Hammond, Charles, of Charles	1	2	3		12
Hobbs, Beal	1	1	2		
Elder, Charles	1	1			14
Green, John	1	1	3		
Elder, Elizabeth	2		3		3
Elder, Elija	1	3	3		1
Thaunton, Joseph	1	3	3		
Fieldings, Jeffery	1	2	2		
Cox, James	1		2		
Barker, Bednigo	3		1		
Stobright, William	4	1	1		
Hobbs, Leonard	4	6	2	2	18
Shipley, Adam	1	3	3		
Shipley, Benjamin	1	1	5		
Shipley, Mary		3	3	1	
Wooding, John	2	2	3		
Weekly, Charles	1	2	3		
Weeks, Ezekel	1	2	3		
Eliott, Daniel	1	1	7	1	3
Whitefoot, David	1	2	4		
Stewine, William	2		3	4	
Howard, William	1				
Negroes, free				5	5
Stinchcomb, Victor		1	2		
Cramblick, Jacob, Snr	1	1	2		
Cramblick, James	1	2	5	2	
Chambers, Amus	1				
Dorsey, Benjamin	1				9
Minchel, Stephen	1		1		
Barlow, Zacariah	4	4	2		
Issacks, Isaac			3		
Bon, Joseph	2	1	2		1
Davis, Thomas	1	2	7		17
Higgans, Joseph	1		1		
Treakle, William	2	3	1		
Leuis, John	1		2		12
Broun, Susanah	1		2		6
Randel, Aquilla	1				
Randel, Nathan	1		1		
Broun, Betty		1	3		1
Randel, John		4	5		1
Davis, Robert	1	2	2		
Davis, Archbad	2	3			10
Cord, Sarah	2		3		
Gather, Ralph	1		1		
Burgue, Robert	1		1		
Evins, Henry	3		2		
Davis, John	2	1	1		2
Burgue, Peter	2	2	1		
Loe, Joseph	2	2	3		1
Broun, Joshua	1	1			7
Nelson, Henry	1		3		
Randel, Beal	1	1	1		
Jones, Samuel	1	1			1
Dorsey, Vachel (Carrols Mannor)	4		7		8
Rathif, Joseph	2	4	5		16
Powers, Stevin		4	5		
Young, William	1	4	3		
Young, Joshua	1	2			
Dorsey, Charles	1	2			32
Worfield, John	1	4	6		
Pumfery, Greenberry	1		5		
Worfield, Richard	1		3		
Forrister, Vincin	1		3		
Bucknoll, James	1		3		
Disney, James	4	2			1
Carey, John	1		1		
Corey, Thomas, Snr	1	3			1
Carey, Thomas, jnr	1	1	6		
White, Elizabeth		1	2		
Disney, John	2	2	1		
Burgess, Thomas	1	2	2		
Philps, Walter	2	1	1		1
Watts, Joshua	1		1		
Ranor, Samuel	1		1		
Ingrime, Snoden	1		1		
Watts, John	1		1		
Watts, Richard			4		
Chancy, Zacariah	1	4	2		
Jones, Richard	2		1		
Widdows, Joseph	2		1		
Mewahaw, Joseph	2	3	1		
Dorsey, Benjamin	2	3	3		18
Frost, James	1		3		
Frost, James, jnr	2		3		
Sewell, James	2		2		
Adair, William	1		2		7
Barry, Bazel	1		2		
Leachfield, John	1		1		
Dunaway, Pearce	1		1		
Ledlow, William	2		2		
How, William		3	2		
Broun, Amos	4		2		
Herculis, Henry	1		4		
Black, Hew	1		4		
Cole, John	1		2		
Spears, Thomas	1	2	3		
Kirk, Thomas	1		1		
Sewell, John	1		2		
Spurrior, William	4	1	6	1	9
Spurrior, John	1	1	2		5
Shepley, John	6	1	8	1	7
Dorscy, Sarah	2		4		7
Hammond, Capt Charles	2	2	3		15
Dorsey, Caleb	1	3	3		37
Howard, Achsah	2	2			9
Dorsey, George	2	2			5
Broun, Samuel	3	4			27
Pue, Dr Michael	3	4	7	1	19
Johnson, Thomas	2	1	4	1	
Martin, Peter	1				

ANN-ARUNDEL COUNTY—Continued.

NAME OF HEAD OF FAMILY.	Free white males of 16 years and upward, including heads of families.	Free white males under 16 years.	Free white females, including heads of families.	All other free persons.	Slaves.
Howard, Joseph	2			4	27
Macgill, Sarah	1			3	25
Worthington, Thomas of Nicholas	1	4	6	1	15
Odle, Richard	1	4	6		10
White, Charles	2	4	5		9
Leichfield, John, Sn.	1		2		4
White, Francis		4	2		1
Litchfield, John, jn.	1	2	1		
Worthington, Thomas, of Jn.	1				12
Worthington, Vachel	1			2	10
Macfarding, Samuel	2	1	3		
Dorsey, Amos	1	1	4		18
Kirby, Joshua	1	1	1	2	
Wilson, William	1		1	2	
Dorsey, Eli	1		2		49
Cass				3	
Davis, Eli	1	5	2		
Deppy, Mary			1		1
Howard, Brice	2	3	7		29
Dorsey, Michael	3		4		7
Talbert, Richard	2	6	3		4
Dorsey, Vachel, jn.	2	1	1	1	17
Bussy, Samuel	1		2		
Frost, John	1	1	4		10
Dorsey, Henry Woodard	1	2	4		
Conroy, Barnaby	1	5	3		
Jones, Christopher	1		2		
Baxter, Patrick	1	1	1		
Grimes, John	1		2		
Parepoint, Henry	1		2		
Read, Jacob	1	5	3	1	
Hobbs, John	2	3	6		
Molhearn, Bernard	1		2		
Dun, Patrick			1		
Hines, Acha	1		1		
Scott, Adam	2	3	2		1
Mathiott, George	6	3	1		
Bolestine, Batholemue	1	3	2		
Gillingham, James	6	2	3		1
Maslan, Isaac	3		3		
Simmons, Abraham	2	4	4		
Talbert, John	1	2	2		
Porter, Nathaniel	1	1	2		
Young, Jacob	1		3		
Young, Richard, Sn.	1	1	4		
Fonel, William	1		4	2	1
Davis, John	1		1		
Wilson, Mathew	1		4	6	
Beall, Russel		2		2	
Frank, Old				2	
Johnson, Joseph	1	1	2		
Kirby, John	1		2		
Young, Richard	3	3	2		
Chamberlin, Sam¹	2		4		
Crumlot, Caleb	2		4		
White, John	2	3	6		
Jones, Jacob, of W.			1		
Jones, Ann, Widdow of W.			1		6
Jones, Elisha	1	2	2		
Stark, Samuel	1		1		
White, Thomas	1	4	3		
Evans, Leuis	2	1	3		
Eliott, Judas	1	1	1		
Wilderman, Jacob	2		5		
Marriott, William	1		2		
Hoof, John	2	1	2		
Green, John	1				
Shutzy, Charles W.	1		3		
Evans, Josep.	2	3	6		
Broun, Valintine	1	4	4		1
Carr, James, Sn.	1	2	3		
Carr, James, Jn.	1	2	3		
Jones, Zinmiah	2	3	3	1	
Dean, Joshua	2		3		
Dean, Robert	1		2		
Harp, Joshua	1				
Harp, Thomas	1		5		
Williams, John			2		
Jones, William of W.	3	4	4		
Cannon, William	2	2	1		
Jones, Samuel	1		5		
Gardiner, Catharine			2		4
Cummins, Margarett	2		3		16
Eliott, James	4	2	2		
Kirby, Moses	1				
Dorsey, John Worthington	1	4	3	1	20
Ridgley, William, jn.	1		5	1	5
Dorsey, Caleb of C Beal.	3	4	3	1	22
Frost, John	2		3		9
Fox, Charles	2	2	5	1	
Rough, Edward	1		1		
Dorsey, Miss Lucey	1		1	1	13
Porter, Charles	2	3	4		2
Shecks, John	2	1	2		
Leatherwood, Thomas	1	5	4	1	7
Dabs, John	1		4	1	
Parepoint, Joseph	1		1		4
Holland, Jacob				2	
Scott, Mary	2		2		8
Bunigin, John	2	1	2		
Parepoint, John	2		3		
Stewart, Robert	2	1	4		
Kelly, Dennis	3	4	6		
Porter, Richard	3	4	6		
Harrison, George	1	2	2		
Conner, William	1	1	1		
Haywood, William	3	2	5		
Smith, Noble	1	2	2		
Elmore, James	1		4	1	
Allibone, Benjamin	1	1	1		
Jones, Agniss			5		
Clarke, Isaac			6		
Gasaway, Nicholas	2		5	1	1
Worm, Jacob			5		
Parepoint, Jemima			1		
Scot, William	2	1	7		8
Shipley, Samuel	3	3	4		
Shipley, Joshua	1	1	1		
Collings, Daniel	1		4		
Wable, Adam	1	2	4		
Martin, Erenius	7	1	5	1	4
Porter, Nathaniel	1				
Hutson, Robert	4		3		
Harvey, Thomas	1	1	3		
Barns, Hew	1	1	2		
Allein, John	1		3		
Crumvel, Olever	1	2	2		
Dorsey, Edward (Iron-head)	4		7	18	64
Elmore, James		2	3		
Riston, Henry	3	1	4	1	5
Griffith, Dennis	3	1	6		
Taylor, William	1		2		
Scott, Richard	1	3	2		
Wade, Walter	4	6	2		
Davis, Joseph	4	1	5		43
Dorsey, Elizabeth			2		
Squires, William	4	1	3		16
Nelson, Henry	1	3	4	5	17
Stringer, Richard	1		4		
Hoofnogan, George	1	2	5	1	4
Griffith, Charles, Jn.	1				2
Haslip, Reason	1	1	5		1
Cadle, Griffith	1	2	3		
Simpson, Sarah	1		3		
Worfield, Richard	2	2	3		
Welch, Ann			1		
Ledlo, William	1		1		
Donaway, Pearce	1		1		
Scott, Samuel	1	5	1		
Pigman, William	1		4		
Maccauley, James	1	2	4		
Carroll, Charles	2	1	3		
Polun, Mary		3	4		
Drummond, Hugh	3	2	3		11
Cole, Thomas	1		4		
Leachfield, William	2	2	2		
Hamilton, John	1		3		
Leachfield, John	1		3		1
Westly, William	1	3	4		
Ridgley, Richard	2		6		24
Davis, Mathias	1	1	3		
Dorsey, Beal	1				22
Ridgley, Sarah	1		4		12
Borry, Bazel	1		2		
Savage, William	2				
Egeland, William	3	1	2		16
White, Joseph	3	4	3		
Bateman, William	2	4	3		11
Hammond, Nathan	1	1	2		5
Dorsey, Loyd	3		2		
Brooks, William	3	1	2		5
Gather, Thomas	1		3		
Edmonson, James	1	2	3		
Wood, Thomas	3	2	2	2	7
Martin, John	1	2	1		
White, James	2	4	5		
Leachfield, William	1	3	2		
Hamilton, John	1	2	2		
Spears, Thomas	2		4		
Gardiner, William	2	1	4		
Thompson, William	2	1	4		8
Dorsey, Nicholas	2	1	4		20
Hobbs, Charles	1		2		
Gozogan, Robert	1				
Ducker, Elizabeth			3	1	7
Duvall, Jacob	4	3	4		1
Sappinton, John	1		4		
Worfield, Vachel	2	1	4		10
Sappington, Caleb	1		5		3
Long, James Disney	1	2	2		3
Clarke, Benjamin	2		5		2
Ridgley, John	2	4	3	1	2
Ridgley, Nicholas	2	3	6		1
Ridgley, Greenberry	2	3	6		
Mitchel, David	2		5		
Disney, Richard, jn.	1		3		
Arnold, William	2		3		
Patteson, George	2		3		
Ham, William	1		4		
Raldings, John	2		5		
Birchhead, Abraham	2		3		
Bedford, John	1		1		
Disney, Richard	1	2	2		
Iiams, John	1		3		4
Purdea, Henry	1		3		
Gather, Joshua	1	2	4		
Rian, Jacob	1	2	2		
Smith, Edward	2		2		4
Porter, John	3	2	2		7
Marriott, Sylvanus	1	1	7		
Danison, Thomas	2		2		
Sappington, Margaret			1		1
Mollinee, Leonard	1		1		3
Sappington, John	2	3	7		5
Wheeler, Richard	3		3		
Worfield, Joshua	1		3		
Danison, Joseph	2		3		
Marriott, John	1		3	1	11
Marriott, Richard	1	1	2	1	7
Broun, Benjamin	1	2	3		2
Case, Thomas	2		3		
Survoy, Sarah				8	
Griffith, Eli	4		2		4
Williams, Benjamin	2	1	4		
Newcomb, Samuel	1				
Yieldhall, Thomas	1				
Butt, John	3	1	1		
Griffith, Charles	3		1		16
Griffith, Robert	1	1	3		1
Watts, Richard	2		1		
Bucknall, James	1		6		
Hood, Robert	1	4	6		
Pumfery, Greenberry, jn.	1		2		
Worfield, John	1		4		
Worfield, Richard	1		2		
Hood, John	1	2	3		
Forrister, Reason	1		2		
Deodiston, William	2		4		
Rolls, Nehemiah	3	1	4		1
Rolls, William	1	3	4		2
Hood, William	1	3	5		
Martin, Richard	1	1	1		
Cunningham, Michael, Jn.	1		1		
Forist, Winson	1		1	2	6
Forister, Jacob			4	3	
Summers, James Dent	1		4		
Worfield, Richard				3	
Collings, Sarah			4		7
Spurrior, Thomas	2	5	4		3
Spurrior, Reason	1		2		
Eliott, John	1	2	2		
Birk, John	1		3		
Whittle, David	1	5	5		
Hood, Liddy			5		
Leatherwood, Mary			5	1	
Birchhead, James	1		3		1
Reynolds, Robert	3		3		
Reynolds, James	3	4	2		
Plummer, William	2	1	2		
Reynolds, Rebecca			3		
Christwell, Andrew	1				
Reynolds, John	1		2		
Britton, James	3		1		
Plummer, Priscilla	1		4		5
Plummer, John	1	3	4		
Forister, John	1		3		
Forister, Joseph	1		4		
Forister, Leak	1		4		
Forister, Jacob	1		4		
Forister, William	2	3	4		
Foster, John	1		4		
Hall, John	1	2	3		
Hall, Edward	1		4		
Walker, James	2		5		6
Forister, Johnathan	1	1	5		
Martin, Richard	1	2	3		
Miles, Samuel	1		1		
Dumer, Thomas	1		4		
Reynolds, Tobias	1	1	4		

ANN-ARUNDEL COUNTY—Continued.

NAME OF HEAD OF FAMILY.	Free white males of 16 years and upward, including heads of families.	Free white males under 16 years.	Free white females, including heads of families.	All other free persons.	Slaves.
Dicas, Jacob	1	3	3		
Plummer, Daniel	1				
Foster, Hannah			2		
Reynolds, Nicholas	1	3	1		
Godman, Samuel	2	4	2		6
Joe, free negro				4	
Sall & family				3	
Bet & family				7	
Tob. & family				6	
Connally, Barnabey	1		3		
Bernet, John	1		4		
Worfield, Nicholas R	1		1		
Foster, Ross	1	2	3	5	27
Bebs, John	1				
Conaway, Robert	2	3	1		
Appyby, Begnnal	1	2	1		
Belt, John Sprigg	2		1		6
Spurrior, Edward	2	1	1	2	4
Ham, Mary		3	1		4
Streeks, Francis	1	1	1		
Waters, Philip	3	1		4	1
Fitzgenior, John	1		4		
Morton, Robert	2				
Dorsey, Robert	2				1
Dorsey, Maj Richard	1	1	5		1
Shellhammed, George	1	1	3		
Magcill, Patrick	1		4		12
Mercer, William	1	2	2		
Lane, James	1	1	2		3
Todd, Thomas	1	2	6	1	
Jenstone, Thomas	1	2	2		
Gulm, Edward	3		2		16
Cooley, David	1	1	2		
Richard, free negro				5	
Cook, James	1	3	3		
Moore, William	1		3		
Maddin, John	1		6		
Boor, Isaac	4	4	4		
Williams, Ennion	4		4		
Johnson, Horatia	1	4	4	2	9
Roberts, Thomas	2		2		
Farebank, John	1		3		
Clarke, John	1		1		
Caples, William	2	2	7		18
Hopkins, David	3	2	7		1
Luster, John	1		1		
Dorsey, Edward, of Jno.	1		2	1	13
Paul, free negro				4	
Betsey, free negro				4	
Igle, John	3			4	
Bayer, William		2	3		
Forrister, Nicholas	1	1	3		1
Forrister, William, jnr.	1		1		
Forrister, George	2	3	3		
Forrister, Benjamin	2		2		2
Gardiner, Mathew			4		
Forrister, John	1	1	1		
Stockston, John	1		1		12
Watts, Samuel	1		2	4	
Barton, Kizy				5	
Gardiner, Nancy				4	
Ball, William	1	1	1		10
Button, Thomas	1		1		
Rush, Stephen	1		1		
Joice, Thomas	1		3		
Ranor, Benjamin	2	1	2		
Joice, Nathan	1		3		
Walker, Susanah			4	7	7
Cromvell, Richard	2	1	2		21
Dorsey, Nicholas	1		2		
Harris, William	2	1	2		
Pitchard, John	2	1	2		3
Mesk, William	1		1		
Sterrets quarter					9
Perry, Samuel	2		3		
Mercer, Peregrine	1		3		
Trayhound, John	1	1	3	3	10
Johnson, Bazel	1	2	2		
Kilso, James	1		2		11
Walker, John	1	1	1		18
Right, Benjamin	1		2		10
Hammond, John	2	4	4		23
Boyer, Nicholas	1		2		
Pattison, Ann		1	2		
Ranor, Benjamin	1	2	2		1
Smith, Daniel	8		3		
Crumull, Thomas		2	3		
Pumfery, William	2	1	5		10
Pumfery, Ebeneser, Snr.	2	2	2		12
Killy, Patrick	1	1	1		
Stewart, Ebeneser	1	5			
Stewart, Joshua	1		1		
Stewart, James	1		5		
Hawkins, Joseph	1		2		
Hawkins, Aaron	1	3	3		
Hawkins, Samuel	1	3			1
Hawkins, Thomas	3	1	2		
Bryan, Liddy			1		
Marriott, Ann			1		
Lynthecum, Amasa	2		2		
Bonner, Mathias	1		2		
Thaunton, William	1	1	2		
Laurance, Francis	1		2		
Hodge, Joseph	1	2	4	1	
Smith, Daniel, jnr	1	1	2		3
Joice, Rebecca	2	1	3		
Cammel, Joseph	2		2		
Hawkins, James	2	2	2		1
Alderidge, Joseph	2		1		
Mewchace, David, jur.	1		1		
Mewchace, David, Snr.	4	1	3		
Dicas, James	1	2	3		
Meak, John	1		1		
Yieldhall, Samuel	2	6	3		3
Cann, Gross				3	
Benson, Richard	1	5	5		
Merrikin, Capt Joshua	2		2		25
Dorsey, Edward, of Jno.	1		1		
Dorsey, Henry, of Edwd.	1	3	2		13
Pumfrey, Edward	2		5		
Stewart, David			1		
Stewart, Charles, son of Davd.	2		1		6
Stewart, Ezekel	2		2		1
Stewart, Ezekel, jur.	2		2		
Ashbough, George	2	4	2		5
Rolis, John	1	3	2		
Berryman, Jane			5		
Northcoat, Thomas	1		1		
Broun, John				5	
Lynthecum, Abner	1		2		
Brewer, John	1	3	4		
Brewer, Nicholas	1	1	5		
Foreman, William	1	1	1		4
Stewart, Joshua	1	1	2		
Vinhams, Nathan	1		3		
Gray, Joshua	2	2	3		2
Apleby, Reason	1		2		
Gray, John	2		2		
Lynthecum, Admiral	1	2	2		
Jacobs, Samuel	1	2	2		
Joice, Jacob	3	2	2		2
Ritchardson, James	1		2		
Laury, Joseph	2	2	4		
Pumfrey, Edward	1	5	2		3
Pumfery, Joseph	1	1	2		
Mathews, Isaac	2		1		
Jacob, Zacariah	3		1		8
Hall, Hannah	1		1		
Fish, William	1		1		
Wood, John	1	2	2		1
Herrington, Thomas	1		4		
Hall, Jess	1	5	4		7
Mayo, Mary	1	3	2		
Fouler, John	2		2		10
Mayo, Thomas	1		1		
Merikin, John	1		4		
Conaway, Charles	1	1	2		
League, James	1	2	2		
Grimes, Vinion	2	1	5		1
Lovet, John	1		2		
Jones, Benjamin	1		4		
Ashpaw, Henry	1	1	2		
Mattimore, James	1		4		
Williams, John	1	1	4		
Marah, William	1	1	4		3
Horner, Sarah	1	2	2		
Jacob, Richard	4	2	6	1	14
Jacob, Dorsey	4	2	3		
King, John	2	3	2		
Mathews, Isaac	2	2	1		
Trotman, John	1		2		
Urqueheart, Jane		3	5		
Gather, Reason	1		5		8
Gather, Seth			4		
Hall, Joe	1	1	2		2
Iiams, Rebecca	2	1	4		
Sintax, John	2	1	3		3
Maccubbin, Edward	1		4		
Godman, Edward	1		3		
Johnston, Benedict		1	1		
Younger, Nehemiah	2	1	4		
Henahall, Ann			2		
Pumfery, William	1	2	2		10
Boon, Richard	2		5		
Williams, Bryan	3	2	4		
Williams, Nathan	2	1	2		1
Williams, Naamond	2		4		
Williams, Nicholas	2	2	4		
Wormsley, Richard	1		2		
Vessels, Shederick	1	2	1		
Ridgley, Mordeaca	1		1	1	1
Boon, John, Jnr	3	2	4		
Boon, John, Snr	5		4		10
Foreman, John	1	1	1		
Stansbury, Joseph	1	1	3		7
Cauley, Jame	1	3	2		
Cromwell, John	2	2	3		
Cromwell, Joshua	2	3	8	1	4
Smith, Reason	1	2	2		
Stevins, John	1	1	2		
Cromwell, Francis	2	2	3		6
Fossell, Thomas	2	2	1		
Robinson, Neal	2		1		
Robinson, Thomas	2		4		
Bonedy, James	1		1		
Kimbles, Roland	1	1	1		
Collings, George	1	1	2		
Jub, Susanah	5		2		
Reaves, John	2	1	4		
Suffield, Samuel	2		1		
Meliar, Jess	1	3	2		
Harris, Isaac	4	1	1		3
Shriver, Jacob	2		1		
Collings, Zacariah	3		3		
Farebrother, Francis	2		2		
Shriver, Francis	2	1	2		1
Foreman, Leonard	2	1	2		
Gray, Greenberry	1		2		
Gray, Elijah	1	1	2	1	5
Foster, Susanah	2		2		
Todd, Lancelot	2				4
Conaway, Vachel					1
Conaway, Asy	1	2	5		1
Gray, Rachel		2	3		
Smith, Milky	2		3		
Todd, Elizabeth	1	2			
Wood, William	2	1	3		
Ashley, Zacariah	3		3		
Crumwell, Neal	1	1	1		
Moore, William	1		1		
Smith, Patty			5		
Crane, Samuel	1	4	3		3
Hermon, William	4	1	3		
Gray, Zacariah	1		3		7
Gray, Sarah	1	1	2		15
Marshall, Edward	1		2		
Phillips, Benjamin	1	1	2		2
Little, Rachel	2		5		
Deny, Mary		2	2		
Hannock, Samuel	1	2	2		
Marsh, Joseph	2	1	2		
Shepherd, Kitty	2		4	1	
Jacobs, Joseph	2	1	4		4
Marsh, William	1		3		
Marsh, Richard	2		2		
Little, Robert	1		5		
Gillis, Kate			1	2	
Phillips, John	1	4	2		
Black, Thomas	2	4	5		
Alwell, Sarah		2	5		
Fox, James	3	1	1		1
Sumbler, Francis	1		3		
Halloway, Daniel	1		5		
Phillips, Paul, Snr	1	1	3		3
Phillips, John	2		4		
Atkinson, Francis	1	2	4		
Anthoney			2	5	
Hincock, Ann	1	3	1		
Shepherd, Nicholas	2		4		13
Phillips, Samuel	1		2		
Hector				4	
Bond, Richard				6	
Gambrel, Reason	1		2		18
Worthington, William	1	2	3		18
Griffith, Henry	1		2		
Hicks, Lasarus	1		2		
Jacobs, Joseph	1	1	6		4
Yieldhall, Samuel	2		6		
Laughton, John	1		2		
Shepherd, Ruth		3	2		
Spicer, William	1		3		
Maccubbin, John	2		3		2
Weeding, Richard, jnr.	1		4		
Shont, Henry	4	1	5		23
Merrikin, John, Snr	1	4	5		11
Spicer, William	1	2	5		
Moss, James	1	7	5		12
Small, Helling	1	4	2		5
Weeding, Richard, Snr.	4	1	3		5
Ridgley, Peregrine	2		4		9
Leader, Mary	1	3	3		6
Rideout, John	3		1		33
Stewart, John	1		1		
Lewis, Sarah	1	2	1		
Wood, Henery	1	1	2		8
Evit, Mary			2		
Todd, Ann	1		1	3	
Watts, Isaac	1		1		10

ANN-ARUNDEL COUNTY—Continued.

NAME OF HEAD OF FAMILY.	Free white males of 16 years and upward, including heads of families.	Free white males under 16 years.	Free white females, including heads of families.	All other free persons.	Slaves.
Allein, John	2	4	3		
King, John	1	1	1		
Hall, Rose	1		1		
Duvall, Zacariah	2		4		11
Duvall, Enus	1	3	1		16
Selby, Ann	2	6	2		
Risten, Richard	1		1		
Smith, Bazel	1	2	2		14
Adams, Joshua	3	1	3		
Maccauley, Thomas	1		3		
Philips, Umphery	2		3		
Philips, Paul	1	1	1		1
Allein, Mary	1		4		
Ray, Tess	1		1		
Jones, Benjamin	1	2	3		
Vessels, Elijah	1	1	3		
Robinson, Elijah	1		5		27
Fetts, Susanah	2		4		10
Pumfery, Walter	1		3		
Maccoy, Alexander	1	1	4		1
Pitts, Thomas	1	1	2		
Fields, Jacob		1	2		
Bazel, James	2		1		
Bazel, Joseph	2	1	4		1
Bryan, John	3	1	1		
Dennison, Aaron	1		6		
Rawlings, Richard	2	1	2		
Hancock, Stephin	2	4	7		3
Butcher, Benjamin	1		3		
Sembline, William	1		4		
Henshaw, Bazel	2		5		
Atwell, Richard	1	2	2		4
Hammond, John	1	1	4		
Penny, Charles	1	2	2	1	2
Ryan, John	1	2	2		
Atwell, William	1		2		
Collings, James	1		1		
Collings, John	1	1	2		
Hancock, Nathaniel	2	3	8		8
Maccubbin, William	2	1	4	1	21
Stevins, Jane					
Burton, William	1				
Fouler, Samuel			2		
Johnston, Benedict	1		2		
Chaney, Able	1	1	2		
Robinson, Charles	2	1	5		10
Johnson, Elija	1		2		
Chaney, Richard	1	1	2		
Johnson, Joshua	1	1	2		
Robinson, Dennis	1	1	2		
Robinson, Richard	1		4		
Vinheard, Abraham	1		4		5
Johnson, Charles	2	1	1		
Johnson, Johnathan	3	1	4		
Robinson, Charles, Snr.	2				
Hefmon, Michael	2		2		15
Waters, Charles	1	1	1		
Lensteed, Elizabeth			4		
Godman, Edward	1		4		
Godman, Tabus	1		4		
Turner, Jane		2	3		2
Todd, Sarah			1		2
Rockwood, Thomas	2		1		
Phelps, William		2	1		
Penny, John	1				
Smith, Topping	1		2		
Robinsons, Vachel	1	3	1		
Edge, Thomas	1	2	1		
Robinson, Luke	2	2	6		1
Hallonhauk, Daniel	1		4		
Maccubbin, Joseph	4				14
Fennel, Caleb	1		2		6
Duvall, Ephram	2	3	3		7
Robinson, Hampton	2		3		
Crane, Ezekel	1	1	4		
Robinson, George	3		2		
Foreman, Joseph	3	3	4		2
Simpson, Mary	2		3		
Holland, Edward	3	2	2		
Moss, Robert	3		5		
Hermon, Susannah	1		5		
Watts, Richard	2	1	1		11
Pinnington, William	2	2	3		
Moss, Richard	1				
Key, Philip	1				9
Watts, Francis			1		
Little, Siss		1	4		1
Riston, Benjamin	2		1		
Spriggs, Samuel	1	1	4		
Gardiner, Benjamin	2		4		

NAME OF HEAD OF FAMILY.	Free white males of 16 years and upward, including heads of families.	Free white males under 16 years.	Free white females, including heads of families.	All other free persons.	Slaves.
Pine, Ezekel	1	1	4		
Baly, Thomas	1	1	2		
Mackey, Stephin	4	2	2		7
Francis, John	1				5
Wakins, Sarah			3		
Sanks, George	3		3		
Hammond, Mary		2	3		6
Hall, Rosanah	2		1		
Boon, Charles	3	5	2		20
Boon, William	2		1		
Taylor, Sarah	2	1	4		
Boon, Stephin	2		2		15
Gardiner, Thomas	1		4		
Hall, Elisha	1	1	1		2
Timmins, Edward	1		5		5
Gardiner, Richard	1	3	2		5
Snoden, Milkey	1		1		
Gardiner, Thomas	1	2	4		
Todd, Ezekel	1		3		
Todd, Thomas	1	1	1		1
Smith, Henry	1		3		
Souards, Daniel	1	1	1		
Souards, James	1		2		
Souards, Solomon	1	2	2		
Brignal, Daniel	3		3		
Adams, Sarah			7		
Mattiore, Thomas	2	2	2		1
Phips, Leuis	1	2	3		
Souards, Daniel, jnr.	1	2	1		7
Stinchcomb, Thomas	2	1	4		1
Kirby, Jane	1		1		
Carroll, Daniel	2	1	2		
Merrikin, John	2	2	3		12
Small, John	5	2	2	5	8
Walker, Ann			4		
Seuell, John	2	1	4	1	7
Marriott, John	1		2		5
Fouler, Hamistual	1		3		1
Dorsey, Henry Hall	2				
Templeman, William	1				
Seuell, Augustine	2	1	2		4
Yieldhall, Sarah	1		1		
Raulings, John	1		2		
Ridgley, Henry	3	2	6		3
Cauling, James	3	2	2		
Gamberil, Benjamin	3		2		
Williams, John	3		2		6
Collings, Richard	1		3		
Tilly, Jasper Edward	1		2		2
Cross, John	1	3	2	2	3
Lusbey, Samuel	1		2		26
Yieldhall, Benjamin, Snr.	2	1	4		
Meak, Joseph, Jnr.	1		2		
Yieldhall, Benjamin, jnr	1		1		
Hammond, Reason					131
Peavie, Daniel		3	3		
Leuis, John	1	1	1		
Higgens, Joseph	2				
Hammond, Philip	2	5	2		90
King, Thomas	1	1	1		
Clarke, Edward	2	1	4		
Hughes, James	2		3		
Kirby, John	1		1		
Harding, Nicholas, jnr	3		1		
Harding, Nicholas, Snr	3		2		3
Davis, William	1		2		
Barntt, Edward	2		2		
Harris, William	1	2	1		
Grovier, John	1		2		
Wilson, John	1	3	3		11
Sheckels, Sephus	2		2		
Ilams, William	1		1		
Ilams, William, jnr	1				
Duall, Howard			1	2	
Hesselius, Mary		1	5	2	8
Lusbey, Venien			1		9
Selby, Margarett	1	2	2		6
Gillis, Margarett			4	1	11
Welch, Elizabeth			2		8
White, Richard	1	2	2		
Johnson, Robert	1		1		
Johnson, William	1	1	3		
Johnson, John	2		2		2
Watkins, Rebecce			2		
Barry, John	1	2	3		
Prout, Ann			3	3	
Johnston, Henry	2	3	3		4
Robinson, Laurance	2	3	4		
Nichols, Robert	1	3	2		
Hunter, James	1		3		

NAME OF HEAD OF FAMILY.	Free white males of 16 years and upward, including heads of families.	Free white males under 16 years.	Free white females, including heads of families.	All other free persons.	Slaves.
Raulings, William	1	1	3		3
Johnston, Margaret			3		5
Leuis, Isaac	4	4	4		11
Millar, Adam	3	3	2		4
Baulding, Tyler	1	2	1		
Sewell, Greenberry	2				
Ryan, William	2	2	2		
Carroll, Charles, Esqr	5				316
Thomas, John, jnr	1	1	2		
Madcap, John			1		
Dorsey, Mary		2	3		12
Severn, Richard Dorsey	1				10
Stansbury, John	1		3		
Gale, Ben				2	
Carman, John	1	1	1		5
Hall, John, Esqr	1		1		38
Mclain, John	1				2
Ewell, Soloman	1	3	2		15
Joice, Phillis					2
Maynadier, Henry			2		26
Williams, Eli		1	1		
Joice, William	1	4	5		11
Brown, John	1		3		6
White, Vachel	1		1		6
Brown, Philimon	1	1	1		
Burton, Elizabeth	1	1	3		
M'Cle, John	1	1	2		
Hall, John (Planter)					19
Marriott, Action	1	2	7		6
Watson, Samuel	2	3			1
Jones, George				1	
Chambers, Ned				1	
Willis, Daniel	2		1		
Yieldhall, Robert	1		2		
Burton, Edwinn	1		2		
Charge, Oliver	1		2		
Roll, —— * William	1		1		
Barker, Dr. Jnr.	1		2		
Meak, Aron	2		3	2	
Wee, —— * Thomas	1	1	2		
Meak, Joshua	1		3		
Ringold, Tom					
Broun, Bazel	1	1	2		14
Worfield, Philemon	4		4		5
Baldwin, James	1	3		6	6
Davis, John	1		1		
Baldwin, Henry	4		4		10
Woodward, William, jnr	1		1		
Woodfield, Thomas	2		1		
Sewell, Sarah			3		
Sewell, Ruth			3		
Raulings, Francis	1		2		9
Raulings, Joshua	1		1		4
Carter, Joseph	1		2	1	
Worthington, Nicholas	2		5		84
Madcap, John	1	1			
Stinchcomb, Charles	1		(*)		
Griffth, William	1		(*)	(*)	
Ridden, Henry	1		(*)		
Deaver, Joseph	1		1		
Selby, Johnathan	1	2	1		6
Cradle, Benjamin	2	3	(*)		(*)
Lusbey, Robert	2		3		7
Howard, Widdow	1	2	2		(*)
Noles, Milkey	3	3	3		
Wootton, Thomas	4	1	3		20
Burgess, Caleb	1		1		
Spurrior, Reason	1		4		12
Worthington, John	1		3		52
Worthington, Brice	1	3	4		
Hall, Richard	4		4		
Pumfery, Vachel					1
Ritchardson, John	1	1	3		
Howard, —— *	1		2		
Roston, James	2	3	13		
Maccubbin, —— *	7	1	7		
Richard, Tires	7	1	2		5
Trout, Sarah					23
Quyron, Afflen	2	1	4		7
Stewart, Capt John	2		2		4
Maccubbin, Charles	1	1			
Mihan, John	1	2			4
Savington, John	1	6	5		50
Galloway, John	7	3	(*)		55
Chew, Majr Richard	1				50
Ogle, Benjamin, Esqr	2	1	4		30
Carroll, Nicholas, Esqr			6		9
Chase, —— * Townsend, Esq	1	1	6	1	28
Stewart, —— *	1	1	6	1	15

* Illegible.

BALTIMORE COUNTY.

BALTIMORE TOWN.

NAME OF HEAD OF FAMILY.	Free white males of 16 years and upward, including heads of families.	Free white males under 16 years.	Free white females, including heads of families.	All other free persons.	Slaves.
McMechan, David, Esqr.	3				1
Crookshanks, Charles	2	1	2		9
Man, Anthony	1				3
Coulter, Alexander	5		1		
Vinaud, Jacob	3				
Solomon, Isaac	3		4	1	1
Kimble, Anthony	3	1	6		
Baker, William	2	5	4		3
Davenport, Jonathan	2		4		
Ruby, William	4	3	4		
Dukehart, Margaret		1	4		
Willson, Stephen	2	2	8		
Patton, Mathew	4	5	5		1
Burland, Richard	2	1	2		7
Bary, Standish	4		2		1
Sanderson, Margaret	5	2	2	2	5
Calhoun, James	3		2		3
Lyons, John	3				1
Harling, Susannah			6		
Riddle, Robert	3	1	1		3
Solomon, Elkin	2	1	1	1	
Dixon, Thomas	3			1	
Ball, William	4	2	1		
Justis, Joseph	3	1	2		
Walsh, Robert	1	1	3	1	3
McKim, John	2		1	2	
Adams, Samuel	2			1	2
Grahame, William	2		1		
Meggs, John	2	1	5		
Falford, Mrs		1	6		
Rodnohor, Jacob	2	2	4	1	
Yelser, Frederick	3		5		
Murray, Edward	1		1		2
Dowig, George		1	1		1
Robinson, Samuel	1	1	2		
Fonerdon, Adam	3	3	7	3	
Wells, Cyprian	3	3	4		2
Purley, Paul	1	1	3		
Usher, Thomas	2	2	3		4
Shaffer, Balzer	1	1	2		1
Meaner, Philip	1	1	1		
Casey, Robert	3	2	4		
Brown, Doctr. Geo.	7	1	6		2
Carl, Charles	7		2		
Highshoe, Philip	2	1			
Baker, John	2	2	4		
Hutton, James	1		2		1
Myers, Jacob	1	3	5		
Townsend, Joseph	6	1	4		
Church, Shepherd	2	1			
Jaffray, James	1				5
Leake, Nicholas	1		2		
Rutter, Thomas	4	1	3	3	
Davidson, James	2		2		1
Diffindaffer, Michael	2	4	4		
Prout, William	2				
Tavers, John	1		2		2
Sterling, James	4	3	4		2
Dukehart, Henry	3		4		
Pratten, Caroline		1	2		
Reddick, Mrs			2		4
Torrence, Charles	2	2	5	1	4
Yates, John	1	3	2		
James, Mrs				1	5
Hunter, George	2		2	2	1
Hoffman, Jacob	4	3	3	1	
Woods, William	2	1	3	1	
Diffendafer, Peter	2	1	2		
Sweeney, Hugh	1	2	4		
Bull, James	5	1	4		
Williams, Joseph	4				
Gilder, Reuben	8				
Mathiot, Christr	2	4	2		
Zolekoffer, Conrad	2		2		
Lindenberger, George	7	3		2	
Adams, William	1		2	1	2
Caustin, Isaac	2	4			
Trice, Harman	1	1	3		
Steward, Captain	1		2		
Goddard, Catharine			1	1	4
Barkley, William	5			1	1
Williamson, David	2	1	4		8
Killen, John	2	1	4		
Slater, William	1		2		
Key, Andrew	3	1	4	1	
Jacobs, Moses	3	1	4		
Dusndre, Charles	3				1
Usher, Abraham	4		1	1	
Shultz, John	1		3	1	
Fisher, James	6	3	4		
Boyer, Louis	2		2	1	
Bryden, James	2	2	2	1	
McCreery, Thomas	3		1		1

BALTIMORE TOWN—con.

NAME OF HEAD OF FAMILY	Free white males of 16 years and upward, including heads of families.	Free white males under 16 years.	Free white females, including heads of families.	All other free persons.	Slaves.
Courtney, Robert	3				
Brown, John	2	4	3	1	1
Reid, John G.	1	2	1	1	
Eichelberger, Martin	1	3	7		
McKim, Robert	2				
Willson, William	8	3	2		
Weir, Charles	2	3	1		
Linwell, John	6	1	3		
May, Benjamin	4	1	2	1	2
Pierce, Humphry	3		2		
Bigger, Gilbert	1	1			
Patten, David	2				
Gordon, John	4	2	4		3
Aitkin, Andrew	1	2	4		2
Hollins, John	2	2	2		3
Lynch, John	1	1	1		2
Barney, Joshua	3	4	2	1	2
Barklay, Hugh	3	4	2		
Slubey, Nicholas	3			2	
Van Bibber, Andrew	3		2		4
Van Wyk, William	2	1	4		3
Sterrett, Deborah	3	3	6	2	3
Sterrett, James	1		2		3
Dulany, Daniel	1		3		
Smith, John	6	1	1		9
Purvianer, Robert	2	5	5		4
Williams, Otho H	3	3	3		
Caulk, Joseph	1	1	2		
Shade, John	1	2	1		
De Witt, Thomas	4	2	2		2
Smith, Joseph	1	2	2		
Ratun, Richard	1	2	1		4
Granger, William	1	2	2		
Joiner, Doctr	1	1	1		
Edwards, Thomas	2	1	4		
Hart, Mathew	1	1	2		
Hornbry, Gaulter	1	1	2		
Keeports, George P	1	1	3		
Fisher, John	2	2	2		
Bantaloe, Paul	2	2	6	2	6
Spear, John	3	1	2		8
Sommers, Martin	1	2	2		
West, William	2	1	5		
Frick, Peter	1	1	5		
Prill, Frederick	1	2	4		
Pencill, Balzer	1	2	2		
McEldry, Thomas	3	2	2		3
Wolfendon, Beachamp	3				
Skerrett, Clement	1	1	2		
Franciscus, George	2		4	1	
Pascault, Louis	2		2		2
Salmon, John	1		2		
Donaldson, Joseph	5	4	4		2
Diffindaffer, Daniel	2		4		
Masters, Leigh	3		1	1	
McFadion, William	3		1		
Dizard, Mrs	6		5		
Smith, Samuel	5	2	6		4
Armstrong, David	3		1		4
Wusenthall, Elizabeth	2		3		
Johns, Aquila	3	1	2		2
Burns, James	3	1	2		
Furnival, Alexander	1	1	5	1	
Griffith, Benjamin	4	3	2		2
Shields, David	9		3		
Mattison, Aaron	5	4	3		
Evans, David	2		2		
Day, James	1		2		
Yelser, Englehart	2	1	7	1	
Hildebrand, Jacob	1		1		
McInheimer, Peter	4	2	2	1	
McInheimer, Mrs	4		2		
Hosselfoos, George	4	2	4		
Rutter, Jonathan	1	1	5		
Luson, Mathew	4	1	1		
Bussey, Edward	1	1	3		
Coates, Jonathan	1		1	8	
Purbury, George G	1	1	7	5	
Saunders, Edward	3	4	2		
Botler, Elias	3	1	1		
Youel, William	1		2		
McJilton, Daniel	2	4	2	1	
Philips, Mary			1		
Hart, John	2	1	2		
Nusser, Jacob	3	4	4		
Hagthrop, John	1	1	4		
McConkey, William	1		1		
Berry, William	2				1
Delaport, Frederick	1		2		2
Jacobs, Joseph	2		2		
Warner, George	1		1		
Brandt, George	2		2		
McDaniel, John	1	1	1		

BALTIMORE TOWN—con.

NAME OF HEAD OF FAMILY.	Free white males of 16 years and upward, including heads of families.	Free white males under 16 years.	Free white females, including heads of families.	All other free persons.	Slaves.
Rossiter, Thomas	1		2		1
Edgar, Mark	1	2	2		1
Clifton, Rosin			4		
Markell, William	1	5	1		
Bahon, Stephen	2	1	4		
George, Joseph	2	1	4		
Goldsmith, Copeland	1	4	4		1
Bonell, Thomas	1	1	1		
Thompson, John	1	2	4		1
Messersmith, Samuel	2		4		
Askew, William	2		2		3
Shepherd, Mrs			2		
Beamer, John	2	3	3		
Bull, John	1	4	2		2
Gohogan, George	1		3		
Hopkins, Gerard	4	2	2		4
Lee, Samuel	1	3	1		
Alter, John	2		3		
Millar, William	6	1	2		1
Leavly, Widow	1	1	3		
Jacobs, Barnard	1	1	3		
Course, Mrs	1				
Ridgely, Mrs	3	1	6		3
Ennalls, Andrew S.	1		1		5
Gonsalcs, Joseph	1		1		
Roach, Honor			1		
Stilwell, ——	1	1	1		2
Shrim, John	3		2		
Malcolm, Mr		1	3		
Clansey, Miles	1		2		
Hauser, Jacob	2	1	2		
Grant, Mr	2	1	4		
McCandless, George	5	1	3		5
Hull, John	2	2	3	1	
Deal, Christian	3	1	5		1
Shellar, John	2	1	2		
Snider, Mrs	1		3		
Cassidy, Mrs	2		2		
Lefever, Nicholas	1	1	3		
Jones, Aquilla	3	1	3		
Knox, Nancy			2		
Garnoch, Nicholas	1	1	2		
Richardson, Enoch	1		1		
Coskery, John & James	3	2	2		1
Morris, Mark	1	2	3		
Ross, John	2		1		
Willson, Henry	3	5	4		4
Scott, James	2		1		
Oldham, John	3	2	1		
Titman, Christr.	1	2	2		
Mosler, James	1		2		
Smith, Nathanl	4	1	2		4
Gibson, Joseph	1	1	1		
Helms, Joseph	2		1		
Neal, Mrs			1		
Tap, Charity	1		5		
Mosier, Philp	3	1	1		
England, Abraham	1		1		
Man, Zachariah	1		1	3	
Draves, Mary			1		
Murray, Thomas	1		1		
Sullivan, Timothy	1	1	1		
Segany, Martin	1	2	7		
Strebeck, Christian	1	1	4		
Swift, Mrs	1		4		
Shartel, Erehart	1	2	4		
Harley, John	1	3	3		
Brown, William	2	1	2		
Troarbach, Michael	2	1	2		
Fable, Mr			1		
Fisher, Robert	1		1	1	1
Kuperts, Jacob	1		1		3
Young, Nanny			1		
Pascal, John	1	1	1		
Coffey, Michael	2		2		3
Smith, John			2		
Stevens, Mrs			2		
Rice, Joseph	3	1	3	1	1
Barry, John	1		3		1
Mitchell, John	1		3		1
Hasselbach, John	1		3		
Hagar, Mrs	1		2		
Taylor, Ara	1	1	2		
Lightner, George	1		1	3	
Shaffer, George	1	2	2		
Solzer, Rudolph	1		3		
Adams, Captain	1		3		
Long, Hugh	1	2			
Philips, Becky	1			3	1
Brown, James	4		3		
Harnett, James	3		1		
Roney, Mrs	2	3	1		
Clarke, James	1				1

BALTIMORE COUNTY—Continued.

BALTIMORE TOWN—con.

NAME OF HEAD OF FAMILY.	Free white males of 16 years and upward, including heads of families.	Free white males under 16 years.	Free white females, including heads of families.	All other free persons.	Slaves.
Brown, Thomas				5	1
Boyd, Mrs			2		3
McKim, Thomas	3	1			
Aiken, George	1	1	3	1	
Lavering, Aaron	1	2	3	1	
Stewart, David	4	1	6		10
Taylor, William	2		1		3
Sommerville, James	3	1	2	1	3
Creevey, Hans	1				1
Buchanan, Andrew	2	2			2
Moale, Thomas	2				1
Sadler, Samuel	1		2		2
Clarke, John	2	1	3		
Trotman, John	1	1			
Goldthwait, Samuel	3		1		
Dixon, John	1		3		
McCausland, Marcus	3	2	2	5	
Sloan, James	22	8	3		2
Tinges, John	2	2	2		
Reburg, Christr	6	6	4		2
Read, John	1		1		
Waters, James	2				
Gittings, Richard	2	2	3	1	3
Hollingsworth, Thomas	2	1	4		3
Hollingsworth, Samuel	1	1	5		4
Cruise, Jacob	2	1	1		
Jordon, Dominick	1	3	4	1	
Evans, Joseph	2		2		
Knab, Jacob	5	2	2		
Davey, Alexr W	2	1			
Crosbie, Josias	3	5	4		
Patterson, William	2	5	3		6
Courtney, Hercules	3	1	1	1	3
McKim, Alexr	2		1	1	
Barton, Seth	3				
Kelso, Joseph	1	1	5		1
Campbell, Archibald	2	1	2		6
Leggett, George	1	2	4		4
Buchanan, George	2	1	2		3
Hogan, Edmund	1	4	3		1
Hartman, Paul	4		3		
McCallister, James	2	1	3		
Cannon, Mrs			3		
Ronan, Dennis	2	1	6		
Mackey, John	1	1	2		
West, Mrs	1	1	2		
Brown, Mr	3	1	2		
Rose, George	1	2	3		
Messoneer, Henry	1				2
Pencil, John	3	3	1		
Atkinson, Mr		1	2		
Nathans, Mr	1		3		
Cain, Edmund	1	1	1		
Squires, Mr	1				
Evans, Elijah	2	2	3		
Tull, Mrs	3		1		2
West, Mr	2	1	4		
Bailey, Samuel	2	1	2		
Beamer, Fredk	2	1	5		
Culverwell, Richd	1	1	5		
Dean, Mrs		1	2		
Holbein, Mr	1				
Hensey, Charles	1		1		
Lebold, Mrs			3		
McLure, John	1				
Wallace, Mrs	2		2		3
Parnell, Edward	2	1	2		
Smith, Thomas	2	2	3		
Welsh, Adam	2	2	3		
Run, George	5	3	3		
Thompson, John	8		3		
McClain, Adam	2	2	3		
James, ——	4	3	1		
Williams, John	10	5	5		
Regan, Richard	1	1	2		
Crockett, Benjamin	1		3		1
Ward, Charles	2				
Stewart, Archibald	1	1			
Wallace, Andrew	2	2	2	1	2
Potts, William	2	3	4		3
Lorman, William	3				
Dent, George	1				
Stricker, John	4		4	1	1
Tyson, Elisha	7	3	5	1	
McConnell, Alexr	1	1	3		
Bridenoter, Adam	1	2			
Barge, Andrew	1				
Lavering, Enoch	2	2	2		
Mitchel, John	2	3	1		
Sydnor, Richard	5		1	1	
Ferrall, Mr	2				
Gilbert, Thomas Prior	4	1	1		
Bousman, Lawrence	4	1	3		
Riddlemoser, Michael	1	3	1		

BALTIMORE TOWN—con.

NAME OF HEAD OF FAMILY.	Free white males of 16 years and upward, including heads of families.	Free white males under 16 years.	Free white females, including heads of families.	All other free persons.	Slaves.
Golding, John	4	3	6	1	1
Pawson, Mathew	1	3	3		4
Fisher, John	2		2		
Eichelberger, Jacob	4	2	2		
Buchanan, James	3		5		1
Smith, William	2		1		5
Galbraith, Margaret			2		3
Littlejohn, Miles	2		1		
Hays, John	3	1	2		1
Kingston, Nathaniel	1	1	4		
Jenkins, Thomas	1		2		
McCurdy, Hugh	2	2			2
Hoffman, Peter	4	4	5		
Taylor, Thatcher	2	1			
O'brian, Charles	1				
Towson, Jacob	6	1	2		
Evans, William	4	1	3		2
Johnson, John	2				
Sadler, Thomas	2				
Owings, Samuel	1		5		3
Rogers, Philip	2	5	9	3	1
Lindenberger, George	5				
Mathews, William	4				
Hepburn, Thomas	1		2		6
Davis, Jacob	2		2		
Kirby, Miss			2		
Gantz, Adam	2	2	6		4
Lavering, Nathan	1	1			
Tilliard, William	1	1	5		
Wall, John	2	1	1		
Deal, Chris	1	1	2		
Garts, Charles	10		3		2
Leopold, John	1		2		
Speck, Henry	6	4	2		
Osborn, James	15	3	3		2
Slagle, Christ	2	1	3		
Hawkins, William	8	6	5		1
Usher, Thomas	2	2			
Falls, Moore	2		2		
Merryman, John	2	1	5		7
Pilgrim, Joseph				2	2
Hillen, John	2	1	5		2
Roadslock, George	2	3	3		
Rousel, Louis	1		4		
Davidson, Job	4	5	2		
Smith, Job	3		3	2	
Hopkins, Mrs	1		2		
Redstone, Samuel	1		3		
Duncan, William	1	2	5		2
Calhoun, Mr	1		4		
Mowberry, James	2				
Jacobs, Samuel	1	2	3		
Ray, William	3	2	1		
White, Henry	1	1	3		
Nayhay, John	2	1	1		
Richardson, Daniel	4	2	6		
Taylor, Mathew	1	1			
Reeves, Richard	1		3		
Comperio, John	3				1
Mainwarring, Jacob	1		2		
Hill, Assa	2		4		
Dennis, Daniel	2	1	3		
McCarty, Daniel	2		3		
Baxter, Jacob	1	4	3		
Grant, Daniel	7	2	6		3
Clark, Ambrose	1	5	4		
Rosenstule, George	1	5	3		
Secamp, Albert	1	1			
Dale, James	7		3		2
Benkler, William	2				
Branson, William	5	2	2		
McCannon, James	8	5	2		2
Goddard, William	5	1	2		2
Brown, David	1		3		
Swan, John	2	2	5		3
Swan, Joseph	1				
Collar, John	1		2		
Buzzard, Michael	1	2	2		
Grubb, Peter	2				
Brotherton, Thomas	3	2	4		
Crowan, James	1		4		
Chesroe, George	1		2		2
Tryall, Joshua	1				7
Frogatt, Richard	1		4		
Bosang, Mrs	2	1	1		
Millar, Mrs	1	1	1		
Glassall, William	1		1		
Piety, Peter	1		2		
Nital, John	1	1	4		
Shepherd, John	1	1	2		
Viney, Mrs	1	2	3		
Armige, Anthony	1	1	3		
Vincent, Samuel	1	1	3		

BALTIMORE TOWN—con.

NAME OF HEAD OF FAMILY.	Free white males of 16 years and upward, including heads of families.	Free white males under 16 years.	Free white females, including heads of families.	All other free persons.	Slaves.
Babarin, Louis	3	1	2		1
Landu, George	3	1	4		1
McConcey, Mrs	1		3		
Lucas, Francis	1	1	4		
Powell, Mrs			4		
Piper, Mrs	2		2		
Henry, Charles	2				
Deshang, Peter	1		4		
Prishoe, Mrs		1	3		
Arsali, Peter	1		1		
Murphy, Peter	2	1	3		
Ford, Mr	1		1		
Thompson, Mr	4	1	1	2	
Creek, Joseph	1	1	2		
Goodroe, Mrs	1		2		
Richardson, Mr	1	1	2		
Granby, Daniel	2	2	3		
Murray, Joseph			6		
Robinson, Archibald	2				1
Weaver, Casper	2	3	3		
Hogner, John	1	3	3		
Lacaze, Doctr	1		2		
Leason, Morris	1	1	1		
Roach, John	3	1	2		
Willis, Mrs			4		
Besho, Paul	1		1		
Trout, Mrs		1	2		
Right, Mrs			1		
Gutroe, Mrs		2	3		
Gold, Peter	2		2		
Gutroe, John	2	3	3		
White, Oliver	1	5	1		
Mercer, Benjamin	1		1		
Purie, Peter	1		1		
Munger, Mr	1		2		
Wells, John	1	1	2		
Shamoe, Mrs	1	1	4		
Young, Edward	1	1	2		
Cruise, Englehard	1	1	2		4
Levant, George	1				
Ilgin, George	1		3		
Fouse, Thoobald	1		2		
Swartz, Charles	2	1	2		
Hammond, William	2		3		7
Grose, Mrs			4		
Parker, Mrs	1		2		
Holmes, Mr	1		1		
Brittan, Molly		3	2		
Downey, Mr	1		1	5	
German, Mrs	1		1		
Wagb, Mr			5		
Minich, Balzer	1	1	2		
Kip, John	1	1	6		
White, Joseph	2	5	4		6
McCaskey, Samuel	1		4		
Uhler, Erasmas	9	2	4		3
Hay, Mr	3	1	2		
Rhodes, Louis	2		4		
Donally, Hugh	1		2		
White, Benjamin				6	
Bankson & Lawson	8	1	1		
Gray, John	10	9	7		2
Gray, Samuel	5	3	3		
Bankson, John	1		2		
Martin, Luther	2		5		6
Lawson, Richard	1				
Deaver, John	1	1	2		
Harnett, John	1	3	1		
Smith, Peter	1	4	4		
McGlathery, John	1				
Fisher, John	2	3	3		
Brown, Jacob	4	1	3	1	1
Leavley, George	6	3	7		4
Nicholson, John	4	7	7		2
Grundy, George	3	3	5		4
Beir, Philip	5	2	6		
Wheelan, Richard	1	2	5		
Clemm, William	5	4	2		1
Hessington, William	3				
Poultney, Thomas	2		2		
Procter, John	4		2		
Smith, Mrs			2		
Leakin, John	3	2	2		2
Rice, Joseph	1	2	4		
Brown, Justis	1	2	2		
Pollock, George	1		2		
Lemane, Joseph	1		2		
Barnaby, Elias	2	1	2		
Fluiry, Sebastian	1		1		
Angel, James	1	2	3		1
Swain, Jeremiah	1		2		1
Clements, John	1		3		
Williams, ——	1		3		

BALTIMORE COUNTY—Continued.

BALTIMORE TOWN—con.

NAME OF HEAD OF FAMILY	Free white males of 16 years and upward, including heads of families.	Free white males under 16 years.	Free white females, including heads of families.	All other free persons.	Slaves.
Allison, Patrick	2		1		4
Bankson, Joseph	4	2	2		
Nusser, Sebastian	2	3	1		
Lasurene, Lane	2	1	4		
Hook, Ferdinand	2	2	1		
Graham, William	1	4	2		
West, Mrs		4	1		
Nidew, Mr	1		2		
English, William	1		1		
Jenkins, Cornelius	1	1	1		
Shoemaker, Jacob	1	2	2		
Davidson, Robert	2		1		
Weaver, Mr	1		1		
Foudeberg, Peter	1		1	1	
Walter, John	1	5	2		
Crouse, John	1		3		
Wolf, George	1		1		
Porter, Mr	1	1			
Eagle, Mrs	1	7	1		
Prout, Mr	1				
Hill, James				4	
Ewalt, John	1	2	1		
Forney, John	4		5	2	
Jeffries, William	1	2	1		
Winklar, Anthony	1	2	2		
Bankart, Peter	1	2	7		
Foreman, Leonard	1		3		
Sellars, John	1	1	3		
Shetough, Mr	1		3		
Moore, Thomas	1		3		
George, Yellow				4	
Simpson, James	3		2		
Sindorf, Joseph	1	2	2		
Hutchings, Darcus	1			4	
Peters, Jacob	2	4	1		
Simmering, John	1		3		
Cansman, John	2	1	2		
Sauerman, Peter	1	1			
Burns, John	1		2		
Purpo, Charles	1		2		
Sellars, John	1	1	3		
Peters, Mr	1		2		
Ash, James	1	1	1		
Herren, Tim	3	1	4		
Herrick, John	1	2	3		
Shalley, Adam	2	2	3		
Shalley, Jacob	1		2		
Vantz, David	1	2	3		
Parker, John	1	2	2		
Wildeman, John	1		2		
Shroat, Christr	1	4	4		
Shroat, John	1		1		
Gill, Mr	4	2	7		
Gerry, Mr	1	1	3		
Curtz, Mr	2	1	1		
Latzinger, Mr	1		2		
Beckly, Henry	1	2	4		
Shareman, Henry	2		3		
Lankart, Henry	1	1	3		
Lutz, Mr	1		4		
Smurk, Mrs		1	4		
Eichelberger, Jacob	1	3	3		
Kerb, Doctr	1		5		
Larsh, Abraham	1		2		
Simpson, James	3		1		1
Munro, Samuel	1		4		
King, Thomas	1	1	4		
Wright, Philip	2		3		
Shirt, Jacob	1		4		
Link, Mrs	1	2	4		
King, Mr	1	2	6		
Painter, Henry	2	1	3		
Lenhart, Henry	4		5		
Larue, John	1	4	2		
Somwall, Balzer	2		2		
Demit, Peter	1	2	3		
Hineman, John	1	2	3		
Simmons, James	1		2		
Zitzel, Jacob	1	1	1		
Argents, Harman	1		4		
Hartman, Christr	1		4		
Trumbo, Adam	1	1	3		
Yantz, George	2		4		
Prosser, John	1		2		
Griffin, Thomas	1	2	1	1	
Hardy, Frederick	1	1	5		
Tool, Thomas	1	1	3		
Walter, John	1	1	2		
Bushey, Philip	2	2	4		
Ebert, Martin	3	2	2		
Detterly, John	1	3	4		
Bankson, James	1	1	4		
Wilmore, Robert	2	1	2		

BALTIMORE TOWN—con.

NAME OF HEAD OF FAMILY	Free white males of 16 years and upward, including heads of families.	Free white males under 16 years.	Free white females, including heads of families.	All other free persons.	Slaves.
Eamle, Widow					2
Nelson, Valentine	1	3	2		
Griffin, Osborn	2	1	1		
Pifer, Mr	2	1	2		
Perry, Nicholas	1		1		
Keim, Frederick	1		2		
Craner, Daniel	2	1	3		
Hynes, Solomon		2	3		
Lenhart, Henry	4	3	4		
Purpoint, John	2		5		
Snider, Valentine	2	3	4		
Kellar, John	1	2	2		
Vaughen, John	1	2	3		
Waggoner, John	1		2		
Cooper, Louis	1	1	2		
Johnson, Polly					3
Henninger, John	1	2	3		
Curtis, John	1	1	3		
Hugsh, Conrad	2	3	3		
Metzgar, Barbara			1		
Megan, Peg	1		3		
Dublin, Thomas	1				4
Puntany, Sarah			1		
Williams, John	1	3	3		
Fry, Andrew	2	2	2		
Yeliott, Jeremiah	2	1	2		5
Millar, Jacob	3	1	1		
Hook, Joseph	1	3	4		
Jones, William	3	2	5		
Millar, John	1		3		
Millar, John	1	1	2		
Pitt, David	1	1	1		
Moore, Jacob	1		2		
Fite, Peter	1		3		
Elberger, Mush	1	2			
Cline, Anthony	1		3		
Donavan, Timothy	1		5		
Clarke, William					6
Boyles, Mrs		2	2		
Sensenauf, Adam	1	3	1		
Pitt, Thomas					5
Neal, Hugh	1		3		
Dutero, George	2	1	4		1
Stevenson, Moses					3
Remain, Daniel	1	1	2		
Zitler, Mrs			1		
Burton, Richard	1	1	3		
Jacobs, Patty					6
Wood, Joseph	1	3	1		
Hose, Frederick	1		3		
Stempter, John	1	1	1		
Millar, John	1	1	3		
Calfons, Louis	2	1	1		
Peters, Henry			2		
Ford, Edmond	1	1	3		1
Brand, Jacob	1		2		
Glen, Thomas	1		2		
Grapewine, Frederick	1		1		
Reese, Frederick	2	2	4		
Gill, Thomas	1		1		
Hazard, William	1		3		
Brothers, Henry	1				1
Saltz, Louis	1		1		
Taylor, Richard	1		3		
Harner, John	1	1	2		
Robinson, John	1	1	1		
Reader, Christr	1	2	2		
Burk, John	1	1	1		
Wearley, George	4	3	4		
Baughman, Henry	1	2	3		
Kain, William	1		1		
Barks, Henry	1	1	3		
Burgan, Mr	1	2	4		
McFelon, John	1		2		
Daniel, Isaac					5
Monday, William	1		4		
Shryock, —	1		4		
Nagle, Mr	1	2	4		
Smith, Samuel	1	3	4		1
Wignell, James	2	3	4		1
Forsyth, Alexander	2	4	4		
Close, Christian	3		2		
Schultz, John	3	1	2		
Stoufer, Henry	3	2	4		
Bixter, Christr	1	4	4		
Emerson, Thomas	2	3	5		
Decker, Frederick	2	3	3		
Myers, Christian	2	1	4		1
Wolsh, Philip	6	1	2		
Pixler, David	1	1	2		
Bausman, Lawrence	3	1	2		
Walter, Peter	1	2	4		
Knight, Absalom	1	2	2		

BALTIMORE TOWN—con.

NAME OF HEAD OF FAMILY	Free white males of 16 years and upward, including heads of families.	Free white males under 16 years.	Free white females, including heads of families.	All other free persons.	Slaves.
Brown, Nut			3		
Millar, Adam	1	1	2		
Wright, Frederick	1	2	4		
Leman, Mr	1		3		
Peter, negro (Chs Wells property)					5
Winchester, William	4	4	5		
Jammison, Adam	1	1	3	3	2
Ralph, John	1		2		
Knab, Christr	1		3		
Cooper, John	1		2		
Wall, John	1		3		
Robinson, Ephrain	2		3		1
Deal, Charles	2	3	1		
Allen, James	1	3	3		
Zitler, Mathias	1	2	2		
Wine, Mr. Chris	2	1	1		
Bringle, Mr	1		2		
Lippe, Mrs	2		3		
Sims, Mrs	1	1	2		1
Mathews, William	1		2		
Foreman, David	3		3		
Curry, Andrew	1		1		
Hyans, Solomon	1		3		
Hancha, Ludwick	1	1	3		
Seekwell, Mrs			3		
Dunwoody, James	1		4		
Daufin, John	1	1	4		
Earnst, Michael	1		4		
Kittleman, John	1		4		
Trumbs, John	1	2	4		
Merrica, Charles	1	5	1		
Russell, John	2	1	3		
Horn, Philip	2		1		
Hawkins, Caleb	2		3		
Granger, Joseph	1	1	2		
Ward, Mrs			1		
Russell, John	1	3	3		
Harry, negro				7	
Chester, Samuel	1	2	3		
Calwell, John	1	2	4		
Kilsheimer, Francis	1	2	3		
Williams, William	1	2	2		
Cole, Joshua	1		3		
Richmond, Samuel	1	3	3		
Bates, John	1	1	1		
Berry, Lary				2	
Larue, Francis	1		1		
Speed				2	
Salter, Ellen		2	5		
Brown, Harry	1	1	4		
Brown, Mary			3		
Ford, Mary			3		
Fletcher, Philip	1	2	1	3	
Wilkinson, Jacob			3		
Manie, Thomas	2		1		
Ott, Frederick	1	1	2		
Wells, Benjamin	1		4		8
Graves, negro				2	
Mohler, David	3	1	3		
Sop, Mr	1	1	2		
Marsh, John	1		2		
Butler, John	1		2		
Ridger, John A	1		2		
Moore, Henry	3	2	3		
Sugart, Philip	1		2		
Livers, Arnold	3		2		
Shartel, John	2	1	4		
Randall, Johnsu	2	1	4		
Thornbury, William					
Sides, Aaron	6	2	3		
Selman, Benjamin	1	1	4		
Fox, Anthony	1		1		
Shook, Mrs			2		
Pugh, Joseph	1	1	2		
McCurdy, James	1		3		
Dougherty, John	1		1		
Shriver, John	1		1		
Etter, Henry	1	3	4		
Stacy, Mathew	1	2	4		
Koontz, Jacob	2	3	3		
Adricks, John	1	2	1		
Smith, Samuel	2		1		
Leland, William	1		1		
Manspiker, Henry	1				
Norman, Henry	1		2		1
Downey, Philip	1	2	2		
Stewart, Charles	1	2	6		
Capton, Henry	1		1		
Price, Daniel	1		5		
Haslet, John	1	1	3		
McCisley, John	2	1	2		

BALTIMORE COUNTY—Continued.

NAME OF HEAD OF FAMILY.	Free white males of 16 years and upward, including heads of families.	Free white males under 16 years.	Free white females, including heads of families.	All other free persons.	Slaves.
BALTIMORE TOWN—con.					
Brown, Benjamin				7	
Walker, James	1		2	2	
Kimblemeyer, Frederick	2		3		
Shaw, Mrs	1	1	2		
Scott, John	1	1	2		
Gilbert, John	1	1	2		
Litzinger, George	1	2	4		
Usher, George	1		1		
Keilholtz, ——	1	2	2		
David, Mathew	1	3	2		
Foss, George	1	3	3		
Carroll, Edward	1	2	2		
Daws, Mr	1	2	2		1
Hammond, Isaac	1	1	4		
Randall, Mrs			2		
Allen, Mrs	1	1			
Hanna, Mrs		2	3		
Bagford, William	1	5	7		
Lynn, David	1	1	2		
Wilkins, Isaac	1	1	1		
McLaughlin, Thomas			1		
Adams, Alexander	3	3	3		
——, William	2		2		
Thompson, William	1	5	4		
Thomas, Joseph	1	2	1		
Groce, Anthony	2		2		
Constable, Thomas	5	2	4		3
Slater, Joseph	1	1	2		
Baker, James	1		7		5
McCabe, John	1		2		
Kenedy, Ariana	1	2	3		
Miller, Frederick	1	3	2		
Apperman, Thomas	1	2	1		3
Dickenson, Gideon	3		3		
Clarke, David	1		3		
Laurence, James	1		2		
Nanny				2	
Hoffman, Andrew	1	1	5		
Higgins, Patrick	1	2	3		
Stifer, Daniel	1	2	1		
Tumbletree, Henry	1	2	3		
Rowe, William	1	2	3		
Etaberger, Wolfgang	1	3	3		
Howell, George	1	1	2		
Shepherd, Thomas	2		3		
Underwood, William	2		4		
Enrood, Bluck			2		
Smith, James	2	3	3		
Constant, Richard	1	1	2		
Morris, William	1	1	3		
Bowers, George	1	1	2		
Underwood, Joseph	1	1	3		
Pluck, Andrew	1	1	1		
Pluck, John	1	1	2		
Bowers, Martin	1	2	1		
Shreck, Dedrick	1	1	3		
Blake, William				2	
Harshman, Henry	1	1	4		
Burgess, Thomas	1		4		
McCallister, John	1	1	2		
Doyle, Joseph	1		2	2	
Strider, Joseph	1	3	3		
Maxfield, Widow			3		
Cheney, Hezekiah	1	3	3		
Newcome, Robert	1	2	3		
Taylor, Hannah	1	1	2		1
Tice, John	3	1	4		
McCloud, Sarah			1	2	
Davidson, James	1	2	3		
Bond, Richard	1		3		
Kuner, Peter	1	2	1		
Knox, John	1	1	1		
Dyer, John	1	2	1		
Musser, Laurence	1		2		
Wood, John R	1		1		1
Jordon, Henry	1	1	5		
Delzer, George	1	2	2		
Hattinger, Michael	1		1		
Millar, Jacob	4	4	6		
Million, Patrick	3		4		
Daws, Francis	1	3	2		
Scott, William	1	1	2		2
Myers, Christian	1		2		
Mullen, Patrick	1		3		
Swann, Samuel	1	1	3		
Brown, Bernage			1		
Conner, John	1	1	1		
Trimble, Isaac	3	2	2		
Worthington, Henry	1	2	3		
Roe, Walter	6	2	3		2
Ireland, Richard	3		2		
Jones, Robinson	6	4	2	1	
Yeiser, John	1	2	3		
Demnitt, Jacob	2	1			
BALTIMORE TOWN—con.					
Merryman, Benjamin	1	1	2		
Yeiser, Philip	1	5	2		
Edwards, James	4	2	2		2
Long, James	1	1	3		4
Martin, Samuel	2	2	1		
Mather, John	2	1	2		
Thompson, John	1		3		
Hill, John	1		1		
Aisquith, William	2	1	2		7
Sanderson, Thomas	1		2		1
Weaver, Daniel	3	1	4		
Apple, Christian	1	1	3		
Perrigo, Joseph	1	1	3		4
Davenport, Joseph	1		3		
Sarah					5
Sulzer, Rudolph	1		1		
Cole, John	1	2	2		
Savery, William	1		3	1	
Dobbins, Thomas	1		1		
Carnahan, George	1	2	2		
Willson, David	3		4		
Carr, John	1	2	4		
Kinah				3	
Richards, Parson	1	1	4		2
Davidson, Robert	2	2	4		
Morris, Samuel	2	1	2		
Shrank, Mrs	2		3		
Storey, Enoch	1	2	3		
Shilling, Michael	2	2	2		
Hahn, John	3		2		
Zedekiah				2	
Western, Andrew	2		2		
Ackerman, George	2		1		
Cruse, Jacob	1		4		
Philips, Mary			1		
Reiley, Stephen	1	2	5		
Cole, Frederick	3		1		
Cole, Godfrid	2	2	1		
Cole, Jacob	1	2	2		
Mull, Jacob	1	2	4		
Gisland, Catharine	2	1	1		
McFadion, John	2		4		
Kelly, Elizabeth		2	7		
Millar, Jacob	1		1		
Toole, James	1		4		7
Vaughan, Isaac	3		2		
Griffith, Nathan	2	1	3	3	
Worsing, James	2		3		
Zigler, Henry	2	3	4		
Everhart, Jacob	1		2		
Woman, William	1	1	2		
Bridenbough, John	2	1	5		
Thompson, John	2		4		
Worm, Thomas	1	2	2		
Ball, Thomas	1		3		
Harris, George	1		2		
Millar, John	3		3		
Thompson, Robert	1		3		
Brown, John	2	3	4		
Roley, John	1		3		
Hicks, James	1	2	7		
Selsar, Thomas	1	1	4		
Brown, William	3	1	6		
Piper, George	1	2	5		
Darling Morris	1	1	2		1
Humphrey, Eleaner			3		
Johnson, Israel H	2		1		
Lucas, Philip	1	2	2		
Jackson, Isaiah	2	2	5		
Myers, Jornia	1		2		
Dulany, Peter	1	2	2		
Wheelan, Jacob	2		4		
Harp, Jacob	2		3		
Forsdile, Standiford	1	2	3		
Hacock, John	1		2		
Dalrymple, John	1	3	3		1
Plasted, Mordecai	1		1		
Hallock, Elizabeth		1	4		
Hambleton, John	1	1	1		
Whitaker, Robert	1	1	2		
Lauderman, Henry	5	1	3		
Nugent, David	1		4		
Stull					2
Harrian, Joseph	2	1	1		
Philip, Jacob	1		2		
Kelly, Rose			3		
Saunders, Edward	1	1	2		
Joice, Joseph	1	1	8		
Eisle, John	1		8		
Harrian, Mary			1		
Carson, Andrew	1	1	1		2
Scott, Andrew	1		1		
Stall, Andrew	2	4	1		
Calvin, Daniel	1		1		
BALTIMORE TOWN—con.					
Gibson, James	1	1	2		
Wheelan, Isaac	1		2		
James, George	3	1	2		
James, Samuel	1		2	3	
Brown, David	5	6	4		
Travers, John	4	1	2		2
Mortimer, Thomas	4		4		7
Shryock, John	1	3	3		
McGinnis, Roger			3		
Zigler, John	1		2		
Kellar, John	1		3		
Chahon, David	1		4		
Stall, George	1		1		
Helmer, William	1		2		
Hettinger, Michael	1		1		
Vinegar, Catharine			2		
Page, John	1	3	1		
Porter, Louis	1	1	4		
Hoban, Conrad	1	2	4		
Fox, Richard	1	3	4		
Davis, William	1		1		1
Myers, Margaret	1	1	5		3
Ben, Negro				4	10
Peters, Thomas	1	1	3		10
Baxter, James	2		4		
Redstone, Samuel	2	1	3		
Jalland, John	3		1		2
Sampson, Jacob	1	2	1	3	
Philpott, Brian	3		3		16
Hollingsworth, Zebulon					
Hollingsworth, Jesse	7		3		5
Graybill, Philip	3		1		2
West, James	3				
Shreader, Henry	4	2	3		
Young, Ann			1		
McEheney, James	1	2	2		
Cochran, James	2				
Finagan, Mrs			4		
Darum, Thomas					
Chaney, Mr	2				
Rutter, Solomon	1	1	4		2
Alcock, James	1				
Alcock, William	1	1			
Alcock, Joseph	2				
Alcock, Mansel	1		1		
Belton, William	4	1	2		
White, Martin	1	2	2		
Ross, William	1				2
Weidner, Henry	1	3	3		
Chequire, Charles	3	1	3		3
Zacharie, Stephen	3	2	3		
Vochez, John	2	2	3		2
De Block, Francis	2	1	4		
McDonough, John	1	5	3		
Tschudy, Nicholas	1	1			
Rebolt, George	4		3		
Mickle, John	2	1	3		
Martin, John	8	4	3		3
Stewart, Polly	1	1	3		
Pilkinton, Thomas	1	2	3		
Fosler, Joseph	1	1	2		
Hardin, Abraham				2	6
Nanny					6
Allen, John	1	1	4		
Shannon, Michael	3	2	5		
McCallister, Mrs			2		
Peck, Nat				6	
Adam				3	
Johnson, Edward	1		4		3
Guttoe, Joshua			1		
Kunor, Mrs			5		
Chase, Samuel	5	2	6		4
Rabourg, William	3		2		1
Brandt, Henry	5	1	3		
Grubb, Andrew	3	6	4		
Benthelm, Frederick	1		1		
Deady, Daniel	2		2		3
Bickham, James	2	2	4		
Zitler, Abraham	4		4		
Didur, Henry	3	3	2		1
Stewart, Richardson	6	2	3		4
Holmes, John	2	2	2		
Poe, David	5		2		4
Moreen, Moses					
Poe, George	1	3	2		2
Preston, William	2		1		
Hart, Peter	2	1	3		
McCoy, John	2		2		
Hammond, John	2	2	2		7
Labes, James	3				
Green, Thomas	1		2		
Stark, John	9	1	3		6
Brown, Jacob	6	4	2		
Weyer, John	2	1	1		

BALTIMORE COUNTY—Continued.

BALTIMORE TOWN—con.

NAME OF HEAD OF FAMILY.	Free white males of 16 years and upward, including heads of families.	Free white males under 16 years.	Free white females, including heads of families.	All other free persons.	Slaves.
Forney, Peter	1				
Lamott, John	1	1	1		
Neuman, Jacob	4	5	4		
Hickley, James	7	2	2	1	
Stigar, John	4	3	4		
Galahan, ——	2	4	4		
Rinacher, George	2		3		
Johnson, Christr	8	4	5	2	3
McIntosh, Duncan	1	1	1		
Harbauch, Leonard	5	8	3	1	
Barney, Mr	1		1		
Cruise, Jacob	2		2		
Ruse, John	2		2		
Newton, William	1		2		
Moore, David	4	2	4	1	1
Lynch, William	3		1	2	
Collins, William	2				
Valck, Adrian	1		5	2	5
Gibson, William	3	3	4	2	5
Puder, Leonard	2	2	4		
Lehnhart, Frederick	1		2		
Noel, Septimus	1		2		2
Tripolot, Mary	1		1	1	
Otterbine, William	1	2	1		
Barachman, Peter	1		3		
Fraser, James	1	1	2		
Waters, Martin	1	1	2		
Burns, John	1		1		
Joiner, Widow	1	5	2		
Piper, Widow			1		
Poe, Mrs			3		
White, Simon	4	2	3		
Small, Jacob	1	1	3		
Fisher, Daniel	1		2		
Kunor, Christian	2	2	2	1	
Henry, Hugh	1		2	2	
Kunor, Melcher	1	2	3		
Armstrong, James	2		3		
Croxall, James	2			6	
Grub, Michael	3	1	4		
Cassell, John	1	1	1		
Lehman, Gerard	1	5	3		
Roberts, George	1	5	4		
Hewitt, Caleb	3	4	4		
Swan, Mathew	1	3	2		
Somwalt, George	1		1		
Thornbury, George	1	1	2		
McSherry, Patrick	1		3		2
Henry, Daniel	1	1	4	3	
Haslet, Moses	2	4	4		
McIntire, Paul	2		1		
Kinsel, Fredk	2	1	4		
Prustman, George	3	5	1		
Weatherburn, John	2	7	1		
Wynkoop, James	1	3	6		
Stevens, Mr	1	1	2		
Irish, Mary	1		2		
Allen, William	1	2	7		
Mitchel, Mr	7				
Kurts, John	1				
Wilson, Thomas	1		2		
Clopper, Cornelius	1	3	2		
Clopper, John	1		2		
Levy, Benjamin			2		
Ridley, Mrs	1		2	3	
Cordley, Michael	2		5		
Myers, Jacob	6	1	3		
Donaldson, Joseph	3	5	4	1	
Johnston, Samuel	2	4	6		
Buchanan, William	3	1	4		
Duffey, Timothy	1	1	1		
Dunk, Peregrine	1		3		
Cox, Mathias	1	1	3		
Ross, Thomas	1		5		
Harris, David	1	1	3	1	
Smith, Mrs			3		
Cochran, Hiram	3	2	2		
Smith, Adam	2	2	2	4	
Morgan, James	1		4		
Simonton, James	2	2	4		
Stewart, John	2	4	4		
Foltz, William	5	4	4		
Fitzsimmons, Mr	1		4		3
Robinson, Andrew	2		1		
Robinson, John	1	1	2		
Neilson, Robert	1	1	2		
Shain, Peter	1	5	2		
Harman, Philip	1		2		
Charles					5
Heiney, Nicholas	1	1	2		
Frasier, Alexander	1		2		
Ballard, Robert	1	5	2		
Boyd, Andrew	2	2	4		
Ross, James	2				

BALTIMORE TOWN—con.

NAME OF HEAD OF FAMILY.	Free white males of 16 years and upward, including heads of families.	Free white males under 16 years.	Free white females, including heads of families.	All other free persons.	Slaves.
Davey, George	4	1	3		
Berkley, Hugh	2	4	2		
Lodiger, Simon	2		2		
Kleckner, Adam	2	2	4		
Spicer, Michael	1	1	2		
Jones, Mr	1		3		
Young, Mrs			2		
Stevenson, Mr	1		2		
Moulton, John	2	2	4		
Stewart, Hugh	1	1	3		
Hartman, Jacob	1		1		
Smith, Job	2		6	2	
Leash, Andrew	1	1	1		
Somwalt, Godfrey	1	1	2		
Hagerty, John	1		2		
Butler, Michael	2	1	2		
Stewart, Robert	2		4		
Marr, Robert	1		1		
Husselton, Mrs	1	1	3		
Barnhart, Jacob	2	1	4		
Dalley, Mr	1		2		
Dagan, George	2	3	2		
Steitz, Mrs	1	2	4		
Earnst, Caleb	1	2	4		
Marshall, Widow			1		
Griffen, Henry	1	1	1		
Williams, Sidney					5
Leland, Widow	1		1		
Sindall, William	1	1	3		
Peterson, Joseph	1		2		
Rheams, John	1	1	1		
Shaffer, Frederick	1	1	1		
Parks, William	1		2		
Peterson, Adam	1	1	1		
Parks, Archibald	1		1		
Wineman, Henry	1		3		4
Hansman, Samuel	3	2	5		
Bondfield, John	1		2		
Buck, John	1	2	4		
Deb					3
Starr, Mr	1	5	1		
Bevins, John	1	2	4		
Wheeler, John	1		3		
Shaw, John	1		2		
Rumage, Nicholas	1		1		
Evans, Henry	1	3	2		
McDermot, John	1	2	2		
Shillingbourgh, Peter	1		2		3
Jones, John	1		2		
Sarah				3	
Harry				4	
Blythe, John	1		4		
Turner, Isaac	1	2	2		
Boos, Adam	1		2		
Frydell, Mr	1	2	3		
Root, Peter	1	2	2		
Havey, Daniel	1	1	2		
Hutton, Richard	1		1	2	
Roose, Margaret			2		2
Cloe					
Moon, William	2	3	5		
Jarvis, William	3	2	7		
Cunningham, James	1	1	2		
Curtain, James	1		2		
Gates, Henry	1	1	4		
Alexander, James	1		2		
Robert					8
Mahoney, Mr	1		3		
Brinigan, Captn	1	1			
Davis, ——			3		
Duffey, Mrs			3		
Hill, John	1		4		
Murray, John	1	3	4		
Conner, James	1	2	4		2
Patterson, John	1	1	2		
Dicks, Isaac	1	4	4		
Broon, James	4	4	4		
Burry, Captn	2	3	1		6
Sellman, William	2		4		
Laferty, Mrs	1	1	4		
Van Bibber, Abram	1		4		12
Ross, Captain	1	4	3		
Anderson, Mrs			3		
Free Negroes				2	
Smith, Philip	1	2	2		
Williams, Edward	2		2		
Curtis, John	1	3	2		
Mack, James	3	2	2		
Cranford, John	1	1	2		
Evans, John	1	1	2		
Gill, John	1		2		
Tudor, Elexis	1	1	2		
Gardner, John	1	2	3		
Oyster, John	2	2	3		

BALTIMORE TOWN—con.

NAME OF HEAD OF FAMILY.	Free white males of 16 years and upward, including heads of families.	Free white males under 16 years.	Free white females, including heads of families.	All other free persons.	Slaves.
Web, Diana				2	
Tims, Mr	1		2	2	
Holton, John	1	2	2		
Hopham, Mr	1	1	3		
Brown, Mrs			2	1	
Nickle, William	1		1		
Burges, Fanny			3		
Kelly, Mrs			2		
Clarke, Rapael	1		5		
Curtis, John	1	1	1		
Nonans, Edward	1		1		
Manheer, George	2		1		
Baker, John	1		3		
Dougherty, Patrick	3		3		
Hussey, George			2		
Adamson, John	1		1		
Willson, Mary			2		
Ellis, John	1		2		
Haman, John			1		
Kenedy, Molly			1		
Fleetwood, Mr	1	1	3		
Robinson, James	1		3		
Dunn, John			3	1	
Wood, John	2		1		
Tamer				4	
Fisher, Catharine	1		2		
Thompson, John	3		1		
Armstrong, Mrs			3		
Small, Conrad	2		3		1
Coulson, Thomas	2	3	3		
Somwalt, Philip	2		1		
Willson, Ann	1		2		
Mitcheson, William	1		2		
Lusk, John	1	2	1	1	
Holsten, Robert	1	2	2		1
Solears, Rebecca			1		
Lusk, John	1		1		
Hart, Mathew			1		
Hamilton, Mrs			3		
Rusk, John	2	2	4		
Donnellan, Thomas	2		3	1	1
McLaughlin, William	2		1	1	2
Hackett, John			2	2	
Fortune, James	14		3		
Shaw, Archibald	2	1	4		
Fisherick, James	4		4		
Jenny, Nathani	1		4		
Fulford, John			2		
Weaver, Miss			3		
Hale, George	2		3		
Cain, Mrs			1		
Fields, William	1		1		
Conway, Robert	1	2	4		
Corathwait, Robert	1	1	1		
Ingram, Samuel	1	1	1		
Ford, Thomas				2	
Senk & York					
Foster, Capt	1	3	2		
Robinson, John	1		2		
Fearson, William			2		
Boles, Mrs			2		
Beck, Thomas	2		3		
McCliny, Roger	1		3		
Bennett, Patrick			2		
Alley, Mrs			1		
Made, John	1	2	1		
Cooper, Thomas	1	2	2		3
Cooper, Jonas	2		3		
Hardy, James	1	2	3		
Townsend, Robert	1		4		
Jones, Daniel	1		2		
Freeland, Mr	1		2		3
Cromwell, Joseph	1		2		
Herr, John	1		2		7
James				1	
Allender, Mr	1		1		
Sutton, Isaac	1	2	2		
Louderman, George	3		2		
Philips, Captn	3	3	2		
Ruse, Adam	3		3		4
Coulter, John	3		3		
Hammond, Mr	1		4		
Willson, Hugh	1	2	2		
Krips, Nichael	1		1		
Denagan, Dennis			1		2
Turner, Francis	2		2	2	
Williams, Hannah			2		
Roberts, Henry	1	5			
Ross, Mr				1	
West, Elizabeth			1	3	
Johnson, Joshua	1	1	3		
Welsbach, John	1		3	1	
Cooper, John	3	2	3		
Burkett, Captn	7		2		

BALTIMORE COUNTY—Continued

NAME OF HEAD OF FAMILY.	Free white males of 16 years and upward, including heads of families.	Free white males under 16 years.	Free white females, including heads of families.	All other free persons.	Slaves.
BALTIMORE TOWN—con.					
Ingram, Moses	1	1	2		
Taylor, Levin	1	1	3		1
Osborn, Samuel	1		2		
Bevins, Mrs	1		1	2	5
Morton, Nathaniel	3				
Gardner, Timothy	2	1	4		
Spencer, Benjamin	1	1	3		1
Willmon, Mr	1		1		
Brown, Dixon	1	1	2		2
Jacobs, William	5	1	2		6
Heyner, Joseph	1	2	3		
Shawnesey, John	1		1		
Dixon, George	1	1	2		
Ross, John	1		3		
Bayan, Charles	1	1	2		
Hatten, Thomas	1		2		
Sheckle,	1		1		
Parrott, John	1	2	2		1
Patterson, James	1		2		
Hollis, Mrs			4		
Hermes, Mary		2	3		
Rains, Harry	1	3			
Tucker, David	1		1		
Chesro, John	1	2	1		
Thompson, Robert	2	1	3		1
McDower, Thomas	2		1		
Flinton, Richard	1		2		
Adamousky, Thadeus	1	2	2		
Leary, Margaret	1		3		
Brook, Catharine			5		
Bingham, Thomas	2		2		
Loney, Kit		1	2		
Wigles, William	2		1		
Butler, Wat			3		
Harrison, Jonathan			2		
Tutsbach, John	10	2	5		
Deiter, Jacob	2	2	2		
Barnard, John	2	2	2		2
Moore, Thomas	1	2	2		
Vanhorne, Gabriol P	8	4	4		2
Bowie, John	2		2		
Dashuld, Benjamin	6	3	3		1
Hamilton, John	3	1	3		
Herbert, Mr	1		5		2
Bias, Joseph	5	1	1		5
Welsh, Edward	5		3		2
Trimble, William	3	3	4		
Brotherson, Capt	2		6		
Boas, Peter	1	4	2		
Small, James	1		1		
Smith, Mr	1	1	2		
Bryan, Mr	1		1		
Bewes, Robert	1		3		
Button, Elias	1		4		
Millar, John	1	1	1		
Quail, John	1	1	1		
Hammond, John	1		1		
Adams, James	1		1		
Joyer, Joshua	1		1		
McDonald, Samuel	2	1	4		
Trimble, Mr	1		5		
Martin, William	1		2		
Hannah, Caleb	1	1	2		
Solears, William	1	2	1		
Wear, John	1		2		
Feral, George	1		2		
Wilson, John	1	2	2		
Box, Mrs			2		
Dawson, William	1		2		
Harrison, Thomas	1	1	2		
Young, Henry	1		2		
Inloes, Mr	1		2		
Luskett, Mrs		2	3		
McKinsey, Benjamin		1	3		
Mahew, William	1		1		
Sellars, William	1		2		
Lee, Mrs		1	2		
Aldersgate, John	5	1	3		2
Mackie, Ebenezer	1		2		1
Foster, Joseph	1	3	2		7
Moale, John	4	4	6		9
Watson, Capt	1	1	4		
Thomas, John	3	2	4		2
Gardner, Anne	5		2		
Kurtz, Daniel	2		5		3
Williams, James	1		5		
Free Negro					
Douglass, George	2	2	2	1	
Van Bibber, Isaac	2	2	4		7
McCreery, William	3	1	5		1
Forbes, James	1	1	2		
James's, Miss			2		
Pamphillion, Thomas	9		3		5
Howell, James	1		4		

NAME OF HEAD OF FAMILY.	Free white males of 16 years and upward, including heads of families.	Free white males under 16 years.	Free white females, including heads of families.	All other free persons.	Slaves.
BALTIMORE TOWN—con.					
Warren, ——	3		2		
Shepherd, Capt	1	1	3		
Tinker, William	3	2	2		
Morris, William	3	2	4		
Ensor, William	2	2	6		
Chase, Thorndick	1	2	3		
Calhoun, Moses	3	1	2		
Rogers, John	1		3		
Hardiston, Benjamin	1		4		
Belt, Walter	1	2	4		
Steel, John	4	2	6		6
Stokes, Peter	1		2		
Phips, Nathl	4	1	3		
Baker, Benjamin	1	3	2		
Grimes, William	1	1	2		2
Dickenson, Edward	1		4		
Griest, Isaac	3		4		1
Hill, Josus	1	2	2		
Davis, Joseph	5		2		
Hays, William	2		1		
Herbert, Edward	1		1		
Hendricks, Absalom	1		3		
Kirwan, John	1		3		
Shreighly, Michael	2	1	1		5
Brown, John	1	2	2		
Trepane, Augustin	1	1	4		
Geddis, James	1	1	2		
Gillard, Thorndick	2	1	1		
Johnston, Thomas	2	3	8		5
Young, John H	3		4		6
Pitt, Ann	1	2	3		
Dunkin, James	2	2	3		
Weaver, John	2		2		
French, Simon	2		4		
McMyer, John	4	1	4		
Jones, Richard	2	3	2		1
Jenny, Ebenezer	2	1	2		
Aisquith, Lester	2		2		
Simpson, James	1		3		1
Free Negroes				3	
Crawley, Mary		1	2		
Britt, Robert	5	1	3		5
Murphy, John	1	1	3		
Burnham, James	1	1	1		
Campbell, Archibald	2		4		
Parmele, John	2	1	4		
Lewis, Elisha	2		1		7
Willson, Francis	2	1	3		
Bryan, Charles	1	1	3		
Tibbett, James	4		2		
Crow, William	6	3	3		
Burke, David	3		2		1
Clarke, Mathew	2	3	4		
Fullerton, William	2		1		
Jackson, William	1		8		
Bias, James	5	2	2		3
Dickson, Brittingham	2		2		
McCaskey, James	3	1	4		7
Jones, John	3		3		
Ellerton, Francis	2	1	2		
Stafford, Patrick	1	1			
Huggins, John	1		2		
Dawson, Sarah			2		
Dorsey, Philip			2		
Kirk, Francis	2	1	2		
Hamilton, James	1		1		
Dixon, John	2	1	1		
Robinson, Thomas	2	3	2		3
Howell, James	1	1	2		
Tillinghast, ——	1		4		
Rogers, William	1		2		
Stoddard, David	21	1	5		25
Johnston, William	4	2	11		4
Tumbleston, William	3	2	3		
Peters, Henry	8	1	1		
Hackthrop, Edward	1		1		
Gilbertthrop, Francis	1		1		
Ganting, John	1		1		
Mathews, Patrick	1	1			
Ballard, Michael	2		3		
Cowen, William	1	1	4		
Minkey, Mary Ann			3		
Mahon, Alme			3		
Willson, John	3		1		1
Logan, John	1		1		
Smith, Godlip	3		2		
Job, Morris	3		2		
Waters, Hezekiah	3	2	5		1
Burney, John	3	3	3		2
Weatherby, William	4	1	3		
Morrison, John	2		3		
Leary, Jane			2	2	
Welsh, Margaret			4	4	
Dean, James	2	2	1		

NAME OF HEAD OF FAMILY.	Free white males of 16 years and upward, including heads of families.	Free white males under 16 years.	Free white females, including heads of families.	All other free persons.	Slaves.
BALTIMORE TOWN—con.					
Bayman, James	1	1	4		3
Prindevill, Garret	17		2		
Gore, Richard	1		2		
Curtis, Eleazer	3	2	5		
Etzberger, William	2	4	1		
McDermot, Thomas	3		2		
Mathers, Joseph	13		4		
Wood, Rebecca	1	2	2		
Bailey, Elizabeth	2	2	3		
Osborn, Jonas	8	1	3		1
Sharper, Jacob	1		4		
Wilson, Mathew	1		3		
Thompson, Lesley	2		2		
Gotier, Edward	1		2		
Ross, Robert	6	2	2		1
Free Negroes				4	
Steel, Peter	1		1		3
Johns, William	5	3	2		
Clarke, Michael	1	1	1		
Deseborough, Lewis	1	1	1		
Peurise, Joseph	1		1		
Travers, Mathew	1	1	2		2
Weary, Peter	2	2	6		
Maden, Eleoner			4		
Stephens, Richard	1	1	2		
Philips, Nathan	1		3		
Ross, Robert	6	2	2		
Cooper, John	3	2	2		
Mitchel, John	2	2	4		1
Green, Mary			2		
Chambers, Thomas	1	1	2		
Perkins, Mary		2	2		
Evans, William	1		3		
Byron, Thomas		1	2		
Wooden, Mary		1	2		
Cornelius, Eleoner		2	2		
Drane, Barbary	1	1	2		
Drayman, William	2	1	2		
Logan, William	2	1	3		
Dort, Robert	1	2	2		
Post, Daniel	5		2		
Hick, Nicholas	4		2		
Cummins, Alexander	18	3	3		
Burrows, Thomas	2	1	2		1
Heddrick, Charles	1				
Otts, William	2	2	1		
Marshall, John	2		1		
Long, Thomas	1		1		
Lockwood, William	1	3	3		
Lewis, John	12	1	4		6
Wells, Hannah			5		1
Davis, Edward	3	4	4		
Swift, Rebecca	3	1	2		
Horseman, John	1		3		
Flax, John	1		3		
Stansbury, Margaret		3	1		
Foy, Eleoner		2	2		
Turner, Francis	1	2	4		
Ferrell, James	4		2		
Winning, Margaret		1	2		11
Free Negroes				5	
Laurence, Richard	6	2	5		4
Bluchroth, Henry	3	1	6		
Hale, Isaac	2	3	1		
Mayho, William			2		
Carr, Peter	1		2		
Bandall, Martin	4		2		
Ritchie, John		5	3		
Young, John	2	1	3		
Harrison, Martha		1	2		
Duforrest, Henry			2		
Johns, Richard	2		1		
Tucker, Edward	5	1	1		
Stevens, William	1		2		
Hale, Jonathan	1	2	2		
Strahan, John	4	1	3		
Chandler, John	1	1	3		
Travers, Pricilla			4		
Goodwin, William	3	5	8		4
Stiles, George	17	2	2		1
Daniels, Anthony	11				
Travers, Wm	8	1			
Fitzimons, John	4		4		
Jones, Daniel	4		4		
Stockett, Captain	5		5		
Foster, Moses	9				
Sharp, Peter	11		2		
Buell, Benjamin	11				
Duncan, James	9		6		
Deland, Thorndick	8	2			
Clarke, Mathew	8		5		
Higgins, John	8		5		
Kerr, Archibald	8				
Reed, James	12				

BALTIMORE COUNTY—Continued

NAME OF HEAD OF FAMILY.	Free white males of 16 years and upward, including heads of families.	Free white males under 16 years.	Free white females, including heads of families.	All other free persons.	Slaves.
BALTIMORE TOWN—con.					
Willson, Hugh	10				
Groves, John	9				
Walkins, John	8				
Murphy, John	6				
Steward, Capt.	13				
Elwood, Captain	13				
Towers, Capt.	13				
Foster, Capt.	13				
Cole, Thomas	15				
Porter, James	14				
Belt, Walter	13				
Dillon, John	12				
Jenny, Capt.	10				
Jones, Levin	8				
Snyder, John	8				
Dillon, James	5				
Reeves, Thomas	5				
Blythe, John	12				
Hill, Josus	6				
Stran, Capt.	10				
Martin, George	10				
Hale, Jonathan	5				
Bias, Capt.	11				
Carry James	6	4	5		
Steward, Cowden	1		5		1
Hoale, Samuel	3	2	5		5
Stevens, Capt.	16				
Welsh, Capt.	9				
M'Cammon, Joseph	7				
Beard, Alexander	6				
Folger, Fred'k	12				
Curson, Richard	3	1	1		4
Cunningham, Capt's	6				
Smith, William	2				
Harrison, James	5				
Sewell, Reverend Mr.	4		1		2
Stetson, Isaiah	2				
Mitchel, Henry	8				
Smith, William	3	2	1		5
Gardner, Obed	6				
Moore, Robert	7				
Dick, William	1		2		
Curtis, Francis					
Conway, John	6				
Maddox, John	4				
Shaney, Daniel	2				
Bodley, Thomas	9	3	3		1
Granger, Daniel	1	2	3		
Orford, Charles	1	1	3		
Martin, Robert	1		3		
Smith, Thorogood	2		4		4
BACK RIVER, UPPER HUNDRED.					
Stevenson, Henry	5	1	2		6
Owings, Richard	2	4	2		3
Maygors, John	2	3	2		
Burnham, John, Jun'	2	1	2		
Cockey, Capt' John	2	2	5		12
Ford, John	1	2	1		1
Perrigo, James	1	2	5		
Stanbury, Richardson	1				1
Cockey, Caleb	2		3		3
Norwood, William	4	3	5		1
Tipton, Mary	1		1		
Wood, James	1	1	3		
Young, John T.	1	1	3		
Bosley, William	2	4	3		5
Wilson, Jacob	2	4	4		5
Peticoat, Dorsey	1		4		
Tipton, Shadrack	1	3	4		
Owings, John C.	2	1	7		10
Bond, John, Jun'	1		3	4	1
Bond, John	1		4		12
Dodd, John	2		3		3
Dunn, Arthur	2	2	4		
Gorsuch, Charles	3	2	2		1
Burnham, John	1	1	5		
Ketchpole, John	2		5		
Wright, Joshua	2	4	1		1
Stockedale, John (Overseer Moale's Quarter)	1	1	3		13
Gist, Cole Thomas	2				8
England, Joseph	1	1	1		
Burnham, William	1	1	1		
Tipton, Aquila	1		7		
Tipton, William	2		4		1
Tipton, Hester		3	4		
Tipton, Joshua	1	1	1		1
Sollers, John	1		4		
Chittam, William	1	1	2		
Hopkins, John's	1	1	2		2
Trimble, Corneleous	2	1	1		
Warrick, William	1	2	4		
Orson (Free Negro)				3	

NAME OF HEAD OF FAMILY.	Free white males of 16 years and upward, including heads of families.	Free white males under 16 years.	Free white females, including heads of families.	All other free persons.	Slaves.
BACK RIVER, UPPER HUNDRED—continued.					
Haile, George, Jun'	4	1	5		1
Haile, Nicholas	1		1		
Towson, Ezekiel	2	1	2		2
Wallace, John	2	1	2		3
Doy'l, William	1	1	1		
Reynolds, Thomas	1		1		
Rees, Daniel	2	2	1		
Chambers, James	1	2	1		
Price, Nehemiah	1		3		1
Cole, Philip	1		1		2
Hunt, Samuel C.	1	3			8
Hunt, Phinehas	1		2		9
Colin, John	2		5		
Bond, Christopher	2	2	1		3
Murphy, John	2	2	3		
Bond, Edward	1	1	2		1
Gent, Thomas	1	2	1		5
Power, Patrick	1		3		
Powell, Mary			3		
Stone, William	5	3	4		6
Pocock, John	1	1	3		
Gott, Richard	2		6		4
Gott, Richard of Sam'l	4	2	6		2
Ford, Thomas of Ste'n	1	3	3		
Stansbury, Thomas (of Jn'o)	1	2	6		5
Stevenson, Josias	2				2
Coward, Fielding	1		4		
Stevenson, William	1	1	1		1
Brown, William	1		2		
Merrit, Charles	1	1	3		
Stevenson, Joshua	2		2		3
Rogers, Mathew	2		2		
Bosley, Joshua	1	3	3		10
Fishpaugh, John	3	5	3		1
Parish, John	1		8		
Caples, George	1		4		
Bowen, Solomon (Jun')	2	1	2		
Bowen, Solomon (Sen')	3	2	4		4
Cockey, Stephen	2				3
Lye, Robert	2	7	1		1
Willson, Thomas	2	1	2		
Jones, Joshua	1	6	4		1
Smith, John	2	3	2		
Wheelor, Nathan	1	2	2		
Parks, William	1		1		1
Setch, John	1		4		
Hill, Richard	1	1	4		
Woodcock, Thomas	1		2		
Mason, Michael	2	3	3		
Leaf, Jacob	2	1	4		
Daughaday, John	3	1	2		13
Price, William	1	4	4		3
Price, Stephen	1		3		11
Fanent, William	2	1	4		
McBroom, John	1	3			
Noonan, Michael	1		1		
Woodyard, Neptune, free negro				3	
Herbert, William	1		3		
Parks, Benjamin	1		2		
Parks, David	3	2	3		
Owings, Edward	3	2	5		10
Price, Benjamin	1		3	4	7
Price, Mordecal	2	4	5		1
Mauford, Stephen	1	1	2		
Fitzpatrick, Nathan	2	1	2		
Stevens, Ambrose	2		4		
Belt, Kitturah	2	3	5		1
Perry, (Free Negro)			1	1	
Jones, John	1		4		
Hopkins, John	2	4	4		8
Cooper, Thomas	2	1	6		
Ambrose, John	1	1			1
Rowles, Patrick	1		3		
Hodges, William	1	3	1		
Tarman, John (Overser James Amos)	4	1	2	1	7
Weir, Thomas	1		2		
Risteans, Georges, Quarter					9
Gist, Thomas (of Wm)	1	2	1		5
Norris, Joseph	1	3	3		
Bush, John	1		3		
Ridgeley, Charles (of Wms Quarter)					8
Lynch, William	1	3	3		
Bowen, Benjamin	1	3	7		5
Bowen, James	2	1	2		4
Blachley, Thomas	1		5		
Green, William	1		3		
Hall, Neal (Jun')	1	2	2		
Sollers, Thomas	1		4		
Haile, Nicholas (of Neal)	3		4		
Gorsuch, John	1	2	6		

NAME OF HEAD OF FAMILY.	Free white males of 16 years and upward, including heads of families.	Free white males under 16 years.	Free white females, including heads of families.	All other free persons.	Slaves.
BACK RIVER, UPPER HUNDRED—continued.					
Gorsuch, William	1		1		
Ogden, Amos	2		2		3
Wyley, Joshua	2	1	6	2	3
Ford, Thomas C. Deye	1	1	2		
Hart, Joseph	1	2	5		1
Owings, Samuel (of Thomas)	1		2		7
Hart, Charles	1	1	3		
Towson, Thomas	1		2		
Hunt, Job	1	2	4		11
Kelley, Thomas	2	3	2		2
Bond, Nichodemus	2	3	4		1
Cockey, John (of Thomas)	2	2	2		2
Pindell, Thomas	1	1	1	1	
Fort, Elizabeth	1	1	4		3
Males, John	1	2	2		
Criswell, William	2		5		
Lynch, Lawrence	1	1	5		
Tye, George	1	1	2		
Harvey, William	1		5		11
Cole, Mordecai	1	2	5		3
Lynch, William (of Robuck)			3		7
Storn, Herculous	1	2	2		
King, Susanah			4		
Bryson, James	2	1	2		1
Bowen, William	3	1	2		
Haile, George (Sen')	4		5		5
Anderson, Robert	2		2		
Cole, William	2	2	6		7
Whiteley, James	2	2	4		
Govane, Mary	1	1	3		6
Deavor, Richard	1		3		
Bowen, Jonas (Jun')	1				5
Tag, Thomas, free			1	1	
Bowen, Nathan	1	1	3		9
Wheelor, John	1	2	5		20
Lux, Darby	2		5		
Clarke, William	2		4		
Cole, Samuel	3	3	4		4
Lorah, Henry	1		2		
Harvey, Thomas (Jun')	1	1	2		
Turnpaugh, Christopher (overseer N. Carrol)	2	1	1		49
Wolf, Michael	2		1		
Coale, Giles	1		4	1	
Kennedy, Martin	1		2		
Harford, John	1	2	1		1
Gill, Stephen G	1	2	1		
Cooper, Stephen	1	2	2		
Chamberlain, Samuel	1		1		
Butler, John (Overseer for Jne Moles)	1	1	2		8
Butler, Elijah	1	3	4		
Colegate, John	1	2	3		10
James (free negro)				3	
Beno (free negro)				4	
George (free negro)				5	
Haile, Neal (Sen')	2		5		
Griffith, Owen	1	2	6		
Drewit, William	1	1	6		
Cole, Samuel (of Christr)	1	1	6		10
Pope, Morriss	1	6	3		1
Gill, John	1		3		4
Cockey, Charles	1	1	2		
Sollers, Mary			3		
Ford, Ruhama	2		3		5
Cockey, Thomas Deye	3	2	2		7
Cockey, Edward	3	2	2		6
Pindell, Eleanor	1	1	1		4
Owings, Urath	3	3	4		12
Sater, Hannah	3		2		10
Sater, Joseph	2	2	2		
Driskell, Jeremiah (overser Rice Caton)	7				12
Brown, John (free Molatto)				4	
Sollers, Benjamin	1	2	5		1
Carnan, Charles	3		5	2	15
Price, William	1		1		
Alwood, William	1	2			5
Draper, Thomas	1		2		
Arnald, Edward	1		2		
Buchanan, Susannah	1		7		20
Gill, John (Sen')	1		1		5
Stansbury, Caleb	1		1		
Beach, John	1	3	5		2
Gore, Michael	2		4		6
Yaun, John	1	2	4		2
Hoop, Michael	2		3		
Frock, John	2	1	3		
Gore, Elizabeth	2	1	5		
Gore, Michel (Jun')	2	2	5		
Groom, Nathan	1	1	2		

BALTIMORE COUNTY—Continued.

BACK RIVER, UPPER HUNDRED—continued.

NAME OF HEAD OF FAMILY.	Free white males of 16 years and upward, including heads of families.	Free white males under 16 years.	Free white females, including heads of families.	All other free persons.	Slaves.
Wheelor, William	1	1	3		
Carnan, Robert N	2	1	5	7	3
Mathews, William	3	1	9		
Peg (Free negro)					5
Mathews, Oliver	3	2	3		
Herbert, William	1		3		
Griffith, Joseph	2	2	2		
Mathews, John	2		1	1	1
Ruth (Free negro)				2	
Nailor, John	3	2	6		
Noonan, Michael	1		1		
Green, Abraham	3		3		3
Daughaday, Richard	2	3	4		5
Gill, John (Junr)	4	7	3		5
Towson, William	9	3	1		12
Paul, Peter	1	3	4		
Burk, Joseph	1	1	2		
Bland, William	1		2	1	
Wheelor, Joseph	2	2	3		7
Philips, William	2		1		
Stoombsbury, William	2	2	5		
Hollyday, John Robert	7	1	11		39
Mops, Federick	1	1	3		
Smith, Joshua	2	3	2		4
Wait, Richard	3	1	3		
Fell, James	2	2	3		
Towson, Charles	1		6		3
Duff, Patrick	1	1	1		
Talbott, Edward	4	1	7		22
Parks, David, Overseer Wm McCullins	1				11
Perigo, Charles	2	2	4		2
Stansbury, Thomas	3		6		10
Chenoweth, William	2	1	2		
Pratt, James	1		2		
Owings, Joshua	1		2		
Wadham, William	1	2	1		
Roberts, Richard	1				1
Russell, Robert	1		1		
Means, Margarett		2	1		
Sweeny, Morgan, Overseer D. McKerr	1	2			5
Wilmot, John	1	1	3		9
Turnbul, Sarah			1		18
Worthington, Samuel	5	2	6		33
Cromwell, Thomas	1		4		14
Merryman, Nicholas	2	3	2		12
Owings, Jane			2		
Chilcoate, Eliezah	2	1	1		
Selman, Vachel (overseer for B. Philiep)	2				10
Chandler, Joseph	1		3		
Anderson, Daniel	1	1	2		
Haile, William, overseer for Richd Johns	1				9
Deye, Thomas C	2		2		40
Dixon, Joseph	1	2	4		
Worthington, John T	1		2		17
Best, George	2		2		
Cromwell, Philip	2				1
Cockey, Thomas of Thos	1	3	1		15
James, Thomas	1	3	2		
Cradock, John	6	1	9		14
Bennit George	1	1	3		
Hopkins, Wm				3	
Cromwell, Nathan	4	5	6		15
George, Frederick	4		3		
Stevenson, Sater	2	3	5		2
Mays, John	4	4	1		
Ridgeley, Charles	34	14	20	3	117
Ridgeley, Rebecca	3		1	1	11
Simon				3	
Cate				4	
Hopkins, Nicholas	1				
Hopkins, Joseph	2		2		2
Whelor, Sarah	1		1		

MINE RUN HUNDRED.

NAME OF HEAD OF FAMILY.	Free white males of 16 years and upward, including heads of families.	Free white males under 16 years.	Free white females, including heads of families.	All other free persons.	Slaves.
Anderson, Benjamin	6	1	6		8
Sheppherd, John, Ser	3	1	5		10
Willey, Greenberry	2	1	5		6
Bosman, Edward	4	1	6		9
Trapnall, Vincent	2		3	2	4
Burk, Mary	1	4	1	1	3
Goodwin, Rachel	4		1	1	3
Foster, George	1	2	3		3
Curtis, Joseph	2	1	2		
Elliott, George	2	1	6		1
Anderson, Thomas	2	5	6		6
Almany, John	1	5	2		2
Anderson, William	1		3		2
Ansell, Benjamin	1		1		
Armstrong, Sollomon	2	2	1		
Anderson, Joshua	1	1	2	2	

MINE RUN HUNDRED—continued.

NAME OF HEAD OF FAMILY.	Free white males of 16 years and upward, including heads of families.	Free white males under 16 years.	Free white females, including heads of families.	All other free persons.	Slaves.
Arms, Thomas	1	4	2		
Bosley, Zebulon	2	4	3		4
Byam, William	1	1	2		
Barnerd, Richard	1	3	3		
Bull, William	3	1	3		
Bosley, James	1	3	6	1	6
Bond, Edward	1		3		
Brown, John	3	2	5		
Bacon, Temperance	1		3	2	1
Boran, Thomas	1	2	5		
Broham, James	1	2	2		
Bull, Jacob	1		3		
Baker, Joseph	1	1			
Baker, John	1	2	6		
Burns, Adam	1	3	5		
Burns, Michel	1	2	4		
Bosley, Elijah	1	2	2	1	12
Bosley, Esekiel	4		6		6
Carman, Andrew	1	5	4		
Cap, Abraham	1		5		
Coggins, Sylvester	1		3		
Cale, William	1		2		
Cundy, Peter	2		3		
Curtis, Daniel	2	2	5		
Contride, George	1		2		
Crouse, Christian	1	3	5		
Coufman, Daniel	2	7	1		
Calder, James	1	1	5		1
Currier, William	1	1	3		
Dyall, Thomas	1	1	3		
Dillon, Andrew	1	4	3		
Dixon, John	1		3		
Dunniek, John	2	3	6		
Dick, Jacob	1	2	3		
Dailey, Jacob	3		5		
Dailey, John	3	3	3	1	
Cane, Henry	1	3	3		
Elliott, James	1	1	6		
Enloes, Henry	2	3	4	2	
Eaton, John	1	3	4		
Elliott, Auther	1	1	2	1	
Elliott, William	1	4	2		
Fuller, Nicholas	1	3	6		1
Fortenbridge, Richard	2		1		
Freeland, John, Ser	1	3	4		
Freeland, John, Jr	1	3	3		
Freland, Morris	1		3		
Freeheart, Joshua	2	2	4		
Fowler, Thomas	2		4		
Fugate, Elizebeth		1	4		
Fugate, Martin	2	1	2		
Gorsuch, Elijah	4				2
Green, Shadrick	1	3	5		5
Green, Isaac	1		1		4
Goodwin, William	3		2		30
Gummor, Thomas	1		2		
Gorsuch, Benjamin	2		5		
Galloway, Thomas	2	2	2		
Galloway, Mary			4		1
Gorsuch, Charles	1	2	2	1	
Gorsuch, David	1	1	2	1	1
Goodwin, James	1	2	2		
Giba, Aron	1	2	3		
Grover, Joseph	2		4	1	
Grover, Benjamin	1	3	5	1	1
Gillish, Robert	3	1	6		
Given, John	1	2	2		
Holland, Josep	1	2	2		1
Hutchins, Nicholas, Ser	1		4		
Hutchins, Joshua	1	4	4		
Hutchins, William	2	2	2		
Hughs, John	4		1		
Holmes, Gabriel	1		3		
Hunt, Thomas	1	2	2		
Hinedle, Michel	1	2	3	1	
Mcgaw, Sarah			4		5
Mutchenor, Christopher	1	1	4		2
Harn, Andrew	1	2	2		
Hand, John	1		6		
Hunt, William	1	2	2		
Hamelton, Susannah	2		3		
Hughs, James	2		2		
Hughs, Benjs	2		1		
Hughs, Thomas	2		1		
Hughs, Zenus	4	3	6		
Hutchins, Nicholas, Jr	2		8		8
Heart, William	1		2		
Hayes, James	3	1	6		
Johnston, Melchezedick	1	6	2		
Johnston, Jacob	3	2	6		
Johnston, David	2	2	4	1	1
Johnston, Luke	2	2	4		
Johnston, Thomas	1	1	2		
Jones, Richard	3		7		7
Johnston, William	3	1	2		

MINE RUN HUNDRED—continued.

NAME OF HEAD OF FAMILY.	Free white males of 16 years and upward, including heads of families.	Free white males under 16 years.	Free white females, including heads of families.	All other free persons.	Slaves.
Jones, Abraham	1	1	2		4
Jones, Alice	2	1	2		11
Jackson, George	1		1		
Kelsey, Thomas	1		2		
Kelsey, William	2	1	7		1
Kelley, Thomas	1		1		
Leach, John	1		2		
Leach, Clement	1	2	3		
Leach, Benjs	1	1	2		
Lipe, John	1	2	2		
Lytle, George	3	6	2		3
Langle, John	1	1	1		
Markey, William	1		3		
Meridith, Joshua	2	1	3	1	3
Meridith, Samuel	1	3	2	1	
Meridith, Thomas	1	2	5		3
Miller, Nicholas	1	3	2		
Magon, John	1	3	4		
Mash, William	1	3	4		
Marris, Samuel, Ser	1		3		
Merryman, Elijah	3	2	4	2	4
McClung, Mary	3		1	1	2
Macboice, James	3		2		
Meeds, John	1		3		
Mannors, Allexandra	1		2		
Morris, Joseph	1		2		
Morris, Samuel, Jr	1	3	3		
Morris, John	2	1	5		
Mooberry, Godfrey	1		1		
McClung, Joseph	1	1	4	2	4
Merryman, John	1		2		
McColough, David	2	6	6		
Norris, James	4		6	1	
Norris, Abraham	1	2	3		
Norris, Mary			2		
Norris, William	1	1	2		
Parrish, Nicholas	3		3	1	1
Parrish, William	2	1	2		
Price, Zechariah	4	3	5		
Pool, John	2	3	6		
Pierce, William	2		4		
Pierce, Thomas	1	3	2		
Parmer, George	1		3		
Pocock, James	2		3		2
Parrish, Edward	2	1	3		
Procer, Isaac	1		3		
Pocock, Jessee	1	1	3		
Pocock, John	1		3		
Price, Thomas	1	1	2	2	
Ryan, Nicholas	1		2		
Richardson, Samuel	3	1	1		1
Richardson, John of David	1	2	2		
Richardson, Thomas	1		2		
Rutledge, Abraham, Ser	3	3	2		7
Rutledge, Abraham, Jar	3	3	4	2	2
Rutledge, Joshua	2		2		4
Rutledge, Peter	1	2	3		
Rockhold, Jacob	3		4	1	
Rutledge, Ephrim	2	2	5		
Rubey, John	1	2	5		
Randall, Charles	2	3	4		
Royston, John	2	2	3	1	2
Royston, Joshua	1	1	2		
Roe, Joshua	1	1	1		
Rutledge, John	2		2		
Rutledge, Thomas	1		3		
Rutledge, Michel	1	1	5		
Royston, Abraham	1		3		
Ryston, William	1	1	2		
Richardson, John	1	1	2		
Sutton, James	1		2		
Stanniford, John	3	2	2		16
Sinklar, William, Ser	2				16
Stanniford, Skelton	1		1		
Stanniford, John of John	1	2	3		6
Stansbury, Dixon, Jar	2	2	4	1	6
Smith, Hugh	3		4		
Stansbury, Dixon, Ser	2	1	7	1	13
Slade, William	3		1		9
Sharpe, Benjs	1		2		1
Shaw, Joshua	1		4		9
Shaw, Daniel	2	1	3		9
Sparks, Joslas	1	3	5	2	
Sutton, Joseph, Ser	2		2		9
Sutton, Joseph	2	3	2		
Sutton, Henry	1	1	4		
Sampson, Isaac	1		2		
Sparks, Francis	1	3	3		
Shores, Richard	1	1	3		
Stanniford, Jacob	1	1	3		
Shipley, Benjs	1	3	5		
Sampson, Richard	3	2	7	1	
Stansbury, Edmond	3	4	4	1	19

BALTIMORE COUNTY—Continued.

MINE RUN HUNDRED—continued.

NAME OF HEAD OF FAMILY.	Free white males of 16 years and upward, including heads of families.	Free white males under 16 years.	Free white females, including heads of families.	All other free persons.	Slaves.
Sampson, Isaac, Jr	1	1	4		
Stanniford, Vincent	2	4	1		
Stevenson, John	1	..	3	2	6
Sutton, Samuel	1	1	4		
Splitstone, Jacob	1	..	3		
Sharpe, Thomas	1	..	1		
Sharpe, Horatio	1	..	1		
Splitstone, Jacob, Ser	5	1	2		
Sheppherd, John	1	2	2	..	4
Sheppherd, Nathan	1	1	3	..	2
Sampson, Richard of Isaac	1	1	1	..	1
Sinklar, William, Jr	2	..	4	..	2
Sampson, Manuel	1	2	3		
Talbott, Benj	1	..	3		
Talbott, Jeremiah	2	4	1	..	2
Talbott, Richard	1	1	4	..	3
Talbott, John	1	3	4	..	2
Talbott, Edward	3	2	4	..	2
Tarmer, Benj	1	1	2		
Tarmer, Jemimah		3	3		
Tilbett, Walter	1	2	3		
Willson, Getting	2	3	1	1	7
Wiley, Vincent	1	6	4	..	4
Wright, Thomas	2	2	7	1	
Wiley, Aquila	2	1	2		
Wiley, William	2	2	4	1	
Wiley, John	2	1	6		
Wye, Richard		..		..	8
Wantland, Thomas	2	..	3		
Wantland, Isaac	1	2	2		
Williams, Thomas	1	3	2		
Weeler, Westener	1	..	5		
Wilson, Jane	2	3	4		
Unimauker, George	1	1	2		
Osborn, James	1	..	3		
Owins, Stephen	1	2	3	..	1
Richards, John	3	..	6		

TWO DELEWARE HUNDREDS.

NAME OF HEAD OF FAMILY.	Free white males of 16 years and upward, including heads of families.	Free white males under 16 years.	Free white females, including heads of families.	All other free persons.	Slaves.
Brown, Abel, Senr	2	..	2	2	18
Barnes, Adam	1	5	2		
Frizell, Abraham	1	1	5		
Brown, Abel, Junr	3	3	4		
Tipton, Aquilla	1	2	2	..	2
Shipley, Absalom	3	..	3	1	1
Shipley, Adam	4	2	3		
Frizell, Absalom	2	1	1	1	
Fonda, Abraham	1	1	3		
Peticoat, Ann		..	1		
Buckingham, Benjamin, Senr	3	1	2	1	
Arnold, Benjamin	2	2	6		
Buckingham, Benjamin, Junr	1	..	..	1	
Griffith, Benjamin	2	3	3		
Brown, Bejamin	2	3	3		
Shipley, Benjamin (Overseer for Benjamin Bebber)	3	4	4	..	12
Young, Benjamin (Overseer for Wm Buchanan)	1	1	2	..	8
Lawrence, Benjamin	5	1	1	..	15
Owings, Beal	1	..	1	1	3
Macken, Benjamin	3	..	2		
Wilson, Benjamin	1	1	6	1	
Woolery, Christopher	1	1	3	2	2
Soter, Charles	2	1	3	..	2
McCarter, Calaham	1	1	3		
Conaway, Charles	3	4	2		
Shipley, Charles	1	2	2	..	1
Evans, Charles	1	..	3	1	
Creamer, Christopher	2	2	3	1	
Pickett, Charles	4	..	7		4
Franklin, Charles	3	4	2		
Brook, Clement, Esqr	2	..	..	..	15
Dorsey, Dennis	1	..	1	..	1
Condall, David	1	1	4		
Buzzard, Daniel	2	1	2		
Dorsey, Deborah	2	1	2	..	3
Barnes, Dorsey	1	4	3		
Macklefresh, David	2	1	5		
Brown, David	3	..	1	1	1
Daten, David	2	..	3		
Miller, Daniel	2	3	4		
Brown, Elias	2	1	1	..	6
Orsler, Ely	1	3	6	1	
Stevenson, Edward	1	..	..		
Stockdale, Edmund H	3	1	5	..	15
Wheeler, Edward	1	3	2		
Dorsey, Elias	4	1	3	..	14
White, Edward	1	2	3		

TWO DELEWARE HUNDREDS—continued.

NAME OF HEAD OF FAMILY.	Free white males of 16 years and upward, including heads of families.	Free white males under 16 years.	Free white females, including heads of families.	All other free persons.	Slaves.
Bennett, Elisha	2	..	1	..	4
Clark, Elisabeth	1	3	4		
Byer, Elisabeth		2	2	..	2
Shipley, Elijah	1	..	1		
Dorsey, Ely, of Ed	1	2	2	..	1
Smith, Elisabeth		2	1		
Trash, Eve		3	3		
Lane, Elisha	1	..	1		
Lambert, Elizabeth		..	6		
Mercier, Francis	1	5	3	1	2
Brothers, Francis	1	1	4		
Dines, Francis	1	..	3		
Snowden, Francis Esqr	1	5	6	2	11
Ogg, George	1	3	2	1	
Adams, George	1	1	2	1	
Shipley, Greenberry	2	2	4		
Grist, George	3	1	1		
Mitchell, Gitting	1	..	3		
Selman, Gassaway	2	1	6	2	5
Cook, Greenberry	2	1	2		
Scrudick, George	1	1	3		
Pool, George (overseer for Ed. Dorsey)					
Buckingham, George	1	2	4		
Swingle, George	1	..	2		
Dorsey, Henry	2	1	1		
Ogg, Helen		2	3	..	16
Greathouse, Harmond	3	..	3		
Kneff, Henry	2	1	3		
Fite, Henry	1	3	2		
Boring, Henry	1	..	3		
Peticoat, Humphrey	2	6	3		
Lindsey, John	2	4	6		
Towson, John	1	3	4	1	
Sowers, John	4	3	4		
Insor, John	1	3	3		
Beaver, John	2	1	2		
Newcome, John	2	1	2		
Parish, John	1	2	6		
Barnes, John	3	1	2		
Ake, John	4	..	5		
Hern, John	4	..	5	2	
Teaner, John	4	4	4		
Cook, John, of Thomas	2	6	4		
Farver, John	1	4	3		
Evans, John	3	..	5	1	
Becraft, John	1	1	2		
Smith, John	1	..	2		
Selman, John	1	2	3		8
Hagar, John	1	..	5	2	
Walker, John	1	3	5	1	
Scoales, John	2	..	3		
Creamer, John	1	5	2		
Frizell, John	3	3	6	1	
Elder, John	3	1	5	1	5
Tucker, John	1	3	5		
Shivers, John	1	1	2		
Gillis, John	2	1	1	1	1
Noah, John	1	2	3		
Jacobs, John	2	2	1	1	4
Jordan, John	4	..	3		
Gardener, John	2	..	2		
Cross, John	2	..	4	2	
Weer, John	1	..	4		
Cook, John	2	..	3		
Brown, John	2	3	3	..	3
Davis, John	2	1	1		
Harding, Ignatius	2	2	4		
Glover, John	5	2	3	1	2
Welsh, John	2	..	1	1	
Hall, Isaac	1	2	1		
Brittan, John	1	2	7	1	
Rowden, John	2	4	4	1	
Lee, John	3	1	3		
Butler, John (overseer for N. Pew)	3	1	3		2
Buckingham, John, Senr	1	..	4		
Buckingham, John, Junr	1	5	4		
Dorsey, Johnza	1	2	3	..	16
Fowler, John	3	3	4		
Mitchel, John	2	..	2		
Magee, James	1	..	9		
Arnold, Joseph	1	4	5		
Dorsey, James, Senr	2	1	3		
Dorsey, James, Junr	1	..	3		
McAllister, James	1	..	3	..	2
Chilcoat, Joshua	1	1	2		
Arnold, Jacob	1	1	3		
Porter, Joseph	4	3	1	..	2
Hawkins, Joseph	3	..	4		
Connor, James (overser for Wm Patterson)					
Hook, Jacob	5	..	2	1	24
Brothers, Joshua	1	..	1		

TWO DELEWARE HUNDREDS—continued.

NAME OF HEAD OF FAMILY.	Free white males of 16 years and upward, including heads of families.	Free white males under 16 years.	Free white females, including heads of families.	All other free persons.	Slaves.
Grimes, James	3	2	5		
Burrier, Jacob	2	2	4		
Manning, Joseph	1	..	4		
Brown, Jacob	3	3	3		
Chapman, Joshua	1	3	3		
Lucas, James	2	4	3		
Hood, James	1	4	3		
Asberry, James	2	1	2		
Dorsey, Josiah	4	..	..	..	3
Beasman, Joseph	2	..	3	..	3
Crow, James	2	3	1	1	5
Bosley, James	3	..	5		1
Wilson, Joshua	1	..	5	..	1
Roach, James	1	..	5		
Harris, Kensey	1	1	5		
Swingle, Leonard	1	2	3	3	
Logsdon, Leurence	1	1	5		
Wagers, Luke	2	2	2		
Have, Ludwick	1	3	4	1	
Barnes, Leonard	1	1	1		
Little, Ludwick	1	2	1		
Goodwin, Menley	1	1	3		
Manaham, Margaret	1	3	3		
Arnold, Mary	1	1	3		
Logue, Mary	1	1	2		
Scanlan, Michael	1	2	1		
Logue, Matthias	1	..	3		
Snowden, Mary		..	3	..	3
Gosnell, Mordecai	1	1	3		
Merryman, Nicholas	1	2	5	..	3
Callder, Nathaniel (overseer for Mr Scott)		..		..	14
Gorsuch, Nathan	1	2	6		
Tevis, Nathaniel	2	3	3	..	2
Munrow, Nathan	2	..	3		
Buckingham, Obadiah	1	3	3		
Dorsey, Orlander G	1	4	3	1	6
Tevis, Peter	3	3	2	1	
Shipley, Peter	1	4	5		
Barnes, Philemon	2	4	5		
McCarty, Partrick	1	1	3		
Lavely, Phillip	2	2	6	1	
Kelley, Patrick	1	..	2	1	
Jarvis, Phillip	1	5	3	1	
Hewett, Rachel		4	1		
White, Richard	2	4	3		
Hammond, Rebekah	1	2	3	..	12
Hammond, Rezen	1	1	2	..	6
Creswell, Richard	1	..	2		
Scoales, Richard	1	2	3	..	1
Griffee, Richard	2	1	6	1	
Stevens, Rezen	2	4	4	1	
Lee, Richard	1	4	1	1	
Condal, Richard	1	1	1	..	3
Barnes, Richard	3	2	2		
Mercier, Richard	2	3	3	..	8
Tevis, Robert, Senr	3	3	5	..	6
Tevis, Robert, Junr	3	3	1	..	7
Major, Robert	2	3	3		
Duffield, Richard	1	2	2		
Hainsworth, Robert	2	1	2		
Smothers, Robert	2	6	2	1	
Owings, Richard Esqr	3	6	3	1	21
Manning, Richard	1	1	3		
Gorsuch, Richard	1	..	3		
Merryman, Samuel	1	2	5		
Gorsuch, Samuel	1	1	5	1	5
Stevenson, Samuel	2	1	1		
Shipley, Samuel	2	2	2		
Grimes, Samuel	1	2	2		
Bennett, Samuel	3	6	1	..	1
Crosson, Samuel	2	1	1		
Gosnell, Sarah	1	4	..		
Manning, Samuel, Junr	1	4	2		
Wheeler, Samuel	1	1	3		
Parish, Stephen	2	4	2		
Glover, Samuel	1	4	5	1	3
Mayhew, Samuel	1	1	3		
Poppam, Samuel	1	2	3	..	2
Caple, Samuel	1	2	2		
Jordan, Thomas	1	1	3		
Job, Thomas	1	6	4	1	
Miller, Thomas	2	..	3	..	3
Franklin, Thomas	1	6	2		
Leakins, Thomas	1	..	6	..	2
Lucas, Thomas, Junr	1	2	2		
Barnes, Thomas (overseer for Jno Hood)	1	..	2	..	8
Bennett, Thomas	3	3	5	..	2
Tevis, Thomas	1	..	4		
Beasman, Thomas	2	1	4		4
Lucas, Thomas, Senr	1	1	4		
Jinkson, Thomas	1	1	5		
Gorsuch, Thomas	1	3	5	..	4
Phillips, Thomas, Senr	7	1	3	..	8

BALTIMORE COUNTY—Continued.

NAME OF HEAD OF FAMILY.	Free white males of 16 years and upward, including heads of families.	Free white males under 16 years.	Free white females, including heads of families.	All other free persons.	Slaves.
TWO DELEWARE HUNDREDS—continued.					
Phillips, Thomas, Junr	1		2		2
Macken, Thomas	1	1	2		
Beers, William	2	3	1	1	
Selman, William	2	1	8	1	
Ogg, William	1		2		
Orsler, William	1	2	2	2	
Anderson, William	1		1		
Bayley, William	1	1	4		
Gosnell, William	1	1	5		
Clark, William	1	5	5		
Hardigan, William	4		3		2
Hydem, William	1	4	3		
Wagers, William	3	1	3		
Bellison, William	3	4	2		
Pierce, Walter	2	4	3		
Thomas, William	2	1	5		
Herrington, William	2	1	1		
Boring, William	2	3	4		
Frizell, William	1	1	2		
Buckingham, William	1	4	4		
Parish, William, of Ed	1	1	3		
Pennington, William	4	1	3		
Buckingham, Zale	1	2	3		
Buckingham, Zebediah	1	1	2		
COUNTY NOT SEPARATED.					
Ambours, Stevins	1	1	4		
Austin, Benjas					3
Arnel, Peter	2	1	6		1
Arnel, Peter, Junr	2	1	3		1
Arnel, Mary			3		
Abit, Wm	2	4	3		
Arnel, Richd	1		2		
Austin, Laurance	3	2	2		
Earnist, Caleb	3	1	4		
Alter, Charles	1		1		
Allen, Jams	1	3	3		
Allen, Hugh	1	2	4		
Allen, John	1		1		
Altony, Thos	1		1		
Armontiage, Wm	1	2	2		
Anderson, Jams	1		2		
Asher, John	1	2	4		
Asher, Abraham	4	3	5		
Arnel, Joshua	2	2	5		6
Andrews, Wm	1	2	4		
Allender, Wm	3	2	3		17
Adams, Jams	1		2		
Allender, Fredarick	3	1	4		
Besard, Jams	3		2		
Butt, Wm	1	1	5		
Baxley, John	4	4	3		2
Bond, Richd, Junr	3		1		1
Butler, Mary			2		
Burk, Margaret	1	1	2		
Beit, Kitterich		3	4	1	
Biogden, Charles	1		2		
Bowing, *——ahue	2	1	3		20
Bowing, Josias	1		2		7
Buckhanan, Arter	2		2		
Bowing, Absolum	1	4	3		
Busk, John	1		3		
Baptist, Hardy	1	3	2		31
Barrell, Thos	1		1		
Brake, Rachal			3		1
Bowing, John	2		1		1
Bowing, Eduard	2		2		7
Batty, John	1	2	3		7
Batty, Fedarick	1	2	2		
Brown, Jams	2		4		2
Bratingburg, Vallentine	1	1	1		
Bumberger, Wm	1	3			
Barkley, Joseph	1	2	2		
Branch, Andrew	1	2	2		
Brown, Nicholes	1		2		2
Burns, Michael	1	2	3		
Bustel, John	1		1		
Burns, John	1	1	2		
Bitient, Lewis	1		1	1	
Bonnars, John	1		2		
Brian, Jams	3	1	3		11
Bowing, John	2	4	4		7
Biddason, Mashack	2	3	2		
Barton, Greenbury	1	3	5		5
Buck, Jams	3	3	1		5
Bacon, Ealum	2	2	2		
Busk, Ruth			2		
Brown, Thos	1	2	1		
Busk, Jams	2	1	2		
Bateman, Henary	1	5	4		
Bell, Henary	1	1	1		
Braun, Wm	3	2	4		

NAME OF HEAD OF FAMILY.	Free white males of 16 years and upward, including heads of families.	Free white males under 16 years.	Free white females, including heads of families.	All other free persons.	Slaves.
COUNTY NOT SEPARATED—continued.					
Buck, Joshua	2	1	4		1
Baly, Thos	2	1	4		6
Bond, Thos	4	4	4		3
Bond, Botaird	1	4	3		
Belson, John	1		3		
Biford, Henary	2		4		
Barton, Silla		1	3		
Biddason, Shadrick	1	1	4		1
Biddason, Thos	1		4		1
Belson, John Junr	1	2	4		
Bishop, Wm	2	3	5		
Backbout, Ann			2		
Biddason, Mashack Junr	1	2	2		1
Buck, Benjas	3	1	3		6
Biddason, Shadrick Junr	2	1	2		
Buck, John	1		3		9
Bazel, Elizabeth		1	3		
Barcks, David	1	2	2		
Bivans, Jesse	1	2	1		
Bivans, Rachal	1	2	5		
Coalget, Thos	3	1	3		4
Clay, Ann			2		
Cuningham, John	1	3	4		
Chinnoth, Arter	1		3		2
Conn, Daniel	1	1	2		
Clorges, John	2		2		
Clorges, Clod	2		3		
Cooper, Jacob	1	2	1		
Cobley, Nicholes	1		1		
Chisley, Rosanah			1		
Conn, Daniel Jnr	3		1		
Constobel, John	1		1		
Cook, Michael	2	2	2		
Cumins, John	1		3		
Clark, John	1	1	2		
Childs, George	1		1		
Clark, Richd	1	1	3		
Chambers, Daniel	2		1		
Other Free Persons				6	
Coaiter, John	3		2		5
Coal, Wm	2	1	6		
Casy, John	1	3	3		
Coal, Nathaniel	1		4		
Curry, Barnet	1	3	2		1
Coal, Saml	2		2		7
Councelman, Geo	2	2	2		
Crowley, Michael	2	2	4		3
Chesley, John	2	1	2		2
Cotteral, Thos	1	5	2		1
Clark, Benjas	1	1	5		
Cotral, Thos			1		
Crumage, Sarah	1	1	2		7
Crooks, Jams	2	1	4		5
Collins, Geo	2		2		
Carter, Richd		2	3		1
Carter, Joseph	1	3	1		
Coal, Richd	1	3	4		1
Cristopher, John	1	1	2		1
Councel, Geo	2		4		
Clark, Samuel	2	1	2		16
Clark, Wm	2		2		
Clark, Saml Junr	1	3	4		4
Carback, Thos	1	3	3		
Carback, Anthony	3	1	3		
Carback, John	1	3	3		
Carback, Valentine	2		1		
Carthrite, Abraham	3	1	2		
Cristopher, John Junr	1	3	3		1
Co, Greenbury	1	3	3		
Donally, Jams	1		1		
Dayly, Wm	1	2	4		
Divers, Daniel	1		2		
Divers, Ann			1		
Divers, Cristopher	2	3	1		1
Dellishier, Cristopher	1	1	2		
Dellishier, Vollentine	1		2		
Duning, John	2	4	2		
Drown, Thos	1	2	2		
Darling, Thos	1	2	2		
Duhurst, Jams	2	3	4		
Diel, Henary	2	7	3		
Dever, Wm	2		2		
Divese, Saml	1		2		
Dunking, Thos	1		1		
Dunmore, the Chevalear	1	1	1		10
Demit, Richd	1	2	2		
Dunavin, John	1	4	2		
Dever, Richd	1		3		
Dever, John	1		3		2
Due, Thos	1		4		
Dury, Jams	1		2		
Dukes, Cristopher	2		5		
Davis, Ann	1	3	5		
Disney, Wm	1	1	3		

NAME OF HEAD OF FAMILY.	Free white males of 16 years and upward, including heads of families.	Free white males under 16 years.	Free white females, including heads of families.	All other free persons.	Slaves.
COUNTY NOT SEPARATED—continued.					
Denton, John	3	1	6		2
Divas, Annias	16	4	4		74
Deen, Manniel	1	2	6		
Dorhordy, Catherener	1	2	2		8
Dever, Ann		2	1		3
Dolany, Daniel	1				
Dolils, Walter R	2	1	2		7
Denton, Wm	2	1	4		5
Edwards, Jams	2				
Egelston, Joseph	1	2	4		
Egleston, Elenor	1	1	2		8
Edwards, Jams	1				4
Evans, Daniel	2	3	7		1
Evans, Saml	1	1	2		
Edwards, John	2	1	4		
Bond, Barnet			2		
Bury, Susanah			1		
Bowley, Daniel	3	2	8		18
Fitchpattareck, Nathan	2	1	2		
Fowler, Zacheriah	1		5		
Fowler, Zachriah	1	1	1		
Fardenworth, Jams					9
Other Free Persons				9	
Farner, John	1	3	4		
Fids, Wm					7
Fitch, Henary	1	1	3		1
Fitch, Thos	1	1	1		
Fitch, Wm	1	1	4		5
Flanagin, John	1	1	3		
Fowler, Isaac	1	2	1		
Flanagin, Hienary	1	2	1		1
French, Otho	2		3		
French, Benjs	1	1	3		4
Hoid, John	1	1	3		
Fifer, John	1		1		
Fitz, Henary	1		7		
Franklin, Thos	1	1	4		
Fitz, Robert	2	1	4		
Fuller, Saml	1		3		
Flitcher, Henary	1		3		
Flitcher, John		4	1		
Fowler, Richd, Junr	1	1	2		
Fowler, Richd	1	5	4		
Fowler, Tamar	1	1	3		5
Franklin, Charles	2	1	3		
Gardner, Wm	1	1	2		
Gardner, John	2	1	2		
Gray, Jams	1				
Gray, Rebecca					
Gray, Epharam	2	1	6		1
Gorsuch, Thos	4	3	3		9
Gardner, Michael	2	3	4		
Grimes, Boston	2		3		
Other Free Persons				4	
Green, Moses	2	1	3		
Green, Joseph	3	1	3		2
Gittecum, John	1	1	2		
Gorsuch, Philip	1		2		
Grayham, John	1	1	6		
Gorden, John	1	2	2		
Gorsuch, John	2		7		4
German, John	1		1		
Gaswick, Daniel	1	2	1		
Grigger, John	1		2		
Grigger, John	1	3	2		
Grigger, Daniel	1		2		
Green, Joseph	1	1	1		4
Green, Ninson	1		2		9
Galloway, Thos	1	2	2		
Graves, John	4	1	2		
Griffin, Thos	2	1	2		
Galloway, Wm	1	1	1		9
Galloway, Jams	1	1	2		7
Galloway, John	1	2	4		5
Gray, Richd	1	2	3		15
Galloway, Moses	1		2		23
Graves, Tobitho	1	2	5		
Gorsuch, Daniel	2	2	2		
Griffin, Joseph	1		1		
Gaugh, Jams	1	1	1		
Griffin, John	2	3	3		
Grundy, Saml	1	1	1		
Griffin, John	1	2	3		
Other Free Persons				14	
Gaugh, Henary D	10	1	8		33
Griffith, John	1	2	3		4
Griffith, Henary	2		4		
Grimes, Reason	2		2		
Gillen, George	2		3		
Gash, Corneduce	2	1	4		1
Grimes, Jams	2	1	4		
Garritson, Job	7	1	7		12
Griggery, James	4		7		
Gash, Nicholes	1	2	4		

*Illegible.

BALTIMORE COUNTY—Continued.

NAME OF HEAD OF FAMILY.	Free white males of 16 years and upward, including heads of families.	Free white males under 16 years.	Free white females, including heads of families.	All other free persons.	Slaves.
COUNTY NOT SEPARATED—continued.					
Hlertipe, Jacob	5	5	5		
Handeon, Mary	1	1		3	8
Horsetiter, Frances	1		4	1	3
Hiser, John	2	2		4	
Hose, John	2		4	2	
Other Free Persons				11	
Hopkins, John	1		4	3	8
Haywood, Wm	4	1	2	2	
Howard, Wm	4	1		5	
Hiderson, Patterick	1	1	2		
Hall, Josias Carvel	1		2	2	9
Hufman, Daniel	1	2			
Hall, Mash	1	2			
Hood, Thos	2	6	1	1	
Hall, Saml	2	1	1	4	1
Hemly, George	2		1	4	
Hooper, Jacob	2	1	4		
Hillen, Solomond	2		3	4	12
Hide, Joseph	1	1	3	2	
Hilton, Sarah	1		1	3	
Holbrook, Jacob	1	2	4	7	
Holbrook, Wm	1	2	4	4	
Holeton, John	1		4	2	
Holton, Abraham	2	1	2		1
Holton, Wm	1	1	2	4	
Herryman, Thos	1		1	4	
Higets, Wm	1	1	1	3	
Hickman, Laurance	1		3	3	
Hambelton, Jams	1	1	1	1	
Hart, Henary	1		1	1	6
Hairs, Mary			1	3	
Hughes, Frances	1	3	2	2	
Hunt, Thos	1	3	3		5
Hammond, Abraham G.	6	1	6		7
Hants, Wm	1	4	2		
Hapins, John	1	1	2	2	
Hapins, Charity	3	3	4	1	
Hayston, John	3	2	1		
Other Free Persons				8	
Hisey, Jacob	1	1	4		
Holbrook, Jane		1	1		
Herryman, John	1	1	1		
Hammond, Wm	1	2	4	1	
Holland, Charles	1	1	4	4	
Hughs, Solomond	1	2	2		
Hughs, Mary	1	2	1	2	
Hilton, John	1		4	6	
Herriman, Joshua	1		1	3	
Herriman, Ann	3		3	3	
Jessop, Wm	3	1	5	2	2
James, Elizabeth				2	
Jones, John	1		2	2	
Jones, Thos	1	2	5	5	
Joyas, Wm	1	2	1	6	6
Junk, John	2	2	2	2	
Johnson, Joseph	2	1	3	3	
Ensor, Abraham	1	3	3		
Jones, Michael	1		3		
Johnson, Thos	1	1	2	5	
Jessop, Charles	8	1	2	5	
Jerry, John	1	1	2		
Ingold, Wm	2	2	2		
Jarman, Philip	2		2		
Jarman, Jane				1	
Jones, John	1	1	3		
Jones, John	1	3	3		
Jarman, John	2	2	4	2	
Jarman, Benjamin	2	1	2	1	
Jarman, Benjan	3		2	2	
Johnson, John	4	1	4		
Johnson, Joseph	4		3	4	
Johnson, John	1	2	3		
Other Free Persons				7	
Jarman, Thos	1	1	1		
Jones, Mary	1		1		
Cilman, John	1	2	2		
Clap, John	1	1	2	3	
Kiser, Gasper	5	5	1	3	
Kelly, Edward	1	1	2	1	
Kofman, Abraham	1	5	1	3	
Lynch, Gray	2		1		
Lavalin, Barry	2	1	1	3	
Lynch, Robuck	2		4		16
Lynch, Pattarick	2	1		6	
Lee, Wm	2		1	4	
Litson, Big	2	1	3	1	
Laurance, Wentel	2		1	4	
Laurance, Farden	1	3	1		
Leat, Simon	1	1	3	3	
Lony, Amus	1		2	2	
Laming, Benjamin	3	1	2	7	
Leakins, Robert	2		2	8	
Long, Robert	2	1	3		
Long, John	2		4	11	
Longland, Joseph	1	1	5	7	
Lowe, Wm	1		2	9	
COUNTY NOT SEPARATED—continued.					
Litsinger Peter	1		1		2
Litsinger, Wm	1	1	3		1
Lee, Aquilla	1	1	3		
Lidard, Thos	3	1	7	7	
Logen, Jesse	1	1	2		1
Ledg, John	1	1	2		
Light, John	1		2	3	
Ledg, Rachal		1	3		
Lodly, John	1		3	5	
Light, Benjaman	2		2	2	
Ledg, Nathan	1	2		5	
Love, Wm	1	2		2	
Lynch, Elenor			2		
McKindles, Robert	2	1	4	1	1
Messersmith, Mathias	2	1	1	1	
Murry, John	2		2	2	1
McGrew, Andrew	1	3	1	2	
Morford, Stephen	1	1	3	1	
Madewell, Alexander	2		2	3	
Miller, George	2	4	2	3	1
McMachan, Wm	1		2	3	
McGuyer, James	1	2			
McCubin, Wm	2		2	2	21
Madewell, James	4	1	1	6	
McMachen, Judah			2	3	
Mitchel, Wm	1		2	3	
Miel, Philip	2	1	2	6	
Mummy, David	1	2	2	2	
Memran, Saml	1		1	6	
Martin, Thos	1		1	5	
McKindles, Wm	1	2		4	
Merryman, Joseph	1		2	3	1
Meedy, Wm	1		2	2	
McGrigger, John	1		1	4	6
Menes, Daniel	1	1	2		
Mummy, Barbary			2	4	
Mummy, Cristopher	1	2	2	5	
Miller, Henary	1		2	3	
Matticks, Wm		4	2	2	
Mully, John	2		4	1	
Morris, Charles	2	1	2	3	
Matthew, Meed	1		3	3	11
Milden, Elizabeth	2	1	1	1	
Marshal, John	1		1	3	
Morgin, Michael	2	1	1	3	
Morgin, James	2	1	4	3	
McCasgay, James	2		2	5	9
Martain, Henary	1		2	4	
Milds, Thos	1		4	2	
Maloney, James	1	2	2	2	
McGuyer, Thos	1		2	2	
McHenary, Daniel	1	2	1	2	
McGriggery, John	2	2	1	4	
Mackaby, John	2	1	2	5	7
McHenary, Daniel	2	1	2	3	
McDoniel, John	2	1	2	5	
McCubins, John	1	2		4	1
Mones, Charles	3		2	1	
Mockabe, John	1			1	
McSwany, Jerrimiah	1	1			
Norwood, Ann			1	5	1
Naylor, Wm	3		1	3	
Nizer, John	1	1	2	3	
Naylor, Wm	1		2	1	
Other Free Persons				12	
Nickels, Nathon	1	1	2		3
Nizer, John A.	1	1	1	3	
Norris, Rachal	1		2	3	
Other Free Persons				13	
Odonneld, John	10		6	36	
Orchard, Thos	1	2		4	
Ostern, Henary	1			4	
Orsburn, Joseph	1			4	
Offall, John	1			4	
Offield, John	1			4	
Orsburn, Joseph	1			4	
Offaral, Thos	1		1	6	
Olover, John	1		1	1	1
Orum, Henary	3		2	6	
Other Free Persons				3	
Philips, Wm	1		1		
Poor, Pattarick	1			3	
Price, Mordaca	2	3	3	5	1
Partaradge, John	1		3	1	8
Partaradge, Wm	2		2	5	
Pierce, John	13	1	6	6	12
Pierce, Charles	6	2	5	5	
Phillps, Nathaniel	2		2	7	
Perrigo, John	1	6	1	4	
Penington, Josias	10	6	2	9	
Pool, Wm	1		1	2	
Potton, Frances	1	1		2	
Pendergrass, Patterick	1		2	2	
Penny, Henary	1		2	2	
Parlett, Martain	1		1	2	
Parlett, Wm	1	3	3		3
COUNTY NOT SEPARATED—continued.					
Parlet, David	2	3	3		
Pocock, James	2	1	2		1
Porter, Jesse	2	2	3		
Paul, Peter	1	2	2	4	
Penny, James	1		2	3	
Pedard, Robert	1		2	3	
Parlot, Wm	1		3		3
Parlot, Martain	1		3	3	
Parlot, David	1	1	3	3	
Pattarige, Dominick B.	1	1	2	3	
Porter, John Messer	1		2		14
Parcks, Aquilla	1	1	3	5	6
Parcks, John	1	1	1	6	4
Parcks, Fredaricks	1		1	6	2
Parcks, Archabel	1		3	6	2
Parcks, Sarah			1	4	
Presbury, George, Jur.	1		2		5
Presbury, Walter	2		4		15
Pick, Robert	1		3		
Patten, John	1	3	2		
Price, Nathaniel	1	1	2	3	
Price, Wm	1		2		5
Price, Simon	1	3			
Parker, Thos	1		2		
Pines, Wm	1	6	4		
Parcks, John	1	2	2		
Ribins, Robert	1		2	1	
Row, John	3	2	1		
Roylons, Wm	2		2	3	
Roulands, Ruth			5	9	
Roulands, Richo	3	1		1	
Rusk, Thos	3		2		
Rogers, James	1	1	3		3
Richards, James	1		3	3	
Renshol, Jesse	1		1	2	
Ryle, Adam	1		1	2	
Ryle, Cunrod	1		2	2	
Roddy, Pattarick	1		2	2	
Ryle, George	1		2	1	
Ross, James	2	1	1		
Rafe, John	1			6	
Ryan, Sarah			1	5	
Robertson, Joseph	1	1		3	
Roberts, Jemina			1	2	
Roberts, Aquilla	1	2	4		
Morris, Wm	1	2	2	4	
Rumplinger, John	1		2	4	
Roch, John	1	3		2	
Read, John	1		2	1	
Rossen, Wm	1		1	2	
Rusk, Thos	1		1	1	1
Richards, Saml	1			2	
Rogers, Benjan	3	1		3	10
Rogers, Charles	3		3	5	
Rees, Geo	1		2	4	1
Robin, John	1	1	1	4	
Ritler, Adam	1		2	1	1
Romer, John	1		3	4	
Rees, Daniel	2	1	2		
Quaner, Bynard	1	1	3		
Read, Wm	4		4		
Right, Wm	4	1	3		
Readeles, Wm	1	2			
Richards, Margaret			2	4	
Richards, John	1	2	4		1
Roberts, Benjan	2		2	4	
Robertson, Charles	2	3	3		3
Richardson, James	1	3	2	5	
Rodes, John	1		2	5	
Roylands, Wm	1	2	2	4	
Rusk, Wm	1	1		4	23
Raven, Isaac	1		2		
Raven, Luke	1	3	1	4	6
Reynor, Tobias	2	1	1		
Other Free Persons				8	
Roberts, Thos	1	2	4		2
Right, Abraham	3	2	8		
Stake, Antony	2		2	5	
Smith, John	1		2	3	
Sap, Daniel	1	6	3		
Stone, Edword	1		3	5	
Simond, Henary	1	1	2	5	
Stansbury, Tobias	3		3	4	14
Stansbury, Mary	2	3	3	4	6
Stansbury, Richo	5	1	1		
Sollars, Joseph	2	1	1	6	3
Smith, John	1	2	2	2	
Sweting, Edword	2	3	4	2	12
Sweeting, Robert	3		2	4	
Shaw, Thos	2	1	2		
Shaw, Night Smith	1		2		9
Shaw, Wm	2	1	2	4	14
Smith, Saml	3	2	4		10
Stansbury, Daniel	3	2	2		9
Sindal, David	1		3		1

BALTIMORE COUNTY—Continued.

NAME OF HEAD OF FAMILY.	Free white males of 16 years and upward, including heads of families.	Free white males under 16 years.	Free white females, including heads of families.	All other free persons.	Slaves.
COUNTY NOT SEPARATED—continued.					
Sindal, Joseph	1		2		
Shaw, Mary	1		2		
Smith, Wm	2	1	3		
Stoph, John	1		3		
Stevinson, Henary	3	3	4		10
Swingal, Peter	1	1	2		
Stewart, Ann			1		1
Sly, John	1		3		
Strider, Joseph	1	3	3		
Stevenson, Mordaca	1	2	2		
Shilling, Tobias	1	3	1		
Shearman, James	1	3	3		
Sindal, Philip	2	3	3		1
Shaw, Matthew	1	4	2		
Swingal, George	1	2	4		
Scott, Rossater	3	2	4		
Stevenson, Wm	1	1	3		2
Stevenson, Geo	1	1	4		2
Stansbury, John	2		2		9
Silby, John	1		4		
Stansbury, Charles	3		2		7
Stansbury, David	3	2	3		
Stansbury, Richd	2	1	2		7
Shaw, Sabey	1	1	1		
Stinchicome, Aquilla	1	3	4		8
Sulagen, Judah			2		
Skinner, John	2		1		20
Stell, Gabrial	1	1	2		
Smitson, Daniel	1	2	1		
Stansbury, John D	1	3	4		2
Spiser, Abraham	1				19
Stewart, Wm	1		1		
Stansbury, Abraham	1	3	4		1
Sanders, Mary	1	3	4		
Other Free Persons				12	
Stansbury, Joseph	1	1	4		8
Stansbury, James	2	1	1		5
Stansbury, Daniel	3	1	2		
Silvester, John	1		4		
Tawn, John	1	2	6		1
Trimbel, James	1	3	3		
Trotton, Susanah	1	1	3		11
Todd, Thos	7	3	2		27
Thronton, Wm	1	1	3		
Tompson, Charles	1	1	3		
Trasy, Benjan	1	4	3		
Taylor, Philip	1	2	3		
Taylor, Robert	1	2	3		1
Tanner, Francis	2	2	2		1
Trasy, Benjan	1	5	3		
Todd, Laurance	3	1	2		
Taylor, Richd	3	2	5		
Other Free Persons				20	
Taylor, Saml	1				
Taylor, Patiants	2	2	4		
Other Free Persons				20	
Taylor, Robert	2	3	4		
Taylor, James	1	4	5		
Tompson, John	1	1	1		
Thornbury, Frances	3	1	1		
Tompson, Mary		1	2		
Tuder, Elizabeth	1		3		
Thrauls, Saml	1		4		
Taylor, Joseph	1		1		3
Todd, Nicholus	1		3		
Underwood, Joseph	1	2	3		
Vanvout, John	2		2		
Vershon, Charles	1		3		
Van bibber, Abraham	2	1	3		16
Varnard, George	2	2	3		
Varford, James	3		3		
Welch, James	1		1		
West, Benjan	1		1		
Wilks, Wm	1		2		
West, Sarah	1	4	1		1
Walters, Jacob	2	1	5		18
Woodard, Timethy	2	2	2		
Wats, Josias	1	2	1		5
Wells, Joseph	2	4	1		
With, Wm	1	1	3		
Wood, Robison	2	1	3		
Williams, Charles	1	4	5		
Williamson, David	1	2	3		
Wilson, Joseph	1	2	2		
Witingburger, Lewis	1	3	1		
Williams, Isaac	1	1	2		
Williams, Geo	4	1	2		
West, Eliga	2		2		1
Williams, Andrew	1		2		
Other Free Persons				12	
Wighter, Henary	7	1	3		
Weatherington, Thos	1	1			3
Willmore, Patiants	1	2	4		1
Woodden, John	5	2	2		7

NAME OF HEAD OF FAMILY.	Free white males of 16 years and upward, including heads of families.	Free white males under 16 years.	Free white females, including heads of families.	All other free persons.	Slaves.
COUNTY NOT SEPARATED—continued.					
Wilcox, Wm	1		2		
Walker, Cristopher	2	3	1		2
Woodcock, Wm	1		2		
Williame, John G	1	1	3		
Other Free Persons				4	
Wots, Thos	1	2	2		4
Wheeler, John	1	1	2		
Walker, David	1	4	1		
Woolerick, Philip	1		6		1
Worral, Wm	1	1	2		
Waller, Bazel	1	1	3		5
Wilson, John	1	2			
Welch, Wm	2		1		12
Waller, Wm	2	4	2		7
Waller, Walter	1	1	2		
Weatherington, Wachael	1				6
Walter, James	4		2		6
Walker, Thos	3	2	1		
Willage, James	2		2		
Wigly, Edword	1	1	3		1
Wilson, Given	1		3		1
Wight, Luke	3		4		2
Wair, Thos	1	2	3		
Wilson, Nichoelson	1	1	4		
Worton, Wm	1		2		
Wigley, Isaac	2	1	3		2
West, Edword	1	4	3		2
Wilson, James	1		1		
Waller, Ann	1	3	3		3
Waller, Wm	1	3	3		1
Woods, Wm	1	2	4		1
Wigley, Edword	1		1		
Waller, Zacheial	1	1	2		
Worrel, Wm	2		2		
Yeats, Thos	6	2	6		5
McLaughlin, Thos	1		1		
Welch, John	2		2		
Chamberlin, John	2	4	5		11
Langdin, Thos	1	1	3		
Hooper, Elizabeth			1		
Cook, James	2	3	2		
Darnil, Henary B	2				29
Roberts, Benjan	2	2	3		
Storm, Jacob	1	2	4		
Gittings, James	3	1	7		55
Chamberlin, Philip	2	1	8		3
Trap, Wm	1		5		
Crumwell, Wm	1		4		12
Hunter, George	2	5	5		
Foster, Abraham	1	1	3		
Law, James	2		4		
Hunter, Peter	1	2	2		4
Ford, Isaac	2	2	2		3
Guyton, Underwood	2	4	4		1
Chamberlin, Thos	1	1	5		
McLaughlin, Denis	1	1	2		
Got, Johnothan	2	2	2		
Cullins, Jerrimiah	3	1	3		
Wilson, Henary	2	1	1		17
Galloway, Aquilla	2	2	4		6
Weel, Saml	2	1	1		
Ellott, John	2		2		
Wilson, John	2	3	3		8
Hooper, Isaac	2	4	2		
Wilson, John, Junr	1		8		2
Right, Solomon	1	4	3		5
Rice, James	3		2		
Enriso, Thos	2	3	3		3
Flutter, John	1		1		
Rigley, George	2	1	4		
Lynch, Hulbrady	1	5	2		1
McCasal, Jacob	3	2	4		
McCasal, Catherener		2	4		
Ellott, Mary			2		
Mayson, John	1	1	1		
Downs, Joseph	1	5	2		
Corbin, Joseph	1		1		1
Woodden, Thos	1	1	3		
Balden, Silliah	2	1	5		1
Comas, Calemin	3	3	3		
Voice, Thos	1	3	6		
Grover, Wm	6	2	4		1
Allen, John	1	5	2		
Allen, Wm	3	1	4		
Wodle, John	1	3	2		
Lynch, Cornelus	3		1		3
McCam, John	3	1	5		1
Hughs, James	1	2	2		1
Weston, Thos	1		3		
Gudging, Sutton	5	3	6		5
Belt, Orashey	2	3	2		11
Mash, Thos	3		3		14
Inlows, James	1	2	6		

NAME OF HEAD OF FAMILY.	Free white males of 16 years and upward, including heads of families.	Free white males under 16 years.	Free white females, including heads of families.	All other free persons.	Slaves.
COUNTY NOT SEPARATED—continued.					
Fitzstue, Geo	2	6	4		22
Hopkins, Zechael	1		3		5
Mash, Joshua	1	2	2		8
Corbin, Abraham	1	3	2		8
Bosley, James	1	2	9		1
Corbin, Joseph	1		1		1
Herriod, Robert	1	3	2		
Allen, Wm	3	1	4		
Allen, John	1	4	3		
Jinkins, Ignatious	1	4	3		14
Thobel, Robert	1		1		
Other Free Persons				7	
Barridy, Edword	1		2		
Hughs, James	1	2	2		
Keal, Fleming	1	4	2		
Backwith, Wm	1		2		13
Sias, James	4	2	2		
Willes, John	1	1	1		
Mash, Thos	1		2		1
Bramly, Wm	1	2	3		
Headington, Elisha	3		4		7
Caywood, Edword	1		1		
Reavs, Thos	2	1	1		
Winks, Joseph	1	2	4		
Boslay, Elizabeth	1	3	4		
Headington, Zebulin	2	2	2		3
Jones, John	1	2	8		6
Jones, Enias	1	2	4		
Ligget, Sutton	3	4	3		
Herrington, Abel	1	4	5		4
Britten, Richd	2	1	6		17
Wells, Richd	1	1	2		
Williams, Thos	1	1	5		
Burk, Mary	1	4	1		2
Green, Venson	1		2		
Hutchings, Thos	2	5	2		8
Jones, Wm	1	3	1		1
Burges, Henary	1	1	1		
Franklin, James	3	1	5		84
Other Free Persons				9	
Barnet, Richd	1	5	1		
Callwell, Thos	1	4	1		
Perrigo, Elisha	1		4		
Frances, Saml	2	8	2		
Connel, Wm	4	1	3		
Gorsuch, Lewis	1	2	4		
Shiers, Nicholcs	1		1		
Standfield, James	1	2	2		
Connal, Charles	1	2	2		1
Chinoth, Richd	1	1	1		
Logus, Richd	2	1	1		1
Anderson, Richd	1	2	2		
Culaston, Jesse	1	3	4		
Fowson, Obidiah	1	4	3		
Neail, John	1		1		
Mayson, John	1	1	1		
Hill, Saml	1	1	5		
Harriod, Richd	1	3	2		
Other Free Persons				4	
Miller, Hannah	1	1	2		
All, Edword	3	2	3		6
Wilson, Robert	3	3	2		
Jones, Eanus	1	2	4		
Green, Bednigo	1		4		
Rylant, Nicholus	1	2	1		
Binnix, Barny	2	2	5		
Perrigo, Wm	1	2	6		1
Burk, Richd	1	1	2		
Jones, Jacob	1	2	3		8
Coal, Thos	3	3	4		
Tuder, Thos	3	2	2		
Woodams, Wm	1	2	1		
Wheeler, Joseph	1	1	2		
Edwords, John S	2		1		1
Whorrel, Amond	1	2	2		4
Nicholson, Benja	6	4	8		14
Other Free Persons				14	
Pegy, Wm	1				
Stansbury, Marryman	1	1	1		
Barber, Daniel	2		2		
Ensor, Wm	3		3		
Welch, Abrialer	1	1	3		
Crosgy, Frances	3	2	2		9
Right, Solomond	2	3	2		5
Murphy, John	1		1		
Hitchcock, Wm	1	1	1		1
Carroll, Henary	1		2		11
Amas, Thos	1	4	3		3
Boyce, Thos	1	3	6		
Lynch, Cornelus	1		1		1
Wotkins, Saml	3		2		6
Comb, Coalman	2	3	3		
Butler, Thos	1	2	5		
Bowlin, Sillias	4	1	5		1

BALTIMORE COUNTY—Continued.

NAME OF HEAD OF FAMILY.	Free white males of 16 years and upward, including heads of families.	Free white males under 16 years.	Free white females, including heads of families.	All other free persons.	Slaves.
COUNTY NOT SEPARATED—continued.					
Rice, James	2	1	2		
Jinkins, Michael	2	2	5		22
Ditto, Abraham	3		2		7
McCheny, Stephen	1	1	4		
Demit, James	2	3	4		2
Ford, Isaac	3	2	3		3
Barry, Elizabeth	2		2		6
Barnes, Wm	1				
Gorsuch, Charles	1	4	4		9
Baker, Nathaniel	2		6		
Guyton, John	2		2		2
Chance, John	2	1	3		3
Standiford, Abraham	1	5	4		
Thomas, Wm	1	3	4		
Hunt, Simond	2	4	5		
McMasters, Alexr	3	1	6		
Woters, Isaac	1	4	3		
Tord, Thos	2	2	2		
Magens, John	2	1	2		
Jones, Thos	1	2	6		
Williams, Robert	1		2		
Wells, John	1		2	1	
Playton, Joseph	1	3	7		
Mitchel, Enock	1	6	2		
Newbury, Joseph	2	2	1		1
Dunaway, James	1	2	2		
Chrisel, Robert	1	2	2		
Other Free Persons				13	
Bain, John	1		2		
Brannen, Thos	1	3	2		
Dowey, James	1	2	3		
Guyton, Benjn, Jr	1		3		
Howard, John B	3				11
Howard, John	1		2		
Paxton, Samuel			1		1
Sanders, Wm	2	1			
Pitcook, Moses	1	2	3		
Sneks, Zacha	3	4	4		
Demit, Wm	5	2	5		4
Paul, Thos	4	2	3		
Bannen, Thos	1	2			
Bain, John	1				
Scroging, Elizabeth			1		
Cursings, George	2	1	3		
Tredwill, Daniel	1	2	3		
Douty, Thos	3		1		
Collins, John	2	2	5		
Howard, Thos G	4	3	7		24
Ostler, Ealy	2	3	6		
Aylor, George	2	2	4		
Allen, Solomond	4	3	4		4
Allen, Patrick	1	1	1		
Askew, Joshua	1		5		3
Ostler, Frances	1		3		
Aylor, Patrick	4	4	1		
Allen, Richd	1	1			
Abrams, Jacob	1	3	2		
Hopkins, Hopkin	1		2		
Rester, Rister F	1		2		11
Elliott, James	3	3	5		
Jones, Watkins	2		2		
Burtin, Wm	1	1	1		
Ligget, John	1	2	3		
Due, Robert	1		2		
Williams, Thos	1		3		
Alburt, Zacheriah	1	1	6		
Antony, Adam	1		2		
Adams, Wm	1		1		
Anglespeger, Frances	2		1		
Alwood, Wm	2	3	4		
Ambers, Wm	1		1		
Allgeriar, John, Junr	1		2		
Other Free Persons				1	
Allgeriar, Jacob	2	1	4		
Alder, Mary	1	1	3		
Anderson, Edword			1		
Almack, Wm	1	2	3		
Armonset, John	1				
Ambis, Wm, Jr	1	4	4		1
Alven, Rafe	1	1	3		
Albaugh, Zacheriah	1	1	6		
Adketson, Joseph	1	1	3		
Arrios, Wm	1	3	2		
Alguiar, John	2	3	7		
Alguiar, Jacob	2	1	3		
Brown, Thos	1	1	4		
Butler, John	1	1	2		
Baker, Nicholes	1				
Baly, Mary	2	1	3		
Baly, Geo	1	2	3		22
Baly, Mary	2		3		
Baly, Ealy	11				26
Brooks, George	1		1		
Baly, Wm	1	1	4		
COUNTY NOT SEPARATED—continued.					
Buchaneneus, Wm, Negroes of					8
Butler, Amond	2	2	2		1
Butler, Amond, Jur	1	4	4		1
Butler, Absolum	1	2	3		8
Bowars, Daniel	4		5		3
Bierly, Ledwick	1		1		
Ball, Edword	1	2	4		
Buckingham, Joseph	1	1	2		
Buckingham, Thos	1		2		
Baker, Nicholes	1	1	4		
Baker, Elizabeth	1	1	6		
Baker, Ealy	1	1	3		
Baly, James	1	1	1		
Baly, Ann	2	2	2		
Baker, Zebulin	1	2	2		
Burk, John	1	2	3		
Brothers, Austin	1	5	1		
Baughman, Henary	2	1	3		
Bardell, Charles	1				
Brothers, Mary			1	1	
Ball, John	1	1	3		
Baly, Thos	1	2			
Barney, Rebecca			2		
Beasey, Wm	3	2	2		6
Brooks, Elizabeth			2		
Baly, John	4	2	3		
Brown, Henary	2	3	2		2
Brown, Wm	1	1	4		
Baker, Henary	3	1	5		
Brown, Wm, Junr	1	1	5		
Cromer, Michael	2	2	1		2
Cromer, Vallentine	1	2	4		
Chinoth, Arter	2	1	7		8
Chinoth, Saml	2	5	3		11
Criswell, Richd	1	3	3		
Chinoth, Wm	1		2		
Cossouer, Jacob	2	2	5		
Crider, Martin	1	2	7		
Coulrider, John	2	2	7		
Carr, Andrew	1	1	5		
Campbell, James	7	3	4		
Cullins, Johnothan	2	2	5		
Cullins, John	1	1	2		
Cullins, Thos	1		4		
Cullins, Isaac	2	2	4		
Cumins, Antony	1		4		
Cob, Zechael	2	3	4		
Cath, Michael	2	3	4		
Cullins, Edword	2		1		
Cross, Joshua	1	2	2		
Coal, Thos	1	1	2		3
Climp, John	1	3	2		
Cooper, John	1		1		
Creemer, Mary		1	2		
Citinger, Jacob	2		2		
Chilcoat, Richd	2		1		
Coal, Morris	2	2	5		2
Chamberlin, Saml	2		3		
Cooper, Stephen	2	2	3		
Crampton, Thos	2	1	3		
Crumwell, John	1		3		3
Clark, Joseph	1		2		
Crage, Robert	1	2	2		
Cable, Robert	1	1	2		
Climp, John	1	2	1		
Coal, Elisha	1	2	2		
Co, Nathaniel					1
Cox, Zebulin	2	4	2		
Carroll, Margaret	4		4		47
Clemmon, Edword	1	4	1		
Clark, Richd	2	1	6		
Clark, John	2	1	5		
Criswell, Benjn	2	1	1		
Cross, John	2		2		
Chinoth, Richd	1		1		
Crumwell, John	1	3	3		
Crumwell, John Go	1		2		
Crafford, John	1	2	3		
Canaday, John	1		5		
Chamberlin, Saml	1		2		
Croxtill, John	4		5	1	4
Other Free Persons				1	
Clemmons, Edword	1	3	1		
Conaway, Thos	2		1		
Credick, Thos	2		1		10
Croxtell, Elenor	2		1		25
Conner, Thos	2				
Craft, Wm	2	3	2		
Crumly, Caleb	2		3		
Cable, Jacob	1	2	2		
Crage, Robert	1	2	2		
Councelman, Geo	2	2	2		
Curtis, Thos	1				
COUNTY NOT SEPARATED—continued.					
Crook, Henary	2	2	2		
Conalin, Antony	1	2	2		
Chapman, Nathan	5	2	5		
Cramer, Felty	1	5	2		
Councelman, Elizabeth	1	4	4		
Councelman, John	1	1	4		
Crook, Saml	1	5	3		
McCray, Saml	1	2	1		
Cook, John	1	2	3		
Cook, Thos	3		3		
Conaway, Richd	1	1	4		1
Carty, Fredarick	1		3		
Creamer, Peter	1	3	3		
Cross, Wm	1	4	4		
Cook, Wm	1	3	3		
Dorsey, Zacheriah	2		2		11
Delworth, Wm	3	1	2		
Delworth, Joseph	2	2	2		
Dashin, Isaac	1				
Draperd, Mary			1		
Dismal, Wm			4		
Dew, Joseph	1		2		
Defy, Alexr	1		2		
Dorsey, Bazel	2		5		1
Demanis, Jacob	2	4	2		
Decker, Jacob	1		2		1
Duning, Benjn	2	1	5		
Duncan, Benje	2	2	4		
Davis, Robert	5	4	6		
Ditto, Jacob	2		2		
Dile, John	1	3	3		
Dick, Jacob	1	3	2		
Dick, Fredarick	2	2	2		
Davis, Wm	1	2	2		
Davis, James	2		1		
Davis, John	1	1	4		
Duton, Edword	1	1	4		
Day, Mark	1	1	4		
Day, Isaac	1	1	6		
Deeds, Philip	1	3	1		
Downey, Thos	2	3	7		
Downey, Walter	1	4	3		
Deams, John	2	2	5		
Dever, Steven	2		4		
Doyal, Richd	1		4		
Dew, Jacob	1		3		
Demsy, John	1	1	1		
Deen, Johnathan	1		2		
Deen, Henary	1		3		
Davis, John	1	1	3		
Dorsey, Elisha	3	1	3		2
Demsy, John	1	1	2		
Davis, Wm	1	3	2		
Epard, John	1	2	2		
Ellicott, John	28	2	7		
Ellicott, Johnothan	2	1	3		1
Other Free Persons				3	
Edwords, Elisha	2	2	2		
Elphant, Andrew	1	1	1		
Epard, John, Jur	1	1	1		
Elzer, John	1	4	5		
Ederrong, Jacob	2	2	4		
Ederrong, Cristopher	2	2	4		
Enzor, Johnothon	1	1	2		1
Eckien, Jacob	1	3	4		
Eckier, Jacob, Junr	1	2	1		
Eckellstpeger, Peter	1	2	3		
Edwords, John	1	2	3		
Estgrig, Daniel	3	2	5		1
Ethard, John	2	1	2		
Enzor, George	3		6		2
Enzor, Darby	3	1	6		
Enzor, Elizabeth	1		2		7
Ephaugh, George	1		2		
Ephaugh, Henary	2	2	7		1
Everhart, Geo	1	2	7		
Emtire, Abraham	2		4		
Elserod, Fredarick	1		7		
Elserod, Fredarick	2	2	2		
Ellisburger, Peter	1	1	3		
Enzor, Nathaniel	1		3		
Estgrig, John	3	2	2		1
Fling, James	1		6		
Frog, Boston	1	3	7		
Ford, John H	1	6	1		4
Fearnott, Andrew	4		1		
Folton, Charles	1		1		
French, Frances	1	1	2		
Ford, Thos	3	1	1		1
Fenton, Charles	3		1		
Fulhart, Philip	2		1		
Frizel, John	2	3	2		7
Fulhart, Jacob	1	1	3		
Fight, Andrew	1	1	3		

BALTIMORE COUNTY—Continued.

NAME OF HEAD OF FAMILY.	Free white males of 16 years and upward, including heads of families.	Free white males under 16 years.	Free white females, including heads of families.	All other free persons.	Slaves.
COUNTY NOT SEPARATED—continued.					
Furney, Daniel	2	1	2		
Fisher, George	2	1	4		
Flutter, Geo.	1	2	2		
Fair, Geo.	1	3	2		
Fight, Wiley	1	1	5		
Fisher, John	1		1		
Fisher, John Junr	1	1	2		
Foster, Francis	2	1	5		
Foster, Nicholas	2	2	2		
Frank, Philip	2	3	4	1	
Franger, Michael	2		1		
Foster, Adam	1	1		1	
Ford, Joshua	1	2	2		1
Other Free Persons				1	
Feather, Philip	1	3	5		
Fisher, Michael	1		3		
Foster, Thos	1	1	3		
Frazer, John	3	2	4		
Foster, Abraham	1		1		1
Ford, Barney	1	2	2		1
Ford, Rashey	1		1		
Fisher, Joseph	4	2	5	1	
Frances, John	1	1	2		
Ford, Mordeca	1	2	1		7
Foubel, Fredarick	1	3	2		
Foubel, Michael	1	2	6		1
Frankford, Henary	2	2	2		
Fisher, Geo., Junr	1		3		
Fisher, Michael, Jur	2	3	6		
Fisher, Leonard	2	1	1		
Fraylor, Uriah	3	1	4		
Freeman, Wm	1		3		
Fairs, Stophal	5	2	2		
Fisher, Geo.	1	3	3		
Feather, Adam	2	1	5		
Farner, James	1		2		
Farden, John	1	2	2		
Foubel, Peter	2	3	1		1
Felty, Felix	1	1	1		
Frayland, Zacheus	3	1	5		
Grand, John	2	3	1		1
Goar, Elizabeth		3	1		
Goar, Michael	2		2		5
Goar, Michael, Jur	1	3	6		
Goldsmith, Thos	2	1	3		
Grough, Adam	2	4	1		
Guivens, Thos	1		4		1
McGraendfield, Cogney	1	1	5		
Goodman, John	1		3		
Greenfield, Michael	1	1	6		
Green, Henary	1	1	3		
Gunnison, Pattarick	2	4	3		
Grier, Michael	4		3		
Gladman, Michael	1	4	5		
Greenwood, Thos	2	2	3		5
Griffith, Johnothon	1		3		
Griffith, John	3	1	1		1
Geoye, John	3		3		
Getter, George	1		1		
Gist, George	1	4	4		
Gumil, Martin	1		1		
Gumil, Cunrod	1	1	2		
Greene, Elizabeth			1	6	
Gain, John	1		1		
Gist, Susanah			3		5
Gist, Joseph	2	3	5		1
Gist, Wm	1		2		5
Gain, Wm	2	1	2		
Goodwin, Daniel	2		3		
Goodwin, George	1	2	2		
Guill, Nicholes	2	1	6		4
Guill, Stephen	1	4	1		6
Guill, Edward	2	1	2		4
Gray, John	1	1	1		
Green, Joshua	1		3		
Gall, Michael	1	1	4		
Grayham, John	3	4	3		
Gain, John, Junr	2	4	2		
Gorsuch, Thos	1	2	4		
Gray, Jacob	1	2	5		
Griffin, Charles	1	2	4	2	
Jenkens, Joseph	1	3	2		
Griffin, Benjn	1	1	1		
Goar, Cristopher	1	3	5		2
Green, Thos	1	4	4		
Greathouse, David	1		1		
Greathouse, Harmon	1	1	1		
Gantz, Adam	2		2		
Gladman, Michael	1		5		
Gilherst, Robert	2	1	3		4
Gusnel, Nicholes	3	1	1		
Gusnel, Hooper	1	1	3		
Gusnel, Charles	1	2	2		
Gusnel, Philip	1	2	2		
Gusnel, Mordeca	1	2			

NAME OF HEAD OF FAMILY.	Free white males of 16 years and upward, including heads of families.	Free white males under 16 years.	Free white females, including heads of families.	All other free persons.	Slaves.
COUNTY NOT SEPARATED—continued.					
Gusnel, Peter	1		2		
Green, Henary	3		2		
Grayham, James	1	5	2		
Gusnel, Greenbuary	1		1		1
Gusnel, Zebulin	1	2	6		
Gusnel, John	2	3	4		
Grayham, James	1	1	3		
Gusnel, Joshua	1	1	3		
Gore, John	1	1	2		
Green, Henary	1	2	1		6
Gilard, John	1		6		
Gray, James	1	1	2		
Gusnel, Philip	1	1	2		1
Guill, Edward	1	1	2	3	
Guill, Benjn	1	1	2	6	
Guttery, Wm	1	2	2		
Guill, Thos	2	2	5	2	
Giles, Benjn	1		2		
Gitter, Peter	2	2	5		
Grayland, Moses	1	3	1		
Hutson, Joshua	2	1	1		1
Hutson, Thos	2	1	2		
Hart, John	1	1	4		
Holms, James	1	2	4		
Hair, Jacob	1	2	3		1
Harvy, Thos	2		3		15
Huets, Randel	2		3		
Hooker, Jacob	3	1	5		
Huffman, Wm	1	4	5		
Henary, Nicholes	1	2	4		
Hust, Benadick	2	2	2		
Harper, Joseph	1	2	4		
Hall, Tilly	1	3	3		
Hilterbrider, Jacob	1		2		
Huden, Wm	1		1		
Hovers, Fredarick	1	8	3		
Hany, Matthias	1	3	3		
Hatler, Frances	1	2	3		
Harris, Geo	2	3	5	1	
Hager, Geo	1		2		
Other Free Persons				1	
Hooker, Thos	3	2	3		
Hooper, Thos	2	4	4		
Hair, Stophal	1	1	8		
Hage, Arter	1	1	2		
Helton, James	1		2		
Hembler, Joseph	1	2	2		
Harter, Frances	1	2	1		
Hennestopal, Jacob	1	2	4		
Hennestopal, John	1		3		
Hennestopal, Barnet	5	2	2		
Holton, David	2		5		
Hager, Geo	1	2	2		
Hayes, Rachal	1		1		
Horn, Adam	1	1	1		
Hayes, Sarah		3	4		
Holms, John	1	1	2		
Hammond, Wm	1		4		150
Highley, Fredarick	2	2	2		
Henary, Isaac	2	2	2		
Harmon, Caleb	2		3		
Hambelton, James	1	1	2		
Hambelton, Samuel	1		3		
Hoock, Jacob	3		3		
Hallow, Philip	3	2	1		
Hammond, Michael	2		4		
Haward, James	2		3		13
Hose, Michael	2	1	2		
Hall, Benjs	1	1	2		
Hobly, Sarah		1	2		
Hollin, John	3		2		
Handcock, Wm	1		3		
Hasting, Joseph	4	1	3		
Huch, Eurath			3		
Huch, John	1		5		
Handily, Lawrance	1		3		
Halfand, Andrew	1	2	2		
Hambelton, Geo	1	1	2		
Hambelton, James	1		1		
Hambelton, Samuel	1		2		
Hambelton, Sarah			1		
Hains, Henary	2		2		
Hickey, Owing	1		1		
Hayworth, Johnothan	1		1		
Hayman, Wm	1	2	2		
Hambelton, Edword	2	3	4		1
Hains, Daniel	2	2	2	1	
Hains, Henary	1	1	4		
Howard, Cornelus	2		3		10
Hammond, Mordica	2	1	6		8
Hessey, Charles	2	3	4		
Hessey, Wm	1	1	4		
Hansey, James	2	1	8		
Hansey, Richd	1	3	5		
Hutson, Joseph	3	4	4		1

NAME OF HEAD OF FAMILY.	Free white males of 16 years and upward, including heads of families.	Free white males under 16 years.	Free white females, including heads of families.	All other free persons.	Slaves.
COUNTY NOT SEPARATED—continued.					
Hutson, Wm	1	4	4		4
Hicks, Abraham	1	2	3		
Hingel, Wm	1		4		
Hall, Henary	3	2	8		
Wisner, Matthias	1	4	3		1
Hitchman, Martin	1	3	2		
Holland, Jesse	1	2	3		
Hair, John	1		8		
Heitrain, Jacob	2		3		
Hilliman, Cunrod	2	2	1		
Hager, Fredarick	1		3		
Harriage, Elias	1		3		
Harriage, Elias, Jur	1	1	1		
Hart, Henary	1		2		
Hust, Aguster	1	3	2		
Hust, Bennit	1		2		
Hust, Bennet, Jur	1		2		
Hust, Michael	1	2	2		
Hawkins, Thos	4	2	3		
Hopkins, Wm	3	1	1		
Hucker, Richd	3	3	9		2
Isarel, Gilbert	1	5	3		
Isarel, Ealy	2		5		
Johnston, Jerrimiah, Jur	1	1	1		7
Johnston, Wm	2	3	7		
Jurden, Diner	1	1	2	5	
Jessop, Margaret			2	5	
Jean, Wm	1	1	2		1
Judah, John	2		3		
Igo, Wm	2	4	5		
Johnston, Timathy	1	2	1		
James, Thos	2	4	6		
Johnston, Thos	1	3	3		22
Johnston, Jerrimiah	3	3	5		13
Josias, Benjs	2	3	6		
Josias, Joseph	2	3	6		
Isarel, Robert	2				
Jones, Richd	9	5	9		17
Kanaday, Thos	1	2	6		
Kanaday, John	1	1	6		
Kinsey, Wm	1	1	1		
Kuth, Wm	1	1	3		
Kelly, Wm	1	1	1		4
Kalbaugh, Cristopher	1	3	3		
Kalbaugh, Henary	1	2	4		
King, Wm	2	4	1		
Keever, John	1	2	1		
Keeth, Wm	1	4	1		
Kenneli, Jacob	1		1		
Keever, Peter	1		1		
Kid, John	1	3	2		
Keeth, Wm	4		4		
Kid, Joshua	1	1	4		2
Grear, Felty	1		2		
Kayher, Samuel	3	1	2		
Karlinger, Cunrod	3	3	1		
Karlinger, Geo	1		2		
Kelly, Thos	2		4		
Kelly, Matthew	2	4	5		
Leaf, John	2	1	4		
Loyd, Stephen	1	1	6		
Litsinger, Henary	1	2	2		
Lemmon, Catherener	1	3	3		
Lowe, Wm	1	3	2		1
Long, Cunrod	1		4		
Lewall, Zacheriah	1		1		
Lewall, Luther	1	3	4		
Lewall, Eathen	3	1	3		
Lewall, Wm	3	1	2		
Lister, Daniel	1	5	5		
Lewall, Henary	1	5	3		
Lance, Elisha	1	2	2		
Lamott, Daniel	1		2		
Lemmon, Alexr	1	1	9		2
Lemmon, Lanly	1	2	2		
Lowden, Thos	1		1		
Lowden, John	1		3		
Lutter, Cristopher	1	1	5		
Lamott, Henary	1	7	3		
Lidard, Thos	1	1	7		
Longwell, Robert	1	3	4		
Lewis, Charles	1		2		
Lyon, Robert	3	2	3		26
Leatherwood, Wm	2	3	3		40
Liner, Peter	1				
Lowerry, Denis	1	1	4		
Lemmon, Wm	1		4		
Leonard, Wordil	1	2	2		
Lee, John	1	4	2		
Lewis, Charles	2		3		
Lewis, John	2	2	3		
Luckis, Wm	1		3		
Lynch, Hugh	1	2	3		
Luckis, Thos	1	1	3		
Lee, Geo	1	1	5		

BALTIMORE COUNTY—Continued.

NAME OF HEAD OF FAMILY.	Free white males of 16 years and upward, including heads of families.	Free white males under 16 years.	Free white females, including heads of families.	All other free persons.	Slaves.
COUNTY NOT SEPARATED—continued.					
Ledwick, Peter	2	3	4		
Littel, Cristopher	2	2	1		
Lockhead, Frances	2	1	4		
Lowerry, John	2	3	6		
Lowerry, Nicholus	3	1	4		6
Layhue, John	2	2	6		
Logden, Thos	1		1		
Lemmon, Jacob	4		5		6
Lane, Richd	1	3	4		2
Lane, Abraham	1	1	6		
Locket, Matthew	1	1	2		
Lane, Richd Junr	1	3	6		
Louderslagel, Philip	1	1	2		
Louderslagel, Frances	1	1	2		
Louderslagel, Geo	1	1	2		
Lemmon, Calem	1	2	1		
Love, Philip	2				10
Lell, Wm	3	3	6		
Matthews, Edword	1	1	4		
Menshe, Peter	1		1		
McCray, Wm, Jur	2		1		2
McGuyer, Peter	1				
Murry, John	2	5	5		
Myers, Geo	1				
McComosky, John	1	2	1		2
Malenea, Denis	1	4	3		
McComosky, Rebecca	1				
McComosky, John	1	1	1		6
Malenea, Geo	2	4	4		
Murry, Wheeler	1	2	3		
McConnal, John	1	1	2		
McClinton, Alexr	1	1	1		
McComosky, Moses	1	5	4		
Merryman, Wm	1	1	2		
Merryman, Wm., Jr	1	1	2		
Merryman, Geo	2	4	5		
Myers, Margaret	1	3	2		
Marky, Henary	1				
Mosman, James	2	3	3		
Mosman, Frances	1	2	4		
Medicoat, Samuel	1	1	4		
Marky, Samuel	1		3		
Malenea, Wm	1	4	4		
Mash, Richd	1	4	4		
Matly, Leonard	1	3	2		
Myars, Isaac	2		5		
Menshy, Peter	1	3	1		
Moor, Geo	1	3	3		
Martain, Geo	2	1	3		
Martain, Jacob	2	2	5		2
Menshy, Philip	2	3	10		
Miller, Peter	1		1		
May, John	1	3	3		
Miller, Thos	1	1	3		
Miller, Elizabeth	4		3		
Mash, James	1		1		
Meeds, James	1	2			
May, John, Junr	1		3		
Morris, Edward	3		4		
McCulaston, James	1		3		2
Matthewis, Thos	7	2	6		
Marvel, Elizabeth			3		
Moke, Henary	1		1		
McCarthey, Calliham	1	2	2		
Merryman, Nicholus	2	2	4		2
Merryman, Saml	2	2	4		
Mitchel, Pattarick	1	1	1		
Miney, John	1	1	1		
McCinsey, Wm	1	2	3		
Mair, Wm	2	4	1		
Miller, Rachal		2	3		
Miller, Margaret	1	1	2		
Mash, Richd			2		
Miller, Joseph	4		5		
Mannun, Saml	2	4	3		1
Moly, Wm	1	4	2		
Mummy, Saml	1	4	3		5
Mulleka, Michl	1	2	2		
Merchant, Joseph	1	2	3		
Muolewain, Wm	1	3	5		1
Morrison, John	3		4		
Madary, Catherener	3	2	4		
Malenea, Peter	1	1	2		
Madary, John	1	3	4		
Madary, Jacob	2	3	3		
Maybary, Catherener		1	5		
Mutry, Rebecca		2	4		3
McCray, Wm	2	1	2		2
Mesemore, Jacob	1	3	1		
Mesemore, Jacob, Jr	1	2			
Myers, Abraham	2		7		
Marky, Henary	1				
Marshal, Wm	1	3	4		4
Marshal, Thos	1	2	7		
Mash, Wm	1	1	2		

NAME OF HEAD OF FAMILY.	Free white males of 16 years and upward, including heads of families.	Free white males under 16 years.	Free white females, including heads of families.	All other free persons.	Slaves.
COUNTY NOT SEPARATED—continued.					
Matthewis, Edword	1	1	3		
Marca, Jacob	1	6	3		
Marshal, Jacob	2	1	6		
Matthewis, Wm	1	3	3		
Norwood, Saml	2	1	2		16
Norwood, Edword	2		5		14
Night, John	3	4	4		
Nash, John	3	1	2		
Nice, Geo	8		4		7
North, Cristopher	1		7		
Noul, Jacob	3	3	3		
Nice, Peter	1	2	6		
Nelson, James	3	2	4		
Neal, Antony	1		2		
Myers, Abraham	2		4		
Murry, Christopher	1	1	3		15
Mitchel, James	1	2	2		
Owings, Caleb	2		6		13
Owings, Caleb	1				22
Owings, Henary	3	1	2		10
Ostler, Wm	1	2	2		
Owings, Saml	7	1	8		13
Owings, Thos	6	3	6		12
Owings, Catherener	1	2	2		
Odle, John	5	1	5		9
Odle, Walter	3		5		15
Owings, Joshua	4	2	4		
Ostler, John	2	3	4		
Ore, John	1	3	3		
Otheryoung, Christopher	2	2	2		
Otts, Peter	4	4	6		
Owings, Stephen	1		1		8
Otts, Barbary		2	3		
Orrick, Andrew	1	2	3		
Oshal, Justice	1	2	3		
Oshal, Jesse	1	4	4		
Orsburn, Joseph	1		4		
Owings, Robert	2	2	3		
Orsburn, Judith	2	2	5		
Otheryoung, Jacob	2		3		
Pits, Lewis	2	3	2		1
Parcks, Philip	4	4	3		
Pluher, John	1	1	2		
Pluher, Jacob	1	3	2		
Perrigo, Moses	1	3	4		
Prichard, John	2	2	4		
Plowman, Johnothan	2		5		
Plowman, Johnothan, Jur	1	3	3		
Plowman, James	1	6	2		
Plowman, Edword	1	4	2		
Peddecot, Dorsey	1	1	4		
Parmer, Geo	1		2		
Purkey, Wm	4	1	4		
Price, Saml	1	1	1		
Pits, Martin	1		2		
Purkey, Jacob	1	5	1		
Parrish, John	1	1	1		
Pen, John	6	3	3		
Pen, Reason	2	3	5		2
Peck, John	1	1	2		
Pemiar, John	1	2	7		
Peacock, Luke	1	3	2		2
Peddecot, Wm	1	2	2		
Peddecot, Adam	1	3	1		
Markins, Elizabeth		2	4		
Morgen, Philip	1	1	1		
Ogg, Wm	1		2		
Parrish, Johnothan	1	1	2		
Parrish, Elizabeth			5		
Parker, Wm	2	1	3		
Pemberton, Henary	5	1	5		
Porter, Greenbury	2	1	2		
Porter, Philip	2	1	8		
Parrish, Comfort	2	1	4		
Parrish, Richd	1	2	4		
Parker, Robert	1	3	3		3
Poneypecker, Wm	1	2	7		
Possom, Charles	2		4		
Pusserham, John	1	2	6		
Picket, Wm	3	3	3		
Other Free Persons				1	
Pussal, Wm	1	2	5		1
Price, Joshua	1	4	4		1
Perrigo, Henary	1	2	5		
Perrigo, John	1		2		
Popalit, Charles	5		4		
Price, Benjs	1		6		
Popalit, Peter	1	1	1		
Popalit, Stophal	1	1	1		
Price, Gist	1	2	1		
Parrish, Mordical	2	4	4		

NAME OF HEAD OF FAMILY.	Free white males of 16 years and upward, including heads of families.	Free white males under 16 years.	Free white females, including heads of families.	All other free persons.	Slaves.
COUNTY NOT SEPARATED—continued.					
Parrish, John	2		3		
Ridgley, Charles	1	5	5		19
Rusk, Paul	1	4	2		
Randel, Roger	1	1	1		
Rennels, Sarah			2		
Roals, Thos	3	2	4		
Randel, John	1		2		
Roles, Ealy	1	1	2		
Roles, John	2	2	5		1
Roles, Jacob	1	2	1		1
Randel, Beal	3	3	6		1
Randel, Wm	1		2		
Randel, Thos	2		5		
Ripe, Michael	1	6	4		
Richhart, John	1		4		
Richards, Richd	1	3	4		
Richards, Saml	1	2	2		
Richards, Nicholus	1	2	1		
Rodes, Stopal	1	2	2		
Richards, Thos	1	1	2		1
Ryan, John	1		2		
Rensher, Moses	1	2			
Richards, Richd	1		2		
Riley, Wm	1	1			
Rayder, Jacob	1	1	2		
Rollands, Wm	1		2		
Rollands, Wm, Jur	1		2		
Ryston, John	2	1	2		1
Riley, Thos	1		1		
Rollins, Abraham	1	1			
Richardson, Wm	1	2	3		
Ruby, Thos	1	6	3		
Richards, John	1		3		1
Roberts, John	1	4	6		
Randel, Richd	1	1	2		
Randel, Aquilla	1	2	2		
Roger, John	1	1	3		
Roles, John	1	4	5		1
Randel, Nicholus	1	2	4		15
Ricker, John	3	2	2		
Rodes, Thos	1		1		
Rusk, Johnothan	1	1	1		
Russel, Cornelius	1		1		
Rister, John	1		1		
Rister, John Junr	1	3	4		
Rister, Philip	2	3	5		5
Riester, Geo	3	2	1		36
Robertson, Wm	1		2		
Right, Jacob	1		2		
Richhart, John, Junr	1	1	2		
Rees, Jacob	1	1	5		2
Riley, Wm	1	1	4		
Renchart, Piter	1	1	1		
Rice, John	1	1	1		
Rogers, Thos	1		3		
Randel, Christopher	1		1		
Rogers, Geo	1	1			
Ring, Stophal	2		2		
Randel, Wm	1	3	1		
Ritter, John	1	1	3		
Ritter, Ledwick	3	3	3		1
Rodes, Stophal	1	2			
Rivel, John	1		2		
Rees, Geo	1		5		4
Switzer, John	1	4	5		
Smith, Henary	1	2	4		
Sank, Geo	1	2	2		
Sugars, Edword	1	2	2		
Sadler, Joseph	2	4	5		
Stinchicome, John	2	4	3		1
Stinchicome, Nathaniel	2	1	6		
Stinchicome, Christopher	2		1		5
Stinchicome, McClain	1	1	4		1
Stinchicome, Saml	2	5	3		
Stinchicome, Thos	3	4	4		2
Stinchicome, Nathaniel	1	5	4		
Stimmerman, Geo	3	2	5		
Stockstill, Thos	1	2	7		
Stockstill, Edword	2	2	5		6
Stockstill, John	2	4	4		4
Slorip, Peter	2	2	3		
Sentz, Adam	2		3		
Starck, Christopher	1		2		
Shaver, John	2	2	6		2
Shaver, James	3	3	2		2
Sherry, Daniel	2	1	5		
Smith, Thos	2		5		
Stilts, Philip	1	3	6		
Stilts, John	1	1	1		
Stilts, Philip	1	1	1		
Sulaven, John	1		4		
Smith, Adam	1	1	4		
Spindel, Nicholus	1		1		
Spindel, Geo	1	1	3		

BALTIMORE COUNTY—Continued.

COUNTY NOT SEPARATED—continued.

NAME OF HEAD OF FAMILY.	Free white males of 16 years and upward, including heads of families.	Free white males under 16 years.	Free white females, including heads of families.	All other free persons.	Slaves.
Spindel, Jacob	2		2		
Bain, Wm	1	3	2		
Spiser, James, Junr	1	2	3		
Spiser, James	3	1	3		1
Himes, Saml	1	2	2		
Ray, Joseph	1	2	3		
Ray, Benjn	2	2	1		
Tyson, Jesse	8	2			4
Newbury, Joseph	3	3	2		
Dewbury, Joseph	2		2		
Cavenhoven, Geo	3	1	4		
Burlocy, Geo	2	1	4		4
Bartin, Ersil	2		7		2
Guynn, Wm	1	3	7		
McLaughlin, John	2		1		
Other Free Persons				29	
Everit, Wm	2	1	4		
Young, Rebecca	1	2	6		15
Paul, John	2		1		18
Bain, John	1		2		
Other Free Persons				16	
Martain, Alex	4		4		
Lynch, Wm	1		2		4
Lynch, Abraham	2	1	3		
Lynch, Mary			1		
Taylor, Wm	1	1	2		
Wheeler, Wilson	2	2	3		
Tuder, John			6		
Luckis, Thos	1	1	3		1
Black, Samuel	1		2		
Dorsey, Nicholus	1	2	3		9
Gaugh, Henary	2		4		9
Nickels, Thos	1		3		
Hickley, John	1	1	3		
Johnston, Robert	1		2		
Cord, Stephen	1	3	2		
Poter, Thos	1		2		
Williams, Thos	1	2	1		
Thorn, John	1	2	3		
Williams, Robert	2		2		
Clayton, Joseph	1	2	7		
Rosenbury, John	1	1	5		
Gittings, Henary	1		4		6
Gittings, James	2	2	4		7
Rosenbury, John	1	1	2		
Cowin, Wm	1		2		
Strowbridg, Elizabeth	3		2		
Hall, Aquilla	4	5	9		35
Hagen, Henary	1	1	4		1
Liggett, James	1	2	4		
Slee, Joseph	1	3	2		12
Weever, Casper	1				
Other Free Persons				2	
Nickols, Thos	1		2		
Greenfield, Feby	2	1	5		
Ridgley, Edword	4				31
Woolf, James	2	1	2		9
Hilton, Joseph	3	1	2		
McGuffin, Andrus	2				1
Dear, Benjn	1	3	5		
Brian, Thos	1	1	4		
Shaw, Robert	2	4	5		
Burtin, Joseph	2	4	4		
Shaw, David	1		2		2
Griffin, Philip	2	5	3		
Proctter, Thos	1		1		
Other Free Persons				3	
Sunderlin, Wm	1	6	8		
Jones, Wm	2		2		11
Crudington, Geo	2	3	6		
Adams, Wm	1	3	2		
Howard, Robert	1	3	2		
Brian, Thos	1	1	4		
Bishop, Wm	1	5	2		
Landon, Thos	1	1	5		
Norwood, Charles	1	2	1		13
Lemmon, John	3	2	3		3
Smith, Andrew	5		6		
Dunaway, Thos	1	1	2		1
Wheeler, Wm	1				4
Brooks, Charles		3	3		
Enson, Abraham	2	2	3		1
Vanghen, Gist	4	2	3		
Lemmon, Joshua	3	2	5		
Coal, Abraham	2	1	4		6
Coal, Abraham, Junr	1	2	2		5
Mays, John	2		3		
Bausley, Caleb	1	3	3		6
Price, Daniel	2	3	3		
Griffith, Abraham	2	4	5		
Scott, Abraham	5	1	3		
Mayson, James	2		4		
Coal, Thos	2		2		19
Horsly, Thos	3		2		
Hunter, Peter	4		2		

COUNTY NOT SEPARATED—continued.

NAME OF HEAD OF FAMILY.	Free white males of 16 years and upward, including heads of families.	Free white males under 16 years.	Free white females, including heads of families.	All other free persons.	Slaves.
Trasy, Nicholus	1		2		
Matthewis, John	2		1		4
Matthewis, Frances	1		3		
Ensor, Geo	5	1	7		2
Ensor, Elizabeth	1		1		8
Ensor, Darby	1	1	1		
Hall, Edword	1	3	2		8
Hall, Wm	1		3		4
Hall, James	1	4	3		3
Hooker, Benjn	3		5		7
Gorsuch, Charles	3	1	7		7
Gorsuch, Charles	1	1	2		5
Means, James	1		1		
Hoy, James	1	3	5		
Gorsuch, John	1		2		11
Price, Samuel	3	4	4		
Price, Mordecai	2	2	4		
Gorsuch, John	2	6	4		
Matthews, Rachal	4	2	3		1
Other Free Persons				4	
Markey, Wm	1		3		7
Price, John	1	1	2		
Matthews, Samuel	3		4		
Other Free Persons				20	
Edwords, Henary	1		1		
Hunt, Robert	1		2		
Harriod, Wm	1	2	2		
Miller, Hannah	1	1	2		
Page, Wm	1		1		
Green, John	3		5		
Purigo, Joseph	2		5		
Other Free Persons				13	
Wheeler, Nathan	2		5		6
Coal, Samuel	1	1	2		
Bradfield, James	1		5		1
Wheeler, John	1		1		1
Rencher, Haziah	1	2	1		
Wheeler, Benjn	1		2		3
Wheeler, Benjn, Jr	1	2	3		2
Wheeler, James	2				4
Carr, James	2		4		
Nailer, Samuel	1		3		
Busby, John	3	2	4		8
Hall, Caleb	6		7		1
Martain, Robert	1		3		
Burns, Robert	3	1	1		
Spindel, Jacob	1		2		
Shall, Joseph	3	2	4		
Stansbury, Joseph	1	5	3		8
Siper, Charles	1		2		
Sentz, Peter	3	1	5		
Sentz, Christopher	7		2		
Shuman, Adam	2	2	3		
Zigier, Peter	1		2		
Smith, Frances			2		3
Silvester, John	1	1	5		
Other Free Persons				6	
Scott, Barnet	1		3		
Sitler, Abraham	1	1	2		
Spiser, Thos	1	3	2		1
Silvester, John	1	1	1		
Scott, Burr	1		3		
Stocket, Wm	1		4		3
Smith, Samuel	2	1	3		1
Shoat, Solomon	2	1	3		5
Shoat, Richd	1	1	3		
Shoat, Edword	1		2		
Smith, Adam	2	7	2		
Simmerman, Geo	2		2		6
Simmins, Thos	1	2	3		
Shipley, Robert	2	2	3		
Shain, Henary	2	3	5		
Sentzes, Adam	1	1	1		
Stump, Tory	1		1		
Sentzes, Adam, Junr	1	2	3		
Seat, Peter	1		5		
Snider, Frederick	2	1	2		
Snap, Peter	2	1	1		
Snider, Martain	1	2	5		
Snider, Frederick, Junr	1		2		
Shade, John	1	2	5		
Shaseler, Jacob	1		3		
Slagel, Elizabeth	2	3	5		
Showar, John	1	1	2		
Stockstill, Edword	2		2		
Storm, Jacob	1	2	6		
Shilling, John	1		1		
Summers, John	3	3	2		4
Simpson, Hannah			6		
Soliars, Frances	1	1	1		13
Skill, Wm	1		3		
Stiger, John	2		3		
Stockstill, John	2	1	3		13
Teal, Geo	1	6	3		
Todd, Benjn	68	3	4		5

COUNTY NOT SEPARATED—continued.

NAME OF HEAD OF FAMILY.	Free white males of 16 years and upward, including heads of families.	Free white males under 16 years.	Free white females, including heads of families.	All other free persons.	Slaves.
Other Free Persons				3	
Traynor, Joseph	1	1	1		
Trayser, Boyal	1	2	2		
Trayser, Benjn	2	2	4		
Trayser, John	3	2	7		
Tryer, Geo	1		2		
Tilman, Jacob	1	1	2		
Tipton, Bill	1	1	2		
Tipton, Garriod	2		1		7
Taylor, Geo	1		2		
Tipton, Bryon	1	2	5		
Tipton, Wm	1	2	3		
Tipton, Johnothan	2		3		
Tipton, Johnothan, Jur	2	3	5		
Trasy, Bozel	3	1	4		
Trasy, Wm	1	1	3		
Trasy, Elisha	2	2	4		
Taylor, John	2	1	1		
Turner, John	2		2		
Thomas, Benjn	1		2		
Taylor, Susanah	1	2	1		
Trasy, John	1	4	2		
Tipton, Samuel	1		8		
Tanner, Geo	3	2	6		
Towson, James	1		3		
Towson, Shade	1	1	2		
Turner, John	3	2	5		
Taylor, John, Jur	1	3	5		
Taylor, Geo, Jur	1	2	1		
Trasy, Walnut	1	4	2		
Trasy, Tage	1	1	3		
Thomas, Daniel	1	1	2		
Trayner, Henary	2	1	6		
Turner, James	2		3		
Trash, Geo	1	2	3		
Turner, Matthew	1	2	2		
Tresel, Peter	1		4		
Upercue, Jacob	1		1		
Upercue, Jacob, Jur	1	4	1		1
Vachal, Shipley	2	2	2		
Vaughen, Gist	3	3	4		2
Vaughen, Christopher	2	1	6		
Vaughen, Kesiah			4		
Vaughen, Richd	2		5		
Vaughen, Benjn	1	2	5		
Varner, Adam	1		1		
Varner, Philip	1		2		
Whiting, Chas	1	6	3		
Walker, Geo	1		2		
Willhaven, Fredarick	1		3		
Wight, Thos	1	3	3		
Weever, Christopher	1		4		
Wellhilm, John	1		2		
Wiley, John	2		2		
Weever, Geo	1	3	5		
Walton, John	2	2	6		3
Wells, Thos	2		2		8
Wills, Levy	1		1		
Walker, Charles	3	2	8		18
Woolf, Michael	1		2		
Wheeler, Mordecai	1	2	3		4
Wheeler, Brian	1		2		
Wheeler, Greenbury	1	2	2		
Wheeler, Wm, Jur	2	1	2		
Weever, John	2	1	4		
Wareham, Henary	2	3	3		
Whipling, Charles	1	4	4		
Weyman, Barrit	1	3	4		
Walton, James	3	1	3		
Wheeler, Richd	1		4		
Wilson, John	1	1	3		
Woolf, Elizabeth	2		3		
Wells, Wm	3	1	3		
Woodcock, Robert	1		1		1
Woodcock, Robert, Jur	1		1		
West, Peter	1	2	1		
Welt, James	2	4	4		
Walker, Thos	2		3		4
Widerman, Geo	1		1		1
Worters, Benjn	1		2		
Wilmoth, Richd	1		2		
Wiston, Joseph	1		1		
Wilson, Hugh		1	3		
Worters, Philip	3	3	3		3
Walker, Charles	4	3	8		11
Weast, Henary	2		2		1
Wilderman, John	1		2		
Wordel, Leonard	1	2	3		
Walker, Jesse	1		2		
Wilderman, Geo	2	5	3		
Williamson, Samuel	1		2		
Weatherington, Thos	6	3	3		38
Worrel, Ann					
Weatherington, John	3		3		10
Worters, Elenor	2	1	4		6

BALTIMORE COUNTY—Continued.

NAME OF HEAD OF FAMILY.	Free white males of 16 years and upward, including heads of families.	Free white males under 16 years.	Free white females, including heads of families.	All other free persons.	Slaves.
COUNTY NOT SEPARATED—continued.					
Wight, Otho	2	4	5		
Worters, Alexander	1	3	5		6
Wan, Edward	1	3	3		
West, Joseph	1	1	1		1
Ware, Wm	3		4		3
Ware, Wm	1		1		1
Ware, Robert	3		6		10
Wheever, John	2	1	4		
Word, John	3	3	4		
Williams, Thos	1	1	1		
Bowar, Martin	1	1	5		
Other Free Persons				10	
Williams, Nicholus	2	1	3		
Williams, Ann	2		5		4
Watts, Richd	1	5	4		
Wheeland, Stephen	1	5	1		1
Other Free Persons				19	
Workinger, Henary	1		3		
Wareham, Henary	1	2	3		
Wareham, Henary Junr	1	1	1		
Wineman, Barnet	2	2	1		
Other Free Persons				14	
Whatson, Wm	1		2		
Wells, Wm	3	1	3		
Winetrod, Henary	1		3		
Wheeler, Geo	1		3		
Walker, Daniel	1	1	4		2
Williams, Mary		3	1		
Wheeler, Elisha	1		3		
Woolf, Valentine	1		1		
Other Free Persons				12	
Wiley, John	2	2	2		
Williams, Benja	1	7	2		
Westley, John	1		1		
Williams, Peter	1		1		
Williams, John	1		3		
Woodden, Stephen	1	5	3		1
Westler, John	1		4		
Willhelm, Henary	1	3	2		
Wheeler, Wm	2	1	3		
Winchester, Richd	5	1	2		2
Wiant, Nicholus	1	3	5		
Wheeler, Richd	1	1	1		6
Other Free Persons				19	
Welch, James	1	4	1		
Willibother, Andrew	1	4	2		
Wheever, Philip	3	2	4		
Wheever, John	2	3	2		
Williams, Thos	1	1	3		
Wilson, Peter	1	1	3		
Young, Walter	2	1	1		
Yhoun, John	2	2	4		2
Young, Mark	2		4		
Younglabunt, Daniel	1	1	4		
Younger, Jacob	2	3	4		
Other Free Persons				18	
Stacy, Wm	7	5	4		1
Shilling, Absolum	1	1	2		
Shilling, Christopher	1		3		
Shaver, Michael	3	4	3		1
Shaver, Aplener	1	2	4		
Seller, Henary	1	2	1		
Swisler Jacob	2	1	3		
Shilling, Wm	1	2	2		
Stiner, Adam	2	2	8		
Singer, Christopher	2	3	3		
Sellers, Paul	3	2	2		
Sellers, John	1		2		
Shaver, Michael	1	2	5		
Shuster, John	1		2		
Sicks, Nathaniel	1	3	3		
Siper, Wm	1	3	3		
Siper, John	1	3	3		
Stormer, Wm	1	2	1		
Steel, Wm	1				
Selman, Wachal	1		2		
Stuben, Henary	2	5			9
Other Free Persons				1	
Soward, Edward	1	2	2		
Summer, Edward	1	1	4		
Story, Thos	1	1	2		
Story, James	1	1	1		
Stevenson, Abraham	1	3			1
Sabry, Wm	1		4		
Sias, Benja	1	1	2		
Stansbury, Caleb	2	2	3		1
Sias, Joseph	3	3	5		
Sias, Elizabeth			2		
Shockney, Pattarick	1	1	1		
Showar, Henary	1	1	2		
Sabel, Leonard	2		2		
Stefly, Jacob	1		2		
Smith, Joshua	1	2	3		
COUNTY NOT SEPARATED—continued.					
Shaver, John	2	1	3		
Shearman, John	1	2	3		
Singston, Stophal	1	1	1		
Shaver, John	1	3	2		
Stansbury, Richd	1	2	3		
Cumins, Antony	2		1		
Culiston, Shedrick	1	1	1		
Culiston, Josias, Junr	1		1		
Cross, Sollomon	1	2	3		
Cooper, John	1	2	1		
Cooper, James	1	1	2		
Coonts, Michael	5		2		
Culaston, Jerrimiah	1	1	4		
Cray, John	4	2	1		
Clark, Joseph	1		2		
Cramer, Henary	3		2		
Coal, John	3	3	4		
Cray, John	2		2		
Cumbly, James	2	4	8		
Crayner, Henary	1	1	1		
Cray, John	1		2		1
Cryses, Geo	1	2	3		
Cramer, Mary		1	1		
Cetinger, John	1		1		
Casaun, Jacob	1	3	4		
Cross, Joshua	2	1	1		
Collins, Edward	1		2		
Crider, Ealy	1	3	4		
Clark, Henary	3	4	4		3
Cox, Jacob	1	1	5		
Cox, John	1	1	2		
Cox, Wm	2		2		
Coltrider, John	2	2	6		
Crise, Henary	2	1	3		
Crider, Mordicai	1		3		
Collet, Susanah		2	5		
Crayton, John	1	1	1		
Clatter, Ann			4		
Chilcoat, Richd	2		3		
Coal, Christopher	1		2		
Coal, Venson	1	2	5		
Culaston, Jesse	1	2	2		
Culaston, Wm	2	3	4		
Citinger, Henary	2	2	4		
Chilcoat, Elias	2	1	1		
Coal, Abraham	3	1	4		
Culastick, John	1				
Cuningham, Wm	1				
Cable, Robert	2	2	4		4
Coal, Abraham	2		2		3
Chilcoat, Richd	2		2		
Corbin, Benja	2	1	3		
Corbin, Elisha	1	1	4		
Coulrider, David	1	5	1		
Creemrine, Abraham	1	3	3		
Co, Mark	1	2	3		
Collet, Abraham	2	3	2		
Collet, Moses	1				10
Cross, John	1	1	2		
Benet, Wm	1		2		
Barnet, John	1	3	1		
Boring, Joshua	1	1	4		2
Thompson, James	1	3	2		
Backer, Geo	1	2	4		
Backer, Wm	2		2		
Burns, John	1	3	5		1
Bowar, John, Jur	1	2	4		
Burns, Adam	1		1		
Backly, Jacob	2	2	11		
Bierley, Peter	1	2	4		
Batcher, Christopher	2	2	3		
Bierley, Cunrad	2	3	3		
Brown, John	2	2	2		
Brown, John, Jur	1	2	5		
Bashen, Antony	1	3	2		
Backer, Geo	2	2	2		
Boring, Absolum	1	1	1		1
Boring, John	1	1	2		
Boring, Absolum, Jr	1	4	4		
Burck, Darby	1	1	2		
Brown, John	1	1	2		
Barney, Wm	1	1	2		
Belt, Joseph	2		1		
Belt, Lonard	4	1	5		
Barret, Edword	2		4		
Boring, James	3	2	2		
Boring, John	1	2	2		2
Boring, Zecheal	1	2	6		
Boston, Joseph	1	3	5		
Bond, John	1		6		
Bosman, Edward	1	3	3		
Brown, John, Junr	1	2	2		
Brown, Geo	2	3	4		
Buher, Henary	1	1	4		
COUNTY NOT SEPARATED—continued.					
Bonggarner, Motlener			2		
Boring, Thos	1	3	1		
Boring, Rheuben	1	2	1		
Brook, Joseph	1	1	2		
Boring, Henary	1	2	2		
Bilzard, John	2	5	3		
Bilzard, Wm	3	2	2		1
Bues, Henary	3	5	1		
Bues, John, Junr	1	3	4		
Bues, John	2	1	3		
Ball, Nathaniel D	1	4	4		
Ball, Wm	3	2	4		
Brian, John	3	3	4		
Ball, John	1	1	7		
Ball, Wm	1	1	3		
Bats, John	1	1	2		
Braker, Jacob	1	2	1		
Baker, Geo	1	3	4		
Burlinger, Joseph	4	2	4		
Beecher, John	1		2		
Beecher, Jacob	1		2		
Boring, Thos	1	1	2		
Benet, Geo	1	2	1		
Banks, John	4	2	4		
Banks, Wm	1	1	1		
Banks, Jas	1	1	2		
Bats, Frederick	3	1	5		
Butler, Nicholus	1	1	4		
Branwell, Henary	1		2		8
Bond, Samuel	3	4	5		
Bently, Zacheriah	1		6		
Baston, John	1		6		
Butler, Joseph	1	2	2		
Brooks, Elizabeth		1	2		
Boards, Philip	4	1	1		
Bever, John	1	2	1		
Busby, John	3	2	9		2
Bever, Christopher	1		2		
Boose, Peter	1	1	3		
Benen, Catherener	2	3	3		
Gorsuch, John	2				1
Gorsuch, Joshua	2				
Gorsuch, Charles	2				5
Storm, Geo	2	1	1		5
Given, John	2	3	5		1
McGaw, Sarah	1	1	1		5
Mintion, Christopher	2		4		2
McBuisey, James	1		1		2
Slade, Thos	1	1	2		1
Slade, Abraham	1	1	1		
Sap, Frances	1	2	6		
Spindel, Jacob	2		1		
Storm, Wm	1	2	4		
Showars, John	2	1	1		4
Sipher, Elisha	1	2	1		
Singer, Christopher	1	2	3		
Storm, Geo	2	3	5		2
Sords, Hugh	1	1	1		
Shaver, Margaret	2	1	4		
Suster, Ledwick	1		2		
Other Free Persons				1	
Reed, John	5		6		
Judy, Martin	3	2	3		
Brown, Luke	1	3	7		
Lewis, Edword	1	1	5		
Reed, Robert	1	3	1		
Lewis, Nicholus	1	2	3		
McCubin, Zacheriah	1		6		17
Mash, Nathaniel	1		2		
Stomper, Henary	1		2		
Mash, John	1	3	4		
Reed, John	2	3	2		
Foreman, John	1	5	4		
Sutherland, David	5	1	5		5
Bond, Benja	1	1	8		3
Upton, James	1		4		
Worrel, Caleb	1	2	4		6
Ramy, Adam	1		6		
Watkins, Wm	3	4	4		
Peacock, Luke	1		2		5
Hany, Richd	1	1	2		
Brackly, Matthias	1		2		
Morris, John	1	1	2		
Cookey, Joshua	2		5		9
Crooks, Henry	3	3	2		
Green, Henary	1	1	3		
Liggatt, Thos	1	1	3		
Zimmerman, Geo	3	2	6		1
Lee, Geo	1		2		
Demit, Stansbury	1		5		
Hissey, Wm	1	3	4		
Robertson, Thos	1	2	2		
Limeburger, Wm	1	2	3		1
Gardner, John	1		3		

COUNTY NOT SEPARATED—continued.

NAME OF HEAD OF FAMILY.	Free white males of 16 years and upward, including heads of families.	Free white males under 16 years.	Free white females, including heads of families.	All other free persons.	Slaves.
Other Free Persons				17	
Limeburger, Andrew	2		2		3
Rith, Frederick W	3				
Simpson, Joseph	1				
Other Free Persons				5	
Hissy, Charles	2	3	4		
Conaway, John	2		2		
Right, Esther	2		2		
Beem, Philip	1	2	2		
Geen, Wm	2	1	2		1
Conaway, Richd	1	1	2		1
Conaway, Ruth			1		1
Cruks, Samuel	1	1	3		
Lowe, Nicholus	3	1	3		1
Gray, James	1	1	1		
Shoat, Edword	1		2		
Demit, Wm	2	1	5		
Ford, Thos	2	1	5		1
Baughman, Henary	1	3	5		
Ford, Thos, Junr	2	2	2		
Howard, Charles	2	2	2		8
Fitzgarel, Richd	1	1	1		
Jones, Elias	3	2	5		5
Morgin, Wm	1		2		
Parrish, Edword	1	2	4		
Jones, Benjn	1		4		1
Jones, Henary	1		4		3
Kelly, Michael	1		1		
Carroll, Daniel	1	1	3		10
Smith, Henary	1	1	4		
Smith, John	2	A	1		
Curnelus, John	2		1		1
Constant, Edword	1		2		
Mink, Thos	1	2	4		
Carman, Patrick	1	2	2		
Smith, Nicholus	3	2	5		
Matthews, Mordicai	1		4		
Mungs, James	1		1		
Green, Nicholus	1	1	2		1
Tuder, Thos	4	1	2		
Bennex, Barney	2	2	5		
Lemmon, Moses	1	3	4		
Morris, Isaac	1	3	4		2
Brian, Luke	1	1	3		
Long, Thos A	1		1		
Tolbert, Venson	1	3	6		6
Corbin, Venson	1	2	6		
Dixson, Geo	1	1	1		
Corbin, Edword	1	3	3		1
Herriman, Geo	3	1	2		10
Collet, Hannah	1	2	3		
Gale, Michael	3		4		
Elfrod, Fredarick	1	1	3		
Mostman, James	1	2	4		
Mostman, Frances	1	2	4		
Tolbert, John	1		2		7
Wells, John	3	1	5		
Perrigo, Wm	1	1	6		1
Burtin, Joshua	1	2	3		
Chinoth, Frances	3		3		
Dixson, Geo	1	1	3		
Burtin, Thos	1	1	3		
Merryman, Cagy	2	2	9		9
Bosley, Elizabeth	1	1	4		2
Bosley, Walter	2	1	4		12
Trapnel, Wm	4	1	5		
Stansbury, Wm	1	3	6		4
Lynch, James	3	2	1		
Bausley, Wm	1	2	2		2
Love, Thos	3		3		10
Price, Benjn	5	1	5		
Gorsuch, Dixson	2				10
Bausley, Greenbury	1		2		6
Ovrick, John	1	5	2		7
Tipton, Samuel	2		2		11
Tipton, Samuel, Junr	2	5	4		7
Merryman, Benjn	2	1	10		
Thomas, John	1		3		
Whating, Thos	1	2	2		
Cox, Joseph	1		2		16
Watson, Archabel	1	1	4		
Gorsuch, Thos	1	2	4		2
Guin, Wm	1		3		
Wain, Jacob	1	4	3		
Hicks, Jacob	1	1	5		1
Hicks, Abraham	1	3	4		
Foster, John	2	3	3		9
Walker, Joseph	2	2	4		
Reed, John	1	1	1		
Drawbridge, James	1		1		
Grumebridge, James	1		1		
Merryman, Nicholus	2		4		22
Ensor, John	2	2	7		4
Stansbury, Joseph	1	5	3		
James, John	2	1	3		3

COUNTY NOT SEPARATED—continued.

NAME OF HEAD OF FAMILY.	Free white males of 16 years and upward, including heads of families.	Free white males under 16 years.	Free white females, including heads of families.	All other free persons.	Slaves.
Chance, John	1	1	3		3
Clark, Benjn	1	4	3		
Baker, Charles	2	3	3		
Green, Clem	1		2		9
Hagen, Henary	1	1	4		1
Peirce, Thos	5	1	1		2
Holland, Samuel	1	2	6		
Allender, Joshua	2		3		
Bussey, Mary			1		9
Allender, Wm	1	1	1		
Holland, John	1		1		
Holland, John, Jur	3	1	3		
Holland, Geo	1	3	4		
Askew, Henary G	1	3	4		
Johnson, David	1	2	1		
Guyton, Benjn	2	1	4		(*)
Guyton, Underwood	4	3	4		(*)
Dives, Christopher	1	4	1		(*)
Askew, Derumple	1	4	5		
Guyton, Henary	4	2	5		4
Johnson, Matthew	1	3	1		
Gordin, Wm	1	1	1		1
Corbin, Naten	1	1	2		
Anderson, Richd	1	2	4		
Stansbury, Jesse	1		5		
Towson, Obediah	1	3	2		
Neal, David	1	2	3		
Frances, Samuel	1	4	2		
Standfield, James	1	2	5		
McCam, John	3		5		
Lynch, Brady	1	4	2		1
Curry, Alexr	1	2	2		
Helton, Aquilla	5	5	4		16
Pindel, Philip	1	2	3		
Smitson, David	1	1	2		1
Price, Wm	1		1		1
Other Free Persons				5	
Helton, Abraham	1		2		
Allen, John	1	5	3		
Wodiy, John	1	3	2		
Naylor, Geo	1		2		
Bussy, Jesse	3		3		16
Butler, Thos	2	4	5		
Weston, Thos	1		3		
McCam, John	4		6		
Helm, Leonard	2		3		7
Helm, Mahary	2	2	3		1
Sinder, Geo	3	1	3		
Frankingburgher, Henary	1		4		
Shavish, Hill	3		3		1
Carvell, Richd	1	2	2		
Burten, Antony	1	2	4		
Studs, Richd	1	1	3		
Biyford, Wm	1	3	5		
Goar, Andrew	2	3	3		5
Cooper, James	2	2	3		1
Gardner, John	3	4	4		
Brooks, Joseph	1		4		
Oram, John	1	5	2		
Lewis, Henary	1		2		
Merryman, Samuel	3				4
Ridgly, John	1		4		8
Armstrong, Michael	2	4	4		
Merryman, Caleb	2		3		8
Jarves, Mead	2		3		
Mummy, John	1	2	2		
Tidy, Wm	3	1	6		
Jarves, Norman	1	1	2		
Road, Richd	1	2	5		
Lingerfelter, Geo	1	2	2		
Summerman, Henary	1	3	1		
Butler, John	1	1	2		
Rock, Thos	1		1		
Wilks, Wm	1		1		
Flold, James	1		2		
Sterrett, Alexr	1	2	2		
Wiler, Geo	9		4		
Smith, Leonard	2		3		
Cross, Ann			3		
Pollck, Wm	6	4	3		
Fravelit, Frances	1	1	2		
Crocket, Thos	1	1	8		3
Inlose, Henary	3	1	2		
Hofman, Michael	1		2		
Tidy, Wm	1	2	5		
Serny, Christopher	1	2	3		
Widly, Wm	1	1	2		
Johnson, Charles	1	1	2		
Gardner, Geo	1	1	3		2
Grant, John	1	3	3		
Demit, John	1		2		
Hofman, Adam	1		3		
Brady, Juda	1	2	3		1
Loos, Arnel	1	1	2		1

COUNTY NOT SEPARATED—continued.

NAME OF HEAD OF FAMILY.	Free white males of 16 years and upward, including heads of families.	Free white males under 16 years.	Free white females, including heads of families.	All other free persons.	Slaves.
Deems, Fredarick	1	4	1		1
Hook, Jacob	1		1		1
Hook, Jacob	2	1	7		
McClellan, Robert	2		1		
Seeny, Hugh	1		3		
Price, Matthew	1		4		3
Price, Amon	1	2	4		
Barger, Peter	2	4	4		
Norwood, Elisha	2		3		
Orms, Samuel	1	1	1		
Willoby, Wm	1	1	1		
Reed, Geo	1	2	2		
Wight, Thos	3	3	4		
Stroud, Wm	1	2	3		
Foulger, Fedarick	2	1	2		1
Gardner, Geo	1	1	2		2
Bell, Richd	3	2	4		2
Brooks, Umphry	1	2	2		1
Brooks, James	1	2	3		
Night, Shorick	1	2	2		1
Ritter, Thos	1		2		
Bell, John	1	2	5		4
Bell, Eviaf	1	1	5		
Night, Jacob	2	1	5		2
Russel, Wm	2	2	4		22
Carny, James	1	1	2		
Hook, Redolph	2	6	3		
Kraner, Michael	1		2		
Kraner, Michael, Jr	1	2	2		1
Rutter, Henary	1	3	4		
Hook, Fredarick	1	1			
Hook, Jacob	2	2	2		
Najet, Samuel	2		2		
Ritter, John	1	2	4		
Taylor, John	1		4		1
Turner, John	4	1	3		1
Tabet, James	1		2		
Laurance, James	1		3		
Welch, Sarah	1		3		3
Jarves, Edword	1	1	2		1
Jarves, Aquilla	1	1	2		
Crampton, Thos	1	1	1		
Stevenson, John	1	4	2		
Boon, John R. C.	1	1	4		6
Smith, John	1	1	3		
Burton, Antony	2				
Young, Elenor	1		3		5
Todd, Thos	1	3	3		12
Wooden, Steven	3	1	3		2
Wooden, Solomond	1		1		
Morgan, David	1	1	2		
Puntney, Elizabeth			3		
Perrigo, Joseph	3	5	2		
Turner, Peter	2		3		
Chier, John	1		1		
Wotham, John	3	1	2		
Causby, John	1		2		
Rutter, Thos	1	2	4		12
Muisher, John	1	3	5		
Owndul, Cunrod	2	2	4		
Right, Joseph	2	3	3		
Woodhouse, Geo	1		5		
Poor, Thos	2	2	4		
Carr, Wm	1		3		
Stinson, Wm	2	2	1		6
Patterson, John	1	1	4		
Wooden, Solomon	1	1	3		4
Plichey, David	2	3	3		
Alexander, Amos	4	1	1		1
McCarter, Wm	1		1		
Chilcoat, Michael	1	1	2		
Chany, Zafiya	1		2		
Miller, Matthew	1	3	3		(*)
Beem, Geo	2	4	6		
Grayham, Wm	1	1	2		
Lee, Samuel	2		3		
Allen, Patrick	1		2		
Craferd, John	1		1		
Langly, Benjn	1	2	2		
Smith, Diner	1		3		
Mace, John	1		1		
Orem, John	1	2	1		
Mash, Wm	1		1		
Barnet, Andrew	4	1	6		
Barnet, Peter	1		1		
Woodard, Wm	3	4	5		6
Armstrong, Michael	3		4		
Jarves, Armon	1		1		
Allen, Patrick	1				
Baly, Thos	1		3		
Words, John	1	2	3		22
Dorsey, John	2	1	3		
Roland, John	1				
Day, Robert	2				5
Evans, Griffith	6	1	1		

* Illegible.

BALTIMORE COUNTY—Continued.

COUNTY NOT SEPARATED—continued.

NAME OF HEAD OF FAMILY.	Free white males of 16 years and upward, including heads of families.	Free white males under 16 years.	Free white females, including heads of families.	All other free persons.	Slaves.
Martin, Jacob	1				
Allbrite, Peter	1	1	2		
Allbrite, John	1	1	4		1
Armetrage, John	1	2	1		
Eagel, Margaret		4	1		
Aidrige, John	2	1	3		
Allen, Michael	2		1		
Bernal, Lewis	3	2	5		3
Other Free Persons				9	3
Belt, James	1	1	1		4
Barker, Henary	1		5		
Bowars, Cunrod	1	1	2		
Burges, W^m	1	2	2		
Brent, W^m	1		2		
Burbian, Charles	4	3	1		1
Bray, Joseph	1	2	3		
Bowing, Edward	1	1	2		
Buckingham, Thos	6	2	2		2
Bowars, W^m	1	2	3		
Bowing, James	1	1	2		
Cheserow, Geo	1	1	2		2
Cruse, Christopher	1	3	1		
Coalman, John	3		1		
Cashshau, Abraham	2	1	1		
Carroll, Mary			1		
Cook, Ambors	1	1	2		
Cartin, Frances	2		5		
Criswell, W^m	1		2		(*)
Calf, John	1	1	2		
Carr, James	1		2		
Coal, John	1	3	2		
Corbason, W^m	2		2		
Cabel, Henary	1		2		
Climer, Catherener	1	1	6		
Coons, Jacob	1	1	1		
Other Free Persons				23	
Dunwooddy, Robert	2	1	2		
Delile, John	1	1	2		
Dugan, Cumbirlin	4	2	5		13
Drake, Frances	1	3	5		1
Deshlel, Frances	1	3	3		
Dyer, Catherener	1		4		
Johnson, Sarah			1		
Edy, Daniel	1	1	3		
Eans, Philip	1		2		
Everit, James	1	1	1		
Other Free Persons				21	
Faints, Jacob			5	1	1
Felton, John	1	1	1		
Ferrel, James	2		2		
Forels, James	1	1	2		1
Fowler, Thos	2		3		
Gantz, Adam	3	2	3		3
Good, Samuel	1	1	3		
Goodino, John	1		1		
Gaynor, Hugh	1		2		
Godfrey, Allen R	1	1	2		
Hagaty, John	1		1		
Hart, Uriah	1	2	1		
Hill, Asa	2		1		
Hoas, John	2	1	4		
Hurly, Patrick	1	1	1		
Hughs, Rich^d	1		4		1
Hodskings, W^m	1		3		
Hook, Antony	3	3	2		1

NAME OF HEAD OF FAMILY.	Free white males of 16 years and upward, including heads of families.	Free white males under 16 years.	Free white females, including heads of families.	All other free persons.	Slaves.
Alter, Christopher	2		3		1
Holman, John	1		5		
Hale, Philip	3	1	5		2
Hodgkings, Thos B	4	1	3		3
Harris, David	1		3		
Hargood, Henary			3		
Hapenny, Patarick	1		4		
Hughs, Christopher	3	4	5		
Harbite, Charles	2		2		8
Harman, John	3	2	2		
Hoas, Fredarick			3		(*)
Hooper, W^m	2	1	3		
Johnson, Sarah			2		(*)
Lewis, Hannah		1	2		
Labuch, Jachues	1		2		2
Lewis, Thos	1		1		
Laurengen, Mary			2		
Lemden, Thos	1	1	2		1
Love, James	1		2		
Hook, John	4		2		
George, Peter	1		1		
Sellers, Henary	1		2		
Ziger, Peter	1	1	2		
Cabel, Andrew	1				
Allen, W^m	3		4		
Burbian, Mary		1	5		
Lock, W^m	1	3	3		
Lupestine, Andrew	1	3	2		
Laurance, Joseph	1	2	3		
Lamott, Daniel	6		1		
Miller, James	3		1		
McCulla, James		1	3		
Miller, Magalen		2	2		
May, Catherener	1		3		
Moquian, W^m	1	2	2		
McCoslin, David	1		6		
McGuier, Mary	2	1			
Mayson, Benj^a	1	2	2		
Musherow, Joseph	2	1			
McHenary, James	2	1	2		6
Mine, Crouts			2	4	
Nogel, Henary	1		2		
Other Free Persons					11
Nash, Thos	2	2	6		
Night, Elizabeth		1	4		
Night, Benj^a	1		3		
Nusser, Jacob	1	1	4		
Norton, Benj^a	2		3		
Odevager, Lucy	1		4		
Orrick, Charles	1	1	2		
Powal, Thomas	1		2		
Barkman, Joseph		3	2		
Philps, W^m	2	2	3		1
Prishon, Nicholus	1		3		
Perry, John	1	2	2		(*)
Peal, Geo	2	1	1		
Richard, W^m	1		2		
Twilenny, Rebecca		2		4	
Other Free Persons				6	
Ray, Geo	3		3		
Rusk, David	1	1	2		
Russel, Alex^r	1		3		
Rangelware, Peter	1		2		
Reed, James	1		3		1

NAME OF HEAD OF FAMILY.	Free white males of 16 years and upward, including heads of families.	Free white males under 16 years.	Free white females, including heads of families.	All other free persons.	Slaves.
Ruseburt, Martin			5		
Reed, W^m	1	3	2		
Shock, Geo	2	1	4		
Smith, Jacob	2		3		1
Sunday, Matthias	1	1	3		
Shier, John	1		2		
Slay, John	1	2	3		
Smith, John	1	1	2		1
Shriver, Jacob	1	2	2		
Shandler, John	1	1	1		
Sitler, Philip	1				
Sherral, Michael	1		4		
Stayton, W^m	1	3	4		
Sulaven, Philip	1		3		
Shanyman, Fredarick	1	2	1		
Smith	43		45		3
Selman, Amzia	1	1	2		
Stiger, Andrew	2	1	2		
Smith, Jacob	1		1		
Simolt, Jacob	2		1		
Tarbait, W^m	1		2		
Turner, Samuel	1		1		
Tatler, Joseph	1	2	2		
Tellen, Peter	1		3		4
Tarny, Philip	1		2		
Turner, W^m	1	1	5		
Trakel, Geo	3		2		
Turner, Rich^d	1	2	2		
Tiart, John	4		2		1
Trash, Jacob	1		1		
Walkins, W^m	1		2		
Other Free Persons				2	
Welch, Edmand	1	3	2		
Widerfield, James	9	2	2		
Williams, Otho	2	1	5		
Woolly, Joseph	1		2		
Waggener, Andrew	1	(*)	(*)	(*)	(*)
Woolford, Stophal	1				
Wight, John	1	(*)	(*)	(*)	(*)
Wich, James	1	1			
Woodserfield, John	1				
Wilks, Joseph	1				
Young, Jacob	1	1	2		(*)
Yelser, John	1	2	3		(*)
Stoph, Philip	1		2		
Piner, Henary	1				
Hicks, Robert	3		3		
Thompson, Cornelus	3	1	3		
Backer, Engain	3				
Other Free Persons				4	
Rogers, Guy	2	1	2		
Fife, James	1		1		
Cowin, Elizabeth			2		
Laggard, Joseph	2	1	2		1
Burbian, Joseph	1		2		
Smith, Henary	1	1	4		
Reed, Hannah			3		
Butler, ——	3		4		
Huggins, ——			4		
Other Free Persons				10	
Widerfield, ——	1	2	5		3
Booth, ——	3				
Capel, ——	1		4		
Green, Thos	1		3		
Parney, Samuel	1	1	5		

CALVERT COUNTY.

[Schedules destroyed.]

CAROLINE COUNTY.

NAME OF HEAD OF FAMILY.	Free white males of 16 years and upward, including heads of families.	Free white males under 16 years.	Free white females, including heads of families.	All other free persons.	Slaves.
Allen, Reubin	3	2	3		
Anthony, Henry	1		2		2
Anthony, Mark	1	1	3		
Austin, Henry	1		1		
Abbot, Jesse	2		2		
Ayres, Abraham	1	2	6	1	
Armstrong, Jno	1		1		
Anthony, Joseph	2	1	4	1	
Anderson, John	2	3	2	1	
Allen, Ann			2		
Allen, Mary			2		
Andrew, James	1	4	2		
Andrew, Jeremiah	1	2	2		
Andrew, David	1	3	2		
Andrew, Isaac	1	2	4		
Andrew, Luke	1	2	5		
Andrew, Richard	1	3	3		
Andrew, Jacob	1	1	3		
Andrew, Beachump	2		6		
Andrw, William	2	4	6		
Andrew, Sarah, of Jno			2		
Andrew, Penelope	1	3	6		

NAME OF HEAD OF FAMILY.	Free white males of 16 years and upward, including heads of families.	Free white males under 16 years.	Free white females, including heads of families.	All other free persons.	Slaves.
Allen, William	1	2	2		
Anderson, Isaac	1	2	1		
Alford, Matthias	1	1	7		
Allcock, Thos	2		2		6
Alford, William	2	1	2		
Andrew Bromwell	1	3	3		10
Andrew, Edward	1	1	3		
Andrew, Mary			3		
Alford, Aaron		2	3		6
Alford, Maccabus	2		3		
Andrew, Mark	2	1	6		1
Andrew, W^m of George	2		3		
Andrew, Jas. Stradly	1	2	2		
Auld, Sarah			2		4
Andrew, Mary, of Geo			2		
Bush, Andrew	1	2	2		
Burton, William	2	1	2		3
Burk, Nathan	2	2	2		
Burk, Elizabeth			2		6
Bright, Thomas	1	2	1		
Bell, James	2	1	2	1	3
Bailey, William	1		2		4

NAME OF HEAD OF FAMILY.	Free white males of 16 years and upward, including heads of families.	Free white males under 16 years.	Free white females, including heads of families.	All other free persons.	Slaves.
Banckes, William	2	1	2		6
Banning, William	2	3	4		7
Barrow, Darcus			2		7
Barrow, John D	5	1	2		
Bush, John	2		3		
Bartlett, James	2	1	4		
Bartlett, Danl	2		2		
Bond, Rachel			3		6
Barwick, Jas	1	4	5	3	2
Brown, Rebe^a			2	3	
Bell, William	2	3	5	2	5
Bowman, James	1		3		8
Bradley, Jno	1	2	3		
Bradley, Sarah			3		
Bell, Robert	2	1	4		2
Boon, Benj^a	2		4		2
Burk, Robert	4	1	3		5
Boon, James	2		4		
Boon, Jas. Junr	2		3		5
Baynard, Danl	1	2	3		
Buckingham, Isaac	2	1	7		1

* Illegible.

CAROLINE COUNTY—Continued.

NAME OF HEAD OF FAMILY.	Free white males of 16 years and upward, including heads of families.	Free white males under 16 years.	Free white females, including heads of families.	All other free persons.	Slaves.
Boon, Isaac					12
Boon, William	1	3	3		
Boon, James, 3d	3		3		
Boon, Jno.	6	1	1		
Boon, Mary	1		2		3
Boon, Jacob	2	3	4		1
Boon, Robert	1		4		
Boon, Izabell		4	2		
Boon, Thomas	4	2	3	1	3
Baggs, Elizabeth	2		1		
Bradley, Henry	1	1	2		
Beaver, James	1		2		
Baynard, Levin	1	2	4		1
Black, Jas. Junr	2	1	4		
Baggs, Tibbles	2		1		
Brown, Jno.		1	1	1	1
Brown, Elizabeth	2	1	5		
Bradley, Thompson	2	2	3		
Bateman, Marg		2	1		
Butler, James	1	4	1		
Beal, Jane		4	1		
Bailey, Nathan	3	1	5		
Banikes, James	1	2	3		
Bright, James	1	2	4		
Birt, William		4	3		1
Birt, James	1	1	3		5
Brown, Joshua			3		
Beazel, Jno	1	2	1		1
Badger, Jonathan	2	1	2		
Brawdy, James	3		2		20
Black, James	3	3	5		6
Baxter, John	2		3		
Broadaway, Robt		2	1		
Blunt, Benjamin	1		5		13
Blades, Arnold	1	2	5		
Bawstick, Thomas	1		1		
Bell, Daniel	1		2		
Bell, William	1	2	3		
Boxwell, Henry	1		2		
Barwick, Margt			2		
Barwick, Henry	1	1	5		
Barwick, James	1	2	2		
Blades, Tilghman	1	1	2		3
Barwick, Sidney	1		1		
Brannon, Matthew	2		3		
Bishop, William	1	3	6		
Baynard, Thomas	3	2	3	1	6
Bruding, Sidney Opis	2	1	8		
Brannock, James	2	1	5		
Bachelor, Penelope			3		
Brannock, Matt	1		1		
Bowden, Edward	1		1		
Berry, William		1	1		
Baxter, Thomas	1		1		
Barton, John	3	4	2	1	
Bending, Thomas	1		3		
Bing, William	2	3	2		1
Bland, Joseph	3	1	2		
Bland, Joseph, Junr	2	1	5		
Bending, Thos	2	1	1		
Brown, Live	2		2		3
Barton, Jno	2		2		
Brown, Jesse	3	1	4		1
Bachelor, Nathan	1		1		
Bachelor, William	3	2	6		2
Brooks, Benjn	1		5		
Banning, Andrew	1		3		
Barnett, Wm	2	1	5		
Barnett, Jane			3		
Barwick, Jno	3	2	2		1
Blades, Jno	2		2		1
Bush, Andrew			2		
Bitteler, Margt			2		
Barton, Edward	1		2		
Body, John	1	3	4		
Blades, Joseph	1	1	1		
Burk, Edward	1	2	3		5
Blades, Levin	3	2	4		
Bartlett, Danl			3		
Baker, Lydia			5		
Bell, George		1	1		5
Blades, Thomas	1	2	2		
Beachump, Ann			3		
Beachump, Jno	3	2	3		4
Blair, Charles			3		30
Blades, Anderton	1	3	4		
Bowdle, Henry	1	3	5		
Brooks, Henry	1	1	1		3
Bitteler, Elizh			3		
Barwick, Fisher	1		4		
Bitteler, Joseph		2	2		
Blades, Mary			3		
Beachump, Jno., Junr	1	1	2		
Casson, Philip	1	2	2		
Cooper, Thomas	3		2		
Cooper, Cloudsbury	2	1	1		5
Critchett, Charles	3		4	1	2
Cooper, John, Junr	2	1	5		1
Cooper, Solomon	2		2		6
Colscott, William	1	5	1		1
Clark, Parrott	1	1	2		4
Carpenter, John	2	1	2		
Cliff, Henry	3		5	2	1
Clark, Joshua	1	2	2	4	11
Coleton, William	1		1		15
Crayner, Emory	1	2	2		
Clayner, Emanuel	2	1	8		1
Chitton, William	4	1	1	1	3
Chilton, Anthony	1		3		
Clough, Delilah			1		
Carney, Mary		1	3		
Colley, Peggy			1		
Cooper, Lydia			3		
Casson, James	1		2		6
Chillcutt, Joshua	2	4	6	1	
Chance, Bachelor	2	1	2		
Chilton, Matthew	2	1	3		
Coulgin, John	1		3		
Carter, Edward	1	2	3		1
Cooper, Benjn	2		1		2
Carter, Edward, Junr		1	1		2
Cannon, William	3		4		1
Carpenter, Robert	1	4	5		
Chance, Tilghman	1	7	3		
Carter, William	3	2	4		3
Courcey, William	2	3	7		2
Clark, William	3		2		
Chance, Peter	1	1	4		
Cearn, Nathan	1		4		
Coxell, Hezekiah	1	1	1		
Courcey, Sarah			3		
Credock, William	2		1		1
Cavender, Mary			3		
Cox, Anthony	2	2	4		
Charles, Levin	3	2	1		
Conaway, Samuel	2		4		1
Courcey, Henry	2		2		
Carne, Thos					3
Chance, Rich.	2	1	1		
Cook, James	2	1	1		5
Cannon, Henry	3		1		
Cornish, Betsey			3		
Cullin, David	2		2	1	
Countis, James	1	2	7		
Copes, Rachel			4		
Copes, John	1	1	3		
Cleaves, Nathan	1		1		
Coventon, Edward	1	1	2		
Comiges, William	1	1	2		
Countis, Peter	1		2		
Clark, Solomon	3		3		
Carey, James	3	2	3		5
Colbreath, Sarah			4		3
Councill, John	1	1	5		
Clements, James	1	2	2		
Cooper, Mark Griffin	2		2		
Chance, Jeremiah	1	1	4		
Camper, James	1	1	2		
Camper, Quinten	1	1	4		
Cox, Joseph	1	2	2		3
Clark, Michael	1	1	2		
Cahall, Clondsbury	1	1	3		1
Cahall, William	1	1	4		
Credock, Margt			3		1
Cahall, John	1	1	2		
Cremcen, Jno. Tayloe			2	7	
Cawsey, Peter T		2	2		1
Carey, William	1		4		
Climer, Francis	3		1		
Carlile, Robert	2		3		
Carlile, Samuel	2	1	3		
Curry, John	3		2		
Colscott, Rolph	1		3		
Carrol, John	3		2		
Cooper, John	1	2	2	2	
Cooper, Stephen	3		4	1	1
Cawsey, Ann			2		
Connelly, Jesse	1	1	2		
Chaffinch, John	1		1		
Chaffinch, Jno., Junr	1	1	3		
Cox, Nancy			4		
Carrol, Sarah			4		
Collison, William	2	5	2		
Collison, Peter	2	2	2		1
Cook, William	2	2	2		
Clark, Richard	2	1	2		
Chuzum, Samuel	1	2	3		
Cocklin, James	2		3	1	
Chuzum, William	2	1	3		
Cork, Mary			4		
Cremcan, Keziah	2	1	3		
Collins, Samuel	3		2	3	
Cork, Peter	3		2		4
Chillcutt, Thos	1	2	4		
Carter, James	2		4		
Clogg, Jenny			2		
Carter, John	2		3		
Clayland, John	4	4	4	8	5
Covey, John	4		4	4	
Corkin, Henry	1	1	2		
Cork, John	2		3		3
Camper, William	2		4	7	
Chillcutt, Thos	3		6	1	
Chuzum, James	1	3	2		
Cremcen, Jno.	3	2	2		
Cooper, Taphanis	4		5		3
Cook, Margt			4		
Cawsey, Beachump	2		2		
Collins, Abraham	4	1	2	2	
Collins, Isaac	3		6		
Cawsey, Solomon	2		3		2
Collins, William	1		2		
Cremcen, Elijah	2	1	6		
Coulburn, Solomon	3		3		2
Clarkson, Richd	1	1	3		3
Carey, Edward	1		2		
Collins, William	3		1		1
Catrip, Thomas	1		2		
Connor, Sarah			1		
Cohee, Amos	2	3	3		
Clark, Caleb	2		5	6	
Connelley, Owen	1	2	2		
Chance, Elijah	2		2		
Cork, Francis			3		2
Cremcen, Noah	1	2	2		1
Cremcen, Curtis	1	1	4		2
Clark, Abraham	1		2		
Clark, William			2		
Corns, Elizabeth			2		
Chiply, John	3	4	7		
Crayner, Joshua	1	3	1		
Chaffinch, Jas	1	2	4		
Connelly, Reubin	1	2	3		
Cooper, Mark			4		
Dwigans, James	3		4		8
Downes, Aaron	2	3	4		
Diggans, John	2	1	4		10
Dwigans, John	2		2	1	10
Downes, Ann			2		2
Downes, Hawkins	3		2		6
Downes, Philomon	2		3		5
Downes, Henry	1	1	2	1	
Delany, William	3		3		
Doroschbroom, John	1	2	3	1	7
Doroschbroom, Matt	2		3		
Diet, Aaron			4		
Due, James				5	
Dawson, Rebk			4		2
Davis, Baptist	2	1	1		
Dill, Joseph	1		3		
Davis, Griffin			3		
Davis, Hannah			1		
Deford, Joseph M	1		1		
Dean, Michael				4	
Dunkin, Elizabeth			3		
Deford, Joseph		4	2		
Donbrano, Thomas	1	2	2		4
Downes, Thomas	1		5		
Dabson, Edward	1		2		
Dill, Philip	1	2	2		
Denney, Samuel	2	1	1		
Draper, Judal		2	1		
Dill, Celia			2		
Dixon, Zebulon			4		9
Dixon, Joseph	1		1		5
Delehay, William	1	1	3		2
Drury, James			4		
Denney, Benjamin	3		5		24
Driver, Matthew	7	1	3	1	10
Driver, Christopher	1	1	2		6
Dixon, Rebk			2		
Draper, William	1		1		
Dwigans, James			2		
Dean, William	1	3	3		
Dixon, James	4		3		
Dillen, John	1	1	3		
Driskill, Laurance	1	1	1		
Delehay, John	1		3		
Dean, Francis	1		2		
Dean, Elijah	1	3	2	2	1
Dean, Mary			2		
Dillen, John, Junr	1		1		
Dillen, James	4		5		
Dawson, John Fork	3	1	6		6
Davis, Lemuel	1		2		
Deal, William			2		6
Dawson, Edward	1	3	4		19
Douglass, Joseph			3		
Davis, Abraham	2	1	3	5	
Dawson, John			2		
Dawson, Elizabeth			1		

CAROLINE COUNTY—Continued.

NAME OF HEAD OF FAMILY.	Free white males of 16 years and upward, including heads of families.	Free white males under 16 years.	Free white females, including heads of families.	All other free persons.	Slaves.
Dawson, William	3		2		
Dill, Adam				7	
Dawson, Noah	2		1		1
Dawson, Daniel	1		1		
Davis, Aquilla	1	2	3		
Dukes, Thomas	3	1	3		
Durgan, John	1	2	4		
Dean, Elizabeth		2	5		
Dean, Sarah		1	2		
Emory, James				3	
Emory, Charles	1	2	2	3	
Emory, Arthur	2	1	4		
Elleckson, John	1	4	3		
Edge, Robert	1	2	3		
Ellett, Francis	1	1	1	1	
Evetts, Lethell	2	2	3	2	
Ewing, James	1	3	5		11
Edmondson, Peter	2		1		14
Edgill, Benjamin	2	3	7		
Eaton, Anderton	1		4		15
Eaton, Jonthan	1	3	5	1	
Eaton, Mary	2		3		8
Eaton, Rebecca		3	3		
Eaton, Levi	1		3		
Eaton, Thos.	1	3	3		
Edgill, Henry	1	3	5		
Edgill, Walter	1		1		2
Evitts, Abraham	2	1	5	1	
Edmondson, William	2		1	1	1
Edmondson, James	4	1	4	1	
Emerson, Samuel	2	1	2		
Eaton, Edward	1	5	3	1	
Edgill, Daniel	2	2	2		8
Floyd, Aaron	1	1	4		3
Fountain, John	4	1	2		10
Fountain, William	1	2	3		
Fields, Esther	2		2		
Flemming, Archibald	1				1
Freeman, Lydia	1	1	2		3
Foster, Nathan	1	1	4		
Frantom, Richard	1	2	2		
Freeman, John	8		3		31
Freeman, Timothy	1		2		
Faulconer, Jacob	3	4	4		
Fairfield, Marian		1	3		
Fearns, Miles	1		1		
Fisher, Richard	1	1	5		7
Forrister, James	1	1	2		
Faulconer, Daniel	1	1	1		
Faulconer, William	1	1	2		
Bantom, Gabriel				8	
Fisher, Samuel	1	1	2		
Fisher, Henry	1	2	1		
Faulconer, Charles	1	2	2		
Fountain, Mary	1		3		20
Fountain, Casson	1	1	2		
Foster, Mark	1	2	4		
Fountain, Thomas	1	1	2		5
Fountain, Samuel	1	1	3		7
Fountain, James	2	4	3		
Fountain, Risden	1	1	2		
Fountain, Roger	1	1	5		1
Flowers, John	1		1		
Flowers, Ellis	1	1	1		
Foster, Stephen	1		1		1
Faulconer, Jacob	2		2		
Fardwell, Jacob	1		1		
Frantom, William	1	1	3		
Frazier, William	2	1	2	2	17
Frantom, Catharine	2	1	3		
Ferguson, Rachel		1	1		
Friend, John				4	
Fiddeman, Hawkins	3	1	3		
Faris, Mary			4		
Flowers, Rebeckah		1	2		1
Fowler, Thomas	3	4	4		
Fountain, William	1	2	2	1	4
Fleharty, James	1	1	3		3
Fountain, David	1		1		
Fountain, Nathaniel	1	1	3		7
Fleharty, Stephen	3	2	4		6
Fleming, John	1		3		
Gordon, Alexander	1	2	2		
Goforth, Jane			2		
Glanden, Hynson	3	1	4		
Green, Valentine	4	2	4		3
Ginn, John	4	3	2		
Green, John	4	2	2		13
Glanden, James	1	1	2		
Glanden, Leben	1		3		
Greenly, Mary			3		
Grigg, John	1	2	2		1
Gland, Joannis	1	1	2		4
Ginn, Joseph	4	4	3		
Ginn, Lott			2		2
Garrott, Matthew	1	2	1		3
Glanden, Elizabeth	1	1	1		

NAME OF HEAD OF FAMILY.	Free white males of 16 years and upward, including heads of families.	Free white males under 16 years.	Free white females, including heads of families.	All other free persons.	Slaves.
Greenage, Sherry				6	4
Griffith, Solomon	4		2		
Green, Nemiah	1		2		
Gouty, John	2		4		
Griffith, John	2	1	5		
Griffith, Alexander	3	4	4		5
Garey, George	1	3	7		
Grayless, Jesse	5		4		1
Grace, Solomon	2	3	5		
Grayless, William	1	2	3		
Griffith, Moses	1	3	3		
Grayham, Thomas	1	2	4		
Green, John Miller	1	2	2		
Grace, Natt¹	1	2	2		
Gouty, Able	1		3		1
Grimes, Marg¹			3		
Greenwell, James	2	1	1		2
Gray, William, Junr	1	3	5		
Glines, Philomon	1	2	2		
Griffith, Nathan	1	3	2		
Gamble, Gideon	1		1		
Gannon, Thomas		3	3		
Gully, Charles	2	3	5	1	
Hickman, Henry	1		3		
Hawkins, Francis					6
Hollond, Ruth			3		
Hardcastle, James	1		4		13
Hall, Thomas	1	2	2		
Hambleton, James	1	2	1	1	
Hicks, James	4		4		16
Hicks, Giles	1	1	2		
Hill, Elizabeth			2		
Hardcastle, John	5	1	2	2	13
Hardcastle, Aaron	1		3		6
Hardcastle, Robert	3		4		14
Hammond, Lucretia			1		
Harvey, Thomas	2	2	5		2
Hunter, Ezekiel	4	1	7		7
Hunter, Ezekiel, Junr	1	2	4		
Holson, William	2	1	4		
Hinsely, Solomon			1		
Holden, John	2		5		
Harrington, Thomas	1	2	3		
Hollingsworth, John	3	2	4		
Hefferson, Robert	1		2	1	
Hignut, Sarah			1		
Higgans, Benjamin			2		
Hopkins, Thomas	2	3	2		
Hardcastle, Solomon	3	3	1		
Harrington, Peter	3	3	7	1	3
Harper, William	4	1	6	1	1
Harper, Samuel	2	2	4		4
Holson, Solomon	1	1	2		
Holden, Calib	2	2	3		5
Holden, Calib, Junr	2		2		
Hutson, John	1	2	1		
Harrington, Abigale	1		3		
High, Alexander	4		4		
Harrington, John	1	2	2		
Hay, William	2	3	2		
Hickey, John	1	3	4		
Hutchings, Thomas	1	2	4		
Hutchings, Jno	2	2	4		
Hobbs, Merrium			2		
Harrington, Philip	3		5	1	
Hunt, James				3	
Hicks, George	1	2	2		
Hubancks, John	1	2	1		
Hubancks, George	1	2	1		1
Hardcastle, Thomas	5	4	4		20
Hutson, Hooper	2	2	2		
Herrington, William	2		2		
Herrington, Henry	2		2		
Harrington, James	1		3	1	
Hughlett, Thomas	5	3	4	1	11
Herrington, David	1	1	1		
Hazlett, Cynthia	1	3	5		2
Herd, Joseph	1	3	2		2
Hutson, John	1		2		
Herd, William	1	3	4		
Hancock, Thomas	1	1	2		
Hutton, William	2	2	3		
Harrison, James	1		3	1	
Horney, James	1				
Harrington, Ann			4		6
Hurry, Thomas	1	2	3		
Hardicane, Robert	1	2	1		
Hollis, Claradine		3	2		
Hobbs, Robert	2				
Harris, James	3		3		
Hignutt, Daniel	1		5		
Harris, Celia	1	2	1		
Horney, Deborough		2	3	1	
Hall, James	1	1	2		
Hobbs, Garey	1	2	2		
Hobbs, Solomon	1	1	2		
Hobbs, Zebulon	3	2	3		

NAME OF HEAD OF FAMILY.	Free white males of 16 years and upward, including heads of families.	Free white males under 16 years.	Free white females, including heads of families.	All other free persons.	Slaves.
Henry, Stephen	1		1		2
Harding, Absolem	1	1	3		
Hubbord, Charles	1	1	1		3
Hall, Felix	1		2		
Hall, Levi	1	1	1		
Herring, Daniel	1	1	1		
Henry, Elizabeth			1		
Heleby, James	2		3		4
Harris, John	4	3	3		
Hubbord, Solomon	1		1		3
Hubbord, Jesse	1	4	3	1	
Hubbord, Thomas	1	5	5		
Hobbs, John	1	5	1		
Hobbs, Mary			3		
Harrison, John	3	1	2		8
Hopkins, Thomas	2	1	5		1
Hobbs, Deborough	2	1	1		
Hooper, John	1		1		3
Hooper, Jno. Junr	1	1	2		
Harrison, Nicholas	1	1	1		2
Hutchison, Archibald	1		2		
Harrison, John	1	1	1		
Hall, Levi	1		2		
Hutchison, John	1	1	3		
Haskins, William	2				15
Hackett, Elizabeth		2	3		
Hobbs, William	1		1		
Hughs, Jonathan	1	1	1		
Harvy, John	1		3		
Harris, Amos	3	2	2		6
Hopkins, James	1	2	3		
Harvey, Samuel	2	1	4		
Hollond, Levi	1	1	4		
Huchings, Aquilla	1		4		1
Harvey, John, Junr	1	4	6	1	
Hollond, Richard	1		5		
Hopkins, John	1	1	3		
Hughs, John	1	1	8		
Hobbs, Joshua	1		1		
Howard, Joseph	1	1	3		
Harper, John	1	1	2		
Jones, John	3	2	3		1
Jadwin, John	2	2	1		
Jacobs, John	2	2	1		
Jackson, Archibald	1	2	3		
Jones, John Hatter	1	2	3		
Jones, John	2		2		
Jakes, Henry	1	1	2		
Jump, Purnell	1	2	1		
Jump, Peter	2	1	5		2
Jump, John	1		2		
Jump, Benjamin	1	3	3		1
Jump, Elijah	2		4		
Jump, Thomas	2		3		2
Jump, William	2	2	0		
Jones, James	1		2		
Jones, Richard	2		2		
Jump, Aliemby	2	4	2		3
Ironsmore, John	2	2	5		
Jackson, Archibald	1	1	1		
Jackson, Edward	1		2		
Jackson, Thomas H.	1		2		
Jackson, Abednigo	2	1	1		
Johnson, Aulbert	1	1	3		
Jackson, Archibald	1	2	3		
Jadwin, Elizabeth		1	3		
Jones, Edward	1	1	6		
Ireland, Abednigo	1	1	4		
Ireland, Shadrach	1	1	3		
Jackson, Peter for Thos. Goldsborough	1				17
Jackson, Civel	3	1	2		
Jackson, Samuel	4		1		5
Jones, Charles	1	3	1		
Jones, James	2		1	2	2
Jackson, William		2	1		
Jackson, Sarah		3	4		
Johnson, James	1		3		
Jewell, William	1		3		
Jewell, George	1	1	3		
Jester, John	1	3	5		
Johnson, Jonathan	1	3	3		
Jewell, William, Junr	1	3	3		
Johnson, Abraham	1		4		
James, Hesekiah	1		4		
Jenkins, Thomas	1	4	4		
Jones, Ebar	2	4	2		
Johnson, Cornelius	1	2	5		1
Jenkins, Ann	1	2	4		
Ireland, Rachel	2		4		
Ireland, Samuel	1	1	1		
Johnson, Mary			4	4	
Jones, Solomon	3		1	2	1
James, Jane			3		
James, Peter			6	6	
In the Poor House	2	1	7		1

CAROLINE COUNTY—Continued.

NAME OF HEAD OF FAMILY.	Free white males of 16 years and upward, including heads of families.	Free white males under 16 years.	Free white females, including heads of families.	All other free persons.	Slaves.
Jones, Hezekiah	1	2	1		
Johnson, Levin	1		1		
Johnson, James, Jun'	2	2	3		
Kemp, Quinten	1	3	1		
Kerby, Mary	1	3	1	6	9
Keene, William	2	3	4		24
Kenton, James	2	2	5		8
Kenton, Solomon	2	2	4		6
Kinneman, Samuel	1	1	5		2
Kinneman, Benj=	1	1	3		
Kinneman, Maryann			3		
Kenton, Margaret			4		
Knotts, William	1	2	4		
Kenneman, Ambrose	3	2	3		
Knotts, David	2	1	4		
King, John	2	1	1		
Knotts, Absolem	1	3	3		
Kenton, Thomas	1	1	4	1	
Knotts, James	3	1	5	1	
Keene, Rev'd Samuel	5		4		24
Kinderdine, Winefred	2		2		2
Kennard, Richard	1				12
Kerby, Calib	1	1	2		1
Kentin, Howell	1	1	1		
Kidd, William	2	3	3		
Kimms, John	1	2	2		
Kelley, W= of W=	1		2		1
Kelley, Dennis	1	2	3		
Kelley, William	1	1	1		2
Kelley, Mary	1	1	3		
Kelley, Dennis, Jun'	1	1	1		
Kirkman, Sarah	2	1	1		
Love, James	3	5	4		2
Loockerman, Jacob	1	1	2		7
Loockerman, Richard	1	1	2		17
Lane, William	1	1	9	1	3
Lane, Nancy			1		
Leaverton, James	5		1		3
Lane, Walter	1	2	3		
Lane, George	2		1		
Lane, Rebeckah			3		
Laremore, John	1	1	3		1
Lemar, James	1	4	1		
Leath, John	3		2		1
Longfellow, Amos	1	2	4		
Lee, John	2	2	4	2	2
Lemar, Whealer	1	1	1		
Lemar, Galley	2	2	4		
Lamdin, John	3	3	4		8
Lazeby, Mary	1	1			
Lemar, Lemuel	1	1	4		
Lane, Francis			1		
Long, Jno	3	3	5		
Lemar, John	1	3	1		1
Long, Thomas	3		1		
Lary, Philip	1	2	3		4
Lecompte, James	2	1	2		3
Lecompte, Thomas	1	1	2		2
Lecompte, Charles			2		7
Lyster, Joshua	3	2	2		
Lane, William			1		
Lucus, John	2	2	2		2
Lucus, Michael	2	3	4		4
Levis, Nancy			3		
Lary, Jonathan	1	2	2		
Lucus, John, Jun'	1	1	2		
Lewis, Thomas	3		2		1
Lucus, William	1		2		1
Lane, Richard	2	1	1		
Eyster, John	1	4	2		
Leaverton, Moses	3	3	3		
Layton, John	3		4		
Lyden, Shadrach	2	2	1	1	
Laurance, Mary		2	1		
Loockerman, Thos. W.			1		15
Layton, John	1		2		
Lord, Perry	1				
Lane, Joseph	1	2	2		
Morgan, Nancy		2	1		
Miller, Susannah			1		
Millis, Edward	1		1		1
Maden, Rabeckah			5		
Morgor, John	1				
McKnees, Partha		1	3		
McKnees, Benjamin	1	1	3		
Mounticue, Jere=	2		3		
Martindale, Henry	2	2	5		3
Millington, James	1	1	1	1	
Malony, Michael	1		1	3	
Malony, Mich'l, Jun'	1	1	3	1	
Malony, Jonathan	2	3	4		
Martindale, Sam'l	4	3	4		4
Martindale, Mary	2	2	3		
Martindale, Esther	1	2	3		
Mounticue, John	1	1	1		
Miller, Thomas			3		
Mason, James	1	2	5		1
Merrick, Izrel	3		2		
More, Benjamin	1		4		
Mason, Henry	1		4	1	3
Mark, Ann		1	4		
Mounticue, Harrison	1	2	2		
Mounticue, Jeremiah	1	2	3		
Magines, Ruth	1	1	4	7	
Matthews, Greenbury	1	1	4		
Martin, George	1		2	4	
Mounticue, Jadwin	1	2	2		4
Mason, William W	3		3		13
Matthews, Henry	2	2	5		
Money, James	2		2	1	2
Mason, Capt. Thos.	2	1	2	3	8
Mason, William	2		3		1
Mason, Sarah		2	3		
Mason, Thos. of Wm	2	1	2		7
Million, Lear		2	2		
Moulden, Elizabeth				5	
McCooms, Barnett	1				
McCooms, John	1	3	3		
McCooms, James	1	1	2		
Meredith, Absolem	2	3	5		
Milbern, Edward	1		3	1	
Minner, Joshua	2	3	2	1	
Minner, William	1		1	2	
Maller, William	1	1	2		
Mounticue, John	1	1	3		
More, John	1	1	1		
McGrann, John	2		1		
Merrick, Izrel, Jun'	2	3	1	1	1
Morris, Elijah	1	1	2		
Manship, Charles	2	3	3		3
Manship, James	1	3	1		
Miller, Killen	1	1	3		
Matthews, Maryann		2	4		
Morgan, Solomon	2	2	3		
Morgan, George	1	2	1		
Moberry, Ann	1	2	6		
Morgan, John	1	2	4		
Mussleman, Peter	1		1		
Mathers, Derby	1	1			
Madden, William	1		1		
Manlove, Mary		1	2		
Morriston, George	1	1	2		
Mitchell, Ambrose	2	2	6		
McKimme, Eliza''	1		3		
McGraw, William	2		2		
Munnett, Abraham	2	2	2		
Mitchell, Andrew	3	1	1	1	3
Morgan, James	2		5		
Minner, John	1	2	1		
Mitchell, John	1	3	2	1	17
Morriston, John	2	3	6		
Manship, Nathan	2	3	4		9
McKimme, Gideon	2	1	4		
Minner, John, Jun'	1	1	1		
Morgan, Mary	2	1	5		
Morgan, John	1	2	3		
Murphy, Thomas	1		2		1
Merrick, William	1	1	3		
McCarter, Dennis	1	1	2		
Charles, Negro				2	
Phillis, Negro				4	
Nicols, Henry	2	1	4		13
Will, Negro				1	
Nutter, Thomas	2	1	3		
Neilson, Rachell		1	3		
Patt, Negro				4	
Noles, William	1	3	4		
Sapp, Negro				5	
Isaac, Negro				7	
Answer, Negro				7	
George, Negro				6	
Nann, Negro				4	
Jacob, Negro				4	
Palm, Negro				9	
Hagar, Negro				1	
Narvell, Robert	2		1	1	1
Francis, Negro				3	
Nucomb, Timothy	1		3		
Lydia, Negro				2	
Beck, Negro				8	
Jack, Negro				5	
Saul, Negro				6	
Susan, Negro				1	
Comfort, Negro				3	
Sarah, Negro				3	
Binah, Negro				3	
Dick, Negro				3	
Nedd, Negro				5	
Sarah, Negro				1	
Sipeo, Negro				2	
Nunam, Sylvester	1	2	4		
Philis, Negro				3	
Nash, Robert	1				
Pegg, Negro				4	
Hannah, Negro				6	
Pheba, Negro				4	
Abraham, Negro				2	
Lennon, Negro				2	
Priss, Negro				3	
Nann, Negro				4	
Nicols, John	2	2	5		1
Nicols, Mary	1	1	1		
Nicols, Joseph	1	1	3		12
Noble, Levin	2		2		4
Nicols, Isaac, Jun'	1	1	2		7
Nicols, Thomas			2		
Nicols, Isaac	1		2		7
Hannah, Negro				2	
Will, Negro				6	
Benn, Negro				5	
Greenage, Negro				3	
Kate, Negro				1	
Jethro, Negro				8	
Precilla, Negro				4	
Sarah, Negro				3	
Draper, Negro				5	
Cuffee, Negro				4	
Daphna, Negro				4	
Henny, Negro				4	
Nunam, Ann	1		5		
Benn, Negro				4	
Noble, Maryann			2		
Nedles, William	1		4	2	1
Nicols, James	2	1	2		1
Nuner, Jacob	3		1		
George, Negro				4	
Nunam, Mary		1	3		
Sam'l, Negro				5	
Jethro, Negro				2	
Overstocks, James	1	4	3		4
Orrell, Thomas	2	3	4		4
Oxenham, Richard	3	2	5		3
Orrell, Francis	2	2	3		4
Orrell, Robert	2	2	2		1
Oldfield, William	2	2	3		
Oram, John	3		6		
Price, Timothy L	2	3	7		9
Price, Isaac	1				
Price, Neal	2		3		2
Price, Henny			3		
Purnell, James	1	3	1	1	
Purnell, Elizabeth		2	2		1
Price, Prudence			3		2
Pratt, Jacob	1		1		
Parr, John	1		1		
Pennington, Thos.	1		3		12
Pratt, Christopher	1		1		
Postlethwait, Robert	2	1	2		3
Porter, Robert	2	2	2	1	
Priest, Esther	2	1	4		
Pierce, John	1	1	3		
Parkinson, John	1	3	3		
Price, Morgan	1	2	8		26
Parrott, Elizabeth	1	1	4	2	
Parmar, James	1	1	2	1	
Purnell, Richard	1	2	3		
Porter, Colliston	1	2	3		
Pinder, Thomas	1	1	3		
Proctor, Mary			3		
Purden, Joseph	2	3	3		1
Protholo, Jane			2		
Pritchett, Noah	1		2		
Poor, Elijah	1		2		
Pippin, Robert	1	3	5		
Pippin, John	1	2	2		
Punney, Henry	1		3		
Purnell, Abraham	1		1		
Price, Jas. (Quarter)					6
Pippin, Elijah	2		2		7
Powell, James	1	3	3		
Poor, John	1	2	4		
Purnell, John	3	4	6		3
Pain, John	1	5	4		
Pain, Sarah	2	1	1		
Pinkins, Vincent	2	2	1		
Pain, Isaac	3	2	2		
Pritchett, Richard	1			3	2
Porter, James	1	2	2		
Pierson, Edward	1	2	3		
Peters, William	3	2	4		2
Perry, Thomas	1	2	3		
Pritchett, Ezekiel	1	3	1	2	
Parker, Allen	1	2	1		
Phillips, Rich'd			6		
Pool, John	2	2	4	2	
Peters, William	3	4	3		
Pritchett, Edward	2	2	3		
Pritchett, John	2	2	5		

CAROLINE COUNTY—Continued.

NAME OF HEAD OF FAMILY.	Free white males of 16 years and upward, including heads of families.	Free white males under 16 years.	Free white females, including heads of families.	All other free persons.	Slaves.
Pavey, Isaac	1		2		
Potts, William	2	3	1		
Pavey, John	1	1	3		
Perry, William	3	1	5		
Perry, John	1	1	3		3
Pinder, Edward	1		1		
Potter, Doct. Zebdiel	4	2	3		16
Powell, Rachael		2	3		
Perry, Thomas	1	1			
Pariah, Susannah			3		
Parker, Mary	1		3		1
Perry's, W= (Quarter)					11
Perry, Edward	1		2		
Perry, Richard	1	2	2		3
Parrott, Thomas	1	1	2		
Pratis, Charles				6	
Prous, John	2	2	4		
Quality, Owen	1				3
Quality, James	1				5
Quinn, John	1	1	1		
Richardson, William	4	4	6		36
Richardson, W= Dover	1		1		9
Richardson, W=, Ex= of Henry Dickinson	1				57
Richardson, Sarah			1	2	
Robinson, William	1	2	3		13
Russum, Triphina	1		4		1
Rathel, Pritchett	1	1	3		
Rollison, James	1		4		
Rice, Sarah		2	4		
Rigiway, John	1	1	3		2
Reynolds, Francis	3			1	
Russum, Nancy			4		
Roe, John, Jun=			2		
Robinson, Rachel	2		7		8
Roe, William	1				
Roe, Thomas	1	2	3		
Roe, John	1	2	7	1	
Rodin, James	3	1	4		
Roe, Abner	1	3	5		
Rouse, Solomon	1		2		
Rouse, Rebeckah		2	2		
Rouse, Susannah		1	2		
Rich, Peter	2	3	6		
Roe, Margarett	2	2	5	1	5
Robinson, James	2		2		
Roe, Thomas	2	1	4		
Rigiway, John	1	2	4		
Ring, Daniel	1	1	4		
Roe, Hugh	1	3	4		
Rash, Martin	1	4	4		
Rigiway, Joshua	1	4	2		
Ratliff, John	2	3	4		
Rolph, James	1	3	1		
Rouse, Benjamin	2		3		
Reed, James		2	3		
Richards, Esther		2	4		
Revel, John		2	2		
Rouse, Sarah		3	1		
Reed, Charles	1	4	4		
Russell, Elijah	1	4	4		
Richardson, John	1	1	2		
Richardson, Edw=	1	1	1		
Richardson, Joseph	1				8
Rogers, William	1		3		
Reeves, John	1	1	1		3
Roe, Obediah	1	3	2		
Roe, Thomas	1	2	4		
Richardson, John	3	2	5		
Ross, James	1	2	2		
Ross, Mary			2		
Rhodes, Henry	1				3
Rhodes, Edward	1	2	2		2
Russell, John	1	2	1		
Ryall, James	2	2	1		
Ross, Levin	2	2	2		
Riggin, Solomon	2	1	1		
Ross, Anthony	2		3		8
Ross, Cain	1	1	3		
Ross, Abraham	1		3		1
Russum, Africa	1	2	2		
Rumble, Mary			3		
Rumbly, Henry	2	1	5		
Reice, Mary		3	3		
Reid, Nathan	1		2		
Ryon, William	3	3	4	1	
Ross, Clement	1		4		3
Richards, Esther			5		1
Ryon, James	1		3		
Rumbly, Lydia	1	2	3		
Ryall, James	1		3		
Sharp, William	1	1	1	1	
Smith, John	1	1	4		
Smith, Levin	2	3	5		
Stokes, William	1	2	2		
Stuart, William	3	4	2		3

NAME OF HEAD OF FAMILY.	Free white males of 16 years and upward, including heads of families.	Free white males under 16 years.	Free white females, including heads of families.	All other free persons.	Slaves.
Skinner, Richard	1				10
Sharp, James	1		3		
Stafford, Zadock	1		4		
Saulsbury, James	1	1	2		1
Sharp, Henry	4	1	4		7
Stuart, Athol	1	2	3	2	
Steth, Jacob	2	2	2		5
Swan, Mary			2		
Saulsbury, William	1	3	2		
Smith, William	2	1	1		
Sellers, Francis	1	1	1	1	2
Swan, James	1		2		
Swan, Thomas	3		1		3
Swan, Thos., Jun=	1	2	1		
Shields, Bennett	1		2		
Saunders, William	1		3		
Sylvester, William	1	1	5		1
Sylvester, Purnell	1	3	4		
Stafford, James	2	3	4		
Shepherd, Elizabeth		2	8		
Shaw, William	2	2	6		5
Sylvester, Robert	2	1	3		1
Saterfield, Maria			2		
Strahon, David	2	1	2		
Slaughter, Stephen	2	1	2		2
Sylvester, Benj=	4	2	2		38
Sylvester, John	1	1	4		
Shoobrooks, Thos	1	3	3		
Stafford, John	2	2	2		
Stareks, William	1	1	1		
Smith, Susannah			3		
Sherwood, Nickson	1	1	3		
Southley, Sam=	2	1	3		
Sylvester, Cloudsby	1	1	3		
Sullivan, Jeremiah	1	1	2		
Skulley, James	1	1	1		
Scott, Thomas	1	1	4		9
Smith, John	1	2	5		
Scoudrick, Charity		1	2		
Story, Nancy	1	1	3		
Swift, Ann	2		4		
Swift, Vincent	2	4	4		3
Stewart, William	1		2		9
Sherwood, Daniel	1	2	3		
Sherwood, Merrium		2	2		
Sherwood, Francis	2	3	2		
Slaughter, Elizabeth			6		
Swift, Thomas	1	3	4		
Swift, Richard	1	3	4		2
Swift, James	2	1	5		4
Slaughter, Natt=	2	3	4		
Slaughter, James	1		2		5
Slaughter, Edward	1	1			
Slaughter, Jno. Jun=	1		4		3
Slaughter, Jno	1		4		4
Sylvester, Henry	1		2		
Sparkes, Daniel	1	2	1		
Stuart, Daniel	1		2		
Swift, David	1	2	2		4
Scott, Jno	1	1	1		
Sorden, Mary	1	2	3		
Strahon, Thomas	2	2	2		
Saulsbury, Nehemiah	1	2	3		
Speerry, John	2		3		
Sparks, Richard	2	1	4		
Saulsbury, Ebenezer	1	3	4		
Swiggate, Harman	2	1	2		
Swiggate, William	2	3	4	1	
Swiggate, Johnson	2	3	5	1	
Swiggate, Henry	4	3	3		
Stafford, Balam	1	1	2		
Stevens, John	1	1	3		11
Staterfield, William	1	3	6		
Smith, Joshua	1	3	6	2	10
Summers, William	3	3	4	2	10
Sangston, Jno. A.	2	1	4		11
Stark, James	2	1	2		
Saulsbury, Jno., Jun=	1		6		
Saulsbury, John	1	2	3		
Summers, Elizabeth		2	4		12
Smith, Thomas	1	2	5		
Stevens, Azel	1	5			
Stevens, Jonathan	1		3		
Stevens, Mary	1		5		
Saulsbury, W= of Jas		2	2		
Sutton, Peregrine	1		2		
Sherwood, William	1	3	1		3
Spence, Thomas	1	1	2		
Simmons, John	1	1	1		
Simmons, Robt	1		3		3
Story, Esther		3	3		
Stanton, Beachump	2		3		
Smith, John	3	1	6		
Stokes, Ann			3		
Sparkland, Samuel	1	2	3		
Stubs, Jno	3		2		

NAME OF HEAD OF FAMILY.	Free white males of 16 years and upward, including heads of families.	Free white males under 16 years.	Free white females, including heads of families.	All other free persons.	Slaves.
Stark, Joseph	2	1	1		4
Sherman, John	2		3		
Sullivan, Owen	1		1		
Sullivan, John	4	2	3		
Stubbs, Henry	2		2		
Sutton, Benjamin	2	1	7		
Sisk, David	4	1			4
Sisk, Jno	3		1	2	1
Satchell, Andrew	1		2		
Suiters, Charles	1	1	2		
Stack, Thomas	1	1	1		
Spence, Patrack	2	2	1		
Smith, Thomas	2		3		
Smith, Ezekiel	2		2		1
Stafford, James	2	3	4		
Smith, Richard	1	1			
Smith, William	1		1		8
Smith, William	1		3		4
Stevens, Elizabeth	1		1	1	2
Stubbs, Nicholas	1	3	2		
Stubbs, John	1	2	4		
Smith, Isaac	1		2		
Sullivane, Mary			2		
Snow, Thomas	2		2		
Summers, James	2		4		5
Sullivan, Sol=	2	1	3		
Sasercon, James	3		3		
Steel, Peter	1		2		
Steel, James	1		2		
Scoudrick, Mary		1	2		
Sewell, William	1		5		
Stevens, Johannah		2	2		
Smith, John	1		3		4
Smith, Edward	1	1	3		
Sherwin, Daniel	1	1	4		
Shanks, Benjamin	1		1		
Swiggate, W=	1				
Stanton, Thomas	2	1	2		
Slaughter, Thomas	1		1		
Towers, James	1		2		
Turner, John	1	2	2		
Tinor, James				2	
Taylor, William	1	1	6	2	
Thompson, Dekar	1		3		15
Tinor, Hannah			2	2	
Tool, James	2	1	4		
Thornton, James	2	1	2		
Thawley, John	1	4	5		
Tolson, James	1	2	2		2
Turner, James	4		5		
Townerd, William	1	1	6		
Trout, Richard	2	1	2		5
Thawley, Edward	1	1			
Thomas, Rebeckah		2	1		
Taylor, Natthaniel	2	1	1		1
Thomas, Philip	1	1	1		
Tharp, John	1		1		
Trusty, Stephen				3	2
Tolboy, William	1	3	3	3	2
Tolboy, Robert	1		3		
Towers, Ann		3	6		
Towers, Thomas	2	3	5		4
Turner, Thomas	1		2		13
Turner, Henry	1	1	4		1
Turner, Henry, Jun=			3		6
Todd, Michael	5	1	3		
Twiford, Jonathan	1	3	2		
Todd, David	1	3	1		
Todd, Nathan	1	3	1		
Todd, Michael, Jun=	1	1	2		1
Thomas, Robert	1	1	3		
Tull, Levin	1		1		
Thomas, Ellis	1	3			5
Towers, Solomon	3	1	6		
Thornton, George	3		5		4
Teakle, Capt. Severn	2		2		13
Vaux, William	2	1	2		1
Vincent, Jeremiah	1	4			
Vickers, Elizabeth			3		
Vincy, James	1		3		
Vinzant, Joshua	1	3	3		
Vincent, Eliab	1	4	5		3
Verden, William	1		4		
Vinzant, George	1	2	3		
Voss, John	1	1	3		1
Vain, Bartholomew	1	2	1		
Vain, John	1	3			
Vain, William	3		1		
Victor, Major	3	3			
Vaulx, John	1		3		5
Valliant, John	1		4		3
Valliant, Daniel	1	2	3		5
Valliant, Thos.	2	1	4		
Vaulx, Sarah			3		
Vaulx, James	1		1		
Walker, Philip	2		2		14

CAROLINE COUNTY—Continued.

NAME OF HEAD OF FAMILY.	Free white males of 16 years and upward, including heads of families.	Free white males under 16 years.	Free white females, including heads of families.	All other free persons.	Slaves.
Willson, Solomon	2	2	4		
Willson, James	2	2	2		
Wadman, Thos.	3	1	2		1
Willson, William	2	2	5		
Willson, James, Junr	2		3		
Williams, Isaac	1		3		
Willis, Andrew	5	6	4		1
Wingate, Thos.	1	1	3		
White, Thomas				3	
Ward, Henry	3		2		
Williams, Rachl		2	5		1
Webber, James	3	1	4		2
Webber, David	2	3	3		1
Winchester, John	3	3	2		
Wootters, Lemuel	2	2	1		
Warner, Richard	2	2	3		
Walker, George	2		3		
Willson, Sarah			3		
Watson, John	1	1	4		
Wakeman, James	1	1	2	1	
Whidby, Joseph	3	2	5		
Whidby, Benjamin	1	2	3		
Winchester, Jas (Quarter)					9
Williams, William	3	1	3		
Whiteley, Robert	1		1		
White, Dr. Edward	2	1	3		
Whiting, David	2		2	1	3
Williams, Jacob	2	3	2		2
Warner, Woolman	1		2		6
Whealer, William	1	1	3		
Walls, John Milbern	1				
Wilson, John	2		3		12
Willson, Benjamin	1		2		7
Wrench, James	1	1	4		
Whiteley, Nathan	4	4	3		3
Walker, Charles	1	1	6		
Watson, Mary			4		
With, William	2	3	5		
Warren, Clark	1	2	3		
Willoughby, Saml	1	3	4	1	
White, John	1		4		
With, George	1		2		
Wright, John	1	1	1		
Willoughby, Sole	2				
Willoughby, Absolem	1				
White, Jno	3	2	4		7
Wherrett, Bennett	1		4		
Wootters, John	1	1	2		
Wootters, James	1		5		
Whiteley, William	5	1	5		12
White, William	2		3		
Williams, Thomas	1	2	2		
Woothers, Solomon	1	1	3		
Whitington, Joseph	1	2	3		
Whitington, Benjam	1	2	3		
Woothers, John	1	1	4		
White, Ann	1	1	1		2
Willson, John	1	1	3		
Woothers, Reubin	1	2	3		
Woothers, Aaron	1	2	3		
Willson, Jonathan	3	3	2	1	1
Willoughby, Prudence	2	4	4		
Warron, Solomon	1	3	3		
White, John	1	1	1		
Willoughby, Eben	1	1	1		
Webster, Hannah			1		
Woothers, Elijah	1	2	7		
Williamson, Elijah	1	1	1		
Wright, John	1	2	3		2
Withcutt, Thomas	1	1	4		
Willis, Richard	1	1	3		1
Willson, Jonathan, Junr	2	2	2		
Williams, Andrew	2	1	4		
Willis, Joshua	5	3	4		2
Willis, Henry	2	1	3		2
Wright, Levin, of R	1	1	1		
White, Nancy			1		2
Watkins, Thomas	4	1	8		
Willis, Elijah	1	1	8		1
Wright, Jas., of Levin	2	2	2		1
Willoughby, Richard	1		2		1
Willis, Sarah		2	5		
Willoughby, William	1	1	5		
Wildgoose, Sarah		1	4		3
Willis, John	3	3	4		6
Woolford, David	1		2		6
Waddle, James	1		2		
Willcutt, Richard	1		2		27
Watson, Mary			2		
White, Thos., Hog Island	1	2	3	1	
Wing, Elizabeth					6
Waddle, Jas., Junr	1	4	2		
Woodle, Jesper	2	1	3		
Willoughby, Wm, Junr	1		3		
Ward, John	1		3		
Wright, John	2	2	3		
Wright, Lemuel	2	1	3		
Wright, Edwd of R	1	2	6		
Wright, Roger	3		2		
Walker, Jno. Carpenter	2		1		
Willis, Thomas	3	4	4	1	
Wright, James	2	4	2		
Wright, Edward, Gent.	2		2		7
Willson, George	1	2	3		
Wright, Jas., of R	1	4	2		
Wright, Calib	1	1	2		
Wright, Jonathan	1	2	2		
Widdit, Rowland	1	2	2		
Williams, William	1	2	2		
Wright, Mary	1	2	2		
Waggarman, Jacob	1		3		
Williams, Isaac	1		1		1
Watkins, Thos., Junr	1	1	3		
Wright, Jacob	1		1		
Wright, Daniel	1	1	3		
Watkins, Joseph	1	1	3		1
Walker, Moses	1	3	6		7
Willis, Thomas	1	1	4		1
Waddle, John, Junr	4	2	2		
Waddle, John	5	1	4		
Williams, Joshua	1	3	2		
Walker, John	1		2		3
Walker, Thomas	1	1	1		1
Willoughby, John	1		1		
Walker, William	2	2	3		10
Willis, Deborough			2		
Whiteley, Byng	1		2		
Ward, Foley		2	2		
Warren, William	1				
Waits, Elias	1				
Wist, Lydia		1	1		
Young, Peregrine	1		2		
Young, Mary	1	1	2		

CECIL COUNTY.

BACK CREEK HUNDRED.

NAME OF HEAD OF FAMILY.	Free white males of 16 years and upward, including heads of families.	Free white males under 16 years.	Free white females, including heads of families.	All other free persons.	Slaves.
Alexander, James	3	2	4		5
Alexander, Jamison	5	3	4		5
Alexander, Isaac	2		1		
Alexander, Mary		2	3		
Artergee, Benj.	2		4		
Alman, Isaac	2		3		8
Adair, Joseph	2	3	2		
Bolding, Noble	1	2	1		
Brevard, Benj.	1	1	5		
Black, David	3	2	3		2
Bouldin, Mary	1	1	7	1	2
Buchanan, Margaret	2		5		
Baker, Henry	1	2	2		
Bowen, Ezekiel	2	3	2		
Beedle, Thomas	2	4	2		4
Bradley, Neal	1		2		
Beedle, Benoni	1	2	2		
Briscoe, Joseph	1		1		1
Bouldin, Richard	3	4	4		8
Beedle, Noble	2	3	2		6
Bouldin, John	2	1	2		8
Bigham, John	2			1	
Brevard, Hannah	1		1	1	1
Chambers, John C	3	1	2		
Cook, John	1		3		
Campbell, John	4	2	3		
Carter, Thomas	2		1		
Chick, Peregrine	1	2	4		
Chick, Nathaniel	1	1	4		2
Clift, William	1		4		
Chambers, Nichs	2		3		
Camlin, James	1		2		
Davis, William	3	5	4		
Elisbury, Benj.	1	1	1		
Ernst, Frederick				1	
Ford, Richd. B	2		3		11
French, Lydia		1	5		
Ford, John, of John	2	2	5		
Foster, James	2	1	7		
Ford, Thomas	2		4		1
Ford, Richard	1	5	3		6
Groves, Jacob	1	1	4		
Gordon, John	1	2	3		

BACK CREEK HUNDRED—continued.

NAME OF HEAD OF FAMILY.	Free white males of 16 years and upward, including heads of families.	Free white males under 16 years.	Free white females, including heads of families.	All other free persons.	Slaves.
Glenn, Samuel	1	2	3		5
Hughes, Samuel	2	1	4		
Henderson, Frisby	2		1		4
Harvey, Phineas				1	
Harley, Mary	3		2		
Hukill, Jeremiah	1	2	4		
Harrison, James	2	2	4		
Hugg, Benjamin	1	4	1		2
Harris, John	1	1	3		
Hughes, Mary			2	1	
Hukill, Jesse	3	2	2		
Holliday, John	1	1	2		
Hammond, Rachel	1		4		1
Harris, John	2		3		
Iler, Stephen	2	1	2		
Israel, Peter	2	3	2		
Jones, Charles	1		1		
Kinkead, John					1
Kilpatrick, Saml	1	1	1		
Lawrence, John	3	2	1		
Logue, Isaac	1		1		
Miller, Benjamin	2		4		9
Murphy, Joseph	1		3		
Miller, Richard	1	2	2		
McDonald, William	3	2	1		1
Nowland, Jacob	1		4		
Penington, Robert	2	1	7		
Pugh, John	1	1	5		
Pearce, Sarah			4		4
Pearce, Benj	2	1	2		2
Price, Thomas	3	4	4		2
Patterson, Joseph	1	4	3		
Quigley, Charles	2		2		
Robinson, Daniel	3	3	5		1
Rose, Sarah			2		
Robinson, Hannibal			2		
Richardson, Micah	4	2	4		14
Sappington, Benjamin	1	1	6		7
Springer, James	4		3		
Salmon, Daniel	1	2	3		
Stalis, James	2	3	4		
Sterling, Isaac	2		3		
Stuart, John, Senr	1	1	2		

BACK CREEK HUNDRED—continued.

NAME OF HEAD OF FAMILY.	Free white males of 16 years and upward, including heads of families.	Free white males under 16 years.	Free white females, including heads of families.	All other free persons.	Slaves.
Stuart, John	1		1		
Shearon, William	1		4		
Thomas, Isaac	2	1	2		
Thomas, Joseph, Senr	2	2	4		
Thomas, William	2	2	3		
Taylor, Soumah	2	3	2		6
Thomas, Aquila	2		3		2
Thomas, James	1	1	3		
Thompson, George	3		4		
Taylor, William	2	1	2		
Tarpey, John	1		2	1	
Thomas, Henry	1	1	2	1	
Turner, Jesse			2		
Thompson, Ephraim	2		2		4
Thompson, Isaac			3		4
Thompson, Samuel	2		2		7
Thompson, Mary			2		1
Thompson, William	1	2	4		2
Veal, Evan	2	5	2		
Whitham, William	3		4		
Wirt, Thomas	5	3	4		8
Wright, Alexr	2	1	5		6
Wallace, Adam					

BOHEMIA HUNDRED.

NAME OF HEAD OF FAMILY.	Free white males of 16 years and upward, including heads of families.	Free white males under 16 years.	Free white females, including heads of families.	All other free persons.	Slaves.
Beedle, John	1	1	2		
Beedle, Elizbeth			3		
Beedle, Saml	1		3		1
Beedle, Raymond	1	1	2		5
Beedle, Benjamin				1	
Beedle, William	1	1	2		
Beedle, Augustine	1	1	2		
Beedle, John	1		1		12
Bateman, Isaac	1		1		
Brewer, James	1		4		
Biggs, Richard	1	1	4		
Cox, Herman	1		2		
Cox, Peregrine	1		2		1
Cox, John, of Benjamin	2		2		3
Cox, John, Junr	4	2	4		20
Davison, Richard	4	1	2		9
Davis, Joseph	1		2		1

CECIL COUNTY—Continued.

NAME OF HEAD OF FAMILY.	Free white males of 16 years and upward, including heads of families.	Free white males under 16 years.	Free white females, including heads of families.	All other free persons.	Slaves.
BOHEMIA HUNDRED—continued.					
Etherington, Barthw	1	3	1	....	9
Etherington, Thomas	2	2	2	....	1
Etherington, Susannah	1	1	2	....	2
Etherington, Sarah	....	....	1	....	4
Forman, Thomas M	2	1	4	....	48
Ford, Joseph	1	....	....	....	29
Ford, Frederic	1	1	2	....	21
Ford, George	3	....	2	....	67
Gooding, Isaac	1	2	1	....	25
George, Sidney, Esqr	2	....	3	....	67
Gofton, John	2	....	1	....	....
Hall, William	1	3	4	....	2
Henry, James	....	....	....	1	....
Hurley, John	....	....	....	1	....
Humphreys, William	1	2	3	....	2
Hendrickson, Augustine	3	3	4	....	7
Hendrickson, Hyland	2	....	....	....	1
Hague, Joseph	3	2	3	....	....
Hukill, Joseph	1	....	4	....	....
Husler, William	1	2	4	....	....
Jones, William	3	2	5	....	....
James, John	2	1	2	....	....
Jones, Thomes	1	1	2	....	....
Jones, Simeon	1	1	1	....	....
Jeffries, William	2	1	3	....	....
Key, James	3	....	1	....	....
Lusby, Edwd	1	3	4	....	....
Lesalle, Mabel	1	....	3	....	....
Lusby, Thomas	2	2	2	....	1
Loague, James	2	....	2	....	....
Lusby, Robert	3	....	3	....	6
Louttit, Mary	....	....	4	....	5
Money, Robert	2	....	....	....	6
Money, Isaac	1	....	2	....	1
Martin, William	1	1	2	....	....
Mercer, John	1	1	1	....	6
Marshall, William	1	1	3	....	14
Moore, John	2	1	2	....	2
Meekins, Joshua	2	5	3	....	....
Morgan, Anne	....	....	1	....	1
Morgan, James	1	2	6	....	3
McDowell, William	3	....	1	....	2
Money, John	4	5	4	....	12
McGuire, George	1	3	3	....	....
Nowland, Peregrine	3	1	3	....	6
Othoson, John	1	2	2	....	1
Owings, Barthw	2	2	6	....	1
Owings, Stephen	2	....	2	....	....
Pennington, Robert	3	2	2	....	5
Penington, Edwd, of Robt	1	....	....	....	....
Penington, John	7	3	5	....	6
Penington, Samuel	2	2	3	....	10
Porter, Benjamin	2	3	4	....	10
Price, Hyland	1	4	3	....	4
Price, Edward	1	1	1	....	13
Parsley, Edward	1	....	5	....	....
Penington, Robert, 3d	1	1	3	....	9
Price, William	2	1	3	....	11
Price, Lewis	3	1	6	....	12
Pearce, William	5	2	4	....	....
Price, John	2	4	2	....	33
Price, Benjamin, Junr	1	....	1	....	8
Price, Thomas	1	1	3	....	4
Price, Benjamin, Senr	3	....	2	....	6
Price, Mary	....	2	3	....	....
Penington, Benj	2	2	2	....	1
Pearce, Henry Ward, Jnr	1	....	1	....	29
Pearce, Henry Ward, Senr	2	1	4	....	39
Price, Andrew	1	2	3	....	1
Penington, Robert, Son Saml	1	....	4	....	8
Redgrave, Issac	1	2	3	....	1
Ruley, Ann	1	1	5	....	2
Roberts, John	1	2	4	....	....
Roberts, Robert	1	1	3	....	....
Ruley, Seth	3	....	1	....	2
Rice, Catharine	1	1	3	....	....
Roberts, Lewis	2	3	3	....	3
Savin, Mary	....	....	4	....	5
Savin, Thomas	1	....	....	....	10
Savin, Edward	1	....	....	....	18
Severson, Thomas	2	2	5	....	7
Sewell, Richard	3	1	5	....	1
Shaw, John	1	3	2	....	....
Stockton, Joseph	3	....	....	....	8
Simmons, Lawrence	1	3	1	....	....
Stanley, Elizabeth	....	....	....	1	....
See, Epraim	2	4	2	....	....
Severson, Hance	1	....	....	....	2
Sullivan, John	1	1	3	....	....
Terry, Vachel	2	1	1	....	11
Veazey, Edward	2	....	....	....	12
Veazey, Doctr Thos B	1	1	5	....	13
BOHEMIA HUNDRED—continued.					
Veazey, John Ward	2	2	7	....	8
Vickers, David	1	....	2	....	3
Ward, Elizabeth	1	1	3	....	12
Wroth, James	1	2	2	....	6
Ward, John, 3d	3	1	6	....	6
Ward, William	1	1	5	....	17
Wiley, John	4	3	5	....	1
Wroth, William, Esqr	3	1	1	....	4
Wrothwell, Joseph	3	2	5	....	15
Walmsley, Thomas K	1	1	2	....	4
Walmsley, Robert C	1	....	1	....	5
Walmsley, Ann	....	1	3	....	5
Walmsley, Thomas	1	....	1	....	1
Walmsley, Rachel	....	1	1	....	2
BOHEMIA MANOR HUNDRED.					
Altham, Spencer	2	2	2	....	5
Beaston, Richard	2	1	6	....	6
Bayard, Benj	2	2	4	....	10
Bowen, Richard	1	2	4	....	9
Beaston, Hester	....	....	5	....	3
Bouchell, John	2	....	3	....	14
Boyles, Rebecca	....	....	2	....	1
Buckworth, Saml	2	2	3	....	....
Bayard, Saml	2	....	6	....	10
Beaston, George	3	2	....	....	5
Boyles, James	2	1	1	....	2
Biggs, Nathan	1	2	2	....	....
Baker, Nicholas V	2	....	2	....	....
Burnham, Thos	1	2	2	....	4
Boyles, Daniel	1	1	1	....	....
Boyles, Adam	2	1	2	....	6
Baker, Eleanor	3	1	4	....	....
Carty, Jere	1	3	2	....	2
Craig, James	3	....	2	....	7
Cochran, Moses	2	....	2	....	7
Corbally, Richd	1	5	3	....	....
Carty, Mary	....	....	2	....	....
Crow, Andrew	1	2	3	....	4
Carty, William	1	3	3	....	....
Craig, William	4	1	3	....	5
Cale, James	1	3	4	....	....
Crow, Margt	....	1	4	....	....
Dean, James	1	....	3	....	....
Dawson, Nathl	1	1	5	....	7
Dawson, William	1	1	2	....	....
Ellsbury, Lambert	1	....	3	....	5
Eliason, Wm	2	....	....	....	....
Ford, Hezekiah	2	1	3	....	4
Ford, Edward	2	....	3	....	12
Faris, James	1	1	1	....	....
Ford, William	1	1	3	....	....
Ford, Jesse	2	1	1	....	3
Grant, Hugh	....	....	....	1	....
Griffith, Benjamin	1	1	2	....	1
Gordon, Margaret	....	1	3	....	....
Gray, William	....	....	....	1	....
Hodgson, John	1	1	3	....	....
Hudson, Jacob	4	2	3	....	....
Hukill, William	2	2	3	....	3
Hooper, Isaac	2	1	6	....	....
Hughes, Andrew	4	4	2	....	4
Hersey, Benjamin	1	2	3	....	1
Hollins, Jonathan	1	....	1	....	....
Hall, William	1	2	1	....	....
Hodgson, Richd	2	2	4	....	7
Jackson, William	3	4	4	....	....
Jackson, Peter	2	3	1	....	....
Kirk, Alexr	2	2	3	....	....
Kleinhoof, Wm	1	1	3	....	....
Knight, John	2	2	2	....	15
Kelly, William	1	1	1	....	....
Lewis, David	1	2	2	....	....
Lawson, Peter, Esqr	5	....	2	....	36
Lancaster, Sinclair	3	1	2	....	1
Lawrenson, James	2	3	5	....	10
Logue, Ephraim	1	1	4	....	9
McLaughlin, Thomas	1	....	2	....	3
Moore, Nathan	3	....	2	....	....
McCleary, John	3	2	5	....	....
Magee, Sarah	1	1	1	....	....
Meekins, Susannah	....	2	....	....	....
Meekins, James	3	1	3	....	....
Mansfield, Saml	2	....	3	....	10
Montgomery, John	2	1	3	....	3
Mills, Mary	1	....	1	....	....
Oldham, Majr Edward	4	2	4	....	21
Oxley, John	1	....	2	....	....
Oxley, James	1	1	3	....	....
Price, Hyland	4	4	4	....	4
Peery, John	1	1	4	....	1
Price, Sarah	2	2	2	....	4
Parrisett, Nichs	1	....	4	....	2
Pugh, Humphrey	2	....	3	....	3
BOHEMIA MANOR HUNDRED—continued.					
Pusey, John	2	1	3	....	....
Richardson, William	2	5	4	....	1
Rider, Joseph	2	....	....	....	10
Ryder, Elizabeth	....	....	2	....	....
Ratcliff, James	3	3	3	....	....
Sutton, Benjamin	1	....	4	....	3
Smith, Margaret	....	....	....	1	....
Smith, Catherine	....	3	3	....	....
Sproul, Robert	1	3	2	....	....
Savin, Samuel	1	2	3	....	....
Simmonds, Benjamin	1	2	3	....	6
Sterling, Ephraim	3	2	4	....	4
Sterling, Robert	1	2	4	....	....
Sluyter, Benjamin	1	1	2	....	12
Taggart, John	1	2	3	....	....
Taylor, William	1	1	1	....	3
Taylor, Joseph, Senr	4	....	4	....	....
Thompson, Susannah	1	1	5	....	5
Vickers, George	2	2	6	....	1
Vandegrist, Pere	1	4	4	....	....
Watson, Lewis	1	....	....	....	....
Whitham, Pere	1	2	3	....	1
Whitham, William	2	....	5	....	....
Wilcox, Stephen	1	1	2	....	....
Wingate, Peter	1	2	1	....	....
CHARLES TOWN.					
Anderson, William	2	1	2	....	2
Anderson, Eliza	1	1	3	....	....
Adair, John	2	1	5	....	1
Beazeley, Edward	2	1	3	....	....
Brumfield, Betsey	....	2	3	....	1
Bailey, James	1	....	4	....	....
Brumfield, Edward	1	2	2	....	4
Bennet, Richard	4	....	5	....	....
Cuningham, David	1	1	2	....	....
Cuningham, Arthur	1	....	1	....	....
Cather, Robert	1	....	....	....	....
Cazier, Abraham	1	1	2	....	....
Cuningham, James	2	1	3	....	....
Collins, Jere	1	3	1	....	....
Ferguson, Agness	....	1	2	....	....
Ferguson, Mary	1	1	4	....	....
Flanagan, James	1	2	2	....	....
Grant, Margaret	2	1	3	....	....
Grant, John	1	....	2	....	....
Grubb, Andrew	1	....	2	....	....
Ginther, Margaret Eve	1	....	2	....	....
Graham, William	1	2	3	....	....
Gerrish, Rachel	....	....	3	....	....
Gilmore, Rose	1	....	1	....	....
Hamilton, Patrick	1	....	1	....	6
Howell, Capn William	1	1	3	....	....
Hassan, Alexander	1	1	1	....	....
Hederick, Sarah	1	2	1	....	....
Hudaburk, John	....	....	....	1	....
Hamilton, George	1	2	3	....	1
Jackson, Sarah	....	3	2	....	3
Jacquett, Peter	1	2	3	....	....
Kilpatrick, Samuel	2	1	1	....	1
Linton, William	1	1	....	....	....
Montgomery, Doctr Hugh	1	1	2	....	3
Miller, Henry	1	....	4	....	....
McCormick, Robert	1	1	1	....	....
McMeans, James	1	1	1	....	....
Menteith, William	2	1	2	....	....
McCullough, Alexander	1	2	3	....	....
McCracken, Ann	....	....	2	....	....
McGill, Saml	3	1	3	....	....
McNair, Samuel	1	....	2	....	....
Norton, Nathan, Esqr	1	....	....	....	....
Notherman, John	1	1	3	....	....
Oldham, Jeremiah	3	....	1	....	....
Owings, Jonas	....	....	....	1	....
Severson, Joseph	1	....	2	....	....
Simco, George	....	....	....	1	....
Templin, James	1	5	3	....	....
Thomas, Edward	1	1	1	....	1
Thompson, Samuel	....	....	....	1	....
Wilson, Andrew	1	1	5	....	....
Wylie, James	2	....	2	....	....
Winchester, Eliza	2	2	2	....	....
Woodworth, Dorcas	....	....	....	1	....
Welsh, James	....	....	....	1	....
Yeomans, Thos	3	2	1	....	....
EAST NOTTINGHAM HUNDRED.					
Askin, Henry	3	1	3	....	....
Askin, Jane	1	....	1	....	....
Brown, Jehu	1	5	3	....	....
Blakeley, Joseph	2	....	2	....	....
Boggs, James	4	....	6	....	....

CECIL COUNTY—Continued.

EAST NOTTINGHAM HUNDRED—continued.

NAME OF HEAD OF FAMILY.	Free white males of 16 years and upward, including heads of families.	Free white males under 16 years.	Free white females, including heads of families.	All other free persons.	Slaves.
Bailey, Anne	1		3		
Bond, Richᵈ, Esqʳ	2	2	5		1
Bond, Samuel	3	3	5		1
Bond, Able	1		3		
Brown, Mercer	1		5		
Brown, Jesse	2	5	6		
Bowen, Benjamin	2	1	4		
Brown, Patrick	1	3	2		
Brown, John	1	1	1		
Chandler, Benjamin, Juʳ	2	3	4		
Corbitt, Esther			2		
Cather, George			2		
Cleland, James	1	6	4		
Cochran, Robert	3	2	6		
Chandler, Benjamin, Sʳ	8	1	3		
Churchman, George	4	1	3		1
Cross, John	4	2	6		
Crigon, Hugh	1		2		
Charles, Jacob	1		1		
Duncan, Andrew	2	3	4		
Derby, Hugh	1	2	2		
Donnally, Edwᵈ	1		2		
Eliason, John	5	1	3		6
Ewing, Robert	2	3	2		
England, John	2	4	4		
England, Samuel	3	3	4		
Ewing, Henry	5	2	6		
Evans, Elizᵃ	2	2	4		
Ferguson, Thomas	1	1	3		
Ferguson, John	1	1	1		
Francis, John	1	2	3		
Gatchell, Nathan	2	2	4		
Gatchell, Jacob	3		3		
Gatchell, Samuel	1	2	3		
Gilleland, Thomas	4	1	5		
Gatchell, Ann			1		1
Grant, James	2		4		
Gilpin, Samuel, Esqʳ	3	1	3		5
Gallagher, William	1		2		
Gold, William	1	2	4		
Hewston, James	2	1	2		
Hindman, James	1	1	2		
Hill, Samˡ	1	2	2		
Hill, John	1		2		
Harvey, Fanny			3		
Hamilton, Elizabeth	1	1	3		3
Haragan, John	1	3	2		
Hamilton, William	1	2	1		
Hull, John	4	2	2		
Harlan, Solomon	2	2	4		
Hutton, John	1	2	2		
Hill, Margᵗ					1
Job, Archᵈ	5		4		
Jones, Amelia		1	1		
Kelly, William	1		2		
Kellan, Jane			1		
Kirk, Elisha	3	1	6		3
Kirk, Levi	1		2		
Logan, Hugh	1	2	2		
Lackland, Jeremiah	1	1	2		
Miller, John	2		2		
McDowell, Thomas	1		3		
McAvoy, Daniel	1	2	1		
MKinley, Alexander					1
McMullen, Robert	1		3		
Mullen, William	3	1	5		
McGee, John	2	1	2		
Manuel, Thomas	1		1		
McCauley, Barney	1		2		
McKey, Capt. James	2	3	2		
McCleland, Thoˢ	3	1	2		
McHaffy, Joseph	3	1	3		3
Moore, William	1	3	3		
Mackey, James	1	3	5		3
Melvin, Hance	2	2	3		
McRuth, Robert	1		1		1
Mathews, John	2	3	5		
McCartney, John	1		3		
Oldham, Edward	3	1	2		2
Ogilvie, John	3	1	6		2
Oldham, Richard	1	5	4		9
Oldham, Ann			4		
Oldham, Thomas	2		4		
Polk, John	1	3	3		
Parker, Joseph	2	1	3		
Philips, John	2	1	3		
Power, Robᵗ	1	4	5		
Perry, David	1	5	2		
Penington, Joseph	1	5	4		
Rogers, Elisha	3	2	6		1
Rogers, Elijah	1	1	4		
Riddle, Humphry	2	2	5		
Rogers, Thomas	9	4	8		
Rowles, Hezekiah	3	2	3		
Reynolds, Thomas	3	2	3		

EAST NOTTINGHAM HUNDRED—continued.

NAME OF HEAD OF FAMILY.	Free white males of 16 years and upward, including heads of families.	Free white males under 16 years.	Free white females, including heads of families.	All other free persons.	Slaves.
Ramsey, Charles	2	3	4		
Rogers, William, Junʳ	1	1	1		
Strachan, John	1	1	3		
Scott, Isaac	2		1		
Shields, William	1	2	1		
Smith, Robert	3		2		
Steel, James	3	5	4		1
Story, Joseph	1	1	5		3
Sharp, Thomas				1	
Steel, Mathew	1		2		
Smith, Robert	3	1	2		
Smiley, William	1		1		
Terry, William	3	4	3		
Taylor, John	1	1	3		
Tanner, Joseph	4			4	
Tyson, Benj	1	2	2		
Thompson, Andrew	1	1	2		
Trimble, James	3	2	6		1
Underhill, Thoˢ, Junʳ	3	1	2		
Williams, Charles	1	1	2		4
White, Abner	2	4	5		
Wilson, George	1	2	5		
Woodrow, Jacob	1	1	1		
Wilson, John	1	5	2		
Whalley, John	1		3		
Wilson, Samuel	1	1	3		
Wallace, Docᵗ Michˡ	3				4
Wilson, Jane		1	2		
Williams, Archᵈ	2	1	1		4
Wilson, Benjamin	3	2	3		
White, John	3	1	3		
Woodrow, Eleanor		2	4		
White, Edward	4	3	5		
White, Jonathan	3	2	5		
Wilson, Thomas, Junʳ	2	1	4		
Wright, William	3	2	4		
Wilson, Thomas	2	1	3		
Witherspoon, John				1	
Wilson, Peter				1	
Wilson, James	1	2	2	1	
Young, Robᵗ	2	3	3		1

ELK NECK HUNDRED.

NAME OF HEAD OF FAMILY.	Free white males of 16 years and upward, including heads of families.	Free white males under 16 years.	Free white females, including heads of families.	All other free persons.	Slaves.
Alcorn, William	1		3		
Arrants, William	1	3	2		
Ashbough, Jacob	2		5		
Anderson, Abraham	1		3		
Aldridge, Samuel	2	1	3		7
Aldridge, Fredus				1	
Alexander, Justis	1		2		
Beedle, Hyland	3	3	3		
Bryson, Ann		1	4		3
Belony, Archᵈ	1	3	1		
Brook, William	1	1	2		
Badcock, James	1		1		
Boyles, Timothy	1	3	2		
Bryson, Richard	1	1	3		
Batten, James	1		3		
Burk, William	1	4	2		
Bradley, George	1		3		
Burgoigne, James	1	2	2		
Bristow, William	1	2	6		
Boyce, Francis	1	4	1		
Barnet, Jane	1	1	2		
Bristow, John	1	2	2		
Bryson, Sarah	1		2		
Currer, Francis	1		2		
Crouch, Edward	1	2	2		
Cumminge, John	1		2		
Cuminge, William	1		4		
Crookshanks, William	2	1	6		
Curlet, John	2	4	2		
Creamer, Philip	2		2		
Cooper, John	1	2	2		5
Cazier, Elizabeth	1	1	5		6
Crouch, Isaac	4	1	6		6
Currer, Sampson	1		3		
Cannon, Patrick				1	
Crouch, James	2	1	3		1
Crabstone, Moses	2	1	6		
Crouch, John	3	2	2		1
Culbertson, David	1	1	3		
Doyle, James					1
Dalrimple, James	1		2		
Donally, Edward	1		1		
Empson, Cornelius	1	4	3		3
Farley, John	1	1	3		
Frew, Alexander	4		3		
Fulton, John	2		1		1
Foster, William	2		3		
Foster, Jesse	2	2	3		1
Foster, James	1	2	3		
Foster, John	1		3		
Ford, George	1		2		42

ELK NECK HUNDRED—continued.

NAME OF HEAD OF FAMILY.	Free white males of 16 years and upward, including heads of families.	Free white males under 16 years.	Free white females, including heads of families.	All other free persons.	Slaves.
Ford, John	2	3	6		8
Crouch, Thomas	2	2	4		3
Crouch, Robert	1	1	4		1
Campbell, James	1	1	1	4	
Cavender, Elizᵃ		1	1		
Gerrish, Edward			4		
Grace, William	1	1	4		
George, Nicholas	1	1	2		5
Hukill, Peter	1	4	2		
Hitchcock, Nicholas	1	3	6		
Hukill, Richard	3	2	4		
Hill, Jonathan	1	1	2		
Holmes, Samuel	1				
Hukill, James	1	1	5		5
Hankey, Morris	1	1	3		
Hyland, Edward	1	4	5		6
Hyland, Jacob	2	3	3		
Hitchcock, John	1		2		
Hill, James					1
Hitchcock, William	1	5	5		
Heath, John	2	2	3		
Hukill, John	1		1		
Hill, George	1	2	1		
Hill, David	1	1	1		1
Hart, Robert	2	3	5		11
Hart, Thomas	1		2		
Jackson, Henry	2	1	4		1
Ireland, Nathan	1	1	4		
Johnston, James	1	7	2		
Kankey, Rebecca	2	2	4		4
Kirkpatrick, John			1	1	
Kankey, Harman	2		4		6
Kelly, Edward	1		3		
Knight, George	2	1	3		
Keatly, John	5	3	2		
Lewis, John	3	2	2		
Lowrey, John	1	1	2		
Lowrey, Ann			2		
Lashley, John			2		
Lewis, Samuel	1	3	2		
Lum, Michael	1	2	5		4
Lorrain, Thomas	1	4	4		
Lowrey, James	1		4		1
Lum, Jacob	3	3	3		1
Lynch, William, Junʳ	1	1	3		1
Lemon, Archᵈ	1	3	3		
Lynch, William, Senʳ	1	2	3		1
Lort, Joseph	2	2			4
Lowrey, Sarah			2		
Hankey, Nicholas	1		2		
Manley, Jacob	2		5		8
McMins, Lydia			1		
Mauldin, William	1	4	3		17
Moody, Alexander	1	2	3		
Moody, John, Junʳ	1		3		
Manley, John	2	1	1		1
Murphy, Thomas	1				
Maffit, William					1?
Manley, John	1	1	1		4
McVea, Passmore	1		1		
Moody, Alexander	2		1		
Milborn, Nicholas	2	2	3		
Maffitt, Thomas, Esqʳ	3		4		
Manley, Jesse	2	2	4		1
McCracken, John	3	3	3		
Nugent, Elizabeth	3	1	3		
Newell, Thomas	1		3		
Nevil, John, Junʳ	1		2		
Nevil, John, Senʳ	2	2	8		1
Owens, Thomas	1	6	2		
Oldham, James	1	1	3		
McIntire, Ann	1	1	1		
Mauldin, William	2	1	4		9
McClure, William	2	1	4		
Masterson, Nicholas	2	1	2		
McKinney, Benjamin	2	1	2		
McDonald, John	1		2		
Moore, William	2	1	4		
Price, Ephraim	2	3	3		3
Philips, Zebulon	1	2	3		
Philips, Nicholas	1	2	3		
Price, Jesse	1	5	2		
Philips, Nathan	1	2	2		
Rutter, Joshua	2	1	3		
Roach, Samuel	2	1	3		
Riggs, Andrew	2	4	3		
Roach, Philip	1		1		
Rutter, Isaac	1			1	
Roach, Richᵈ					1
Rynard, John	1	1	4		
Rose, Henry	2	1	1		
Redman, Robert	1	4	4		
Rutter, Rachel	1	3	3		
Stalcup, Margaret	3	2	3		
Stoops, William	1	2	3		1

CECIL COUNTY—Continued.

NAME OF HEAD OF FAMILY.	Free white males of 16 years and upward, including heads of families.	Free white males under 16 years.	Free white females, including heads of families.	All other free persons.	Slaves.
ELK NECK HUNDRED—continued.					
Smith, Joshua	3	3	4		
Stedham, Henry	1	2	1		
Shinson, Martin			1	1	
Simpers, Sarah			1	4	
Simpers, Jacob		2	1	1	1
Smith, Samuel	1		3	2	
Simpers, Thomas	1	1	2		
Simpers, Richard	1	1	2		2
Segars, Mary			5		
Smith, Michael	1	2	2		
Simpers, William	2		5		
Smith, Henry	2	5	3		
Thackery, Thomas	3		7		13
Trump, John	4	2	1		
Veazey, William		2	1		2
Young, Ann	1	1	2		
Waram, James	1	3	4		
Wingate, Edward			4		
Watson, William	1	1	3		
Wallace, Hugh	1		3		
Wilcox, John	1	1	3		
MIDDLE NECK HUNDRED.					
Beedle, Wilmer	1		1		
Ballard, Jonathan	2	1	2		
Blanchford, Richard			1		1
Beaston, Fras	1		1		49
Council, Edwd Carey	2	2	2		2
Dixson, Thos	2	1	3		
Flintham, Benjamin	2	1	4		6
Lynch, Rosannah	2		4		
Lynch, Catharine		1	2		
McKelvin, Benjl				1	
McAvoy, Nichs			2		
Nugent, Mary	1	1	6		
O'Donald, James	4	2	3		3
Penington, Atkey	2	2	4		
Ryland, John	3		2		
Sappington, Thos	1	3	2		7
See, James			2		
Ward, William	1	1	4		8
Walmsley, John	2	3	5		2
Walmsley, William	1		1		
NORTH MILLFORD HUNDRED.					
Armstrong, William (b.s.)	2	1	6		1
Alexander, George	1	1	7		5
Alexander, James	1	2			
Alexander, John	2		2		
Alexander, Sarah	2		4		
Alexander, Josiah	3	2	6		
Andrews, Zachs	2	1	2		
Alies, John	2	1	2		
Alexander, Isabella	1	1	9		
Ash, George	2	2	3		
Armstrong, Thomas	1	2	3		
Anderson, John	1	2	3		
Armstrong, Ann	1		2		
Armstrong, Willm, Junr	1	1	2		1
Armstrong, Jas	1		1		
Ash, Nichs	1	5	2		
Bowser, Wm	1	1	2		
Bradley, James	1	1	1		
Bonsal, Jane	1	1	2		1
Briscoe, Peregrine	4	1	2		
Black, Hugh	1		5		
Buchanan, John	2	2	4		
Boyd, Sarah		2	4		
Boyd, John	2		1		
Brooks, Barnaby	1		3		
Boyd, Mary		1	3		
Bailey, Charles			2		
Bolton, Joseph	1	1	4		
Bennet, Henry	1	2	2		
Booth, Jonathan	5	2	7		
Boucher, Joseph	1		4		
Bean, Nathan	2		1		
Belveal, Mary			3		
Barnard, Joshua	1	2	3		1
Barnaby, John	2		2		
Baxter, Joseph	3		3		
Barroll, William	2	3	7		
Bird, Thomas	2		3		
Bird, Mary	3		10		
Briscoe, Samuel	2	1	6		
Buchanan, James	2	3	5		1
Brown, James	1				
Booth, Ebenezer	2	3	3		2
Cumings, William	2	2	3		
Crow, Rebecca			2		
Conway, William	1	1	6		

NAME OF HEAD OF FAMILY.	Free white males of 16 years and upward, including heads of families.	Free white males under 16 years.	Free white females, including heads of families.	All other free persons.	Slaves.
NORTH MILLFORD HUNDRED—continued.					
Couden, Revd Jos	1	2	4		11
Caruthers, Francis	2	2	2		
Caruthers, Walter	2	4	5		2
Caruthers, Francis, Sr	1	4	1		
Clark, Elizabeth			1		
Carion, William	1	1	3		
Cumings, William	1	1	3		2
Cochran, James	1	1	2		
Clark, Joseph	1		3		
Clanahan, Samuel	1	2	5		
Cloward, William, Sr	1	1	3		
Cloward, William, Jr	1	1	3		
Cuningham, Mathew	1	4	3		
Callender, John	1	1	4		
Costard, Thomas	1		4		
Cashore, William		1	3		
Cumings, James	1	3	3		
Cumings, Samuel	3		2		
Devinney, George	3	3	4		
Dysart, Archd	3	6	2		
Delap, John			1		1
Dixson, Samuel	3		3		
Doublard, Anthony	1		2		
Domegan, William	1	4	3		6
Dull, Leonard	1		1		
Dutiway, Anthony	1	1	2		
Davidson, Agness	3	1	2		
Davidson, William	2	2	3		1
Davidson, James	2	2	3		
Davidson, John	1	2	3		
Davis, Levy	1	2	1		
Evans, John	3	3	3		3
Evans, Cole Saml	2	1	5		8
Egnar, Peter	2	5	2		1
Everitt, Benjamin	3	1	2		
Evans, Peter	3		2	3	
Emmit, Rebecca		2	1		
Falls, Fras	1		1		
Fulton, Hugh	3	4	2		
Fife, Grace	1		5		
Fields, Comfort		1	5		
Fee, John	1	5	2		
Finley, Robert	1	1	2		1
French, Joseph	1	1	1		
Gault, Andrew	1				
Galbreath, John	2		1		
Galloway, John	1		3		
Garrett, James	1	2	2		
Gilpin, John	6	3	4		4
Gold, William	2	2	5		
Gray, Starrett	2	1	3		
Gillespie, John	1		1		
Gwyn, John	1		1		
Gottier, Francis	1	1	3		
Giles, Thomas	2	2	4		
Hollingsworth, Jacob	2		3		11
Harding, Reuben	2		3		
Hollingsworth, Zebulon	4	3	4		8
Hessinger, Peter	5		4		
Hill, Agness	2		1		
Hill, Sarah		2	2		
Hill, John		2	3		
Hibbits, James	1	3	2		
Henry, John		2	2		
Henry, William	1	3	2		
Howard, William	3		2		
Holmes, William		1	2		
Hewit, Samuel	6	3	5		2
Haggarty, Andrew	1		1		
Hollingsworth, Henry, Esqr	5	2	8		23
Hollingsworth, Mary			1	3	
Houch, Andrew	1	1	2		
Hugg, William	4	3	3		1
Harvey, Andrew	1	1	7		
Hayward, Robert	1				1
Heinholdt, Johant	2		1	1	
Hasell, Ann		1	1		
Henry, William		1	1		1
Handy, John	1	2	3		
Higier, Frederick	1	2	4		1
Hall, James	1		2		
Harris, George	2		2		4
Poor house	10	3	17		
Hutchinson, William	1	2	4		2
Hersey, Isaac	1	2	1		
Hibbits, Robert	1	2	4		2
Jones, Ester			1	3	
Jones, James	1	2	3		
Johnson, William	4	1			
Jordan, John		2	3		
Johnson, John	2	2	3		
Jewell, Cornelius	2	1	1		
Irwin, Susannah			1	3	
Jacobs, Thomas	4		1		4

NAME OF HEAD OF FAMILY.	Free white males of 16 years and upward, including heads of families.	Free white males under 16 years.	Free white females, including heads of families.	All other free persons.	Slaves.
NORTH MILLFORD HUNDRED—continued.					
Jamison, William	1	1	3		
Kilgore, James	1				2
Kilgore, William	1	1	3		
Kinkead, Alexr	1	1	4		3
Kerr, George	2	3	6		1
Kerr, Robert	1	1			
Lackey, Thomas	2		4		
Lutton, James	1	1			
Leach, John	1	6	1		
Longwill, Robt	1	2	7		2
Lewis, Richd	3	1	8		2
Lawson, George	1	2	2		1
Lowrey, Jane		4			
Longwill, William	1	5	3		
Mitchell, William	1		3		
Moore, Aaron	2	1	1		
Moore, Alexander	1	1	1		
McCausland, Thos	1	1			
McIntire, John	1	2	4		
McCleland, James	1		2		
McNeal, James	1		3		
McCoy, William	1	1			
McHugh, Eliz	5		3		
Meban, Edward	2	1	4		
MHalan, James			1		1
Means, Benjamin	2		1		
McCoy, Henry	1	1	1		1
McCutcheon, John	2	3	2		
McCaskey, William	1	1	2		
Mackey, Martha	3	1	2		3
McCleland, Jane			1		1
McFann, David	2		2		
Monagal, Hugh	1	5	2		
McColgin, Susannah	1		2		
Menough, Isaac	1		1		
Mullatt, Peter	1	1	2		
Mitchell, John	2	1	3		
MKinsey, Benjamin	1		1		
Mahalan, James	1				1
Miller, Lewis	4	4	3		4
Miles, Isaac	2	2	3		
Murray, John	1	1	3		
Mitchel, Rudulph	1		2		
McGowan, Hector	1		2		
McDonald, Alex	1		1		
Mitchell, Doct Abs	1	3	4		5
McAvinch, Edward	1		1		
Means, John	2	2	3		
May, Robert	10		3		20
Meeks, Thomas	1		3		
McLaughlin, Owen	1		5		
Nowland, Michael	5		2		
Nutt, William	1		5		
ONeal, John	1	1	2		
Peery, James, Junr	1		2		
Polk, Samuel	1	1	3		
Pile, Abraham	1	2	6		
Pennywill, Sampson	1		1		
Parker, Samuel	1		2		
Pusey, Israel	2	2	2		
Partridge, Francis	2	1	4		
Paulson, John	1	2	4		
Post, Cornelius	1		1		
Passmore, Rebecca	1		5		
Parker, Samuel, Senr	2	1	5		
Philips, Joseph	2	4	2		
Philips, Thomas	1	4	3		
Parker, Evan	1	1	3		
Quail, Robert	1				
Rudulph, Tobias, Esqr	4	1	3		11
Robinson, Catharine	1	1	2		
Rudulph, Jacob	1	2	4		4
Rudulph, John	2	1	3		
Ricketts, Benjamin	2	5	3		3
Roy, Robert	2	1			
Robinson, John	1		2		
Rusier, John	1	2	3		
Robinson, Henry	4	2	3		1
Rose, James	1	1			
Rayall, Samuel	1				
Ricketts, David	3	1	4		4
Ricketts, John	3	1	1		10
Ramage, James	2		1		
Reynolds, Henry	2	4	4		1
Read, Alexander	2	3	1		1
Read, Thomas	1		2		
Roney, Patrick	1		2		
Robinson, William	1		2		
Smith, David	2	4	3		3
Singleton, William	2	1	1		
Scott, John	1		2		
Simpers, Thomas	1	2	2		17
Sharp, Thomas	1	1	2		5
Sharp, Jehu	1		2		
South, Hezekiah	1		2		

CECIL COUNTY—Continued.

NAME OF HEAD OF FAMILY.	Free white males of 16 years and upward, including heads of families.	Free white males under 16 years.	Free white females, including heads of families.	All other free persons.	Slaves.
NORTH MILLFORD HUNDRED—continued.					
Scott, John, Junr	1	2	4		
Scott, William, Junr	1		3		
Scott, Mary	1		4		1
Sears, Capn John	3	2	2		3
Springer, Joseph	1		1		
Shields, Archd	1	1	5		8
Smith, Francis	1	1	2		
Springer, Peter	2	1	1		
Sharp, Frances			3		
Scott, Mary	1		2		
Scott, Thomas	2	3	5		
Scott, Moses	3		5		
Tool, Andrew	1	1	1		
Thomas, Christopher	2	3	3		
Thompson, Robert	1	1	2		
Todd, William	1		2		
Towers, Andrew	2		1		
Tedford, John	1	3	1		
Tyson, Levy	2		1		
Tuten, George	1	3	2		
Turner, Andrew				1	
Taylor, Richard	1	1	1		
Taylor, Moses	1		2		
Thompson, William	3		4		
Vinney, Hugh	1	1	3		
Updegrove, Richard	2	2	4		
Wallace, Joseph	1		1		
Whan, Samuel	1	3	4		1
Weir, Edward	3	1	2		
Wilson, William, Junr	2		1		
Work, George	1	1	3		
Wilkinson, Joseph	1		2		
Wilson, Alexander	2		2		
Woolaston, Joseph	2	2	2		
Wilson, William	4		3		
Wilson, William Cooper	1		2		
Walker, Andrew		2	1		
Williams, Thomas	3		2		
Wilson, Philip	1	1	2		
Wilson, Levi	1		2		
Wilson, William	1	1	5		
Wallace, Doctr George	2	1	2		3
Winters, Danl	2	1	3		
Woodrow, Benjamin	1		4		
Wherry, Jesse	2	1	1		3
Watson, Francina		3	2		
Wimble, John	2	2	3		
Wade, John	1		2		
Worth, Joseph			3		
Watson, Mary			2	1	
Wilson, John, Senr	3	2	7		1
Walmsley, Robert	1	2	1		1
Wilson, Benjamin	1	3	3		
Work, Alexander	1	1	4		
Weiser, Jacob	1		4		
Wilson, Samuel	2	7	3		2
Wilson, James	1	1	3		
Wilson, Benjamin	1		1		
Wilcox, Elizabeth	2	4	3		
Work, Samuel	1	4	2		
Cooley, William	1	1	2		
Cook, Archd	1	1	2		
Campbell, James	2	2	7		
Crosby, Jesse	2		1		
Cochran, Alexander	1	2	1		
NORTH SASSAFRAS HUNDRED.					
Archibald, Ebenezer	2	1	1		
Airicks, Joseph	1		2		
Burns, Sarah	1	2	3		
Bryan, John			1		
Beard, Lewis	3		2		12
Broxen, Thomas	2	2	2		1
Beedle, Stephen	1		6		8
Burk, William	1		2		
Bohaney, William	1		5		
Costillo, Evan	1	1	5		
Cline, Philip	4	1	5		
Cleaves, Joseph	1		2		
Conray, Daniel	2		1		
Covington, Nathl	1		1		26
Carty, John	1		6		6
Cauk, Isaac	2		3		
Cradock, Richard	1	3	3		2
Cradock, Daniel	1		2		
Caruthers, William	4	1	3		1
Coleman, Charles H	1		3		
Forbes, Daniel	1	4	3		
Fitz Gerald, John	3		4		
Fulton, Doctr James	3		2		9
Gears, John	2	1	3		25
Gribbin, Henry	1	2	1		

NAME OF HEAD OF FAMILY.	Free white males of 16 years and upward, including heads of families.	Free white males under 16 years.	Free white females, including heads of families.	All other free persons.	Slaves.
NORTH SASSAFRAS HUNDRED—continued.					
Hersey, Thomas	1	7	1		
Hanson, John	2	2	4		1
Hodgeon, Robert	7		1		1
Hedges, Rebeccah			1		7
Kirk, Garret	1	1	3		
Lyon, Barthw	1	3	3		
M Kinney, John	3		4		
Massey, John	2				3
Mahaney, William	3		2		
Morton, John	1		1		1
Mathews, Doctr William	5		2		25
M Kinney, Thomas	2		1		1
Meekings, Peter	2	1	4		2
Massey, Sarah		1	3		
Mackey, John				1	
Nowland, Benjamin	2		2		9
Nowland, Jesse	2		2		6
Penington, Elizabeth	1	1	4		
Penington, Joseph	3	1	2		6
Robinson, James	1	2	3		
Rigs, Daniel	1	1	4		
Ryland, Sylvester	3				
Ryland, Rachel		2	4		
Ryland, Fredus	3	1	3		10
Ryland, Benjamin	1	2	3		13
Savin, William	1		2		9
Shelly, John	2	2	2		4
Sappington, John	1	1	3		
Smith, William	2	1	1		
Savin, Peregrine	2				14
Starkey, William	1	3	2		1
Tull, Thomas	4	1	3		
Thomas, Joseph	1	1	6		
Webb, Benjamin	1	2	6		
NORTE SUSQUEHANNAH HUNDRED.					
Alexander, Arthur	3	2	2		
Aiken, Robt	2		2		2
Barrett, Mary	2	2	4		22
Blake, Isaac	1	1	3		
Beaty, Samuel	1	2	3		
Bell, Robert	2	2	7		
Boyd, Alexander	3	4	3		
Baker, Nathan	3	3	1		
Brooks, John	3	3	4		
Bonner, Robert	3		4		
Boyd, John	1	1	1		
Boyd, Francis	1	1	4		6
Clark, Samuel	1	3	2		
Corbitt, Joseph	1		2		
Clemings, John	1				
Cazier, Susannah	1		2		
Campbell, Grace		1	2		
Carnahan, Robert	3	3	4		
Chandlee, Thomas	2	1	4		
Chew, Nathan	3		2		7
Crowley, John	2	2	2		
Corbitt, Jane			2		
Cole, Philip	15	2	5		31
Catts, Michael	1	1	5		
Creswell, John	1	1	1		6
Campbell, Catharine	1	1	4		
Currer, William	2		3		
Currer, Jonathan	1		2		
Dallam, John	1		5		
Dixon, William	2	2	3		
Dempsey, Luke	1	1	2		
Evans, John	1	2	3		
Ewing, Thomas	1	1	6		4
Evans, Amos	1	1	5		
Elder, James	2		2		1
Evans, Robert	2	2	5		9
Finley, Robert	3		4		1
Finney, Robert	2		5		
Foster, Benjamin	2	2	2		
Foster, Archd	3	1	4		
Ferguson, James	1	1	4		
Gatchel, Jeremiah	2	2	4		
Gover, Robert	1				21
Gibbony, Alexr	1	1			
Glasgow, Jonathan	1		1		1
Griffith, William	2	4	5		
Green, Edward	2		3		
Gillespie, James	2		3		5
Gay, Samuel	1		2		1
Green, James	1	1	3		
Greer, John			2		
Gibson, Martha	2	2	5		
Hartshorn, Majr John	2	2	3		6
Hitchman, William	2	2	4		2
Hunter, James	3	1	4		

NAME OF HEAD OF FAMILY.	Free white males of 16 years and upward, including heads of families.	Free white males under 16 years.	Free white females, including heads of families.	All other free persons.	Slaves.
NORTH SUSQUEHANNAH HUNDRED—continued.					
Honyman, Margaret			3		
Holliday, Clement					4
Harry, William	2	3	3		
Howard, Simeon	1	3	2		
Horner, Stephen	1	2	5		
Happersalk, John	1		2		
Johnson, Isaac	2		1		
Jackson, Edward	4	3	2		
Knox, Robert	3	2	1		
Lockwood, Mathew	1	1	6		
Kidd, Martha	5		4		
Kidd, George	1	2	3		2
Kelly, Thomas	4		5		1
Kennedy, Thomas	1		2		
Kerr, Nathl	2		5		
Kerr, John	1	2	4		
Kelly, Hannah			2		
Lusk, John	2		1	1	
Lesslie, George	2	1	3	1	1
Lyon, John	2	1	4		
Lyle, Henry	2	1	4		
Lyon, Hugh	4		5		
Little, William	4	3	5		
Miller, John	1		4		
McCrea, Hugh	7		4		
McMullin, James, Sr	3				
McNeely, Joseph	1	1	5		1
Muir, John	1		1		
Murry, Daniel				1	
McGonegal, John				1	
McCullough, William	3	2	4		
Mulveen, David	3	1	1		
McMullen, Robt, Junr	3		2		
Moore, Margt			5		
Mitchel, James	2	6	3		19
MoCoy, John	7		8		9
McMaster, Robert	3	2	3		
Morrow, Robert	1		3		
McFee, Malcolm				1	
Miller, Samuel, Esqr	5	3	3		4
McHarrie, John	4	3	2		2
McCall, John	4	3	3		
Murphy, John	2		2		
Mitchel, Mary		2	1		
Miller, Henry	1	3	2		
Nesbit, James	1	3	4		
Nesbit, Robert	1	2	4		
Orr, James	2	5	2		2
Owens, David					
Patton, William	4	2	3		
Patton, David	1		3		6
Porter, Capn Robt	1	4	4		1
Prig, Joseph	6		1		
Peters, William	1	1	3		
Perry, Edward	1		2		
Porter, Eleanor			2		
Patterson, John	1	1	6		9
Patterson, William	1	3	2		
McMullen, Samuel	2		1		
McMullen, Saml, Jun	2	3	3		
McMullen, Robert, Sn	1	2	3		
McCracken, James	1		2		
Mahon, William	1	1	5		7
Rogers, John	1	1	3		
Regan, James			2		1
Reynolds, Jacob	3	1	5		
Reynolds, Richd	1	3	3		2
Rawlings, Greenbury	1		4		3
Rawlings, John	2	1	2		
Rowlands, John	3	1	2		7
Rowlands, James	3	1	2		
Read, John					
Rutter, Richard	1	5	1		
Robinson, William	1	5	1		
Ryan, John	2	1	3		1
Stormons, Nathan	1	1	3		
Spear, James	1	1	6		
Sutton, Stephen	1	1	1		9
Stump, John	1	1	1		25
Stokes, Frances			4		
Steel, James	2		1		2
Sterrett, John	3	2	4		1
Simmons, Thomas	1		5		
Tower, John	1	1	5		
Taylor, John	1	2	4		
Tallum, John	3	1	4		
Taylor, Thomas	1	2	3		
Thompson, James	2		1		
Taylor, Moses	1		1		
Thomas, Philip, Esqr	3	2	5		43
Thomas, John Chew	2		2		27
Thomas, Richard	2	2	5		51
Whitelock, Charles, Jr	1	2	3		

CECIL COUNTY—Continued.

Name of head of family.	Free white males of 16 years and upward, including heads of families.	Free white males under 16 years.	Free white females, including heads of families.	All other free persons.	Slaves.
NORTH SUSQUEHANNAH HUNDRED—continued.					
Whitelock, Charles	4	4	3		1
Watson, Isaac Decoo	1		2		
Weir, Andrew	2	1	2		
Wood, Joseph	1		2		
Weir, Robert	1	2	1		
Williams, Doctr John	1		2		1
Williams, John	1	2	4		
OCTORARO HUNDRED.					
Arbuckle, Joseph	1				1
Brown, Jeremiah	1	3	3		
Bell, Archd	1		2		
Brown, Thomas	2	1	4		
Cromwell, Vincent	3	3	4		
Cromwell, John H	1	2	8		11
Connor, Jacob	4	2	3		
Conn, Robert	1		1		
Dunbar, Andrew	3	1	5		
Dorsey, Stephen	1	2	1		6
Ewing, William	1	3	2		
Ewing, Nathaniel	1		1		7
Ewing, Patrick, Esqr	2	1	5		3
Fulton, Alexr	1	3	4		1
Franks, Ann			2		
Greave, John	3		5		
Gillespie, Mary		2	3		5
Guy, Margaret			6		5
Gillespie, Nathl	1		1		6
Glenn, John	2	3	4		
Gorden, John	1		3		
Gillespie, William	2	3	6		7
Hall, Elihu, Senr	3	1	4		17
Hall, John	1	3	2		2
Hall, Elihu, Junr	1	1	5		10
Harris, William	1	1	7		
Henderson, Augustine	1				
Hillis, Abraham	3	4	2		1
Helm, Michael	1	2	4		1
Hughins, John	1		2		
Hill, Richd	1	4	3		
Keith, Robert	1	1	3		
Love, James	2		4		1
Lafferty, Edward	1	4	3		
Love, Robert	2	1	2		1
Low, William	4	1	4		
Lynch, William	1		2		
Lynch, John	1	2	4		
Moore, James	1	2	5		
Mehony, John				1	
Mackey, William	1	1	1		1
McCleary, Samuel	1	2	5		
McLaughlin, Colin	1	2	3		
McLean, John	1		1		
McCoy, John	1	2	3		2
McDowell, Thos	1	1	2		
McDowell, Elizabeth			2		
McHallam, James	1	1	2		
Moseley, Jacob				1	
Neal, John	1	3	4		
Porter, Stephen, Esqr	2	2	3		3
Physick, Henry	3	2	3		2
Porter, James	1	2	1		
Porter, George	1	1			
Porter, Samuel	1		2		5
Polk, James	1		2		
Porter, James Leiper	2		3		10
Rawlings, Joseph	1	1	2		3
Roach, Frederick	1	3	2		
Read, Robert	1	2	4		
Rowland, Robert	1	1	7		3
Scott, Thomas	1	3	5		
Sims, James	2		1		3
Smith, Edward	1	2	1		
Stephenson, Joseph	1	5	1		
Smith, Robert	1	1	2		
Shears, John	1	1	1		
Short, Edward	1		1		
Thomas, Isaac	2		1		
Tingus, Peter	1		1		
Welsh, William	1	1	4		
Walker, Isabella		1	1		
Waters, Allen	1	3	4		
Lucy				2	
Ogle, Benjamin				1	
Chatham				1	
Hannah				2	
Bryson, Rebecca				1	
Bet				1	
George				1	
Bryant, Hannah				11	
Duke				7	
Ned				1	
Henny				1	
OCTORARO HUNDRED—continued.					
Will, Blue				3	
Monnie, John				1	
Phillis				1	
Pere				2	
Vallow, Stephen				7	
Vallow, Robert				6	
Mounts, Alexander				1	
Moses				4	
Manuel				3	
Clark, John				3	
Hunter, Thomas				1	
Dinah				5	
Primus				1	
Flora				1	
Tom				1	
Lynn				1	
McDonald, Chas				1	
Vallow, Henry				1	
Pere				3	
Jack				1	
Amie				7	
Matilda				3	
Nelly				1	
Isaac				1	
Maronn, John				1	
Anderson, Susannah				4	
Rachel				3	
Solomon				1	
Morrison, Rachel				1	
Grey, William				1	
Gibbs, John				1	
Ben				1	
Eve				6	
Dide				2	
Sall				2	
Dingle, Ben				1	
Sarah				1	
Lambert				1	
Price, Jere				1	
Dinah				5	
Joe				1	
Jacob				1	
Londonderry				1	
Poll				1	
Charles				3	
Gibson, Richard				5	
Susanah				4	
Poorhouse				4	
Peter				1	
Isaac				1	
Saml & Wife				2	
Ruth				2	
Jack				2	
Eliza				1	
Hester				1	
Jere				4	
Lucy				1	
Moore, John				3	
Uncle Toby				1	
Poll				1	
Lerry, Benj				1	
Elimas				6	
Isaac				1	
Phillis				1	
Nance				1	
Moses				1	
Bess				4	
Tom				4	
Cato				5	
Benjamin				10	
Hammond, Mary				9	
Aaron				1	
Jack				1	
Peter				1	
Rachel				1	
Cato				1	
Gale, Capn				8	
Cassandra				1	
Hopkins, Edwd				1	
Sylvester				1	
Bob				1	
Hannah				1	
Combolt, Princess				1	
Abraham				1	
Bill				1	
James				1	
Amelia				1	
Comber				1	
John				6	
Bill				1	
Flora				1	
Thomas, Surey				5	
Fowler, Freeman				1	
Duke				2	
OCTORARO HUNDRED—continued.					
Dover				4	
Pompey				3	
Nell				1	
Sarah				1	
James				1	
Chance				1	
Phillis				4	
Ruth				2	
Jeoffry				6	
Hannah				3	
Nance				1	
Caesar				2	
Williams, Joseph				3	
SOUTH MILLFORD HUNDRED.					
Armstrong, Thomas	1	1	2		
Anderson, John	3	2	5		
Armstrong, John	1	4	1		
Ball, George	2	3	3		
Berry, Richard	1	1	1		
Boyd, Mary			3		
Bell, James	3		2		
Baldwin, Peter	1		1		
Bultiel, Ann		1	3		
Boyd, John	1	2	5		
Brown, William	1	2	2		
Brown, Hugh	2	2	2		
Barr, Robert	1	3	3		1
Batchelor, David	1	1	1		
Brown, John	1	4	2		
Badger, Charles	1	2	2		
Baker, Mary		1	3		
Blackburn, Robert	1		1		1
Culberson, Richard	1	1	4		
Cochran, John	2		2		
Culley, George	3	2	3		
Chaslor, Jacob	1		1		
Crooks, James	2	3	6		
Cook, James	1	2	2		
Campbell, John	1	1	2		
Delap, William	1		1		
Dobson, Adam	2	3	3		4
Evans, Mary		4	3		
Fulton, William	2	7	3		
Fleck, John				1	
Foster, William	1		2		
Glass, John	2	1	4		
George, John	1	5	2		
Gillis, Samuel	1			5	
Griffith, John	3		3		
Hall, Andrew	1	1	1		
Holt, Isaac	2	3	2		6
Hansel, Mathias	1	2	2		
How, Samuel	1	3	4		
Hemphill, Robert	2	3	4		
Henry, Stephen	1	4	2		
Hugabaugh, Isaac	1		2		
Hull, William	1	1	2		
Hall, Isaac	2	1	1		
Harvey, William	1	1	1		
Hannah, Joseph	1		1		
Harvey, William, Junr	1	1	1		
Hemphill, James	2	1	1		
Johnson, William	2		3		
Johnson, Matthias	2		2		
Johnson, Josiah	1	5	3		
Johnson, Levi	2	3	6		
Lowther, William	3		5		
Lutton, Robert	1	1	1		1
Low, John	1	3	2		
Lucans, John	1		2		
Lidworth, Patrick	1	2	1		
Morgan, Jacob	1	2	1		
Mathews, Mary		1	2		
McLaughlin, James	1	1	3		
McCauley, James	3	3	4		
MKewn, Samuel	2		4		1
Miller, Thomas	3		5		
McVea, Daniel	1	1	1		
McCreery, John	3	3	6		
McNinch, John	1	1	2		
Miller, Samuel	1	2	2		
Miller, William	2	3	3		
Moffitt, Samuel, Esqr	3	3	5		3
McCaig, James	1	2	4		
Mahon, William	1	3	3		
Mahon, John	1		1		
Nash, John	2	1	4		
Nash, John, Junr	1	1	1		
Nowland, John	3		2		
Patterson, Robert	2	3	4		

CECIL COUNTY—Continued.

NAME OF HEAD OF FAMILY.	Free white males of 16 years and upward, including heads of families.	Free white males under 16 years.	Free white females, including heads of families.	All other free persons.	Slaves.
SOUTH MILLFORD HUNDRED—continued.					
Passmore, William	3	3	3		1
Piper, Samuel	1	1	3		
Read, Andrew	2	4	5		
Rumsey, Henry	1		2		12
Richardson, Thomas	1	1	3		
Rogers, Samuel	3		1		
Ricketts, John	1	3	3		
Ricketts, Sarah			2		
Smith, Robert, Junr	1	1	2		
Smith, Robert, Senr	4	2	3		1
Smith, Joseph	2	2	6		2
Shields, Francis	1	1	4		
Short, William	2	1	6		
Short, Adam	3		1		
Short, Thomas	4		9		
Simpers, John, Junr	3		2		9
Spence, John	1	3	1		
Smith, Robert Cooper	4		1		
Thompson, Isaac	1	2	1		
Tyson, Benjamin	1	1	7		
Wallace, Thomas	3	2	6		6
Willson, Thomas, Senr	5	1	2		1
Work, James	3		3		
Wilson, Thomas, Junr	2	2	4		
York, Benjamin					
SOUTH SUSQUEHANNAH HUNDRED.					
Alexander, Arthur	2	2			
Abrahams, Richard	2	1	5		
Arnott, Samuel	1		2		
Atchinson, John	2		1		
Alexander, Justis	1		2		
Alexander, John	1	3	4		
Bassett, Richard	1	1	1		
Beard, Doctr John	3	1	3		
Brookins, Charles	2	1	3		4
Bashford, Francis				1	
Brumfield, John				1	
Baker, Jeremiah, Esqr	2	1	4		10
Brown, Alexander	1	1	6		
Baker, John	2	3	5		
Chapple, John	1	2	3		6
Caruthers, William	3		1		4
Couden, Samuel	1		1		
Caldwell, Robert	1		2		
Crookshanks, John	5	1	1		
Caruthers, William, Junr	1		2		
Carswell, John	2	1	3		
Cather, John	3	1	4		
Cord, Thomas	5			7	
Channel, John, Senr	3			3	
Channel, John, Junr	2		2		
Cosgrove, Michael	1	2	2		
Crosson, Hugh	3	1	2		
Campbell, James				1	
Currer, Jeremiah	1	3	3		2
Currer, Elijah	1	1	1		
Chambers, William	1	1	4		
Costelo, Francis	2	2	6		
Cameron, John	2	4	4		
Corbitt, William	1		6		
Cuningham, Isabella	1	2	2		
Cassady, William	1		1		
Dolan, James	1	1	3		
England, Joseph	1	2	3		
Edmiston, Joseph	1	1	1		
Edmison, William	2				
Elliott, Joseph	1				
Fox, Philip	2		8		
Foy, Patrick	1	2	3		
Farley, John	1	1	4		
Gillespie, Daniel	1	3	2		
Green, John	2	2	2		
Glenn, Jacob	1		3		3
Gardiner, James	5	1	4		
Hall, John	2		1		3
Hill, Robert	1		1		
Hartshorn, Thomas	5	1	4		
Hamilton, Robert	1	2	2		
Holland, John	2	2	3		2
Huston, William	1		4		
Hederick, George	1	2	3		1
Hall, Mary	3	2	1		
Howell, Lydia	2		2		
Jones, Samuel	2	4	4		
Jack, John	2	1	1		
Janney, Thomas	3		2		
Janney, John	1		2		
Johnson, Isaac	2		2		
Matthews, David	1	1	2		
Marshall, William	1	1	2		
Garigal, Samuel			4		
SOUTH SUSQUEHANNAH HUNDRED—continued.					
McVea, Jacob, of John	2	4	3		
MDowell, William	2	1	3		
Kilpatrick, William	1	3	5		
Kerr, James				1	
Kinley, Daniel	1		1		3
Kelly, John	1	2	3		
Kirkpatrick, John	1	2	1		1
Loubinswiler, Jacob	1	4	2		
Lackland, James	1	3	2		
Lane, Gilbert	1				
Lynch, John	1		3		
Logan, Mathew	1	1	1		
Logan, Samuel	1	3	3		
Lesslie, John	1		2		
Leslie, Robert	1	1	2		
Lackland, Nathan	1	1	1		
McBride, Archd	1	1	1		
MVea, John	2	1	1		
McCullough, Samuel	2		3		1
McCleary, Thomas	3	3	3		
MKewn, Samuel	3	1	2		2
MLaughlin, Mathew				1	
McVea, Daniel	2	3	3		
MVea, Jacob, of John	2	4	2		
Morrow, James	3	2	5		
McCauley, Daniel	2	2	4		
Milligan, James	4	1	6		
McKewn, William	1	3	4		
MKewn, John	2	1	4		
MVey, Edward	1		1		
Miller, Isaac	1	3	2		1
McDowell, William	1	1	3		
McCoy, Alexander				1	
McGarrity, Richard	1	2	4		
McIllwee, John, Junr	1	1	4		
McCaul, John	3	3	2		
MIllwee, John, Senr	2	1	2		
McCullough, William	1		1		
Neal, Charles	1	1	1		
Oldham, Joseph	1	2	2		
Oldham, Jacob	1		2		
Orrick, James, Esqr	2		1		4
Oldham, Zebulon	1	2	3		1
Orr, Robert	2		2		
Owens, Francis	1	4	3		
Patterson, Samuel	2	3	3		3
Pugh, Patience	1		2		
Peagrim, Elizabeth	1				
Russell, Thomas	2	5	3		
Russell, Ann		2	5		16
Riddle, Robert	1		1		
Read, William	1	1	2		
Ramsey, Nat, Esqr	3		2		26
Sheredine, Daniel	6				41
Slyer, John	2	2	3		4
Sourbright, George	2	3	3		
Stephenson, William	1		4		
Smith, Robert	1		1		
Stephenson, John	2	2	8		
Sadler, Henry	1	1	4		
Severson, Stephen	1	2	1		
Smith, John	1	2	3		
Taylor, Charles	1	1	1		
Taylor, John	1	1	3		
Thomas, Capn William	1		3		7
Trump, Abraham	1	3	2		
Thompson, John	3	2	1		
Underhill, Thomas	2	1	3		
Wilson, Margery	1		3		
Willocks, William	1	1	3		
Williams, Basil, Esqr	1	4	7		14
Wilson, John Mason	1		2		
Wilson, John Weaver	1	3	3		
Wilson, Andrew	1				
Williams, Thomas	3	6	5		2
Winkles, George	1	2	3		2
Watson, Joseph	1	4	6		1
Willocks, Andrew	2	2	2		
Willocks, James	1		3		
Wilson, Thomas				1	
Whitaker, Ralph	2	5	2		
Taylor, Thomas	1	2	3		
Taylor, James	1		1		
Thompson, James	1	1	3		
WEST NOTTINGHAM HUNDRED.					
Alexander, James	1		1		
Allen, William	1		3		
Allen, James	2	4	6		
Adams, Mary				1	
Booth, Edward	1	4	3		
Baker, Nathan	1	5	3		
Barnes, James	4		1		5
WEST NOTTINGHAM HUNDRED—continued.					
Borland, John	1	3	4		
Barclay, William	1		3		
Brown, Jacob	4	8	4		
Butterfield, John	3		3		
Brackley, Joachim	2		3		
Booth, William	1	1	2		
Bryson, William	3	2	2		
Briesland, William	1	3	2		
Brown, Joseph, Junr	2	1	4		
Brown, Samuel	4		6		
Brown, Elisha	3	1	5		
Brown, Robert	3	2	2		
Brown, William	1	2	5		
Brown, Joseph, Junr	2	1	4		
Baker, Thomas	1	4	3		
Blackburn, John	1	2	2		5
Brown, Joseph, Senr	2	1	4		
Bernard, Thomas	2	1	3		
Brown, Saml (Weaver)	2		1		
Crawford, John	1		1		
Crawford, James	1		1		
Caldwell, Joseph	1	1	1		
Connolly, Michael				1	
Cummings, James	2	5	3		1
Caldwell, Thomas	2	1	2		
Curl, Margaret			2		
Curl, James	1		2		
Coale, William	1	7	3		
Cookson, Samuel	2		3		
Coulson, Joseph, Junr	2	3	4		
Coulson, Joseph	1	2	4		1
Coulson, John	4	4	6		2
Dixson, John	2	3	4		
Death, Elizabeth	1	3	2		
Douglass, James	1	1	2		
Dick, William	1	1	2		
Ewing, Amos	3	1	5		
Edmiston, Alexn I	2	1	2		3
Evans, James	1	4	3		2
Eakins, Susannah			1		1
Eagon, James	1	5	4		
Edmiston, David	3	3	2		
Ferguson, John, Junr	2	1	4		
Ferguson, John, Senr	1	2	2		
Giuney, Timothy	2		2		
Hagin, Solomon	1		3		
Harland, Doctor	4	1	5		
Hall, Colo Elihu	1	3	5		9
Hall, Richard, Esqr	1		2		4
Harris, Nathan	2	3	5		
Harris, John	1	2	3		
Harris, Elisha	1	1	3		
Haines, William	4	4	5		
Hasson, Benjamin	1	3	2		
Haines, Job	4	6	6		
Haines, Jacob	3	3	8		
Hindman, Samuel	3	1	6		
Hindman, Mary	1		2		1
Haines, Isaac	3	1	4		
Heron, Capn Jas G	2	1	8		10
Johnson, William	4		3		2
Job, Daniel, Senr	4	3	5		
Knight, William	2	5	5		
Knight, John	1	4	6		2
Kirk, Abner	2	2	5		2
Kirk, Eli	1	2	3		
Kirk, Jacob	1	1	5		
Love, Rosanna	1	2	3		
Lafferty, Jackson	2	2	4		
Long, Alexander	2	3	3		
Leaney, Peter	1	2	1		
McClure, James	1		2		
Maxwell, James				1	
Meloy, Sarah			1		
McCullough, John	4	1	5		2
McClean, William	3		3		
Moore, Robert	2	2	2		
Maxwell, Isabella	3	1	6		
Mullen, Andrew	1		1		
McCardle, Terence	1	1	2		
McDowell, Thomas	1		3		
Mifflin, John	2	1	1		1
Mask, Isaac	3	1	3		
Miller, John	1	3	3		
McKleheany, William				1	
Nesbit, Joseph	2		2		
Nesbit, Alexander	1	2	1		
Polk, David	2		2		1
Patton, James	3	1	3		
Peoples, Samuel	1		1		
Patterson, Moles	3	1	3		
Palmer, Richd	1	1	2		
Patton, Thomas	2	1	7		
Ray, George	1	1	2		
Reynolds, Israel	3		2		

CECIL COUNTY.—Continued.

WEST NOTTINGHAM HUNDRED—continued.

NAME OF HEAD OF FAMILY.	Free white males of 16 years and upward, including heads of families.	Free white males under 16 years.	Free white females, including heads of families.	All other free persons.	Slaves.
Reynolds, William					
Rankin, Thomas	2		1		3
Reynolds, Samuel	4		1	6	5
Ray, James	1		2		5
Riley, Thomas	1	1		1	
Reynolds, Jacob, Junr	1			1	
Ryley, John	2			1	3
Ramsey, Andrew	2		2		3
Ramsey, James	1			2	
Reynolds, Joseph	2		4		5
Reynolds, Stephen	2	1	1		4
Reynolds, Stephen, Junr	1		3		2
Reynolds, David	1			2	
Reynolds, Levy	1	1		4	
Reynolds, Jacob	1	3		4	
Reynolds, Jesse	2	2	5	7	
Rich, Sarah				4	1
Sidwell, Margaret	1	1		4	
Sinclair, Aaron	1			1	
Sidwell, Elisha	2	1	1		
Sidwell, Jacob	2	1		3	
Sidwell, Joseph	1	1		3	
Waram, Thomas	1	1		3	
White, Joseph	1	2		3	
White, David	1	3		3	
Woodrow, Simeon	1	5		3	
Walker, William	1	4		1	
Walker, John	1		3		1
Woodrow, John	1	1		3	
Woodward, James	1	1	1		
Walker, Andrew	3	3		1	

WEST SASSAFRAS HUNDRED.

NAME OF HEAD OF FAMILY.	16+ M	<16 M	Females	Other free	Slaves
Abbott, Jacob F	2		2		4
Abbott, William	1		3		14
Allen, Mordecai	1		1		
Allen, John	1		3		
Benson, Benjamin Junr	1	1	3		
Benson, Benj. Senr	2	1	3		6
Bellew, Eliz			4		
Bevins, James	2		4		
Beedle, Alice		2	2		
Barnaby, William	4	1	3		
Benson, John	1	1	1		5

WEST SASSAFRAS HUNDRED—continued.

NAME OF HEAD OF FAMILY.	16+ M	<16 M	Females	Other free	Slaves
Brown, Martha			2		
Cosden, James	4	2	3		3
Cox, John	4	4	3		
Craig, Blanche	1	2	3		3
Coursey, William				1	
Campbell, William				1	
Cowarden, James	1		4	1	
Cann, Jane		3	2		1
Cuningham, Mary		1	2		
Connolly, John	2		3		
Coppin, Mary	2	3	2		
Cosden, Jeremiah	2		2		
Crangle, James	1	2	2		24
Davis, Thomas	1	1	1		
Dennis, Araminta		2	1		
Davis, William	3	1	1		7
Dorrell, Eliz			2		2
Etherington, Spencer	1		2		2
Feddis, Jonathan	3		7		
Farran, James	1	3	2		2
Fields, Christopher	2		2		10
Fackney, John	1	1		3	
Ford, Nathaniel	1		3		1
Forden, Thomas	1		5		3
Greedy, Rebecca			7		
Gears, Benson			5		
Hedrickson, Matthias	2	1		3	
Hendrickson, Matthias, Jr	1	1	2		
Hendrickson, Ann				1	
Helmstuft, William					1
Hendrickson, Henry	1	3	1		
Hendrickson, Barthw	1	1	7		5
Hendrickson, William	1	1	2		
Hares, Doct David			2		7
Hall, Francis			2		6
Hayley, James	1		3		
Hayes, Richd	1	2	4		
Hanson, Rebecca		1	3		4
Jones, Thomas	3		4		
Jervis, John	1	1	4		
Longfellow, Gideon	1	1	3		14
Mercer, Ann		2	1		
McKillegan, Morris	3	1	2		5
Money, Benjamin	2		1		
Miller, John	2	1		4	2

WEST SASSAFRAS HUNDRED—continued.

NAME OF HEAD OF FAMILY.	16+ M	<16 M	Females	Other free	Slaves
Morgan, Thomas	1		2		
McCleland, Nathl	1		3		
Murphy, Francis	1	2	3		
Milligan, Robt, Esq	1		3		34
Nicholas, John	1		3		
Neilson, William	5		3		9
Penington, Hyland	3	5	4		
Penington, William D	1	2	4		
Penington, Henry	1		2		
Price, Rebecca	1	5		5	
Price, Henry	1	1	2		
Price, John Hyland	5	3	3		17
Penington, Robert	1		1		
Penington, Henry	1	2	4		
Penington, Joseph	1	2	1		
Penington, George	1		3		
Porter, Capn James	3	1		9	
Prushaw, Nicholas			1		
Pearce, James	1	1	1		
Price, Richard	2	1	5		4
Parsley, Thomas	3	4	2		5
Pearce, Thomas	3	2	4		23
Robinson, Thomas	1			1	7
Robinson, Benjamin	1		1		
Robinet, Richard	1	3	3		
Richardson, William	1	2	2		
Savin, Richard	1			1	
Savin, Augustin	1	5		3	19
See, Benjamin	1				6
Sheppard, Mary			1		
Stoops, Peregrine			1		
Stephens, Thomas	2	2	5		7
Thompson, John	1		2		
Tully, Rebecca			2		
Tippings, James	1	2	2		1
Veazey, Rebecca	1		4		10
Williamson, Alexr	1	2	2		11
Wingate, Hezekiah	1		4		2
Wingate, Peter	1	1	6		
Welsh, Philip	1	3	6		
Ward, Peregrine	1		1		
Wiley, William	1	1	1		35
Ward, John, of Pere	4	1	2		
Welsh, William	1		1		13

CHARLES COUNTY.

NAME OF HEAD OF FAMILY.	16+ M	<16 M	Females	Other free	Slaves
Adams, George	3		2		3
Acton, James	3		3		
Adams, Adam, Free Negro				2	
Adams, Henrietta			5		7
Allen, Zechariah	1	2	5		7
Adams, Ignatius	3		3		6
Adams, Richard	3	1	2		7
Adams, Benj	1		1		11
Adams, Samuel	1	1		4	
Adams, Leonard	3		1		
Arvin, Thomas, Junr	1	4	4		
Armes, Stacey		1	3		
Adams, Ann (Mulatto)				7	
Anderson, William					
Acton, Osborne R	2		3		
Arvin, Thos, Senr	2	1	2		2
Arvin, Edwd	2	1	3		1
Arvin, Joshua	1	4	4		
Askin, Eliz			1		1
Acton, Henry, of Jno	1	3	4		
Acton, John	2		1		5
Acton, John, Junr	1	2	6		
Adams, Jas (Oversr for Saml Edelen)			2		11
Athey, Hezer	1	3	2		
Atchinson, John	2		2		
Ash, Charles	1		5		
Ash, William	1		5		
Atchinson, Joshua	2	1	1		
Adams, John	2	4	1		11
Adams, John R	1		4		12
Anderson, Jonathan	1	1	3		9
Anderson, Joseph	1		3		4
Anderson, Benj	2		2		
Alexander, James	2		1		1
Allbrittain, William	1	2	4		1
Adams, John, Junr	1		2		
Adams, Joseph (Nanjemoy)	1	2	5		2
Adams, Zeph	2	3	3		
Anderson, James	2		2		

NAME OF HEAD OF FAMILY.	16+ M	<16 M	Females	Other free	Slaves
Allen, Joseph					
Allbrittain, Charles	1	4	3		1
Adams, Ann (Mulatto)	1	1	4		6
Amory, Samuel	1	4	1		14
Allen, Francis			1		
Allen, George	1	2	4		
Allen, William (of Jas)	1	3	1		5
Anderson, Hendley (Mulatto)				1	
Allen, James	1		4		
Allen, William	2		2		5
Adams, Rhody		3	2		3
Adams, Charles	1		2		
Allen, William	1	1	5		
Adams, William	2		5		12
Armstrong, Robert	1		4		
Adams, George	1	1	2		
Adams, Richd, Senr	1	5	1		
Bryan, Stripling				1	
Burch, Jonas	1	2	2		14
Briscoe, Walter	2		5		20
Barber, Cornelius (Newpt): Perugin Callhill, Overseer					13
Boarman, Ralph	1		5		39
Berry, Thomas	2	1	3		3
Barnes, Humphry, of Richd					1
Boswell, Ignatius	1		4		3
Barnes, Henry	4	1	1		18
Bowie, John	1		4		4
Boswell, Walter	1		4		4
Boswell, George	2		3		6
Boswell, Joseph	1		3		2
Boswell, Sarah			3		9
Boswell, Edward	2		4		
Blair, Matthew (Mercht)	2	3	4		
Brawner, John C	4				
Brawner, Henry	1	2	4		4
Brent, Chandler	2	3	3		29
Brent, Ann			2		5
Butler, John	2	3	4		
Barnes, Matthew	3	1	5		2

NAME OF HEAD OF FAMILY.	16+ M	<16 M	Females	Other free	Slaves
Bradley, John	1		1		
Boswell, Sarah (Widow of Wills)	1		5		10
Boswell, Edwd W	1	1	5		3
Bullman, Thomas	1	1	5		
Bush, John	2		3		7
Boswell, Elijah	2		2		6
Boswell, Josias	1	4	2		2
Bell, Basil	1		3		13
Burgess, Thomas	1	1	4		3
Brawner, Benjamin	1	1	6		6
Boswell, John, of Matthew	2	2	4		9
Burrows, John	1		4		9
Burrows, Samuel	1		5		
Brent, Robert	1	3	7		29
Boswell, Milley		2	4		
Brooke, John	1	2	6		24
Bruce, John	1	2	2		16
Bateman, Benja, Senr	1	1	1		
Beavin, Walter (Newport)	1		1		3
Beavin, Leonard (Newport)	1		1		3
Brooke, Baker	1	1	2		20
Brady, Gerrard	1	3	5		
Bond, Thomas	3		5		6
Barron, Nathaniel	1	5	2		
Brady, Owen	1	1	5		
Blandford, William	1	1	7		6
Beall, Thomas	1	1	6		4
Bannister, Richard	1		2		
Brown, Catherine	2		3		36
Brown, Doct Gustavus R					37
Baggett, Ignatius	5	2	4		2
Bean, John	1	2	2		
Beane, Leonard	1		3		5
Boarman, James, of Edwd	2		4		5
Berry, Pryor	1	2	4		
Berry, James	1	1	4		1
Beavin, Joseph	1	1	4		2

CHARLES COUNTY—Continued.

NAME OF HEAD OF FAMILY.	Free white males of 16 years and upward, including heads of families.	Free white males under 16 years.	Free white females, including heads of families.	All other free persons.	Slaves.
Blandford, Richᵈ	1	1	2		4
Blandford, Elizᵃ		1	2		4
Blandford, Charles	2	2	3		1
Blandford, Ann	2		5		4
Beavin, Matthew	2	2	4		4
Beavin, Paul (Mulatto)				1	
Boon, Nicholas	3	4	4		13
Boon, John	1		5		5
Boswell, Thomas	1		3		
Bryan, Lewis	1	2	1		1
Bryan, William	1	1	1		
Been, Benjᵃ	1				
Brenighan, Zechaᵃ	2		3		
Berry, John	1	2	3		3
Berry, Elizᵃ			1	2	
OBryan, William	1		2		
Berry, Samuel	1	4	3		2
Berry, Humphrey	2		1		12
Berry, Joseph	2		5		
Berry, Benjᵃ	2	3	6		2
Berry, Hezekᵃ	2	3	3		4
Boon, Walter	1	1	2		
Beale, Charles	2	2	3		8
Beale, Sarah			2		2
Brent, Richᵈ	2	2	2		14
Beavin, Benjᵃ	1	3	4		7
Beavin, Richard	3		1		10
Beavin, Paul	1				
Beavin, James (Mulatto)				1	
Beavin, Wheeler	2	1	4		1
Beavin, Richard, of Basil	3	1	2		3
Beavin, Elizᵃ (Widᵂ of John)		2	3		
Beavin, Susanna (Mulatto)					1
Butler, Charles (Free Negro)					1
Billingsley, John	1		4		10
Beavin, Hezᵃ	2	2	3		10
Beavin, John	1	5	4		5
Brent, Charles	2	4	5		21
Burch, Edward	1	2	3		9
Burrows, Zephaniah	2		3		
Branson, Leonard	1		2		
Burrows, Gabriel	2	1	1		
Brown, Richᵈ (Free Negro)				1	
Burch, Walter (of Oliver)	1	5	2		15
Brimhall, Jeremiah	1				3
Barker, William	2		1		7
Barker, William, Junᵣ	1	1	2		5
Boarman, Leonard, Junᵣ	1		1		16
Boarman, John	1	3	5		16
Boarman, Mary Ann	1		1		27
Boarman, Leonard	1		1		12
Boarman, Mary (Wid of Geo)	2		3		28
Boarman, Eleanor			1		10
Burkells, William	2		4		3
Bryan, William (Mulatto)				1	
Boarman, Joseph	1		2		14
Burch, Richard (of Oliver)	1	4	5		
Burch, Justinian (of Oliver)	1	5	5		9
Butler, Jacob (Mulatto)				1	
Burch, Oliver	1		2		9
Burch, Henrʸ (and a Mulatto Boy to be Free at the Age of 21 years)	1			1	
Butler, Josias (Mulatto)					5
Boarman, Thomas J.	5	1	1		18
Boarman, Duke	1				
Boarman, John (of Thoᵃ James)	1		2		3
Boarman, Joseph	3	1	2		12
Bolling, Thomas	1				10
Bolling, John	1	1	3		5
Bolling, Catherine	3		3		11
Boon, James	2	3	4		6
Bolling, Francis	1				14
Boarman, Jane (Widow of Thoᵃ James)			2		15
Boarman, Ralp of Thoᵃ James					
Boarman, Henry	1		2		12
Boarman, Mary (Widᵉ of James)			1		23
Butler, Rhody (Mulatto)				1	
Brightwell, Richard	1		3		4
Bryan, Basil	1	2	3		

NAME OF HEAD OF FAMILY.	Free white males of 16 years and upward, including heads of families.	Free white males under 16 years.	Free white females, including heads of families.	All other free persons.	Slaves.
Bryan, Mary Ann	1	2	2		1
Bryan, John	2	2	5		
Bryan, Ignatius	2	1	5		
OBryan, James	1	1	1		
OBryan, Josias	1	4	3		
Burch, Jesse (Mill Wright)	3	2	2		5
Brimhall, William	4	2	5		2
Brightwell, Robert	1		3	3	
Barron, Catharine			1		
Barron, Thomas	2		2		9
Burch, Jonathan	2	2	2		15
Brawner, Barton	4	3	4		8
Brawner, William	1	2	3		13
Brawner, John	2		2		7
Barnes, William (Junᵣ)	1	2	1		
Barnes, William, Senᵣ	3	4	4		1
Barnes, Godshall	2	2	1		1
Bell, Edmund G	1	1	2		
Bowie, Abraham					
Bowie, Mary Ann	2	1	5		1
Barnes, Catharine			2		8
Barnes, Richard			4		22
Bateman, James	2	1	1		
Branson, Leonard	1	1	1		1
Barber, Cornelᵃ (at his Quarter in Pickawaxen: Jonᵃ Higg, Overseer)					9
Boarman, Eleanor (Pickawaxen)		2	2		11
Bateman, Richard	1		3		1
Boarman, Edward	2	1	1		3
Burrows, Samuel (Free Negro)					1
Bateman, John	1	1	2		
Bateman, George	2				1
Bateman, Elevin	1	1	1		
Bateman, Jesse	1		4		1
Brooke, Matthew	1		4		
Bateman, Judith	1	4	2		3
Burridge, Nenyan	1	4			
Bateman, John, Senᵣ	1		3		
Bateman, John, Junᵣ	1		1		3
Blockstone, Samuel	3	4			
Bryan, William (Mulatto)				1	
Barjona (Free Negro)				1	1
Bateman, Thomas	2		1		1
Bruce, William	1	1	1		5
Bowie, Rhody	2		6		
Bowie, Meredith	1	2	2		2
Brawner, Joseph	1	4	2		
Brawner, Shadrac	4	4	6		
Bruin, John	1	1	1		1
Brawner, John (Junᵣ)	1	2			
Brown, Joseph	1	1			
Benson, Benjamin	1	1	1		12
Brooke, Thomas	1		2		
Blockstone, Joseph	1		2		
Burges, Mary		2	2		
Brawner, Edward	1	4	2		
Bowie, Benjamin	1	1	2		
Brawner, Isaac	1	1	2		2
Bailer, Andrew	1	5			24
Burrows, Charᵃ (at Jnᵒ Taylor's Quarter)	1	3	4		54
Burchill, Charles	1	2	2		1
Bradshaw, Jeremiah	1	2	3		
Bowie, James	2	3	3		5
Bowie, David	1		3		1
Barker, William	2	2	2		
Barker, Elizabeth			2		
Basten, William	1	2	6		
Beck, Francis	1	1	4		3
Brawner, Williamᵃ Junᵣ	1		3		8
Barkslay, William	1	1	2		3
Basten, Matthew	1		2		
Baker, Jane			2		
Crismond, John M	2	1	1		1
Crackells, Thomas	1		2		12
Cooksey, Jesse	1	2	6		1
Punch, William Clements	1		2		
Coombes, Richard	1	1	5		7
Cahoo, James	1	4	1		
Clements, Edward	2	1	1		
Carrington, John, Senᵣ	2		2		6
Carrington, Mary	2		1		
Cope, John	2	1	3		2
Clements, Beavin	1	1	4		
Clements, John, of Josᵖ	1		1		
Craik, Adam	2				1
Chandler, Stephen	2		3		9
Cawood, Benjamin	2	1	4		32
Cox, William, Junᵣ	2	4	5		13

NAME OF HEAD OF FAMILY.	Free white males of 16 years and upward, including heads of families.	Free white males under 16 years.	Free white females, including heads of families.	All other free persons.	Slaves.
Cooksey, Hezekiah	2	2	3		7
Chandler, Samuel	1				
Chapman, John, Senᵣ	2		1	1	21
Clements, Leonard (of Walter)					
Clark, Richard (Mulatto)				1	
Clements, Joseph	1		5		8
Clements, John A.	2	1	5		
Clements, Leonard, Senᵣ	2		2		7
Copher, Matthew	2		3		1
Clark, Elijah	2	3	3		4
Chapman, Hendley	2		1		7
Cox, Hugh	2		4		12
Clements, John (Swamp)	2	5	5		7
Crismond, Joseph	3	3	6		
Copher, John	1		1		
Clements, Francis (of John)					
Bennett, John C	1		3		
Cox, Samuel	1		2		21
Chandler, John	2	2	1		4
Craik, William, Esqᵣ	1				23
Cox, John (of Richard)	1				
Cox, Richard, Senᵣ	1		6		
Clements, Edwᵈ (of Wᵐ)	2	2	2		1
Crismond, Aaron	1				
Crismond, John	1		2		
Cox, John, Senᵣ	1		5		
Coomes, Joseph	1		2		15
Clements, Eleanor			1		2
Clements, Sarah				1	
Cartwright, Gustavus	2	1	5		13
Curtis, Samuel (Free Negro)				2	1
Causin, Gerrard B	1	3	4		75
Cotterell, Burford	2	3	3		15
Chinn, Thomas	2	3	4		3
Compton, William, Senᵣ	1		3		9
Collins, Samˡ	3		2		1
Clements, Walter	1	4	3		4
Cain, Francis	1				
Cooper, James	1				
Clements, Charles (of Charles)	3	1	5		
Carrington, John, Junᵣ	1		3		
Clements, John F.	1		3		
Cook, William	1	3	3		9
Cook, Robert	1		1		4
Beavin, Clement	1		3		
Conway, John	1		1		
Coombes, Sarah		1	3		
Courts, Charles	2	3	6		
Cawood, Woodward	1	2	2		2
Coombes, Joshua	1		4		
Clements, John, of Francis	1	1	3		16
Clements, Mary	2	3	3		61
Clinkscales, John	1	1	3		
Carter, William, Mulatto				1	
Clements, William, of Jacob	1		4		1
Clark, Elizabeth, Mulatto				5	
Cobey, William	1	1	2		
Clements, Walter (Cornwallis Neck)	3		3		9
Clements, Walter, of Walter	1	1	3		6
Chapman, Susanna	5		1		33
Conner, Joseph (Mulatto)				1	
Clements, Charles, of Walter	1				
Cox, Francis	1		2		2
Conner, Michael L.	1				
Clements, William, Senᵣ	1	2	5		3
Conner, Owen	1	1	3		
Clements, Elizabeth			1		
Chapman, Sarah, Widᵉ of John			3		22
Clements, Bennadicter	1	4	4		
Cohooe, Elizabeth	1	1	4		
Canter, William, Junᵣ	3	2	2		7
Canter, William, Senᵣ	1		2		9
Courts, George (Free Negro)				1	
Canter, Isaac	1		2		2
Courts, Ann (Mulatto)				1	
Chatham, James	1	4	5		
Cohooe, Sarah (Mulatto)				2	
Craycraft, Bladen	1	3	3		3
Cooksey, Philip	3	1	2		3
Cooksey, Jonathan	1		5		1
Callicoe, Joseph	1	1	5		

CHARLES COUNTY—Continued.

NAME OF HEAD OF FAMILY.	Free white males of 16 years and upward, including heads of families.	Free white males under 16 years.	Free white females, including heads of families.	All other free persons.	Slaves.
Canter, Susanna	2	1	2		5
Canter, Joseph	1	1	1		6
Callico, Thomas	1		1		
Callico, James	3		4		
Cooksey, Thomas	1		3		4
Carrol, Samuel	1	1	5		1
Corry, Elizabeth			3		7
Cooksey, Ledstone	1	3	3		
Cooksey, Jesse	1	2	6		
Cooksey, Henry	3	4	2		15
Collins, George (Mulatto)				1	
Cooksey, John	1	1	3		6
Conyham, James, Mulatto				1	
Carrick, Joseph	1				6
Clements, Henry	1				
Clark, Elizabeth			1		1
Callico, Monica			1		
Callico, James, of Peter	1	3	5		3
Canter, Truman	1				
Callico, William	1	3	6		
Clinkscales, Adam	2		6	2	
Callico, Henry	2	1	2		
Callico, James	1	2	1		
Canter, James	2	2	4		1
Canter, Leonard	1	1	2		3
Cahoo, James	1	1	6		
Chunn, Zachariah	1	2	4		7
Chunn, Lancelot	3		1		1
Colley, James		1	1		
Carrington, Samuel	1	3	3		
Clements, Samuel	2	4	4		
Clements, Zachariah	1		1		
Cato, George	2	3	2		4
Carpenter, Viney		1	4		
Clark, George	1	3	1		
Clements, John (at [?Richᵈ Barnes])	1	1	5		
Carter, Charles (Mulatto)				1	
Causin, Ann		3	3		
Contee, Benjamin, Esqʳ	1		5		48
Cotterell, James	1	1	1		11
Cotterell, Benjamin	1		1		5
Courts, William	1	1	3		39
Crain, Elizabeth	2		1		24
Chunn, Mary Ann	1	2	7		10
Connor, Dennis	1	1	1		
Chunn, Levi	1	1	1		14
Call, Samuel (Free Negro)				1	
Compton, Revᵈ John W.	2		1		6
Campbell, John, Esqʳ	1		4		54
Cotterrell, Thomas	2	4	3		4
Carter, Hannah (Mulatto)				4	
Cope, Thomas	1	1	1		1
Cody, Matthew	1		2		1
Cavender, Ann		1	6		
Clinkscales, Adam	2		4		2
Coby, John	2	2	3		8
Clements, John, of Jnᵒ, Senʳ	1		2		4
Carroll, Samuel	1	1	3		
Cock, David & Geo. (Free negros)				3	
Clark, William	1	4	3		
Carpenter, John	1	1	3		
Courts, Benjamin	1	2	2		
Carroll, Richard	1	2	2		
Carpenter, William	1		2		
Chinn, Robert	1				
Dodson, William	4	3	4		6
Dagg, John	2	1	1		1
Dixon, John C	1	1	1		2
Dixon, Francis	3	1	11		
Davis, Benjamin	2	3	2		8
Dodson, Barton	1	2	6		1
Darnall, Benjamin	1	1	3		
Davis, Eleazer	1	4	3		6
Douglass, Thomas	1	2	5		1
Day, Benjamin (Mulatto)			6		
Doyne, Ann			3		6
Doyne, Joseph	1				
Dixon, John	1				4
Douglass, Benjᵃ, of Jnᵒ	2	1	2		11
Dunning, John	1				
Downs, William, Junʳ	1	2	1		4
Davis, Mary		1	2		
Dixon, Mary			4		1
Dement, Joseph	1	1	1		1
Digges, Henry	6		3		52
Dyson, Thomas A	3				
Dodson, Jacob	1	1	4		11

NAME OF HEAD OF FAMILY.	Free white males of 16 years and upward, including heads of families.	Free white males under 16 years.	Free white females, including heads of families.	All other free persons.	Slaves.
Douglass, Jesse	1		1		1
Doyne, Robert	1	1	2		14
Dement, Charles	2		4		6
Dement, Edward, Junʳ	1	3	2		1
Dement, Edward, Senʳ	1		2		1
Dent, Peter	3	1	2		5
Duley, Benjᵃ	2		3		
Dent, Henry, of Geo	2				10
Deakins, Edward	3	3	6		6
Dyer, Jeremiah	1	3	6		10
Dunning, Nathaniel	2				1
Darnell, Thomas	1	2	4		
Duggins, Robert	1	1	5		
Downs, William, Senʳ	3	1	5		3
Dixon, George	2	4	3		2
Dent, Capᵗ John	1	1	1		17
Dent, Marshall	1		2		21
Dixon, George, Junʳ	2		3		9
Dulany, Daniel	1	1	1		
Diment, John	1		3		
Downs, William, Junʳ	3	2	2		
De Jean, Alexdʳ	2		1		10
Dement, William	1	2	5		6
Dent, Ann	2	2	3		5
Day, Vinney (Mulatto)				4	
De Mar, Joshua	2	2	4		
De Mar, Francis	1	1	2		
De Mar, William	1	1	2		
Douglass, Benjᵃ, of Charles	1	5	4		2
Dorrett, Aaron	1	2	4		
Duggins, Robᵗ Jun	1				
Dent, Capᵗ Hezekiah	2	4	4		21
Dent, Thomas H	2	1	5		2
Dent, Michael	1	1	1		5
Dent, Joseph M	1	2	4		2
Dent, William	3		5		4
Dent, Gideon	1	1	3		8
Dent, John Brewer	1	1	3		1
Dent, Zachᵃ	1		2		3
Dent, Benjᵃ	1	2	3		
Dent, Titus	1	2	3		3
Davis, Abraham (Mulatto)				7	
Dent, Hatch of John	1	1	3		7
Dent, John, Senʳ	1				7
Dent, John, of Jnᵒ	1	1			7
Davis, Eleanor			1		
Davis, Zachariah	2		5		12
Davis, Lyddia	1		3		
Davis, Jesse (Carpenter)	1				
Darnal, Catherina Mulatto				1	
Davis, George	1	2	3		
Dent, Henry (Newport)	1				2
Davis, Randall	1	1	3		
Davis, Joseph	2		2		
Davis, William	2		2		
Davis, Philip	1	1	2		10
Dyson, Gerrard	1	5	4		1
Davis, Benjamin, Senʳ	4		1		24
Davis, William, Junʳ	1	2	5		1
Dent, Revᵈ Hatch	1	3	4		11
Dement, Edward	1		2		19
Dement, John	1	1	3		1
Davis, Kenelm	1	1	3		
Dyson, Geo	2	1	2		8
Davis, Eliza	2		4		
Dyson, Bennett	2		4		18
Dent, George, Esqʳ	1	2	8		20
Delozier, John, of George	2	2	2		
Dean, George	2		1		
Delozier, John, of John	1				
Day, William (Mulatto)				1	
Day, Henrietta (Mulatto)				3	
Demar, John	1	2	5		
Demar, Daniel	2	3	2		
Davis, Elizabeth	2		4		1
Davis, Jeremiah	1	3	4		
Dent, Eleanor	1		3		31
Douglass, Joseph	1	1	6		10
Dutton, Zachᵃ	2	1	5		3
Dorrett, William	2		4		
Diggs, Ann of Jnᵒ	2		3		14
Dooley, Thomas	1	2	3		1
Dutton, Notley	1				20
Dutton, Notley, Junʳ	1	3	3		2
Dutton, Gerrard	3		3		2
Dunnington, Peter	3	2	2		1
Dunnington, William, Junʳ	1	1	3		
Davis, Richard, of John	1	2	3		
Delozier, Thoˢ	2	2	5		1
Dyal, Willᵐ (Overˢ for Geo. Mason)	2	3	4		10

NAME OF HEAD OF FAMILY.	Free white males of 16 years and upward, including heads of families.	Free white males under 16 years.	Free white females, including heads of families.	All other free persons.	Slaves.
Dyal, Joseph	1	1	2		
Davis, James, of Henry	2	2	2		5
Dent, Warren, Esqʳ	1		4		34
Davis, Isaac	1		2		2
Donnison, Joseph	3				
Dent, George (Nanjemoy)	2	1	9		38
Dunnington, Rebecca	2		5		
Dunnington, Chloe			5		
Dunnington, George	2	3	5		15
Dunnington, James	1		3		8
Dunnington, William, of Wᵐ	1	2	3		2
Dunnington, William, Senʳ	1		1		10
Dunnington, Francis	1	4	3		5
Evans, Hezekiah	1	1	1		
Edelen, Francis, Junʳ	1		3		3
Edelen, Joseph	1	1	2		
Edelen, John	2	6	3		15
Evans, Thomas	1	1	1		1
Evans, Elisha (Overseer for Jˢ Simms)	1				20
Evans, John	1				
Enias, Charles	3		1		
Edelen, Basil	2	2	2		21
Easten, Clem (Mulatto)				1	
Edelen, John B	1	1	3		10
Edelen, Jane	1		2		2
Edelen, Richard	2	1	3		30
Estep, Richard	1	3	2		6
Estep, John	1	4	1		4
Edwards, Hezekiah	3	2	5		1
Edelen, James	2	2	4		4
Edelen, Francis	1	2	4		7
Edelen, Oswald	1	1	2		7
Edelen, Susanna			3		6
Edelen, Edward	1	3	1		11
Edwards, Sarah		1	8		3
Easton, Samuel (Mulatto)				1	
Eliett, Thomas	1		2		
Eglinton, Barnaby	2		3		
Eanis, David	2		1		
Eliett, Thomas	2		1		
Evans, Hezekiah	1				12
Evans, Jesse	1	2	4		
Eliett, Richard	1	2	1		
Elgin, Robert	1	3	4		8
Elgin, William, Senʳ	6		3		29
Elgin, Francis	2		1		4
Ferguson, Robert	3				4
Fernandez, Chloe			3		13
Franklin, Zephᵃ, Junʳ	1	1	1		3
Featt, Jane (Free Negro)				1	
Fowke, Gerrard	1	2	3		49
Franklin, William, Junʳ	1	2	3		2
Flurry, William	1	2	4		1
Fowke, Roger	1	3	2		13
Farrell, James	1	3	4		
Franklin, Francis B	1	1	1		29
Fitzgerald, Thoˢ	1				
Freeman, Nathan	2	1	2		19
Flowers, David	1	1	2		2
Ferguson, Jonathan	2		4		
Ford, Ann			2		13
Freeman, Moab	2	2	2		
Freeman, James	1		1		
Ford, John, Senʳ	2		4		16
Farrell, Charles	1	5			
Frazer, Ann			3		
Fendall, Mary		1	3		13
Franklin, John, Senʳ	1		3		
Fenwick, James	2	4	2		50
Freeman, Richard	1	1	4		
Ford, Ninian (Mulatto)				2	
Ferguson, Sarah			3		3
Farrand, Elizabeth			5		
Farrand, Zephaniah	1	2	1		1
Ferrand, Timothy	1	2	3		
Franklin, William, Senʳ	1		3		1
Franklin, Edward	1		1		
Franklin, Priscilla			1		15
Franklin, James	1	1	2		3
Franklin, Zephaniah	4		3		10
Franklin, William, Junʳ	4	1	3		2
Flurry, Edward	4		2		1
Flurry, John	1	3	2		1
Flurry, Edward, Junʳ	1	2	5		2
Franklin, Hezekiah	1	3	2		3
Farrell, John	3		1		
Fowler, Ann		1	2		21
Fendall, Samuel	1	2	3		5
Fisher, John C	1		3		
Farr, John	1				
Farr, William	1		2		7

CHARLES COUNTY—Continued.

NAME OF HEAD OF FAMILY.	Free white males of 16 years and upward, including heads of families.	Free white males under 16 years.	Free white females, including heads of families.	All other free persons.	Slaves.
Fearson, Walter	1	2	3		
Fearson, Joseph	1	1	1		39
Friend, Daniel	1		5		3
Ford, Chandler	2	2	7		17
Fendall, Benjamin	1	3	3		26
Franklin, Noah	1	3	1		
Fairfax, Sarah	2	2	4		1
Frawner, Cecily (Mulatto)				2	
Ford, Phillis (Free Negro)				1	
Flannagin, Barton	1	4	3		4
Fulcer, William	1	2	4		
Fitzgerald, John	1	1	3		
Fowler, Elizabeth		2	2		
Flannagan, Ann		1	4		1
Fleming, Mary	1	2	4		15
Forbes, John	7	3	3		68
Goodrick, Mary, Junr			3		
Gilpin, Thomas	1	3	4		10
Green, Henry	1	6	2		8
Green, Clare	1		1		
Gray, Sarah			5		
Garner, Charles	3		1		12
Green, Peter	2	1	5		7
Garner, John	2	1	5		6
Goodrick, Charles	1				2
Goodrick, Mary, Senr			1		
Gray, Hannah			2		31
Gray, Joseph	2	3	4		9
Garber, Bennett	1				
Green, Eliz	2		2		14
Griffin, William S	1	1	2		2
Griffin, John	2	4	3		
Gray, James	2		2		1
Gray, William	1	2	3		1
Goodrick, Walter	2		1		10
Green, Charles, Senr	1				11
Green, Giles, Senr	2				11
Green, Giles, Junr	1	2			5
Griffin, Lancelot	1	1			5
Griffin, Ann		1	5		5
Griffin, Sarah			5		5
Griffin, James	1	1	2		
Green, John, of Francis	1		4		1
Glasgow, John	1		3		
Glasgow, Thomas	1		3		
Green, William	1		2		
Green, Nicholas	2		1		16
Gambra, Richard	2	2	1		
Gates, James	1		6		
Green, Melchizedec	1		1		
Gates, Leonard	2		4		
Guy, William, Senr	2	1	4		2
Guy, John	1	3	6		
Guy, William, Junr	2	1	5		
Griffiths, Thomas			6		
Gates, Joanna			3		
Green, Austin	2	1	2		14
Grant, Eliz		1	2		1
Green, Eliz	2		1		4
Gibbons, Francis	1	4	4		
Gill, Adam	1		3		
Gates, William	1	3	2		
Gittings, Thomas	1	1	3		
Gardner, Ignatius	1				14
Gardner, Capt John	1				10
Gardner, Richard	2	3	3		14
Gibson, John	2	1	5		1
Grify, Mary			1		5
Grindall, William	1		1		11
Gladding, Robert	1		3		10
Gill, Lydia		1			10
Garner, Joseph	1		3		15
Gardner, Charles	1		3		5
Gardner, Francis	1	1	3		17
Gardner, Henry	1				4
Gibbons, Nehemiah	1	5	5		2
Gardner, William	1	3	1		14
Gibbons, Jeremiah	1	3	2		32
Gibbons, Thomas	1		1		11
Gibbons, William	1		5		
Guy, Francis		2	8		
Gates, Edward	1	2	4		8
Gill, Robert	1	3	4		
Good, Ann			4		
Good, Oswald	1	1	5		
Gill, John	2		6		
Glasgow, Allen	1		1		
Goodrick, Eliz			8		
Gray, George (Newport)	1		3		
Golding, Mary			3		1
Golding, Robert	2	3	5		
Gray, Margaret			1		
Gray, John N	2	1	2		1
Gray, Jeremiah	2	1			11

NAME OF HEAD OF FAMILY.	Free white males of 16 years and upward, including heads of families.	Free white males under 16 years.	Free white females, including heads of families.	All other free persons.	Slaves.
Gray, Williamson (Nanjemoy)	2	2	1		
Glover, Philip	2		2		4
Gwinn, Benjn (Jne Clegget, Overseer)	1				15
Gwinn, Eliz			2		10
Joy, Joseph	3		4		1
Gibson, John, of Wm	1				9
Goose, James (Mulatto)				1	
Garner, Capt. Hezekiah	1	2	3		11
Gray, Edward	1	2	3		
Gray, (Serjt) Benjn	1				4
Gardner, Jane		2	2		
Gardner, George	2	3	1		5
Gray, George (Nanjemoy)	1		3		
Groves, John	1	2	6		
Groves, William	1	2	3		
Green, John (at Meeks Mill)	1	2			
Garland, William (Nanjemoy)	1		3		48
Gray, Andrew	2	2	4		
Gardner, Theophilus	1		2		
Griffiths, John	1		2		
Groves, Abednego	1		2		
Griffin, Richard	1		2		
Green, Samuel	1	1			
Griffiths, Zachariah	1	1	4		
Griffiths, John, Senr	1	2	6	1	1
Gilbert, Joseph	1		2		
Groves, Eliz			2		
Griffin, John (Nanjemoy)	1		2		
Hayley, Sarah (Mulatto)					5
Harley, Jonathan	1	1	1		
Hays, Vinney		3	2		1
Howard, Benjamin	2	3	3		1
Hall, Richard (Mulatto)				6	
Hamilton, Bennett	2	3	6		13
Hartsgraves, George	2	1	6		13
Hunt, William	1		2		
Hamilton, Alexander	1	1			
Hanson, John, of Jno	2				14
Hay, William, Senr	3	1	3		9
Hay, Thomas	3	1			
Hayley, Dorothy			3		
Hanson, Walter, Junr	1	1	1		13
Hunt, Joseph	2	8	4		1
Hunt, Mishach	1		1		
Hanson, Theophilus	1	2	3		23
Higden, Frans, Senr (Newport)	2	1	6		6
Hopewell, Thomas	3	3	2		13
Hutchinson, George	1	2	4		27
Hanson, Saml, of Wm	1	1	2		9
Hawkins, Francis	1		1		13
Haslip, Samuel	1	3	3		8
Harrison, Thomas	2	1	2		12
Hand, George (Mulatto)					1
Hand, John (Mulatto)				1	
Hanson, Samuel, of Walter	1				4
Hicks, Thomas	1	1	2		
Hill, Lydia		1	1		
Huton, George	2	1	4		14
Hawkins, Alexdr H. S	1	1	4		21
Holden, James			2		4
Holden, Chloe			2		
Hawkins, Elizabeth	2	2	3		115
Hawkins, Smith	1		1		
Hanson, John, Senr	1		3		12
Hanson, Henry M	1				7
Hawkins, Susanna					11
Hawkins, Jane			1		5
Hawkins, Caleb	1	1	4		4
Hill, Leonard	1	1	2		2
Harboard, James	1	1	3		4
Harley, Henry (Mulatto)				5	
Hanson, Hoskins	1	3	4		32
Hungerford, Ann (Mulatto)				2	
Hamilton, Patrick	2		1		6
Hamilton, Edward	1	2	4		14
Hanson, Major Samuel					
Hawkins, Catherine (Newport)			1		9
Halkerston, William	1				
Haydon, Joseph	1		3		
Huntington, John	1	1	4		2
Haydon, James	2	4	4		2
Hindman, John	2				2
Hennekin, John	2	1	3		3
Huntington, William	1				
Huntington, Edward	1	1	2		
Hall, John	1	1	2		1

NAME OF HEAD OF FAMILY.	Free white males of 16 years and upward, including heads of families.	Free white males under 16 years.	Free white females, including heads of families.	All other free persons.	Slaves.
Hampton, Casey	1	1	5		39
Hawkins, Ann			5		3
Howell, Mary Ann			3		
Hamilton, Ignatius	2	6	4		
Harvin, Thomas	2	5	4		
Hunt, James	1	2	3		2
Howell, Samuel	1		5		
Howell, Mary			1		65
Hagan, Jonathan	1	1	1		
Hunt, Jonathan	1	1	6		
Hill, Joseph	1	1	3		2
Hunt, Silvester	1	1	1		
Hetchinson, James	1	6	2		
Hanson, Walter, Senr, Esqr	2		4		20
Hagan, Henry	1	2	2		45
Hatcher, John			5		1
Hanson, Samuel, Senr, Esqr			2		26
Hutchinson, William	1				
Hall, Elizabeth			3		6
Hamilton, Duke	2		5		3
Hughs, Charles	1	3	3		
Hunter, David	1		2		
Hicks, John (Mulatto)					1
Henderson, James	1				
Hickey, Francis	1	1	3		2
Hazard, Michael	1	3	8		
Hagan, Ralph	4		4		7
Hagan, Benjamin	3		5		1
Higden, William	1	2	2		
Hill, Thomas	1		4		
Higdon, Richard, Junr	1	1			
Hamersley, Francis, Newport (Bennett Warthen, Overseer)					
Higdon, Leonard B	3	3	3		4
Hardman, Thomas	1				
Hill, William (Mulatto) Newport				6	
Hancock, William	1	4	7		2
Hancock, Abraham			3		
Hill, Monica			1		
Harvin, Zephaniah & Henry Parker Apprentice to the said Harvin	2				
Holland, John	2	3	1		
Hobbs, Isaac	1	1	1		
Harvin, Allen	1	3	1		7
Hagan, Joseph, of Wm	1	1	2		4
Hagan, Joseph, of Jno	1		1		
Hagan, William, of Wm	1				
Harvin, Roswell		2			
Harvin, William	1		3		
Hagan, James, of Igns	1		3		1
Hagan, Benjamin (Newport)	1	2	4		
Harrison, William (Newport)	1	2	4		10
Hunt, Elijah	2	2	2		
Hilton, Thomas	3		4		
Higgs, George	2	2	4		
Higdon, John B	2		3		
Huntington, Luke	1	3	7		1
Haslip, John, of Henry	1		1		1
Haslip, Henry	1	2	4		
Howard, Thomas G	1		1		
Hart, Michael	1	2	3		3
Haslip, John, of Robert	1		1		
Haslip, Robert, Senr	1		3		11
Hifield, Thomas	1				5
Hubbard, Edward	1	2	5		5
Hancock, Josias	1				5
Higgs, Jonathan	2	1	3		31
Hamersley, Henry					
Hand, Jane (Mulatto)				6	
Hargus, Joseph	2				5
Hungerford, Jane			3		13
Hungerford, Thomas	3	1	3		19
Harris, Thomas (Pickawaxen)	1	4	4		24
Hancock, Thomas	1		3		7
Hill, William (Mulatto) Port tobacco				8	
Harley, Sarah			1		
Haslip, Richard	2		6		
Haywood, Samuel	2		2		
Howard, John	1	1	4		3
Halford, John (Free Negro)				1	
Hudson, Richard	2		2	1	
Hyfield, Frederick	1				5
Harrison, Revd Walter	1				21
Harrison, Joseph White	1		7		5
Hamilton, Eleanor Ann	1		7		5

CHARLES COUNTY—Continued.

NAME OF HEAD OF FAMILY.	Free white males of 16 years and upward, including heads of families.	Free white males under 16 years.	Free white females, including heads of families.	All other free persons.	Slaves.
Harrison, Grace				5	30
Harrison, Ann	1	1	2		19
Hatcher, Ignatius	1	3	3		1
Hamilton, William (Nanjemoy)	1		2		
Hanson, Samuel, of Saml, Junr	1	1	1		5
Hudson, Caleb	1	1	1		4
Johnson, John	1	1	3		
Jackson, William (Mulatto)					13
James, John	2	1	2		
Jackson, James (Mulatto)				1	
Jenkins, Mary	1		2		12
Jackson, Zachariah (Mulatto)			1		
Jenefer, Doctor Daniel	2	1	3		38
Johnson, Ann	2		1		8
Jameson, Benj	1				15
Jameson, John	1	4	2		2
Jenkins, Edward	2		5		14
Jenefer, Danl, of St Thomas Jenefer, his Quarter Port Tobo Parish, Edwd Herrick, Overseer					20
Johnson, Archibald	2				12
Johnson, Walter	1	2	3		4
Johnson, Rachael		1	2		
Johnson, Hezekiah	3	4	3		12
Jameson, Walter	1	1	4		25
Jenkins, George	2	1	4		16
Jackson, Samuel (Mulatto)				4	
Jackson, Barton (Mulatto)				2	
Jackson, John (Mulatto)				4	
Jones, William (Nanjemoy)	3	4	2		
Jones, Richard	1	1	2		
Jones, James	1	2	2		1
Johnson, Joseph	1		5		2
Johnson, Susanna			5		2
Jones, William, Junr	1	2	3		
Jackson, Susanna (Mulatto)				4	
Jackson, John B. (Mulatto)				2	
Jenkins, William	1		2		
Jameson, Samuel	1				5
Jameson, Henry J	2		2		
Jameson, Ralph	1				7
Jameson, Sarah	1		3		26
Jameson, Leonard	1		5		3
Johnson, John, Senr	2	3	4		12
Johnson, John, Junr	1		3		1
Johnson, James	1		3		13
Jackson, Abednego (Mulatto)				4	
Jameson, Henry	2				2
Johnson, Jacob (Nanjemoy)	1	1	4		
Jenkins, Thomas (Cob Neck)	2	6	2		20
Jones, Samuel	1	3	3		20
Jones, William	1	3	3		6
Joy, Ann			3		
Jenkins, Abednego			3		5
Jones, John Court, Esqr	3		1		
Jenkins, John (Cob Neck)	2	2	3		
Jenkins, William	1	1	1		
Johnson, William (Posey's Mill)	1				
Jones, Benjamin	2	2	2		
Jenkins, William (Mulatto)				9	
Jones, Joseph	1	4	2		
Johnson, James (Millwright)	1	1	1		
Jackson, Thomas	3	3	2		3
Jenkins, Elevin	1		2		3
Husk, Elizabeth	2	1	5		
Hurry, John	1	1	2		3
Hurry, William	1	2	1		
Howard, John	1		4		
Harris, John, Junr	2		2		
Hannon, Henry	1	2	2		
Hannon, Walter	1		2		
Kersey, Mary			4		
Kellow, Thomas	1	1	4		3
Kitchen, William	1		2		
King, William	1	2	1		
Kennaham, John	1	6	1		1

NAME OF HEAD OF FAMILY.	Free white males of 16 years and upward, including heads of families.	Free white males under 16 years.	Free white females, including heads of families.	All other free persons.	Slaves.
King, John	2		3		7
Keech, George	2		3		10
King, Jane			1		5
Kerrick, Edward	1	1	5		1
Kersey, Daniel M	1		1		1
Keech, George, Junr	1		1		
Kidwell, Thomas	1		2		
Kennyham, Patrick	1		2		
Kendrick, Zachariah	1	1	2		4
Kennia, Ignatius	1		2		
King, Aquila	1	3	3		4
Kennia, John, Senr	1	3	4		1
Keech, Margaret			4		1
Kirkpatrick, William	1		1		2
King, Rebecca	1		5		15
King, Williamson	1		3		7
Kennedy, William	1	1	4		5
Kennedy, Clement	2		4		11
Kelbard, Thomas	2		4		
Kelbard, John	1		3		4
King, Benjamin (Nanjemoy)	1	1	2		1
Laymond, Charles S	2	1	6		
Lindsay, William	2		7		
Layman, John C	3		2		
Latimer, James, Junr	2		5		
Lovelace, William	2	6			8
Latimer, Judith			2		14
Lowe, Ann		1	2		3
Luckett, Samuel, Junr	1	3	3		4
Lomax, Thomas	2		5		
Lamaster, William	2	1	1		
Luckett, Notley	2	1	5		
Lewis, George	1	5	2		
Lawson, Robert	1				48
Luckett, Benjamin	1		3		
Lanham, Moses	1	1	3		
Luckett, Joseph	3				8
Latimer, Ann	1		3		
Laymond, Capt John	3		2		
Layman, William	1		4		
Lewis, Benjamin	2		3		2
Luckett, George	2	4	1		2
Linkin, Eleanor (Mulatto)				3	2
Lomax, Benjamin	1	6			
Lanham, Sarah		1	1		
Luckett, Ignatius, of John	1				1
Lewis, John	1	3	3		
Labrador, John	1		2		
Luckett, Thomas	1	1	6		11
Langley, John (Fuller)	2	4	3		
Lomax, Luke	1	4			
Leigh, William	1	2	3		
Leigh, George, Esqr	1		1		12
Lenkin, Townly (Mulatto)				6	
Lenkin, Henly (Mulatto)				6	
Lush, William				7	
Love, Samuel	1		1		
Langley, William	2	3	3		
Langley, Joseph	2	5	3		
Lyon, John	1	3	4		
Letcher, Leonard	2	2	4		5
Lyon, Henry	2	2	5		9
Leech, Thomas	1	2	2		
Levi, Anthony	1		3		
Lyon, Leonard	2	2	3		10
Lyon, James	2	3	7		4
Lomax, John (Nanjemoy)	2	1	5		
Latimer, Ann (Widow of Marcus)	4	2	5		15
Laidler, Robert	1	1	3		13
Lovelin, Moab	1		3		
Lomax, Stephen	1		1		
Lancaster, John, Junr	1	3	2		13
Lancaster, Thomas	1		2		24
Langley, Joseph (Cob Neck)	3	2	5		11
Lancaster, Joseph	3		5		14
Lancaster, John, Senr	5	1	2		53
Laidler, John	1		3		9
Luckett, Thomas, of Thomas	1				1
Luckett, Margaret	1		5		13
Luckett, Samuel, of Igns	1	2			
Lutwyche, Thomas	1		1		12
Landergin, Thomas	1	1	1		1
Lazarus, Mary (Free Negro)				1	
Maddox, Cornelius	1	2	3		
Merrick, Thomas D., Esqr	2		1		6

NAME OF HEAD OF FAMILY.	Free white males of 16 years and upward, including heads of families.	Free white males under 16 years.	Free white females, including heads of families.	All other free persons.	Slaves.
Miller, Christopher	1		4		
McBride, John	1				
Matthews, Ignatius	8		1		15
Moore, Aaron	3				1
McLaurin, Jane			1	2	
Miles, Walter	2	1	2		6
Maddox, Hendley	2	1	2		
Mankin, Richard T	1	1	2		5
McCray, Philip	1		3		1
Moreland, Stephen	1	1	6		
Martin, Michael	3		1		9
Moreland, Richard	1		4		12
Moreland, William	3	7	2		6
Morris, William	4	2	5		2
McDaniel, Isaac	2				2
Mudd, James, Senr	2		1		4
Macpherson, Samuel	3				8
Munro, Thomas	2	3	2		1
Morris, Jacob	3				7
Maddox, Susanna			1	2	
McBane, William	2	3	6		2
Mudd, John, Junr, of James	3		1		
Manning, Walter	3		1		4
McDaniel, Zachariah	3	1	4		17
Manning, Deborah	1	1	2		6
Mayhall, John (Mulatto)				1	
Morrison, William	1		5		1
Mitchell, Samuel	1	2			1
Mayhall, Robert (Mulatto)				9	
Meekhum, Samuel	1		3		
Millar, Alexander	1		1		
Mitchell, Bennett	1	5	5		23
Mitchell, Rachael					11
Maddox, Elizabeth	1		3		1
Muncaster, James	1	4	4		13
Millstead, Matthew	3	6	3		
Macpherson, Walter, Junr	2	1	2		8
Maddox, Hendley, of Ben	2	6	4		2
Mudd, Smith	2	2	5		3
Miles, William	1	2	6		
Murray, Philip A	2	3	5		
Macpherson, John					16
Macpherson, Capt William	1	3	6		22
Martin, Thomas	2	3	3		6
Mudd, Joshua	2		3		12
Murray, William	2	3	2		
Miller, John	1	2			8
Moran, Luke	1		2		
Money, Isaac	1	2	2		
Marshall, Samuel	1				3
Martin, Zachariah	2	1	4		12
Martin, Leigh	1		1		10
Monk, Jane (Mulatto)			3		1
Manry, Ignatius	1	3	4		
MacDaniel, Charles	2		4		2
Maddox, Henry	1	1	5		13
Molyneaux, Revd Roberts					64
Miles, Edward	6		4		12
Miles, Nicholas	2	2			
Morris, James, Senr	1		3		
Moreland, Henry A	1				
Murphy, Hezekiah	1		3		
Maddox, Notley, Senr	2	1	3		7
Montgomery, Eleanor	2		1		
MacGlue, Elizabeth		1	4		
Macpherson, Lieut Mark & Company	26				
Miles, Joseph	1	2	6		6
Mudd, Jeremiah	1		7		1
Muschett, Mungo	1	1	2		17
MacCoy, Mary			7	1	
MacDaniel, Theophilus	1	1	7		
Mitchell, Captain John	2	1	5		21
MacBane, John	1		5		
MacDaniel, Archibald	1		5		
McDaniel, Allen	1	2	7		3
MacDaniel, Daniel	2	1	6		3
Moreland, Zachariah	2		8		
Middleton, Horatio	1				20
McEvoy, John	1		1		
Marshall, Thomas, Senr	2		3		14
Marshall, John, of Thomas	1		1		
Macpherson, Basil	1		1		5
Marshall, Thomas Hanson	1	1	3		49
Munroe, Thomas	1	2	3		1
Munroe, John		3	4		
Macpherson, Walter, Senr	2	3	6		23

CHARLES COUNTY—Continued.

NAME OF HEAD OF FAMILY.	Free white males of 16 years and upward, including heads of families.	Free white males under 16 years.	Free white females, including heads of families.	All other free persons.	Slaves.
Moore, James	1		1		13
Moreland, Samuel	1	1	2	4	
Moreland, Mary	1		2	4	
Miles, James	1		2	6	
Middleton, James, Senr	2		4		49
Middleton, James, Junr	1	1			14
MacDaniel, Nathaniel	1		3		
Montgomery, Joshua	2	1	7		
Montgomery, James	1	2	2		
Moreland, Jacob	1	3	4	2	
Miles, Eleanor	1		2		
Miles, Edward, of Henry	2	3	5		1
Miles, Barton	1				
Maddox, Edward (Nanjemoy)	2	3	1		3
Maddox, Henry (Nanjemoy)	1		1	3	7
MacDaniel, Rebecca		1	4		
Middleton, Theodore	1	2	1		5
Middleton, Smith	1				10
Mudd, Mary	1		5		6
Moore, Matthew, Senr	1				
Montgomery, Mary	1		3		1
Montgomery, John			4		
Montgomery, Henrietta			3		
Montgomery, Rebecca		2	3		
Miles, Nicholas	1	1	2		
Miles, Henry	1	1	2		5
Mudd, Roswell	1	1	3		
Moreland, Isaac	1	3	5		
Moreland, Theophilus	1	2	3		
Moreland, Patrick	2		1		2
Martin, Mary	2	1	4		
Moreland, Richard, Junr	2	1	9		
Montgomery, Thomas	1	2	3		
Moreland, Philip	1		2		
Moreland, Joseph	1		2		2
Moreland, James	1	2	2		
Mahorney, Millborne	1		2		
Moore, Matthew, Junr	1	3	5		
Moore, Elijah	1	3	4		1
Montgomery, Barnaby	1	3	3		
Mahorney, Basil	1	1	2		
MacDonnaugh, James M.	1		1		8
McCoy, Johnston	1		2		8
Mudd, James, Junr		3	2		7
Macpherson, William H.	1		7		11
Macpherson, Kitty G.	1	4			9
MacAtee, Susanna			2		
MacAtee, Mary	3		2		2
Marshall, Phillip	1	1	3		12
Mohorn, Velindar			2		
McAtee, John, Senr	2		4		4
McAtee, Thomas, of John					
McLean, William	1	3	2		1
Mason, Wm Pomonkey (Qua. James Lorney Overseer)	1				5
Marbury, Francis H.	2	1	1		10
Marbury, Henry	1	1	2		6
Moreland, William	1		3		
Mudd, Richard	3	1	4		11
Mudd, Bennett	1				
Mudd, Henry J. (of Thos)	2		3		12
Mudd, Mary	1		5		11
Mudd, Henry T.	1	3	3		7
McDaniel, Jonathan	2	1	4		
Mudd, Ann	1		2		
Mudd, Henry, Senr	2		5		9
McGruder, Mary (her Qua^r no Overs^r)					7
Moran, John, Senr	1		3		
Maddox, James, Senr	1	1	2		
Moran, Severil	3	2	2		13
Moran, Gabriel	4		3		11
Moran, Andrew	4		3		10
Macpherson, Elizabeth		1	4		
Morris, Ann			4		
Marshall, Benjamin	2		6		
Mollahorn, John W.	2		4		
Murphy, Daniel, of Ja^s	2	5	4		
Mattingley, Ralph	1	1	2		
Mudd, Bennett, Nport	1				
Mason, John	1	1	1		
Macpherson, Capt Alexander	1	3	5		18
Midley, John	1	3	3		12
Morris, Joshua	1	1	3		
Montgomery, William	3	1	2		1
Montgomery, Joseph	3	2	6		
Murphy, Walter	3		1		1
Massey, Mary			2		
Montgomery, Charles	1	2	1		1
Moore, Jane			3		
Murphy, Nathaniel	1		1		9
Molton, Joseph	1	4	2		8
Molton, George	1	2	2		4
Moran, Jonath^e	1		4		4
Moran, Charles	2	1	3		17
Moran, John	2	1	6		7
Monroe, John			4		
Molton, Elizabeth			4	2	7
Murphy, Samuel	1	3	3		3
Matthews, Thomas	1	3	3		6
Murphy, Daniel, Senr	4	2	5		9
Mattingley, Zach.	1		3		
Mankin, William, Senr	3	1	3		
Maddox, Noah	3	1	3		2
Mason, W^m (his qua^r, Jno Delozier, overseer)					20
May, William	2		6		
Maddox, Henry (Nanjemoy)	1	2	3		1
McConchie, William	4	3	7		50
Marshall, Robert	1	2	3		16
Mastin, Huse	1	1	3		26
Mahorney, Clement	1	2	3		1
Maddox, Eleanor		1	4		11
Minitree, Paul	2	2	4		8
Marshall, Thomas	1		4		13
Maddox, John (Pickawaxen)	2	1	4		24
May, Richard	2	1	1		1
Marshall, John, Senr	2		4		23
Marshall, William, Senr	2		4		14
Read, Tobitha			3		2
Macmillion, William	2	3	3		
Martindale, Elizabeth	2		4		
Miller, George	2	1	1		
Muschett, Capt John	1	4	4		17
Millstead, Elizabeth		1	4		
Millstead, Samuel	2	4	5		
Millstead, Thomas	1	1	4		
Maddox, Samuel	1	2	4		2
Maddox, Basil			3		
Moredock, Samuel	1	1	3		
Maddox, John (Chickamuxen)	2	3	3		15
McAtee, Sarah			3		2
Macpherson, John, of Danl	3	1	4		
Marr, Martin	1		4		
Millstead, William	2		4		12
Maddox, John, of Jno.	2		3		2
Marstin, Jane	1	1	4		
Mason, Lott	1		5		3
Moredocke, James, Senr	1	3	4		
Maddox, James, of Ja^s	1	2	4		
Marshall, William, Junr	1		2		5
Macpherson, Samuel Hanson	3	1	3		12
Middleton, Samuel	1		3		32
Mason, Martin (Carpenter)	3		2		27
Meek, John B.	3		2		
Mitchell, William	2	1	3		
Maddox, Len.	2	2	3		
Mayhew, Catherine	2	4	2		5
Moredocke, Godfrey	2		2		1
McGregor, Walter	1		4		
Millstead, John B.	1	1	4		1
Moredock, William	2	1	4		
Moredock, William, Junr	1		1		
Maddox, Richard	1		5		
Maddox, Rhody	2	2	5		5
Martin, Allen	1		4		
McPherson, Daniel, of Daniel	1	1	4		
McLeannam, John	1	1	3		1
Millstead, Noah	1	2	4		
Mason, Richard	7	1			24
Mankin, Charles	2	3	5		14
Norder, William	1	1	3		1
Nally, Shadrac					
Nace, Negro, the property of Thomas Young, prince Geo. County, & his family					3
Newman, Edward			4		
Notier, Michael	1				
Nellson, Thomas	2	1	5		10
Knott, Justinian	2	5	4		4
Nettle, James F.	1	4	4		
Nally, Dennis	2		4		
Newman, William	2	4	4		1
Nally, Leonard	1	2	2		6
Nally, Gustavus	2	1	2		
Nally, Susanna	2		4		
Nottingham, Eleanor	2	3	4		
Noble, Zachariah	1		4		
Noble, William	1	1	2		1
Nally, William	1	2	7		
Nally, Barnaby			3		
Nally, Thomas			3		1
Nally, Thomas, Junr	2		2		3
Newman, William (Mulatto)				4	
Newbury, John	1		2		
Nellson, Joseph	2	2	7		2
Nellson, Frederick	1	1	1		3
Nicholson, Henry	1		5		
Nally, John	1	2	3		1
Nettle, Thomas	1		3		
Norwood, Garner	1	3	4		30
Neale, James	1	2	2		20
Neale, Bennett	1		3		
Neale, Edward	1	2	4		18
Neale, John (Cob neck)	3	1	4		18
Neale, Joseph (Cob neck)	2	3	7		13
Nellson, John	2	2	2		1
Neale, Sarah	1	2	2		
Nellson, Thomas, of Thos	1	2	2		2
Nally, Richard	1		3		
Noiry, Daniel	1	2	3		10
Nellson, Hannah (Mulatto)				1	
Ovenbread, William	1	2	2		
Ostree, Thomas	2	2	3		1
Ogle, Benjamin	2		1		
Ostree, Philip	1		2		
Owen Joseph		3	2		3
Owen, Elizabeth		1	6		9
Ogden, Jonathan	2		3		
Osborne, Thomas	1	3	2		2
Osborne, Rhody			2		1
Osborne, Jeremiah	1	3	3		
Osborne, Walter	1		1		2
Owen, Richard	1		3		18
Ogden, Benjamin	1	3	3		
Osborne, Henry	1	3	2		
Oden, John	2		3		
Oden, Isaac	1	5	3		2
Oliver, William			2		1
Oliver, James	1		1		
Othrington, Caleb (Mulatto)				8	
Oden, Elias	1		1		5
Posey, Henry of Humphrey	1	1	2		10
Oakley, John	1	4	3		2
Oakley, Joseph	1		5		1
Osbourne, Thomas, Junr	1		5		
Pickerell, Samuel	1	2	4		
Pickerell, Joseph	1		4		
Padgett, James	1		2		4
Power, Joseph	2		3		
Peers, Nicholas	2	2	4		4
Price, Thomas	2		4		4
Poston, William	1		6		
Permition, James	1		2		
Posey, Thomas	1		2		5
Posey, Henrietta			4		3
Power, Mary Ann		1	5		
Philips, Isabell			1		
Proctor, Leonard (Mulatto)				1	1
Penn, William (Nport)	1	2	3		1
Pye, Walter	2	2	1		14
Philpot, Hanson H.			4		5
Pyles, Revd Henry (N^port)	1		2		28
Parnham, John, Esqr	2	2	3		26
Proctor, James (Mulatto)				1	
Penn, Mark H.	2	1	3		
Power, John	1		5		9
Porteus, Martha			4		
Pickerell, John	1	5	4		
Padgett, Joseph	1		1		1
Padgett, Benj^s of W^m	1		4		
Padgett, Eleanor			4		1
Padgett, Benj^s of Ben.	1		2		
Padgett, Benj^s	1	5	2		
Padgett, John	1	2	3		
Padgett, Henry	1		3		1
Padgett, Eliz.	1	2	5		
Padgett, Jonathan	1		3		
Padgett, Aaron	1		5		
Pye, Joseph	1		3		10
Pye, Charles	4		3		23
Perry, Sibba	1		3		
Peacock, John	1	1	1		6
Proctor, Thos & Samuel Collins (Mulattos)				12	
Pierce, Charles	1		4		1
Pierce, John	1	2	2		2

CHARLES COUNTY—Continued.

NAME OF HEAD OF FAMILY.	Free white males of 16 years and upward, including heads of families.	Free white males under 16 years.	Free white females, including heads of families.	All other free persons.	Slaves.
Parker, Jonathan	2	1	3	...	3
Power, Jesse	1	1	3	1	...
Paddy, John	1	2	1	5	...
Perry, Edward		4	5		...
Perry, James A	1				...
Perry, Hugh (Benedict)	1	4	4	...	3
Proctor, Charles (Mulatto)					7
Penny, Ann (Mulatto)					1
Posey, Elizabeth (Newport)	1		2		12
Proctor, Joseph (Mulatto)					6
Proctor, Francis (Mulatto)					6
Proctor, Michael (Mulatto)					1
Proctor, Eleanor (Mulatto)					2
Proctor, Thomas (Mulatto)					5
Proctor, Henry (Mulatto)					6
Poston, Benjamin	1	1	5	...	1
Proctor, Milley (Mulatto)					1
Proctor, Tenney (Mulatto)					1
Proctor, Isaac (Mulatto)					1
Proctor, Jennett (Mulatto)					1
Proctor, Elizabeth (Mulatto)					1
Proctor, Chloe (Mulatto)					1
Proctor, Jacob (Mulatto)					1
Paddison, John	1	1	2	...	
Poston, Priscilla	1	...	2	...	10
Poston, Mary	1	...	3	...	4
Poston, Bartholomew	1	...	1	1	1
Poston, Solomon	1	3	3	...	
Poston, John	1	1	2	...	4
Proctor, William (Mulatto)					5
Plummer, Judith	1	4	2	...	
Proctor, Susanna (Mulatto)					1
Penny, Sarah (Mulatto)					3
Price, Zachariah	1	1	3		13
Penn, Major Jerred	1	1	3		41
Penn, Mark	2	5	2		...
Penn, Stephen	1		4		...
Philpot, Elizabeth	2		2		...
Penn, John	1	1	7		2
Posey, Belain	1	6	3		23
Penn, John	1	1	5		...
Posey, Rhody	1	1	3		...
Posey, Benj, of Uzziah	1	1	3		...
Posey, Benj Y	1	1	3		7
Price, Henrietta	1	1	1		...
Posey, Thomas, of Thos	1	1	1		...
Posey, James	1		3		...
Posey, Elizabeth		1	3		...
Perry, Francis	1				...
Posey, Jacob	1		1		...
Posey, Francis	1				...
Picking, John	1	1	1		...
Posey, Mary Ann		1	5	3	2
Posey, Burdett	1	2	2		...
Perry, John	2				...
Posey, John	2				...
Perry, Robert	1	1	2		2
Posey, Rogor	1	2	1		...
Posey, George	1	3	2		...
Posey, Thomas	2		2		...
Posey, William	1	2	3		...
Perry, Mary			2		...
Posey, Humphrey	3	2	6		4
Picking, Sarah	1		2		...
Perry, Thomas	1	2	2		8
Posey, Uzziah	1	2	2		...
Perry, Hugh (Nanjemoy)	1	2	3		...
Philberd, John	1	1	3		1
Posey, Ann	1	1	3		...
Quade, Thomas	1	2	4		...
Queen, Walter	1	4	4		12
Queen, William	1		6		18
Ruston, James (Mulatto)					3
Russell, James	3	...	2	...	4
Russell, Thomas	1	1	1		4
Robinson, William (Son of Ben)	3	2	3	...	6
Ray, Charles (Mulatto)					4

NAME OF HEAD OF FAMILY.	Free white males of 16 years and upward, including heads of families.	Free white males under 16 years.	Free white females, including heads of families.	All other free persons.	Slaves.
Reeder, Richd R	1	1	5		21
Riney, James	1	1	3		5
Richardson, Josias W	1		3	4	
Robey, Zachariah	1	3	4		
Robey, Benjamin, of Richard	1	1	6		
Robey, John, of Richard	1		3		8
Robey, Samuel, of Richard	2	5	4		
Ridgate, Elizabeth		1	3		12
Robey, Hezekiah	1		2	1	
Robinson, William	1	1	4		
Robey, Alexander	2	4	3		5
Robey, Barrack	1	1	1		
Robey, Basil (Poor House)	6	8	20		9
Rains, Robert (Mulatto)				5	
Rock, Charity		2	4		2
Reed, Thomas	2	1	4		
Robey, Jesse	1		2	2	
Rogers, Robert	1	2	8	...	11
Ray, Daniel (Mulatto)				2	...
Reeves, Bennett, Newport	2	2	2		
Robertson, Mitchell	2	1	2		4
Reeves, William	1		1		5
Reeder, Benja	3		3		11
Ray, James (Mulatto)				5	...
Robey, Jeremiah	1		2	1	
Robey, Samuel, of John	1	1	1		
Robey, Lessly	1	1	4		6
Robey, John A	3	1	4		
Robey, Joseph	1	1	3		1
Robey, Jacob	1		3	1	
Robey, Leonard, Senr	2	1	4		
Robey, Richard, Senr	2	1	4		5
Robey, Barton, of Richd	2	1	4		
Robey, Thomas	2	4	4		2
Robey, William, Senr	1	4	2		
Robey, Aquila	1	2	6		5
Robey, John N	2	2	2		8
Reeves, Upgate	2	2	2		1
Robey, Penelope			3		
Rawlings, Sarah	1		2		
Reeves, Hezekiah	1	2	1		26
Robertson, James	1	2	2		5
Roberson, Benjn	1	1	4		4
Reeves, Courtney	1		2		31
Robey, William, of Richard	3	4	4		1
Richards, Richard	3	4	1		
Richardson, Mark	1	3	3		
Richards, William	1	1	3		
Roberts, Henry	1		5		
Reeder, John	1	3	5		
Ray, Thomas (Mulatto)				6	...
Richards, Samuel			2		2
Robey, John, of Josias	1		4		1
Roe, William	1	4	3		2
Rowland, John	3		3		
Robertson, Elijah	1		3		
Risen, Elizth			3		
Robey, Joshua	1		4		1
Richards, Thomas	2	1	6		6
Rawlings, Martha			3		
Rutter, Joseph	1		1		
Reeves, Leonard	1	3	3		
Reeves, Samuel	1	4	6		3
Robertson, William G	2	3	5		
Richardson, Luke	1	1	2		
Robertson, William (Pickawaxen)	1	2	5		1
Rebbitt, Francis	1	1	3		
Ratcliffe, John	1	4	3		
Reeves, James	1		3	2	
Rock, James	1				
Reeves, Thomas	1	4	9		
Russell, John	1	1	6		
Risen, Peter			3	3	
Risen, Ann		2	3		3
Renn, John	1	2	3		
Ratcliffe, James	1	1	4		2
Robertson, William (Nanjemoy)	2	2	5		1
Ratcliffe, Quinton			3		
Ratcliffe, Shadrac	2	2	3		
Ratcliffe, Joseph	3	5	6		
Risen, Chandler	1		4		
Ratcliffe, Samuel	1				
Ratcliffe, James (Carpenter)	1				
Ryan, Ignatius	2			5	32
Robertson, John	2	2	2	...	24
Rye, John	1	2	4		...

NAME OF HEAD OF FAMILY.	Free white males of 16 years and upward, including heads of families.	Free white males under 16 years.	Free white females, including heads of families.	All other free persons.	Slaves.
Risen, Philip	1		6		
Rye, Rawley	2	3	3		
Rye, William	1		4		
Risen, Lancelot	1	2	4		
Rice, William	3	1	1		
Rye, John	1	1	1		
Ratcliffe, Burdett	1	1	1		6
Ratcliffe, Ignatius	2	6	2		4
Ratcliffe, Francis	1		2	1	
Ratcliffe, Rhody	2	3			1
Rye, Warren	1	3	3		1
Ratcliffe, Winnefort	2		2		5
Shelton, John S	1	1			12
Sewall, Charles	2		2		27
Simpson, Ignatius	2	1	3		8
Stone, Thomas, Senr	1	2	3		15
Sandiford, Thomas	3		4	4	4
Smith, Sarah			1	1	1
Smith, Elizabeth	1		3		2
Stockett, Thomas	1	1	2		3
Semmes, Marmaduke		2	4		19
Stuart, Ignatius	1	1	2		1
Stonestreet, Edward	1	1	2		2
Smoot, Edward, Senr	1	1	4		19
Sanders, Thomas	1	1	5		
Smith, Walter	5	3	5		8
Smoot, Josias	1	3	1		22
Sanders, Edward	2	1	2		5
Stone, William, Senr	2	2	5		8
Sanders, John	2	3	7		9
Shurden, John	1		3		
Simpson, Thomas	1	1	1		9
Stewart, Henry	2		6		
Semmes, Ignatius	3	1	5		13
Smith, Josias	1		6	5	
Simpson, Charles	1	3	3		15
Semmes, Bennett B	1		3	1	6
Swann, Charity (Mulatto)				1	...
Swann, Elizabeth (Mulatto)				5	
Swann, Linder (Mulatto)				1	
Swann, Eliz, Junr (Mulatto)				1	
Semmes, Jame, of Thos	1		2		1
Stone, Hanson	2	1	2		10
Stone, David	2				9
Swift, Gordon (Virginia), no Overseer					7
Stone, Mary	1		2		23
Smallwood, Capt. Thomas	2	1	2		7
Smallwood, Ledstone, Junr					
Smallwood, William M	2	1	2		7
Stuard, Ann	1				
Shackorley, William	1		4		4
Smithson, William	1	4	3		
Semmes, William, Sen	1	2	4		1
Smoot, William B. (of Thos)	3	4	2		16
Scott, James	1	5	3		
Skiffington, Roger	1				
Smallwood, Ledstone, Senr	1	1	4		
Smallwood, Pryor, of Ledstone	2	1	7		1
Simpson, Henrietta			4		
Smallwood, Bean (of Pryor)	1				
Swann, William (Mulatto)				3	...
Scrogin, Dorothy			5	4	
Shikerley, Thomas	1		2		6
Shervin, Mary	3		1		19
Stone, John H., Esqr	3		6		24
Stone, Walter	3		2		
Semmes, Robert D	3	2			10
Semmes, Mary			4		7
Scott, John Day	1		4		7
Shepherd, Francis	3		5		7
Sly, Robert (Newport)	2	1			11
Smoot, Isaac	4		9		
Semmes, Mark	4	3	5		10
Sute, Walter	1	1	4		2
Scallion, John	1		3	3	
Scott, James (Newport)	1	3	3		5
Scott, Christian			3		8
Simpson, Catherina			3	3	
Simpson, Thomas (Newport)	1		2	1	2
Swann, Edward (Senr)	3	2	3		
Semmes, Thomas (Port Tobacco)	2	3	9		23
Smith, Henry	1	1	1		...

CHARLES COUNTY—Continued.

Name of head of family.	Free white males of 16 years and upward, including heads of families.	Free white males under 16 years.	Free white females, including heads of families.	All other free persons.	Slaves.
Smallwood, James	1	2	4		9
Simpson, Joseph	1	3	1		
Smith, James	1		4		3
Smith, Electius	1		1		3
Smith, Elizabeth	1	2	4		5
Smith, Basil	1	2	4		9
Sansbury, Isaac	5	2	6		9
Stuart, William	1	4	3		1
Simpson, Thomas	1	1			
Smallwood, Susanna	1		2		6
Smallwood, Walter	1				4
Smallwood, Henry	1		2		1
Smith, Thomas (Blacksmith)	3	2	5		
Smallwood, Ann			1		12
Smallwood, John, of James	1		2		
Spalding, Basil	2		4		19
Spalding, Edward	1		3		6
Spalding, Basil, Junr	1	1	2		4
Sinnett, (Major) Robert)	2		3		28
Swann, Samuel, Junr	2	1	3		2
Smith, Vernon	1	4	3		5
Sanders, Bennett	1	1	6		1
Steward, Philip	1				33
Smallwood, Ann (Widow of Jno)		1	4		3
Slater, Samuel	1		4		
Slater, John	1		6		1
Smallwood, Basil	1	1	2		1
Stone, John, Senr	1	1	2		9
Sullivan, John	1				
Smith, Clement	1	3	4		7
Stonestreet, Henry	2	3	3		17
Slater, William	1	3	1		5
Smith, Simon	1	3	6		3
Smallwood, Thomas, of Thos	1	1	6		
Smallwood, Hezekiah	1	1	4		1
Smallwood, Pryor, of Thos	1				
Smallwood, Bean, of Thos	1	2	4		
Savoy, William (Mulatto)				5	
Savoy, Archibald (Mulatto)				9	
Shaw, John (Pomonkey)	1	2	2		
Shaw, William (Pomonkey)	1	1	5		
Stoddert, Thomas	1		1		
Stoddert, Elizabeth			2		5
Stamp, John	1	1	3		1
Smith, Henry (Bryantown)	1	1	1		1
Smith, John (Benedict)	2		1		7
Smith, Jane			1		2
Smith, John L	1	2	2		
Shepherd, Philip	1	1	4		
Sothoron, Levin	3	1	3		13
Slye, John	1				
Sothoron, John	1				20
Smith, Charles S	1				10
Smith, Henry (of Charles)	2		1		14
Smith, Richard	1	3	1		
Shanks, John	1	1			3
Sothoron, Henry G. (his Quarter at Benedict: Leonard Branson, Overseer)					23
Smoot, John N	2		6		9
Smoot, Hendley	2	2	7		14
Scott, Crecy (Mulatto)				1	
Simms, John	4	2	4		1
Sinclair, Mary	2		4		3
Simpson, Rachael			2	1	
Savoy, Martha (Mulatto)				2	
Sute, John	1	2	5		1
Simpson, John L	1	1	3		1
Simmonds, Samuel					
Steward, Henry (Benedict)	1		3		
Sanders, Ann (Widow of Joshua)			2		28
Scott, Joshua (Mulatto)				3	
Spalding, Ignatius	2				15
Smoot, Arthur	1	2	4		5
Smoot, Barton	1	2	1		
Beager, Benjamin	1		1		
Semmes, Edward	1				5
Smoot, Mary			2		2
Shickleworth, John	1	1	4		
Smoot, Samuel	1		2		4
Savoy, Francis (Mulatto)				1	

Name of head of family.	Free white males of 16 years and upward, including heads of families.	Free white males under 16 years.	Free white females, including heads of families.	All other free persons.	Slaves.
Sothoron, Ann			1		9
Scallion, Peter	1	1	4		
Swann, James	2	3	2		
Swann, Chloe	1		3		1
Swann, Thomas	1		7		
Swann, Samuel H	1	1	1		1
Swann, Charles	1	1	5		
Somerville, Philip	1	1	2		
Swann, Thomas (Senr)	1	3	4		
Steward, George	1	1	2		4
Steward, Walter	1	6	4		
Smallwood, Mary	3	2	6		
Swann, Mary, Junr (Mulatto)				11	
Speake, John, Senr	1		2		
Sanders, Jordan	1	2	5		
Shaw, Sarah	1	1			
Stone, Matthew	1				5
Swann, Jennett (Mulatto)				4	
Smoot, Alexander	2	3	1		9
Smith, James	2	2	4		
Smith, John	2	1	3		1
Smoot, William, of Edward	2	3	4		10
Smoot, John, Senr	2	4	4		11
Smith, Elizabeth	1	1	1		6
Scrogin, Barton	1	1	2		
Simms, Mary (Pickawaxen)			5		6
Smith, John (Cob neck)	1	1	5		2
Shaw, William	3	1	6		7
Simpson, Jane (Pickawaxen)		1	4		4
Swann, William (at the mill)	3		2		14
Scott, John	1	1	3		2
Scott, Samuel	1		2		10
Shanna, James	1		4		
Smoot, William of Wills)	2	2	4		4
Sutherland, Ignatius	1	2	4		
Skinner, Jeremiah	2		5		5
Stromatt, Capt John	2		5		8
Speake, Hezekiah	1	1	3		1
Stoddert, Major William	1		1		23
Simms, Thomas (Nanjemoy)	1	5	1		7
Skinner, Walter	1	1	1		
Simms, Joseph (of James)	1	4	3		12
Sothoron, Walter	1	2	2		7
Skinner, Elisha	1	1	2		1
Smoot, Eleanor			2		
Smoot, Richard	1		3		
Steward, William (Nanjemoy)	2	4	6		1
Smallwood, (Genl) William	1	2	5	7	56
Speake, Capt Joseph	1		4		8
Speake, John T	1				9
Speake, Henrietta		1			9
Speake, Capt Frans	1	1	3		15
Skinner, Thomas (of William)	2	2	3		
Skinner, Thomas (of Thomas)	1	2	6		
Skinner, John, Senr	1	2	4		
Speake, Henry	3	1	4		13
Skinner, Edward	2	1	2		
Skinner, Jesse	1		1		
Skinner, James	1		4		6
Skinner, Manning	1		3		1
Simmons, Aaron	1		2		5
Smith, John (Nanjemoy)	1	2	3		1
Skinner, John (Junr)	1	2	3		
Shields, Thomas	1	3	7		
Skinner, Joseph, at Wm Jones	1				
Stone, Samuel, Senr	2	1	2		8
Sisson, Caleb	1		2		1
Smith, Eleanor (Mulatto)				4	
Skinner, Hezekiah	1	2	6		
Strange, Charlotta	1		1		24
Simms, James	2	5	1		18
Smoot, William Barton (of Charles)	1	2	4		26
Thompson, George (Shoemaker)	2		2		
Turner, John B., Esqr	1	3	2		1
Turner, Zephaniah	2	2	3		15
Tuson, Robert (Mulatto)				5	

Name of head of family.	Free white males of 16 years and upward, including heads of families.	Free white males under 16 years.	Free white females, including heads of families.	All other free persons.	Slaves.
Timms, Charles	2	3	3		2
Timms, John	4	3	6		2
Tier, William	2	1	3		9
Tier, Charles	2		2		8
Tier, Francis	2	1	2		5
Tier, Joseph	2	1			9
Thompson, Matthew	1	1	6		
Thompson, Joseph Green	1	1	2		21
Tier, Sarah (Mulatto)				1	
Tubman, Eleanor	1			1	10
Tubman, Samuel	1	1	2		8
Thompson, John B	1	2	2		25
Thompson, Joseph	2				
Taylor, William (Mulatto)				5	
Thompson, Thomas (Mulatto)				1	
Thompson, Alexander (Mulatto)				1	
Thompson, Mary (Mulatto)				4	
Tier, Ann	2	2	3		6
Taylor, James	1	2	3		6
Thompson, James	2	3	3		1
Thompson, George			2		4
Thompson, Ann			2		
Thompson, Ann (Junr)			2		
Turner, Samuel	4		5		3
Thompson, Thomas	1	3	7		
Tench, Joshua	1	1	4		3
Thompson, Smallwood	2	1	1		2
Thomas, John Mattoman	1	1	4		
Tench, Thomas	1	1	2		
Tyler, William	1	2	3		13
Thompson, Charles	1		1		6
Thompson, John (of George)	1	1	4		5
Thompson, James, of Jas	1	1	1		3
Turner, Jonathan	1	2	5		2
Taylor, John	1	1	1		
Tubman, Richard	4	2	3		13
Thompson, James	1				
Thompson, Leonard	2	4			1
Timpson, Benjamin	3		4		1
Thompson, John (Bryan Town)	1	2	2		1
Turner, William	1		3		12
Thomas, Kenelm	1	1	4		7
Taylor, Mary	2		3		
Thompson, Thomas	2	2	5		
Tubman, Henry (Quarter)					12
Thomas, Mary	1		1		6
Thomas, Nathaniel	1	1	2		7
Thomas, James, Junr	1	1	2		7
Thomas, James, Senr	1				8
Thomas, Catherina	2	2	5		4
Thompson, Henry (Mulatto)				6	
Thompson, William (Mulatto)				1	
Thompson, Joseph (Mulatto)				1	
Tench, Leonard	1		1		2
Turner, William (Junr)	1	2	2		2
Turner, John	1	1	1		
Turner, Williamson	1	1	9		
Turner, Randliff	3	2	9		1
Thompson, Ann (Mulatto)				1	
Thorn, Absalom	2	3	3		3
Thorn, Elizabeth	1	1	3		
Tippett, Ely	1	1	2		
Tubman, George	1	1	1		22
Thompson, Mary (Chickamuxen)			3		
Timms, Joseph	1	1	2		
Turvey, Joshua	1				
Taylor, Henry	1	1	3		1
Thomas, Philip	1	3	5		10
Tomkins, John	1		4		1
Thompson, Joseph	2	6	3		19
Thomas, William (Nanjemoy)	1				
Thompson, Leonard (Nanjemoy)	2		4		1
Taylor, William (Chickamuxen)	1		5		13
Thompson, Thomas (Chickamuxen)	2	4	3		1
Thomas, William (Senr) (Chickamuxen)	1		4		
Thomas, Clem	1	4	2		1
Templeman, John	1	1	1		

CHARLES COUNTY—Continued.

NAME OF HEAD OF FAMILY.	Free white males of 16 years and upward, including heads of families.	Free white males under 16 years.	Free white females, including heads of families.	All other free persons.	Slaves.
Turner, Joseph (Port Tobacco)	1	4	5		11
Thomas, Colo John (Nanjemoy)	2		2		24
Taylor, William (Nanjemoy)	1	1	4		
Thompson, Ann (Nanjemoy)	1		2		
Talmash, Judith	3	1	3		1
Taylor, Sarah		1	3		
Thompson, Alexander M	1		1		
Thompson, William	1				
Williams, Jeremiah	1	1	1		
Wedding, Philip	2	1	3		
Ware, Edward Scott	2	2	4		
Wallace, Judith	1	3	3		4
Wages, Mary			1		
Wright, Thomas	1				
Wheeler, Richard	1		3		1
Wheeler, Charles	1				7
Webster, Thomas (Mulatto)				3	
Wheeler, Clement	2	1	4		7
Welch, William	1		1		
Wheeler, Ann	2		1		7
Ware, Francis M	2	1	1		5
Wills, John Baptist	2		3		4
Warthen, Priscilla		3	1		
Ware, Francis (of Jacob)	1	2	3		
Ware, Jacob	2		2		
Weems, Revd John	1	1	2		5
Warthen, William	2	3	5		1
Whitter, William	1				5
Whitter, Buckley	3		5		
Wheeler, Ignatius	1	2	3		13
Warthen, Ignatius	1	5	1		
Wills, Ignatius I	1		2		5
Ware, Colo Francis	1		4		18
Wheeler, William	1				18
Wood, James (Newport)	2		5		4
Wood, Philip	2	1	4		8
Watts, Doctor Willm (Quarter)	1				5
Warthen, Baker J	1	1	4		
Wildder, Margaret		1	4		7
Wiseman, Zachariah (Mulatto)				1	
Warthen, Bennett	2	1	5		2
Warrington, James	1				
Windsor, Mary			1		1
Winter, John	2		1		22
Winter, Capt Walter	1	4	6		14
Winter, Elizabeth			1		12
Warder, William	1				
Williams, John	1	2	3		1
Wedding, Thomas	1		3		2
Wedding, Thomas, Junr	1	3	2		1
Wight, Isle of	1	1	3		5
Wright, John	1	1	3		
White, William	1	3	3		2
Wedding, John, Senr	1	3	8		
White, John	1		4		
Wilkinson, Alexander	2				8
Wilkerson, Walter	1	1	6		1
Willett, George	2	3	3		
Wedding, William	2	1	7		
Wheeler, Ignatius (Junr)	1		4		
Welch, Edward	1	3	3		
Wilkerson, Bennett	1	3	2		1
Willett, James	1	3	2		
Wood, James (Son of Sorrow)	5		1		25
Williams, John (Mulatto)				1	
Welch, George	1	1	2		1
Wood, John (of Richard)	1	1	4		
Ward, Thomas	1		7		5
Wood, James (Pomonkey)	2		1		1
Wright, Joseph	1	2	1		2
Wright, John	1				2
White, John	2				
Wood, Margaret	1		2		13
Wood, Peter	1	2	2		16
Wilkinson, Capt William	2	3	5		29
Whetely, William	1	3	3		16
Whetely, Francis	1	3	2		7
Wallace, Cornelius	1		4		4
Wallace, Richard	1		2		6
Wood, Benjamin	3	1	5		8
Waters, Randolph	1		2		2
Williams, John, Junr	1	2	4		1
Warthen, Marma D	1				
Wathen, Barton, Junr	1	2	2		2
Warthen, Clement	1	1	7		
Warthen, Bennett, Junr	4	3	6		3
Whetely, Mary			2		
Wathen, Martin	3		3		2
Williams, Salary			1		
Whetely, Francis	3	1	4		7
Wathen, Barton	1	3	4		2
Waters Gustavus	1	2	1		2
Waters, James, of Joseph	1	2	4		3
Waters, Joseph	1	2	4		7
Waters, James (fuller)	4	1	5		2
Waters, Edward	1	2	2		1
Waters, Zephaniah	2	1	3		3
Weatherington, Richard	1	2	5		1
Waters, Thomas	1	5	3		14
Waters, Mary			3		1
Waters, William	1	2	4		2
Wallace, James	1				
Waters, John C.	2	2	7		24
Weatherington, James	1		1		
Wheelan, John	1		1		7
Wood, Margaret, Junr		3	2		1
Watson, James	2	3	5		4
Wiseman, James (Mulatto)				1	
Wood, Leonard (Newport)	1		6		13
Wood, (Doctor) Gerrard	1	3	1		13
Ward, Mary		1	4		5
Wheeler, Benedict	1	3	3		12
Ward, Ignatius	1	3	3		2
Ward, John (of Augustus)	1		2		9
Ward, Susanna	2		3		5
Williams, Jeremiah	1	1	1		
Wildair, John B	1	2	3		4
Windsor, Zachariah	1	1	6		
Wildair, James	2		1		9
Wood, Jane (Mulatto)				5	
Winman, Edward	1				
Warder, James	2	2	4		
Warden, Acey	2		3		6
Wheeler, Samuel	1	2	3		5
West, Henry	1		5		
Woodward, Henley	2		1		7
Whaland, Jeremihah	1	2	2		
Woolford, Vinney			3		
Woodward, Samuel	2	1	2		2
Wright, Mary	1	1	4		
Winter, Walter (Nanjemoy)	3		1		12
Williams, Elizabeth			1		3
Wapole, George	3	1	2		
Wapole, John	1	2	5		
Wright, John L	2		2		3
Wright, Gorry	1				
Wapole, George, Junr	2		2		
Woodward, William	1	2	2		
Wapole, James	1	1	5		
Wapole, William	1		4		
Wheatley, Samuel, Negro & family					3
Woodward, John	1		1		
Wright, John (Nanjemoy)	1	2	2		
Williams, John (Overseer for Wm. B. Smoot)	1	1	3		
Vincent, Philip	2		3		
Vincent, Rhody	1	1	5		
Venables, Mary	1	2	6		1
Venables, Ezekiel	1	2	1		1
Voulls, James	2	1	3		
Vane, William	1		6		
Vincent, William	1		2		8
Young, Robt (his Quarter) Jas Chatham, Overseer					9
Yates, Josias	2		1		1
Young, Elizabeth		1	1		8
Yates, Elizabeth			6		65
Young, Joseph	1	1	3		13
Yates, Charles	1	2	5		12
Young, James	3	2	2		
Upton, William (Mulatto)				3	
Vardin, John	2	3	4		8
Vane, John	1		4		1
Spalding, Edward (Negro)					2
Jenifer, Daniel, Esqr	1				22

DORCHESTER COUNTY.

NAME OF HEAD OF FAMILY.	Free white males of 16 years and upward, including heads of families.	Free white males under 16 years.	Free white females, including heads of families.	All other free persons.	Slaves.
Earle, Thomas	2	1	2		
Muir, Thomas	1	1	5		5
Jones, William, Jur	3		2	1	11
Standley, Robert				3	
Stanford, Thomas	2		1		6
Marshall, Theophilus	2	3	4		9
Tootell, John	4	2	3		11
Hodson, James	3	2	2		17
Pritchet, Elijah	2		6		6
Freeman, John				2	
Pitt, ——*	1	3	3	2	2
Pitt, ——*	1		3		5
Bassett, Nicholas	1	3	3		
Jones, Nancy		1	5		
Lingril, William	3	2	3		3
Stinson, Samuel	1	2	2		
Sullivan, James	2	1	3		
Wirt, E——*		1	1		
Web, Molly		3	3		
Walters, Levin	1	3	1		2
Dawson, Diah	3	3	4		
Smith, James	1			1	1
Shanton, John	1	2	3		1
Cavindor, Thomas	1	4	4		
Hooper, Henry	2		3		
Lee, Thomas	1	3	5	1	1
McCollister, Nathan	1	2	2		
Lane, Solomon	1	1	2	3	2
Whelar, Thomas	1	2	4		
Dawson, Joseph	2	6	2		2
Mills, David	1		4		3
Hayward, Alen	1	2	3		1
Wheelar, William	1		3		
Hayward, Levin	3	2	3		1
Anderson, Henry	1	1	3		8
Keys, Mary	2	1	3		
Keys, James	4	4	4		1
Poorhouse, P. Beaston, overseer	5	6	12		2
Beaston, Peregrine & his family	1	3	1	1	
Layton, ——*	2		4		6
Smith, Thomas	1		2		
Robertson, John	1		2		22
Vincent, Margaret	2	6	4		2
Cummins, James	3		5		2
Hamilton, Elizabeth	3	1	3	1	3
Vincent, William	1	3	2		2
Dodson, Joseph	4		2	1	2
Blake, William	1		3		
Vane, Henry	1	3	3		
Phillips, William	3	1	3		1
Trego, Newton	3	1	2		12
Woodards, Ailse	1	1	3		1
Hubbert, John	1		1		
Lecompte, Paris	1	2	2		1
Hubbert, Lydia			3		
Vincent, Stephen	2		5		
Sherman, Stephen	1	1	1		
Hurst, Samuel	1		2		7
Cook, John	3	4	4		7
Woodard, Ailse			1		
Phillips, Joseph	1	2	2		2
Owens, John	1		5		
Sherman, Benja	2	2	2		
Jones, Levin	1	3	2		
Rawley, Walter	3	6	4	5	1
Lecompte, John	2		2	15	1
Handley, Handy	4	1	4		4
Hodson, John H	1		3		14
Lecompte, Joseph	1		3		2
Lecompte, Levin	2	4	2		4
Lecompte, Levin (of Jno)	2	2	4	5	1
Hodson, Elizabeth	1		3		22
Jones, John	1	4	3		1
Ward, Thomas	1		3		
Herron, Elizabeth	3	3	10		26
Yates, Joseph	2	6	3		6
Rawley, William	1	2	1		6
Baley, Levin				3	
Barnet, Thomas	2	2			13

* Illegible.

DORCHESTER COUNTY—Continued.

NAME OF HEAD OF FAMILY.	Free white males of 16 years and upward, including heads of families.	Free white males under 16 years.	Free white females, including heads of families.	All other free persons.	Slaves.
Layton, Nellie	1	2	4		
James, Obadiah	1	1	3		11
Gibson, Sally		2	4		
Manning, Anthony	2	1	6		19
Cave, Benj.	1	3	6		2
Ward, James	1		3		3
Arnet, Thomas	1	2	2		1
Rachel, Free				6	
Orum, Levi	3	3	5		
Taylor, John	1		1		
Harvey, David	2	6	4		4
Moyain, Thomas	1	1	2		
Rue, Jesse	2	4	4		2
Carroll, Denton	1	2	3		17
Smith, James	1				8
Ayres, James	2	2	2	1	11
Hodson, John	2	2	2	1	5
Hodson, Ann			4	5	12
Keys, John	1	2	1	1	2
Brumigem, John	2	1	3		5
Greenwood, John	1	1	1	1	
Delehay, Moses	1		3	3	2
Hayward, William	2				
Carey, Collins	2				
Keys, William	2		1		5
Delehay, William	1	4			3
Tucker, William	3	1	3		4
Delehay, Ann S.	1		3		1
Coleston, John	1	3	3		
Dawson, Elizabeth		1	3		
Harris, William	1	1	1		
Whelar, Mary			1		
Craft, Allis	1	1	1		
Paul, Ralph		1	2		
Airey, Tho Hill	2	4	3	24	
Ward, George	1	1	4	6	1
Perry, Betty			3		
Griffin, Amos	1	3			
Whelar, Mary Ann			4		
Clarriaje, Peggy			1		
Dawson, —*	2	2	3		
Earle, Gramtom	2	3	2		3
Rose, Betty		1	2		
Keys, Francis	1	1	3		
Paul, Mary			1		
Carroll, Patrick	4	3	2	1	1
Owens, Owen	2	1	4		3
Hughes, Harry			3	2	
Hughes, James			2	4	
Dawson, Thomas		1	3		
Low, Isaac	1	1	2		11
Hale, Edward	1		2	1	1
Harvey, Zadick	1		1		
Dawson, Joseph	1	1	3		5
Bruffet, Gardiner	2	2	6		1
Hooper, Henry Q	1		3		26
Ball, Levin	1				4
Martin, Thomas	2	1	1		17
Stevens, Sarah	2	2	1		2
Stevens, Levin	2				7
Scott, John	3	4	6		7
Parks, Mark	1	1	1		8
Merrick, John	1			6	1
Stevens, Edward	1				2
Boze, John	1				1
Breerwood, John, Jur	2	2	3	1	
Riggin, Jerry	1	1	3		
Bramble, Edmondson	2		2		
Breerwood, Thomas	1	2	2	7	1
Standley, Allse				2	
Brawdis, Edward	4	3	2	1	13
Brawdis, Tabitha	1		4		11
Burris, John	2	1	4		3
Johnson, Shadrick	1				
Foxwell, Edward	1		2		
Willey, William	2		2		
Willey, Edward	2	3	1		
Eailston, John	1	2	2		21
Bestpitch, Jonathan	3	2	5		8
Summers, Park	2	4	3		
Summers, Jacob	2		3		
Rachel, Free				1	
Hight, Joseph	1	3	4		2
Gonter, Jabus	1	3	4		
Reed, William	1	2	2		
McGraw, Levin	1	1	3		
Bestpitch, Rachel	2	1	2		1
Keene, Ezekiel	2	1	2		10
Hughes, James				1	
Insley, Joseph	2	2	2		
Insley, Andrew	1		1		
Tom, Free			1	1	
Firman, William		2	4		4
Batsey, Richard	1		4		3
McCartee, Samuel	1		4		
Stafford, Thomas	2	1	4		8
Bramble, Gabril	2	1	4		8

NAME OF HEAD OF FAMILY.	Free white males of 16 years and upward, including heads of families.	Free white males under 16 years.	Free white females, including heads of families.	All other free persons.	Slaves.
Boyle, Anthony	1	1	2		7
Patison, Ataway	2	2	2		7
Woolen, Levin	4	1	6		4
Breerwood, John	3		3		8
Lane, Dennis	3		4		3
McCartee, John	1	1	2		
Martin, Richard	1	3	1		11
Warren, William	2		2		3
Mereign, Moses	2	3	4	1	1
Ruke, Ezekiel	1	3	4		
Hicks, Thomas			3		10
Partridge, Jonathan	1	1	1		8
Saunders, Leah			5	4	
Mills, James	2	2	1		10
Busick, Edward	1	2	1		1
Mills, John	1	1	2		
Porter, Levin	2		2		6
Murray, Rosannah		2	2		
Wheatley, Nehemiah	1		3		20
Greenfield, Ford	1				
Vincent, Salisbury	1	1	1		2
Eaton, Edward	1	1	4		
Richardson, Henry	1	1	2		
Richardson, Thomas	1	1	2		
Johnson, William	1	6	4		
Standley, Ezekiel				4	
Buley, Mikey			2		
Simmonds, Thomas	2	1	3		
Delchay, Christopher	1	1	4	1	15
Bendel, Mathew	1	2	1		
Simmonds, Andrew	1	2	5		4
Simmonds, Levin	1	1	2		
Parker, Daniel	2	4	2		20
Standley, George					1
Dawson, James	1		3		
Vallent, Benjamin	1	1	2		
Whelar, Thomas	1	2	3		
Molesworth, James	1	1	2		
Vallent, Bennet	1	2	2		
Lecompte, Charles	3				20
Hardin, Jesse	1	2	2		
Hubbert, Thomas	1	2	2		
Hooper, Henry	2	2	2		
Rotin, Richard	2	1	3		
Cottril, William	2	1	7		
Hooper, Thomas	1	1	2		
Troth, William	1	2	1	1	
Layton, Mary	2		4		
Bowdle, Thomas	1	2	7	8	
Bowdle, Henry	2	3	4	4	
Rose, Joseph	2		4		
Lewe, John				3	
Powel, Henry	1		1		10
Dickinson, Ann	1	2	2		20
Dean, —*	1	1	1		
Ennalls, Joseph	1	3	3		21
Insley, Solomon	1	3	2	2	
Smith, Thomas	2				
Travers, Henry	2	1	3		13
Travers, Levin	2			1	4
Elliott, Hooper	1	3	2		1
Dolny, John	4	3	3		2
Blamer, Sally		1	2		
White, John	1	3	2		
Badley, William	1	2	2		
Badley, Thomas	1		2		
Hicks, John	1	2	4		
Stevens, Thomas	1	2	3		2
Cotter, Sally					2
Cook, Molly			4		
Stevens, Cail	1		3		
Moluck, Roger					6
Moluck, Moses			1	3	
Whitehicks, Richard					7
Samboe, Free					5
Hooper, Roger	2		2		10
Newton, Milkey	4	2	4		9
Newton, Edward	1	1	1	1	1
Newton, Nimrod	2	3	3		
Hutchison, John	1	2	5		2
Thomas, Levin	1	2	3		
Tryor, John	1	1	2		
Satchel, Thomas	1	2	1		
Sherwood, Philip	3				
Stevens, Thomas	3				1
Lee, Christopher	1		2		
Swiggate, James	1		1		
Reed, John	3		1		4
Downey, Timothy	3				
Ferman, John	1				
Vickers, —*	1		2		
Meloy, —*	2		2		
Sulivane, —*	2	2	3	6	11
McCollister, Henry	1	2	4		1
McCollister, David	1	1	1		
McCollister, Garrison	1	1	1	1	
Badley, Nathan	2	1	4		

NAME OF HEAD OF FAMILY.	Free white males of 16 years and upward, including heads of families.	Free white males under 16 years.	Free white females, including heads of families.	All other free persons.	Slaves.
Dean, William	1	4	3		1
Moore, John	1	3	3		
Badley, Lucy			3		
Williams, Luke	1		1		
Benston, Lovey		1	2		
Baltimore, Mary	1	1	1		
Web, John	2	1	6		
Littleton, Betsey	1		3		
Littleton, Thomas	1	2	4		
Littleton, Molly			4		
Hall, Molly	1	3	3		
Standley, James				6	
Walker, Nat.	2	3	1		
McCollister, Andrew	1	1	4		1
Morris, Edward	1	4	3		1
Davis, Thomas	1	2	5		5
Cook, Molly			2		
Bonevill, Hall	1	1	1		5
Gibs, Sam		1	1	1	1
Farara, Barbary			1	1	
Noble, John	1	1	6		5
Hodson, Levin	2				4
Hayward, Hannah			1		7
Brannick, Sarah			1		
Gray, Betsey			1	2	
Crawford, Wallace	2		2		8
Crawford, Joseph					
Hubbert, Peter	1		3		3
Piercey, William	1	1	4		6
Ewing, Robert	1		1		13
Jones, Benjamin	1	1	1		
Walston, —*	1				
Lecompte, Samuel	1	3	5		
Standley, Sladdy				1	5
Billings, William	1		1		
Bramble, Peggy		3	4		
Cox, Natty	2	1	4		
Bramble, Thomas	1	2	4		
Cox, John	1	1	2		
Hubbirt, John	1	1	2		
Whitehicks, Betsey				1	
Dent, Beckey			1		
Dent, Priscey			1		
Lane, John	1	3	4		
Norman, William	1	3	2		1
Cornish, Sam				4	
Hooper, John	1	2	3	1	
Delehay, Nancy			3		4
Hubbert, Becky	1		2		
Higgins, Henry	1		2		
Gilbert, Gracy		1	4		
White, Sally	1		3		11
White, Betsey			2	3	6
Cornish, Anney				7	
Shehan, Thomas	3	1	3		3
Stevens, John	1	1	3		13
Baynes, John	1				
Sullvane, James	3		5		26
Cummins, Andrew	1				42
Green, Esther			2		
Wright, Cannolly	1	1			4
Daffnny, Rhody			1		1
Pritchet, Arthur			4		4
Pattison, William	1		4		6
Wheatley, Edward	1	1	4		1
Stevens, James R.	1		3		12
Wheatley, —*			2		
Bramble, Moses	1		4		2
Vane, John	1	3	2	1	
Canter, Isaac	3	2	2	1	
Beetpitch, Leah			1		
Hobbs, James	1		1		
Herlock, John	1	2	4		1
Herlock, William	1	2	4		6
Smoot, Rosannah	1		2		6
Lairy, John	2		3		2
Nicolls, Daniel	3	2	3		20
Foster, Joseph	1		1		
Pritchet, Thomas	1		3		2
Jacobs, Jacob	1	1	1		
Cows James	1		7		
Airey, Nancy			1		7
Dines, Jerry	3	2	4		2
Firbus, Ephraim	3		4		3
Thomas, William	3	1	4		2
Herlock, William	2		4		3
McCollister, Esther			3		
Payne, Cain	2		1		2
Payne, Mary		1	4		2
Wingate, Zebulon	1	3	2		2
Dun, Gilbert	1		1		
Carroll, Charles	1	1			
Stevens, John	2	1	1		3
Carroll, Lancy	2				
Low, Reubin	1				
Carroll, William	2	2	3		
Carroll, Dan¹	1	2	2		4

* Illegible.

DORCHESTER COUNTY—Continued.

NAME OF HEAD OF FAMILY.	Free white males of 16 years and upward, including heads of families.	Free white males under 16 years.	Free white females, including heads of families.	All other free persons.	Slaves.
Whealton, William	2	1	4		2
Wolen, William	1	3	3		
Thomas, John	3	2	3		2
Bell, Isaac	2		2		22
Low, William	2	3	4		
Herlock, Thomas	1		4		1
Williams, —*	2	1	4		
Herlock, Jery	1		4		
Low, Isaac	1	2	5		1
Wall, Rody			4		
Payne, John	1		4		
Gambel, Molly			4		
Herlock, Jonathan	3		4		7
Moore, Reubin	1		4		
Tinsley, Thomas	1	1	4		
Dunaway, Sally		1	1		
Bell, Arthur	1	1	4		3
Hardin, Judy	1		4		
Payne, Joseph	1	4	7		
Cockerin, James	1	1	3		
Payne, James	1	3	1		9
Charles, Isaac	2	3	3		
Adams, George	1		4		
Charles, Jacob	2	1	2		
Stack, Elizabeth	1		1		1
Charles, John	1	1	1		
Charles, Solomon	2	1	2		
Wright, Lovey	1		3		
Kinnemont, William	2	4	3		
McFarlin, John	1	2	2		
Noble, Joshua	1		2		
Connolly, William	1	4	2		
Connolly, Thomas	1	2	4		
Everington, William	2	1	2		2
Sam, Free				5	
Lewis, Abraham	4	1	2		2
Wheatley, Anthoney	1	3	4		
Low, James	1	2	5		
Buthel, Moses	1	1	4		
Foxwell, Richard	2	3	1		
Medford, —*	1		2	1	
Wright, —*			4		
Brown, Euliston	1	1	3		
Tootell, Thomas	1	2	1	1	7
Foxwill, Charles	1	1	4		
Wheelar, Joshua	1		4		
Bright, Benjamin	2	3	3		
McGher, Samuel	1		4		4
Busick, Betty			4		
Sullvane, Bridget			4		
Lord, Sally			3		
Brown, Charles	1	2	4		9
Cockerin, John	1	3	5		
Andrew, Mary	1	1	2		
Gray, Matthew	1		4		
Carroll, William	1	1	3		1
Carroll, Samuel	1	1	2		
Gray, Thomas	2	3	4		
Cockerin, Rachel	3	2	6		2
Cockerin, James	1	1	4		1
Nicolls, Thomas	2	1	4		
Dean, Sophia			2		
Rowans, Francis	1		1		
Warington, Nathaniel	1	1	2		1
Dean, Edward	1	1	2		
Hubbert, Daniel	1	1	1		
Russum, Mitchel	2	1	3		19
Bell, Daniel	2	1	2		
Kelley, Dennis	2	1	2		15
McKenzie, Thomas	2		2		
Corns, John	1	3	4		
Dodson, George	3	3	5		4
Shehan, James	1	5	1		
Brumwill, Sheddin	3	1	7		3
Kenard, —*	2		5		
Nicolls, —*	1	3	4		
Robertson, Stanley	1	2	4		
McCollister, James	2		1		
McCotter, John	2				3
Trul, Nancy	1		4		
Trul, Nancy, wid* of A.	1	1	4		4
Howeth, Sewel	1	1	3		
Andrew, Nehemiah	1	1	6		
James, Walter	1	3	2		
Willis, Jarvis	1	1	3		
Henry, Ezekiel	1	1	3		
Thompson, Thomas	1	3	2		6
Trul, George	1		4		
Trul, John	2	2	2		7
Medford, Nathaniel	1	1	4		5
Medford, William	1		4		8
Cockerin, Marjaret	1	1	1		
Bonner, William	1	4	3		1
Godin, Daniel	1	2	3		
Low, Isaac	1	1	5		16

NAME OF HEAD OF FAMILY.	Free white males of 16 years and upward, including heads of families.	Free white males under 16 years.	Free white females, including heads of families.	All other free persons.	Slaves.
Anderson, Thomas	1	4	5		6
Trippe, Margaret			2		29
Robertson, William	1				4
Carter, Jerry	1		1		3
Small, William	1		2		11
Harrington, Nathan	1		3		7
Nash, John	1	3	2		
Murriah, Free					3
Sarah, Free					2
Wicket, Leah			2	5	1
Wicket, William	1	2	4	2	
Carmine, Joseph	1		2	2	
Collisson, Benjamin	3	1	2	5	
Grasyer, Edward	2	3	4	2	
Carroll, —*	1		2		
Wright, Elisha	1	1	3		
Wright, Jacob	1	1	3		
Wright, Samuel	1	5	1		
Dean, Elijah	1	3	3		
Cockerin, William	1	1	4	1	
Eccleston, Sarah	1				3
Carter, Catron			2	2	
Logan, Isaac	2				
Eccleston, Sarah		1	3		17
Sherman, Seth	1		2		1
Henry, Molly	1	1	2		4
Moore, James	1	1	6		
Keys, George	1	1	2		
Connolly, Kul	1		1		
Cook, Nelly			1		
Becks, James	1	3	1		
Murray, David	1	1	2		
Williams, Thomas	1	1	5		2
Tineley, Joshua	1		2		4
Patison, John	1		1		
Frasier, Levin	2		5	1	
McCollester, Betsey	1		3		
Hubbert, Siney		1	2		
Norman, Thomas	1	1	2		
Badley, Thomas	2	3	3		3
Eccleston, John	1		3		13
Ennalls, Thomas	1		1		11
Dean, John	1		1		5
Richardson, Rebecca	1	2	6		37
Stevens, John	2		2		1
Sullvane, Timothy	1				
Lord, —*	1	3	6		
Tanner, Vinson	2	1	3		
Wheatley, William	1		6		
Messick, Luke	1	1	6		
Briley, Thomas	1	1	2		2
Chipman, Paris	2		2		1
Messick, Benjamin	1		2		
Henderson, Polly		3	2		
Fletcher, Bat	1		4		2
Jones, Ezekiel	1	2	3		
Fletcher, William	2	2	4		1
Morine, Babel	1	3	4		
Jones, Covinton	1	1	1		
Messick, Lewis	1		3		
Cavindon, Isaac	1	1	4		
Wheatley, Ezekiel	1		4		
Morine, William	1	2	2		
Elliott, John	1	3	5		1
Shehee, Daniel	1		2		
Shehee, Daniel, Jur	1	2	3		
Wheatley, William	1		4		1
Wheatley, Charles	1	1	4		2
Wheatley, Isaac	1	2	2		2
Badley, Elizabeth	1	1	4		
Badley, Nathan	1		2		
Wheatley, William	2				
Gale, George	2				8
Twiford, John	2	1	5		11
Turpin, John	1		2		6
McFarlin, Levin	1	3			
Murfey, James	1		3		
Murfey, William	1		1		
Thomas, Allen	1	1	2		
Dean, —*	1		4		
McWilliams, —*	1		4		
Willen, Hopkins	1		3		
Wilson, Jesse	1				
Melican, Betty		3	2		
Melican, Patiener	1		2		
Russel, Jean	2	1	2		
Russel, William	1	1	2		
Smith, Nancy	1	2	2		
Mills, Mary			1		
Jacobs, Jonathan	2		3		1
Tucker, James	2	4	6		
Dean, William	1	1	1		
Smoot, Henry	1	3	4		10
Shanks, Abner	1	2	4		5
Worton, Benjamin	1				

NAME OF HEAD OF FAMILY.	Free white males of 16 years and upward, including heads of families.	Free white males under 16 years.	Free white females, including heads of families.	All other free persons.	Slaves.
Mills, John	1	1	1		
Passipa, Moses	1	2	2		
Vansickle, Gilbert	3	2	2		
Dean, John	1	1	3		
Bramble, David	1		4		
Smoot, John	4	4	2		41
Crapper, John S.	1		3		9
Connolly, Elijah	1				
Stokes, Valentine	1				
Chilent, Thomas	1				
Henry, James	1				
Stokes, Valentine, Senr	2		3		
Connolly, William	1		1		
Connolly, Patrick	1		3		
Taylor, —*	1	2	4		2
Moore, William	1	1	4		
Outerbridge, James	1	1	5		
Insley, Thomas	4		3		
Willin, James	1	1	1		
Dean, Noble	1	3	2		
Harper, Beauchamp	2	2	5		7
Dean, Frederick	2		4		
Vickers, John	3	2	3		
Wheatley, William	1	1	3		1
Briley, Margarit	1	3	1		1
Frampton, John	1	3	3		
Wright, James	1	3	3		
Willis, Shaderick	1	1	5		
Cannon, Tubmon	2	1	1		
Frampton, Huberd	2	1			
Jones, Daniel	1		3		
Handley, Handy	1		2		
Melican, Elizabeth		3	1		
Wilson, James	2	2	7		7
Wright, Isaac	2	2	3		4
Wright, Jacob	1	2	4		5
Handley, Sally	1		5		
Cole, Edward	1		1		
Adams, Charles	1	2	2		5
Adams, Edward	5	1	2		2
Harrison, John	2	5	2		1
Sterling, Josiah	1	1	1		4
Stewart, Jonathan	1		1		
Brannick, John	1		1		
Goslin, —*	1	2	2		
Dill, Milly		1	2		2
Charles, Willis	1	2	2		
Connolly, Thomas	2		4		
Connolly, Keil	1	2	1		
Williams, Jesse	1	2	3		
Williams, Job	2	3	6		
Delaney, James	1		2		
Vanner, John	2		1		
Burns, Nancy			2		
Ramble, William	1		2		
Smith, Matthew	4	2	4		14
Rowans, William	2	3	3		
Wales, John	2	3	6		
Wright, Constant	1	2	3		
Hacket, Thomas	1	3	3		
Wall, Ezekiel	1	2	4		2
Elbert, Solomon					2
Green, Thomas	1		4		
Herrington, Ezekiel	1	4	4		
Herrington, Thos	1	1	2		
Herrington, William	1	1	2		
Herrington, James	1	1	2		
Sherwood, Benjamin	1		2		
Stevens, Hacket	1	3	3		
Bramble, David	1		3		
Wall, William	1	4	2		
Aleoke, Samuel	2		3		14
Ennalls, —*	2		3	22	
Ennalls, —*	2		3		14
Mitchel, John	1		3		19
Daffin, Charles	1	3	3		37
Hooper, William	1		2		35
Marshall, Levin	1		1		10
Granger, James		1	1		
Rawlins, Hudson	1	4	5	1	2
Wicket, James	1	3	5	1	
Wicket, Joseph	1	3	5		
Melvil, Sarah	2	3	5		7
Medford, Betsey	2	3	1		1
Brandis, William					
Hicks, Ann	2				22
Hooper, Mary			4		21
Suvil, Thomas	1	4	3		
Hicks, James	1	4	1		3
Mills, William					
Ennalls, Anne	1		6	1	20
Hooper, John	1	1	3		32
Merrick, William	1	1	3		
Lord, John	1	3	5		
Kirbey, Joseph	2	3	5		

*Illegible.

FREDERICK COUNTY.

NAME OF HEAD OF FAMILY.	Free white males of 16 years and upward, including heads of families.	Free white males under 16 years.	Free white females, including heads of families.	All other free persons.	Slaves.
Dixon, Thomas	1		2		
Stevenson, Richard	1	1	1		
Schools, Thomas	1	2	4		
Arnold, Anthony	3		3		
Ackerman, George	3	3	6		
Arnold, John	3		2		
Arnold, William	1	2	3		
Bennet, Benjamin	1	1	1		4
Baxter, Benjamin	1	3	3		
Brower, Emanuel	3	3	3		
Becraft, George	3	2	6		
Butt, George	4	1	2		
Baker, Henry	1	2	2		
Britewell, John	1		2		
Boiler, Joseph	2	2	2		
Beall, John, Junr	1	2	4		
Butler, John	3	1	4		2
Bond, Nicholas	3	1	3		1
Bale, Peter	2	3	4		
Boyer, Philip	2		4		
Barnes, Philip	3	2	5		
Boarden, Sephous	3	4	2		
Babs, William	2	2	4		
Boddington, William	1		1		
Brightwell, William	1	1	3		
Crumbecker, Abraham	2	3	3		
Clary, Benjamin	2	5	1		2
Crumbecker, Catharine	2	1	4		
Clarke, Clement	1	2	7		
Clary, David	2	3	3		2
Crawford, David	2	5	3		
Crowl, Devalt	1	4	5		
Crawford, David, Junr	1	1	2		
Cooper, George	1	1	3		
Coagh, Henry	2	3	3		
Clew, Henry	2	2	5		
Craybill, John	1	1	3		
Campbell, John	4	2	7		
Cummins, James	1				1
Crawford, James		2			
Crawford, John	2				
Cumpston, Margaret		1	6		
Crowl, Margaret			2		
Chapman, Nathan	1	4	2		1
Craybill, Peter	2		3		
Couden, Sarah			1	1	
Compton, William	1		3		
Clary, William	1	4	3		
Cummings, William	3	2	4		7
Clarke, William	1	3	3		
Davis, Adam	2	3	6		
Davis, Amos	2	3	6		9
Devilbiss, Casper	4	4	4		
Duttero, Conrod	5	3	7		2
Dorsey, Daniel	1	3	6	2	21
Dorsey, Elizabeth		4	2		5
Dorsey, Eli	1	4	4		13
Dorsey, Eli (of Edwd)	4		1		1
Davis, Garret	2	7	1		
Deale, George	2		2		
Durbin, John	1	2	2		
Danner, Jacob	4		4		
Dorsey, John	2	3	4		4
Dodson, John	1	1	1		
Deale, John	1	3	4		
Dimsy, John	1	3	3		
Deakus, John	1	3	4		
Davis, Philip	2	3	4		
Danner, Samuel	1	4	5		
Dorsey, William (of Thos)	3		2		1
Dickenstreet, William	3		4		
Evans, Ezekiel	2	2	5		
Etaler, John	2	2	2		
Engler, Jacob	3	7	1		
England, John, Junr	2	5	4		
England, John, Senr	1	1	1		
Everly, John	1	3	2		
England, Jacob	1	4	3		
Ensey, Jacob	2	2	8		
Farquhar, Allen, Junr	2		1		
Farquhar, James	1	4	3	1	1
Farquhar, Samuel	3	4	3	1	
Farquhar, William	4	1	5	1	
Farquhar, William, Junr	1	1	2		
Flegle, Felty	1	2	2		
Goslen, Amos	1	1	2		
Gloss, George	1		5		
Gist, Joshua	3	6	6		8
Gilbert, Jacob	2	1	2		
Gosnel, Joseph	2	2	15		
Grimes, Joshua	2	2	5		
Gittinger, John	2	3	4		
Grimes, Nicholas	1	1	4		
Gardner, Tobias	2	2	3		
Greenwood, Yost	2	2	4		1
Hockman, Mary	2		3		
Harkman, Abraham	1		2		
Hardy, Arnold	1		2		2
Hall, Benjamin	2	4	6		5
Hoss, Margaret	3		3		
Howard, Ephraim	1	1	6		12
Hosplehorn, George	1	1	3		
Hans, George	2	5	5		
Hope, Esther			2		
Hartsock, Henry	2	3	4		
Hull, Jacob	2	3	5		1
Hans, Jacob	1	5	3		
Hibbert, Joseph	2	3	5		
Hinkle, John	2		5		
Hockman, John	2		2		
Hammond, John	1	4	2		12
Howard, Joshua, Esqr	2	4	6		10
Harrison, James	2	4	1		
Hans, Joseph	1		3		
Hensy, John	1	3	2		
Hosplehorn, Ludwrick	1	1	1		
Hans, Michael	2		4		
Howard, Martha	1	2	1		
Hans, Nathan	3		2	1	4
Hoy, Nicholas	3		2		
Hobbs, Nicholas, Esqr	3	5	5		19
Harris, Nathan	2		3		16
Hammond, Vachel	2	6	3		11
Isenburg, Enoch	2	3	1		
Isenburg, Gabriel, Junr	1	1	2		1
Justice, Griff	2	3	4		
Justice, Elizabeth			4		
Israel, John, Junr	1	1	2		1
Israel, John, Senr	3	1	7		
Isenberg, John	2	3	3		
Isenberg, Jacob	1	3	5		
Justice, Jesse	1	3	3		
Justice, Margaret			1		
Isenberg, Nicholas	1		3		
Keller, Daniel	2	2	2		
Kiger, John	2	2	3		
Kensler, James	2	1	7		
Kiger, Leonard	2	2	5		
Kemp, Peter	3	1	4		3
Knight, Samuel	1	1	4		
Lemmon, Adam	1	1	2		
Lavely, Christian	1	1	4		
Landis, Henry	3	4	3		
Lemmon, Jacob	1	5	1		
Lookenpeale, Jacob	1		3		
Lawrence, Martha		1	3		10
Lookenpeale, Peter	3	1	2		
Leatherwood, Samuel	1	2	6		
Lard, William	1	1	4		
Markley, Adam	1	1	3		
Miller, Benjamin	2		1		
Markley, Ephraim	2	4	2		
Murray, Edward	2	2	5		
Moyers, Peter	1	2	2		
Miller, Geo	1	2	6		
Markley, Gabriel	1	1	4		
Moyers, Henry	2	1	5		
Maynard, Henry	1		2		5
Murray, James	1	3	8		
McDaniel, Joseph	1	1	4		
Myers, John	1	3	4		
Maynard, John	4	1	4		3
Mumford, John	4		2		2
McDaniel, James	2	4	3		
Miller, Joseph	2	2	1		
McDaniel, Redman	2	1	1		
Merryman, William	1	1	3		
Merady, Simon	1	3	3		1
Moore, Tobias	3	3	4		
Madcap, Thomas	2		4		
Meeler, Ulrick	3	3	3		1
Murkle, William	3	3	2		
Nicodemus, Henry, Senr	3		7		
Norris, John	2	3	4		
Norris, John, Junr	1	1	1		
Nicodemus, John	2	4	7		
Nichols, James	1	3	2	2	1
Ovelman, George	2	1	2		
Orr, John	3	1	4		
Orbit, William	3	2	4		
Onseller, Sarah	1	2	2		
Polston, Andrew	2		4		
Prude, Conrod		4	6		
Polston, Cornelius	3	5	3		
Pusey, George	1	1	5		
Poole, Henry, Senr	7	3	5		10
Parish, Gilbert	2	2	4		
Polston, James	2	4	4		
Parish, Richard	5	4	3		
Peter, Warner	1	1	1		
Plain, David	3		5		
Writing, Andrew	2		2		
Richards, Aaron	2	5	4		
Root, Daniel	2	2	3		1
Rinehart, David	2	2	3		
Rip, Henry	3	1	5		
Rifle, Jacob	2	3	4		
Stoner, Ann	4		3		1
Selman, Adam	2	3	2		
Spoon, Conrod	1		4		
Stoner, David	1	1	1		
Stevenson, Daniel	2	6	4		
Stevenson, Edward	25	1	8		
Swadener, Elizabeth	2		4		
Stoner, John		3	3		
Stripe, Jacob	2	5	2		
Smith, Jacob	2	3	4		
Spurrier, Levin	2	2	3		
Strouse, Nicholas	2	1	5		
Soam, Peter	2	4	4		
Stripley, Peter	1	2	5		
Simpson, Richard, Senr	4	1	3	1	5
Stringer, Richard	2	1	3		3
Smedley, Samuel		2	4		
Shepherd, Solomon	3	3	4	1	
Spurrier, Thomas	2	2	3		
Shipley, Uriah	2		3		
Smouse, Henry	2		2		
Tagan, Jacob	2	1	4		
Talbot, James	1	2	3		
Umstead, Nicholas	2	4	11		
Upcraft, Robert	1	5	5		
Warman, Andrew	2	3	4		
Riting, Andrew	2		4		
Wood, Basil	1		2		2
Wood, John	1	1	2	1	5
Warfield, Elizabeth	1	5	4		9
Winters, George	3	2	2		
Welsh, Henry	2	2	3	1	1
Warman, Henry	2	2	6		
Willets, John	2	2	3		
Wright, Joel	2	3	5		1
Waggoner, John	5	3	5		
Worman, Jacob	2	3	4		
Wells, Joseph	1	2	4	5	13
Wood, Jonathan	2	2	5		
Wood, Joseph	2		4		
Wood, James	2	2	4		
Winters, Jacob	2		2		
Wood, Joseph	3	5	5		4
Wolfe, Martin	2	3	3		
Wampler, Peter	2	3	4		
Yorgen, Henry	1	1	2		
Yon, John	1	4	4		
Young, Philip	1	4	4		
Overholts, Isaac	2	2	6		
Nieuman, Frederick	2		3		
Will, Henry	1				
Light, Judy			4		
Crowl, Henry	1		4		
Merchant, Charles	2		2		
Crocher, George	2	1	2		
Squires, Michael	2		6		
Dorsey, William, Junr	2		2		1
Swadner, Andrew	1	1	1		
Wampler, David	1	2	1		
Yond, Jacob	1		1		
Bailey, Joseph	1		1		
Shipley, Vachel	1	5	3		10
Cummings, Robert	1		1		
Crumbecker, John	1		1		
Bear, Michael	1		1		
Rodepouch, Frederick	1		1		
Madding, William	2	2	4		
Herring, John	3	2	5		
Murray, Eli	1	1	1		
Herring, Elijah	1	1	5		
Condall, William	1		5	1	
Adams, Richard	3	3	5		4
Albaugh, Christian	3	1	3		
Albaugh, David	3	1	3		
Albaugh, John	3		5		
Andis, Matthias	1		4		
Andis, Martin	1	3	4		
Albaugh, Peter	3	3	4		
Albaugh, Philip	1	3	2		
Andis, Paul	1	1	2		
Albaugh, William	1	1	2		
Albaugh, William, Junr	1	3	2		
Albaugh, Zachariah	2	2	1		
Bentley, Abner	3	3	2		
Bostian, Anthony	1	3	5		4
Beamer, Adam	4	4	6		
Barnhart, Benjamin	2	1	6		
Bolsell, Charles	3		6		
Barrack, Christian	2		3		
Buzzard, Daniel	2	4	4		3

FREDERICK COUNTY—Continued.

NAME OF HEAD OF FAMILY.	Free white males of 16 years and upward, including heads of families.	Free white males under 16 years.	Free white females, including heads of families.	All other free persons.	Slaves.
Boyer, David	2	2	1		
Bentley, Elijah	1		1		
Baker, Frederick	1	1	2		
Bierly, George	2	2	3		
Barrack, George	2	1	2		5
Barrack, Frederick	2	1	1		
Brown, Hannah		4	5		
Barrack, Henry	2	3	2		
Beamer, Henry, Junr	3	2	2		
Bostian, Henry	1	2	4		
Browning, Jeremiah	6	2	8		
Beard, Margaret		4	2		
Barrack, John	1	4	4		1
Barrack, Jacob	2	4	4		
Beatty, James	3	1	7		11
Brightwell, John	2	1	4		
Boiler, Joseph	2	1	4		
Barrack, Jacob (of Wm.)	1	4	3		
Barker, John	1	2	5		
Baker, Joseph	1	1	2		
Barrack, John, of Jnr	1	3	4		
Beall, John	4	3	10		
Baker, John	1	2	2		
Bryan, James	1	1	1		
Burrier, Leonard	4	1	4		
Bentley, Levi	1		1		
Barnet, Luke	2		2		
Bailey, Major Mountjoy	7	2	5		10
Bostian, Michael	1	1	4		7
Brashears, Nathan	3		3		
Burket, Nathaniel	2		4		
Boone, Nicholas	2	3	6		
Beard, Peter	3		1		
Barrack, Peter	3	1	1		5
Barnett, Robert		3	1		
Bucken, Robert	3	1	1		
Baker, Samuel	1	5	5		
Bentley, Solomon	2	5	4		
Boyer, Teterick	1		2		
Barrack, William	2	1	3		
Beatty, William, Esq	4	8	4		12
Brawner, William	2	3	4		1
Campbell, Ann	1	1	2		
Cline, Adam	1	4	2		
Cregar, Adam	3		4		
Cassell, Abraham		4	1	2	
Crapster, Abraham	2	1	2		2
Cron, Alexander		4	3		
Cregar, Conrod	3	2	3		1
Cumber, Christian	2	5	4		
Crumbaugh, Conrod	1	6	4		
Clance, Charles	2	3	3		
Carmack, Evan	1	5	5		
Cramer, George	2	5	3		3
Cregar, George	2	2	3		
Curts, George	1	1	2		
Cramer, George	2	1	2		
Curtis, Henry	1	2	3		
Cregar, Henry	2		1		
Cookerly, John	4	2	2		2
Carmack, John	1	3	3		
Cooper, John	3	1	1		
Crum, John	7	1	2		
Colleberger, John	2		1		
Cramer, John	1	4	1		1
Crum, John, Junr	2	2	4		
Campbell, John	1		2	1	
Cumpston, Mary		2	5		
Crow, Michael	1	2	3		
Campbell, Martha	1	2	3		
Crowell, Margaret			1		
Copple, Nicholas	2	1	4		
Cramer, Peter	3	2	1		
Clapsaddle, Paul	4	2	4		
Compter, Peter	2	2			
Coale, Richard	6	2	6		23
White, Benjamin	2		5		
Cook, Samuel	3	1	3		7
Carmack, William	3	3	5		
Crum, William	3		3		
Cramer, William		4	6		
Duttero, Jacob	5	3	6		
Delaplane, John	3	4	4		
Devilbiss, John	1	1	1		
Delaplane, Joseph	1	5	2		
Devilbiss, John	1	1	3		2
Dahoof, Nicholas	2		3		
Deale, John	1	2	3		
Dolhammer, Uly	1	2	2		
Dick, Peter	3		3		
Dern, William	2	3	2		2
Dorsey, William	2	3	5		22
Eckhart, Anthony	3	1	4		
Eader, Abraham	5	2	4		
Eader, George	1	1	3		
Epperly, Jacob	3		3		
Epperly, Jacob, Junr	1	1	3		
Epperd, Philip	3	1	4		
Fogle, Baltzer	1	2	1		
Fox, Baltzer	2	1	7		
Fox, Casper	1	3	1		
Fundebaugh, Catho			3		
Fundebaugh, David	1	2	3		
Fundebaugh, Daniel	1	2	3		
Fogle, Matthias	1	5	1		
Fox, George	2	2		4	
Fogle, Henry	2	2	1		
Flenner, John	2	2		4	
Filler, Jacob	1		4		
Fundebaugh, Lazarus	1	2	6		
Fox, Michael	1	2	4		
Friese, Michael	4	1	5		
Fox, Matthias	1	3	6		
Fox, Peter	2		4		
Fishburn, Philip	2	1	8	2	1
Fine, Peter, Senr	1	1	3		
Fulton, Robert	3			5	
Gaver, Christian	1	1	6		
Graybill, John	2	1	10		
Grimes, John	1	2	2		
Gilstons, John	1	2	1		
Grabs, John	2	1	3		
Grimes, Martin	3		3		
Garver, Martin	2	1	2		
Gassaway, Robert	2	3	5		1
Garver, Samuel, Jun	2	2	4		
Garver, Samuel, Senr	3	2	2		
Grimes, William		2	5		
Gilmore, William	1	1	3		
Half, Abraham	3	1	2		4
Hufford, Christian	2	3	5		
Harker, Cornelius		4	4		
Hosselton, Edward	1	4	3		
Hover, Elizabeth		3	4		
Condell, Zachariah	1	1	1		
Hawk, George	2		2		
Hartsock, George	3	2	3		1
Holle, George	1	3	1		
Hoff, Garret	2		2		
Himes, Henry	1	2	3		
Herd, Jacob	1		3		
Hines, John	1	8	3		
Hartsock, John (of Nichs)	2	2	4		
Harlin, Joel	2	2	4		
Hooper, James	1	3	5		
Hardman, Michael	2	3	2		
Hedge, Mary		2	2		
Hoover, Mary		1	2		
Hartsock, Elizabeth		2	2		
Hufford, Philip	1	3	4		
Hawk, Paul	1	1	6		
Hedge, Peter	2	3	4		
Hines, Philip	2	1	2		
Hone, Samuel	1	3	2		
Howe, Samuel	1	4	2		
Hammer, Tobias	2	3	5		
Iler, Conrod	2	5	5		
Jumper, Christian	2	1	2		
James, Daniel, Senr	4		4		24
Iler, John	2		4		
Keller, Jacob	2	2	2		
Jacobs, Philip	2		6		
Jones, Richard	2	2			1
Johnson, William	1	3	3		
Knave, Bostian	3	3	3		
Kitterman, Christian	3		3		
King, Charles	1	3	4		
Kelleberger, George Adam	4	4	5		
Kitterman, George John	2	3	3		
Coonts, George	1	3	1		
Keller, George	2	2	1		
Keller, Juliana	1		3		
Kinzio, Henry	2	4	5		
Klise, Henry	2	1	4		
Lemon, Adam	1	2	2		
Link, Adam	3	2	1		2
Lenginfelter, Barnet	2		2		
Ludith, Daniel	2		3		
Lutz, George	5	3	5		1
Lock, John	3	3	3		
Logmire, John	2	1	3		
Lease, Jacob	1	3	3		
Late, Michael	4	3	3		5
Lemon, Peter	1	3	3		
Longsworth, Solomon	1	3	4		
Lamar, William	3		4		10
Leace, William	3	3	3		
Musgrove, Benjamin		4	6		
Mort, Conrod	1	1	3		
McBride, Daniel	1	2	3		
Myers, Frederick	2		3		
McMin, George	1	3	4		
Miller, George	1	2	4		
Maynard, Henry			4		7
McMullen, Mary	3	2	4		
Loyd, Thomas	2	1	1		
McKenzie, John	2		4		
Miller, John	1	1	4		
Melton, Joseph	3	2	4		
Mumford, Jacob	2	2	6		
Mort, John	2	4	2		
Marks, John	1	2	2		
Mensher, John	3	4	5		
Miller, John	1		2		
Moyer, John	1	5	3		
McKenzie, John	1		2		
Mort, Matthias	2		2		
Mills, Richard	1	2			1
Miller, Sarah		2	4		
Maynard, Thomas	1	3	3		6
Mock, Valentine	1	3	4		
Moore, William	1		4		
Naylor, Alexander	1		3		
Norris, Benjamin	1	2	4		
Need, Christoper	2		3		
Nelson, Henry	2	5	7		1
Nashbaum, John	2	4	7		
Noland, Michael	1		2		
Ovelman, Henry	2		2		
Ovelman, Jacob	2		2		
Occerman, Jacob	3	2	4		
Orand, Jacob	2		2		
Ovelman, Michael	2		4		
Pettinger, Benjamin	2		4		
Beltzer, Christopher	2	4	5		
Poole, Conrod	2		5		
Pettinger, Danl, Jun	2		3		
Stoner, David	2	2	2		
Phillips, John	1	3	8		4
Pettinger, John	1	3	4		
Pagan, John	2		2		1
Powright, Lawrence	1	1	1		
Pringle, Margaret	1	1	5		
Putsebaugh, Peter	2	1	2		
Pettinger, William	1	2	5		
Runner, Abraham	3		6		
Rheam, Baltzer	1		4		
Riddle, Benjamin	1	5	1		
Richards, Caleb	1		2		
Root, Daniel, Senr	3	1			1
Richards, Catharine	2	1	2		
Rye, Henry	3	1	4		
Read, Henry	1		4		
Rasler, Henry	2		4		
Renner, John	2		8		
Ringer, John	1	4	8		
Rheam, John	2	1	5		
Rhodes, Jacob	1	3	4		
Ringer, Jacob	2		4		
Rasler, Michael	1	3	3		
Reynolds, Thomas	1	1	3		
Renner, William	1	2	6		
Roy, William	1	2	5		
Stutt, Adam	1		2		
Smith, Adam, Junr	2	1	2		
Smith, Adam, Senr	3		2		
Sponseller, Andrew			1		
Strine, Adam	1		3		
Simpson, Basil	1	2	4		9
Snyder, Baltzer	1	3	1	1	
Sailer, Christian	4	3	3		
Smith, Christian	1	4	4		
Stevens, Charles	2	4	3		
Sailer, Daniel	1		3		
Sowers, Frederick	3	2	4		
Sappington, Doct. Francis B	1	2	2		11
Stitely, Frederick	1	2	5		
Sensen, George	1		4		
Shank, George	2		5		
Shoemaker, John	2		3		
Stitely, Jacob, Junr	1		2		
Sowers, Jacob	1		2		
Stoner, Jacob	3		7		
Stutt, Catharine			1		
Stouder, John	1	4	3		
Stephenson, John	1		2		6
Snider, John	2	2	3		
Stoner, John	1	2	2		
Snouk, John	1	3	3		
Sleets, John	1		3		
Simmons, Jacob	1	2	3		
Steele, James	4	3	2		
Smith, John (Tanner)	2		2		
Stitely, John	1		5		
Stitely, Jacob	1	1	4		
Stoner, John, Junr	1	1	1		
Snider, John, Junr	1		4	6	
Sim, Joseph	2	1	1	1	34

FREDERICK COUNTY—Continued.

NAME OF HEAD OF FAMILY.	Free white males of 16 years and upward, including heads of families.	Free white males under 16 years.	Free white females, including heads of families.	All other free persons.	Slaves.
Shroyer, Leonard	1	3	2		
Shank, Michael	1	4	2		
Swamley, Margaret			1		
Spensinger, Michael		2	1		
Strihe, Peter	1	1	3		
Smith, Peter	3	4	4		
Stephens, Peter	2	3	5		
Smith, Philip	5	3	6		
Smith, John (of Philip)	1		1		
Snouk, Peter	1	2	2		
Stimble, Peter	1	3	5		
Sim, Patrick	3	2	2		37
Storep, Peter	5	3			
Simpson, Richard, Jun.	2		2		2
Sowers, Sophia	1	1	4		
Stallions, Samuel	1	3	3		
Springer, Susanna	1	2	3		
Sheredine, Upton, Esq.	2		1		25
Smith, William	2		4		
Sim, William	5				13
Sim, Anthony	2		1		10
Waters, Azel	1		7		4
Warfield, Alexander	2				9
Wood, Abraham		3	4		
Winebrenner, Anthony	1				
Waters, Andrew	2	2	2		
Waggoner, Adam	2				
Warfield, Basil	2		1		
Williams, Edward	1	4	1		
Wind, George	1		3		
Wickham, Henry	2	1	7		
Warfield, Henry	1		1	1	3
Wolfe, Jacob	3	1	2	1	1
Wood, Joseph	3	1	3		2
Whiteneck, John	1		2		
Werns, Jacob	1		3		
Wetsell, Jacob	1	4			
Wolfe, Mary	1		4		
Weaver, Philip	2	3	4		
Wickham, Robert	1	2	5		
Walse, Samuel	1	2	2		
Whitecraft, Samuel	1	1	4		
Wyer, William	2	4	3		
Yandis, Daniel	2	3	1		
Yandis, John	1	4	4		
Young, Philip	4	4	4		
Arnold, Archabald	1	3	3		1
Arter, Daniel	2	5	5		
Appler, Jacob	2	2	4		
Angel, John	1	2	2		
Adams, Joseph	2	2	6		
Arter, Michael	2	2	3		
Angel, Philip	2	2	3		
Addelspurgor, Thomas	1	2	2		
Barnhart, Anthony	1	2	2		
Black, Adam	1	5	3		
Benson, Benjamin	5	5	2		
Brininger, Casper	3	1	2		
Bower, John	2	5	5		
Beeler, Daniel	1	2	5		
Bost, Felty	1	1	2		
Brown, Geo	4	1	3		
Barnover, George	1	6	2		
Bosley, Gideon	2	4	4		
Brown, John	2		7		
Blueback, Benjamin		1	2		1
Brown, Joshua	1	3	4		
Brasilton, Isaac	2	2	5		
Bumbgardner, John	3	3	4		
Bishop, John, Sen.	1	3	6		
Burgoon, Jacob	3		6		
Bricker, John	1	2	2		
Brothers, Jacob	1		2		
Booker, John, Jun	1		3		
Baum, John	1		3		
Buffington, Jacob	2	2	5		
Bricker, Jacob	1	1	3		
Booker, John, Sen.	1	3	1		
Brothers, John			3		
Boyer, Mary	2		7		
Bumgardener, Michael	2	4	3		
Bruce, Norman	3		2		24
Babylon, Philip		3	1		
Beam, Philip	2		3		
Baum, Peter	1	2	2		
Beard, Paul	1	3	2		
Bowers, Stephen	2	1	6		
Colclaysier, Daniel	2	7	5		
Shadd, Daniel	1				
Cover, Eve		1	3		
Cresman, Frederick, Jr.	1	2	5		
Cresman, Frederick, Sen.	4	4	1		
Cassel, Jacob	2	4	4		
Coe, John, Sen.	2	3	2		
Clemson, John	2	3	4		
Coe, John, Jun.	3	5	3		
Crowl, Michael	1	4	4		
Coontz, Mary	2		2		
Crouse, Philip	2	2	7		
Cruise, Paul	1				6
Comp, Peter	1	2	4		
Chadd, Samuel	1	4	4		
Durbin, Benjamin	1	4	8		
Drumbar, Conrad	1	1	3		
Deverbaugh, Christian	2	1	4		
Dahoof, Christian	1	3	4		
Dern, Frederick	2	4	4		5
Dutters, John	1	3	2		1
Devendall, John	3	2	3		
Davis, John	1		2		
Dodson, Michael	2		2		
Dell, Nicholas	2	6	5		
Durbin, Thomas	4		3		
Durbin, Susanna	2		4		
Durbin, Thos Bond	2	2	4		
Durbin, William	2	4	6		
Egg, Jacob	1		7		
Erbaugh, Margaret	1	1	3		
Estep, Thomas	2	1	2		
Eckler, Jacob	1	2	2		
Estep, William	2	3	5		
Erbaugh, Wendle	2	1	3		
Farquhar, Allen	6	5	2		
Flegle, Charles	1	3	5		
Fisher, David	3	3	4		1
Frock, Daniel	2	4	3		
Flegleson, George, Jun.	2	1	3		
Fisher, Geo	1	4	6		
Featherbin, Jacob	1	1	5		
Ferguson, John	4	2	6		
Freeman, Jacob	2	1	6		
Fringer, Jacob	2		3		
Fuss, John		1	2		
Flegle, John	1	2	3		
Firmwalt, Lawrence	3	5	5		
Farquhar, Moses	2	2	2		
Foutz, Michael	2		2		
Fisher, Mary	2	2	5		
Fogle, Michael	1		2		
Furney, Nicholas, Sen.	1	1			
Fuss, Philip	1		3		
Flegle, Valentine	1	2	1		
Gist, David	1				7
Grandadam, Francis	2	2	1		1
Gramer, Jacob	2	4	5		
Gist, John	1				2
Gwynn, John	1	2	3		
Greenhalt, Jacob	2	2	3		
Hawn, Andrew	2	3	5		
Heener, Conrad	2	4	6		
Hyter, Phoeby	2	2	6		
Hartsock, Daniel	2	2	2		
Hawn, David	1	3	4		
Hodgkiss, Edward	1	2	3		3
Havener, Geo	2	1	2		
Heldebright, Geo	2	1	2		
Hawn, Geo	2	1	2		
Humbert, Geo	2	3	3		
Hand, Henry	2	4	5		
Harsh, Harman	2	3	6		
Hyner, Herbert	4	2	8		
Hoffman, Henry	2	1	7		
Heldebridle, Jacob	1		3		
Hyde, Jonathan	2		3		
Hichew, Jacob	3	2	4		
Harman, Jacob	2	1	4		
Hull, John	2	1	11		
Hecker, Barbara	1		3		
Heldebridle, John	1	2	2		
Hepner, John	3	2	1		
Harman, John	2		4		
Hawn, Jacob	2		2		
Hawn, Jonathan	1	4	4		
Havener, Michael	1		6		
Hagrader, Mary	3		2		
Hand, Matthias	1	3	4		
Hans, Martin	1		3		
Hans, Mordecai	1	2	3		
Hines, Martin	4		3		
Hichew, Philip	4	3	1		
Hendricks, Meriah	2	1	1		
Hand, William	1	1	4		
Haslet, William	1	3	1		
Jacobs, John Conrad	1	1			
Kline, Daniel	4		2		
Kemp, Judith		1	2		
Koons, Abraham	1	3	2		
Kephart, David	6	3	4		
Keefer, Frederick	1	5	3		1
Kirby, Joseph	1	3	4		
Keys, John	3	4	5		
Kesler, John	4	2	3		
Kirtsmiller, Leonard	2	1	3		
Kibler, Michael	1		1		4
Kenworthy, William	3	4	6		
Leppo, Mary			3		
Lease, Conrod	1	3	1		
Laugh, David	1		1		
Lemon, Solomy			3		
Lambert, Geo	1	2	3		
Lemmon, Jacob	2	3	5		
Logsdon, John, Jun	2		3		
Lambert, John	2		4		
Logsdon, John, Sen.	3	1	3		
Lister, John	1	2	3		
Lane, John	3	2	3		
Lister, Nicholas	2	1	5		
Lamb, Pearce	1	1	5		
Miller, Abraham	2		4		
Moore, Abraham	3		7		
Myerly, David	2	2	4		
Majors, Elias	3		12		7
McKenzy, Ell	1	3	3		
Myerly, Geo	2	2	3		
Myers, Geo	2	4	4		
McKensy, Henry	2	3	4		
Matthias, John	2	4	4		
Maxwell, William	1	2	7		
Miller, John	2	2	5		
Myers, Jacob	1	2	4		
McHaffy, Jane		1	3		
Mitting, John	1	5	1		
Marker, John	2	2	3		
Majors, Nathaniel	1		4		
Moser, Peter	2	1	6		
Mony, Richard	2	1	2		
Myers, Mary	4	2	2		
Utto, William	5	2	2		
Perkinson, Edward	2		4		
Pepple, John	3	4	4		
Painter, John	2		2		
Piper, Jacob	2		2		
Pepple, Jacob	1	2	4		
Pheasant, Samuel	2	3	2		
Powell, William	2	5	4		
Reece, Andrew	2		4		
Rowland, Abraham	2	1	3		
Roop, Joseph	2	1	2		
Rick, Christopher	1	3	1		
Roberts, Henry	1	3	4		
Russel, Jacob	1	3	3		
Richardson, John	4	3	3	1	
Runkles, Jacob	2	3	6		
Reece, John	2	1	1		
Right, John	3		4		
Ritinger, John	2		4		
Ritingmyer, Michael	2	1	5		
Reniker, Paul	2	5	5		
Roberts, William	1	3	5		4
Hardman, John	4		4		
Stultz, Conrod	1	1	7		
Stevenson, Charles	2	1	4		3
Sullivane, Cornelius	1	5	3		
Shriver, David	5	4	4		6
Spangier, Geo	3	7	3		
Stevenson, Henry	3	1	5		4
Sill, Henry	2		4		
Shearman, Jacob	3	1	4		2
Snuffer, John	2		6		
Snider, Jacob, Sen.	1		4		
Snider, Jacob, Jun.	1	4	2		
Slick, John	2	1	4		
Sharret, John	1	3	2		
Slife, John	1	3	3		
Shriner, John	2	3	2		
Stem, John	2	2	6		
Smith, Tice	2	2	4		
Smith, John	2	3	4		
Simmons, Isaac	1	3	4		
Switzer, Lud.	2	4	7		
Sap, Leonard	2		4		
Sigerfors, George	3		1		
Switzer, Matthias	1	2	5		
Shirvy, Modelena	1		5		
Smith, Mary	2		1		4
Shriner, Peter	3	3	4		
Stults, Mary	3	2	6		
Snarr, Philip	2	4	4		
Shoemaker, Peter	1	2	1		
Lane, Peter	1	2	1		
Stuller, Ulrick, Sen	3	2	6		
Stansbury, William	2	3	4		
Stevenson, William	1	3	3		
Smith, William	2	3	5		
Slick, William	1	1	7		
Sowers, William	3	1	5		
Taney, Frederick	1	4	2		
Talbot, Ann		2	3		
Uler, Andrew	2	3	1		

FREDERICK COUNTY—Continued.

NAME OF HEAD OF FAMILY.	Free white males of 16 years and upward, including heads of families.	Free white males under 16 years.	Free white females, including heads of families.	All other free persons.	Slaves.
Wigart, Andrew	4	2	2		
Winters, Geo	1		2	1	1
Wentz, Frederick	1		2	3	
Wygart, Geo	3	2	2		
Werner, John	3		6		
Wright, Joseph	3	1	6		
Weaver, John	1		2		1
Wells, James	4	2	2		5
Woolery, Jacob	1	1	1		
Wampler, Lod	2	3	4		
Waggoner, Michael, Senr	1		6		
Waggoner, Michael, Ju	1	2	6		
Werble, Philip	1	2	4		
Warner, Peter	1	1	1		
Wilson, Thomas	1			4	2
Wymert, Valentine	6	3	4		
Winchester, William	6		5		
Young, Andrew	1		2		
Yengling, John	2	4	3		
Zacharias, Daniel	1	2	4		2
Werner, Elizabeth	1	3	4		
Smith, John	1	1	2		
Durbin, Mary	2	1	3		
Thirkpine, John	1	1	3		
Bishop, Vachel	1	2	3		
Mikesell, Jacob	1	2	5		
Pepple, Peter	1	4	4		
Bower, Geo	1		2		
Ford, Stephen	1		1		
Jones, William	2	1	2		
Winegardner, Conrod	2	1	3		
Koldenbaugh, Andrew	2	2	4		
Reid, Hugh	3	2	8		9
Michaelhein, Francis	3	2	3		
Sell, Adam	1	2	3		
Sunbrun, Charlotte			3		
Stoneycypher, Martin		1	2		
Serr, James	1		2		
Sanbach, Francis	1	2	1	1	
Sell, Henry, Junr	1		1		
Getty, Francis	1		1		
Reeves, Prudence	1		1		
Myers, Nathan	3	2	3		
Cromer, John	1		2		
Powder, Jacob	2		1		
Winchester, Stephen, Esqr	2				
Crawford, John	1				
Lowry, John	1				
Eckart, Geo	1				
Harker, Julot			3		
Winters, Adam	3	3	2		
Bricker, Henry	4	1	4	1	34
Welsh, Thos	4	4	1	3	
Shad, William	1	1	3		
Oustler, Ormond	1	3	3		
Rader, Jacob	1	3	1		
Anders, John	1		2		
Colleberger, Jacob	1	4	2		
Cremian, Charles	1		4		
Hareh, Conrod	1		1		
Cookerly, Jacob	1		1		
Wood, John	1	2	4		1
Bishop, John	1		2		
Isenberger, Nicholas	1	1	2		
Nickey, David	2	1	2		
Wilson, William	4	3	8		
Richards, William	1				
Kitterman, John	1				
Warfield, Absolom	1				2
Wright, Anthony	1	1	1		
Barnes, James	1	1	3		
Thomas, John	1	1	3		10
Erbaugh, William	1				
Ritinger, Ann		1	5		
Hawn, John	2	3	2		
Harlin, Daniel	3	2	1		
Hall, James	2		1		
Smith, Middleton	4	1	4		
Wickart, Christian	1	5	4		
Way, Arnest	1	2	3		
Good, Jacob	1		1		
Kise, Abraham	3	1	5		
Myers, George	1		1		
Gassaway, Samuel	1	1	2		
Albaugh, Daniel	1		1		
Cyphered, John	1		1		
Stidley, Frederick	1	2	3		
Bostion, Philip	1		3		
Bower, Abraham	1	1	4		
Smith, Christian, of Wm	1		4		
Stricker, Jacob	1	1	1		
Dean, John	1		1		1
Fine, Philip, Jun	1		1		
Smith, Henry	1	2	3		
Borice, Laurence	1		1		

NAME OF HEAD OF FAMILY.	Free white males of 16 years and upward, including heads of families.	Free white males under 16 years.	Free white females, including heads of families.	All other free persons.	Slaves.
Hodges, Andrew	1				
Arnis, Jacob	1		1	2	
Wood, Charles	1		1		
Binger, Michael	2	1	3		
Beamer, Matthiss	3	1	2		
Helvory, Edward	3	1	2		
Gorson, Charles	5		5		
Link, Thomas	1		1		
Newport, James	1	3	3		
Fine, Peter, Junr	2	2	5		
Gay, Henry	1		4		
Burket, Joseph	1		2		
Lath, Henry	1		2		
Umber, William	1	3	2		
Borell, George	3	1	3		
Witting, Sarah	2		4		
OBryan, Terence	1	2	5		
Baker, Francis		1	3		
Whitmore, George	1	3	3		
Slice, Thomas	1	2	6		
Fuss, Conrod	1	2	2		
Beklote, John	1	1	2		
Steller, Ulrick	1	1	1		
Deale, Leonard	1		2		
Cramer, Jacob	1		2		
Richards, John	1	1	3		
Tate, Mathew	2	1	1		
Allison, John	2	4	3		1
Addison, Robert	1	4	1		
Anderson, William	1	3	6		
Biddle, Andrew	2	4	6		
Buzzard, Andrew	3	6	5		
Ransburg, Aaron	1	3	3		
Burket, Christian	1	2	3		
Beall, Tabitha			5		4
Busey, Charles	1	5	5		22
Beall, Elisha	2	1	6		10
Burket, George, Junr	1	1	2		
Boyer, Hobertus	2	2	2		1
Brandensburg, Jacob	2	2	2		
Barnes, John	2		2		
Beall, Joseph	2	2	6		
Beall, John	2	2	6		8
Bear, John	2	4	2		
Beall, Nathan	2	4	3		5
Boggis, Samuel	1	5	3		18
Burgee, Thomas	2	3	6		
Baldwin, Thomas	1	1	9		6
Brashears, William	2		6		
Ballinger, Cassa	2		6		
Clay, Adam	2	4	5		
Cheney, Charles		4	3		
Cook, George	1	2	4	1	14
Cutsell, Peter	1	3	6		
Clay, John	1	2	2		
Covel, Johnr	1	1	8		
Clary, John	1	1	4		
Camp, Peter	2	3	3		
Connor, Thomas	1		4	2	3
Cain, William	2	4	4		
Cecil, William, Senr	1		2		
Carvil, William	1	1	2		1
Cox, William	1	2	2		
Cecil, William, Jur	1	6	1		
Duval, Benjamin	2	6	3		1
Dorsey, Basil	2		3		18
Dorsey, Edward	2	2	3		10
Dunning, James	1	2	3		
Duvall, Mary		6	2		
Davis, Richard	4	3	3		13
Darnall, Thomas	2	5	2		18
Duvall, William, Senr	1	1	2		
Duvall, William, Jun	1	6	3		
Edelen, Christopher	1	3	5		
Edmondson, Roger	3		5		1
Fogle, Adam	2	2	4		
Falkner, Gilbert	2		4		2
French, Israel	1		2		
Fowler, John	1		2		
Fair, Michael	2		3		
Freeman, Richard	4		3		3
Fowler, Zadock	1	2	3		
Griffith, Caleb	1	2	2		
Griffith, Elisha	2	2	1		4
Green, Francis	1	4	5		
Gibson, Hannah	1	2	2		
Gabble, Joseph	1	1	2		
Gardner, John	2	1	2		3
Griffith, Orlando	5		3		9
Griffith, Philip	1	3	3		
Grover, Thomas	1	1	3	1	
Hardigel, Catharine		1	3		
Hyat, Eli	2	2	3		
Harding, Elias	1	1	3		2
Hobbs, Greenbury	1		3	1	4
Hobbs, John	6	3	3		2

NAME OF HEAD OF FAMILY.	Free white males of 16 years and upward, including heads of families.	Free white males under 16 years.	Free white females, including heads of families.	All other free persons.	Slaves.
Hall, Joseph	1	1	2	1	4
Hinton, John	2	1	2		
Hyatt, Meshech	3	1	2		6
Hall, Nicholas	2		4		10
Hillery, Osborn	2		1		
Hillery, Ralph	1	1	3		4
Herner, Richard	1	1	3		
Holland, Ruth			2		
Hammett, Robert	4		3	1	4
Howell, Stephen	2	2	4		
Hennis, Samuel	2	1	4		
Hillary, Thomas	1	2	4		
Hobbs, William	2	2	2		17
Hall, William	1	1	4		12
Hall, William Murdock	1	1	4		16
Harding, Zephaniah	1	1	5		5
Jacobs, Daniel	1	1	5		1
Ingman, Edmund		4			2
Ijams, John	1	1	3		11
Ijams, Plummer	1	1			1
Ijams, Richard	3		2		3
Johnson, Roger	4	5	4	2	29
Kirk, Benjamin	2	2	2	1	1
Keepers, Isaac	3	3	2		
Koontz, John	2	4	5		
Kendel, James	6	3	4		
King, John	3		3		1
Kinley, Shadrach	3		3		
Linton, Benjamin	1	2	1		
Leggs, Charles	1	1	2		
Luther, George	1	4	4		
Linton, Jeremiah	1	1	4		
Luther, Jacob	1	1	5		
Leak, James	3	6	4		
Linton, Samuel	1		3		1
Linton, Samuel, Jun	2	2	3		
Linton, Zachariah	2	4	2		2
Mussetter, Christian	1	1	3		
Mahony, Daniel	2		5		
McDonald, Francis	1	1	6	1	2
Mobler, James	1	1	5		
Macelfish, John	2		2		14
Macelfish, Jane		2	4		5
Moore, James	3	1	3		
Mobley, Lewis	1	1	3		19
Mossetter, Michael	1	2	3		
Mealy, Michael	1	2	2		
Maynard, Nathan	2		2		11
Maclefish, Philip	1	3	4		4
Murrel, Robert	1		1		
Maynard, Richard	2		2		
Maynard, Thomas, Senr	1	2	1		10
Mitchell, Thomas	1	1	2		
Mark, Thomas	1	2	4		
Morsell, William	1	1	5		1
Murphy, William	3	2	3		13
McLain, William	2		3		9
Norwood, Jeremiah	3	1	2		1
Newcomer, William	3	5	2	2	
Night, William	2	1	1		
Orland, Andrew	2		1		
Orinand, Michael	1		2		
Plummer, Abraham	1	1	5	1	1
Pourtney, Anthony	3	5	5		1
Plummer, Isaac	1	2	4		
Plummer, Joseph	1	2	7		2
Plummer, Jessee	1	1	2		
Plummer, Joseph (of Sam1)					
Patterson, Joseph	3		6		
Plummer, James (of Sam1)	1	3	2		
Plummer, Moses	1		2		
Plummer, Robert	2	1	1	1	1
Plummer, Samuel	2		5		
Plummer, Sarah		2	4		
Petser, Samuel	1	1	4		
Plummer, Thomas	4	1	9		1
Purdie, William, Senr	4	1	1		
Pencoast, William	1	1	4		
Plummer, Yate	2	3	5		
Plummer, James (of Thos)	1	3	2		1
Ramsour, Adam	1	1	2	2	
Rine, Casper	2				
Ruliff, Gilbert	2				
Ramsower, Henry	1	2	2		
Richardson, John	1	2	5		1
Rate, James	1	3	4	4	4
Ragan, John	4		2		
Rine, Michael	4	3	5		
Roberts, Richard	2	1	2		
Roy, William	1	1	3		
Simmons, Belinda	1	2	4		7
Shelman, David	1		4		
Smith, George	3	3	7		

FREDERICK COUNTY—Continued.

NAME OF HEAD OF FAMILY.	Free white males of 16 years and upward, including heads of families.	Free white males under 16 years.	Free white females, including heads of families.	All other free persons.	Slaves.
Snider, Jacob	2	1	1		
Snider, Jacob, Junr	2	2	4		
Silver, Margaret	1	2	3		
Sadler, Michael	1	3	7		
Sane, Philip, Junr	1	4	4		
Sprigg, Thomas	1	4	5		12
Stevens, William	2	2	1		5
Talbot, Benjamin, Senr	1				
Turner, Charles	3	1			
Talbot, John	2	1	6	1	
Talbot, Joseph	1	1	4		
Topery, Joshua	2	3	5		4
Taylor, Isaac	2	4	5		
Tomlinson, Jessee	3	3	6		
Turner, John	1		2		
Turner, Philip	1		2		
Taylor, Henry	2		5		
Turner, William	3	4	4		
Turner, William James	1	5	3		
White, Elisha	1	2	3		
Winter, Frederick	1	1	4		
Wolf, Henry	3		2		
Ward, John	1				1
Warfield, John	1	1	2		
Warter, Job	2		3		8
Wilson, Isaac	1	4	2		2
West, Joseph	2		2		
Williams, John	1	3	5		
Webber, Robert	1		5		
Waters, Samuel	2		3		
Wheeler, Samuel	1	3	1		
Wilkes, Thomas	3	1			
Wood, William	2		1		
Webb, William	2	2	1		
Rippen, Thomas	1	3	2		
Wilson, John	1		2		
McDaniel, Ann	1	1	1		
Swindley, Danl	1	2	1		
Waggoner, Joseph	1		4		
Lett, Elijah				6	
Lett, Aquila				5	
Sigfrids, Godfrey	2		1		
Sprigg, Thomas	1	5	2		
Smith, Jeremiah	1				
Boone, Jacob	1				
Norris, Edmund	2		5		
Glover, John	2		1		
Hilton, Susanna		1	2		
Taylor, Charles Philpot	2	2	5		1
Johnson, William	1	1	1		
James, Samuel				9	
Cole, Dennis	3	2	3		
Han, Lewis	1		2	1	
Roseberger, Frederick	2	1	3		
Hagerman, John	2	1	1		
McCain, John	1	3	2		1
Button, David	1	3	2		
Graybill, Jacob	4		6		
Adkins, William	1	1	6		
Nublock, Geo	2	1	2		1
Ragan, Daniel	2		2		
Brayfield John	1		1		1
Ford, Joseph	2	1	2		
Hayes, John	1	2	2		
Smith, John Hamilton	1		2		8
May, Benjamin	2		2		
Baker, John	2	1	1		
Smith, Isaac	3				
Shafer, Stephen	2		2		
Griffith, Patty		1	2		
Yingling Adam	1	1	1		
Sigfrid, Geo	1	3	4		
Connor, Edward	2		2		
Griffin, William	1	1	4		
Waugh, William	2	1	1		
Shrieves, William	5	1	2		31
Clothes, Geo	1		2		
McGee, John	1		3		
Smith, James	1		3		
Clance, John	1	2	3		
Jones, John	2		1		
Littlejohn, Geo	3	3	3		
Door, William	1	1	2		
Tobine, Michael	1		2		
Shanks, Ignatius	1	1	2		
Barnot, James	1		1		
Wheeler, Robert	2		3		
Styer, Jacob	1	4	4		
Hurly, James	2	2	4		
Perry, James	2	1	1		2
Kirk, Thomas	1		4		
Knight, Joshua	1		1		
Knight, James	1		1		
Wayman, John	1		1		
Brush, John	1	3	4		
Macelfish, Charles	1	1	1		7
Bennet, John	1	3	2		
Busey, Henry	1	3	4		
Price, Thomas	2	3	4		
McAtee, James	4		3		
Purdie, William, Junr	1	2	2		
Bradey, James	2	1	4		
Estep, James	2	1	4		
Finch, John	1	1	1		5
Fineheart, Massey	1	3	2		
Milla, John	1				2
Jones, Joshua	1		5		
Gosling, Henry	1	1	1		
Stattings, Phineas	1	1	3		
Lett, Jemima	2	1	3		
Martin, Charles	1	3	4		
Selman, Thomas	2	2	2		
Scruble, Henry	2	2	5		
Daker, Henry	1	1	3		
Clarke, Richard	1	1	2		
Hillery, Margaret		1	3		
Hillery, Jeremiah		1	3		1
Brasford, Thomas	1		3		
Hill, Anthony					8
Ryan, Thomas	1	2	1		
Jones, Zachariah	1	5	2		
Howard, Charles	1	2	2		7
Duvall, Mareen	2	1	2		3
Vanfenson, Arnold	2	3	5		1
Jones, Lewis	2		6		
Simpson, Amos	2	1	2		
Lar, Henry	1			1	6
James, Samuel	1		2		5
Bryan, Josiah	1		2		
Rop, Mary		1	3		
Collins, William	2	2	1		
Lanthrow, George	1	1	3		
Duvall, Lewis	2	2	4		6
Adams, Martin	1		2		
Adams, Thomas	1	1	4		
Angel, Charles	1		4		
Armstrong, James	2	3	3		
Agey, Jonathan	1	3	5		
Alexander, Thomas	1	2	4		
Andrews, William	1	3	4		
Bower, John	1	1	5		
Biggs, William, Senr	4		2		
Beamer, Philip	3		2		2
Black, Andrew	2	1	6		1
Barr, Archabald	1	1	3		
Bouden, John	1	3	3		
Biddle, George	1	2	2		
Brooke, Ralph	1	1	3		13
Bowersock, Geo. A	2	5	6		
Bigsler, Samuel	2	3	5		
Bankard, Jacob	1	3	3		
Baker, John	4	4	12		
Black, Frederick	4	4	6		
Baldwin, Elijah	2	4	4		
Baldwin, Daniel	2	4	5		
Bushman, Henry	3		2		
Brooke, Roger	2	2	2		19
Buchanan, Doctr John	2	4	1		1
Bentley, Eli	2	3	4		
Boyle, Daniel, Esqr	1				1
Burke, John	1	3	4		
Barnhart, Michael	2	2	5		
Biggs, Jacob	2	4	4		
Beam, Peter	2	2	2		
Clunt, Jacob	2				
Cornell, Richard	2	3	6		
Cover, Yost	1	2	5		
Cover, John	1	3	6		
Collendine, Jacob	1	3	3		
Crouse, Valentine	1	2	7		
Cress, Valentine	2	3	4		
Clunt, Andrew	2	3	4		
Conly, John	2	2	4		
Coonts, Henry, Senr	2	2	3		1
Kesselring, Lodowick	1	6	6		
Cornell, Benjamin	2	6	6		
Coontz, Paul			6		
Crapster, Rudolph	1		5		
Cramer, Casper		3			
Craglo, George	1	1	3		
Crouse, John, Senr	4	1	3		
Crabbs, George	2	1	3		
Cover, Earhart	1	3	3		
Clunt, Adam	2	4	3		
Coontz, William	2	3	3		
Clabough, Frederick	1	3	4		
Crowl, Peter	1	2	2		
Cover, Jacob	2	2	1		
Cover, John, of Fredk	2	2	1		
Clabough, Charles	1	1	1		
Davis, Phineas	1	1	4		
Eickard, Joseph	2	3	2		
Erb, Christopher	3		3		
Erbaugh, Laurence	3	3	11		
Eckard, Michael	1	2	4		
Elder, Thomas	1	4	5		3
Elder, Francis	1	2	4		1
Eckis, John	1	5	3		
Evans, John	1	4	3		
Estep, James	1	3			
Fickle, Jonathan	1		3		
Furney, Abraham		4	5		
Fickle, Matthias	1	3	2		
Furney, Philip	1	4	3		
Ferguson, Samuel, Junr	2	1	2		
Ferguson, Samuel	3		2		
Fare, Charles	2	4	3		
Fletcher, Jacob	3	5	4		
Fuss, William	2	1	7		
Fringer, Nicholas	2		2		1
Good, George	2		6		
Groff, John, Senr	7		2		
Galt, Matthew	2	7	2		
Groff, John, Junr	1	2	3		
Gwinn, John, Esqr	1				1
Good, Adam	2	1	3	2	4
Gordon, Joseph	2		2		1
Good, Eleanor			2		1
Gilleland, Hester		1	2		
Hesson, Wendle	4	4	4		
Hesson, Baltzer	1	2	6		
Herner, Michael	2	2	3		
Hammer, Francis	2	3	4		
Harris, John	2	1	5		1
Honewalt, Lodowick	1	1	2		
Hainds, Edward	1	1	3		
Heck, George	3		3		
Hubbert, Peter	2	2	5		
Hubbert, Philip, Jun	1	1	1		
Hammer, Jonas	1	3	3		
Hull, Andrew, Senr	1		2		
Hawn, Lodowick	1	4	5		
Harris, Thomas	1	1	6		1
Herner, Christian	1	5	2		
Hill, Abraham	1	1	5		
Hill, James	1	2	4		
Hess, Charles	1	1	2		
Hill, Richard, Senr	1		2		
Hill, Isaac	1		3		
Hill, Richard, Jur	1	2	3		
Hill, William	1		3		
Hagan, Patrick	2	3	4		
Hughes, John	2	2	5		3
Herner, George	2	4	2		
Hubbert, Philip	1	1	2		
Hull, Andrew, Jun	1	4	2		
Hill, Joseph	1	2	2		
Iron, John	3	3	6		
Jameson, Robert	3	3	4		
Inch, Peter	2	3	2		2
Jones, John	1	2	3		
Jones, Thomas	1	2	4		
Keefer, Henry	2	1	4		
Kesier, Jacob	2	1	4		
Key, John Ross, Esqr	3	3	1		26
Carr, James	3		5		
Kelly, George	3	3	4		
Laney, John	3		4		
Lingenfelter, Daniel	1		2		
Lingenfelter, Valentine	1	3	1		
Lemon, John	3		4		
Leech, Benjamin	1	1	6		
Love, Robert	1	1	3		
Lynn, Nicholas	1	2	4		
Long, Daniel, Senr	3		2		
Lynn, Michael	1	1	7		
Leech, James	1		1		
Lewis, Sarah			4		
Lingenfelter, Geo	1	1	4		
Logan, Andrew	1	3	4		
Love, James	1	1	4		
Long, Peter	2	1	2		
Munshour, Nicholas	2	2	3		
Markland, John	2	1	3		
McKaleb, Joseph	2	3	2	1	2
Michael, Peter	1	1	1		
Miller, Jacob	3	1	5		
Matthias, Joseph	2	2	9		
Miller, Stephen	3		6		
Midhour, John, Senr	3	2	1		6
McPherrin, Samuel, Senr	2		2		
McPherrin, Samuel, Jur	1	1	2		
Mefferd, John	4	3	7		2
Miller, John	2	1	5		
McAlister, Alexander	2	1	3		
McCune, Samuel	2	1	6		
Marks, Peter	2	3	4		
Martin, Jacob	1	1	4		
Miller, Martin	2	4	6		
Miller, George	2	2	3		
Miller, Martin, Jun	2	2	2		
Martin, Geo	2	2	3		

FREDERICK COUNTY—Continued.

NAME OF HEAD OF FAMILY.	Free white males of 16 years and upward, including heads of families.	Free white males under 16 years.	Free white females, including heads of families.	All other free persons.	Slaves.
Moaler, Jacob	3	2	5		
Moaler, Solomon	1	2	2		
Majors, James	4	3	4		1
McPherrin, William	4	1	5		
Moritz, Jacob	1	2	3		
McComb, William	2	2	3		
Newcomer, Samuel	2	2	6		
Need, Magdalena	2		4		
Nall, Philip	2	3	4		
Nichodemus, Valentine	1		3		
Null, Valentine	2				
Null, Wendle	3		2		
Null, Michael	3		2		2
Nell, Philip	1				
Nipple, Stephen	1		6		
Null, Jacob	2	1	2		
Nutter, Zacob	1	1	2		4
Noel, John	1	2	7		
Orendorf, Peter	2	3	4		
O'Hara, Henry	2		5		1
Oler, Peter	4		4		
Oler, Geo. Adam	1	2	4		
Putonberger, Michael	3	3	4		
Poor, Abraham	1	2	2		3
Poorman, John	2	2	5		
Pettit, James	2	1	3		
Phillps, Reese	1		2		
Paxton, William	2	2	3		
Paxton, Thomas	2	3	7		
Peale, David	2	3	2		
Pole, Thos Samuel	1	2	3		3
Panter, Henry	2	3	3		
Rice, George	2		1		
White, William	1	3	4		
Rinedollar, Geo	1		4		
Rinedollar, Henry	1	3	2		
Rosenplot, John	2		4		
Rice, Casper	3		4		
Rinehart, George	3	1	5		
Reed, Jacob	2	1	5		
Rinehart, Felty	1		1		
Rudicill, Tobias	4	3	6		
Reece, John	1	2	5		
Real, Michael	1		2		
Rinedollar, Matthias	1	3	4		
Rice, Andrew	1	2	2		
Rudolph, Peter	2	1	4		
Rogers, Owen	2	1	5		
Rutcorn, Christian	2	1	6		
Slider, Peter	2		4		
Swyer, Matthias	4	1	3		
Six, Henry, Senr	1	2	3		
Six, Geo	1	4	2		
Shealy, Christian	1	6	3		
Sane, Philip	1		1		
Shiner, Philip	4	1	1		
Shroyer, Matthias	3	2	3		
Stump, George	1	3	3		
Smeak, Simon	3	3	5		
Stagner, Peter	2	4	3		
Stump, Leonard	2		1		
Slider, Simon	2	6	6		
Shull, Stephen	2	4	6		
Shull, John	4	5	3		
Stonecypher, Daniel	6	2	4		
Sink, George	1	2	4		
Stimble, Jacob, Senr	4		4		
Storme, John	4		3		
Smith, Capt John	2	1	2	1	7
Shroyer, Jacob	2	3	5		
Sheets, Jacob, Junr	1	1	1		
Sheets, John	1	1	1		
Sparkes, Joseph	1	1	3		
Spalding, Henry	1	5	4		1
Smith, Jacob, Senr	2		3		
Smith, Jacob	1	1	3		
Sharrer, Lodowick	2	4	3		
Six, John	1	3	3		
Shrader, John	1	3	6		
Shaner, Peter	2	3	1		
Shilling, John	1	2	3		
Storme, Joseph	2	2	4		
Varterbaker, Jacob	1	2	4		
Shaw, Victor	2	9	4		
Six, Philip	2	2	3		
Sunbreen, John	2	4	3		
Shunk, Peter	1	4	3		
Sharrer, Tobias	2	1	3		
Sterling, Jonathan	1		2		
Troxall, Jacob	1	3	4		
Taney, Joseph	1	2	7		11
Duttero, Conrod	2		3		
Trucks, John	2		4		
Thomson, Hugh	3	5	6		
Trucks, Geo	2		4		
Welty, John	3	2	3		
Wimmer, Abraham	4	1	3		
Wilson, Caleb	2	1	8		
White, Andrew	2	2	8		
Will, Nicholas	1	2	3		
Wolfe, Christopher	2		4		
Will, George	1		3		
Wyvilla, Stephen	4	3	5		
Westbay, Hugh	3	2	6		
White, Abraham	2	2	5		
Woolart, Ludwick	1	2	2		
White, Christopher	2	1	3		
White, Henry	2		4		
Yengling, Frederick	2		7		
Yengling, Margaret			2		
Yengling, Jacob	1	6	4		
Smith, Doct. Joseph Sim	1		3		1
Crapster, John	3	4	3		
Woodrow, John	2	1	3		
Medzler, Nicholas	1	1	3		
Bristo, Samuel	1	1	3		
Adams, Ann			2		
Hart, Philip	4	1	5		
McSherry, Barnabas	1	1	1		4
Lufft, George	1		1		
Swope, Henry	2				
Wait, Joseph	1	4	3		
Cornell, Jacob	2				
Need, Geo	1	1	2		
Kennedy, Henry	1		2		
Fisher, Christian	1	1	4		
Crawl, Peter	1	1	2		
Scepter, Joseph	1	1	3		
Stemble, Jacob, Junr	1	1	1		
Arnd, John	1	1	4		
Pepple, William	1		4		
James, Thomas	2	2	4		
Myers, Jacob	1	1	6		
Baker, Frederick	1				
Mantle, Michael	1			3	
Little, Joseph	1	2	2	1	
Staples, William	1	1	2		
Brednick, Henry	1				
Shonce, Christopher	1	3	1		
Price, Benjamin	1	1			3
Sponceller, William	1	2	4		
Smith, John (Cooper)	1	2	4		
Dennis, Jacob	1	4	1		
Burgman, Christopher	1	4	6		
Frank, Geo	1		3		
Rimby, Peter	1	3	2		
Marshall, William	2		4		
Dunn, Robert	2	1	1		1
Crouse, John, Jun	1	2	2		
Charlton, John Usher	2	1	2		3
Rudicill, Jacob	1	1	2		
Copeland, Philip	3	1	5		
Good, Isaac	1	1	1		
Baker, Henry	1	2	4		
Knox, John	2	1	4		
James, Samuel	2	2	1		
Britton, William	2		3		
Ryley, Doyle	1		3		
Sink, Jacob	1	2	2		
Walker, William	1	4	3		
Quinner, Jacob	2	1	2		
Hammer, Michael	1		3		
Lee, Dudley	1	3	1		
Davis, Elizabeth			1		
Butler, Thomas	1	1	5		
Derr, Jacob	2	4	6		
Goshour, John	1	1	1		
Seipe, Henry	2		3		
Conrod, Jacob	2		3		
Cuddy, Henry	2		3		
Wyer, John	1	2			
James, John	1	3	2		
Angle, Jacob	2	1	2		
Stump, Adam	2		5		3
Erb, John	2		5		
Agle, Peter	1	2	2		
Ambrose, Catharine	2	1	3		
Ayle, Daniel	1	2	3		
Anderson, Edward	1	2	3		14
Byerly, Jacob	2		3		
Bine, Adam	2	1	4		
Beall, Basil	1	4	8		12
Beall, Collimore	3		2		1
Bouse, Christian	2		2		
Brunner, Elias	3	3	4		
Bear, George	3		4		1
Beamer, Henry	2	2	5		
Beit, Hickison	2	2	5		9
Bruner, John	2		4		2
Biggs, John	2	1	3		
Bear, John	1		2		
Bringle, Laurence	3	1	3		
Bookey, Matthias	3	1	3		
Bruner, Stephen	3	3	5		2
Brawner, Thomas	2		5		
Crickbaum, Conrod	2	1	3		
Coon, Christian	2	3	5		
Clise, Frederick	1	4	5		
Coontz, George	1	3	5		
Clem, George	1	1	3		
Coppersmith, George	1	1	2		
Cross, Henry	1	1	4		
Calflesh, John	3	1	2		
Colour, Jacob	1	3	6		
Cregar, John	1	2	5		
Crowl, Isaac	2	1	3		
Crist, Jacob	5	2	1	1	6
Calf, John	1	1			
Cattero, Jacob	1		2		
Culh, Isaac	1		2		
Cregar, Laurence	1	6	2		7
Carey, Mary	3		1		6
Christ, Michael	2	1	7		5
Crowl, Nicholas	2	1	2		
Collins, Hodijah	1	2	5		2
Crist, Philip	2	3	4		1
Cregar, Valentine	2	3	3		
Crum, William	2	3	3		5
Derr, Bostian	2	3	1		7
Devoyer, Edmund	1		2		
Devilbiss, George	4	5	3		2
Domer, George	2		3		
Donnehow, Hugh	1	5	4		
Delander, John	1		3		
Devilbiss, John	1	2	4		5
Derr, John Martin	3	1	7		
Derr, George	2	1	2		
Deane, Robert	2	2	5		
Elder, Guy	2	3	9		2
Elder, William, Junr	1	2	4		1
Freshower, Adam	1	2	5		
Flemming, Arthur	1	2	3		4
Fouts, Baltis	2	2	4		2
Fowler, Clement	2		4		
Fouts, Henry	3	1	3		7
Faro, Henry	2		2		
Flannagan, Hugh	3	1	3		
Fralick, Henry	1		5		
Freshour, Mariah		4	2		
Freck, Jonathan	1	2	3		
Flemming, John	1	2	4		8
Flannagan, Lackland	1	2	2		2
Frecker, Philip	1	2	5		
Flemming, Thomas	1	2	2		
Funderburgh, Walter	2	2	3		
Grosheng, Abraham	2	4	3		1
Getsingtanner, Baltser	2	4	2		
Gilbert, Barnet	2		2		
Getsingtanner, Christian (of B.)	1	2	1		
Gauk, Christian	1	1	4		
Gantt, Fielder	2	1	2		6
Getsingtanner, Jacob, Senr	1		3		
Getsingtanner, Jacob	1	3	3		3
Getsingtanner, John	2	1	4		2
Gritchshall, John	2		4		
Green, Samuel	2		2		9
Goodman, William	1	1	2		2
Holts, Benedict	3		2		
Hinkle, Baltis	3		2		
Hull, Benjamin	1	2	5		
Head, Biggar	1	3	5		3
Hedge, Charles	1	1	5		
Heffner, Catharine	1	2	4		
Herring, Casper	2		4		
Hildebrand, Erasmus	3	3	5		
Heffner, Frederick	1		6		
Heffner, Frederick, Jun	1	5	4		
Holtsman, Frederick	1	4	6		
Helman, Harman	1	1	6		
Jackson, Henry	1	5	4		
Haff, Jacob	1	2	5		3
Houk, John	1	2	2		
Hedge, Jacob	1	1	2		1
Holts, Jacob	1		2		
Heckathon, Jacob	2	4	2		
Housman, Jacob	2	3	1		
Holtsman, Jacob	2		2		
Highfield, Jonathan	3	6	6		2
Holtsman, Jacob, Jun	1	3	2		
Hinkey, John	1		2		
Hildebrand, Mary	2	1	5		
Hedge, Mary	1		5		
Hope, Michael	1	4	5		
Hefner, Michael	1		5		
Hefner, Michael, Jun	1	1	5		
Houk, Peter	2		2		
Holmes, Peter	1	2	6		
Harrison, Richard	5		6		1

FREDERICK COUNTY—Continued.

NAME OF HEAD OF FAMILY.	Free white males of 16 years and upward, including heads of families.	Free white males under 16 years.	Free white females, including heads of families.	All other free persons.	Slaves.
Head, William	2		2		1
Head, William, Junr	2	2	6		1
Johnson, James, Esqr	9	1	3		65
Julian, John	2	4	3		
Ikenbread, Mary	1	2	2		
Johnson, Thomas, Esqr	18	1	5		38
Knouff, Adam	1	2	2		
Kemp, Frederick	2	4	4		
Kemp, Henry	2	3	4		
Kelly, Hugh	1				
Kemp, John	2	1	5		
Kiger, Leonard	2		5		
Kemp, Peter	3	2	6		1
Livers, Anthony	3	3	1		10
Lefever, Christian	2	2	5		
Linebaugh, Christian	1		6		
Lefever, Elias	3	4	2		
Licklider, George	1	3	2		
Lemon, Jacob	1		2		
Late, Leonard	2	4	2		
Livers, Nathaniel	1	1	1		
Licklider, Peter	1	1	2		
Lilly, Richard	3	1	3	2	5
Lilly, Thomas	1	1	1		3
Morningstar, Susanna	1		4		
Miller, Anthony	2	2	6		
Miller, Abraham, Senr	5	1	7		
Moore, Alexander	1	3	4		
Myers, Bostian	3	4	4		
Miller, Daniel	3	4	4		
Measle, Frederick	1				
Main, George	1	3	1	1	
Myers, George	2	3	5		
Marshall, James	2	1	4		8
Miller, Jacob	5	2	4		7
Magill, John	1		2		7
McDonald, Jacob	1	1	5		
McDonald, James	1				
Miller, Jacob, Jur	1		2		
Moser, Leonard	1	2	2		
Morningstar, Philip	1	3	2		
Myers, Stephen	3	3	6		
Ogie, Alexander	4	2	2		
Ogle, Jaros	2	5	3		3
Prutsman, Daniel	1	2	3		
Prutsman, Elizabeth			3		
Pentz, Jacob	2	1	4		
Pup, John	2		1		
Pingley, Christian	4	3	4		
Patterson, John	1	2	6		
Prutsman, John	1	2	4		
Price, Philip	3	4	5		
Pup, Peter	1		2		
Price, Thomas	6	1	5		8
Ramsburg, Adam	1	1	3		
Reece, Adam	1		2		
Reece, Adam, Junr	1	3	4		
Ridge, Benjamin	1		2		
Ramsburg, Christian	2	2	2	4	
Ridge, Ephraim	2	1	3		
Rob, Frederick	3	1	1		
Ream, George	1	2	6		
Reynolds, Hugh	4	4	4		4
Ramsburg, John	4	1	3	2	1
Ramsburg, Jacob	2	6	3		
Reed, John	2	4	3		
Ringer, Matthias, Junr	2		3		
Ringer, Matthias	1	1	1		
Rogers, Patrick		2	4		
Ridge, William	1	3	2		
Snouk, Adam	2	1	6		
Souder, Adam	5	1	4		
Stull, Adam	2	3	6		
Stoner, Benedict	2		6		6
Simmon, Baltis	1		1		
Shoup, Christian	1	2	2		
Springer, Christian	2	3	3		
Stull, John	2	1	3		
Shryock, Christian	2	2	3		
Shiff, Godfrey	1	2	5		
Shafer, Conrod	2	1	5		
Shryock, Daniel	3		2		
Stofer, Elias	2	1	4		
Shriver, Frederick William	1	4	1		1
Shoup, George	2	3	2		
Shofe, John	3	5	3		
Giddy, Peter	2	1	3		
Scis, Geo	2		2		
Simmerman, Geo	4	1	2		
Shaver, Geo	2		4		
Staley, Henry	1	3	4		
Stuffle, Henry	1	3	3		
Shaffer, John	2	2	4		
Shaver, Jacob	1		2		1
Staley, Jacob	2	2	2		

NAME OF HEAD OF FAMILY.	Free white males of 16 years and upward, including heads of families.	Free white males under 16 years.	Free white females, including heads of families.	All other free persons.	Slaves.
Staley, Joseph	1	5	6		
Stoner, John	6	4	5	2	4
Sin, Jacob	1		4		
Shitoacre, John	2	1	3		
Smith, Joshua	1		1		
Smith, John	3		2		
Staley, John, Junr	2	5	2		
Spoon, John	2	4	3		
Shingle, Laurence	2	3	7		
Storme, Magdalena		1	3		
Staley, Melchor	1		5		
Smith, Matthias	2	2	7		
Shoup, Matthias	1	2	7		
Sheon, Nicholas	2	2	7		
Sin, Elizabeth			4		
Staley, Peter	1	2	5		3
Shaver, Peter	2	1	1		
Scis, Paul	1	1	1		
Smeak, Simon	4	6	3		
Selby, Samuel	4	1	7		7
Shelmerdine, Stephen	3				7
Shryock, Valentine	1	4	3		
Smith, William	1	3	6		
Streaver, Yockman	2		4		
Thomas, Christian	1	4	5		2
Thomas Francis	1		7		6
Troxall, Frederick	2	3	5		
Tuttero, George	2	1	3		
Tuttero, George, Junr	1	1	3		
Trout, Jacob	2	1	4		
Totfer, Peter	1	1	4		
Troutman, Peter	2	2	4		4
Westenhaver, Christian	2	2	2		
Weelfy, David	2	1	4		
Whetcroft, Edward	3	3	2		
Woolhide, Frederick	2		1		
Woolhide, Frederick, Junr	1		4		
Woodrick, Geo	2	4	5		
Weller, John, Jur	2	3	3		
Weller, Jacob	3	4	3		1
Weller, Jacob, Jur	1	5	4		1
Wood, Richard	1	1	3		
Werner, Jacob	1	1	4		
White, Joseph	1				
Wolf, Peter	5	1	6		1
Woolhide, John	1	3	6		
Young, Casper	1	2	3		
Young, Daniel	1	2	3		
Young, George	2	3	5		
Young, John	2	4	2		
Yont, John	3	4	3		
Yesterday, Michael	2	2	3		
Young, Peter	2	1	4		
Waggoner, Adam	2		3		
Biggs, Benjamin	2		4		
Crawford, Moses	1	5	5		
Troxall, David	1	6	6		
Jones, John	2	4	3		
Etsler, George	2	1	2		
Barnhart, David	2		1		
Stoner, Casper	1		2		
Thomson, William	1		5		
Boyd, Abraham	1	1	2		
Brawner, Elizabeth	3	2	2		4
Montgomery, Edward	1		3		
Wright, Henry	2	3	2		
Wolf, Simon	2		1		
Ocker, Christian	3	3	8		
Noah, Conrod	1	2	1		
Fox, Henry	2		4		
Coplin, Philip	3	1	5		
Shuman, Jacob	1	3	6		
Miller, John	1	3	2		
Pot, Benedict	2		2		
McGill, Patrick	1	1	1		7
Crama, Jacob	1		1		
Smith, Nicholas	3	1	3		1
Pharoah, Leonard	1	2	2		
Mullen, Nicholas	2	4	2		
Stokes, James	2	2	2		
Lickfetter, George	2	2	2		
Girton, Sylvester	1	1	2		
Noland, James	2		2		
Rady, Henry	1	2	5		
Windsor, Modelena			2		
Streavy, Paul	2	4	3		
Eden, Robert	1		1		
Fogleson, George	1		2		
Crafts, Thomas	1		2		
Ketterman, Stoffel	1		1		
Shringer, Matthew	1		1		
Cannen, Jacob	1		1		
Livers, Thomas	1	1	5		
McCusick, John	1	2	1		
Barnet, Luke	1		1		
Westford, Thomas	1		1		

NAME OF HEAD OF FAMILY.	Free white males of 16 years and upward, including heads of families.	Free white males under 16 years.	Free white females, including heads of families.	All other free persons.	Slaves.
Fuller, Samuel	1	2	3		
Rock, John	1	2	5		
Orbit, Philip	4		3		
Durst, Henry	1	3	4		
Watson Samuel	1		3		
Goodman, Philip	2	2	2		
McKensie, David	2	1	2		
Reckard, John	1		3		
Walter, Jacob	1	1	2		
Shriver, Henry	1	5	2		
Fortune, Charles				2	1
Durst, Philip	1	1	6		
Goodman, William, Jun	3	4	4		
Bevengton, Henry	1	2	4		
Westerhaver, Christopher	2	2	3		
Loudenbaugh, Conrod	2	2	1		
Kemp, Frederick, Sen	1		4		
Barnhart, Geo	1		4		
Haldebrand, Joseph	1	1	2		
Hester, William	1	1	2		
Wortakel, Geo	2	3	3		
Ambrose, Henry	1	2	3		
Allison, James	2	2	2		
Armstrong, John	3	1	2		
Artman, Michael	1		2		
Artman, William	2		9		
Blackburn, Alexander	1	2	4		
Boon, Abraham	1	1	1		
Briner, Abraham	1		5		
Sweeny, John	2	2	4		
Bryan, Edward	3	1	1		
Braner, Henry	3				
Brown, Joseph	3		4		
Crise, Henry	4	1	5		
Bruner, Peter	1	2	4		
Buzzard, Peter	1	2	3		
Brown, Robert	1	2	3		
Bouser, Stophel	2	2	2		
Brown, William, Jur	1		2		
Brown, William	2	8	5		
McCormack, Daniel	2	1	4		
Collins, Humphrey	1	4	4		
Crabbs, Henry	4		7		
Cooper, James, Junr	3		1		
Crist, Jacob	2	4	6		
Knouff, John	1	2	3		
Knouff, John, Junr	2	2	2		
Calf, John	3	1	2		
Crabbs, John	3	5	4		
Calf, Jacob	1	2	2		
Crist, John	2	5	2		
Clabough, John of Jno	1	4	4		
Cooper, James	2		4		
Kemp, Lodowick	2	4	4		
Copeland, Matthias	2	4	5		
Coon, Philip	1	2	4		
Croan, Robert	1	2	4		
Cleland, Samuel	1	1			10
Carrick, Samuel	2		2		6
Currans, William	3	1	1		
Delositer, Daniel	1	1	8		
McDonald, Samuel	2	2	8		
Davis, Thomas	2	1	1		
Elder, Arnold	1		2		7
Elder, Charles	6	2	3		7
Elder, Elisha	1	3	3		4
Elder, William, Junr	3	3	3		
Elder, Phebe	3	1	2	1	
Elder, Clementina	2	1	1		6
Emmit, Samuel	2	1	2		6
Elder, William, Esqr	4	3	7		2
Emmit, William	3	1	5		
Fevery, Jacob	2	2	3		
Faris John	1	2	3		
Flora, John	3	3	5		
Fleck, Lucas	3	3	3		1
Fry, Martin	3	3	6		
Freck, Philip	1	2	2		
Flemming, Robert	2	5	3		3
Fream, Richard	2		2		
Gordon, Daniel	2		2		
Grove, Henry	1	1	5		1
McGary, John	1	1	4		
Gump, John	2	2	4		
McGorgan, John	2	1	1		
Gates, Jacob	1	1	5		
Hill, Abraham	4	1	3		
Hofman, Adam	2		3		
Hagan, Alexander	2		3		
Hoover, Christian	2	4	3		
Hockensmith, Conrod	1		2		
Harbough, Christian	1	4	2		
Henning, Casper	1	2	3		
Hobbs, Charles	1	3	3		2
Hammer, Jacob	1	1	4	1	

FREDERICK COUNTY—Continued.

NAME OF HEAD OF FAMILY.	Free white males of 16 years and upward, including heads of families.	Free white males under 16 years.	Free white females, including heads of families.	All other free persons.	Slaves.
Hockensmith, George..	2	2	6		1
Harbaugh, George.....	4	4	3		
McHenry, Henry......	1	3	4		
Hoover, Hans Wendle..	3		4		
Harbaugh, Jacob.....	2	6	6		
Harbaugh, John......	1	5	1		
Hammer, John.......	1	4	4		
Hornacre, Isaac.....					
Hayes, Jonathan.....	3	1	3		6
Hockensmith, Jacob...	3	3	6		
Hughes, James......	3	1	5		
Hoover, John.......	1	2	4		
Hughes, Joseph.....	1				1
Harbaugh, Lodowick..	3		4		
Hockensmith, Michael.	3	5	5		
Harmar, Marks......	4		4		
Patterson, Thomas....	2	3	4	1	
Jennings, Richard....	1	1	2		
Koon, Christian.....	2	3	3		1
Kill, George.......	1	5	4		
Keever, Lodowick....	1	2	4		
McKeen, William.....	2	1	2		
Love, Benjamin.....	2	3	4		
Love, David.......	3	1	2		
Loy, Frederick......	1	5	4		
Lynn, Henry.......	3	2	4		
Love, Hugh.......	1	6	3		
Linebaugh, Jacob.....	2	2	6		
Livers, Mary.......	1	1	2		2
Lips, Philip.......	1	2	3		
Lemmon, Richard....	1	2	3		
Muckaberry, Abraham.	1		3		
Messner, Christian....	1	1	2		
Marker, Catharine....	1	1	3		
Matthews, Conrod....	1	5	6		
Martin, David......	2	2	4		
Miller, Frederick....	6	2	7		
Messner, George.....	4	5	6		
Matthews, Henry....	1	3	6		
Matthews, John, Jun ..	1		3		
Martin, Jacob......	1	5	3		
McMahen, James.....	3		3		
Morrison, James.....	3	2	4		
Matthews, John.....	2	4	6		
Minute, James......	2	4	5		
Miller, Lodowick....	1	4	3		
Martin, Matthias....	3	1	7		
Miller, Philip......	2		5		
Matthews, Philip....	3	5	4		
McAtee, George.....	1		3		
Maxwell, Thomas....	2	1	2		
Murdock, William....	1		1		1
Meredith, William....	1	2	6		
Nusey, John.......	1	1	3		
Nickum, John......	3	3	3		
Oler, Andrew......	3	2	1		
Overholts, Abraham...	2	2	4		
Iler, Frederick.....	2	4	6		
Hover, George.....	1	1	3		
Ott, Geo........	1	1	6		
Hover, Jacob......	1	5	3		
Ogle, Joseph......	1		3		
Oyler, Jonas......	1	2	3		
Ott, Jacob.......	1		3		
Oler, Laurence.....	2	5	3		
Ott, Michael......	2		1		
Oler, Philip.......	1	3	4		
Ott, Peter.......	1	2	4		
Ott, Abigail.......			2		
Ott, Geo., Junr.....	1	2	3		
Parks, James......	2	2	6		
Proutman, Jacob....	2	3	6		
Porter, Nathan.....	1	2	3		1
Patterson, Nathaniel..	2	1	2		3
Row, Arthur......	3	5	4		
Robinson, Charles....	2	3	6		
Ritter, Elias......	1	5	1		
Row, George......	1	3	4		
Rosier, Henry......	1	3	3		
Riffner, Henry.....	1	3	3		
Ringland, John.....	1	1	3		
Ryan, James......	1	7	5		
Ramsay, Joseph.....	3		5		
Rosebaugh, Isaac....	1		1		
Riffly, Jacob......	1	1	4		
Row, Michael......	1	2	4		
Ryley, Thomas.....	4		2		
Roberts, William....	3	2	3		
Slush, Andrew.....	3	3	5		
Smith, Amos......	1	3	4		6
Stewart, Alexander...	2	1	3		1
Smith, Christian....	3	3	4		
Slonacre, Christian...	1		6		
Smith, Daniel......	1	2	4		1
Sheets, Frederick....	1	3	4		1
Smith, Geo........	1				1
Smith, Geo., Jun....	1	4	2		
Stringer, Geo......	1		1		
Shroyer, John (Tanner)	1	3	3		
Shroyer, John, Senr...	2	3	2		
Smith, Jacob......	1	7	2		
Smith, John......	2	1	2		1
Stevenson, James....	1	2	6		
Sheets, Jacob......	5		3		
Stoner, Jacob......	1	1	6		
Snider, John......	1	1	5		
Shields, James.....	1	3	4		
Stevenson, John....	1	1	2		
Stricker, Michael....	2		2		
Smith, Michael.....	2	2	1		
Smith, Matthias....	1	3	2		
Shaver, Peter......	3	2	6		4
Shaver, Philip.....	1	1	2		
Singer, Samuel.....	1	1	4		
Steckle, Simon.....	1		2		
Shields, William....	3	1	3		5
Sweny, William.....	1	5	2		
Thomson, Ralph....	3	3	7		
Thomas, Christian...	1	3	2		
Tanner, David.....	1	2	3		
Thomas, Jacob.....	1	1	2		
Thomas, Isaac.....	1		2		
Troxall, John......	1	3	5		
Troxall, John, Junr...	3	3	6		3
Toughman, John....	1	6	3		
Tanner, Jacob.....	1	1	2		
Troxall, Jacob, of Peter.	1	2	1		
Troxall, Peter.....	3	1	2		
Thompson, William...	4		6		
Valentine, Henry....	1		1		
Valentine, Jacob....	1	3	4		
Valentine, John....	1	2	1		
Whitmore, Abraham..	2	1	5		
Williard, Andrew....	1	3	4		
Whitmore, Benjamin..	2	2	4		
Whitenhaver, Christo- pher........	2	4	2		
Wolf, Daniel......	2	2	4		
Whitmore, David....	2	2	6		
Weaver, Geo., Jr....	2	1	2		
Whitmore, Henry....	2	2	2		
Williams, Henry....	2	2	1		3
Whitmore, Jne.....	3	2	2		1
Wilson, Joseph.....	3	4	5		5
Withero, John.....	2	4	5		
McWilliams, John....	1		5		
Williard, John.....	1	6	1		
Wilson, Michael....	1		1		3
Williard, Peter.....	1		2		
Williard, Philip....	1	3	2		
Renit, Robert.....	1		1		
White, Sarah......	1		3		1
Wilson, Thomas....	1	5	3		3
Young, John......	1	2	1		
Zacharious, Mathias..	1	2	3		
Newman, Jacob.....	2	1	1		
Hoptman, Henry....	1		2		
Little, Barnet.....	1		2		
Cockran, Daniel....	1	2	2		
Cridler, John......	2	3	2		
McDonald, Margaret..			3		
Shields, William, Jnr.	1	3	1		
Dugan, John......	1	1	4		
Sook, Henry......	1		2		
Nunemacker, Philip ..	2		1		
Hoover, Jacob.....	1		1		
Simmon, Jacob.....	3	3	2		
McGuire, Ross.....	2		2		
Bonor, Geo.......	1	2	3		
Canon, Mary......			2		
Buchanan, William...	1				
Nelson, Peter......	1		3		
Richard, John.....	1	1	2		
McKain, William....	1	2	2		
Wright, Joseph.....	1	3	3		
Smith, Thos......	1				
McIlroy, James.....	1		1		
Beale, Geo.......	1				
Keever, Jacob.....	1	1	3		
Keever, Abraham....	1	3	2		
Koefer, Casper.....	1				
Iser, Geo........	1	3	6		
Burk, James......	1	1	1		
Hanups, Michael....	2		1		
Matthews, Chidley...	2		1		
Connor, James.....	1	3	8		
Whitmore, Benjamin, Jr	1	1	3		
Clarke, Joseph.....	1	1	1		
Boos, John.......	1		5		
Fulam, John......	1		3		
Calf, John, Senr....	3		3		
Frame, Geo.......	1		1		
Harbaugh, Jacob, Jr..	1	2	1		
Nelson, Roger, Esqr...	1	1	2		8
Ridge, Cornelius....	2		1		
Dunning, Patrick....	1	1	1		
Kiser, Decus......	3		9		
Hardmar, William...	2		3		
Douglas, Thos Fogerty	1	2			
King, Jacob......	1		3		
Turnbaugh, William..	2	1	3		2
Moore, James.....	1	1	2		
Taney, Henry.....	1		3		
Whitmore, Jacob....	1		3		1
McNeale, Archabald..	1	3			
Webb, Benjamin....	1	1	2		
Thomson, Jno. of Wm..	2	5	3		
Sage, Samuel.....	1	1	2		
Flora, Abright.....	1	3	2		
Davis, William.....	1	4			
Shadd, Philip.....	1		6		
Williams, Jacob....	1		1		
Harshman, Wm.....	1	3			
Grove, John......	1		3		
Swope, Barnet.....	1	4	4		
Lowry, David.....	3	3	2		3
Hardy, Solo......	2		4		
Cron, Michael.....	1	4	3		
McFear, Patrick....	2	1	1		
McLaugin, James....	1	1	1		
Kile, William.....	1		1		
Kennedy, Ann.....	1		2		
Sweney, Edward....	2	3	2		
Crawford, John....	4	3	2		
Erbaugh, Jacob (of Lodo).......	1	2	1		
Smith, Christopher...	1	2	5		
Smith, Peter......	1		1		
Jones, David......	1	1	5		
Bryan, William.....	1	1	2		
Beaty, Jacob......	2	2	5		
King, Geo........	1		1		
Fulham, Jno......	1		1		
McKissick, Margt....	1		1		
Funk, Rudolph.....	1	1	5		
Bever, John......	1	1	1		
Craling, Teteril....	1		1		
Caster, Thos......	1	1	2		
Stuffy, Andrew....	1	1	2		
Stulk, James......	1	4			
Averly, Adam.....	2		2		
Arnold, Andrew....	3	3	5		1
Ankrom, Aaron....	1	3	2		
Ambrose, Christopher.	1	2	4		
Shalt, Elizabeth....	1	2	4		
Arnold, Henry.....	3	2	2		
Ashmond, Henry....	1	2	3		1
Ambroser, Henry....	1		4		
Ambrosier, Henry, Senr	1	2	3		
Albright, Henry....	2	2	3		
Arnold, John......	2	1	4		
Artman, John.....	2		3		
Alexander, Jacob....	2	1	3		
Averhart, Jacob....	1		3		
Ancrum, Jacob.....	3	2	5		
Ancrum, Richard....	1		1		7
Alexander, Valentine..	1		2		
Buger, Barthe.....	1		7		
Buzzard, Cathe....			7		
Baker, Conrod.....	2	2	2		
Bizar, Daniel.....	2	3	6		
Buger, Daniel.....	2	1	6		
Butler, Edward....	4	1	6		5
Byser, Frederick....	1	4	3		
Barger, Frederick....	4	2	3		
Bowersmith, Geo....	1	4	6		
Bigly, Henry, Junr...	1		1		
Brodeback, Henry....	2	1	2		
Bowsinger, Henry....	1	2	3		
Biggerly, Henry, Senr .	2	2	3		
Blessing, Jacob.....	1		2		
Belt, Jeremiah.....	2	2	9		25
Bergeseer, Jacob....	1		1		
Byser, Jacob, Junr...	2	1	4		
Bartholomew, John...	2	3	3		
Buzzard, Jacob.....	1	3	4		
Burton, Elizabeth...			5		
Burton, John.....	2	1	5		
Byser, Jacob.....	2	1	5		2
Bricket, John.....	1	2	5		
Beckenbaugh, Leonard	2	6	4		
Bower, Noah.....	1	2	3		
Bambridge, Peter....	4	2	5		1
Buzzard, Samuel....	2	3	5		
Brown, Stoffel.....	2	3	4		
Beard, Samuel.....	1		3		
Brandenburg, Samuel.	2	1	6		
Bower, Peter......	1		5		

FREDERICK COUNTY—Continued.

NAME OF HEAD OF FAMILY.	Free white males of 16 years and upward, including heads of families.	Free white males under 16 years.	Free white females, including heads of families.	All other free persons.	Slaves.
Boalus, Valentine	1	1	2		
Brandenburg, Wm	1	3			
Beaver, William	1	3	4		
Brandensaurg, William, Jr	1	1			
Beckwith, Benjamin	2	2	4		2
Blickenstaff, Yost	2	2	3		
Kern, Adam	1	1	2		
Coplintz, Adam	1	1	1		
Crone, Conrod	2		1		1
Craft, Frederick		1	2		1
Cost, George	3	1	5		
Custard, Geo	1	4	5		
Cannon, Geo	1	3	4		
Cassel, Geo	2	4	1		
Colman, Henry	2	4	2		
Coplintz, Harman	1	2	4		
Coplinger, Jacob	1	2	4		
Carnes, John	2	1	7		
Cain, John	3	2	2		
Coons, Jacob	1		4		
Colman, Joseph		1	3		
Cost, Jacob	3	3	2		2
Carter, John	2	3	4		
Carn, Jacob	3	2	3		
Callaman, John					9
Coller, Michael	2	4	4		
Collins, Matthew	1	2	4		
Cloninger, Philip	2	4	2		
Coplintz, Peter	1	4	2		
Cline, Peter	1	4	2		
Cassel, Thomas	1	5	5		
Devar, Abraham	2	5	5		
Duttero, Baltser	2	5	5		
Downing, Benjamin	1	3	3		3
Deloyder, David	1	3	5		1
Delashmut, Elias	2	3	5		
Drill, Jacob	3	4	4		1
Dettro, John	1	2	3		
Deloyder, Jacob	1	1	1		
Deloyder, John	2	1	1		
Dobb, Jacob	2	4	5		
Isburn, Robert	1	2	2		1
Everett, Valentine	2	2	5		
Fry, Anough	1	1	7		
Fluke, Barbara	1	1	3		
Funier, Henry	1	1	3		
Fluke, Henry	1	1	1		
Fisher, Henry	1	3	6		1
Frasier, Henry	3	2	2		
Failing, Henry	1		3		
Funk, Peter	2	1	3		
Fuiwiler, Jacob	2	1	1		
Fluke, John	1		1		
Fluke, Barbara					
Frazier, Jonathan	1	6	3		8
Fisher, Peter	1	2	3		
Fink, Philip, Sen	4	1	2		
Fuiler, Robert	1	3			
Frazier, Thomas	2	4	3		21
Ferguson, William	2		4		
Frazier, William	1	3	2		1
Fox, Frederick	3	3	5		
Garret, Barton	3	3	3		14
Gaver, Daniel	1	2	1		2
Garsinger, David	2		3		
Kernhart, George	1	3	4		
Gittings, Jeremiah	1	3	7		14
Gwinn, Joseph	1	4	6		11
Grosnickie, John	1	1	4		
Grove, Jacob	1	2	2		1
Gilbert, Jeremiah	1	1	3		
Garver, Michael	1	2	5		
Gisert, Melcher	1		2		
Gaver, Peter	4	2	9		
Grosnickie, Peter	1	3	7		1
Gilbert, Thomas	1	2	3		
Misker, Valentine	1	1	5		
Herring, Adam	1		3		
Harshberger, Barnabas	2	3	1		
Harshman, Christian	2	1	6		
Howe, Caleb	1		1		1
Hay, Daniel	1	4	3		
Hook, Daniel	1	2	2		13
Hinklehouser, Deterick	2	1	3		
House, George	2	3	3		
Hillary, John	3	1	4		19
Hedge, Joseph	3	3	4		
Holland, Jonathan	1		1		
Hook, James	2				26
Hackney, Jacob	2	3	1		12
Haverley, Michael	1	1	1		
Holland, Otho	3		5		
Hutral, Peter	1	2	1		
Hawk, Peter	1	1	1		
Hodge, Shadrack	1		3		
Harrison, Thomas	1	5	5		
Hawkins, Thomas	1	1	3		29
Hagerty, Thomas	2	3			
House, William	2		4	1	6
Iseminger, Adam	1		5		
Gough, Adolph	2	1	4		
Ireland, Alexander	3		8		
Jameson, Benedict	3	1	3		27
Johnson, Joseph	2	3	4		
Johnson, John	1	3	5		
Ireland, Jonathan	2	2	3		
Johnson, Robert	1	2	2		
Johnson, Thomas	1	3	6		
Knouff, Adam	5	1	5		
Kugle, Adam, Senr	2		4		
Kesler, Andrew	3	5	3		
King, Andrew	1	2			
Kemp, Conrod	3	1			3
Kephart, Jacob	1	2	4		
Kenough, Henry	1	2	4		
Kier, Jacob	2	3	4		
Killer, Jacob	2	7	5		
Kefauver, Jacob	2	3	3		
Keller, John	1	3	3		
Keller, Philip	2	1	2		
King, Mary	1		1		
Knife, Michael	1				
Knife, Michael, Junr	2		3		
Kefauver, Philip	2	1	4		
Keller, Philip, Senr	4	4	2		
Kefauver, Peter	1	1	2		
Keale, Peter	1	4	2		
Lemaster, Abraham	2		4		
Leakin, Abraham, Senr			2		
Leatherman, Daniel	1		4		
Leatherman, Godfrey	1	2	5		
Lighter, Henry	1	5	2		
Long, John	1	2	5		
Laurence, Jacob	2	1			
Leaken, John	2	1	10		
Lamb, John	1	5	3		
Ludy, John	1	5	2		
Lemon, Lodowick	1	3	4		
Lemar, Richard	3	1	5		
Long, Stoffel	2	3	4		
Lee, Thomas Sim, Esqr	8	3	4		119
Luckett, William, Esqr	2	4	4		15
Linginfelter, Valentine	1	1	6		
Mensh, Adam	2		1		
Main, Adam	1	1	2		
Mockett, Andrew	1	1	3		
Miller, Conrod	1	2	4		
Moser, Conrod	1	2	5		
Morgan, Conrod	1	3			
Mathery, William	1				
Miller, Elizabeth		1	3		
Maine, Frederick	1	3	3		
Miller, Frederick, Junr	2	2	2		
Michael, George	2	1	3		
Miller, Frederick	1		4		
Maine, George	2	3	7		
Markell, George	2	2	4		
Marker, George	1	3	4		
Miller, Henry	2	3	4		
Moyer, Joseph	3	1	3		
Messeburg, Jacob	1	1	1		
Moser, John	2	2	1		
Miller, John	2	1	5		
Miller, Michael	1	1	2		
Miller, Nicholas	1	3	3		
Miller, Peter	4	3	3		
Mitchell, Peter	3	5	2		
Magruder, Samuel	2	1	2		3
Mitchell, Stophel	2	1			
Mitchell, Theodore	1		6		5
Mock, Thomas	4	5	5		
Moser, Valentine	2	1	5		
Moser, Valentine, Junr	1		5		
Moothers, Valentine		2	3		
Magruder, William, Esqr	2		4		14
Marlow, William	3	1	4		
Neff, Adam	3	4	1		
Nisewarner, Christian	2	2	8		1
Neff, Daniel	1	1	2		
Nicholson, Francis	1	1	2		
Neff, Henry	1	1			
Neff, John	1		2		
Nisewanger, John	2	4	7		
Osterday, Christian	3	2	2		4
Ogden, Joseph	2	1	2		
Osterday, Christian, Junr	1	1	5		1
Peckenbaugh, Susanna		3	5		
Philpot, Barton	5	2	6		11
Philpot, Charles	2	1	6		2
Poe, George	2	1	4		
Powlas, George	1		6		
Pepper, Henry	2	1	5		
Prather, John	1		4		
Prather, Enoch	2		1		1
Putman, John	1	2	6		
Powlas, Nicholas	3	2	5		
Putman, Philip	3		5		1
Philipp, Samuel	2	3	6	1	
Philpot, Zachariah	2	2	3		2
Routsong, Adam, Junr	3		3		
Rawlings, Aaron	3	3	6		
Rice, Benjamin	2	2	6		
Ricker, Conrod	3	1	2		
Rouderbush, Daniel	2	4	2		
Ramsburg, John, Junr	1	2	3		
Roud, Henry	2	4	3		
Redburn, Henry	3	2	8		
Richards, Jacob	2	2	3		
Ridgely, Jacob	1	5	3		1
Riddlemoser, Michael	2	4	6		
Ruble, Peter	1	4	6	1	
Rodenpeier, Philip	1				
Rechard, Peter	2	1	4		
Ridgely, Richard	1		4		2
Rudy, Peter	1	3	4		
Rice, Ann	1		3		
Smith, Andrew	1	1	3		
Smelser, Adam	2	2	2		
Shoemaker, Christian	2	4	6		
Shryer, Christian	2	4	4		
Shrader, Conrod	1	2	3		
Stottiemyer, David, Ju	1	1	2		
Swaggert, Daniel	2	3	2		
Stottiemyer, Devalt	1	2	4		
Sheon, David	2	4	1		
Sueman, Eleanor	2	4	5		
Staley, Elizabeth					
Stemple, Frederick	4	4	3		3
Shaaf, George	4		3		
Shaveler, George	4	4	3		
Stockman, George	3		4		
Smith, Henry (of Henry)	1	3	1		
Staley, Henry	1	1	2		1
Smith, Henry	1	1	4		
Shrader, Henry	2	2	6		
Elifer, John	2	4	4		
Shean, Jacob	3		4		
Shank, John	1	6			
Smith, Jacob	3		6		
Saggersy, Jacob	1	3	3		
Shemmy, John	1	2	3		
Shryer, Jacob	1	1	4		
Stone, John	2	4	5		
Sheffer, John, Junr	1	2	4		
Smith, John, of Jacob	2	2	5		
Smith, John	4	1	2		
Sheckles, John	2	4	1	1	13
Simmons, James	2	4	6		4
Serjeant, James	1	2	2	3	
Stombie, Joseph	1	2	4		
Speelman, Jacob	2	2	4		
Staley, Jacob	2		2		
Swearingon, Joseph	1	2	2		2
Smith, John	1	2	3		
Smith, Leonard	3	2	3		
Sturm, Jacob	3	2	2		
Swinburger, Michael	1	2	3		
Swearinger, Margaret		1	2		
Shafer, Philip	1	1	5		
Shunk, Philip	1	5			
Sensebaugh, Peter	3		4		
Sommers, Jacob	3		3		
Sergeant, Snowden	4	3	3		
Sweringen, Thomas	2	2	5		
Sommers, Valentine	1	4	2		
Shilkinack, William	2		2		
Smith, Mary	2	1	3		
Tusnier, Andrew	1	2	1		
Thrasher, Benjamin	1	2	4		3
Tenbell, Isaac	2	2	5		
Tenbal, Jonathan	1		4		
Turner, Jacob, Junr	1	1	4		
Titous, Jacob	1	1	5		
Turner, Jacob	1	1	5		
Thomas, Jacob	1	3	5		
Toms, John	1		5		
Thomas, Leonard	1	5	4		
Troutman, Michael	5	6	4		9
Trine, Susanna	1		2		
Trett, Paul	1	6	3		1
Toms, Samuel	1	2	8		
Templing, Samuel	2	2	5		
Thresher, Thomas	2	2	5		4
Toms, Wm	2	5	6		
Tucker, Wm	2	5	5		
Wortal, John	2	2	5		
Uhiry, Henry	1	1	2		
Uhiry, Michael	1	3	2		

FREDERICK COUNTY—Continued.

NAME OF HEAD OF FAMILY.	Free white males of 16 years and upward, including heads of families.	Free white males under 16 years.	Free white females, including heads of families.	All other free persons.	Slaves.
Wiles, George	1		1		
Weaver, Daniel	1	1	4		
Willard, Davolt	2	3	4		
Wells, Ducket	2	4	4		
Wilyard, Elias	3	5	6		
Winbegier, Francis	2	2	5		
Weaver, George	1	1	3		
Whiskey, Margaret	1	3	3		
Westman, Jacob	5	3	4		
Westenberger, Jacob	1	2	3		
Westherfield, Jacob	1	3	4		
Whip, Jacob	2		1		
Weakly, James	2		2		
White, James	1	4	3		
Weadle, Jacob	2	4	3		
Holsopple, Mary	1	4	5		
Wilyard, Philip	3	2	5		
Widle, Peter	3	1	2		
Wiles, Thomas	1	4	1		
Young, Conrod	2	2	3		
Yost, George	3		3		
Young, John	6	1	3		
Yoney, John	1	3	2		
Yates, Ignatius	1	1	6		
Yost, Lodowick	2		3		
Yoney, Peter	2	3	3		
Condell, William (of Davy)	2	1	2		
Mullineux, Robert	2	1	2		
Wade, John	1		3		
Wheeler, Richard	1	3	4		
Barnet, Jacob	1		3		
Parish, Gilbert	2	1	3		
Dorsey, John (of James)	2				
Justice, Ezekiel	1		1		
Cook, Casper	1	3	2		
Crain, Robert	2	1	3		
Cockran, Robert	1	3	3		
Devoy, John	1		3		
Richards, Joshua	1	2	2		
Clary, William	1	2	3		
Franklin, Charles	1	4	3		
Baney, George	1	2	3		
Dorsey, David	1	1	2		
McLain, Joseph	2	1	2		
Crone, Robert	2	1	3		
Norton, Isaac	1	1	2		
Heck, Daniel	1	1	5		
Myers, Peter	2	2	2		
Philbel, William	1	1	2		
Sile, Conrod	1	1	2		
Potter, William	1		2		
McKee, Samuel	1	2	4		
Rister, Samuel	1		2		
Cornicle, Danl	1	1	2		
Kelly, Thos	1	1	1		
Clary, David	2	1	1		1
Plaster, Joseph	1		2		
Whitehead, Joseph	1	2	1		
Geering, John	1		1		
Poole, Henry, Jr	1		1		1
Mason, Robert	1		1		
Smith, Jacob	3	1	2		
Wood, Henry	1		2		4
Brightwell, Richard	1		1		1
Wright, Joseph, Junr	2	1	1		
Runey, John	1		1		
McMahens, James	1		1		
Black, John	1		1		
Redick, Leonard	4	2	5		
Shoester, Joseph	1		2		
Roberts, William	1		2		
Umstead, Enoch	1	1	2		
Dage, Jacob	1	4	4		
Beatty, William	1	4	4		
Justice, Aquila	1	2	2		
Dodson, John	1	3	4		
Isenberger, Henry	2	3	3		
Davis, Gilbert	2	3	3		
Davis, Francis	2	1	3		
Ball, Henry	2	3	4		
Richardson, John	2	1	2		
Bab, John	1		2		
Lavely, Jacob	1	1	4		
James, William	1	4	4		
Koontz, Henry	1	4	4		
Leek, William	1		1		
Parron, Samuel	1	4	2		
Nelson, Burges	1	1	3		
Stormes, Isaac				2	
Beckworth, Mary		1	5		
Pepple, Abraham	1		3		
Beaverd, John	1	1	3		
Dahoof, Henry	2		2		
Farver, Margarett	2		1		
Shethouse, Peter	1		2		
Gather, William	2	4	6		9

NAME OF HEAD OF FAMILY.	Free white males of 16 years and upward, including heads of families.	Free white males under 16 years.	Free white females, including heads of families.	All other free persons.	Slaves.
Wayman, Thomas	1	1	5		
Hargwager, Henry	1		2		
Snider, Peter	1	2	3		
Stringer, John	1		2		3
Rister, Michael	1	2	4		
Adams, Joseph	2		1		
Fulker, Christopher	1	2	2		
Castleburg, Benja	2	1	6		
Ingler, David	1	4	4		
Girty, George	1	2	5		
Poonsock, Jacob	1	1	1		
Pringman, Michael	1		1		
Faw, Abraham	3		1		2
Snertzell, Geo. W	1		4		5
Pifer, Philip	4	2	4		
Hisler, Nicholas	3		2		
Margin, John	1	1	2		
Swartz, Valentine	1	1	2		
Hickson, Thomas	6	3	2		
Olix, Michael	3		3		
Adams, George	2	3	3		7
Bear, Jacob, Senr	1		2		1
Bear, Jacob, Jur	1		2		
Baltzell, Jacob	2	6	3		
Weaver, Christian	2	2	4		
Schley, Thomas	3	2	1		
Ogle, Thomas	1	3	3		1
Evit, Woodward	2	1	3		
Steiner, Jacob, Jur	4	1	3		
Ebert, Adam	2	1	1		
Shelman, John	2		3	1	2
Gombar, Jacob	1	1	3		3
Ingle, Peter	2		2		
Wondenbarker, Adam	2	5	3		
Stoner, Christian	4	1	7		2
Burket, Geo	1		1		4
Tillard, Edward	1	2	3		11
Martz, Geo	3		2		
Spangler, Geo	3	1	1		1
Carn, Michael	1	4	2		
Adams, Valentine	2	2	2		
Hart, Christian	1		3		
Shull, Catharine	1	2	3		
Himes, Lawrence	1	2	3		
Reel, Frederick	1	5	2		
Ramer, Michael	4	3	2		
Bookey, Matthias	4		3		
Ketsinderfer, John	1	2	2		
Haas, Michael	6		5		1
Brunt, Stoffel	1	1	2		
Cossell, Daniel	1	1	4		
Miller, Andrew	1	1	2		
Croy, John	1		2		
Bruner, Catharine			1		
Callister, Sarah		1	2		
Moyer, Michael	1	3	4		
Measle, Jacob	2	2	2		
Measle, Casper	1	2	2		
Judy, Martin	1		2		
Bierly, Frederick	4	2	4		1
Gombar, John	1		1		
Yontz, Catharine		1	3		
Adlum, John	1	3	5		
Bargor, Philip	2	5	1		
Risner, Tobias	2		2		
Tice, Nicholas	1	3	6		
Shankneer, John	1		3		
Winemiller, Henry	1	3	1		
House, William	1		1		
Coonts, Baltser	1		2		
Bogan, Frederick	1	2	2		
Heck, Margaret		1	3		3
Crabb, Thomas	1		1		
Bonnet, Christian	1		2		
Mantz, Peter, Esqr	3	3	4	1	6
Mantz, Casper	1		2		
Delacour, Joshua Fredk	1	1	2		
Schley, John Jacob	1	5	3		2
Schley, George Jacob	5	2	4		
Lontz, Leonard	2	4	6		3
Shull, Frederick	2	4	4		1
Waugh, William	2		4		
Wise, Mary			2		
Mantz, David	5	2	7		
Mantz, Francis	4	3	6		2
Charlton, Eleanor	5		3		
Shell, Charles	5	3	5		1
Lynch, Susanna	1		2		
Hower, Nicholas	6	2	4		2
Koons, Henry	1		3		
Vanhorn, Benjamin	1		3		
Hoffman, Jacob	1		3		
Parks, John	3	2	3		5
Prangle, Christian	3		3		
Fessler, John	3	1	3		
Hanson, Jane			1		17
Harrison, Catharine	4	1	2		3

NAME OF HEAD OF FAMILY.	Free white males of 16 years and upward, including heads of families.	Free white males under 16 years.	Free white females, including heads of families.	All other free persons.	Slaves.
Thomas, Doct. Philip	5	1	2		4
Potts, Sarah			2		4
Neale, John	1	1	2		4
Shew, Jacob	1	1	2		
Somersett, Thos	2		2		
Winter, John	1		1		1
Lingenfelter, John	1		1	1	
Kline, Mary	1	2	3		
Kline, Frederick	1	1	1		
Bear, Geo. Junr	6	1	2		1
Houser, Michael	3	3	4		
Duvall, Samuel	2	1	2	1	2
Howman, Peter	2	4	2		
Shiner, Adam	1	2	3		
Shiner, Valentine	2	1	3		
Testel, John	1		1		
Young, Jacob, Esq	1	3	3		4
Dyer, Martha			3		3
Hower, Daniel	6	2	6		
Crush, Conrod	4	1	8		1
Coonts, Henry, Sen	1		2		1
Barnhold, Ann			7		
Candle, Jacob	2	2	6		1
Pence, George	2	5	5		
Ingle, Peter, Junr	2		2		2
Buchers, Richard		5	2	2	
House, Thomas	2		4		
Burkett, John	1		4		
Smith, James	1	2	2		2
Wandell, Jacob	2	1	5		
Bear, Catharine			4		1
Riggs, John	1	1	4		
Mackey, Robert	1		2		
Clements, William	2		2		5
Williams, John	1	2	4		
Waling, John	3	2	1		
Brim, Henry	1		1		
Gilleland, Philip	1	1	2		
Gatrell, Charles	1	1	2		6
Hollow, Christopher	1		2		
Peters, John	1	1	2		
Hollow, John	1	1	2		
Hollow, Michael	1		3		
Hollow, Michael, Junr	1		3		
Speaker, John		1	2		
Hollow, Godfrey	1	2	3		
Lott, Philip	2	1	5		
Rate, Alexander	1	1	3		
Crise, Henry	1	1	2		
Johnson, Doct. John	1		2		2
Wane, Isaac	3	2	4		
Gross, Sarah			2		
Durf, Jacob	2	3	5		
Quicksel, Mary		3	2		
Coller, Jacob	3	1	2		
Ironmonger, John	1	1	2		
Hall, John	1		2		5
Lewis, Jacob	1		1		
Kline, Stephen	1		2		
Kimes, Henry	1	1	3		
Hutchin, John	1		1		
Kerr, John	1		1		
Waters, George	1	1	2		
Brown, Simeon	3	1	2		
Thomas, Wm	1		2		8
Murquit, Michael	1	2	2		
Norris, Samuel	1	3	2		
Levy, David	19	4	11		
Waters, Peter	3	1	2		
Beatty, Thomas, Esq	2		2	1	8
Kisinger, Francis	2		2		
Levy, Jacob	1		2		
Thomas, Samuel	1	3	4		4
Taylor, Thomas	1	3	2	1	
Goss, Gideon	1	2	4		
Metzker, Jacob	2	2	4		
Wisher, Christian	1		2		
Hinghew, Frederick	1		4		
Shelman, Jacob	5	1	4		2
Nixendurf, Samuel	1		1		
Pence, Margaret		1	4		
Hersheyer, Adam	1	3	4		
Bear, Henry		4	1		
Snider, George	1	1	3		
Storm, Leonard			3		1
Madery, Nicholas	2	2	3		
Baltzel, Christian	1	2	3		
Penders, Jacob	1	1	1		
Luckess, Luck	1	1	1		
Bear, William	2	3	3		
Fie, Joseph	2	1	1		
Bruner, Jacob	2	1	3		
Wigel, John	2	1	3		
Adams, Jeremiah	1	1	4		
Baltzer, John	2	1	4		
Kipelrinjer, Martin	1		1	3	
Wesenger, Peter		3	1		
Tolks, Catharine		1	3		

FREDERICK COUNTY—Continued.

NAME OF HEAD OF FAMILY.	Free white males of 16 years and upward, including heads of families.	Free white males under 16 years.	Free white females, including heads of families.	All other free persons.	Slaves.
Walker, John	1	2	1		
Mates, Michael	2		5		
Hardman, Christian	1	2	2		
How, George	1	3	2		
Smith, Peter	1	2	3		
Kesmer, Michael	2		3		
Half, Margaret		3	3		
Hoffman, George	1	1	2		
Oliz, Adam	1		2		
Englebright, Conrod	3	4	2		
Shaaff, Casper	2		2	5	
Wints, Jacob	3	1	1		
Fielding, Michael	1	1	4		
Crook, Revd John A	1	1	3		
Hocks, Frederick	1	1	3		
Stuner, Frederick	2		2	4	
Boyd, Andrew	1	2	3		
Clark, James	2		2		
Rinehart, George	1		2		
Shafer, Henry	1	1	2		
Low, Jacob	1	4	2		
Bartman, Christophel	1	3	15		
Snider, Jacob	1	2	5		
Dunuman, William	1		1		
Hain, Jacob	3	4	3	4	
Fink, Adam	1		2		
Fox, Elizabeth	2		2		
Stoore, George	2	1	1		
McGrah, James	1		1		
Juright, Justice	1	1	2		
McDanel, Alexander	1	1	2		
Kephart, Peter	3		3		
Gipps, Nicholas	3		3		
Richer, Henry	1	2	3		
Morhefer, Peter	1		3		
Heckman, Stephen	1		4		
Brown, Godfrey	2	2	3		
Devilbiss, Christopher	1	1	4		
Pringle, Christian	2		3	1	
Smith, Philip	2		7		
Dull, Joseph	1	4	2		
Kulp, Michael	1	3	1		
Kulp, Michael, Jur	1		2		
Miller, Conrod	1		1		
Graybill, Peter	1		1		
Mahoney, Sophia		1	2		
Frombech, Revd Jacob	1		1		
Baker, Mary	1		1		
Fultz, Margaret	1		1		
Row, Michael	1		2		
Guyer, Adam	2		1		
Charles	1	1		3	
Shanhols, Frederick	1	1	3		
Shultz, Catharine			2		
Grossman, John	1		1		
Simmerman, John	1	1	4		
Leap, William	1		4		
Eberts, George	1		2		
Cain, Jacob	1		2		
Staufer, Daniel	1	3	3		
Titlow, Christian	1		4		
Forble, Jacob	1		4		
Brown, Michael	1	1	2		
Hoffman, George	1		2		
Davis, William	1		1		
Balsel, Jacob	1		1		
West, Jacob		3	2		
Harding, Richard	1	1	1		
Roads, Barbara			3		
Row, James	1		3		
Proder, Conrod	1	1	3		
Neghalt, Nicholas	2	1	3		
Walter, Jacob	1		2		
Stalkman, Catharine			2		
Everhart, Michael	1	1	3		
Aunbert, Christian	1		3		
Limbreck, Daniel	1		3		
Hebert, Catharine			4		
Weaver, Michael	1	4	2		
Coffman, John	1	3	3		
Kitwilder, Jacob	1	2	3		
Whitmore, Michael	2		3		
Keller, Catharine			5		
Lilly, Samuel	1	1	2		2
Bonum, Malachia	1		1	7	
Keller, Jacob	1	3	3		
Conrod, Elizabeth	1		7		
McKan, Bartholomew	1	2	3		
Henry, Conrod	1		3		
Tetlow, Abraham	1	3	3		
Bowly, Jacob	1	2	4		
Bowly, Charles	2		2		
Snodyell, Jacob	3		2		
Wilson, Thomas	3		2		
Cronise, Henry	2		2		
Getert, Valentine	2	1	2		

NAME OF HEAD OF FAMILY.	Free white males of 16 years and upward, including heads of families.	Free white males under 16 years.	Free white females, including heads of families.	All other free persons.	Slaves.
Foley, Henry	2	2	3		
Conrod, Henry	3		2		
Cronise, John	3	4	2		
Fie, Henry	2	1	1		
Shavock, Adam	1	3	2		
Lice, Erasmus	1		2		
Bruner, Peter	1	1	2		
Common, Geo	1		2		
Frangie, Laurence	1		4		
Nuse, Michael	1	4	2		
Sheffy, Adam	1		4		
Eckart, Christian	1		3		
Campbell, John	2	1	2		
Hostetter, Henry	1		3		
Haven, Catharine			2		
Butt, John	1		1		
Smith, John	1	1	4		
Gardner, Lewis	1		1		
Craglow, William	1	1	1		
Gunsaw, Geo	1		2		
Young, Andrew	2	1	2		
Fauble, John	1	1	4		
Hardman, Joseph	2		4		
Brangie, George	2	1	2		
Bontz, Adam	1		2		
Bradley, Thomas	1	1	4		
Bell, Bubby			1	2	
Shiseler, Jacob	2	2	2		
Bontz, Henry	2	2	1		
Roar, Rudolph	2	3	4		
Dull, Conrod	2		6		1
Shultz, David	1		1		
Durf, Samuel	1		1		
Klienhart, Francis	2	1	1		
Keisler, George	1		2		
Roar, Jacob	3	1	5		
Wise, Jacob	1		1		1
Ramsburg, John, Junr	2	1	1		
Bartle, Jacob	1		2		
Watts, Martin	4		4		
Ritchie, William, Esqr	2	2	2		3
Ritchie, Abner	1		2		
Dyer, Edward	1	1	1		3
Cary, John Dew	1		1		
Riley, Patrick	1		1		
Connar, William	1		1		
Roar, Philip	3	2	2		
Bruner, Modelena			3		
Lowe, Andrew	5		3		
Ogle, Benjamin	3	1	3		3
Butler, Richard	2	1	1		3
Fisher, John	2		4		3
Gombar, John, Junr	1	4	3		
Miller, Jacob	1	2	2		
Booker, Frederick	3		2		
Steiner, Jacob		2	5		1
Kenop, Mary			2		
Bruner, John	1	1	1		
Meddert, James	2	3	5		
Miller, Samuel	2		3		
Miller, Godlip	2		5		
Norris, Barnet	2		1		
Sealer, Henry	1		1		
Trisler, Michael	2		5		2
Leatherman, Henry	1		2		
Battsell, Michael	2	4	7		
Hoffman, Jacob	3	1	1		
Kephart, John	3	1	7		
Shine, Philip	3		4		
Coon, Henry	1	2	1		
Baker, Christian	4		3		
Mires, Jacob	2	1	6		
Garnhart, Henry	2	2	2		
Grove, Rachel	1		4		
Hoofnogle, Peter	1		2		
Semmer, Elizabeth	1	4	2		
Keller, Adam	1		2		
Ott, Michael	1	1	2		
Guyer, John	2		2		
Getsentanner, George	4		2		
Booker, John	1	2	3		
Hoffman, George	1		3		
Lombrick, Michael	2	2	3		
Prangle, Christian	1		4		
Borham, Mercy	1	1	4		1
Baker, Peter	1		2		
Fye, Simeon	1	3	8		
Chopper, Philip	1		8		
Houk, Jacobs	1		2		
Road, Christian	1		1		
Filker, Jacob	1		2		
Elkmand, Mary			2		
Simmon, Jacob			1		
Miller, William	1	1	2		
Bear, George		1	2		
Knouff, Jacob	1	1	2		

NAME OF HEAD OF FAMILY.	Free white males of 16 years and upward, including heads of families.	Free white males under 16 years.	Free white females, including heads of families.	All other free persons.	Slaves.
Elbert, Catharine		5	2		
Lear, Daniel	3	3	2		4
Brothers, Henry	3		1		
Hole, Jacob	2	3	5		
Baltzel, George Jacob	2	4	2		4
Buckias, John	2	1	3		
Gipps, Abraham	1	2	1		
Shafer, Philip	2	3	1		
Minshel, Joshua	3	3	2		
Fluke, Peter	2	1	1		4
Tyler, Doctr John	4	3		6	
McCleary, Henry			3		
Ritchie, Mary			3		1
Runkle, Revd William	4	2	3		
Hirley, Frederick		1	4		11
Beall, Wm M., Esqr	2		3	4	6
McPherson, John, Esq	2	2	4		19
Murdock, George, Esq	2	6	6		2
Mantz, Isaac	2	2	2		2
Ritchie, John	1	1	5		
Hoffman, John	2	2	5		2
Woodward, Benedict	4	2	2		23
Johnson, Baker, Esq	2	5	4		22
Potts, Richard, Esq	2	4	7		
Shields, Patrick	1		2		
Hunter, William	1		4		
Springer, John	1	1	4		
Rights, Anthony	1	2	6		2
Wells, Thomas, Junr	1		1		
Paxton, Nathaniel	1		4		
Holland, Wm	1		4		
Bear, Hugh	1	2	4		
Priner, Abraham	1	1	2		
Brown, Robin	2		5		
Angle, Peter	2		5		
Angle, George	1	2	5		
Brade, George	1		2		
Miller, John	2	3	4		
Knu, George	2		4		
Hale, George	3	3	4		
Mullen, Nicholas	1		3		
Bell, Nathaniel	1		3		
Brothers, John	3	1	3	1	11
Graham, John	3		3		4
Hatherly, Benjamin	2		4		
Clark, James	3		4		
Mire, John	2	4	4		
Moyer, Joseph, Junr	1		2		
Moyer, Peter	2	1	2		
Miller, John	1	1	1		
Stottlmyer, George	1	1	3		
Stottlmyer, Jacob	2	1	3		
Hoover, Jacob	1	1	1		
McClary, Wm	1		3		
Glasby, Mathias	1	1	5		
Kerr, Thomas	1		2		
Eitly, Wm	1		2		
Ford, John	1	2	2		3
Holliday, John	2	1	2		
Spake, Conrod	1		3		
Peter, Enoch	2		2		
Yates, Thomas	2	1	3		
Morrow, Peter	1	2	2		
Young, John Jacob	1		3		
Burn, Henry	1		3		
Brandenburgh, George	1		3		
Stimmer, George	1	3	2		1
Yudy, Philip	2		2		
Melcher, Philip	1	1	1		
Reed, Jacob	2		3		
Boghier, Peter	1		4		
Conrod, John	1		4		
Rerter, Feity	1		1		
Michael, Conrod	1		3		
Limmon, John	1		1		
Liver, Nicholas	1		1		
Lenmon, Abraham	1		4		
Lambert, Joseph	1	3	1		
Digman, Anne			3		
Baker, Adam	1	3	3		
Iford, Jeremiah	1		2		
Allsock, John	1		3		
Baker, Martin	1	1	5		
Storm, Wendle	1		1		
Kirfover, Nicholas	1	2	2		
Peckenbaugh, Peter	1	2	3		
Adams, Stophel	1	1	4		
Loufer, Frederick	2		2		
Horine, Tobias	1		1		
Summers, Jacob	1		2		
Braize, John	1	3	2		
Mitchel, Leonard	3	1	2		
Hale, Thomas	1	1	2		
Wolfly, David	2	4	3		
Sheredine, Paul	2	1	2		
Earl, James	1		5		

FREDERICK COUNTY—Continued.

NAME OF HEAD OF FAMILY.	Free white males of 16 years and upward, including heads of families.	Free white males under 16 years.	Free white females, including heads of families.	All other free persons.	Slaves.
Gaston, John	2		2	1	
Sims, Thomas	2	3	4		
Bread, George	2	2	5		
Hiltebrand, Henry	2	2	3		1
Hurley, William	1 2	1	3		
Kensler, Uley	1 2	1	2		
Noland, James	2		1		
Selby, William	2		1		
Combs, Henry	1		4		
Show, Conrod, Junr	1 1	1	4		
Philips, James	2		4		
Tobridge, John	2	2	3		
Leather, George	2 2		3		
McGorvin, Dennis	1		3		
Hershberger, Henry	2	3	2		1
Nichols, Philip	1	2	1		
Martin, Jacob	2	2	3		
Lantz, John	1		4		
Philler, Henry	1				
Davis, John	1				
Krumer, Adam	2	1	2		1
Toole, James	1 1		5		
Hessler, William	1 1	1	2		
Thresher, Elias	1 1	1	2	1	
Lamar, William	1	4			5
Lamar, Lemack	1 1	1	4		
Hagan, Andrew	1		2		
Deaver, Michael	1	3	2		
White, John	1	1	2		
Leakins, Daniel	1	1	2		
Leakins, Abraham, Jr	1		3		
Haney, John	1		1		
Howard, Elizabeth		1			
Clary, Wm	2		3		
Rice, Joseph	2		3		
Perrill, Thomas	1	1	2	1	
Callaman, Moses	2		2		
Mansfield, John	1	2	2		
McCormack, John	2		4		
Sergeant, Sarah	1		2		
Brent, George	1	4			
Cox, Elisha	1				
Frasier, Sarah		2			
Frasier, John	2		4	1	3
Gittings, Colmore	2			1	6
Shingle, George	2 2	2	5		4
Smith, Patrick Sim, Esq	3	2	7		24
Frasier, Sarah		2	7	5	2
McLamar, Archibald	1	2	1		2
Reynolds, James	32		3		7
Goodwin, Richard	1	1	2		
Farthing, Aaron	2				
West, Erasmus	2				2
Clark, John	1		2		
West, Thomas	1	2	1		
West, Joseph	2		4		3
Trenton, Richard	2				14
Smith, Sampson	2 1				
Hinton, John, Jur	1		4	5	
Vickery, George	1		1		
Denny, Stophel	1		2		
Blessing, George	1	1	2		
Porter, Samuel	1		2		
Allhough, Simeon	1	3	4		
Wiles, James	3		4		
Engle, Peter	2		4		
Yousl, George	2 1	2	3		
Sombower, Adam	1	2	2		
Carver, Michael	1	1	4		
Eller, Elizabeth	1		4		
Paker, George	1	2	1		
Fink, Philip, Junr	2 1	3	3		
Korr, Casper	2	3	1		
Comb, Henry	1		5		
Miller, George	1		3		
Wiseman, Conrod	1		3		
Arnold, David	1	1	1		
Harley, Joshua	1	1	5		
Young, Henry	1	5	5		
Alexander, Henry	1	2	1	1	
Jacobs, Joel	2	1			3
Young, Jacob (of Conrod)	1		6		
Firestone, Nicholas	1	2	4		
Barnes, Nachel	1	1	1		
Hardman, Daniel	1	3	5		
Helker, Christian	1		1	1	
Yerrick, John	1	1	1		
Clipper, Felty	1		3		
Beckett, William	2	3	1		
Smith, John (of Jno)	2		2		
Phelps, Eli	1		2		
Giseberd, Andrew	1 1		3		
Organ, Thomas	1	1	2		
Marlow, Thomas	1		2		6
Keller, John	1		1		
Shafer, John, Jur	1		1		
Yandes, George	1	1	2		
Foutch, John	1	1	2		
Drine, Susanah	1	1	1		
Keller, Philip, Jur	3		2		
Powell, Thomas	1		2		
Mottor, Valentine	1	3	2		
Mottor, Henry	1	2	2		
Snuer, Henry	1	3	4		
Stone, Jacob	1	2	5		
Jackson, James	1	3	2		
Snerr, Henry	1	2	5		
Stottelmire, David, Jur	1	2	5		
Gelashee, Mathew	1	5	5		
Sheuman, Aaron	1	1	5		
Tarr, Philip	1	2	5		
Smeltzer, Andrew	1	2	3		
Lezer, Zachariah	1	3	3		
Coons, Thomas	1	3	3		
Houp, Nicholas	1	3	3		
Behind, Jacob	1		3		
Briger, Peter	1	3	3		
Ulith, Jacob	1	2	3		
Reed, Jacob	1	3	3		
Bambridge, Absolam	1	1	3		1
Dutterson, Jacob	1		1		
Dull, Peter	3		4		
Eicker, Barnabas	1	1	1		
Miller, George	2	2	5		
Heck, Andrew	1	1	1		
Boutsong, Adam, Junr	3		4		
Luser, Daniel	2	4	1		
Smith, Jacob, Junr	2		6		
Kugle, Adam	1	2	2		
Kugie, John	1	1	2		
Bagle, Henry	1	2	2		
Bockman, Andrew	1	2	2		
Shuffler, Peter	1	2	4		
Sheffer, Peter	1	2	1		
Daily, John	1		1		
Toms, Jacob	1		2		
Sommer, Christian	1	1	2		
Dusinger, Jacob	1	4	3		
Toms, Abraham	1	1	4		
Holsoppie, Fredrick	1	1	2		
Dubie, Isaac	1	4	3		
Leatherman, Joseph	1	2	2		
Blukenstaff, Ulerick	1		3		
Main, John	1	1	3		
Lopp, Henry	2	3	1		
Mark, Joseph	2	4	6		
Mires, Jacob	1	1	6		
Carringer, David	1	1	3		
Boohoup, John	1	3	1		
Brown, Peter	1				
Arnold, Zachariah	1	1	1		
Arnold, Samuel	1		2		
Gaver, John	1		3		
Brake, Peter	1	3			
Stile, Philip	1		1		
Hobrick, John	1		1		
Rice, Michael	1	2	1		
Niceinger, Magdalena			3		
Smith, Conrod	1	1	2		
Williams, Daniel	1		1		
Hargess, Elizabeth			4		
Smith, Michael	2		4		
Fock, Hugh	2		5		
Hobrick, John	1	1	2		
Kisler, Henry	1		2		
Koons, Jacob	1		3		
Michael, Lodwich	1		2		
Hutt, Samuel	1	2	2		
Orr, Nicholas	2		2		
Leister, George	2		4		
Daganhart, Christain	2	3	5		
Babylon, Philip	3	1	2		
Bakely, Henry	2		5		
Kimes, Jacob	2		4		
Matteny, George	2	4	3		
Harine, Lodwick	2		2		
Fester, Daniel	1		2		
Collins, Mathias	1	1	2		
Moyer, Samuel	1		2		
Esburn, Jane			5		
Hedge, Shadrack	1	2	2		
Cornickie, John	1		3		
Shewen, Cornelius	1	1	2		
Walter, Michael	1	1	2		
Chicote, James	1	1	3		
Helms, Nicholas	1	2	3		
Durbin, Cornelius	1		2		
Heavner, Andrew	1	1	1		
Snider, John	2		1		
Watkins, Samuel	1	2	1		
Culp, Philip	1		1	1	
Oliver, Thomas	2 1		1	2	
Pulbough, Joseph	1	1	5		
Paddy, William	1		2	4	
Else				2	
Halns, Nathan	1	3	2		
Harrisson, Benjamin	1	3	2		
Light, Elizabeth			4		
Colden, Jacob		6	2		
Mackable, Allen	2		4		12
Murray, Edward	2	2	3		
Fluhart, Stephen	2 1	1	2		1
Elliott, Thomas	1 1	2	3		
Jones, Thomas	1	3	2	3	
Lamar, Thomas	1		2		
Swomley, Daniel	1		2		
Hughes, Jesse	3	1	4		
Wessley, Henry	1	2	2		
Hall, Gabriel	1	1	2		
Barnes, Elisha	1		2		
Farmer, William	2	3	4		
Bean, Walter	2	1	3		
Pennybaker, Samuel	1		3		
James, John	1	1	1		4
Hardinger, Christian	2		3	1	
Gist, Jonathan	2				2
Wright, Samuel	1		2		
Wright, William	1		1		
Hutton, Joseph	1		2		
Ovelman, Jacob	1	4	3		
Flenner, Daniel	1		3		
Barnhart, David	1		2		
Poling, Elias	1	1	5		
Kump, Peter, Junr	2		2		
Bayplot, John	2		2		
Emery, John	1	6	2		
Arthur, Frederick	3		5		
Beak, Jacob	2	2	2		
Franklin, Thomas	1	3	4		
Lescalute, William	1	2	2		
Crawford, James	3		3		
Daddiaman, Jacob	3	3	2		
Cassel, Henry	1		2		
Moon, Matthias	1		3		
Wampler, Jacob	1		2		
Hoff, Leonard	1		2		
Fowler, James	1	2	3		
Hilbert, Margaret			2		
Flegie, John	1		2		
Crisher, Nicholas	1		1		
Myers, Joseph, Junr	1	1	2		
Owings, Beale	1		1		6
White, Ann			2		
Riley, John	1	2	4		
Casner, William	1		4		
Crawford, Elias	1		2		
Montgomery, Thos	1		1		
Hollingsworth, Jacob	1		1		
Stem, Matthias	2	1	4		
Ogly, Peter	1	3	1		
Cover, Abraham	2		5		
Fuss, John	1		2		
Brown, Ann			5		
Winters, John	1		3		
Halns, William	2	3	2		
Wright, David	2	4	3		
Wright, Henry	1		2		
Toole, Catharine			2		
Sloregenhoupt, Philip	1	4	5		
Angel, Jacob	2		2		
Yengling, Jacob	2 1		2		
Goodley, Henry	3	1	2		
Moyers, Joseph, Senr	2		5		
Roadpouch, Frederick, Ser	2	2	5		
Kemp, Mary		1	3		
Chadd, William	1		1		
Ford, William	1		2		
Stephenson, Maryman	1		1		
Burns, George	1	4	5		
Estep, Zachariah	1		4		
Long, Jacob	1		1		
Mikesell, John	1	3	1		
Fivecoat, Peter	4		3		
Fester, George	2		3		
Hafley, Stephen	2	3	3		
Bishop, John, Jur	1		2		
Hawk, Peter	2	5	1		1
Heck, John	1	1	4		
Rife, Christopher	1	3	5		
Hoyer, Jacob	1		3		
Riffle, Ludwick	1	3	3		
Trisnen, Philp	2	3	3	5	
Tomlin, Hugh	1	1	3		
Baltsell, Jacob	2	1	4		1
Rue, Jacob	2		3		

FREDERICK COUNTY—Continued.

NAME OF HEAD OF FAMILY.	Free white males of 16 years and upward, including heads of families.	Free white males under 16 years.	Free white females, including heads of families.	All other free persons.	Slaves.
Keele, Henry	3	1	1		
Linebaugh, Adam	1	1	3		
Anders, Herbert	1	1	2		
Bloom, Adam	1	1	4		
Linebaugh, Samuel	1	1	5		
Overholtz, Isaac	1	2	4		
Black, Abraham	1	1	2		
Thomas, Isaac	2	1	2		
Hamilton, John	2	1	1		
Snouk, Adam	2	1	2		
Thomas, Amos	1		6		
Dennis, Jacob	2		1		
Eichelberger, Leonard	1	5		4	5 1
McAnair, Samuel	3	1	5		
Reynolds, James	1	2	3		
Parsons, Robert	1		4		
Nail, Jacob	1		1		
Nail, Daniel	1	2	2		
Miller, John, Junr	1	2	1		
Wise, John	1	2	3		
Wine, Michael	1	2	5		
Crawford, Moses	2		5		
Bankard, Henry	1	5	1		
O'Hara, Daniel	1		4		
Wile, Peter	1	2	6		
Cress, Simon	1		3		
Stonecypher, Jacob	1	3	1		
Cornelius, James	1		2		
Duttero, Frederick	1		2		
Curran, Michael	1		4		
Worshall, Augustus	3	2	4		
Glass, Samuel	1		1		
Kennedy, Mary		2	6		
Ormant, Mary			1		
Bowen, Christopher	1	2	1		
Yengling, Christopher	1	3	3		
Osler, Ormond	1		3		
Bankard, Abram	1	1	2		
Crawford, James	4	1	1		
Fromback, John	2		1		
Kepler, George	2		3		
Hichen, Jacob, Junr	2		3		
Teter, Jacob	2	1	3		
Sheets, Martin	1	1	3		
Farah, Charles	1		3		
Cloud, Mordecal	1	1	3		
Shanam, Catharine	4	1	4		
Carver, John	2	1	4		
Spigler, Israel	1	5	3		
Helbert, George	2	1	1		
Hope, William	1	1	5		
Summerman, Michael	1	2	2		
Pate, Edward	1		4		
Waters, Dyer	1	1	5		
Bageunt, William	1	1	5		
Fisher, William	2	3	2		
Turner, Solomon	1		2		
Lear, Garrett	1	1	3		
Dun, Barnet	1		8		
Finch, Thomas	3	1	5		
Barnes, Edward	1	1	7		
Bannister, James	2	1	1		
Hetherly, Benjamin	1	1	3		
Faikner, Alexander	2		3		
Mason, Jonathan	2	2	5		
Barnes, David	1		5		
Harris, Elizabeth	1		2		
Roberts, John	1	1	2		
Hersey, Christopher	1		1		
Turner, Thomas	2	1			
Deuker, John			4		
Plummer, Eleanor			4		
Shryock, Daniel	1	1	6		
Clark, Joshua		3	1		
Blohorn, William	1	3	6	1	
McElfresh, Henry	1	1	1		
Plumer, Jonathan		3	3		
Shriner, Peter	2	1	3		
Barker, Fielder	1	1	3		
Dorsey, Evan	1		2		
Beavington, Henry	1	3	2		
Wolf, John	2		4		
Sommers, Thomas	2		1		
Sheets, Henry	2	2	4		
Linger, John	1	2	2		
Ungelby, Zachariah	2		2		
Davis, Barnet	2	4	6		
Ingham, Joshua			4		
McKader, Sarah			4		
Strevert, Edward	1	1	3		
Flemming, Thomas	2		3		
Manklin, Benjamin	1		2		
Wallace, Robert	1	1	2		
Hilton, John	1	2	6		
Todd, Alexander	3		2		
Arnold, John	3		2		

NAME OF HEAD OF FAMILY.	Free white males of 16 years and upward, including heads of families.	Free white males under 16 years.	Free white females, including heads of families.	All other free persons.	Slaves.
Selman, Gassaway	3	2	4		5
McDudel, John	2		4	3	
Brian, James	2		5		
Davis, Luke	2	2	5		1
Gist, Elizabeth		5	2	5	
Holler, Peter	2	2	2		
Smith, Henry of Nics	2	2	1		
Booghler, Jacob	1		3		
Clark, John	1	4			
Hamer, George	1	3			
Kline, George	1	3			
Pathoover, Edward	1				
Smith, Francis		4	5		
Cassberry, Jesse			4		
Fitchtuck, John	1		3		
Ward, Francis	1		1		
Warren, James	1		1		
Smith, Leonard	1		1		
Broadband, Joseph	1		3		
Miller, John	1	1	1		
Smith, Joshua	1	1	1		
Stouder, Joseph	2		4		
Philberger, Frederick	1		3		
McBee, Hugh	1		3		
Wright, Joseph	5	3	6		
Ford, John	1	1			
Athey, Wilson	1	1	2		
Modden, William	1	1	2		
McCulloh, Lewis	1	1	2		
Deal, Benjamin	3	1	2		
Ake, Jacob	1	3			
Neal, Dennis	1		4		
Spund, Joseph	2		2		
Stowder, Joseph	2	4	7		
Carr, John	2		4		
Ihleburger, Frederick	1		1		
Seagler, Jacob	1	1	3		
Elder, Joseph	3	2		1	
McLocklin, James	1		2		
Williams, Clement	3	2	9		2
McLocklin, Alexander	1		4		
Brian, Martin	1	2	4		
Morrow, Archabald	2		2		
Rakus, Henry	2	1			
Kupers, Isaac, Jur	1		1		
Yist, Philip	1		8		
Huccie, John	1	2	8		
Martin, James	3	2			
Setdown, Elizabeth			1		
Honeburger, John	1		2		
Magawer, Patrick	1		2		
Mourer, Conrod	1				
McDear, Patrick	1	1	2		
O'Neal, Archabald	1	3	2		
Sawer, Adam	1	2	2		
Cough, George	1		2		
McClue, William	1	1	2		
Streaer, Jacob	1		2		
Mayer, John	5	1	8		
Heatch, Elizabeth		3	5		
Stoop, Margarett					
Canadey, Ann	1	1	1		2
Webbs, Benjamin	1		1		
Landey, Richard	1		4		
Hunter, William	1		4		
Mefford, Philip T	1		4		
Secafuse, John	1		4		
Snider, Christopher	2	1	3		
Shover, George	2	1	3		
Oldam, William	1		3		
Collard, Joseph	2		3		
Feaster, George	2	2	3		
Beall, Theadore	1	2	3		5
Tabler, Jacob	1	3	2		
Jacove, Jacob	1		2		
Thomas, William	1	3	2		
Matnews, John	1		8		
Mower, Andrew	1	1	5		
Long, Jacob	1	3			
Segafuse, Peter	1		3		
Calfleash, John	1	1	4		
Alexander, John	1	1			
Fitzgerald, James	1	1	2		
Richardson, Richard	3	2	6	4	
Altow, Priscilla				7	
Armstrong, Priscilla				7	
Thomas, Daniel	2	2	3		1
Arthur, Henry	2	2	3		
Custard, Manuel	1	4	3		
Longsworth, Robert	1	4	3		1
Adkins, Charles	3	1			
Summerwell, James	3	1	2		
Wertz, Michael	1				7
Davis, Ignatius	1	1	2		7
Perry, Sarah	2	2			
Scoggins, Ann					6

NAME OF HEAD OF FAMILY.	Free white males of 16 years and upward, including heads of families.	Free white males under 16 years.	Free white females, including heads of families.	All other free persons.	Slaves.
Briscoe, Robert	2		2		
Martin, John	1	3	6		
Tabler, Michael				5	
Lett, Rosalin	2		2	5	2
Jacobs, Richard	2		2		
McDaniel, Mary	1	1	3		
Dulen, Francis	1		3		13
Harding, William	1	1	5		13
Magruder, Susannah		3	5		
Hill, Thomas			4		2
Stewart, Posey		3	4		5
Hill, Joseph	3	4	2		5
Simmerley, Mathias	2	2	3		
Grosman, Simon	1	3	4		
Howard, Joseph	2	1	3		10
Marshal, William	2		6	1	
Cumbridge, George			3		
Thomas, John	1		5		
Perril, Basil		3	3		
Yesterday, Martin	1	5	5		2
Perril, Samuel	1	1	5		
Ball, Daniel	1		3		
Carns, Jacob	2		3		
Canadey, Soloman	1	2	2		
Lett, Zakariah	1		3		
Thomas, William (of Wm)	1	2	2		
Lett, Daniel	1	2	6		
Stewart, Benjamin	2	1			4
Lewis, David	2		4	2	
Thomas, Levy	1		2		
Wheeler, Robert	1	1	4		
Hilton, John	1		4		
Lett, Robert	1	1	3		2
Durm, John	1		2		11
Cumpton, John	1		2		11
Harding, Gary	2	4	1		4
Chism, John	6	2	4		9
Dawson, Nicholas	2	4			1
McDead, Robert	2	2			1
Chism, Thomas	2		3		
Jacobs, William	2	3			8
Goodman, Joseph	2	1			
Jacobs, Benjamin	2	2			8
Jacobs, John	3	3	2		
Ball, John	1		2		
Carnegie, Catharine	3	1	2		
Linpley, John	3	1	3		2
Limpley, Peter	3	1	6		
Cruso, Robertson	1	1			4
Coblin, James	1		3	3	8
Dunkin, Theodore	3	1			
Stover, Philip	3	4	1		8
Noland, Philip	1		3		
Anceli, Priscilla			3		
Hughes, Levy	4		5		
Hekerthrow, George	2		6		
Yesterday, Margaret	2		1		
Nicholas, John	3	1			
Davis, Walter	2		4		
Fogle, Christian	2		1		
Howard, Cornelius	4		2		
Thomas, Gabriel	4				
Brandensburgh, Frederick	2	4	5		5
Darnall, John	2		2		45
Darnall, Henry, Esqr	3	2			20
Proof, Jacob	1		5		
Parnell, Bedwell	2	1	5		1
Prush, David	2		4		
Nashorn, Conrod			4		
Nashorn, Paul	1		3		
Nashorn, John	1	1			4
McClain, William	3		5		
Whip, John	2	2	5		
More, John	1	5	5		
Farthing, James	2	5	4		
Leather, John, Junr	2		5	1	1
Leather, John	2	2	3		
Beall, James	2		5		
Shafer, Adam	3	1	3		5
Beall, Nenian	2		2		
Cramer, Mary	1	1	2		
Shiveley, John	1	1	1		
Johnson, Joshua	2	1	2	1	
Hagerty, John	2	2			
Zealer, Yost	2	1			
Hargat, Abraham	3		2		3
Whip, Martin	3	1	2		
Jose, George	3	1	2		
Marker, Christian	1		2		
Fest, Michael	3		2		
Thomas, Gabriel (of Feity)	1	5	2		
Nicholas, George	3	1	2		1
Paggett, Josiah	1	1			

FREDERICK COUNTY—Continued.

NAME OF HEAD OF FAMILY.	Free white males of 16 years and upward, including heads of families.	Free white males under 16 years.	Free white females, including heads of families.	All other free persons.	Slaves.
Renner, William	3		3	3	2
Odd, Robert	3	2	3		4
Winepegler, Henry	2	3	1		
Winepegler, George	2	1	3	6	4
Hofman, Adam	1		4	6	4
Baggal, Benjamin	1	2	2	4	
Cramer, Casper	3		1	6	
Collins, Patrick	3	1	2	6	1
Masteller, George	2	2	8		
Stoher, Michael	2	2	7		
Hill, Henry R	2		4	2	
Hill, Penelope	2	2	2		
Pepper, John	4	1	1		
Hill, Benjamin	1	4	2		
Pepper, John, Junr	1	1	1		
Hill, Robert	1	4	1	5	
Dashnall, George	4	2	5	3	
Carperton, John	1	1	1		
Hardman, Nicholas	1	2	2		
Tarlton, Jeremiah	2	1	4		
Briscoe, Ralph	3	4	4		7
Kile, John	4	4	4		3
Everhart, Lawrence	4	2	4		
Head, Richard	4	1	1		
Cassiman, William	1		3	2	
Beaumont, William	2	1	4		
Marshal, Alexander	2	1	4		2
Firestone, Mathias	1	4	5		
Shriner, Peter	1	1	2		
Storp, George Adam	2	2	7		
Kephart, Simeon	2	3	2		
Williams, William	2	2	2	1	5
Everhart, Peter	2	2	4		
Jeffison, Henry	1	2	4		1
Fife, Jonathan	2	4	2		
Thomas, Edward	2		2		13
Thomas, Benjamin	3	6	6		2
Davis, John	2	4	2		
Harrisson, William	2	1	3		
Davis, Nathaniel	2	3	5		
Pagget, Josiah, Jun	1	1	4		
Nelson, Arthur	1	1	2		14
Brookover, Thomas	1	2	3		
Quyan, John	1	2	1		
Fryer, Richard	1	2	1		
Stevenson, Richard	1	1	1		
Duncan, William	3		4		
Coy, Christopher	1		2		
Tucker, Stephen	2	1	2		
Hatting, John	1	2	2		
Collins, Robert	2	1	2		
Genkins, Joab	1	5	5		4
Livers, Thomas	2	2	3		
Cating, Joshua	2	1	3		
Cheeseman, Frederick	1	1	1		
Dawson, William	1		2		
Warfield, Anne		1	4		
Fox, Henry	2		4		
Woodman, Thomas	1	1	4		
Ridgeway, James	1	3	4		
Briner, John	1	3	2		
Nichols, James	1		2		
Lamb, Henry	2	3	2		
Carter, John	3		3		
Delashmet, Lindsay	2	3	2	1	35
Delashmet, Basil		2	6		5
Thomas, Rebeccah		1	2		8
Dillon, William			2		
Smith, Henry	2	3	2		5
Gisberts, Gisbert	5		5		
Hill, Thomas	1		2		
Smith, Joseph	2	3	1		
Michael, Andrew	4	1	3		
Michael, William	4	1	3		
Johnson, John	5	2	2		13
Johnson, Thomas	2	1	1		7
Tansey, Lidia	1		4		
Hill, Joseph	3	1	2	1	1
Burger, William	1		2		
Pagget, William	2	1	2		
Watkins, Christopher	1	3	2		
Sedge, Henry		1	3		
Bright, Sarah		1	4		
Thomas, John	1	3	2		
Wortz, Michael	1	1			
Gant, Margaret			2		
Thomas, George	1	3	2		1
Gyer, George	1	2	2		
Thomas, John	1	1	2		
Vatgin, Stephen	3	1	1		
Morris, Jonathan	1		2		
Darnall, Philip	2	1	2		3
Smith, Joseph	2	1	1		9
Howard, James	1		2		
Howard, Edward	1	2	5		
Thomas, Valentine	2	5			
Thomas, Gabriel, Jur	5	1	5		

NAME OF HEAD OF FAMILY	Free white males of 16 years and upward, including heads of families.	Free white males under 16 years.	Free white females, including heads of families.	All other free persons.	Slaves.
Thomas, Stofel	1	1	2		
Ramsberg, George	2	2	5		1
Lonk, Christopher	1			5	
Wolf, Adam	4		4		
Show, Conrod	3		3		
Whiskey, Augustus	1	1	4		
Whip, Tobias	1	4	4		
Wren, Catharine	1	1	4		
Simmerman, George	1	2	2		
Briar, Godfrey	1	2	5		
Lawfer, Chanta	2	3	5		
Stubs, Catharine			2		
Songor, Stephen				5	
Ott, Barnet	2	3	5		
Toup, George	3	3	5		
Simmerman, Michael	1		3		
Simmerman, John	1	2	3		
Fukney, Peter	1	2	5		
Fouts, William	1	3	3		
Shots, Michael	5		4		
Busson, Benjamin	2	1	2		
Breiner, Stephen	1	2	4		
McCusey, John	1		3	1	
Kufer, Christian, Junr	3	4	4		1
Kufer, Christian	1	1	2		
Moseback, Henry	1	3			
Foutz, Michael	1	1	1		
Watgain, Christian	1		1		
Kemp, Lodwik	4	1	4		5
Howser, Margaret			3		
Kemp, Catharine		2	5		
Harget, Peter	2	2	5		
Hatter, George	1	2	6		
Chattel, Thomas	1	2	2		
Powers, John	1	1	1		
Hime, Andrew	2	4	6		
Renner, Michael, Junr	3	2	3		
Pagaent, William	3		4		
Smith, Jacob	1		3		
Bost, Michael		4	5		
Wooman, Christian	1	2	5		
Smith, Jacob	1		2		
Dutterow, John	1		2		
Toffler, George	2	1	2		
Randal, Samuel	2		2		
Loffer, Lodwick	2	1	3		
Loffer, Michael	1		1		
Statzler, George	1		1		
Goldshine, Arnes	1	2	3		
Whiskey, Margaret	1		3		
Parsins, John	1	4	3		
Tabler, William	1	5	4		2
Renner, Charlotte			5		
Furtney, Catharine			2		
Furtney, Daniel	1	4	2		
Furtney, Peter	1	2	4		
Jones, Thomas	1	2	3		1
Renner, Isaac	1		3		
Tatler, Melcher	1		2		
Hoffman, Francis	2	1	2		6
Hoofer, Leonard	1		3		2
Williams, Elizabeth			2		
Coutz, Devalt		1	2		
Collier, Edward	2		1		
Ungerfer, Frederick	2	1	2		
Swadner, Henry	2	1	1		
Shreader, John George	1	3			
Williams, James	1		3		
Edzler, Daniel	2	1	3		
Gliston, John	3	2	3		
Shivers, Richard	1		1		
Medoo, Henry	1		1		
Taylor, Conrod	1	1			
Wallace, Samuel	1		3		
Hart, Ellis	1	1	3		1
Boyer, John	1		2		
Bankard, Christopher	1	3	3		
Steel, Abraham	1	1	1		
Gun, Alexander	2		2		
McKenzie, Thomas	2		2		
Gahart, Adam	1		3		
Dagan, George	3	1	3		
Wolfkill, John	1		2		
Hasler, Urith	1		5		
Cola, William	1		2		
Comber, Christian	2	2	5		
McKaleb, David			2		
Gesty, Jacob	1		1		
Boran, Lawrence	1	1	3		
Rife, Christian	1		2		
Kins, John	1	3	2		
Meyors, Robert	1		2		
Snosinger, Joseph	1	1	2		
Stoner, Christian	1		2		
Miller, Michael, Jur	2	2	3		
Nestor, Jacob	1	3	1		

NAME OF HEAD OF FAMILY	Free white males of 16 years and upward, including heads of families.	Free white males under 16 years.	Free white females, including heads of families.	All other free persons.	Slaves.
Baker, Henry	1	2	4		
Lambert, Peter	1	2	2		
Slush, John	1	1	2		
Slumer, George	3		3		
Luster, Michael	3	2	1		
Sole, Peter	2	4	4		
Tetrick, Martin	2		2		
Beard, Frederick	2	2	1		
Gettes, Alexander	2		2		
Lenport, George	3		2		
Traxall, Jacob, Jur	3		3		
Utto, Peter	1	1	4		
Fox, John	1		4		
Sargent, George	1	2	5		
Hiter, William	1	1	1		
Thompson, William	1	1	3	1	
Moyer, Christian	1		2		
Ugly, Peter	1	1	3		
Colterbaugh, Frederick	1		5		
Lickfetter, Joseph	2	5	5		
Sandbaugh, Philip	1	1	2		
Herrin, Daniel	1	1	3		
Miller, Robert	1		2		
Michael, William	1	3	2		
Garver, Martin	2		3		
Rylett, Edward	1	2	2		
Overholse, George	2	1	3		
Citterman, John	1				
Sanders, Samuel				7	
Athey, Jacob	1		3		
Sepherd, John	1		3		
Naw, George	1	2	3		
Combaugh, Michael	1		2		
Beans, Francis	1		2		
Stallions, Benjamin	3	1	1		
Myers, William	1	1	3		
Lean, John	2		4		
Goswell, Charles	1	2	4		
Sponseller, Jacob	1	2	2		
Dail, John	1	1	2		
Witseller, John	1	1	2		
Boon, Charles	1	1	2		
Swadner, John, Jur	1	1	2		
Mett, Francis	1		1		
Crice, John	1		1		
Sawers, Balser	6	1	4		
Browning, Benjamin	1	1	5		
Bowden, John, Jur	1	1	3		
Butler, William	1		2		
Hartsock, John	1		3		
Dutero, George	1		3		
Develbiss, George	2		3		
Hemp, Philip	3	2	2		
Cromer, Jacob	1		3		
Myers, Stephen	1		2		
Beamer, Henry	1	1	2		
Beamer, Tice	1		3		
Barrack, William	1	1	2		
Ernst, Jacob	1		2		
Wallis, Elizabeth			2		
Wallis, Renchart			2		
Mills, John	2		2		
Cain, John	1		2		
Gay, Henry	1	3	3		
Mirlvey, Michael	1		1		
Holliway, Edward	1	1	2		
Burrier, Philip	2	2	2		
Fine, Philip	1		8		
Albaugh, Daniel	1	1	4		
Win, John	1	1	4		
Eader, Jacob	2	2	4		
Leakins, William	1		4		
Nelson, William	1	1	4		
Devine, John	1		3		
Davden, William	1		2		
Dean, John	1		2		
Young, Nicholas	1	1	7		
Bower, Abraham	1		2		
Smith, John	1		2		
Hall, John G	2	3	5		
Snider, Philip	3	1	5		
Root, Daniel, Jur	3	1	5		1
Nave, Balser	2		2		
Deal, Samuel	1		2		
Horine, Daniel	1	1	2		
Everley, George	1		2		
Lutz, Nicholas	1	2	2		
Copple, Philip	1	2	2		
Fogle, Henry	1		2		
Screwel, George	2		2		
Barrack, Peter	1	2	2		
Custus, Henry	1	2	3		
Simpson, Benjamin	1	3	1		
Shafer, Jacob	1				
plus, William	1	1	1		
Neal, Alexander	1	3	1		

FIRST CENSUS OF THE UNITED STATES.

FREDERICK COUNTY—Continued.

NAME OF HEAD OF FAMILY.	Free white males of 16 years and upward, including heads of families.	Free white males under 16 years.	Free white females, including heads of families.	All other free persons.	Slaves.
Hardman, Henry	1	2	6		
Brothers, John	1		2		
Fisher, Philip	1	1	1		
Tipple, John	1		4		
Luccessle, Michael	1	1	1		
Fisher, Henry	1	1	1		
Climmer, Laurance	1	1	6		
Habb, Richard	2		5		
Frickburger, John	1	1	1		
Frost, George	1		3		
Semmer, Adam	2		5		
Parret, Peter	2	1	1		
Adams, George	1		4		
Carter, John	1	4	4		
Holce, Nicholas	3	1	2		
Fagler, Henry	1	1	4		
Bore, Michael	2		2		
Hox, Mathias	2	4	4		
Linebaugh, John	1		2		
Bent, Samuel	1				
Flemming, Joseph	2		2		3
Martz, George	1	2			
Cline, Nicholas	1	4			
Gessenger, Charles	2		4		
Angel, Peter	1		2		
Kelse, Eccard	1	1	2		
Hedge, Andrew	1		2		
Candler, Jacob	3		4		
Trimble, Michael	1	4	2		
Hefner, Cutlip	1		1		
Wedrick, Marten	1		1		
Brushier, Stephen	1		2		
Spealman, Laurance	1	1	2		
Crust, Henry	1	1	4		
Dorchey, John	1		4		
Larkins, George	1		1		
Grose, Henry	2	2	3		
Creaver, Varney	2	6	3		
Doratha, Patrick	1	3	2		
Mathews, Peter	1		2		
Flanagan, Malachia	1	2			
Brice, John	1		4		
Sowder, Adam	1		2		
Genspur, John	1		2		
Mullan, Nicholas	1	3	3		
Frink, Henry	1	3	2		
Ball, William	1		3		
Haheooh, Frederick	3	2	2		
Simmerman, George	3		5		6
Lap, William	1		4		
Kell, Henry	3	2	1		
Caldwell, James	2	1	4		
Creager, Daniel	1		4		
Haslet, William	1	6	1		
Defauld, Rachel		1	1		
Knox, James	1		4		
Rekenbaugh, George	1	1	2		
Lindsay, Oliver	1		5		
Favonite, Henry	2	6			2
Nuse					2
Hoffman, Nicholas	1	1	3		
Clem, Henry	1	3			
Boyer, Michael	2		2		
Cashier, John	1		1		
Haws, John	1		2		
Reidenhorn, Barnet	1		3		
Connelly, Hugh	1	3	2		
Nale, Bosteon	1	1	2		
Landers, Roger	1	3	4		
Sailor, Frederick	2		2		
Moser, Michael	1		2		
Lidd, Henry		2	2		
Shafer, Eve		2	7		
Coons, Nicholas	1	2	2		
Snider, Lodwick	1		5		1
Livers, Elizabeth	1		1		
Livers, Ignatius	2	2	1		
Nacvicker, Armibald	1	1			7
Bell, Cephas	1				3
Calbek, Andrew	1	1	4		
Avery, George	1		4		
Beckwith, Lamach	1		1		2
Lisler, William	1	2	6		
White, Elisha	1	2	4		
Strisler, John	1	2	3		
Salmon, Edward	1	3	2		
Groshart, Adam	1	3	1		
Lilly, Henry	1		1		
Gantney, Adam	1		1		
Cephas, Frederick	2		1		
Valette, Alexander	1		1		
Pierpont, Amos	1		1		
Miller, Jacob	1		4		1
Coons, Jacob	1	3	4		
Willer, Mathias	1	3	5		
Willer, John	1	1	3		

NAME OF HEAD OF FAMILY.	Free white males of 16 years and upward, including heads of families.	Free white males under 16 years.	Free white females, including heads of families.	All other free persons.	Slaves.
Willer, Daniel	1	1	3		
Atman, William	2	2	2		
Stoner, Henry	1	1	2		
Sham, Peter	2	1	1		
Miller, John	4		4		
Waggoner, Joseph	1		3		
Brand, Christopher	1		4		
Chunk, Joseph	1	2	2		
Yanser, Christopher	1		3		
Crobough, Lodwick	1	2	2		
Hoffman, Frederick	1	1	8		
Janeth, Thomas	1	2	6		
McDaniel, Francis	1		3		
Carter, Solomon	2		6		
Powel, William	2		4		
Creager, John	2	1	3		
Springer, Edward	1		2		
Lambert, Christopher	1		3		
Miller, John	1		2		
Peter, Frederick	1		1		
Smith, John	1		2		
Cryer, William	1	2	2		
Campbell, James	1		2		
Grushong, John	1	2	2		
Simmers, Thomas	1	2	3		
Clem, Michael	1				
Hanley, Stephen	1	2	4		
Creager, Adam	1	1	5		
Harp, John	3	1	5		
McAfee, Daniel	1		4		
Livers, William	1	3	3		
Rife, Henry	1		1		
Fry, Jacob	1	2			
Wolf, George	1				
Cromer, Frederick	1	1	2		
Bush, John	1	1	2		
Fry, Daniel	1	2	3		
Pherson, Leonard	1	2	1		
Hoofer, Jacob	1		3		
Hardy, William	1	5	5		
Recop, Susanah		1	2		
Caughman, Jacob	1		2		
Willer, Jacob	2	3	5		
Willer, Jacob, Jun	2	1	2		
Anders, Lawrence	2		2		
Willers, John, Sen.	4	2	6		
Penser, Godfrey	1	2	5		
Yost, John	3	1	3		
Coons, George	3	3	5		
Williams, Clement	3	3	9		2
Tallhill, Henry	3		1		4
Johnson, Peter	1	1	2		
Cantour, Christian	1				
Siss, Godfrey	1		2		
Prutsman, Lodwick	1		2		
Pelshill, Uly	1	1	2		
Cannon, Adam	1	3	2		
Shoup, John	1		1		
Thompson, Leck			6		
Haffler, Jacob	1	1	1		
Rass, Daniel	1	1	2		
Carver, Jacob		3	6		
Riffle, Joseph	2	4	3		
Dumburger, Mary			4		
Noel, Blosius	2	6	2		
Miller, Henry	1	1	2		
Stoner, George	2		2		1
Flower, Nicholas	1		5		
Case, Robert	1	6	5		
Bushman, Jacob	1	1	4		
Blates, Frederick	2		4		
Darr, George M.	2		3		
Merring, Wolfgang	2	4	6		
Snider, George	2		6		
Miller, Henry, sen.	2		4		
Algier, Rachel	1	3	4		
Eck, Conrod	1	4	4		
Master, Rinehart	1	4	6		
Shoup, Henry	1	2	2		
Navel, Peter	1	1	3		
Septer, Frederick	1		2		
Septer, John	1	1	3		
Brown, Jacob	2		3		
Fisor, Jacob	1		6		
Fisor, Nicholas	1	1	4		
Mertz, George	1		2		
Long, Conrod	1	2	2		
Blair, Samuel	5				
Brown, Peter	1	4	3		
Wimast, Henry	1		5		
Varner, Adam	1	3	2		
Brown, Daniel	2		2		
Lingenfelter, Christian	1		1		
Keifer, Philip	2	1	1		
Springle, Peter	1				

NAME OF HEAD OF FAMILY.	Free white males of 16 years and upward, including heads of families.	Free white males under 16 years.	Free white females, including heads of families.	All other free persons.	Slaves.
Snider, Catharine	1	2	4		
Study, Lodwich	1	3	6		
Rice, Thomas	1		6		
Routsong, Conrod	1	2	5		
Yingland, Abraham	1	1	2		
Yingland, John	1	2	5		
Leister, Conrod	2	1	2		
Study, Martin	2		2		
Long, John	2		2		
Miller, Philip	1		2		
Tannin, Aquila	1	2	2		
Cromrind, John	1	4	5		
Daman, Frederick	2	1	4		
Yonker, Jacob	1	1	2		
Ettinger, Jacob	1	2	4		
Starner, Christian	1		2		
Feeser, Adam	1	1	3		
Carter, Susana		1	1		
Mixel, Peter	1	1	2		
Kemp, John	1	1	3		
Sailor, Henry	1	1	2		
Lingenfelter, Peter	1	2	4		
Lingenfelter, Michael	1	1			
Henlsh, Jacob	2	1			
Miller, Jacob	2		2		
Hanes, John	2	3	2		
Beagle, Nicholas	1		2		
Dill, Esther			3		
Dill, Nicholas	1	1	1		
Gilbert, Rachel			3		
Gilbert, Francis	1	2	3		
Erehart, George	2		3		
Beagle, Tobias	2		3		
Houke, Jacob	2		3		
Linderman, John	3	3	4		
Coons, Henry	1	4	6		
Smith, Jacob	1	2	5		
Wolf, Andrew	1	3	6		
Norris, Nathaniel	1		3		
Switzer, Rudolph	2		6		
Moyer, Daniel	2	2	5		
Helchew, Nicholas	1		2		
Harrisson, Benjamin	1	3	2		
Strine, Jacob	1	4	4		
Shoemaker, Jacob	1	4	4		
Mort, Peter	2		8		
Springer, Jacob	1	2	6		
Fogle, Frederick	1	5	5		
Larkins, John	1	1	4		
Sponseller, Jacob, Jur	1	3	2		
Watt, Thomas	1	1	3		
Rippin, Thomas	1		1		
Doan, Hezekiah	1	2	2		
Shittinhelm, Frederick	1		3		
Jumper, Jacob	3	1	2		1
Jumper, Mary			2		
Litt, Henry	1	3	4		
Fox, Casper	2	1	3		
Erbin, James	1	5	1		
Hammond, Ormand	1	1	2		12
Johnson, Robert	11	1	10		
Hickenmiller, John	1	1	1		
Miller, Devalt	1	2	5		
Miller, John	1	1	3		
Miller, Peter	2		1		
Amelung, John Frederick	7	1	10		4
Gripencurl, Diderick	2		2		
Harpoke, John F. C.	2	2	5		
Messing, Christian	2	4	3		
Cramer, Balth	1		4		
Muller, Jacob	1	1	2		
Brandt, Christian	1	1	1		
Balheim, H.	1	3			
Messenkop, C.	1		4		
Giseler, George	1		2		
Eccerhart, Martin	1	4	2		
Becel, Carl	2		6		
Impson, H. Wm	1	1	3		
Cocklenkerg, Adam	1		3		
Stanley, Thomas	3		3		
Metzger, John	3	1	2		2
Apel, H. Wm	2		2		
Bear, Gorg	1				
Madery, John	1	3	7		
Becker, H.	1	3	2		
Schade, John Julius	1	2	1		
Burshank, Wm	1	2	2		
Giseler, John	1	2	2		
Horn, David	1	2	4		
Meinhard, Jacob	1	3	5		
Rund, H.	1		1		
Gabler, H. Wm	1		4		
Wend, Henry	1	2	2		
Rodensick, Henry	1	2	2		

FREDERICK COUNTY—Continued.

NAME OF HEAD OF FAMILY.	Free white males of 16 years and upward, including heads of families.	Free white males under 16 years.	Free white females, including heads of families.	All other free persons.	Slaves.
Brauner, Frederick	1	1	1		
Feurhacke, George			2		
Sengstake, Philip	1	1	1		
Wollsmecer, H	1		1		
McKogh, P	1		1		
Will, H	1	3	3		
Seitz, Henry	2		1		
Knop, Carl	1		1		
Ellengenger, Christian	1		3		
Moor, Wm	1	1	2		
May, Benjamin	1		2		
Bodence, David	1	3	2		
Weiss, L	1		2		
Bosenberg, Henry	1	2	1		
Hiegeman, John	1		2		
Pole, John	1	2	3		
Hahn, Lud	1		2	1	
Hohne, Loohnd	1		1		
Tuppel, Christian	1		1		
Bader, Anton	1				
Triemer, Lem'preeth	1		1		
Sekildler, I	1				
Bohn, Otto	1				
Schemich, Casper	1				
Preine, C	1	2	1		
Smith, Math	1		1		
Kespel, Bell	1		1		
Clark, James	1	2	3		
Sherder, H	1	1	2		
Gerhard,	1		1		
Week, Michael	1	1			
Runecker, H	1		1		
Kramer, George	1		1		
Grambo, H	1		3		
Hartman, I. I	1	3	2		
Erhart, Carl	1	1	1		
Kluet, John	1		4		
Schreiler, Henry	1		3		
Smith, Andrew	1				
Smith, Aloysius	1				
Haupt, Math	1				
Haase, I	1	1	1		
Iter, Anton	1		1		
Croehan, J. M	1		3		
Hane, Jacob	1				
Tupir, Revd	1				
Neith, Lorentz	1				
Bouche,			1		
Stouver, John	1		1		
Erb, Peter	2	1	4		
Finefrock, Henry	1	3	5		
Boyer, Henry	1		2		
Boyer, John	1		1		
Wively, John	1	1	4		
Fox, Henry	1		1		
Epley, Jacob	1	2	2		
Fumenfeiter, Pheonix	2		5		
Smith, George	1		1		
Wolf, Michael	2	3	1		
Markle, Nicholas	1		2		
Boyer, Henry, Senr	3		3		
Shilling, Conrod	2	1	2		
Sheets, Peter	2		2		
Shilling, John	1		2		
Morris, Benjamin	1	2	1		
Soyer, John	1				
Crabb, Ralph	2	2	1		3
Mahoney, James H	2		2	1	9
Regden, John E	1				

HARFORD COUNTY.

NAME OF HEAD OF FAMILY.	Free white males of 16 years and upward, including heads of families.	Free white males under 16 years.	Free white females, including heads of families.	All other free persons.	Slaves.
Smithson, William	1	1	2		16
Jones, Gilbert	2		2		2
Gibson, Thomas	1		2		2
Penkney, William	1	1	2		3
Reardan, John	1	2	4		
Rockhold, John	2		5		
Maulsby, David	1	2	4		
Maulsby, William	3	3	2		
Moore, James, Goal	3	1	4		3
Johnson, James	3	1	1		1
Bond, Samuel	3		3		2
Baker, James	1		4		
Caulder, John	2	1	1		
Bond, James	1				8
Hannah, James	1	4	2		
Norris, Benjamin	1	2	4		
Robinson, Mary					1
Guyton, Mary		1	3		
Hughs, Esther			2		
Hughs, William	2		1		
Mackis, Mary		1	1		
Aldridge, Sally			1		
Bunting, Billy D			1		5
Peters, Samuel	1		3		
Rutter, Thomas	1		4		
Bond, Dennis	2		4		12
Norris, Jacob	2		4		8
Gallion, Widw Rachel			4		
Norris, Eliza		2	6		6
Norris, Susanna			6		
Norris, John	3	2	5		3
Morford, Isaiah	3	1	2		3
Robinson, William	3		2		1
Morford, Thomas	1		2		2
Anderson, William	2	3	4		
Robinson, Richard	3	2	6		2
Spencer, Enoch	2	1	2		
Hanway, David	2		1		
Carlile, Lanclet	2	2	2	3	1
Thompson, Thomas A	2	3	7		4
Norris, Edward, of Jo	1	3	5		1
Garrettson, James	3		2		4
Allworth, Benja	3	1	2		2
Amos, James, Senr	3		1		23
Johnson, Matthew	1	3	2		
Williams, Abraham	1	2	1		
Hawkens, Charles	1				
Rose, Aquila	2		4		
Parker, Edward	2	2	4		6
Corbin, Jacob	2	1			
Freeborn, John	1		1		
Parsons, Abner	1	1	1		
Dunsheath, David	1		1		
Barton, James	5		3		1
Barton, James, Son of Jmᵃ	2	1	2		
Williams, Divid	2	1	1		
Fips, John	1	2	3		
Cullom, William	2	1	2		
Cullom, Jerimiah	1	1	2		
Prewett, John	1	2	3	3	
Raldin, William	1		3	3	
Polson, John	4		5		
Bull, William	4	1	5		4
Richardson, Wm	3	2	4		7
Richardson, William, Junr. p	1	1	1		
Whiteford, David	1	2	5		
Jenkens, Eliza		1	2		
Rutledge, Jacob	2				5
Pearse, Hugh	2	1	4		
Parker, John	2	4	3		
Taylor, John, of Charm	2	1	1		2
Spencer, Abel	2	2	5		
Galloway, Absalom	2	2	1		1
Taylor, Charles	1	1	3		4
Maul & Churchman	3	2	1		
Standiford, Samuel	1	1	3		1
Hutchens, Samuel	1	1	3		
Amos, Mord	1	3	3		4
Durham, David	2	5	4		
Johnson, Thomas	2		3		13
Jones, William	3	1	3		
Leese, William	1	1	1		1
Comas, James M	2	2	7		9
Trapnall, James	3		2		9
Vance, Samuel	2		3		
Connell, Bartholomew	2	3	4		1
Taylor, Thomas	1		4		1
Vance, James	1		3		
Moore, John	1	1	1		2
Barnett, James, Junr	1	3	3		
Mountgomery, John	5	1	2		
Osbon, William	2	3	3		15
Gryton, John	2	3	1		
Jarvis, James	1	1	3		
Bussey, Bennett	2	3	4		5
McNair, Archd	1	2	2		
Cunningham, John	1		3		
Jarvis, Solomon	1	2	1		
Rose, Joseph	2	4	4		1
Ward, James	1	3	4		5
Johnson, Bernard	2	1	2		2
Adams, John	1	4	2		
McComas, Moses	2	2	2		5
Bond, Buckler	2	2	4		7
Mathews, Capn Bennett	2		2		7
Carr, William	1		2		
Dyer, Joseph	1				5
Henderson, Doctr Philᵖ lip	2	3	5		10
Preston, James	1	5	2		1
Jackson, John	1	1	2		
Wilson, John	2		7		
Amos, William	3	2	4		
Amos, Mauldon	2	4	3		7
Bull, Jacob	4	1	3		8
Rush, Jacob	3	2	5		
Freeman, Thoᵃ	1		1		
Cox, Eliza			1		
Norris, Wm, of Jo	2	2	4		1
Harry, David	1	3	3		
Cann, Robert	2	1	5		
Ford, Wm	2	1	3		
Ford, John	1	3	2		
Norris, Joseph, of Jmᵃ	1	3	2		
Gardener, Thomas	1	2	2		
McComas, Daniel	1	4	3		
Caldwell, Samᵗ	2	4	3		3
Richardson, Thomas	2		3		1
Davis, George	1	2			
Dawes, Mary					1
Lancaster, Nathan	1	2	2		
Ragan, Danᵗ	1	1	1		
Shimon, Wm	1		1		
Williams, Peter	1	1	2		
Rose, William	1		3		
Jones, Amos	1	1	3		
Whitson, Benjᵃ	1	2	2		
McComas, James	1	1	3		1
Amos, James, of M	2	1	2		
Amos, Mord., Senr	3		4		2
Bentley, Joshua	2	2	5		
Jones, Isaiah	1	3	4		
Craven, Andrew	1		2		
McCanney, Hugh	2	3	5		
Morford, Obadiah	2		2		
Corbin, John	1	2	3		
Amos, Benjᵃ	5	1	6		9
Parker, Aqᵃ	2	3	6		4
Hutchins, Richard	2	3	4		
Ashmead, John	3		3		
Draper, Simon	1		1		
Gibson, Joshua	4	1	8		1
Kenedy, John	2	2	3		
Bond, John, Senr	1		1		4
Scott, Danᵗ	1	1		1	5
Holland, Francis	1	1	2		14
Taylor, Walter	1	1	2		3
McComas, Danᵗ	1		2		
McComas, John	5	2	4		6
Guyton, Joshua	2	3	4		
Patterson, William	2	3	5		
Hays, John	2		1		6
Poteet, James	2		2		
Poteet, Thoᵃ	1	5	1		
Miles, Joshᵃ	2	5	1		
Hermer, Michael	2		3		
Parker, Martin	2	3	4		
Bond, Thoᵃ, of Dnᵗ	1	1	1		8
Daws, Benjᵃ	3				
Jarrett, Abraham	1	4	2		7
Hitchcock, Assel	1		2		8
Doran, John	5	1	2		7
Marshal, Samᵗ	1	1	4		
Renshaw, Phillip	1	1	2		
Hitchcock, Assel	1		2		8
Hitchcock, John	1		4		
Hitchcock, Isaac	1		3		
Hitchcock, Wm	1	5	3		
Amos, Fredᵃ	1		1		
Davis, John	1	1	1		4
McGidegan, Thoᵃ	1		2		
Barton, William	2	2	2		7
Rockhold, Tood	1		2		
Parsons, Isaac	1		2		
Miles, Aqᵃ	2	4	3		1
Skeventon, James	4	2	2		
McComas, Alex	2	1	2		6
Riddle, Ricᵈ	2	1	3		
Rigbie, James	3		5		
Preston, Thoᵃ	1	1	3		
Grear, Aqᵃ	2	1			
Amos, Joshᵃ	2		2		2
Gordon, Wm	1	1	7		1
Jones, Joseph	1	1	2		1
Chalk, Abᵐ	1	1	6		
Merrett, Sarah		1	1		
Rain, Samᵗ	1	1	2		4
Fendley, James	2	1	1		
Kirkwood, Robᵃ	4	1	2		

HARFORD COUNTY—Continued.

NAME OF HEAD OF FAMILY.	Free white males of 16 years and upward, including heads of families.	Free white males under 16 years.	Free white females, including heads of families.	All other free persons.	Slaves.
Harris, Jmª	1		3		
Meads, James	1	5	3		
Glann, Wm	1	1	3		2
Johnson, John	2		2		
Smith, Thoª	1				1
Barnett, Thoª	2	1	4		
Henderson, Francis	2	2	3		
McGovern, Mark	2	1	2		
Gormley, Owen	1				
Agan, Ricd	1				
Briarley, George	1	1	4		
Callan, James	1	1	3		
Cox, Thoª	2	3	5		
Wilgus, Jmª	2	1	5		
Thompson, Jmª	2	2	3		1
Anderson, Hugh	1		4		4
Rutlege, John	5	1	3		11
Amos, Wm, Junr	3	5	4		5
Turner, Andw	2	3	4		
Patterson, Wm	1	6	4		
Scarff, Jnº	2	2	3		
McMulin, Patrick	1	1	3		
Demos, Jno, Junr	1	4	4		
Demos, John	1		2		
Creswell, John	1	1	1		
Jones, Wm	2	1	4		
Cretin, John	1		4		2
Cretin, James	2	1	2		2
Huston, Wm	1		1		
Huston, Mary		1	4		
Hughes, Saml	1	1			
Watt, Joseph	1		3		
Smith, Nathan	2	2	2		8
Denbow, John	2	1	6		2
Gordon, Francis	1	1	4		
Norris, Geo	3		4		
Goins, Jmª	2	2	4		
Knox, Geo	1				
Mosman, John	2		1		
Bay, John	1		2		
Black, John	1	3	2		
Bell, John	2	3	5		
Woodsworth, Thomas	4	2	6		
Ayres, Thoª	3	2	4		1
Mallick, Jnº	1		2		
Hitchcock, Josiah	1	4	4		
Kerns, Wm	3	2	4		
Coleman, Geo	1	2	4		
Clark, Robt	2	4	7		
Wilson, Benjª	1	1	4		16
Fulton, John	3		5		
Preston, Benjª	3				6
Asten, Joseph	3	4	4		3
Whitaker, Josª	2	2	6		5
Wilson, Humphrey	2		1		
Fencham, Edwd	1		1		
Whitaker, Jnº S	1	3	3		
Waters, Robert	2	4	7		
Crosby, Jnº	1	3	3		
Stockdale, John	1	5	4		
Whiteford, Hugh	1	1	1		5
Wiley, Nat	6	1	2		
Threadway, Danl	3		2		
Wilson, Jnº	3	3	6		
Canady, Jmª	2	2	5		
Creig, Pierce	1	5	1		6
Garrett, Henry	1	3	7		
Sheridine, Jmª	1	1	3		
Clark, Davd	3	4	6		4
Rigdon, Alex	3	4	4		10
Whitford, Robt	3		7		3
Allen, Jmª	1	2	4		
Thompson, Andw	2	2	6		1
Clendening, Jmª					
Montgomry, Thoª	1				1
Green, Benjª	3	2	6		7
Gray, Jnº	2	4	4		
Norris, Alex	2	4	7		
Norris, Thoª	6	4	4		
McGaw, Saml	1		1		
Shields, Paul	2	1	1		
Maulsby, David	2	2	3		1
Whitaker, Isaac	2	1	4		
Gasts, Thomas	1	3	2		4
West, James	1	2	2		
Donavan, Joseph	1		2		1
Saunders, Joseph	2		3		
Ward, Jnº	2	2	3		2
Couler, Jonas	2	2	3		
Brown, Solomon	3	1	3		
Elliott, Ann		2	2		
Hope, Thoª	3		3		
Garrett, Wm	1		4		6
McIlvain, Archd	1	1	1		
Everett, Isaac	2	4	6		
Thompson, James	1	5	2		

NAME OF HEAD OF FAMILY.	Free white males of 16 years and upward, including heads of families.	Free white males under 16 years.	Free white females, including heads of families.	All other free persons.	Slaves.
Williams, Wm	1	1	2		
Machis, Isaac	3	1	1		
Ned, Negro					6
Gleed, Jmª	1	2	1		
Threadway, Edwd	1	2	2		
Jarrett, Jesse	2	2	5		6
Gorden, Charles	1	3	2		
Reese, Jnº	1		2		
Maulsby, Benjª	1		3		
Galaspy, Charles	2	3	2		
Turner, Thoª	1	1	7		
Rutledge, Wm	1	2	2		
McCoy, Andw	3	2	2		
Weston, Jnº	2	1	2		8
Lancaster, Jesse	2	3	3		
Norris, Wm, Senr	4	2	3		3
Pocock, Danl	2		4		5
McLennon, Natª	1	1	1		
Whiteford, Jnº	2	1	1		
Hutchins, Saml	1	1	3		
Green, Joshª	1				
Renshaw, Joseph	3	1	8		11
Dearmatt, Mary			2		
Grafton, Wm	3	3	2		1
McMullen, Jnº	1		3		
Gibson, John Lee	5	2	5		32
Patterson, Saml	1	6	3		
Norris, Capn Aqª	2	5	4		
Slade, Wm	1	4	2		1
McComas, Jmª	3	3	3		
McComas, Alex	1	2	2		2
Watt, Joseph	2	1	3		
Fenley, Jmª	2	1	4		
Magness, Elizª			2		
Magness, Moses	2	5	2		
Keign, John	1	3	2		
James, Walter	3	2	4		
Long, John, Senr	1	1	2		
Anderson, James	1	3	2		
Sharp, Thoª	3	1	2		
Greenfield, Wm	1	3	2		
Brook, Geo	1	1	1		
Hannah, Jnº	1		1		2
Scott, Andw	1	1	2		
Todd, Patrick	1		1		
Smithson, Achd	1	1	3		5
Hines, Laurence	1	1	1		
Rutledge, Shadrick	1		3		1
Paine, Jnº	2		4		
Hughs, Jnº	1	1	3		
Barrett, Jnº	1	4	5		
Turnpaw, Jn	1	1	2		
Parsons, Jn	2	1	2		
Dungan, Abel	1				
Allen, Jn	3	3	3		
Rigdon, Wm	2		3		
Reese, David	1	1	1		
Bull, Waltr	2		2		3
Thoª, Abel	1	2	4		
McClasky, Joseph	1	2	1		
Lancaster, Natª	1		3		
Dyer, Joseph	1	4	4		3
Ady, Wm	1	4	3		
Wheeler, Ignª	3	3	7		44
Jones, Elizª	1		1		
Schofield, Jnº	1	2	1		
McDade, Neal	1	1	1		
Hayly, John	1		1		
Smith, Nath	2	3	2		
Perry, Wm	2	2	4		
Perry, John	1	1	3		
Perkins, Charles	2	3	3		
Smith, Wm	1	2	5		
Smith, John	1	2	3		
Jackson, Jamª	2		1		
Rigdon, Baker	1	3	3		
Evans, Evan	1	2	4		
Morgan, Robert	1	3	5		15
Prigg, Edwd	1				15
Flowers, John	1	1			
Walters, Thoª	1	1	6		
Walters, John	1	2	1		
West, Luke	1	2	4		
Tower, Negro					5
Pegg, Negr					5
Rogers, Rowland	2	3	5		
Hannah, Esther		2	3		
Wells, Wm	2				1
Coop, Hannah			2		
Thomas, Elizª			2		
Gilmore, Wm	3		1		11
Norris, Danl	1	1	2		
Poor house, At the					33
Bradfd, Wm	3	1	6		2
Amos, Robt	4	1	7		9
Archer, John	7	5	2	2	7

NAME OF HEAD OF FAMILY.	Free white males of 16 years and upward, including heads of families.	Free white males under 16 years.	Free white females, including heads of families.	All other free persons.	Slaves.
Maria, Negro				2	
Maguire, John	1	2	8		
Norrington, Francª					
Amos, Jmª, Junr	3	4	5	1	9
Davey, Thoª	2	2	4		
Robinson, Joseph	2	2	5		
Webb, Saml	3	1	4		5
Morris, Robt	1				
Thompson, Danl	1		6		
Cooley, Richd	1		2		1
Waters, William	2	1	1		
Brownley, Joseph	1	4	5		6
MComas, Edwd D.	2	4	3		2
Downs, Thoª	1				
Lyon, Elijah	1				1
Gib, John	1		1	1	1
Townsley, Wm	1		2		
Antle, John	2	1	3		
Reese, Joseph	1	1	2		
Sewel, John	1	3	3		12
Webster, Micl	1	3	3		
Weir, John	1	2	1		1
Carroll, John	1		2		
Pocock, Danl	1	1	2		
Renshaw, John	1	1	4		
Channell, Edmd	4	1	1		
Watson, Wm	1	2	3		
Richardson, Saml	1	1	4		
Threadway, Thoª	1	5	2		
Bull, Jacob, Junr	2	3	2		4
Bull, Jnº of Edwd	1				3
Bull, Jacob	1	1	2		2
Webster, Isaac	2	3	5	2	7
Sinclear, Jnº	2	6	2		2
Whitson, David	1	1	2		1
Turk, Esau	3	2	4		
Bodkin, Robt	3	1	5		
West, Nathl	1	4	4		
Preston, Barnard	3	4	3		9
Thompson, Thoª	3	1	8		
Johnson, Mosª	2	1	4		6
Everett, John	4	1	4		
Hughs, Thoª	2	2	6		
Allender, Wm	3	1	7		8
Robinson, Wm	2	1	3		
McCord, Arthur	1		5		
Reed, Thoª	1		3		
Law, Jmª	1		5		
McClentock, Mat	1		1		
Norris, Jnº, Senr	1	1	1		3
Wheeler, Joseph	1	3	2		15
Wells, Wm	2		1		
Lytle, Wm	1	3	3		
Moore, Edwd	1	2	2		
Martin, Wm	1	3	3		
Cowan, Robt	1	2			
Everett, Jmª	1		6		
Rhodes, Benjª	1		1		
Bull, Edwd		4	4		
Scarff, Jnº	1	2	2		1
Weir, Jnº Barr	1		3		
Magness, Moses	1	4	1		
McFadden, Wm	1	1	1		
Billingslea, Walter	1	4	2		2
Townsley, Joseph	1	2	3		
Perry, Wm	1	2	3		
Cooley, Ricd	1				
Long, John, Junr	1	1	3		
Bay, Wm	1	2	3		
Bay, Hugh	1	1	3		
Dever, Hugh	1	5	2		
Vanclief, Mary		2	3		
Ruff, Richd	1	1	1		4
Baker, John	1	2	2		3
Wright, Thoª	1	2	3	1	5
Street, John	3	3	3		
fuller, Henry	1	3	3		
Scott, Aqª	1	1	3		
Williams, Wm	1	1	4		
Robinson, Wm	1	2			
Tolbott, Edwd	1	1	4		6
Scarff, John	2	3	5		1
Street, Elizª		3	1		
Jones, Benjª	3		4		
Montgomery, Jnº	1	1	4		
Barnett, Jmª	3	1	2		2
Elliott, Edwd	2	1	1		
Elliott, Thoª	1	1	2		1
Rogers, Benjª	1	2	4		
Brady, Hugh	1	2	5		
Carlin, Geo	1		2		
Hayley, Danl	1	2	2		
Webb, Saml	3	2	3		7
Albert, Jn.	1		1		
Erwin, John	1	1	2		
Lewis, Jesse	1		1		

HARFORD COUNTY—Continued.

NAME OF HEAD OF FAMILY.	Free white males of 16 years and upward, including heads of families.	Free white males under 16 years.	Free white females, including heads of families.	All other free persons.	Slaves.
Fullard, Henry	2	3	3		
Hays, John	1	4	3		
Perry, W^m	1	3	1		
Jewel, Rich^d	1		3		
Price, Eliz^a	1		3		
Barnhouse, Franc^s	1		1		
Taylor, W^m	1		1		
Rigdon, Stephen	1				3
Rigdon, Ann			1		9
Barnhouse, Jm^s	1	1	2		
McKinsey, Roderic	1	3	2		
James, Negro				2	
Harry, Negro				3	
Mathers, Mic^l	6	1	9		3
Pitt, W^m	1		2		
Riley, James	1	3			
Nation, George	3		3		1
Bradford, W^m	1	5	3		6
Jem, Negro				1	
Mose, Negro				5	
Sam, Negro				10	
Crosby, W^m	1	1	3		
Stallion, Jacob	2	4	2		
Waters, Godfrey	1	1	4		5
Ellis, John	1	4	3		3
Webster, Saml	2	2	7		7
McLaughlin, Geo	3	4	3		2
Webster, Jno. Lee (Q^r)					21
Hart, Robt	1	3	4		
Quinlan, Jm^s	1		4		
Sherwood, W^m	1	2	3		
Thomas, Giles	1	1	3		
Johnson, Jno	1	3	5		4
Kennard, Mat	2		4		
Morsell, Benj^a	2	1	4		
Saunders, Joseph	2	1	3		
Hairgrove, Thos	2		4		
MComas, Jno	2	1	1		
Osbon, Benj^a	2		2		
Osbon, Saml	2	2	2		1
Monk, John	2	2	4		2
Weatherall, Jm^s	2	2	2		
Hassett, W^m	2	1	2		1
Cook, Alex	2	7	1		
Hall, Jacob	2	2	1	1	
Brown's, Mary			1		4
Harper, Rich^d	2	1	2		
Sellers, Paul	1	1	1		
Reardan, Ozias	1	3	4		
Browning, Perry	1	2	3		
Norris, Jno	1		3		
Troyloe, Negro			2		2
Davidson, Jesse	1	1	2		1
Carter, John	1		2		
Ruff, Henry	6	1	3		10
Baker, John	1		4	1	
MGaw, Jm^s	1		1		
Rampley, Jm^s	1	2	6		
Madden, Jm^s	1	2	1		
Moore, Dennis	1		1		
Anderson, Jm^s	2	4	3		4
Miles, Thos	2	3	2		
Batey, W^m	2	2	2		
Lemmon, George	1	3	2		3
Briarly, Robt	1		2		6
OConner, Mic^l	1		2		
Briarly, Robt	1		1		
Creig, Saml	1	1			
Treadway, Thos	1	5	1		
MComas, Aaron	1	1	1		
MComas, Jno	2	4	1	1	7
MComas, W^m	1	2	1		
Letty, Negro				4	
Sampson, Negro				5	
Ganley, W^m	1		2		
Trons, Rachel		1	2		
Hooper, Abm	2	1	3		1
Collins, Henry	1		3		1
Nichols, Jm^s	1		2		
Gorrell, Thos	1	1	2		
Ellis, Henry	1	1	4		
Miles, Joseph	1	1	6	3	
Amos, W^m	3	4	4		
Bodkin, Robt	1		6		
Visage, James	1		4		
Cowan, Ed^d	1	2	3		
Stewart, John	1		3		
Askins, Saml	1	3	1		
Brimage, Geo	1		3		
Kelly, Arthur	1	1	2		
Dick, Negro				6	
Sam, Negro				2	1
ONeal, John			1		
Gordon, Jm^s	1				
Carr, Margrett			3		
Huff, Jno			1		

NAME OF HEAD OF FAMILY.	Free white males of 16 years and upward, including heads of families.	Free white males under 16 years.	Free white females, including heads of families.	All other free persons.	Slaves.
Thomas, Giles	1	1	3		4
Chew, Thos	1	2	2		3
Downey, W^m	1		2	4	3
Downey, Saml	1	2	2	4	4
Hamilton, Jm^s	2		4		
Jenkson, Robt	1	2		2	
Smith, Nath^n	1	1	2		
Palmer, W^m	1		2		
Barnett, Jm^s	4	1	2		2
Harris, Robt	1	1	2		6
Foster, Thos	1		2		1
Foster, Jesse	1	1	2		
Balderson, Jacob	2	3	5		
West, Joseph	2		2	1	
Green, James				1	
Kelly, Jm^s	2	2	3		1
Roach, David	1		3		
Cunningham, John	1		3		
Balderson, Isaiah	3	3	3		
Aston, Jm^s	1	1	2		
Pain, Eliz^h	1		3		
Day, John	2	1	3		1
Rougan, Thos	1	5	1		
Litten, Jno	1	1	1		
Bodkin, Robt	2	1	4		
Stokes, Joseph	1		1		
Osbon, Alexand^r	7	1	3		
McNare, Arch^d	1	1	7	5	
Darrah, Jno	1	2	4		
Barnett, Jm^s	1	3	4		
Sedgwick, James	2	4	6		2
Moore, W^m	2	5	3		2
Warner, Isaiah	2		5		
Anderson, James	1	3			
Rigdon, Benj^a	1		3		
Love, John	4	2	3		
Wells, W^m	1	1	4		11
Singleton, Jno	1		4		
Cox, Israel	1		3		
Palmer, Saml	2	1	3	1	4
Reese, Hannah			3		
Mcfadden, Jno	1		3		
Scarborough, Saml	1	1	3		
Scarborough, Jno	2		6		
Scarborough, Ecludus	1		3		
Scarborough, Joseph	1	4	1		
Scarborough, Thos	2		3		
Scarborough, W^m	1		3		
Scarborough, Ecludus Senr	1		2		
Smith, Nathan	1	1	2		2
Palmer, W^m	1		2		
Forsyth, Saml	1	4	4		2
Lindsay, Eliz^a			4		
Albert, Phillip	3		2		
Lynch, Matthias	1		4		
Sedgwick, Benj^a	1		1		
Morrison, Matthew	1		2		
McNab, Jm^s	3	3	2		
Montgomery, Thos	2		4		
Montgomery, Robt	2		2		
Daggs, Jm^s	2	3	3		
Pettigrew, Jno	1	1	5		
Hamilton, Jonathan	2		9		
Henry, Isaac	1		3		
Sloan, Patrick	1		3	1	
Bennington, W^m	1	1	3		
Mooney, John	3	3	7		
Doherty, Jm^s	1		3		
Bold, Cooper	1	3	3		
Williams, W^m	4		3		
Barnett, Joseph	1	1	3		
McMullen, W^m	1		2		
Lukens, Moses	1		3		
Lukens, Benj^a	2	1	6		
Volton, Jm^o	2	2	2		
Henderson, Jm^o	1		2		
Ogle, Geo	3		3		
Flanagan, Mary	1	3	3		
Gordon, Jm^s	2		4		
Everett, Jm^s	2	2	2		
Ruth, Jacob	2		5		
Murphy, John	2	1	1		
Kent, Jesse					
Cooly, W^m	1	1	2		1
Jones, Ann			2		
Jones, W^m	2	2	8		
Webb, John	1	3	5		
Hueston, Jm^s	1	3	3		
MGeough, Jm^s	1		3		
Smith, Patrick	2	1	1		
Gibson, W^m	1		2		
Whiteford, John	1	2	5		
Pool, Mary		2	2		
Chalk, John	2		3		
Chalk, Geo	2	6	3		5

NAME OF HEAD OF FAMILY.	Free white males of 16 years and upward, including heads of families.	Free white males under 16 years.	Free white females, including heads of families.	All other free persons.	Slaves.
Kelly, Thos	1	1	1	1	
Carter, Dennis					2
Jarrett, Bennett	1	1	1	1	
Whiteford, Jno, of Robt	2		1		
MGeough, Eliz^a	5		2		
Amos, Mordecai, of M	1		1		
Perry, John	1	2	2		
Dever, Jm^s	1	4	2		
Jones, Benj^a	1		3		
Jones, Isaac	2	3	5		
Dever, Sarah			5		
Gladen, Jacob	3	2	2		
Gladen, Jno D	1	2	1		
Gladen, Jm^s	2		1		
Wilson, Arch^d	1	1	5		
Ingram, John	2		4		
Foster, Saml	2		2		
Foster, Saml	2		2		
Foster, Jno	2		2		
Foster, Mos^s	1	1	2		
Kilbreath, A^b	2	3	2		
Halkins, W^m	2	3	1		2
Jones, Benj^a	1		2		
Whiteford, Hugh	2	4	3		3
Whiteford, W^m	1		1		
Right, John	1	4	1		
Bundle, Henry	1		5		
Morrison, Mat	1		5		
Neal, John	2	4	2		
Tarbert, Jm^s	1		3		
Watt, Jno	1	1	2		
Taylor, W^m	1	2	1		
Moreans, W^m	1		1		
Cammel, Jm	2		2		
Smith, Sm		1	1		
Canada, Hannah			3		1
Lee, John	1	1	2		
Howlett, Jm^o	1		4		
Dickson, Margret			2		
Burnhouse, John	1		1		
Burnhouse, Franc^s	1		1		
Lewis, Jno	1		1		
Burk, Jno	1		1		
West, Jonath^s	1		1		
Watson, Jno	1	3	2		
Heslet, Jm^s	1		4		
Lewis, Geo	1	4	4		
West, Enos	2	3	4		
West, Nathan^l, Sen	1	2	2		
Sewel, Thos	1	2	2		
West, Franky	1		4		
Guffey, John	6		2		
Clendeuen, Jno			6		6
Jeffrey, Negro				1	
Trainer, W^m	1		2		
Hughston, Hugh	1	2			
Jackson, Mary		1	1		
West, Thos	1	4	3		
Stroud, Thos			4		
Norrington, Mary			4		
Evens, Even			2		
Thomewould, Jno, of D.	1	3	2		1
Cain, Patrick	1		5		
Bryarley, Hugh	4	1	1		3
Carey, Jno	1		5		
Reed, Thos	1		1		
Blaney, Mary			6		4
ONeal Bennett	1	1	3	1	
Key, Jm^s	1	3	1		
Thompson, Josh^a	1	3	1		
Coats, Jotham			3		
Clark, John			1	1	
Muberry, Robt	1	1	2		1
George, Negro				1	
Evans, Even	1	2	4		
Dick, David	1	3	4		
Jewel, Rich^d	1	2	5		
Hays, John	1		5		
Coin, Dominack	1	1	4		
Robinson, Arch^d	1	4	3		3
Golden, Jno	1		3		
Gelaspy, Jno	2	4	2		
Jones, Isaac	1		2		
Richardson, Henry	2	3	3		3
MCormuck, Geo	1		3		
Cowan, Robt	2	2	4		1
MCormuck, Jm^s	1		4		
Reside, Edward	3		5		
Wiley, Nathaniel	1		2		
Smith, Valentine	2	1	2		
Porter, Alex	1	2	2		
Halkings, Thos	1	5	4		
Johns, Pricilla			2		
Steel, Margarett	1		2		5
Hay, Thos			1		
Alexander, Jm^s	1		2	1	

HARFORD COUNTY—Continued.

NAME OF HEAD OF FAMILY.	Free white males of 16 years and upward, including heads of families.	Free white males under 16 years.	Free white females, including heads of families.	All other free persons.	Slaves.
Alexander, Jane	1		3		
Alexander, Andrew	1	1	3		
Alexander, Jno	1	2	6	1	
Clark, Jms	2		5		5
Mitchel, John	2	1	5		
Hervey, Archd	1	1	4		
Mitchel, Thos		1	2		
Allen, Rebecca		2	4		
Allen, Jms	1	2	2		
Stroud, Thos	2	1	5		
Green, Bennett	2	3	5		
Huskins, Thos	1	1	1		
McMurrin, Thos	2	3	1		
Warrick, John	1	2	1		
Cariton, John	1		2	1	
McCulter, Robt	1		1		
Baten, Jms of Jno				5	
Flatt, John	1	5	2		
Davidson, Wm	2	2	1		
MConklin, Hannah		3	1		
Briarly, Henry	1	3	5		5
Allmen, John	1	5	3		
Bay, Hugh	2	4	4		
Heaps, Achd		3	2		
Heaps, Robt	3	2			
Roberts, John	1		4		
Darienton, Joseph	1		1		
Gulliver, Thos	1	1	4		
Armstrong, John	1	3			
Marchall, Saml	1	1	3		
Hodkins, Joshua	1		1		
MColister, Jms	1		2		
Bullock, John	1	2	3		
Hughs, Aram	2	1	2		
Toland, Benjn	1		2		
Patterson, John	1	2	3		
Madden, Jms	2		2		
Patterson, Mary			2		
Burns, Thos	1	2	6		16
Green, Henry	4		7		12
Cooper, Henry	1		7		6
McAtee, Elizh	3	3	2		
Bowen, Elisha	1	3	2		
Forward, Saml	2		2		
Piles, Ralph	3		2		
Reed, Peter	1		2		
McThany, Matw	3	3	2		
MCoy, Robt	4	2	2		
MCoy, Wm	1		1		3
Forwood, John, senr	1		4		
Hartley, Wm		1	5		
Rattican, Jms	1	1	2		
Bowman, Sylvester	1				10
Wheeler, Benjn	2		3		19
Wheeler, Thos	1		3		6
Wheeler, Josiah	1		4		7
Waters, Henry	4		3		
Carroll, Wm	1	1	1		
Moore, Edwd	1	2	2		
Martin, Wm	1	2	4		
Preston, Bernard, Senr	2		1		
Ruff, Heny, Senr	2		1		8
Ruff, Heny, Junr	1				1
Flanagan, Edwd		2	5		7
Criswell, Robt	1	1	1		
Manahan, Arthur	1		1		
Quinlan, James	2	1	1		
Cummings, John	1		1		
Slack, John		1	9		
MDonald, Elizh			4		4
Harry, Negro				2	
Mcfadden, Wm	1	1	2		
MVay, Jno	1	1	1		
Hart, John	3		4		
Townsley, Jno	1		4		
MClentock, Matw	1	1	3	1	1
Hays, Archer	1	3	2		6
Screrwood, Wm		2	4		
Manahan, Barnard	1		1		
McClure, Richd	1		1		
Townsley, Wm	1	3	4		
Taylor, Wm	1				5
Duglass, Danl			3		3
Webster, Richd	3	4	3		
McIntire, John	1		3		
Webster, Jno, of Richd	1		3		
Curry, Jms	2		3		
McAdoo, Jno	2		3		7
MLaughlin, Geo	3	1	2		
Wilmott, Richd	1		2		10
Hatwell, Wm	1		3		
Wiggins, Saml	1	2	1		
Young, Alex	1	4	3		
Waters, Walter	1		3		2
Kirkpatrick, Hugh	3		3		
Lee, Letty			2		
Billingslea, Jms	2		1		2
Billingslea, Ruth	3		1		5
Copeland, John	2		4		8
Jervis, Jms, Senr	2	2	3		
Crwford, Robt	3	2	3		
Quinlan, Phillip	3	3	6		3
Cain, Jms	1	3	2		6
Lytle, Wm		3			10
Wheeler, Bennett	2	2	2		
Dunson, Thos	1	1	2		
Lee, Saml	2	1	6		16
Antie, John	1	2	2		1
Lee, Parker H	1	2	4		17
Doherty, Saml	1	2	4		10
Brownley, Joseph	4	3	5		7
Gibb, John	1		2		1
Creighton, John	1	1	3		3
Hardy, Benedict	1	2	2		3
Morris, James	1		1		
Simms, Ralph	1		2		
McClain, Jms	2	2	4		
Howlet, Andw	2		2		
Fullerton, John	1		4		
Steel, Jms	1		2		5
Jones, Aqa	1		6	4	
Weeks, John	1	1	3		
Morrison, Ann			2		
Mcfadden, John	3	2	2		
Barclay, John	2	5	2		4
Howe, Wm	2	3	4		
Patterson, Saml	1		3		
MCullough, Robt	1	2	3		
Hervey, Archd	1	3	1		
Cretin, Robt	1	1	3		
Cretin, John	1		1		
Burk, Berry	1		2		
MMullien, Patrick	2	1	1		4
Scoggns, Cylvester		1	2		
Gawley, Jms	1		2		
Bramage, Jms	2	3	3	1	
Arue, Michel	1	6	4		
Denny, Jms	1		2		
Heaps, Robt	1	3	2		3
Bossley, Winston	2	2	2		
Hueston, Wm	1	2	1		
Semmes, Andw	1		2		
Gormley, Owen	1				
McClane, Jn	2	1	3		
Shinnard, Wm	1	1	5		
Hadley, Wm	1	2	1		
Ayres, Stephen	1		1		8
Denny, James	1				
McCullough, David	1	4	4		
Armstrong, Nehemiah	1	1	1		
Armstrong, John	1	1	2		
Slade, Ezekiel	1		3		
Shaw, Henry	3	2	3		
Irwin, James	1		3		
Fosset, Henry	1	3	6		
White, John	1				
Miles, Jno	1		3		2
Wright, Elisha	1		2		
Moore, Docr Jms	1	1	2		
Kennedy, Thos	1	1	2		
Read, Thos	1		1		
Wildgoose, Wm	1			2	
Semmes, Jane	2		1		3
Slade, Dixon	1		1		
Smith, Peter	1	1	4		
Shores, Richd	1	2	4		
Ballentine, Thos	1				
Pocock, Danl	1	2	1		
Downs, Saml	1	2	3		
Pocock, Joseph	1	2	3		
Roe, Wm	1		4		
Russell, John	1	4	5		
Smith, Jno	2	2	2		
Smith, Wm	1	1	3		5
Smith, Sam	2	3	4		
Rigdon, Baker	1	2	1		
Jackson, Mary			3		
Cole, Mary	1		3		
George, Negro				1	
Crall, Phillip	3	2	4		3
Roach, David	1		7		
Miller, Joseph	4	2	3		1
Grafton, Wm	4	2	3		
Baker, Nathl	1		2		1
Robnson, Joseph	1	4	4		
Grafton, Aqa	1	1	1		1
Grafton, Nat	1		2		
Grafton, Danl	1	2	3		
Grafton, Sarah			3		
Clark, Wm	2	3	2		
Clark, Wm, Jnr	2	1	1		
Baker, Christian	1	1	1		
Grafton, Saml	1	4	2		1
Thomas, John	1	2	6		
Thomas, Eliza		3	6		
Coop, Jams	3	1	6		
MCrorey, Ralph	2		1		
Stroud, Rachel	3	2	6		
Elliot, Saml	1	4	3		
Smith, Catharine			2		
O'Danl, Constantia			2		
Adams, John	1	4	4		3
Baker, John	2	2	3		
Scott, Nat	2		4		
Rigdon, Wm	1		4		
Ayres, John				1	
McConnell, Saml				1	
Ronds, Mary		1	5	6	
Jack, Negro				5	1
Amy, Negro				1	1
Jack, Negro				1	1
Henry, Negro				1	
Onsal, John				1	
Carty, Saml				1	1
Packhaver, John					
Curley, Danl	1	2	2		
Garrett, Wm	1		5		1
Myars, Henry	2	4	1		1
Roundtree, Thos	1		3		2
Amos, Mary	5		3		
Davis, David	3		5		1
Varney, Jms	2	2	4		
Monohan, Barney	1		3		
Amos, Geo	2	2	3		
Scott, Mord	1	2	2		
Baker, Wm, of Cs	2		1		
Doran, John	7	2	4		6
Glenn, Wm	2		3		
Gardner, Geo	2		4		
Carter, John	1	2	4		
Watkins, John	1		2		
Watkins, Isaiah	1		2		
Dover, Aquila	1	4	2		
Jarrett, Henry	1		2		
Jack, Negro				1	
MCrery, Benjamin	2		7		
Bankhead, Hugh	2	2	1		2
Massey, Aqa	3		3		3
Willot, Saml	5		3		
Leonard, Edwd	2	2	7		7
Street, Thos	6	2	1		
Street, David	2		3		2
Street, John	2		3		2
Watt, Robt	2		2		3
Ward, John	2	1	7		
Ward, James	1		5		
Swan, Fredk	1		4		
Street, Thos	2	4	1		
MCullah, John	2	2	2		
Webb, Saml	2	2	2		
Barrett, John	2	3	4		
Harper, Geo	1		4		
Walking, Elijah	1		1		
Gladen, Thos	2		2		2
Montgomery, Jms	2		2		
Anderson, Jms	1	3	2		2
Montgomery, Thos	2		3		
Foster, Wm	3		3		
Glaspy, Jms	1	3	3		
Mannen, Alex	2		2		1
Golden, John	2	2	2		
Webb, John	2	3	6		
Perry, Wm	2		2		
Evirn, James	2	2	1		
Dawson, Wm	2		4		
Gordon, James	2		4		
Glaspy, John	1	3	3		
Fortune, Negro				2	
Shields, John	1	2	3		
Dixson, Rachel		1	4		
Carr, Robt	1	4	2		
Perry, John	1	2	1		
Townsley, Joseph	1		2		
Wilmer, Godfrey	1		2		
Street, Danl	1	1	3		
Geo					
Weathers, Saml	2		4		6
Billingslea, Walter	1	1	2		
Ivy, Joseph	1		3		
Jewel, Geo	3	3	3		
Thomas, John	3	1	3		1
Serjeant, Wm	1		1		
Rutlege, Eliza	1	1	2		
Hall, Wm	1	1	5		17
Taylor, Thos (S. C.)	1	1	6		3
Elliott, Robt	1	3	3		
Clark, Wm	3	3	3		4
Wily, Matw	1	3	3		1

HARFORD COUNTY—Continued.

NAME OF HEAD OF FAMILY.	Free white males of 16 years and upward, including heads of families.	Free white males under 16 years.	Free white females, including heads of families.	All other free persons.	Slaves.
Billingslea, Walter	2	3	2		1
Hunter, Wm	1	1			
Slades, Ezekiel, Sen	3		2		1
Hickley, Geo	1	3	2		
Bond, Ralph	1		2		4
Darby, Negro				1	
Dick, Negro				3	
Rencher, Robt	1	2	3		
Wilson, Wm	1		3		16
Amos, Elisa		1			
Briarley, Richd	2		1		
Patterson, Saml	2	1	2		
Dunsheath, Wm	2		3		
Bankhead, Wm	2		1		
Reardan, John	1	2	2		
Shian, Henry	1	4	2		
Burges, Joseph	1	1	3		
Tardy, John	1	4	2		
Bond, Thos	3	2	6		21
Prusia, Negro				2	
Ben, Negro				6	
Mason, John	2	4	4		
Jones, Wm	4		3		5
Standiford, Saml	1	1			3
Slade, Ezekiel	3	2	4		3
Coleman, Saml	3	7	3		6
Nelson, Robt	2	1	4		3
O'Neal, Francis	1		2		
Christie, Gabriel	8	3	5	4	6
Forwood, Jacob	2	1	4	1	14
Body, Bery	1	1	4		
Melhoof, John	2		3		
Dunk, Thos	2	1	3		
Penny, Charles	2	1	1		
Yokely, John	2		3		
Warham, John	1		3		
Hailey, Wm	2	1	2		
Kingsley, Saml	1		3		
Allander, Nicholas	1		3		
Williams, John	1	2	3		
Watkins, James	1			1	
Burns, Andw	1		2		
Armstrong, Solomon	1	2	3		
Bear, John	1	4	3		
Hoofman, Christr	4		1		
Carver, Henry	3	3	2		1
Bayard, Peter	4		2		
Thompson, Mary			2		1
Myars, John	2		1	4	
Dunn, Mary		1	3		
Coale, Wm	2	1	2		2
Morgan, Wm	4	1			
Levy, Christopher	5	3	3		
Chamberlain, Paul	1	1	1		
Smith, Saml	2				
Wilson, Andw	2	2	4		
Hall, Sarah		1	3		21
Barney, John	2		4	2	3
Porter, John	4	4	2		
Sutter, Nicholas	1	2	4		
Folden, John	1		3		
Cooleg, Abraham	1	1			
Greenfield, Jacob	1		2		
Davis, Elijah	1	1	2	1	14
Giles, Thos	2	3	3		26
Williams, John	1	1	5		
Burnside, Joseph	1		4		1
Sewlovan, John	1	3	4		
Greves, Robt	1		4		
Donovan, Jas	1	2	2		
Durbin, Danl	1	2	4		15
Jay, Stephen	3		3		6
Bradley, John	2		3		
Hoofman, Wm	1		3		
Dorsey, Greenberry	2	3	5		16
Boyd, Jas	1		3		
Culver, Robt	1	3	5		
Harson, John	2	1	6	1	3
Willingsford, John	1	1	2		
Bonister, Wm	4		3		8
Hollis, Wm	2	3	6		4
Taylor, Isaac	1	2	6		
Philips, Jas	1	3	7		39
Pritchard, Jas	1	1	2		
Ashley, Thos	1	2	4		
Turner, Danl	1	2	1		
Grace, Aaron	2		1		
Matthews, Milca	3		2		12
Adkin, Greenby	2	1	1		
Baty, Archabald	2		2		4
Neilson, John	2		2		4
Brown, John	1	1	5		5
Chancey, George	2	1	3		23
Webster, Joseph	1				
Hollis, Amos	1		2		5
Hollis, Martha	1		3		
Vanstkell, Henry	1	3	3		14
Richards, Jas	2		1		
Kinnon, Saml	1	1	2		
Pasterfield, Jas	1	2	2		
Thompson, David	3	4	5		6
Newland, Hannah		3	4		
Dickson, Margaret			3		
Marings, John, negro				4	
Pening, Harry, negro				5	
Evins, Wm	1	2	2		
Hage, Jas	1	1	2		
Bond, Jas	1	1	2		1
Bradley, Nichos	1	1	2		
Stephenson, Jas	1	1	4		1
Shady, Francis	1	1	1		
Everitt, Thos	2				
Feather, Matthias	1				
Thompson, John	2	1	2	7	6
Collings, John	1	1	3		1
Michael, Balsher	3	5	5		6
Michael, Jas	2		2		
Weatherals, Jas	2	1	2		8
Mattles, Roger	1		3		
Chew, Joseph	1		4		
Scarf, Benjn	1		4		10
Day, Maryann			4		
Thomas, John	1	2	3		
Ford, David	1	2	2		
Strickland, Henry	1	4	2		
Scott, Walter	1	1	1		1
Durram, Thos	2	1	2		
Durram, Wm	1	2	2		
Cochran, Isaac	2	4	4	1	
Strickland, John	2	3	2		
Scott, Robt	1		2		
McComas, Alex	1	1	1	1	
Baker, Wm	1	1	4		2
Taylor, Robt	1	2			
Daley, Jas	1	1	3		4
Gifford, Joseph	1	1	5		4
Bond, Jas	1		1		
Cord, John	1		2		
Deweast, John	1		2		
Hall, John	1				7
Jones, Isaac	2		1		
Wilson, Wm	1	1	1		6
Smith, Jonas	1	3	2		
Baker, Wm	1	1	4		2
Hoten, Wm	3	2	2		
Little, Jas	1	2	2		11
Little, Jacob	1				2
McGaw, John	5	1	2		
Dorsey, Frisbey	2	2	6		7
Hill, Harmon	1	2	2		
Steel, Abram	3	3	3		
Little, George	1	2	2		15
Everitt, Joseph	2	2	3		23
Chancey, Benja	1				6
Cord, Amos	2	8	4		
Jiant, Isaac	2	2	2		
Kimble, Giles	1	1	4		
Collins, Jacob	1	3	3		
Kimble, John	1		1		
Riddle, Andw	1		3		
Wilton, Philip	1		2		14
Chancey, John	1	1	2		4
Powel, Wm	1		2		
Wilmore, Saml	4	2	3		8
Woodland, Jonathr	2	3	3		
Barnes, Amos	1	3	3		6
Combes, Utery	1	1	2		
Ford, Jas	3	4	3		
Hill, Tower, negro				3	
Combes, Jacob					
Ford, Alexr	1	3	3		
Murphy, Wm	1	1	2		
Cottee, Edwd	1	3	3		
Dawson, Abrm	1		2		
Carty, Jas	1	4	1		
Denny, Jas	1	4	5		
Dawson, John	2	1	5		
Judd, Wm	3	1	4		
James, Thomas	1		1		
Judd, Joshua	1	2	5		
Judd, Danl	1		2		
Harper, Wm	1	1	2		
Doll, Andw	1		1		
Howard, John	2	1	2		
Gallaugher, Elizabeth	1	1	3		5
Dawson, Jacob	1	1	2	1	
Hall, Wm	2	3	7		32
Hall, Parker	1				10
Howel, Saml	2	3	4		
Ross, Robt, negro				5	
Jolly, Martha			1		17
Griffith, Saml	2	5	6		38
McCowin, Michl	2	1	2		
Simmons, Wm	1	2	2		
Richardson, Jas	1		1		2
Hawkins, Richd	1	4	5		2
Johns, Natl	3	1	4		
Morgan, Ruleph	2	3	4		2
Chesney, Jas	2	3	2		
Bailey, Saml	1		2		
Ewing, Jas	2		2		
Jeffry, Robt	3				6
Stephenson, Rachel	3	1	4		7
Cain, Aquilla	1	2	5		
Morton, Martha	2	1	1		
Green, Isaac	2	1	7		
Gilbert, Micah	3	1	4		4
Judd, Danl	2	3	3		
West, Enoch	2	1	4		
Molton, Matthew	1	3	2		
Gilbert, Parker	4	1	5		3
Bailey, Josias	1	5	2		2
Hanson, Edwd	1	1	2		6
Armstrong, Isabella	1		2		
Price, Robt	2	3	3		
McGaw, Jane	4		6		
Debruler, Anthy	1		3		
Griffith, Hannah	1		2		
Childes, Benj	1	3	1		
Gilmore, Saml	1	1	1		
Rea, George	2	2	5		
Bailey, Aquilla	2	2	1		
Hubboard, George	1		1		
West, Thos	2	1	3		
Cox, Wm	1	6	5	1	5
Bell, Jas	3	2	5	1	2
Pitt, Thos	2	1	2		
Green, Edwd	2	2	5		
Bayard, Jas	1	5			
Hartgrove, Richd	2	4	2		
Mading, Mary	1				
Armstrong, Levina			2		2
Jeffry, Elizab	1	1	2		
Lowman, Francis	1	2	2		
Martin, Wm	2	2	2		
Tipton, John	1		4		
Boles, Thos	1	4	4		
Bowman, Henry	1	1			
Irvine, John	1		2		
Maxfield, Wm	1		2		
Bradley, Edwd	1	2	4		
Tipton, Gabriel	2	2	1		1
Shannon, George	2	2	1		
Kelly, Thos	1		2		
Cortany, Thos	4	2	2		
Palodon, Negro				1	
Ectison, Nicholas	2	1	2		
Hopkins, Charles	1	1	2		
Mitchell, Wm	3	2	7		
Mitchell, Kent	1	1	1		3
Lee, Charles	1	1	1		4
Mohon, John	3	1	4		
Barnes, Wm	2		2		
Stewart, Elizab			1		4
Donovan, Danl	2		2		
Bunton, Wm	1		2		
Jeffry, Thos	1			1	6
Gover, Saml	1	3	4	1	6
Cannon, Moses	2	2	5	2	1
Cowen, Wm	1	1	1		
Wood, Moses	4	1	1		1
Smith, Jonat	4	1	1		
Monaghan, Barney	1	1	1		
Stienson, Jas	1		2		
Nickles, Jas	1	2			
Collings, Morris	3		3		
McCracken, John	3	1	3		
Smith, Wm	2	3	4		
Hannah, Wm	4	2	1		1
Mitchell, John	2	4	4		
Bayles, Natl	1	1	5		
Craigs, John	1		3		
Barnes, Bennett	1	4	3		
David, Negro				2	
Stump, John	2	1	6	3	
Wilson, John	4	2	5	3	
Carter, Saml	3	1	7		
Rankin, John	2	3			
Stephenson, Thos	3		1	2	
Nickleson, Jas	1		2	1	
Jollys, Edwd	5		3	5	11
Dampier, Negro				3	
Nero, Negro				5	6
Judy, Negro					
Knott, Wm	3	1	2		
Arnold, Wm	1	4	2		
Brown, John	1		2		3
Sarah, Negro				3	7
Stpio, Negro					
Kenly, Richd	1	2	3		2
Kenley, Daniel	1	1	1		3

FIRST CENSUS OF THE UNITED STATES.

HARFORD COUNTY—Continued.

NAME OF HEAD OF FAMILY.	Free white males of 16 years and upward, including heads of families.	Free white males under 16 years.	Free white females, including heads of families.	All other free persons.	Slaves.
Ward, Edwd	1		1		6
Christie, Chas	1				
Wilson, Thos	1	1		5	
Johnson, Charles	1	2	2		
Prigg, John					3
George, negro				5	
Boatswain, negro				3	
Wallis, Sam1	2	1	2	3	
George, Negro				7	
Randol, Robt	9	1	3		
Brannon, Wm	1	1	6		
Deaver, Hugh	1	4	3		
Ward, Richd	1	5	2		
Limus, negro				2	
Clarke, John	1	1	5		
Gover, Robt	1		3	9	
Tower, negro				8	
Sulivan, Owen	1	2	1		
Ashley, John	1	1	2		
Holiday, negro				4	
James, negro				2	
Pompey, negro				4	
Cesar, negro				5	
Wilson, Joseph	1		1	3	
Husbands, Elizabh			4	7	
Jacob, negro				3	
Duke, negro				4	
Crawford, Freeborn	1		2		1
Dullim, John	2	3	4	4	
Peter, negro				2	
Harry, negro				8	
Crawford, Jas	1	1	5		4
Irvine, John	1	1	5		
Cherry, Robt	3	1	4		
Coale, Philip	2	2	6	4	
Prevard, Chas	5	3	3	1	
Sam, negro				7	
Jones, Reuben	1	3	5		
Murry, Jean	2	1	4		
Rodgers, Joseph	2	2	4		
Bailey, Caleb	1		2		
Coale, Skippeth	1				
Hopkins, Garritt	1	3	5		4
Roach, David	1	7			
Crooks, Alex	1	1	1		
Dickson, Henry	1	3	2		
Taylor, Andw	1	1	2		
Warner, Cudberth	1	4	5		
Warner, Joseph	2		1		
Warner, Croswol	2	2	4		
Warner, Aaron	1		1		
Eli, Joseph	1	1	2		
Eli, Wm	1	1	3		
Fisher, Jas	1	3	4		
Lennon, negro				5	
Mingo, negro				1	
Mitchell, John		2	2		
Fisher, Sarah					9
Fisher, Thos	1	1	1		
Morgan, Robt	1		3		
Morgan, Lidia			2		
Armount, Thos	1	2	1		
Wigans, Joseph	2	2	5		
Barnes, Job, Jr	1	2	4		2
Barnes, Job	1		5		
Day, Elijah			3		
Cromwell, Fenicia			1		
Morgan, Hugh	1	1	2		
Will, negro				3	
Jacob, negro				5	
Rigby, Jas	2			4	
Buck, negro				5	
Tower, negro				8	
Jacob, negro				8	
Massey, Isaac	2		3	8	
Aaron, negro				8	
Prevail, Gideon	1	3	4	1	
Hopkins, Joseph	4	2	4	11	
David, negro				7	
Jean, negro				5	
Harris, George	1				
Weatherinton, John	2	3	6	1	9
Dullim, Margaret		1	3		
Jack, negro				6	
Wilson, Peter	1	1	3		
Wilson, Benjs	1	5	5	3	
Hopkins, Fanny			1	2	
Prigg, Wm	3	2	1	4	2
Wells, Jean			2	2	
Wells, Richd	1		2		
Morton, Stephen	1	3	5		
Coale, Skippith	3		3	11	
Gordon, Aaron	1	3	5		
Benjamin, Joseph	2	3	3		
Peter, negro			2		
Kerrigan, Edwd	1	1	1		
McClean, John	1		1		

NAME OF HEAD OF FAMILY.	Free white males of 16 years and upward, including heads of families.	Free white males under 16 years.	Free white females, including heads of families.	All other free persons.	Slaves.
Cornelius, Robt	1		3		
Bagley, Wm	2		3		2
Boles, Mary	1	3	4		
Herod, Henry					
Miller, Mary		1	1		
Sam, negro				6	
Hawkins, Robt	2		2		1
McGin, Arthur	1	4	2		
Wilson, Wm	3	2	6	11	
Divine, Mich1	1	1	4		
Coale, Sam1	3	4	3		
Ell, Hugh	2	2	4		
Coale, Wm	1	2	7	7	
Jenkinson, Robt	1	1	3		
Creighton, Patk	1	4	1	1	
Curry, John	4	5	4		
Smith, Wm	1	2	2	8	
Middleditch, Nichas	1	2	2		
Hall, Thos	7	4	2	57	
Sam, negro				1	
Hamby, Sam1	1				
Tasker, Ann			4		
Stableton, Joshua	1	5	2		
Hawkins, Sam1	1	1	5	2	
Johns, Hosia	2		1		
Husbands, Joshua	2	3	6		
Brown, Freeborn	1	2	4	6	7
Smith, David	1				
Worthington, Esther		1	2		
Divine, Chas	1		2		
Webster, John L	2		7	73	
Spreasbanks, Jackson	1				
Thompson, Jas	3	2	1	2	
Gover, Sam1	4	4		52	
McCaskey, Wm	1		2	1	
Barnes, Hosia	1		2	1	
Brown, Mary	1	2		10	
Donovan, Jno	1	5	2		
Boyce, Roger	2		2	30	
Clining, Wm	1	1	2		
Gray, Jas	1	2	3		
Henderson, Nat	1		2		
Gilmore, John	1		2		
Riddle, Wm	4		4	1	
Taylor, Rachel	1	5	2		2
Perryman, Isaac	4	1	3		2
Cunningham, Jas	1	2	2		
Perryman, Martha	1	2	2		
Knight, Thomas	3	1	4		2
Knight, Wm	1	2	1		
Knight, Light	1		2		
Miller, Sam1	1	2	3		
Hopkins, Sam1	2	4	4		
Glen, David	2	1	4		5
Craton, Pat	1	4	2		
Barnes, John	1	3	2		1
Gallion, John	1	2	3		
Cooley, John	3	7	2		3
Horner, Wm	2		3		
Gilbert, Philip	1	2	3		
Crawsen, Richd	2		2		1
Horner, Jas	1	2	3	1	
Donovan, Wm	1	2	2		
Gilbert, Mary	1		1		
Crawson, Richd	1	1	2		
Crawson, John	1		2	2	
Edwards, Jas	1		3		
Andrews, Abraham	1	1	3		
Varchworth, Wm	1		4	1	1
Fletcher, Benj	2	1	2		
Chisholm, Thos	3			18	
Mading, Jas	1		3		
Vandigrif, George	2	2			
Baily, Sam1	1	3	6		
Coale, Ephraim	1	2	4		
McGill, Wm	1	3	2		
Grunly, Sam1	1	3	3		
Cahill, Bary	1		3		
Deaver, Wm	1	2	1	1	
Mitchell, Sarah	1		1	1	1
Donovan, Philip	1	3	10		
Mitchell, Gabl	2	3	3	1	
Mitchell, Rachel			2		
Osburn, Ann	3	1	2		
Knight, Jonathan	1	2	1		
Porter, Wm	1		1		
Gilbert, Thos	1		2		
Gilbert, Mich1	2	2	8		
Layar, Andw	1		2	2	2
Everitt, Benj	2	2	4	3	6
Jeffrey, Wm	1		4		
Barnes, Gregory	3		5		
Barnes, Ford	1	1	2		
Barnes, Gregory, Jr	1		1		
Barnes, Richd	2	1	1	1	
Mitchell, Thos	3	3	4		
Ward John	1	1	4		

NAME OF HEAD OF FAMILY.	Free white males of 16 years and upward, including heads of families.	Free white males under 16 years.	Free white females, including heads of families.	All other free persons.	Slaves.
Loftin, Willi	1	4	5		
Williams, Morris	1	1	3		
Pybus, John	2	2	4		
Bailey, Joseph	2		2		
Evit, Wm	6	1	1	1	2
Green, John	1				
Thompson, Edward	3	2	4		
Price, Wm	1	1	2		
Smith, Thos	2	3	5		
Deaver, Aquilla	1	3	3		
Spencer, Henry	1		2		
Chandley, Wm	1	4	5		
Kelly, Alex	2		2		
Goodwin, Margaret	1		2		
Touchstone, Henry	1	1	2		
S.lvers, Amos	2		2		
Trago, John	2	4	3		
Brody, Matthew	3		3		
Lee, John	1	2	2		
Donovan, Thos	1	1	2		
Arnold, Ephrm	2		3		
Coale, Jane			2		
Coale, Thos	1	2	1		1
Houk, Mich1	1	1	1		
Stephenson, Jas	1	1	2		
Cortany, Thos	4	4	5		
Brewer, Jas	1	2	2		
Brown, Thos	1		2		
Judd, William	2	2	2		
Kenley, Sam1	1	3	4		1
Brown, Jacob	2	3	2		
Bailey, Mary	1	1	4		
McCarty, Jacob	1		2		
Noble, Mark	1	2	2		
Gilbert, Charles	2	2	7	1	13
Barnes, Jas	1	1	5		
Ward, Wm	1	4	5		
Mitchell, Hannah	1	2	2		
Sappington, Richd	1	4	3		1
Caroll, Wm	2	4	2		
Knight, Hannah	2	2	2		
Lynch, John	1	1	4		
Smith, Hugh	1	3	4		2
Cochran Andw	2			1	3
Smith, Thos	4		5		
Pat, negro				7	
Hill, Geo., negro				7	
Paraway, negro				8	
Adam, negro				3	
Valentine, negro				2	
Maria, negro				5	
Botts, John	2	3	5		5
Williams, Wm	2	3	4		
Richard, negro				3	3
Hughes, Sam1	2		2		13
Taylor, Jane	2	1	2		
Charles, negro				2	
Calhoun, Wm	1	1	3		
Smith, B. S., Wm	4	1	5		35
Sampson, Thos	3	1	2		
Slack, Jacob	1	1	4		
Bowler, Peter	1	3	1		
Cowen, Thos	1		1		
Inks, Mary		2	2		
Bradford, Jas	1	1	2		
Calender, John	1	1	1		
Hall, Jas W	1	2	4		25
George, negro				1	
Quay, Thos	1		2		
McCaskey, Corn1	1	2	5		
Deaver, Micajah	1	2	3		
Barnes, Ruth	2		3		3
Bayles, Daniel	2	3	2		1
Pore, Richd	1	1	1	1	
Hughes, John E	2	1	4		10
Touchstone, Sarah	1	1	4		
Orr, John	1		3		
Brogan, Ann			2		
Hardy, John	2	1	2		
Coop, Orasha	1	3	2		
Gorrel, John	1		2		
Durbin, Jas	1		2		1
Curson, Jas	1		1		
Gilbert, Taylor	3		5		2
Gilbert, Chas	1	5	2		
Boner, Jas	2	3	6		
Edwards, Jas	2	2	2		
Culver, Benj	3		4		
Wilts, John	3	3	3		
White, Richd	1	3	6		
Lucky, Wm	5	2	5		5
Hooper, Nicholas	1	4	1		
Dives, Wm	1	4	1		
Smith, Sam1	1	1	1		
Freland John	6	16	6		10
Giles, Johanna			3		6
Dawson, Jessee	1	1	3		

HARFORD COUNTY—Continued.

NAME OF HEAD OF FAMILY.	Free white males of 16 years and upward, including heads of families.	Free white males under 16 years.	Free white females, including heads of families.	All other free persons.	Slaves.
Steel, John	1	2	3		
Collin, Ephraim	1	3	3		
Fie, Mary	2	2	3		
Truelove, Ann		1	3		
Carlile, John	1	1	3		7
Grace, Negro				5	
Cord, Aquillo	1		2		
Stolenger, Geo	1	1	3		
Lovit, Wm	2	2	3		
Combess, Martha			2		
Gallep, Daniel	9	2	6	1	1
Jinkins, Enoch	5		3		
Trewax, Jacob	3	3	1		
Murphy, Timothy	1	1	1		3
James, negro			3		
Ceser, Negro			5		
Dick, Negro			4		
Redding, Jas			1	1	
Deaver, Jas	2	4	4	1	2
Tush, Saml	2	4	4		
Fowler, Saml	3	2	7		
Martin, Edwd	1	2			
Kimbil, John	2	3	5		
Kimble, Sarah		2			4
Cowen, Susana			2	1	
Dorsey, Matthew	2	1	2		
Kimble, Maryann	3		2		
Chance, Alexr	1	1	4		
Harry, Negro				4	
Jack, negro				5	
Garritson, Jas	1	2	6	1	3
Wheeler, Margaret			2		1
Meeks, Rebeckah	1	1	2		
Johnson, Jas	1	5	1		
Homer, Hester			3		
Fowler, William	1	2	2		
Spreesbanks, Benj			2		
Mingo, negro				2	
Smith, John			1		
Thompson, Edwd	3	1	2		6
Thompson, Ingere	3	1	3		
Smith, Basil	2	1	3		
Thomas, Evan	1	1	2		
Brewer, Henry, negro				3	
Armstrong, Jas	1	1	2		
Taylor, George	1	1	2		
Ann, Negro				1	
Garritson, Garrit	1	1	5		5
Mink, Mary			1		
Pike, Hutchen	2	1	2		
Allen, Nichl	1		2		
Ned, negro				2	
Musberry, Wm	1	1	1		
Oliver, Jas	2	1	3		
Barnes, Wm	2	1	2		
Dullam, Jas	4	5	6		17
Dullam, Richd	5		2		26
Sipio, negro				7	
Smith, John	1	3	2		
Brevat, John	1		3		
Whiley, Chrisor	3	1	4		
Easton, George	1	4	2		
Voilet, negro				2	
Lisby, Susan			2		2
Webster, Isaac	1		2		2
Philler, negro				2	
Hector, negro				3	
Dick, negro				3	
Blackstone, Elijah	1				1
Caroll, Elizab					5
Tate, Chas	1	23	1	3	2
Orr, Jas	1	2	2		
Murphy, Henry	1	3	4		3
Ruff, Daniel	2	5	3	2	
Toy, Joseph	2	4	2		
Bull, Richd	2	1	2		3
Carty, Mary	1	1	2		
Packsword, Saml	1	2	1		
Joe, Negro				3	
Peter, Negro				1	
Com, negro				7	
Tom, Negro				4	
Charles, Negro				3	
Greves, Wm	1	5	2		6
Durham, John	2	3	7	1	7
Butler, John	2	3	2		
Price, Jas	3	1	2		
Sanders, Robt	3	6	3		7
Jewell, Wm	1	1	3		
Howard, John	1	1	3		
Ford, Mary	1	1	3		
Chambers, Wm	1		1		
York, Jas	1	2	1		
Carter, Francis	1		1		
Durbin, Sine	1		3		
Bond, Jas	1		2		
Monk, Richd	1	1	4		6
Hutson, Jas	1	1	2	1	2
Colegate, Richd	2	1	2	2	11
Morris, Wm	1	2	1		
Coulter, Corbin	1	2	1		1
York, Wm	1	1	4		
York, George	3	4	3		
Hall, Martha	1	3	4		
Mills, Thos	3	2	4		1
Debruler, Jas	1	4	4		
Howard, Bery	1	1	2		
Horner, Nichos	1	2	2		
Truss, Wm	2	2	1	1	
Daws, Isaac	2	1	3	2	
Daws, Abraham	2	1	1		
Brasher, Robt	1	1	1		
Harry, negro				1	
McComas, Nichos D	1	1	2		8
Dungan, Jessee	1	1	2	1	
Jack, negro				1	
Sparks, Abraham	1				
Hersey, Natl	1	2	1		
Hughes, John	1	2	6		
Burket, Elizab	2		3		16
Chilson, Mary	1	3	5		
Sutton, Saml	3	2	2		
Martin, Andr	1	2	3		
Marittee, Matthew	2	1	3		1
Debrulor, Wm	1	2	1		2
York, George	1	2	1	1	
York, Edwd	2	1	3	1	
Wilson, Wm	4	3			7
Sinclar, Alexr	1		3	1	5
Illii, Thos	3	2	4		
Spencer, Patrick	1	1	1		
Hill, Jas	3	4	4		
Dawny, Thos	2	3	5		
Hall, Daniel	1	1	1		
Stronge, Thos	3	3	3		7
Day, John	1	3	3		10
Vanhorn, Peter	1	2	3		
Ricketts, Saml	1	1	3		14
Duffery, Thos	2	2	1		
Allender, Jane	1	1	3		2
Webster, Michl	1	1	3		
Hutchison, Vincent	1	1	2		
Thomas, negro				8	
Dorsey, John H	2	1	3		11
Maxfield, Jacob	1				7
Legar, Benedt	2	2	2		1
Vanhorn, Martha	1	2	3		
Wiles, Thos		3	2		
Hamilton, John	4	2	2		12
Deford, Saml	2	2	2		
Howard, John G	3	1	4		
Jones, Morgan	3	1	4		3
Hynson, Benjn	2	1			10
Debrulor, Geo	2	4	3		6
Day, Edwd	1	3	3		2
Worters, Chas	1	1	5		
Bayles, Augustine	1	1	1		5
Brown, John T	1	1	1		4
Timmons, Edwd	1	1	2		
Horner, Jane	1	1	3		
Arnold, Prudence		1	1		
Will, Negro				1	
Worsters, Stephen	1	3	2		9
Newell, Jas	3	1	2		
Bond, Jacob	2	3	3		18
Timmons, Thos	2	3	4		
Dutton, John	2		1	6	1
Biggs, Nathaniel	1		4		
Belinder, Negro				7	1
Sutten, Reuben	2	6	3	1	
Roberts, Bellingsby	2	1	1		
Roberts, John	1		4		
Dickson, Wm	1	1			2
Allender, John	1		2		
Wain, John	1		2		
Davis, Margaret			3		
Dowly, Daniel	1	2	2		
Fipps, Joseph	4	1	2		
Smith, Wm	1		2		
Brown, Ben—negro				4	
Crouch, Thomas	2	1	2		
Allen, Avarilla	2	2	4		
Fisher, Ann	1	1	2		
Harrison, Alexr	2		2		
Bennet, Jas	2		2		
Hay, John	1	2	3		5
McGowen, Juda			3	1	
McGowen, John	4		4	4	
Hunter, Joseph	1	2	3		
Tolbay, Zephaniah	1	2	2		
Durham, Zachariah	1	1	4		
Nickels,		1	3		
Dickson, Wm	1	1	6		
White, Stephen	1	1	6		
Corbin, Thos	1		1		
Brown, Thos	1				
Rumsey, Benj	4	1	2		26
Rumsey, John	1		6		41
Walden, John	1	1	2		
Hall, Benedt E	3	2	6		43
Michael, John	2	1	2		2
Maxwell, Moses	2			2	17
Hall, Josias	1		3	3	18
Cline, John	1	1	1		
Jones, Griffith	1	3	7		1
Rutton, Lemuel	1				
Jane, Negro				5	
Johnson, Archibald					
Hill, Harmon	1	2	5		
Taylor, Jas	2		3		
Whitaker, Hezekiah	1	1	3		5
Fair, Robt	1	2	3		1
Rachel, negro				6	
Green, Nathl	2				12
China, Thos	1	2	3		
Jack, negro				6	
McClane, Mary			4		
Drew, Jas	1	2	5		3
Pratt, Nathl	1	2	5		
Brady, Nichos	1	1	5		
Trissler, Valentine	1	1	3		
Loney, Wm	2	3	4		14
Sarah, Negro				3	
Will, Negro				1	
Razin, Sarah		1	2		
Manus, Negro				1	
Warfield, Henry	1	4	3		5
Tush, Rachel			1		
Osburn, Jas	1	3	5		17
Hollingsworth, Jas	1	5	2		
Pritchard, Obediah	1				
Jones, Robt	2	2	2		3
Hanson, Averilla	2		3		6
Hollis, Clark	2	3	4		
Cowley, Thos	2	2	4		
Nass, Elizabeh			3	1	
Drew, Anthony	1	1	3		12
Drew, Sarah		1	2		8
Brisco, Joseph	2	2	2		3
Hamon, John	2	2	2		7
Osburn, Wm	2	3	5		14
Wallingsford, Benjn	1	2	3		
Stephenson, Jas	2	2	4		
Ruff, John	2		2		13
Mingo, Negro				2	
Cuff, negro				3	
Greenfield, Thos	1	1	6		10
Johnson, John	1	2	3		
Jack, Negro				2	
Lester, Norris	1				3
Lester, Wm	1				6
Hanson, Saml	1	1	5	1	2
Deamour, John	1				
Galilon, John	1				
Buck, Mary			2		
Johnson, Ann					
White, Jonathan	1		4		
Rary, Jas	1	1	2		
Gasaway, Nichos	1		2		10
Edwards, Thos	1	1	2		
Hair, Thos	1	1	2		
Taper, Thos	1		1		
Webb, Henry	1		6		
Carter, John			3		
Norris, John	1	2			
Kelly, Valentine	1	1	3		
Stiles, Eliza	1	2	4	2	3
Gilbert, Nichs Jr	1				2
Bowman, Henry			2		
Hopkins, Rachel	2	2	9		
Mohan, John Jr	1	1	2		
Rigden, Charles	1	4	6		
Harbert, Richd	1	5	3		
Mason, Peter	1				
McComas, John			2		
Bet, negro				2	
Joe, negro				5	
Belinder, Negro				4	
Robinson, Abram	1	3	5	2	
Cato, negro					
Nevell, Moses		2	4		
Judd, Wm	1	3	2		
Hoof, Abraham	1	3	2		
Dann, John	1	1	1		
Burton, Jane			1		
Daugherty, Hugh	3	1	2		
Herbert, Benjn	1	1	2		
Engrim, Jas	1		2		
Armstrong, Hessey			1		
Herton, Wm	2		4	5	1	1
Hinds, George	2	2	4		

HARFORD COUNTY—Continued.

NAME OF HEAD OF FAMILY.	Free white males of 16 years and upward, including heads of families.	Free white males under 16 years.	Free white females, including heads of families.	All other free persons.	Slaves.
Tom, negro				7	
Perry, Thos	1	1	1		
Boyce, John	1	5	3		
Debrulor, Jacob	1		1		
Cochran, Wm	1		1		
Davis, Amos	1		5		
West, Michl	2		3	3	
Neevers, Jas	4	2	4		
Day, Joshua	2	2	2		
Hollins, Wm	1	1	2		
Webster, Jas	1		3		
Corruthers, Robt	1	1	3		
Tipton, Richd	1		2	3	
Brooks, John	1	1			
Dale, John	1	5	2		
Robinson, Daniel	1	2	5	4	
Richhouse, Peter	1	2	3		
Brooks, John	2	3	4		
Smith, Wm	2	1	1	8	
Debrewler, Fanny			4		
Barns, Nehemiah	1	2	1		
Gordon, Eleaner		4	4		
Brown, Margaret			2		
Debrewler, Anthony	1	2	2		
Lee, Jas		2	2		
Henson, Herry	2	2		5	8
Murphy, Wm	1	3	3		
Cullings, Morris	1				
Wooley, John	4	1	3		
Caroll, John	2	3	2		
West, Enoch, Jr	1		2		
Dick, Negro				3	
Touchstone, Henry	1	2	2		
Gallion, Saml	1	7	3		
Cromwell, Wm	2	1	1		
Bennet, Wm	1	2	1		
Pritchard, Obadiah	2	1	5	2	
Pritchard, Jas	5		1		
Rees, Abraham	2		2		
Wood, Wm	4	3	5		
Mitchell, Micajah	1	2	5		
Johnston, Tobias	1		3		
Tagart, Saml	1		4		
Anderson, Danl	3	3	7		3
Donovan, Danl	1	3	1		
Greenland, Richd	1	4	3		
Judd, Danl	1	1	2		
Gallion, Joseph	6	1	5		
Graham, Jas	1				
Judd, Joseph	1		3		
Walker, Elioner	2	1	3		
Deaver, David	1	1	5		1
Durbin, Cassandra		1	3		5
Ewings, Jas	1	2	3		
Butler, Wm	2	3	3		
Spencer, Jas	1	3	4		
Smith, Jas	2		2		
Relly, Wm	1				
McDaniel, John	1				
Logan, Michl	2		3		3
Patterson, George	2	1	5		32
Hall, Elizabeth			7		
Hall, Mary			1		5
Sam, Negro					1
Elbin, John		2	3		
Thomas, Saml	1	1	3	1	19
Sipio, Negro				3	
Stump, Henry	4	1	3		8
Cunning, Hugh	2	1	3		
Gorrel, Abraham	2	3	2		
Gorrel, Wm	1	4	3		
Gorrel, Jas	1		3		
Gorrel, Joseph	1	1	1		1
Kelly, Thos	1				
Chandley, Susanh			1		
Shay, Isabella			1		
Spence, Richd	2	2	4		
Everatt, John	1	4	1		
Jane, Negro				6	
Richard, Negro				4	
Cato, Negro				1	
Jack, Negro				3	
Wilsen, John	2	1	4	6	1
Miller, Joseph	3	4	4	7	
Husbands, Jeshua	3	2	2	2	
Coale, Saml	2	4	3		
Coale, Isaac	2	1	3	2	
Smith, John					1
Easulion, Abrm	1		2		
Silvers, Benjn	1	4	3	1	
Ramsay, Wm	3	1	1		
Bailey, Saml	1	3	6		
Wilson, John	3	2	3		1
Spencer, Herry	1	2			
Weatherinton, Chs	2		5		12
Jolly, Elizah	2		5		6
Smith, Ralph	2		3	1	1
Seaton, Wm	1	3	2		
Ned, Negro				3	
Morgan, Wm	1	2	8		31
Chesney, Richd	1	2			
Chew, Thos	1		1		2
Francis, Chas	1		2		
Lee, Saml			1		4
Davis, Joseph	2	1	8	1	1
Beshony, John	2		1		
Warnack, Philip	1		5		
Cook, Sarah	2		2		
Pirkins, Solomon	1	1			
Martin, Robt	1	3	3		

KENT COUNTY.

NAME OF HEAD OF FAMILY.	Free white males of 16 years and upward, including heads of families.	Free white males under 16 years.	Free white females, including heads of families.	All other free persons.	Slaves.
Yeates, Donaldson	3	4	3		6
Cotton, David, negro				7	
Limus, Negro				2	
Turner, John, Junr	1	3	4		9
Wheelock, Alpheus	2		2	1	
Rasin, George	1	2	5	1	8
Miller, Charles, (S. P.)	1		2		7
Howard, Benjamin	3	3	4	1	2
Logan, Michael	2		3		
Corse, Michael	2		3		7
Greenwood, Jacob	2	1	2		1
Hepbron, John	6	2	3		6
Parsons, John	3	2	2	3	
Jones, Thomas	1		4		3
Wroth, James	2		3		7
Budd, Samuel	1				
Duncan, James	1	1	4		5
Crane, David	3	5	3		3
Miller, James	1	1	6		8
Bordsey, Hannah	1		2		18
Gale, Rasin	6	3	4	1	8
Edwards, Thomas	4	3	3	4	
Howell, William	1		3	5	2
Tilden, John	2	1			4
Hastings, George	1				26
Harkness, William C	2	4	4		
Angier, John	3	1	3	1	6
Tilden, William B	1	1	2		3
Corse, James	1	2	3		4
Medford, Thomas	3		5		15
Usleton, Francis	1	2	4		3
Cann, James	3	4	4		9
Chandler, Jane		1	3		5
Howell, Barsheba		4	3		1
Lamb, John	1	3	5	3	6
Gale, George, negro				5	
Cunningham, John, negro				5	
Underhill, Joseph	1	1	2	1	3
Jackson, Richard	1		2		1
Redding, Mary		2	5	1	10
Price, Edward	1	2	4	1	
Crew, Edward	1	2	2		5
Embleton, William	3		1		31
Denning, John	2	3	3		2
Duyer, John	2	2	4		5
Collins, George, negro				1	5
Rasin, Warner	3				7
Hayrfoot, Mary, neg				3	
View, Topmain, neg				3	
Hales, Isaac, neg			4	1	
Copprell, Isaac, neg			3	1	
Nallor, Rachael, neg			2		
Moore, George	3	1	5		6
Keley, James	2	2	4	3	
Martin, Judom, nego				4	
Chandler, Nathaniel	1	1	3		
Cæsar, Negro				2	
Medford, Marmaduke	2	2	4		10
Ridgley, Abraham	1		1	2	1
Burchiner, William	3		2		3
Everitt, St. Leger	3		4	1	5
McDaniel, Duncan	3	1	3		
Meeks, Robert	1				5
Brooks, Temperance			2		2
Meeks, Mary			2		3
Culbert, John	2	1	2		
Worrell, Edward	1	1	2		7
Williams, Joseph	2	1	2		7
Dunn, James (C. T)	6	1	2		5
Hodson, Jonathan	3	2	3		5
Skarvin, Francis	1	2	4		8
Hurt, John, nego				2	2
Cuff, John, nego				4	1
Ford, Isabella		1	2		3
Parks, John	1	4	2		
Lamb, Susanna	3		3		7
Smith, Benjamin	2	3			
Lamb, Joshua	2	3	2		6
Briscoe, Sarah	1	1	3		
Myers, James (Ret.)	2	2	5	1	38
Medford, Susanna	1	2	3		9
Beck, John (S. W.)	1	2	3		20
Terry, Benjamin	1		2		12
Gale, Phebe	1	1	5		
Gale, William	2	2	3		7
Crow, Thomas	2	2	7		15
Woodall, Joseph	2	1	5		
Derrah, Jack, Negro				1	3
Pearce, William (Hop.)	1	2	6		31
Browne, Joseph (Qet.)	1	4	3	1	15
Jones, Jesse	1	1	4		
Thomas, Joseph E.	2	2	5		
Groome, Charles	2	1	7		22
Boyle, Elisabeth			7	1	
Duyer, William	3	2	3	1	1
Duyer, Susanna		4	5		2
Jeffur, John	1				
Phillips, Henry	1	1	1		1
Thomas, Rachael, neg				5	
Thomas, Grace, neg				3	
Dugan, William	2	6	4		1
Juffen, William	1		2		3
Peacock, Richard (W.)	2		3	1	3
Younger, Joseph	3	2	3		
Randall, James	2	1	2		6
Lamb, Daniel	5	2	1		
Ashley, Sophia	2		1		
Kennard, John	1	3	2		13
Corneggs, Jessee (S. P.)	2	2	4		3
Harris, Joseph	2	2	5		2
Gale, John (of B.)	1		1		3
Gale, Barsheba	1	1	3		4
Corse, Caesar, neg				8	
Redgrave, Elizabeth		2	4		
Gardner, Israel	1	1	3		
Greenwood, Joseph	3	1	5		
Turner, Daniel	2	2	6		8
Lamb, Cato, negro				7	2
Davis, Sarah			1		2
Cobourne, John	1	1	2		3
Clark, William	1		7		
Griffith, Samuel	2		3		14
Sessmonda, Rachel, neg				1	
Hozier, Samuel	1	1	3		6
Colemon, William	1	2	4		4
Ashley, John	2	1	8		4
Bowers, Ann	1	1	4		3
Nailer, Sampson, neg				4	
Haynes, Gideon	3	1	3		6
Lamb, Peerce	3		4	5	
Stockett, Margarite			1	1	
Myers, Jeremiah, neg				6	
Corse, John	3	1	1	2	
Mifflin, Hannah, neg				3	
Mifflin, Bebecca, neg				3	
Cole, William	1		3		
Lamb, George	1	2	5		4
Ford, Jere	1	2	5		16
Manley, James	4		4	1	3
Newell, John	2	4	4	1	13
Hill, Ann					
Buchanan, Robert	2		3		19
Rasin, Joseph, Jr	2	2	2	2	10
Effie, Araminta			2		
Bruisebanks, Francis	1	1	5		
Roberts, Samuel	1		5		
Flaharty, Michael	2				2
Briscoe, Moses					7
Greenwood, Jacob, negro				3	2
Hewitt, Thomas	1		2		
Norris, James	1	2	1		1
Duegan, Phillip	2	4	4		4
Rasin, Robert, neg				4	
Ingle, John	1	1	2		
Gale, John, of S	2	1	2		29
Foard, Robert	1	1	3		1
Hart, John	1	1	5		1
Greenwood, Joseph, Ju	1	1	5		13
Cooper, Peregrine	1	1	3		1
Willson, John (S. of G.)	1	4	4		16
Massey, Jessee	1	1	2		7
Kennard, Richard	3	1	1		4

KENT COUNTY—Continued.

NAME OF HEAD OF FAMILY.	Free white males of 16 years and upward, including heads of families.	Free white males under 16 years.	Free white females, including heads of families.	All other free persons.	Slaves.
Cox, Mark A.	1	1	4		26
Foreman, Hannah	1	1	3		
Foreman, Charles	1	1	2		6
Moore, Simon	1	5	4		
Byson, Nate, neg°				2	1
Jeffers, Simon, neg°				6	
Hamilton, Ann		3	1		
Elliott, Joseph	1		6		2
Golding, Samuel, neg				2	5
Lynch, Edmund	1	3	5		2
Turner, Margrete, Neg°				4	
Bennett, Samuel			2		2
Ringgold, Elias	1	2	3		1
Gooding, James	2	1	5	2	5
Pearce, Thomas, Ju.	1		5		4
Ricketts, Nathaniel	2		4		6
Wroth, Kinrin, Jr.	3	2	6		12
Hackett, Isaac	2	4	4		4
Rasin, William B.	2	1	1		4
Logan, Peter	1			1	1
Wroth, Kinrin	2	3	5		16
Lussinbey, William I.	1		3		
Willis, Amos	1		1		2
Willis, Richard	1	4	2		3
Dudley, Joshua	2		2	6	
Chew, John	2			1	
Frazier, John	1	2	4		7
Gale, Rasin, Jr.	1	1	1		2
Sutton, Edward	1		1		
Robison, Abraham	1	3	1		
Thomas, Hannah		2	3		1
Roberts, Temperance	1	1	3		1
Constable, John	1		1		
Williams, Thomas, Neo				2	
Constable, Margarite		2	4		
Boiling, Benjamin				4	13
Hart, Richard	1	1	4		
Wilkinson, Cassandra			1		2
Hart, Joseph	1				
Price, Moses		2	3		
Hepbron, Thomas	1	2	1	1	
Monk, William, Neg				3	
Trulock, Henry	2		4		7
Maxwell, Margarete		2	4		21
Shirky, Charles	1	1	5		1
Porter, John	2	1	3		2
Gale, Cæsar, Neg				3	
Comegys, Jonathan	1	2	6		5
Pearce, Thomas	1	1	2		
Hammond, Samuel	1		2		13
Everitt, Hales	1		2		
Greene, Christopher	1	1	3		
Ringgold, James (C.T.)	2	1	8	1	31
Watts, Ann	1	2	3		
Buchanan, James				9	
Meeks, Aquilla	2	4	5		
Hanson, Catherine	1		4		11
Gale, George	1		3		
Jones, Jacob, Ju.	1		3		4
Haywood, Francis	1		4		
Beck, James	2				1
Kennard, Daniel (W.)	1	1	1	6	
Betts, William	1		3		1
Redgrave, Sampson	1	2	5		4
Ford, William	1				4
Beck, John (B. L.)	2	3	1		
Everitt, Thomas, Neg°				1	
Beck, Edward (W.)	3	1	3		
Ricketts, John	3	3	3		4
Herring, William	1	3	4		
Moore, John (W.)			1	6	
Kennard, John Tilden	3	2	1	19	
McKinley, Sarah	1	4	5		
Kennard, Stephen	2	3	8	1	2
Crouch, Nehemiah	1		3		4
Kennard, Nathaniel	1		3		
Copper, Charles, Jun°	2	2	3	1	4
Alford, Aron	2				
Cork, Moses, Negro				3	4
Alford, Moses	2				5
Hamar, William	3	2	1		
Cork, Jacob, Negro				3	6
Randall, Robert	2		5		3
Foreman, Jacob	3	4	4		
Willson, Sarah (W.)	2	2	5		1
Lensman, John	2	2	2		
Copper, William, Jr	1	1	1		4
Copper, James	1	2	2		
McCoy, Absalom	2	1	4	3	13
Kennard, John (B. L.)	1		2		
Sherein, William	1		2		
Hopkins, Daniel	1	1	2		
Night, Mary		2	3		
Loftes, John	1		2		
Thomas, Mary	1		2		

NAME OF HEAD OF FAMILY.	Free white males of 16 years and upward, including heads of families.	Free white males under 16 years.	Free white females, including heads of families.	All other free persons.	Slaves.
Lowman, John, Ju.	1	1	1		1
Jones, Jacob (W.)	1	3	6		1
Smith, Samuel (W.)	1	1	3		3
Niell, Charles, Jr.	1	7	1		2
Reed, Ann	1	1	2		3
Parker, William	1	2	2		
Wapping, John, Neg					18
Wilson, David	1		3		1
Darington, James	1	1	3		2
Hanson, Gustavus	1	1	1		1
Covington, Mary			3		
Smith, Simon (W.)	1	2	3		6
Armstrong, James	2	4	2		1
Arno, Benjamin	2	1	1		
Arno, Jeremiah	1	1	5		
Atwood, Isaac	1	1	3		
Briscoe, William	1	1	5		5
Briscoe, Jacob	4	2	3		2
Boyer, Ruth	1		5		13
Browne, John	1	1	2		
Bostick, Elenor			3		2
Bantham, Elisabeth	1	1	3		4
Bantham, Henry	2	1	2		3
Bantham, Araminta			4		2
Boots, William	4	4	2		1
Bradshaw, William	1	5	3		3
Blackston, John	1	3	3		4
Briscoe, Alexander	3	3	5		79
Boyer, Thomas			2		
Blackston, James	2		1		11
Boyles, Robert		2	3		
Barnes, Martha	1	2	2		
Barris, William	1		2		3
Beedle, Spencer	2	2	1		2
Bostick, Eli	2	1	4		5
Brooks, Jacob	1	2	3		
Blackston, Lewis	2		5		9
Blanchfield, James		2	1		4
Massey, Mary			4		
Beedle, Mary			2		4
Bagwell, Smith	5		1		2
Briscoe, William, Ju	2		1		8
Brady, —*	2	1	1		
Bailey, —*	1	1	1		9
Bostick, —*			2		
Boyer, —*	1	1	2		
Baird, —*	1	1	3		
Bantham, —*	1		3		1
Bobart, —*	1		2		
Tittle, Lazarus	2	2	3	1	
Greene, Mary			4		
Cannaday, Cuffy, Neg				2	
Tittle, John	1	2	3		
Elborn, Sarah		1	3		
Graves, Elisabeth, Neg				2	
Davis, John	1	3	2		
Kaley, Jane			3		
Bailey, Rachel, Neg°				1	
Griffith, Thomas (P.)	1	1	2		
Benton, James (C.T.)	1	1	1		
Ellison, Thomas	1	1	1		
Reece, Amy, Neg°				2	5
Pepper, Peter, Neg°				3	
Dove, Dolly, Neg°				3	
Bantham, Nancy, Neg°				1	
Harding, Susanna, Neg°				1	
Nicols, Henny			2	2	
Thomas, George	1		2		
Hopkins, Edward	2	3	2		
Palmer, John	2		2		1
Dawson, Isaac	2		2		
Reed, Robert	1	2	4		1
McNamarre, Timothy	1		1		
Hartley, John	3	2	2		
Sudler, Mrs. (C. T.)			4	2	7
Lorain, Thomas	3	1	3		1
Dee, Elisabeth			2		
Harding, Mary			2		
Reed, John (C. T.)	1	1	2		
McIntire, Patrick	1		2		
Lusbey, Joseph		1	4		
Rolph, John	2	2	5		7
McCurtin, Daniel	3	4	3		
Claypoole, James	2		3		5
Hull, David			3		
Deford, Thomas	2		1		3
Sturges, John	2	1	4		2
Mantle, Christopher	2		3		1
Anderson, John (C. T.)	1	1	3		
Ringgold, Mary (C. T.)	4	1	3	1	11
Ringgold, Anna Maria (C. T.)	1		3		5
Dunn, Mrs. (C. T.)		1	3		6
Hoops, William	2		2		
McKinney, William	4	2	5		1

NAME OF HEAD OF FAMILY.	Free white males of 16 years and upward, including heads of families.	Free white males under 16 years.	Free white females, including heads of families.	All other free persons.	Slaves.
Anderson, Joe, Neg				7	1
Crudginton, Mary			2		
Wickes, John	1	1	5		2
Cavilier, Charles	1	1	1		
Sharpless, Robert	1	1	3		
Walear, Mary			3		
Farrier, James	2		2		
Sampson, William, Neg				2	1
Lennox, James	2	2	2		
Burnes, Robert	1		3		7
Hoffman, Daniel	6	3	2		
Arthur, James	1	2	2		
Smith, James (S M.)	8	2	2		1
Farree, James	2	1	6		
Chew, Samuel	2	2	5		19
Hynes, James	1		5		
Maxwell, Alexander	4		5		2
Skinner, Benjamin	4		1		3
Carvill, John	1		2		3
Sullivan, Ann		2	3		
Browne, Darky, Neg				3	
Ashmore, Tobias	3	2	1		
Rankin, Samuel M.	1		1		
Benson, Benjamin (Over P.)	15	16	28	13	
Given, William	2		2		
Nicholson, John	1	2	2		8
Hadley, Samuel T.	2	4	1		
Chaplain, Phillip	4	5	1	1	
Dooley, William	5	1	5		3
Scott, John	1	1	4		5
Scott, Elisabeth		1	8		11
Brooks, Phillip	1		2		1
Houston, James	6	2	2	1	3
Punney, Sarah			2		
Voorheese, John	2	2			6
Carmichael, Mary	1		2		3
Nichols, Jere	1	2	3		7
Mansfield, James	1	2	5		13
Piper, James	1	1	2		4
Lethebury, Pere	1		4	1	6
Mansell, William	1		4	1	
McGuinn, Donald	2	1	2	1	2
Anderson, Robert	3		1	1	2
File, Henry, Neg				2	
Burniston, William	2		4		2
Jones, Isabella (of C.T.)	6	2	1	1	5
Slubey, William	1		3		
Hackett, Charles	2		2		
Tilden, Marmaduke (Qet.)	2	2	1	3	11
Ringgold, James, Ca.	1		2		12
Tilden, Marmaduke (Wort)	2	1	3		12
Dearmote, Michael	1				
Tayler, Phillip	1				13
Tayler, Mary			2		8
Carvill, Ann	2	1	4		14
Hanson, George	1		1		12
Barrott, William	1		2		
Lynch, James	1	3	2		
Redding, Nathaniel	1		1		7
Ferguson, Elisabeth		2	4		
Ingram, Edward	3	4	4		3
Gilcrest, Thomas	3		2		11
Ringgold, Josiah	3	2	2		20
Tilghman, Matthew	2	2	4		12
Ringgold, John (C. T.)	2		2		
Ferguson, Colon, J°.	1		2		3
Chambers, Benjamin	2	3	3		13
Hands, Thomas B.	1	1	3		
Morrison, Ann	1		1		2
Smith, James (Farlo.)	2		1		4
Smith, James (C. T.)	1	1	5		22
Greene, John	1		2		4
Willis, John	1	2	4		3
Apley, Edward	1		4		
Bacon, James	1	1	1		
Lorain, John	9		3		3
Worrell, Thomas (C.T.)	2	3	6		6
Worrell, Mary			3		2
Russell, William	2	3	5		2
Collins, William (C. T.)	1		2	3	1
Parker, Phillis	1		1	1	
Danskin, Mary	1	1	4		
Griffen, Peter, Nego				5	
Halbert, Simeon	1	1	4		
Shamer, Martin	1	1	2		
Chaplain, Samuel	1		2		1
Matslor, Daniel	1	1	2		
Wickes, James	3		3		
Veazy, Elizabeth (C.T.)	2		3		4
Kemp, Martha	2	1	4	1	2
McGinnis, Daniel	5	1	2		1
Wheeler, Charles	1	2	2		

* Illegible.

KENT COUNTY—Continued.

NAME OF HEAD OF FAMILY.	Free white males of 16 years and upward, including heads of families.	Free white males under 16 years.	Free white females, including heads of families.	All other free persons.	Slaves.
Cordon, Barsheba			2		1
Heeter, Arthur	1		2		
McLure, Thomas	1	4	1		9
Roberts, William	1	1	2		
Gamble, Thomas	1	3	1		2
Hebrew, Santo, Neg°				1	4
Flatman, John	2	1		1	4
McClaine, Mary			3	1	
Alley, John		2	3		12
Greene, Alexander	2	1	2		2
Wales, James	2	2	3		1
Bordley, John	2		3	5	12
Scone, William	1		2		11
Jackson, Petty	1		2		4
Piner, Sarah	1		3		20
Debnam, Benjamin	1		2		
Fray, Elizabeth			2		
Jones, Catherine, Neg°			4	1	
Cline, John	1		1		
Cowden, Deborah, Neg°				4	
Arnold, Rebecca		1		4	
Sheppard, Margarete, Neg°			3	4	
Goforth, John	1	2	5		
Perkins, William	2	1	3		1
Earle, Ann	3	1	2		4
Ringgold, Doct. William	2	1	4	1	2
Cockerton, Robert	1		1		
Tighman, James	5		8	1	12
Tighman, Richard, 4.	1	1	10	1	14
Anderson, Robert, Jr	1		1	1	4
Forbes, William	1		1		
Boustred, Joseph	1	2	4		1
Willmer, Simon	1	5		1	19
Miller, Richard, 3.	1		1		1
Anderson, James M.	2	2	4		19
Collins, William, Jr	1		1		
Ringgold, James (Forest)	1	1	4		10
Blakeway, John					
Daniel, Negro				2	3
Dollis, Mary	2	1	3		
Donaldson, Isaac	1	2	1		
Denning, Daniel	1	1	2		
Due, Martha			1	2	
Dalley, Elijah	2	3	1		1
Day, John	2	1	5		8
Moore, Daniel, Neg				5	
Empson, Thomas	2	2	3		2
Eccleston, John	3	1	2		27
Enos, Richard	2		2		
Earle, Hannah			2		
Everitt, Benjamin	2	1	3		8
Foreman, Bartus	2	2	5		
Flynn, John	1		2		
Fields, Benjamin	1	2	3		
Francis, Rebeccah		1	2		
Fagan, Catherine			2		
French, Zerobable			2		2
Ferguson, Daniel	1	5	5		
Forrester, Temperance	1	1	3		4
Freeman, Edward			1		9
Freeman, Isaac	3		3		29
Gallelee, Thomas	1		3		
Greenwood, James	2		4		4
Geddes, Robert	1	1	3		4
Graham, Rebeccah			2		8
Gray, John	2		3		
Grindage, William	1	4	3		12
Glenn, Nathaniel	1	1	1		
Glassford, Martha		2	3		
Glenville, William	1	2	5		10
Greenwood, Daniel	1		7		14
Galloway, Nancey, Neg				2	
Gay, Rachel		2	6	4	1
Gilbert, John	1	1	2		1
Harvey, Archibald			5		1
Harford, James	1	1	4		
Harris, John	2	1	2		
Hull, William	2	1	5		3
Useleton, Robert	2	1	2		1
Hickman, John	1	3	5		1
Hill, William	1		2		1
Hyneon, Mary			1		1
Hudson, Phillip	1		1		6
Hall, George	1	1	2		1
Graves, James H.	1	1	2		4
Hall, Thomas	1	1	2		1
Hatcheson, James	2	1	1		4
Hynson, James	2		2		8
Jury, Lewis	2	2	2		1
Jarvis, Mary			3		2
Johnson, Edward	1		1		
Jones, Charles	5	1	3		1
Ireland, William	1	1	4		9
Johns, Enoch	1	2	2		3
Jones, James (Far.)	3	1	3		9
Judea, negro				2	
Jones, Magarite			2		
Jeons, Charles	2	2	3		3
Knock, Ellsabeth	1	1	3		
Knock, Henry (of W.)	2				1
Keine, Samuel	5				1
Lynch, John (+ roads)	2	2	1		
Kirk, James	1	3	2		
Kelly, Thomas	1	4	2		
King, Daniel	1	2	2		
Kelly, William	3	3	3	5	4
Lessley, Rachael			3		1
Larrimore, Daniel	1	1	3		
Laurence, John	1	2	3		
Logan, Samuel	1		2		
Lynch, John (C.)	1	2	2		1
Little, John	2		2		
Lennon, Samuel	1	1	2		
Mann, George Vansant	2	1	3		13
McGan, Michall	1	2	3		
Moffett, Richard	3		2		18
Moffett, Moses	1	2	5		
Moffett, George	2	1	1		7
Mann, William	2	4	2		
Matthews, Henry	1	1	4		
Merrill, William, Jr	1	4	3		
Moore, George	1	1	2		1
McDonald, William	1	3	2		1
Jones, Benjamin	1	5	5		3
Maxwell, William (of R.)	2		1		5
Margarett, Negro					3
Massey, Mary		2		5	(*)
Mitchell, John	2	2	3	(*)	(*)
Morrison, John			3	(*)	(*)
Massey, Hannah			2	(*)	(*)
McMullen, Andrew	1	1	2	(*)	
Merritt, William	2	1	4	(*)	(*)
McCaskey, James	3		1	(*)	(*)
McGinnis, Casparus	4	2	4	(*)	(*)
McGee, Mary			1	(*)	
Massey, Elijah, Jr		1	2	(*)	
Massey, Elijah	2	1	4	(*)	
Newcomb, John	1		1	(*)	
Moffett, Richard (of G.)	1		1		
Moffett, Jessee					7
McKenny, David	1	4	2		
Niccoson, William	1	3	1		
Noble, Margarett			4		
Newcomb, John	1		3		
Niele, Charles W.	1	2	3		
Nicholsen, William	2	3	2		5
Noland, James	2	3	2		11
Moffett, Robert	1	1	2		2
Brooks, John	2	3	6		37
Newcomb, George	1	3	3		10
Newcomb, William	1	2	3		
Palmer, Benjamin	3	2	6		4
Paul, William	1	2	1		
Parker, Derrack W.	1	1	3		5
Price, Feregrine	1	1	1		
Page, Aquilla	1	2			
Parsons, Levring	1		1		
Phillips, John	1	2	2		2
Pearce, Isabella			2		
Pope, William	6	3	2		5
Palmer, William	1		2		7
Pearce, James	4	1	5		36
Rawlings, Thomas	3	1	3		7
Redgrave, James	3		3		
Rogers, William	2		5		
Reyner, Ebenezer	2	3	6		16
Woodall, Thomas	2	2	4		
Robinson, Daniel	2		1		
Richardson, Matthew, Jr.	1	2	5		1
Rumsey, John	2	1	5		6
Rasin, Joseph (G. T.)	2		5		1
Redgrave, Joseph	2	1	3	1	7
Rasin, Sarah			3		12
Rutter, Francis	3	2	4		4
Scott, Lambert	1		2		4
Saunders, Abraham	2	2	2		1
Smith, George	2	1	2		3
Stoops, Nicholas	1	2	2		7
Sutton, Samuel	1	2	4		9
Stavely, James	2	1	1		
Simpson, David	1	1	1		
Stuart, Ruth	1	1	3		8
Smith, John	1	1	3		5
Gamble, Darius	1		4		4
Frisbey, Elizabeth	2		4		15
St. Clair, Alexander			4	3	
Phillips, John, Negro				2	
Hull, Daniel	1	3	2		
Newmen, Richard	1	1	4		
Moore, William	1	2	1		
Carter, William	3		3		1
Proone, Rebecca			2		
Phelps, Mary		2	2		
Bryon, John	1	1	2	5	1
Young, Grace, Neg°				5	1
Robinson, Rachel, Neg°			4		
Rumney, Joseph	1	3	3		
Willis, Simon	1	1	1		
Punney, Martha			3		
Hyland, John	5	2	4		2
Fendall, John	1	1	1		
Whaland, John	1	2	3		2
Tray, Philip	1	2	2		7
Frisbey, John	1	2	3	2	28
Whaland, Owen	1		3		1
Kendall, James	1	1	3		
Garnett, Joseph	3	4	3		11
Baker, Ann	1	1	4		5
Rollings, Sella	2	1	1		6
Caulk, John	1				
George, Robert	3	1	6	8	
Browne, Margarite, Neg				6	
Love, Robert	1	3	1		
Mason, Chester, Neg				3	1
Beck, Edward, (Qet.)	2	2	2		15
Miller, Mary			4	4	23
Stableford, Thomas			4		9
Headon, John	1	1	3		
Jordon, Elisabeth			2		8
Browne, Nicholas	3	2	5	4	
McFall, Mary			2		
Simmonds, Sarah (Qet.)	4	1	4		3
Hanvey, John	2	1	2		3
Thomas, Samuel, Jr, (Qet.)	1	1	2	5	
McKeel, Samuel	1		1		
Browne, David	1	1	3		
Froth, Phillip, Neg				3	
Cruikshanks, Hannibal, Neg				4	
Pearce, Charles	2	1	5		1
Downey, John	1	1	2		
McLane, Douglas	1		5		
Curry, Robert	3	2	2		3
Kennard, Daniel (Qet.)	2		4		2
Gidley, John	2		3		
Useleton, William	2	1	3		
Smith, James (Qet.)	1	3	1	1	
Milton, Martha			6	1	
Comegys, Jesaee (Qet.)	3	1	2	2	4
Maslin, Frances	2	1	3		
Clark, Elijah	1	2	3		1
Beck, Simon (Qet.)	1	2	3		
Jacobs, Bartholomew	1	2	3		1
Dickson, William	2	2	3		
Smith, Thomas (Qet.)	1	2	3		
Clark, Sarah			3		
Gilbert, Lewis, Neg				1	7
Elly, John, Neg				8	1
True, Hamutt, Neg				2	
Stiles, Rachael, Neg				1	
Sullivan, David				1	1
Kendall, John	1		1	1	
Warrens, Elisabeth, Neg				2	
Berry, William, Neg				3	
Launch, Samuel, Neg				5	
Niele, Charles	3	1	15		6
Covington, Joseph	2	1	2		
Stephens, Esther	2		3		
Byrom, John	2		2		
Pearce, Rebecca	1	1	4		
Young, William (Qet.)	2		4		
Comegys, Edward (Qet)	3	2	4	2	9
Wilkins, Barlus	1		1		6
Few, William	3	1	4	2	1
Willis, Martha			2		
Hegginbottom, Benjamin	1		5		
O'Heron, Patrick	1	5	1		
Rolph, James	2		2		
Browne, Morgan	3	3	3		10
Sutton, John	1	6	3		12
Crouch, Samuel	1	6	3		2
Barrett, Margaret	1	2	4		
Clark, Jeasee	1	5	2		
Hadaway, Robert	1	2	5		
Night, William					
Stuart, John (Qet.)	2	6	4	8	2
Frisbey, William (Qet.)	1	6	1		13
Froth, Jane, Negro				7	
Browne, George	1	3	4	1	1
Shaves, Ruth	1	2	3		3
Browne, John	1		2		

* Illegible.

KENT COUNTY—Continued.

NAME OF HEAD OF FAMILY.	Free white males of 16 years and upward, including heads of families.	Free white males under 16 years.	Free white females, including heads of families.	All other free persons.	Slaves.
Browne, James	1		2		1
Anderson, George, Neg.				1	2
Sheaf, Jacob, Neg.				5	
Ignatius, Neg.				3	8
Murray, James	1	2	2		
Laurence, Thomas	1	2	1		
Perkins, Daniel					4
Matthews, William	3		3		1
Smith, Simon, Jr.	3		1		17
Dudley, Samuel	1	2	3		4
Wright, Benjamin	1		4		6
Williams, Chester, Neg.				2	
Fellon, Rachel, Neg.				5	1
Silvey, William	1	1			
Cannady, William	2	1	2		7
Apsley, Thomas	1		2		
Ward, Joseph	1				5
Blackston, Joseph	2	4	3		4
Gibbs, Ann		1	4		1
Boddy, John	1				13
Turner, Edward	1				36
Higginbottom, Jane			1		
Granger, Thomas	1	3	5		11
Elijah, James, Negro				5	
Willson, Jane	1	1	3		
Thomas, Samuel (B.)	1	1	1		1
Copper, William	1	1	3		4
Bolton, Anthoney, Neg.				1	4
Niele, James	2	1	3		2
Stump, Hannah			5		
Nicols, Daniel	1	2	3		
Carroll, Edward	1	2	3		4
Carroll, Rebecca	2	4	3		
Harris, William	1	1	2		1
Start, Solomon	1	1	2		
Legg, Margarett, Negro				4	
Massey, John	1	1	3		
Jones, William (W.)	2	2	5		2
Phillips, James	1	1	5		
Thomas, James	1	1	1		1
Browne, William	2	1	2		4
Longfellow, Permelia	1		4		
Denning, Daniel	1		2		19
Frisbey, Martha		1	3		8
Rollinson, James	1	3	3		6
Frazier, James	1	1	3		
Glenn, Martha			3		
Swift, John	1	1	5		2
Vickars, James	2		3		
Denson, John	1		3		
Scott, John, Neg.				5	10
James, Thomas J.	2		2		10
Hawkins, Elisabeth		1	3		
Coleman, Nathan	1		3		2
Gilbert, Thomas	3	2			13
Simmonds, Rachel, Neg.				1	
Beck, Samuel	1	1	4		9
Beck, Thomas	2		4		5
Vickars, Rachael	1	3	3		2
Hurt, James	1	2	2		2
Perkins, William (St. J.)	1		1		
Sheppard, York, Neg.				2	1
Hurt, Joce	1		2		3
Smallwood, Joseph, Neg				2	
Leas, Jonas, Neg.				5	
Graves, Harry, Neg.				9	
Davis, Judea					
Chilon, Hannah, Neg.	1		1		
Hadley, Daniel	1		3		
Smith, Sarah		1	3		
Ward, Hannah	1	1	3		
Edes, Hannah	1		3		
Comegys, Gideon	2	2	6		13
Dunn, Michael	3		2		6
Dunn, Darius, Jr.	1		1	1	5
Colemon, James (Cct.)	1	2	6		
Fry, William	1	5	2		
Bogue, William	1	3	3		
Gulck, Mary		1	3		
Cannon, Edward	1	3	4		
Waram, Valentine	1	2	4		
Nemore, Elsey			4		
Mason, William	1	2	5		
Maslin, James	4	3	4		
Maslin, Thomas	3	5	4		5
Collins, William (Cct.)	2	2	3		2
Kendall, William	1	2	7		5
Dunn, Mary, Neg.				4	3
Elborne, Hannah	1	2	4		
Maslin, Brelain	1				17
Nicholson, Thomas	1	2	7		10
Burk, John	2		3		9
Reed, Phillip	2				5
Dempster, Robert	2	1	3		
Maslin, John	5	1	1		2
Ringgold, Doct. John	2		1		11
Smith, Nathan	1		4		6

NAME OF HEAD OF FAMILY.	Free white males of 16 years and upward, including heads of families.	Free white males under 16 years.	Free white females, including heads of families.	All other free persons.	Slaves.
Smith, Hynson	2	1	3	1	5
Davis, Robert	1		3		
Tucker, George	1	2	3		
Frisbey, James	1		6		30
Frisbey, Elisabeth		3	4	1	18
Copper, Darius	1		3		8
Wilson, Sarah			3		1
Lane, Richard			2		1
Hollace, James	1				
Hague, Mary		1	4		
Dowland, Thomas	1	2	4		
Moore, John (B.)	2		1	3	14
Cannon, James	1	1	3		31
Ashley, David (B. S.)	3	3	3		
Lowman, Jessee	1		1		3
Miller, Richard	2		4		30
Miller, Samuel	1	3	4		5
Nabb, Elisha	1	1	4		7
Glenvill, James	1	1	4		9
Spear, James	1	2	(*)		4
Soaper, Elisabeth	2	1	3		
Scott, Timothy, Neg.				5	
Sampson, Sarah, Neg				3	
Sappington, Thomas	3	5	2		
Smith, Oliver	3	1	9		10
Jones, John, Negro				1	
Spearman, William	1	1	9		10
Simmonds, Gilbert	4	1	4		15
Simmonds, Thomas	1	2	1		
Simmonds, William	1	1	2		
Simmonds, Richard	2	2	3		4
Simmonds, Lambert	2	1	4		3
Simmonds, David	1	1	4		
Sampson, Mary, Neg				3	
Saunders, Hannah			2		3
Shawhawn, Frederick	1	2	2		
Smith, William	1	2	1		
Shawhawn, Charles	1	1	2		
Stiles, Reuben	1	2	3		1
Smith, John	1		2		
Smith, James	3		5		11
Sewell, Thomas	2	4	2		5
Sewell, John	2	2	3		1
Turner, Eben	3	2	2		8
Thomas, William (M.)	3	2	3		14
Tate, Thomas	1		2		3
Taylor, Abraham	1	1	2		
Turner, John	3		4		
Thomas, John	2	1	2		6
Tygert, John	1	4	2		1
Thomas, James (U. C.)	2	4	3		
Tippins, James	1	2	2		5
Todd, Samuel	1	2	5		
Vansant, Benjamin	4		3		
Vansant, George (of B.)	2		3		
Vansant, John	1		5		7
Vansant, Cornelius	3	2	2		10
Vansant, William	1	2	2		
Vansant, Christopher	1	1	1		1
Vansant, Joshua	2	3	6		11
Wright, Norris	1		5		
Whittington, Christiana		1	2		5
Woodall, Frances			2		
Woodland, Abraham	1		2		10
Wright, Margarett	4	1	4		7
Woodland, John (of W.)	1	1	3		3
Wright, Edward	1	1	1		7
Ward, Moses	1		4		
Woodall, John	1		1		8
Woodall, John, Jr	1		3		
Woodall, William	1		4		
Welch, Mary			3		
Wadey, Sarah		1	4		
Wyett, William	5	1	4		
Wadey, Berry	1	1	2		
Wallis, John	2		7		3
Woodland, James	1	2	2		12
Woodland, Mary		2	2		
Willson, John, Jr	2		1		
Willson, John		3	2		7
Wise, William	1	1	4		
Willson, James		2	5		
Willson, Ann			5		
Woodland, James (C.R.)	1	1	2		9
Wilmer, Jonathan	1		1		
Welch, Mary (H. S.)		3	2		6
Wallace, William	1		4		
Whittington, Thomas	1		2		
Wallace, John	2		3		
Ward, Mary			2		
Earley, John (Over)	1		2		9
Briscoe, Joseph	1	2	2		
Comegys, ——*	2	2	2		12
Riley, ——*		2	3		8
Mansfield, ——*	1	2	5		
Hurt, ——*	1	1	2		
Caton, William	2	3	3		5

NAME OF HEAD OF FAMILY.	Free white males of 16 years and upward, including heads of families.	Free white males under 16 years.	Free white females, including heads of families.	All other free persons.	Slaves.
Hynson, Pere	1		3		1
Heath, Jessee	1	2	3		3
Smith, George	1	2	2		
Jones, James (B.)	2	2	2		9
Massey, Joseph	2	1	3		
Massey, Daniel Toes	2		3		8
Greenwood, Rebeccah	3	3	4		1
Smith, Margarett			2		
Fisher, Daniel	1	1	2		
Brooks, Seth	1		1		
Rees, George			2		
Lennon, Francis	3	1	1		1
Willson, Solomon	2		1		
Hendrickson, William	1	4	3		
Isaac, Mulatto				4	
Ferguson, Colen	2		2		9
London, Negro				5	
Ellis, William	1	4	2		
Haire, Stephen	1	2	1		
Basser, Christopher	1	2	4		
Maddin, Margarett		2	4		
Congo, Negro				9	
Mandear, Joseph, Negro				6	
Jeffrey, Negro				5	6
Johnson, Josiah	2		4		4
Redgrave, Wineford		1	3		
Cole, Benjamin	1	1	7		
Billy, Negro				4	
Malley, Robert	2	4	3		
Stanley, Isaac	1	2	5		
Fowler, Patrick	2		4		
Stanley, John	1	1	2		
Will, Negro				6	
Roper, John		1	3		
White, John	1	3	4		
Dodson, William	1	3	4		
Sudler, Emory					11
Smith, Daniel	1	2	1		4
Boots, Alphonso	1		1		1
Willis, Joel	2	2	3	1	6
Wallace, Samuel	1		4		
Bramble, James	1	2	5		
Peacock, Richard (N.)	1	2	3		6
Myers, John	2	2	2		12
Knock, Elisabeth		1	3		
Myers, John, Jr	1	2	5		
Knotts, Samuel	1	2	3		
Toney, Anthoney, Negro				1	3
Charington, John	1	8	4		
Pender, William	1	1	3		
Roles, John	1	1	3		14
Wickes, Simon, Snr.	2	1	5		14
Glenn, William	1	1			11
Colemen, Charles	1	1	2	1	4
Reynolds, Hugh	1	1	1		2
Ambrose, Matthew	1	1	1		9
Miller, Nathaniel	2		5		22
Fellingham, Benajah	2	2	1		
Ward, Mole, Negro				3	
Foster, Maria					
Underhill, Michael	1	1	1	2	21
Greenfield, Robert	1	1	2		
Kelly, Hannah			2		
Granger, William	2		4		15
Kelly, John	1		4		13
Elliott, John	1		2		
Kelly, William	1		2		
Cannell, Isaac	1		2		5
Ringgold, William (B.S.)	1	1	2		12
Waltam, John	2		2		11
Lloyed, James	1	1	6		41
Berry, Maney		2	4		1
Beck, Samuel, Jr	2	1	5	1	
Beck, Joshua	1	1	2		
Bowers, James	1	1	2		14
Hale, William	1	1			17
Ayres, William	1	1	4		3
Griffith, Mary			4		
Olliver, Matthew, Neg.				2	
Caten, Thomas	2	1	1	6	3
Due, Samuel, Neg.				6	
Henry, James	1		1		
Dennison, William	1	3	3		
Thompson, William	1	1	1		
Deane, Matthew	1	1	1		
Bibbons, Elizabeth		1	2		
McKenney, William (S.)	1	1	2	2	
Perkins, John	1		2		
Mungan, Samuel	1		2		
Berry, Caly			1		
Mungan, Sarah		2	4		
String, William	2		3		
Smith, Stephen	1		2	1	3
Groome, Daniel	2	3	3		10
Willson, William (S.C.)	1		3		10
Dunn, Darius	1	2	3		8
Miller, Walter	3	2	2		12

* Illegible.

KENT COUNTY—Continued.

NAME OF HEAD OF FAMILY.	Free white males of 16 years and upward, including heads of families.	Free white males under 16 years.	Free white females, including heads of families.	All other free persons.	Slaves.
Miller, Thomas	2	1	4		20
Blackston, Stephen	2	3	5		9
Ricaud, Richard	1	1	3	1	20
Tharp, John	5	1	6		14
Page, John	1	2	5		19
Jones, John (S. C.)				1	
Murray, William, Neg					
Clark, James	1	3	1		
Gibbs, George	1	3	(*)		
Bradshaw, James	1	2	8		
Blackstone, Richard	1	1	(*)	(*)	
McGilton, John	1	1	(*)		
Bishop, Phillip	2	3	1	(*)	
Farmer, Thomas	2	3	(*)	(*)	
Hurt, Morgan	2	3	(*)	(*)	
Miller, Charles (D.)	3	2	(*)		
Meeks, St. Leger (D.)	1	1	(*)		
Copper, James (D.)	1		(*)		
Kirkwood, Peter (D.)	1	2	(*)		
Copper, Robert	1	2	(*)		
Roberts, John	1	2	3	(*)	
Copper, George	2	2	(*)		
Smith, Zachariah (R.H.)	2	1	2	(*)	
Grace, Negro					
Coley, Nathan	3	1	2		
Colemen, Charles	2	1	2		
Askey, Pere	1	3	4		
Berrymon, Sarah, Neg					
Hodges, James	5	1	1	2	
Cennolly, Laurence	2	1	2		
Early, Edward	1	2	2		
Earley, Benjamin	1		2		
Higginbottom, Olliver	1		2		
Crisp, John	1		2		
Ury, Thomas	3	2	2		
Worrell, Thomas (B.)	4	3	1	1	10
Cleaver, John	1	2	4	1	
Hyland, James	1	3	1		
Dunn, Hezekiah	1		5		12
Summers, Robert	1	1	3		
Hopkins, Joleph	1	1	3		
Ashley, David	1		2		
Colemen, William (Ect.)	1	2	2		
Colemen, Hezekiah	1	1	3		
Frazier, Hugh	1		2		
Frazier, George	1	3	4		
Duncan, Alexander	2	2			
Byrom, Ann		1	2		
Jerom, Thomas	1	5	2		2
Benton, Hannah		1	3	1	
Miller, Thomas (Ect.)	1		5		
Hodges, Samuel	1	1	2		19
Eagle, James	1		3		25
Willcox, Henry	1		2		21
Ringgold, William (Ect.)	1		3		16
Williamson, James				8	14
Williamson, Rebeccah			3		7
Browne, Joseph (Ect.)	1	2	2		
Stephens, John Toppin	2	6	2		
Gooding, William	4	3	3		35
Smith, Thomas (Ect.)	4	2	8		6
Crabbin, William	1	5	5		
Bryon, John (Ect.)	4	1	3		4
Smith, Archibald	4	3	2	1	
Durdon, William	1	1	1		8
Wickes, Joseph (Ect. I.)	1	2	1		8
Mansfield, Thomas	1		4		8
Chambers, Charles	1	1	4		
Jones, David	1	1	4		
Merchart, George	1	1	2		
Noland, Alexander					
Hynsen, Benjamin (Ect. I.)	1	1	2		9
Tilden Charles (Ect.)	1		1		20
Hynson, Hannah	1		3		20
Copper, William (Ect.)	2				10
Hynson, Mary (of I.)	2		5		8
Hatcheson, Nathan	2		4		
Nelson, James	1	1	1		
Beck, Edward (B. L.)	1	2	1		10
Beck, John (R. H.)	1		1		2
Crouch, James	1		6		1
Ury, John	1		2		
Copper, Rebecca			2		
Berryman, Elisabeth	1		3		
Coshlow, John	1	1	3		
Geary, Hannah			3	1	
Hailley, John (Pet.)	1		1		
Brice, Judea			5		11
Harragan, Mary			7		
Spencer, Richard	1	4	4		17
Saunders, James (Pet.)	1		6		
Martin, James	2		3		
Skinner, James	2	2	3		
Glenn, Jacob	1		3		
Reed, Amos	1		1		
Gresham, Thomas	2		3		16
Morgan, Charles	2	1			1

NAME OF HEAD OF FAMILY.	Free white males of 16 years and upward, including heads of families.	Free white males under 16 years.	Free white females, including heads of families.	All other free persons.	Slaves.
Hynson, John	1	1	3		1
Hanson, George A	1	2	2	2	7
Benton, James	1	1	2		
Crouch, Mary	2	1	5		9
Bennett, Solomon	2		5		3
Duffey, John	1	1	1		
Ashley, James	1	3	1		
Coleman, Darius	1	1	5		
Wharten, Sarah			6		
Sterling, John		4	6		7
Smith, Jeffry, Neg				4	
Crouch, John	2	2	3		
Clark John (Pet.)	3	2	5	1	
Holtzmon, Henry	2	1	2		
Copper, Charles	1	2	4		
Hynson, Charles (L. B.)	4		4	2	9
Patience, negro				2	1
Hynson, John Carvill	3	2	2		17
Brice, Richard	4	2			7
Taylor, Samuel	1	4	4		7
Lett, negro				4	
Hynson, Richard	3	1	5	1	14
Caeraday, Frances			5		1
Hanson, Benjamin		3	5		12
Shaw, William	1	2	3		2
Jackson, Samuel	1		4		
Massey, Fanny			4		
Crow, Thomas, Jr	2		1		
Dunn, Robert	2	1	5		18
Hudson, Samuel	1	2	2		
Dunn, Elisabeth	1		2		5
Reardon, Thomas	1		3		
Eagle, Henry	1		3		10
Wicks, Joseph, 3rd	1	2	2		20
Browne, William F.	2	3	2		20
Brice, William	2	1	1		
Magner, John	2	1	2		
Cannaday, Samuel	1		3		
Alford, Rachael			3		
Hall, John	1		3		1
Wilmer, Blackston	1	2	6		21
Wicks, Jacob, negro				5	
Wilmer, William	1	3	1		13
Tillingham, Richard	3	2	4		
Strong, William, Jr	2		2		10
Ronell, William	3				
Stanley, Richard	3		5		
Browne, Hannah			4		
Martin, Elisabeth	1	2	3		
Anderscon, William	1	2	2		
Saunders, John	3		3		6
Little, Aranninta			4		12
Beazley, Benjamin	1	1	2		
Fay, John Thomas	1	1	2		
Parsons, John	2		5		
Mott, Henritta	1	2	6		
Carroll, Daniel			2		
Niccoson, Ann				3	
Will, negro				4	
Trusly, Will, co.			3		
Davis, Nathan			3		
Jones, John	1		2		12
Steward, William	2	2	2		11
Jester, Jonathan	12		2		
Candyche, Nicholas	1		2		
Fowler, Thomas	1	2	2		2
Shawhawn, Isaac	2	1	3		
Scaggs, Richard	2	2	2		6
Parsons, Abraham	1		4		
Denning, Martha	1	1	2		
Scone, George	1		3		8
Burgiss, John	2		3		8
Beazley, John	1	2	3		
Davis, Morris	2	1	3		20
Hall, Cuthbert	4	4	3		11
Glasgow, William	2	2	1		1
Hendrickson, Thomas	2		4		
Webb, David	2	2	4		5
Knotts, Absalom	2	6	2		
Keslitt, Mary	1		1		6
Vansant, Ephraim	1	1	1		
Jacob, negro				4	
Vansant, George, of E.	1	4	1	1	3
Porter, Joseph	1	1	5		
Peters, Jonathan	1	1	1		
Hill, Robert	2		3		
Woodale, Allsen	1	2	3		
Tucker, Isaac	1		2		
Clark, William (Forest)	1	2	4		
Wallace, Elisabeth		1	2		
Pennington, John W.	3		2		
McCay, Alexander			2		1
Ireland, Ellener			2		
Ward, Thomas		2	5		
Palmer, Bartlet (O. T.)	1	2	2		
Webb, Robert	2	1	1	3	
Myers, Luke	2	2	3		4
Hollingsworth, Sarah	1	1	3		

NAME OF HEAD OF FAMILY.	Free white males of 16 years and upward, including heads of families.	Free white males under 16 years.	Free white females, including heads of families.	All other free persons.	Slaves.
Smith, George	1	2	2		1
Flynn, John	1	1	2		
Turner, William	1	1	1		7
Jobson, Jonathan	3		4		1
Patten, John	3	1	2		
Townsend, Jehu	2		4		17
Fields, William, Over	2				
Barry, Hannah			2	4	3
Perkins, Thomas	3	1	3	3	
Maxwell, John	2		2		8
McDowell, Thomas	2		4		2
Pell, William	1	1	4		
Mansfield, William	1		6		
Pennington, James	2	1	2		9
Richardson, Matthew	2		4		
Rough, John			1		1
Noland, Jessee	1		2		
McCay, Jessee				2	
Ben, negro					
Bailey, James	1	2	1		
Maxwell, William	2		3		5
Maxwell, Robert (of B.)	2		3		6
Lamb, George	3	3	3		5
Comegys, Jacob	3	3	5		5
Morris, Samuel	1		2		
McCay, John	1	1	1		14
Boyer, Augustine	1		2		5
Knock, Nathaniel	1	1	5		
Redgrave, Abraham	1	1	3		4
Medford, George	1		2		
Cooper, Elisha	2		2		7
Williamson, John	2	1	1		
Cuff, negro					
Willson, Francis	2	1	4		1
Gibbs, Coffee, neg					
Dudley, John, neg					
Mott, William	2	2	3		10
Myers, Luke					2
Conarding, Judea, nego					
Foard, Joseph	4		2		
Parker, James	1				3
Goff, William	1		1		1
Thrift, John	2	1	5		
Hackett, Ann Martha			5		
Armington, Frederick	2	2	4		
Pope, Samuel	1		2		5
Knock, Henry	1		2		5
Stavely, Ann			2		6
Simms, Edward	1	1	3		14
Massey, Elisha	2		4		15
Freeman, Jacob	1	3	8		46
Wilmer, John Lambert	2	2	4		13
Woodland, John (C.R.)	1	1	5		27
Black, George	3	5	1		
Browne, William	3		3		(*)
Spencer, William	1	1	1		(*)
Perkins, Isaac	1		1	4	(*)
Tennant, James	1	1	4		(*)
Turner, Joseph	1		4		(*)
Turner, John (H. C.)	3	1	1		3
Black, Charles, nego				3	
Caffee, negro					7
Wethered, Richard	1	2	3		
Garland, John	1	1	2		
Vansant, Hannah			2		
Sharper James, neg					
Taylor, Henry				2	
Smith, Robert, Over	(*)	(*)	(*)	(*)	
Halcheron, Vincent	(*)	(*)	(*)	(*)	
Woodall, Rebeccah	(*)	(*)	(*)	(*)	
Severe, Peter	1			2	
Henrickson, John	2		3		
Plank, George	2	2	3		
Barris, Benjamin	1		3		7
Welch, James	2	(*)	2		
Vansant, William	1		3		16
Willson, William	1	2	2		1
Fox, John					
Jane, negro					
Freeman, Robert	3	1	1		4
Harrison, Elisha	2	1			(*)
Willson, George	1				(*)
Burchinall, Jeremiah				(*)	(*)
James, negro				(*)	
Jack, negro				(*)	
Middleton, Joseph	2		(*)	(*)	
Osborn, Samuel G.	1	(*)	(*)	(*)	
Copper, John				(*)	
Greenwood, Daniel (C. R.)				(*)	
Howard, John	1	2	(*)	(*)	
Griffith, Luke	2	4			
Everill, John, negro				(*)	
Graves, Richard	3	1	4	2	(*)
Vandyke, Mary	3		1		(*)
Harrowood, Robert	2	1	2		(*)
Knock, Henry	2				(*)

*Illegible.

MONTGOMERY COUNTY.

NAME OF HEAD OF FAMILY.	Free white males of 16 years and upward, including heads of families.	Free white males under 16 years.	Free white females, including heads of families.	All other free persons.	Slaves.
Stoddert, Benja	3	1	4	1	13
Forrest, Uriah	2		3	1	5
Gover, Capt Robt	14	1			
Bond, Capt William	15	2	2		
Bunker, Capt Samuel	7	2	2		1
Butler, Mrs Mary					5
Munk, Edward				4	
Lounds, Francis & C.	2				4
Thompson, George			3		1
Crookshanks, John	2	1		4	
Welsh, William	5	1	1	4	
Kelley, Hugh	1	1	1	2	
Smallwood, William	1		1	4	
Rezener, Eliz		1	1		
Hall, Federick				6	
Warring, Marsham & Henry	2	1		4	
Gregg, Joshua	1			2	
Mim, Elenor			1		
Perry, Saml W	1			2	
Gantt, John M	1			2	1
Worthington, Charles	1	1	3		5
Corcoran, Thomas	8	1	2		
House, John	1	1	2		1
Ellenwood, Benja	1	1	2		1
Davidson, Samuel	2				1
Peter, Robert	4	4	2		16
French, George	1	4	6		8
Slater, Thomas	1	2	4		
Dunlop, James	1				6
Beale, Col. George	3	1			4
Roden, Richd				1	
Lawder, Thomas					3
Richards, Edward	1	1	2		
Duvall, Saml	1		2		
Duglass, James	1	1	2		
Balch, Stephen B	1	3	2		8
Doyle, Alexr	4	3	5		
Moore, James	1		1		1
McCoey, Robt	2	2			1
Masha, William			3	1	
Clagett, Judson & Zadook	2	1			1
Magruder, Brooke	1	3			4
McKever, Wm					
Carlton, Joseph	3		2		
Orme, Lucy			2		1
Lanston, Thomas	2	1			1
O Neill, Bernard	3		4		18
Mountz, Jno	4	3	2		1
Jones, Jno	1		4		
Connelly, Thos	2		4		
Gilpin, Notley	2	2			
Kurtz, Christian	3	4			1
Heter, Coonrod	3		1		
Lamy, James			2		
Smith, Jno	1	3	2		
Brookes, Walter	4				
Beale, Thos of Geo	1		3		11
White, Capt Andrew	4	1	1		
Rose, Capt Jno	13	3			
Magruder Capt Jame	7		2		
Buchannen, Capt Jame	11				1
Peirce, Thomas	1	1	3		
Peirce, Benja N	1		2		5
James, James	1		2		
Borer, Peter	3	5			
McHenry, Mary		5	4		
Easterday, Daniel	1		2		
Sholtz, Henry	1	1	3		
Wheland, Mechael	1		2		
George, Edmond	1	1	2		
Satorius, Charles	1	1	1		
Newton, Arnold	1		6		
Baker, Barton	2	1	3		
Dunbough, E.	1	1	4		
Davis, Charles	1	2	4		
Dodson, Jno	1		4		
Moran, Jame	1	1			
Lacey, Benjamin	4	1	4		
Crage, George	1		1	1	
Cookendorfer, Leonard	1	2	4		
Kelpatrick, Wm	1		3		
James, Jno	1		2		
Lystor, James	1		2	4	
Rigdon, Thomas	1	4	2		
Sloyle, Jno	3	1	2		
Ross, William	2		2		
Hennage, William	1		2		
Bryan, Dennis	1	1	2		
Connely, Timothy	1		3		
Stephens, George	2	3	1		
Grear, Alexr	1			1	
Simms, Jos	2		2		
Barkley, Thomas	2	2	4		7
Dunlap, John	2		2		2
Casanave, Peter	2	1			2

NAME OF HEAD OF FAMILY.	Free white males of 16 years and upward, including heads of families.	Free white males under 16 years.	Free white females, including heads of families.	All other free persons.	Slaves.
Hilsemer, Geo	2		4		
Mim, Peter	2	1	2		
Smith, Mary			3		6
Trutton, Lucy			5	1	
Pegg	1				
Gardiner, Jame	6	3	4		2
Burk, Jacob	3		2		
Ulghon, Robert	1	1	4		
Sutton, John	1	1	2		
Reintzel, Valentine, Senr	2	1	1		
Dawson, Jno	2		1		
Conner, Jno	1		2		
Connell, Jno	2		1		
Calder, James	3		1		
Melvin, James	2	3	2		
Moore, Wm B.	1	2	2		
Pringle, Jno	7		1	1	
Johnson, Gerrard	1		3		
Flarharty, Jame	2	1	1		1
Noles, Henry	1	2	1		
Keplin, Jno	2	2	2		
Smith, Alexr	2	1	1		
Dunnevin, Dennis	1		1		
Riggs, Jacob	1		1		3
Bowman, Peter	1	2	1		
Cornish, Ann			2		
Murphey, William	1	1	2		4
Fowler, Elisha, Senr	1		1		
Fowler, Elisha, Junr	2	1	2		
Gibbs, Joseph	1	2	2		1
Purnell, Ann			1		
Hill, Thomas	1		1		
Branham, Jeremiah	1	2	2		
Turnbull, Jno			1		
Kookendorfer, Federick	2				
Runtzel, Valentine, Junr	3		1		
Simpson, James	3	2	3		
Lard, John	3		1		1
Horse, Jno P	1				
Beale, Hezekiah	1		1		
Magruder, Wm B	3	3	3		8
King, Wm Mercht	3		3		
Branham, Thomas	3	1	3		6
Hope, Betty			2		1
Crouse, Dorus	1		1		
Hardman, Henry	2	1	5		
Gaddis, David	1	1	3		1
Waninbury, Andrew	5	1	3		4
Anderson, George	1	1	2		
Williams, Saml	1	1	3		
McGill, John	1	2	3		5
Munk, William	1	1			
Estave, Andrew	2		1	3	
Shanks, Michael	11	4	5		
Paull, Nicholas	3		4	1	
Thompson, Richard	3	1	3		2
Duncasties, Elij	3				8
Naler, William	4		6		
Schley, Thomas	4	1	1		6
Allison, Elenor		2	1		
Wineburger, George	3	1	2		2
Fura, Charles	4		2		
Brond, Henry	3		1		1
Murdock, Wm	2	1	4		
Smith, Walter	2	3	3		5
Walker, George			1		
Ober, Richard	2	1	1		
Brown, Capt Heugh	2		4	1	1
Aruin, William	1				
Esburn, Jane			5	1	
Johns, Capt Richd	2		1		4
Linebors, Nicholas	1	2	3		
Harper, John	2	1	2		
Threlkeld, John	1				41
Betty, Charles	10	2	3		4
Suter, John	5	3	5		4
Fura, Thomas	5	1	2		
Robertson, William	2	2			5
King, George	2		2		
Linhan, James N.	2		1		10
Linhan, N	2	1	2		
Magruder, Charles	2		3		
Magruder, Patrick	2		5		2
Denes, Manuel				3	
Louns, Benja				5	
Moore, Nelly				5	
Murphey, William				3	
Grunnel, John	1	1	2		
Stephens, Peter	2	1	4		
Deakins, William, Junr			3		8
Williams, Elisha O.	2		3		
Chew, Casandra				3	4
Carlile, Henry	6	2	1		
Moore, William	1	1	2		
Thompson, Joseph	1	1	3		
Olenner, John	1		2	1	
Waters, Moses	2		1		

NAME OF HEAD OF FAMILY.	Free white males of 16 years and upward, including heads of families.	Free white males under 16 years.	Free white females, including heads of families.	All other free persons.	Slaves.
Williams, Robert					
Gosler, Anthony	1		1	7	
Mim, James	3	1	1	2	
Wilson, Daniel	1			1	
Russel, Philip	1		2	2	6
Carney, Matthew	1			2	
Gosler, Margret			1	2	
White, Jane	2		5	3	1
Clagett, James	2	1			4
Burapt, Benja					1
Beall, Brooke					8
McGuire, Mary	1	2	1		1
Gray, Jno			4		
Keeling, Matthew	1		2		
Grimes, Mary			2		
Bryan, Ruth			2		
Lucas, Henry	2	1	2		
Upperman, Henry	1		2		
Sants, Robert	2		2		
McClain, Mrs					
Burman, Jno	1	2			
Truman, Saml	1	1	1		
Carroll, Bryan	2				
Jones, John	2		1	4	
Houser, Martin	2	3			9
Robertson, George	2		3		13
Lutze, Henry	2		2		
Thomas, Samuel, 3rd	2	2	2		13
Moore, Silvanus	1		2		1
Brooke, Samuel				6	
Dunn, John (overseer for Wm Robertson)	1	1	1	6	10
Beall, Cephas	2		3		
Holland, Martha			3		8
Belt, Joseph L	2	2	3		16
Vile, George (overseer for D. Crawford)	1				
Owen, Edward	2		3	2	43
Clagett, Walter	2	1	2		10
Tilles, William	1		2		
Tennery, John	1		2		
Russel, John	2	3			
Heugh, Sarah			4		23
Clagett, Martha			2		16
King, Benja	2	1	3		17
Magruder, Samuel B	2	2	1		
Roads, Nicholas	2		1		
Barber, Eliz			5	2	5
Belt, Joseph	1	2	4		2
Belt, Medelton	1		2		9
Beeraft, Peter	1	1	1		
Windham, William	3	3			
Flint, Thomas					3
Smith, Rebecca			2		11
Magruder, Ninian	1	2	4		10
Magruder, Edward	2		2		
Chamberlin, Clement	1	1	1		
Wade, William	1		3		
Holmead, Anthony	1				
McPherson, Saml	2		3		21
Clarke, Henry	4	2	3		16
Sissel, Sabret	5		2		6
Gattrell, Lucy			1		19
Beale, Jeremiah (overseer for T. Snowden)	1	3	1		19
Osburn, Mary	3		2		
Oasburn, Archabald	2		2		1
Lucas, Jonathan	1	2	2		
White, Basil	3		3		
Lanham, Henry	3		4		
Pearce, Isaac	2		4		
White, Mary			3	1	
Graves, Lewis	1				2
Doras, Frank				7	
Graves, Benja	2	2	2		
Wilson, Jacob	2	1	1	5	
Stallens, Joseph	2		2		5
Bloin, William	1		2		
Atkins, Joseph	2		2		
Collins, Joshua	1	2	3		
Clarke, Thomas	2	2	4		
Tuell, Henry	1	2	4		
Free, Nicholas	2		2		
Lanham, Shadrack	2	1	3		
Tucker, William	2		2		
Collins, Zachariah	1		2		
Keeth, Richd	1	1	2		1
Collins, John	1		1		
Lanham, Henry, Junr	1	1	2		
Lanham, Nathan	2		3		
Crown, Joseph	2		1	3	
Beale, Robert	2		2		
Greentree, Benja	1	1	4		3
Harress, Aron	1	2	7		1
Beale, Zachariah	1		7		5
Beale, Jean	1		5		10
Harris, Zadock	1	4	5		5

MONTGOMERY COUNTY—Continued.

NAME OF HEAD OF FAMILY.	Free white males of 16 years and upward, including heads of families.	Free white males under 16 years.	Free white females, including heads of families.	All other free persons.	Slaves.
Trundle, Thomas	1	1	3		19
Moran, Perry	1	1	2		
Burch, Edward	1	2	3		
Wheatley, John	2	2	5		
Alby, Joseph	2	4	3		
Tracy, Philip	2	1	2		
Boland, Thomas	1	2	5		
Wade, Hezekiah	1	2	3		
Montgomery, Ignatius	1		3		
Davis, Mary	2		2		
Gladman, John	1		2		
Mitchell, Capt Jne	2		2	1	17
Jones, Henry	1		2		2
Terrel, John	1		2		
Thrasher, William	3	1	4		
Wallahan, John	2	1	3		
Lee, James	1	3	2		
Robertson, Alexr	2		5		
Beale, Richd (of Wm)	2		2		
Crushley, Richard	1				
Gadding, Joseph	1		1		
Gadding, Wm H	2	1	1		
Wilson, Thomas	3	1	5		
Summers, Dent	3		1		5
Tuell, Patrick	3	2	3		
Tuell, Roger	2	1	5		
Whaland, Michal	5		3		
Ledan, Nicholas	5	1	3		
Whaland, Matthew	1	1	3		
Nicholason, Richard	1	1	3		
Whaland, Nicholas	1	2	3		
Whaland, James	2		1		
Cohoc, Roger	1	1	2		
Haney, James	2	1	4		
Stutt, John	2		2		
Kesner, John	1	1	2		
Carroll, Daniel, Esqr	3		3		53
Leddean, Jno	1	2	2		
Ball, Richard	1	1	4		
Johns, Thomas	1	1			30
Richards, Jacob	1		2		
Richards, Matthias	1		1		
Syears, William	2	1	3		
Perry, Erasmus	1	4	5		22
Nicholls, Thomas, Senr	3	1	2		15
Harding, Edward	1	2	4		9
Harding, Basil	2	1	2		7
Duvall, Marun	2		2		5
Taylor, Ann			2		
Moore, William	1	1	5	1	4
Harding, Charles	2		1		
Bernard, Tho (Overseer for Kipburn)	1		2		27
Richards, Sarah			3		
Butt, Hasel	1		3		3
Litton, Michael	3	2	3		14
Wilcoxon, John	2	2	6		42
Swearengen, Thomas	2	3	6		21
Prather, Walter	1	3	4		4
Swearengen, Thomas, Junr					
Fields, George	1	1	1		
Swearengen, Obed	1	1	3		
Swearengen, Saml	1		2		3
Swearengen, Elenor	1	1	3		3
Norman, Catharine				6	
Hall, Joseph	1				
Willett, Edward	2	2	5		5
Harriss, Barton	2		1	3	
Harris, Nathan	1	2	3		
Austine, Thomas	1		4		
Linsted, Thomas	1				
Gatton, William	4	2	3		5
Fitzgerrold, John	1		1		
Beckwith, Charles	2		2		1
Potter, William	2		2		
Beckwith, George	2	1	1		
Prather, Aron	5	2	3	1	
Boyd, Susanah	1				
Boyd, Benje	1		2		2
Jennings, John	2	1	6		
Beckwith, William	3	1	2		9
Watson, Henry	5		2		8
Prather, Azariah	2	2	4		2
Croford, Robert	2		3		2
Ward, James	1	2	2		
White, Nicholas	1	4	2		
Higgins, James	2	1	4		10
Higgins, Benje	1		1		
Jones, Charles (of Jne)	2	2	5		1
Lynn, Elizr	1		2		12
Thompson, James	1	1	2		
Beale, Lloyd	3	1	7		10
Frank				2	
Brown, John					4
Hayse, James	1	1	1		
Butt, Rignal	1	2	4		

NAME OF HEAD OF FAMILY.	Free white males of 16 years and upward, including heads of families.	Free white males under 16 years.	Free white females, including heads of families.	All other free persons.	Slaves.
Gates, Edward	1	1	5		1
ODancil, Michael	2		3		
Williams, Barbara	1		1		11
Williams, William P	3				2
McDane, James	1	2	3		
Jordon, Ann		1	3		
Davis, John V	2	1	5		
Cashall, George	1	2	5		
Grant, William	2	3	3		
Butt, Aron, Junr	1		1		
Glass, Saml	5		1		
Shaw, Basil	2	1	1		
White, Alexander	1		1		
Moore, Mordeca	4	1	3		
Hocker, Nicholas	1	3	5		7
Hocker, Margaret			2		7
Sullivan, John	1		2		
Ridgeway, William	2		1	1	1
Knott, Thomas, Junr	2		1	1	1
Bryan, Richard	2		1		
Cyrus					6
Oliver, Joshua	1		2		
Jones, Edward	2	3	5		
Deckerson, Seratt	2	3	2		1
Warfield, Brice	3	3	5		3
Collins, Elijah	1		1		1
Collins, Thomas	1		5		
Winsor, Nary	1		2		
Pigman, Nathaniel	1	2	3		6
Walker, George	1	1	4		1
Readman, Francis	2	2	3		
Magruder, Zadock	1	2	7		26
Magruder, John B	1	1	1	2	5
Jordan, James	1	1	9		
Magruder, Jeffery	2		1		6
White, Ann	1	1	1		
Shaw, Stephen	1		1		9
Moses				4	
Coxon, John, Junr	1	1	1		4
Ricketts, Merchant	1	3	6	2	2
Ricketts, Nathan	1		1		
White, Samuel	1		2		14
Berry, Mildred			1		4
Adams, Edward	1	5	3		
Duntis, Dennis	2	1	1		
Woods, Thomas	2		2		
Tucker, William (W)	2		2		
Current, James	1	2	2		
Foyed, Lake	2				
Wilcoxon, George (Overseer for H. Easton)	1	1	5		11
Berry, Richard	2	3	8		18
Berry, Jeremiah (of Richd)	1		2		6
Beall, Archibald	1		2		8
Leek, John	1		1		1
Gardner, Thomas	2	3	3		
Seeders, Bennett	1	5	3		4
Weeden, William	1	1	3		3
Tolson, James	1	3	3		1
Ewell, John	1	2	5		
Mason, Archibald	1		2		1
Gaither, Samuel	1	2			
Stanton, Patrick	4	1	1	3	
Moore, Saml	1	1	3		
Orme, Philip	2	2	4		8
Evans, Basil	1		3		
Warfield, Zachh	1				1
Snell, George	5	2	1	1	3
Welsh, Richard	2	2	3		7
Beall, Edward	5	3	3		2
Bowan, John	1	2	5		
Anderson, Stephen	2		2		
Jones, Richard	1	1	2		3
Thomas, Evan	2	2	3		
Jackson, Joh	1		1	5	
Wilson, James	1		1		1
Bash, William				4	
Hennis, Sarah			4		
Peach, Samuel	1	1	1	2	
Dunahoe, Ann	2	1	4		
Connerly, Michael	2	4	5		
Connerly, John	2	5	4		2
Jarbo, Gerrard	2	3	3		1
Beall, Lawson	1		4		
Myers, Solomon	2	2	2		
Henry, Thomas	2	1	3	3	
Holmes, William	1	1	3		
Estep, Eliza, Junr	1	1	5		30
Estep, Eliza			5		
Pock, Felter	2	1	2		7
Armstrong, Will				7	
Reason				2	
Mitchall, Walter	2	4	3		
Mitchall, Morris	1	3	2		
Waters, Benje	3	1	4		5
Waters, Richd, Senr	1		1		3

NAME OF HEAD OF FAMILY.	Free white males of 16 years and upward, including heads of families.	Free white males under 16 years.	Free white females, including heads of families.	All other free persons.	Slaves.
Waters, Richd	1	1	3		
Brashers, Morriss	2		5		
Brashers, Morriss, Junr	1	2	5		
Waters, Thomas	3		1		5
Browning, Edward, Junr	2		4	1	
Browning, Edward	2	3	3	1	1
Tucker, John	2		4	1	
Mitchall, Nathan	1		1		1
Burton, Jacob	1		5		
Burton, Basil	2	2	7		
Lansdale, Walter	2	1	2		
Jackson, Nicholas	1		3		
Fossit, James	1		4		
Lazear, Thomas	3	6	2		
King, Alice			2		
Harvey, Allen	3	2	7		
Tempelton, John	1		1		
Westley, Humphrey	1		2		
Hopkins, Philip	1		2	6	
Fitzgerrold, Clement	1	1	6		
Pock, Philip	1		2		1
Marke, Robert	2		8		
Cheney, Henry	1	2	2		
Murphy, Joshua	2		1	1	
Virlinda					6
Case, James	1	4	1		
Wheeler, William	2	4	3		
Case, Shadrack	1	2	2		
Culver, Henry	1		3		16
Holmes, Essabella	1		7		16
Gladman, Michal	1	1	2		
Tomlinson, William	2	1	3		
Dunn, Benje	1		2		9
Dunn, Augustus	1	2	2		11
Berry, Jeremiah	2	4	4		10
Fightmaster, George	1	4	5		
Berry, Benjn	1	4	3		8
Thomas, Richard, Senr	2		1		54
Thomas, John	1	2	2	10	
Mills, Jesse	2		3		
Baley, Basil	1	1	5		
Bailey, Nicholas	2	2	2		
Sutton, Robert	2	2	5		1
Hedly, Jacob	2	1	2		
O'Neill, William	2		2		18
O'Neale, Wm, Junr	2		1		
Ward, John	2	3	4		
Henley, Wm					
Fisher, Martin	2	3	3	1	12
Fisher, Wm	1		2		8
Ducker, Jeremiah	1	4	3		13
Godman, Wm	1	1			1
Crown, Josh	2	3	4		
Aldridge, John	2	1	4		6
Burriss, Charles	2		4		2
Burriss, Thomas	1	3	6		
Ball, James	1	1	5		
Carter, Samuel	1		1		
Wallace, James	2	2	4		22
Magruder, Enrich	2	2	2		9
Wallace, William	3	2	1		9
Gittings, Benje	3		8		
Kesner, Henry	1	1	2		5
Kesner, Federick	1		1		
Beanes, John	1		5		
Colliar, Wm, Senr	2		3		5
Colliar, Wm, Junr	2	2	3		
Lezear, Abednego	1		5		
Ducy, Richd	1	3	5		2
Shearlock, James	1	1	1		6
Holt, Laurance	1	1	2		6
Wilson, Wm	1	1	2		5
Beall, Daniel	1		4		
Beall, Margaret			3		8
Wilson, Wm B	1		4		
Clagett, Nathan	1	3	1		
Magruder, Nathaniel (of N)	1	1	2		2
Whetzel, Frederick	2	2	6		
Spalding, Richd	2	3	2		
Spalding, Enuch	1	1		1	1
Jones, Michael				4	
Lewis, Richard	1				
Magruder, Joseph	1	3	5		13
Aulry, William	1		3		
Mudd, Wm, Senr	4		1		13
Magruder, George	1	2	1		5
Beale, Brooke, Junr	1		1		12
Nixon, Jonathan, Junr	1		2		7
Nixon, Jonathan, Senr	2		2		
Beall, Sarah	2		1		28
Nixon, Hugh	1	2	1		10
West, Sarah			1		
Beall, Tyson	3		5		
Hoskinson, John	4	1	5		1
Sims, Marmaduke	2	1	4		1

MONTGOMERY COUNTY—Continued.

NAME OF HEAD OF FAMILY.	Free white males of 16 years and upward, including heads of families.	Free white males under 16 years.	Free white females, including heads of families.	All other free persons.	Slaves.
Butt, Aron, Senr	1		2		1
Downs, Henry	2		5		
Madden, James	1	3	3		
Bowie, Allen	1		3		
Allison, Charles	3	2	3	3	30
Lane, Hardage	6	5	5		19
Sims, Joseph M.	2	1	2		5
Tucker, Thomas, Senr	3	1	4		7
Yost, Philip	1	3			
Ray, John	4		3		
Ray, Wm	2		2		6
Magruder, Basil	1	2			8
Wilson, Charity	2		3		20
Fitzgarrold, Edward	1	1	6		1
Edwards, Benja	3	3	6		17
Nalley, Saml	2	2	3		
Lanham, Aron	2	2	3		
Jones, Mary			5		12
Elliott, Richard	1	2	3		3
Beall, Benja	1	2	4		
Offutt, Zachh	1	2	4		15
Hennes, Benja	1	2	3		
Blacklock, Richard	1	1	3		
Greenfield, Thomas G.	1	1	3		4
Greenfield, Walter	1		4		
Greenfield, Charles	1		3		4
Culp, George	3	2	3		1
Clagett, Josiah	1				5
Clagett, Ann	2		1		8
Willett, Ninian	2	2	4		12
Moore, James	2		4		2
Chapell, Archibald	3		5		
Galworth, John	1	3	5		
Galworth, Gabriel	1		1		
Greene, Ann	1	1	3		1
Harben, Elisha	1	6	4		
Lewis, Absolum	2	2	4		
Offutt, Capt Nathl	1	4	4		
Offutt, Saml	4	4	8		12
Evans, Jane			3		2
ORiley, Henry	2				
Thompson, John	1	1	2		
Magruder, Levin	4		8		11
Davis, Walter	1	5	4		
Offutt, Zadock	1		4		
Offutt, Wm (of Ja)	1	3	4		4
Jones, Charles C.	3				
Langton, James	1		4		
Langton, Thomas	2				
Day, James	1				
Gassaway, Charles	3	6	6		5
Mollehone, Jas, Senr	3	1	3		15
Warthan, Henry	2		3		
Cissell, John	1	1	5		
Offutt, Thomas	2	1	2		
Offutt, George H.	1	5	1		5
Offutt, Wm, 3rd	1		1		11
Offutt, James (of Wm)	2	2	1		9
Peake, Thomas	1		2		
Garrott, Saml	1	2	5		
McCloud, Mary		3	5		
Easton, John	2	2	2		
Harpe, Josiah	1	2	3		
Harpe, Wm	2	1	6		
Ray, Benja	4	4	4		4
Heater, George	4	4	4		
Dowden, Zachariah	2	1	7		3
Moran, Joseph	1	3	3		
Straney, Nicholas	1		2		
Hill, John	1		2		
Hill, Susannah	1	6	2		
Wootton, Richard	1		2		24
Jones, Nathan	2	4	3		
Edmonstone, Thomas	2	4	3		7
Wheeler, Edward	1		4		18
Waters, Josephas B.	1	2	7		1
Browning, Jeremiah	1	3	7		
Jones, Evan	2	4	4		
ONeale, David	2	1	5		
Barnes, Joseph	1	4	6		10
Matthews, John	2		2		
Beall, Clement	2	1	2		12
English, King	1	2	3		
Valencear, Francis	1	2	3		
Ricketts, Wm	3	4	2		9
Golden, John	1	1	4		2
Sparrow, William	1	3	2		
Balley, John, Junr	1	3	6		
Gilham, Thomas	1	2	2		
Harper, John	1		2		
Leach, William, Junr	1		2		
Leach, William	3	1	6		
Craford, James	3		2		
Tucker, John, Senr	1	2	2		1
Dawkins, Thomas	2	1	2		
Chalmbers, Jno (of Wm)	1		2		

NAME OF HEAD OF FAMILY.	Free white males of 16 years and upward, including heads of families.	Free white males under 16 years.	Free white females, including heads of families.	All other free persons.	Slaves.
Briggs, Robt	2	1	4		
Quary, Henry	1	1	3		
Quary, Daniel	1	2	2		
Clifford, Hugh	1		3		
Allen, Alexr	1		3		
Bonifield, Saml	4	3	2		13
Bonifield, John	1	1	5		
Orme, Eli	1	5	6		
Hobbs, John	1	5	2		1
Henry, Johanah		2	5		
Trundle, Jos ah	1	5	7		
Jones, Westly	2	3	6		
Nicholls, Simon	2	1	3		6
Offutt, Eliz	2		3		
Austine, Zachh	2	2	3		14
Worland, Charles	1	2	3		9
Offutt, William	2	3	3		8
Dunn, William, Junr	1		3		
Dun, Wm, Senr	1		2		6
Wilmott, Thomas	1	2	4		2
Newton, John	1		4		7
Simmes, Joseph, Senr	1	1	4		5
Simms, Elexas	1		3		
Dent, John	1	2	6		
Beall, Kinsey	3		1		5
Randal, John	1		3		
Hobbs, Eliza		2	1		5
Beall, Joseph			3		5
Beall, Robert A	4	2	3		14
Beall, John	1	3	4		4
Beall, Zepheniah	1		4		11
Beall, Zeph (of Jams)	1		3		2
Cross, Thomas	3	1	6		
Mason, Alexr	1		3	6	5
Robey, Leonard		3	5		5
Robey, Berry	3	2	7		
Lazenby, Saml	3	1	4		
Fitzgerrold, John	1	2	3		
Holland, Mary			3		1
Willson, Alexr	3	1	3		
Shaw, Rebecca	2	1	1		6
Soaper, John	2	1	1		
Lazenby, Margreat			3		
Beall, Jereh (of Jas)	4		4		8
Clagett, John (of Thos)	2	1	8		10
King, Samuel	1		4		
Richard	1		2		
Elder, Johanah			2		
Hughs, Edward	2		4		
Caywood, Wm	2	1	1		
Langton, James, Senr	1		2		
Lansford, James	2		3		
Drane, Thomas	3	1	3		10
Parker, Wm	2		2		12
Busey, Saml	2	1	2		7
Busey, John	1	3			
Tucker, Walter	3		3		
Tucker, Erasmus	1		2		
Tompson, Agness			2		
Fling, James	1		4		3
Chalmbers, Wm T	2	2	4		1
Chalmbers, Henry, Senr	2	3	3		
Delleha, Thomas	3	3	3		
Duley, James	1	2	4		12
Stiles, Thomas	2		3		
Stiles, John	1		3		
Riley, Hugh	4	2	4		13
Greenfield, Thos S.	4		4		9
Pelly, Harrison	1		2		3
Goldsberry, Jonathan	3	1	2		7
Jarvis, Garrott	2		1		
Ogdon, Joseph	2		5		
Wood, Lashly	1	1	5		
Cloud, Abner	5	2	2		5
Smith, Ignatius	1		4		3
Lee, Daniel	1	3	4		
Lee, John	1		2		
Lee, James	1	4	2		
Stiles, Wm, Senr	1		2		
Alphin, Edward	1		4		
Prather, John S.	2	4	2		
Ellis, Philip	1		2		7
Gingle, George	1		2	12	
Craber, Philip	1	2	3		
Robinson, Basil	2	1	3		
Nicholls, Saml	3		5		
Camppell, John	2		4		9
Pritchett, Elias	2	3	5		
Braddock, Thomas	2	3	2		
Stallings, Fenenias	3	4	1		
Smith, David	1		2		
Collins, Hezekiah	1	2	2		
Lepoon, Francis		1	2		
Fenicks, John	2	2	5		
Wisener, David	2	2	2		
Collins, John	2		2		1

NAME OF HEAD OF FAMILY.	Free white males of 16 years and upward, including heads of families.	Free white males under 16 years.	Free white females, including heads of families.	All other free persons.	Slaves.
Murphey, John	3	1	4		
Offutt, James, Senr	2		4		25
Austine, Alexr	2		4		
Wade, William (P.)	1		2		3
Offutt, Mordeca	1	2	2		10
Ridgeway, Robert	2	7	7		
White, Joseph	2	1	2		7
Ridgeway, Isaac	2		2		
Fleming, John	1		2		2
Fleming, James	2	3	3		15
Robins, John	2		2		
Magruder, Margaret			1		
Duley, Barton	2	1	5		9
Magruder, Hezekiah	1		1		11
Ederstone, Thos (of Thos)	2	4	3		5
Smith, Hannah			2	5	
Ederstone, Wm	1	3	2		1
Clements, Francis	3		4		9
Bogle, Ann			2		
Steele, Wm, Senr	4	2	2		
Montgomery, Jno B.	3		2		
Sholds, Philip	3		2		
Wade, Abigeri			2		4
Baker, John	3		2		
Madden, Benja	3		2		
Garvis, Elenor		1	2		
Tounsend, Henry	1	1	3		13
Hously, Robert	2		3		
Hurdle, Robert	2	1	2		
Balding, Thomas	1		2		1
Bond, John	2		1		
Lee, Lucy			2	9	
Sparrow, Thomas	2	2	2		1
Sparrow, Jonathan	2	4	4		
Moland, Wm	2	2	4		
Sparrow, Solomon	1	2	5		
Clarke, Jemima			5		
McWear, Wm	1		5		
Magruder, Wm O	2		2		25
Scott, Thomas	3		2		8
Garner, Joseph	1	6	2		
Roberts, Margreat	2	4	1		9
Hawkins, Dorothy			2		19
Hawkins, John	1		1		
Hurdle, Susanah			1		
Southerland, Alexr	3		2		
Elliott, Saml	2	3	2		
Rose, Lunix	2	3	2		
Whitenhouse, Daniel	2		3		
Tophouse, Francis	1		4		
Linch, Patrick	2		4		
Gatton, Wm	2	3	2		
With, Andrew	2		3		
Scott, Walter	1	1	2		
Offutt, Thomas, Senr	1	3	5		9
Offutt, Levin	1		2		2
Magruder, Nathaniel	1		1		12
Magruder, Walter	1	1	1		7
Fields, Wm	1		4		
Carrol, Peter	1		2		
Casey, Daniel	1	2	2		
Griffith, George	1	2	3		
Dyer, Saml	1	2	4		
Dudley, Richd	2		4		
Shealds, Thomas	2	1	4		
Magruder, James	1		1		3
Tracy, Charles	1		4		
Tracy, Alexr	2	1	3		8
Soper, Charles	2		5		
Noc, Peter	2	2	3		8
Coombs, Leonard	1	2	2		1
Roberts, Richd	1	2	5		
Roberts, Rebecca	2	1	5		
Chalmbers, John (of H.)	1		3		
Ogden, Annanias	1		3		
Campbell, Alexr	3	2	5		
Campbell, John	1	1	4		
Mudd, Ann	2	1	1		3
Cross, Humphrey	2	1	2		
Elliott, Joseph	1		2		
Fagan, John	2		1		
Smith, William	1		3		
Evans, John	1	2	4		
Madden, John	2	6	5		
Butler, John	1		2		
Clarke, George	1		3		
Laws, William	1		1		
Barker, Jonathan	1		3		
Biggs, Saml	1	1	3		
Biggs, Henry	1		2		
Fields, Matthew	3		2		
Fields, Abraham (of Jn)	2	1	3		
Duley, John	2		3		
Boswell, Leonard	1		3		
Conway, Adderson	1	1	3		

MONTGOMERY COUNTY—Continued.

NAME OF HEAD OF FAMILY.	Free white males of 16 years and upward, including heads of families.	Free white males under 16 years.	Free white females, including heads of families.	All other free persons.	Slaves.
Cissill, James	1	1	1		6
Willson, Thomas	1	2	1		8
McCue, John	1	1	3		
Br.an, James	2	1	6		
Brusan, Richard	2	1	3		
Wheeler, Leonard	1	1	3		
Tramell, Samson (Quarter)					13
Barker, Annanias	1	1	3		
Marber, John	1	2	4		
Chaimbers, Ann			5		7
French, Benjˢ	1		2		
Beall, Brook					14
Donely, Bernard	1		2		
Cradock, Charles	1		1		
Murphey, Mary		6	1		
Ogdon, John	1	2	4		
Clagett, Samuel	1	1	2		7
Turner, Samˡ	3		4		20
Davis, Robert	1	2	2		
Lackland, James	2	2	3		6
Lanham, Richard	1	3	3		
Orme, Archabald	2	1	3		17
Kennedy, David	2		1		
Gaither, Johns	2	1	3		2
Threlkild, Jane			3		9
Nicholls, William	2				
O'Nel, John	2		6		
Pee, William	3	2	2		10
Allison, John, Senʳ	3	2	3		9
Fitzgarrold, Jnᵒ (Shoeʳ)	1		1		
Ogden, Mary			1		
Penifield, Thomas			1		
Ray, Joseph	1	1	1		
Austine, John	1	4	1		1
Pritchett, Wᵐ	1	1	5		
Smith, Sisseley	1		1		8
Smith, Joseph			3	3	
Taylor, John	1	1	5		
Jenkins, Josᵇ	1	3	1		
Kenda, John	2		2		
West, Richᵈ	1	1	2		2
Adams, Alexʳ	2		2		1
Clements, Bennett	1	3	3		
Connerly, Philip			1		6
Farmer, Richard	1	1	2		
Allison, James	3	3	2		
Gatton, Zachᵇ	1	2	7		
Smith, Nicholas	1	1	3		
Childs, Wᵐ	1	3	3		7
Allison, John, Junʳ	2				
Ford, Hezekiah	1	1	2		
Blaidlock, Thomas	1	1	2		10
Boone, Isaiah	5	2	5	2	
Brookes, Wᵐ	1		4		
Deselum, Moses	1	4	3		
Gatton, Lucy			4		
Magruder, Samˡ W	3	4	2		17
Ray, James, Senʳ	2		2		8
Cheshire, Burch	2	2	7		3
Adams, Stephen	3		4		4
Clements, Wᵐ	3	1	1		
Armsey, John	1	1	1		2
Cookendorfer, Michael	4		2		4
Boyer, John P	2	3	3		
Waggoner, Christian		1	4		
Ray, Mary			4		
Rumington, John	1	4	4		
Janes, Edward	1	2	4		
Needham, Wᵐ	1		1		
Nicholls, Henry	1	1	2		1
Gilham, Thomas (Miller)			4		
Roustage, Wᵐ	1		1		
Shaw, James	4	4	6		
Moore, Benjˢ	1	5	4		
Parker, Baron				5	
Oden, Elie	2		2		6
Noles, James	1	1	1		
Carroll, Elizᵃ		3	3		9
Harven, Nailer		3	1		1
Williams, Leonard	1	1	5		
Williams, Elizabeth	1	2	6		
Downes, Joseph	2		6		
Ratliff, Francis	1	2	4		
Cooke, Joseph	1		2		
Newton, Gabriel	1		3		
Newton, Archᵈ	2	4	3		
Newton, Clement	1		4		
Smith, Barton	1				4
Hoskinson, Elisha	2		2		
Ratliff, John	1		1		
Hill, Humphey				8	
Orme, Jeremiah	3	3	8		26
Wilson, Lancelot	8	1	5		
Wilson, Zadock	1	4	2		11
Lansdale, Isaac	1		3		4
Harriss, Nathan (N.W)	1		4		

NAME OF HEAD OF FAMILY.	Free white males of 16 years and upward, including heads of families.	Free white males under 16 years.	Free white females, including heads of families.	All other free persons.	Slaves.
Thorn, Thomas	1	3	2		
Black, John	3	3	4		
Woolf, John	1		2		
Rennolds, Ella			2		
Willson, Jnᵒ (of Henry)	1	3	2	5	2	3
Wilson, Verlinda	1		3		3
Biggs, Thoˢ	1	1	1		
Perry, Joseph	1	1	3		13
Hoskinson, Josiah	2	1	6		
Wilson, James, Junʳ	1		1	1	1
Beddo, Absolam	1	1	8		10
Daws, David	1	1	1		
Wilson, James	2	1	3		
Lanham, Stephen	1	1	1		1
Ray, James	1	1	1		
Soper, Charles, Senʳ	1		3		4
Selby, John	2	2	6		3
Ray, Wᵐ, Senʳ	1	1	4		
Ingleton, Joseph	1	1	3		
Ford, Rachel					3
Downs, Zachᵇ	1	4	4	2	
Percy, Joshua	1	1	3	6	
Marlow, Samuel	1	3	3		
Barnes, Richᵈ W	1	2	6		2
Gattrell, Joseph	2	3	2		7
Tylor, Jervis	1	2	2		
Beall, Samuel	1	3	2		5
Bill, Richard	1	2	2		
White, Benjⁿ	1	2	5		
Orme, Pressilla	1		2		7
Beggerly, David	1	2	8		
Beggerly, Henry	2	5	6		
Davidson, Henry	2				11
Duvall, William	1		2	1	3
Chapell, Thomas	1	1	4		1
Becraft, Benjˢ, Senʳ	2				19
Wilcoxon, Lewis					8
Gittings, Kinsey	1	1	1		
Belt, Leonard	1				8
Glass, William	1		2		2
Sullivan, Timothy	1	1	2		
Beall, Alexʳ	1	1	2		1
Beall, George, 3ʳᵈ	1	2	2		7
Nivet, Thomas	2	5	3		
Morriss, Randal	1	1	2		
Carman, Thoˢ	1	1	2		
Beall, Ann			2		8
Brown, John	1		2		
Beall, Colˢ George					20
Moore, George	1		1		26
Jones, Charles (C. D.)	1		1		
Diggs, William (of Jnᵒ)	2		1	1	41
Dennis, Jnᵒ	1	1	1		
Clarke, Hanah		1	3		
Audd, Joseph	1				17
Tuttle, Baptist	2	4	4		
Tucker, Joseph	2	1	4		
Collins, James	2	4	3		
Proctor, Thomas	1	1	1		
Cure, John	1	2	3		
Tuttle, Wᵐ	1	3	4		
Burch, Zaphaniah	1	5	4		
Cramphin, Thomas	2				32
Chessley, Thomas			3		29
Chesley, Alexʳ	1	1	3		7
Janes, Henry	1		3		7
Murdock, Jnᵒ, The Estate of					44
Turnbull, John	6	2	1		13
Offutt, Zaphaniah	1	2	3		5
Offutt, Sarah	1	2	4		2
Benton, Joseph	1	2	7		14
Benton, Wᵐ	1	2	7		2
Benton, Erasmus	1	2	2		1
Sedwick, Wᵐ	1	2	5		1
Sedwick, Jnᵒ	3	2	4		
Prather, Barach	1	3	7		2
Crown, Lanslot	1	2	3		
Mudd, Richard	1	3	4		6
Davis, John	1	2	2		
Worthington, Charles					7
Sansbury, Thomas	1	5	2		
Pigno, Nicholas	3	2	2		
Selbey, Thomas, Junior	2	6	6		1
McGrath, William	1				
West, Joseph	1	1	3		
Beckwith, John	1		5		5
Watts, John	1	2	3		9
Ricketts, Benjamin, Junʳ	1		1		9
Ricketts, Jacob	1	2	2		
Crown, Gerrard	1	2	3		
Ward, Joseph	1	2	2		2
Vinson, John	2	1	6		5
Wheeler, John H.	2		4		9
Fields, James	2	2	4		1
Pack, William, Senʳ	3	2	3		2

NAME OF HEAD OF FAMILY.	Free white males of 16 years and upward, including heads of families.	Free white males under 16 years.	Free white females, including heads of families.	All other free persons.	Slaves.
Williams, Nolinder			2		7
Warfield, John W	2	2	5		10
Thompson, William	3		4		
Belt, John					10
Mackall, Benjamin	1	2	7		5
Pack, Thomas			2		4
Penn, Benjamin D	1		2		5
Clagett, Joseph	1	2	2		7
Reeder, Simon	3	4			
Ellis, Zachariah	1		3		5
Medley, John B	3	1	1		7
McDermet, Patrick	2	4	4		1
Perry, Zadok	1	6	2		1
Fyffe, James	1		4		
Kelly, Joseph	1				7
Alnutt, James	1	1	3		4
Walter, David	4	1	6		8
Alnutt, Jesse	1	2	2		5
Martingale, James				5	
Dawson, Nicholas L.	2	3	4		6
Alnutt, Lawrence	1	3	7		6
Alnutt, James	1	3	4		8
Fields Abraham	6	2	4		
Thomas, David	2		4		4
Kelly, Benjamin	2		2		
Kelly, Thomas	2	1	1		6
Mackey, Priscilla		1	2		3
Rawlings, Thomas	1				6
Suter, George		2	2		
McCartey, Daniel	1	2	4		
Jones, John, 3ᵈ	1	2	7		3
Vears, Edward	1	1	3		3
Nears, Elijah	1	1	3		5
Scrivner, John	1	3	7		6
Leach, Thomas	2	4	6		
Waters, Basil	2			4	
Perry, Charles	2	2	6		17
Tayler, John	1	1	4		
Jones, John	1	3	2		
Wade, John	1		4		
Crawford, John Sutton	1	5	4		2
Norman, Basil				8	
Anderson, John	1	2	2		7
Malone, John	1	1	1		
Wallace, William					1
Bowie, Doctʳ John					1
Martin, Honore	3				
Summers, John	1		1	1	1
Simmons, Henry	1		1		
Willson, Thomas P.	1				
Beckwith, Samuel	2		3		
Hamilton, John G	3				
Forde, James	3				
Dayly, Bryan	2	2	3		3
Summers, Caleb	2	2	3		2
Richards, William	2	3	3		
Hopkins, Richard	1				
Jenkins, Philip	1	2	3		1
Hargarly, James	1				
Holland, Solomon	1				
Conner, Richard		1	3		11
Wilson, Joseph	2	2	3		3
Perry, James	1	3	6		12
Hays, George B	1	3	6		10
Jarrett, William	4	3	4		10
Hays, Leonard	1	2	3		2
Hutton, Joseph	1		2		
Thompson, John	1	1	2		
Corkeran, Joshua	1	2	3		
Bowman, George	2	4	2		
Thompson, Clement	1	1	1		
Holland, George	3		2		1
Samuel	2		2		
Chambers, Elizabeth			4	4	
Linthicum, Slingsbey		3	2		1
Johnson, John	1	1	3		
Johnson, Thomas	1	2	2		
Johnson, Thomas	2	1	5		2
Gee, George	1	1	4		
Gus, Joseph	1	1			
Macklefish, Richard	3		4		8
Holland, John	1	1	2		3
Tayler, Aguila	1		1		
Holland, John	1	1	2		1
Holland, Stephen		2			2
Gartrell, Sarah			2		7
Parsley, Thomas	1	2	3		
Gattrell, Aaron	2	3	3		15
Gattrell, Francis	3		4		
Shadburn, Ann			4		
Penn, John	4		4		
Welsh, Elizabeth	1	1	1	1	13
Musgrove, John	1	1	4		
Nicholson, Joseph	3				
Gaither, Henry	3	1			5
Shifty, Harman	3		3		
Moore, Robert	1		1		

MONTGOMERY COUNTY—Continued.

NAME OF HEAD OF FAMILY.	Free white males of 16 years and upward, including heads of families.	Free white males under 16 years.	Free white females, including heads of families.	All other free persons.	Slaves.
Prather, John	1				4
Gaither, Daniel	2				
Burriss, Henry	1	2	2		
Burriss, Charles	1	2	3		
Bevin, William	2		1		
Thompson, Henry	2	1	2		
Garner, Benjamin	2		3		
Garner, Peter	2	2	4		1
Garner, Benjamin	1	1	1		
Shearman, Richard	1	1	4		2
Bevin, Henry	2	3	4	1	7
Thompson, James	2	4	3		
Thompson, Henry	2	1	4		
Thompson, John	1	2	3		
Smith, Daniel	3	3	5		3
Hughes, Benjamin	2	1	4		
Redman, Jesse K.	1	1	3		1
Bowman, Jacob	3	2	5		2
Baker, John	2	6	2		
Stephens, Richard	4	2	3		
Collins, Thomas	3		4		
Davis, Thomas	1				6
Famare, Lawrence	1	2	2	1	
Blowers, Benjamin	1	2	4		
Welsh, Harmutel	1		5		14
Price, Richard	2	5	3		
Gee, David	2		7		2
Thomas, Ann			4		
Waters, Mary	1		2		10
Holland, Arnold	1	1	4		11
Eliett, John	3	1	6		
Brooke, Gerrard	1	1	1		5
House, James	2		2		
Lucas, John	1	3	3		
Chambers, John	2	2	5		3
Windsor, Basil	2	2	6		
Leach, William	2	3	5		
House, John	1	4	5		5
Barnett, William	1	1	5		2
Chambers, Josias	1	1	2		
Gray, John	1		4		
Fitzgerald, Walter	1				
Pigman, Joshua	2	2	3		1
Phips, William	2	1	3		
Machbey, Zachariah	1	2	7		
Barren, Rachael	1	4	3		
Redman, Benjamin	1	3	6		7
Pigman, Nathaniel	2	1	3		5
Pigman, Joseph	2		2		
Waters, Nacy	1		2		4
Peddicort, Jasper	5	2	5		
Crow, Edward	6	3	6		10
Crow, Mrs.	1		5		7
Saffell, Joshua	3	3	5		
Magruder, Ninian					4
Wilson Zadok	1		3		
Ricketts, John	1				
Green, John	1		4		
Green, Clement	2	1	2		1
Davis, Griffeth	2	2	10		
Davis, Levi	2	2	4		4
Kely, Benjamin	5		4		
Ricketts, Basil	1		3		1
Ricketts, Sarah	1		3		
Fish, William	2		3		
Davis, William	1	1	3		1
Davis, Charles	1	2	3		13
Cooke, Elizabeth	2	3	1		5
Lowery, William	3	1	3		1
Ricketts, Anthony	4		1		2
Morgan, Richard	1	1	3		1
Shearwood, John	1	1	3		
Easton, John	1	1	2		
Elliott, Jacob	1	3	3		
Easton, Giles	1	4	1		
Holland, Rachael				6	
Cooke, Nathan	3				11
Duke, William	2	4	8		
Dickerson, Zadok	1	3	3		6
Moore, Isaac	2		3		1
Collins, James	2	2	2		
Moore, Thomas	2		2		
Moore, John	3	3	2		
White, Joseph	2	5	4		
Belt, Sarah	1		4		2
Waters, Richard, Sr.	2	1	1		9
Waters, Doct. Richard	2	1	1		12
Carry, James	1	1	1		10
Dorsey, Joshua	1				12
Gray, Benjamin	1	2	5		
Gray, William	2	1	6		
Selbey, Thomas, Sen.	1	1	1		1
Selbey, Zachariah	1	4	1		
Cattero, Charles	2	1	4		
Adamson, John	1	2	3		1
Goulding, Samuel	1	1	5		
Hodge, Charles D.	1			2	30
Beall, James, of James	2	3	5		6
Dowden, Michael A.	3		1		5
Johns, Aquila	1				19
White, John	1		6		3
Ryan, William	1	1	4		8
Diggs, Edward	1				3
Garrett, John	2	3	1		11
Gartrell, William	1		4		
Darby, Samuel	1	4	4		
Darby, Caleb	1	3	3		2
Linthicum, Zachariah	4	1	7		8
Hempstone, Townley	1				
West, Thomas	4		2		
Poor-house	5		17		
Nicholls, Thomas	4	3	5		
Anderson, Bennett	1	2	1		
Valentine, George	1	2	1		
Wheat, Joseph	1	1	2		3
Case, Brock	2		3		
Catlett, Alexander	2	6	2		11
Brooke, Mary	1		6		7
Dorsey, William H.	4	3	5		18
Atkerson, John	1		1		
Thomas Richard, Jun.	2	1	2		16
Brooke, Basil	1		2		12
Howard, Thomas	2		6		
Marquiss, Ann	2		6		1
Howard, Jacob	3	1	3		
Beall, Brooke	1				
Artis, James	1	2	4		
Jordan, James	1	1	7		
Thompson, John F.	2		4		
Casey, Alice		1	5		5
Reed, Benjamin	2	3	2		
Fryer, Walter	1	4	4		1
Smith, Bennett	1	1	1		
Walkins, Leonard	1	3	2		
Trail, Osburn	1	2	3		
Poole, Joseph	2		3		
Poole, John	2	3	1		
Tucker, Jonathan	2		6		7
Higden, John	1	2	2		
Higden, Thomas	2	5	5		3
Case, Israel	2	6	1		
Hocker, William	1	2	4		4
Higden, Benjamin	2	3	4		
Magruder, Robert	1				8
Trail, James, Jun.	2	5	5		2
Miller, Christ.	1	3	3		
Hathman, George	3	1	4		
Clagett, John	2	2	2	1	1
Glaze, Charity			3		
James, Thomas	2	5	3		
Rawlings, Aaron	2	1	2		
Chiswell, Joseph N.	1	3	8		7
Stimpson, Solomon	1	1	2		15
Dunn, Hugh S.	1		3		2
Tomlin, Hessey		1	3		
Hays, Levy	2	4	2		
Welsh, William	2	1	1		
Truman, Aaron	1	1	3		17
White, Walter	1	4	4		
Warren, John	1	1	2		3
Smith, James	1	1	2		
Smith, George	1	1	1		
Plummer, Zepheniah	1	2	2		
Money, Abraham	2	5	3		
Jones, Sarah	1	4	2		23
Jones, Benjamin W.	1		1		
Cawood Stephen	2	6	5		2
Luckett, David	2	1	3		12
Fowler, Jeremiah	2	2	8		28
Harriss, Edward	1	1	3		
Williams, John	1	1	3		
Roads, Charles	1		2		
Burnes, William	1	2	3		2
Myers, John	1	1	3		
Gaskins, John	1	2	4		
Wheeler, Samuel H.	2	3	3		18
Allison, Mrs.	2		2		6
Allison, Hendry	1		2		8
Knott, Basil		1	2		
Hickman, Joshua	1	1	4		4
Fowler, Elisha	1	1	4		7
Clements, Bennett H.	3		2		5
Bullin, Priscilla			5		
Beard, Jane			3		5
Knott, James	1	1	3		4
Yates, Robert	1	2	6		
Kno bs, John	1		1		
Williams, Rezin	1	1	3		
Yates, Thomas	1		3		4
Beall, Thomas B.	1	4	2		6
Evans, John	1	1	2		
Russell, Henry	1	1	5		
Huff, Robert	2		3		
Smallwood, William	2	6	3		
Wright, George	1		3		
Knott, James	1		2		
Miles, Benjamin	1	1	4		1
Wheeler, Henry	1	1	4	3	
Collyer, William	3	5	3		
Tucker, Randal	1	4	3		
Neill, Barton	2		6		
Atchison, William	3		3		
Swan, Susanna			1	2	2
Allison, Samuel	1	2	2		
Hardey, Fielder	1	1	3		
Williams, Rezin	1	1	3		
Green, Robert	1	1	4		1
Hocker, William	3	1	3		1
Coats, Robert H.	1				
Trundle, Thomas	2	4	4		9
Green, Philip	3	4	4		5
Hunter, Joshua	2	1	3		
Byrn, Matthias	1	3	2		4
Barlow, Zachariah	1	2	3		1
Hickman, Elihu	1				6
Edwards, John	3		3		1
Ogden, Mary	1		3		1
Wilkerson, William	1	3	2		11
Ogden, Charles	1		2		
Newman, William			1	3	
Shelton, Clementine	2	2	3	1	
Shelton, Joshua	2	1	4	1	1
Mathews, Thomas	1		1		
Newman, Benjamin	1				10
Ellis, Shadrick	1	2	3		
Myers, Conrod	1	1	1	1	
Greene, Benedict	1		4		
Green, Thomas	2	1	5		
Collins, Elizabeth			2		
Campbell, Aenias	1				5
Atchison, Samuel	1	1	2		
Wood, Zepheniah	3	1	1		3
Palmere, Elijah	2		1		
Wilson, George	1	4	4		
Riggs, Thomas W.	2	1	7		
McGlauchlin, Henry	1	1	4		
Trail, Francis	1	2	2		8
Birdwhistle, Thomas	6	3	3		8
Murphey, Thomas	1	1	4		
Lone, Thomas	2	1	4		
Jones, Margaret	2		4		
Williams, Jacob	2	1	5		9
Williams, Samuel	2	1	5		
Smith, William	1		3		11
Veirs, John	2	1	1		7
McDade, Daniel	2	3	6		
Doraty, Philip	2	3	6		
MDade, John	1	3	2		
Thompson, John B.	1	5	3		
Perry, John	2	5	3		5
Brashears, Charles	1	1	3		7
Waters, Isaac	1	4	6		
Jones, John	3	1	6		1
Allison, Posey	1	3	3		
Hocker, Samuel	2	4	4		
Dawson, Thomas	2		2		11
Dade, Townsend	1	1	1		4
Knott, Lewis	1		1		
Knott, Cuthbert	1				
Vears, Elisha	1	1	2		2
Street, Francis	3	2	3		
Drake, Robert	2	2	1		
Umpstead, Abraham	1		1		
Gott, Richard	1	1	1		9
Harriss, Samuel	2		2		5
Wilson, Robert	2		3		3
Johnson, Samuel	2	3	4		2
Nicholls, William	2		3		
Dyson, John B.	1		2		
Nicholson, Nicholas	1		2		
Mitchell, Ninian	1		2		
Heighton, Joseph	2	4	4		6
White, Benjamin	2		2		
Riggs, Ruth	2		3		
Heighton, Josiah	1		2		
Reneger, Joseph	1	2	2		
Hilton, Andrew	1		2		
Kenada, Morgan	1			1	
Murphey, Dunkin	1		2		
Wilson, Mathew	3	3	3		11
Wilcoxen, Jesse	3	3	2		
Richards, John	2		4		
Carlisle, Daniel	2	3	4		
Benfield, Samuel	2		4		
Plummer, Jeremiah	2	4	6		
Rincy, John	2	4	4		
Hilton, Moneca	1		1		1
Murphey, Francis	1	4	1		
Wathan, Gabriel	2		2		
Wathan, Edward	2	2	2		3
Allin, Thomas	1				

MONTGOMERY COUNTY—Continued.

NAME OF HEAD OF FAMILY.	Free white males of 16 years and upward, including heads of families.	Free white males under 16 years.	Free white females, including heads of families.	All other free persons.	Slaves.
Howard, George	5	1			9
Hays, Notley	1		2		2
Wivell, Edward H	3	1	4		
Ennis, John	1	3	5		
Harriss, John	1	1	2		1
Burnes, John	1	1	2		2
Wathan, Ignatius	4	5	6		
Norress, Solomon	1	3	3		5
Bennet, James	3		1		
Harriss, Nathan	2	3	3		1
Harriss, Joseph	2	2	3		1
Hilton, James	1		3		
Harriss, Barton	1	1	2		2
Hays, Thomas	2	4	5		
Hays, Richard	1	1	3		
Griffeth, Zadock	2	3	4		
Tayler, Richard	3	2	2		
Nelbours, Nathan	4	3	3		
Hays, Elizabeth		2	5		2
Hays, Thomas	1	2	2		
Duckett, Isaac	2	4	4		
Nelbours, Fleet	1	1	2		
Burch, Jesse	1	1	2		3
Wilcoxen, William	2	1	1		8
Owen, Anny	2	1	2		9
Veach, Nathan	1		2		
Hilton, William	1	2	4		1
Talbert, James	1		2		
Talbert, Thomas	2	2	5		
King, William	2	3	6		
King, Enoch	1		1		
Sarjent, John	1	4	1		1
Hemstead, Christian	1		1		
Wilson, Hezekiah	2		3		1
Mahar, Daniel	1	2	2		
Jones, Hamsbury	1	1	2		
Douglass, Samuel	3	3	5		3
Medley, John L	1		2		2
Cowley, Henry	1		2		1
Alhorn, John	2	1	2		
Thompson, Basil	2	2	1		
Hoggins, Peter	3		5		4
Shaw, John	1	3			
Williams, Thomas	1	1	2		
Self, John	1	1	2		2
Trale, John	1	1	5		
Riggs, John	2	2	4		
Davis, Joseph	1	1	1		
Harbin, Joshua	1		6		
Edwards, Samuel	1		2		
Ray, Nicholas	3	4	5		8
Hoggins, John	1		2		
Davis, Ephraim	2	1	6		
Adams, John	2	1	2		
Young, Adam	2		4		
Clagett, Ninian	1	2	3		7
Medley, Mary			4		
Perry, Hannah	3		3		7
Fennell, Stephen	1	1	1		
King, George	1	2	1		
Head, Ignatius	1		1		
Bryan, Dennis	1		1		
Berditt, Samuel	1	2	2		
Smith, Basil	2	2	5		
Berditt, Benjamin	2	1	4		
Holland, Mary	1		2		
Harriss, Josiah	2		3		
Poole, Basil	2	2	7		
Holland, Nathan	1		1		
Barber, John	5		4		2
Barber, John	1	1	2		
Holland, William	3	1	3		1
Holland, Richard	1	3	3		
Perry, William	1		1		
Mobley, Archibald	1	2	2		
Mobley, William	1	2	2		
Walker, Elisha	1	2	1		
King, Edward	1	2	4		11
Miles, Charles	1	2	4		
Mobley, Levin	1	2	3		
Mobley, William	1	2	4		
Browning, Verlinder	1	1	4		1
Shelton, Thomas	1	2	3		
Lewis, Jeremiah	2	3	4		
Watkins, Nicholas	1	3	4		
Lewis, Margaret			1		
Summers, Paul	1	1	4		
Lee, William	1	1	3		
Lewis, Stephen	1	1	3		
Potter, William	1	1	3		1
Ellis, John	1	3	6		
Harvey, William	2	3	6		
Beall, John	1	6	3		
Winrot, Francis	1	5	5		
Harvey, Charles	1	1	4		
Richards, William	3	1	6		
Browning, Jona, Junior	2	5	4		

NAME OF HEAD OF FAMILY.	Free white males of 16 years and upward, including heads of families.	Free white males under 16 years.	Free white females, including heads of families.	All other free persons.	Slaves.
Browning, Jona	5	1	1		1
Browning, Archibald	1	2	2		
Browning, Elias	1		5		
Hinton, Thomas	1	6	4		
Laton, Alsford	1	1	1		2
Laton, Uriah	1	4	1		
Hinton, William	1		1		
Turner, John	1		3		
Eades, Jacob	1	2	2		
Soper, Basil	2	4	6		2
Hobbs, Samuel	2	3	0		1
Bradford, Barsheba		1	2		
Riley, Zachariah	1	2	4		
Fields, John	1	1	3		
Holland, William	1	1	5		1
Barnes, Thomas	2	4	4		
Lewton, Isaac	1	3	5		
Riley, Jeremiah	2	1	2		3
Batson, William	1		2		
Collins, Edmund	1				
Murrey, John			1		
Moobey, Enoch	1	2	1		1
Merkbey, Brock	1	1	5		1
Griffeth, Benjamin	2		3		6
Plummer, Philemon	1		2		6
Hungerford, Charles	1	1	7		29
Waters, Zachariah	2	2	2		10
Redman, Charles	2		2		
Redman, William	1	3	4		1
Greene, Richard	1	1	6		10
Crow, Samuel	2				8
Dyson, Samuel	1	3	5		7
Darby, Basil	1	1	2		7
Griffeth, Joshua	2	1	3		4
Griffeth, Henry	1				18
Griffeth, Henry, 3d	1	2	1		17
Griffeth, Samuel	2	6	3		8
Gaither, Beale	1				1
Gaither, Gerrard	2	1	1		1
Evely, John	1	3	1		
Burriss, Basil	1	2	4		1
Smith, Thomas	2	1	2		
Flood, Philip	1	1	3		
Duvall, Frederick	1	3	3		
White, John	1		1		2
Boran, Thomas	1	1	2		
Lowry, Dennis	1	2	3		
Beall, Alexander	3	4	7		
Harvey, Basil	2	4	3		
Turner, Daniel	1	2	3		
Lazier, Henry	1	2	6		
Frizzell, Jacon	1	4	1		
Lazier, Jacob	1	1	4		
Watkins, Jeremiah	3	1	2		2
Penn, Edward	2	1	4		5
Rigney, Terence	2	1	4	3	
Barney, James	1	1	2		
Cane, Thomas	2		2		
Whelan, Daniel	1	3	2	1	12
Haden, George	2		2		10
Purdey, Richard	2		3		10
Riggs, Samuel	2	6	5		10
Riggs, Thomas	1	1	1	6	1
Riggs, John	2		2		7
Penn, Caleb	4	2	3		
Penn, John W	1	2	1		5
Hillary, Henry	1	1	1		15
Lyles, Richard	1	2	3		11
Dorsey, John	1	1	1		
Read, Thomas	2	1	3		8
Weeden, Thomas	4	2	4		
Crow, Joshua	3	2	2		6
Waters, William	2		3		11
Aldridge, Thomas	2		3		13
Jones, Richard	1		4		8
Willett, Edward	2		3		
Musgrove, Nathan	3	1	5		17
Dyson, Mattox	2		3		2
Dyson, Bennett	1	1	2		
Ricketts, Thomas	1	1	3		
Vinson, William	1	3	4		2
Warren, George	1	2	2		1
Gatton, Richard	1	2	3		
Kirk, Thomas	2	2	2		2
Kirk, Thomas, Junior	2	2	2		
Kenny, David	1	2	4		
Daley, John	1	1	2		
Dyson, Philip	1	3	4		1
Porter, Nathaniel	1		2		
Gaither, Martha			2		7
Veirs, William	1	1	3		10
Callyhorn, John	4	1	2		
Mulliken, Archibald	2	5	4		1
Veirs, Hezekiah	1	3	5		1
Hoyle, Leonard	1	3	5		
Dyson, Basil	3	2	4		1
Compton, Joseph	2	2	3		

NAME OF HEAD OF FAMILY.	Free white males of 16 years and upward, including heads of families.	Free white males under 16 years.	Free white females, including heads of families.	All other free persons.	Slaves.
Spencer, James	1	2	2		4
Mitchell, Ninian	1	1	5		
Magruder, George	1	1	2		3
Tennely, Josiah	1	1	2		9
Warren, Mary			2		
Thompson, Basil	2	2	2		15
Lewis, William	3	2	5		
Brunner, Peter	1	2	4		
Morton, Thomas	1	1	1		16
Hope, William	1	1	4		
Barney, James	1		1		
Norriss, William	1	1	3		6
Reed, Alexander	1	1	4		
Reed, George	1		2		1
Reed, John	2	2	1		3
M⁰Dade, Patrick	2	2	1		
Veach, Hezekiah	2	1	4		3
Deakins, Francis	1		1		12
Talbott, Charles	1	1	1		
Marstiller, Nicholas			1		
Walker, Thomas	2	2	2		
Willett, Griffeth	2	3	3		2
Harwood, Samuel	1	2	4		17
Luckett, Levin	1	2	2		14
Pearce, Peter	1		1		
Lanham, Catharine			3		
Trundle, John	2	4	5		16
Hogan, Elizabeth		1	1		
Jears, William	2	1	1		
Veach, John	3		3		
Roach, Richard	2	1	3		
Belt, Carlton	2	3	3		22
Hardey, Ashford D	1	1			4
Beall, Levin	2	1	2		7
Wilson, Wadsworth	2		1		10
Veach, Thomas	4		3		7
Hoskinson, Josiah	1	4	5		
Hoskinson, George	1				
Horkins, George	3	2	3		1
Brashears, Charles	3	3	3		4
M⁰Dade, Patrick	2		2		
Bird, Francis	1		2		6
Dyson, Erasmus	1	1	3		2
Swann, Israel	1		3		5
Gatton, James	3		3		5
Gatton, John	1	2	1		
Wood, John	1		3		
Reed, Jonathan	1	3	4		1
Phillips, Jesse	2	2	3		1
Hoskins, Hugh	2	4	4		
M⁰Dade, Philip	1	2	2		
Read, James	1	1	1		1
Williams, John	4	1	1		
Harding, Edward	1	1	2		
Shekle, John	1	2	2		
Cowley, Thomas	3	3	5		6
Young, John	3	3	1	6	7
Southerland, Alexander	1		4		
Lingenfilder, Michael	1	3	2		
Broome, Thomas	2	1	1		9
Thomas, Hezekiah	1		4		12
Stone, Nehemiah	1	1	3		10
Peerce, William G	1	1	5		10
M⁰Dade, John	1		2		
Gentle, Stephen	3		3		
Yates, John	1	2	2		2
Rayman, William	1	1	1		4
Wayman, John	2	1	1		6
Lovelace, Alkana	1		3		
M⁰bride, Lazarus	2	1	3		8
Williams, Walter	1	2	1		8
Magruder, Zadok	2	2	4		10
Hickman, William	2	4	6		20
O Neall, Lawrence	1				
Higdon, Peter	1				
Marlow, James			1		
Dowden, Mary			3		3
Harding, Elias	3		2		14
Harding, Nathan	1	1	2		5
O Neale, Henry					8
Whittaker, Alexander	3	4	5		28
Curry, Thomas	2	1	4		
Harwood, John	2	3	4		14
Quynn, John	1	1	2		2
Shekles, John	1	2	4		
Shekles, Abraham	1	3	1		1
Shekles, Richard	1	2	2		
Beard, John	2	3	3		4
Dyson, Roswell	2		4		2
Compton, William	1	4	1		8
Compton, John	2	4	1		8
Burgess, Philip					
Hickman, Elizabeth	2	2	4		5
Pearce, John B	2	1	4	4	10
Thomas, Martin	2	1	4		
Spates, Robert	2	2	4		
Smith, Samuel	2	7	3		

MONTGOMERY COUNTY—Continued.

NAME OF HEAD OF FAMILY.	Free white males of 16 years and upward, including heads of families.	Free white males under 16 years.	Free white females, including heads of families.	All other free persons.	Slaves.
Beeding, Edward......	3	2	4		
Fisher, Martin.......	2	2	1		2
Collins, Richard.....	2	1	3		
Piles, James........	2	1	5		5
Beall, Robert.......	1	2			1
Beall, Thomas.......	1		4		3
Walker, Thomas.....	2		2		
Hickman, Joshua....	1	1	2		
Fletcher, Thomas....	3	2	4		18
Beeding, Thomas....	5		4		3
Grace, Mary........	1	1	1		
Beeding, Joseph....	1	4	3		6
Knobbs, George....	1	1	2		
Fletcher, Ann......			1	3	
Trammell, Sampson..	1	2	3		11
Athen, Samuel......	1	2	3		
McDade, Daniel.....	1	3	3		
Fletcher, George....	2	2	5		
Walter, Levi.......	1	1	4		
Stephens, James....	1	2	5		4
McGinnis, Neill.....	2	5	3		8
Hickman, Jesse.....	1	1	3		14
Davis, Baxter......	1	2	4		
Steell, James......	2	1	5		
Lovelace, Zadock...	2		3		
Gentle, Stephen....	3		2		
Gentle, Mary.......	1		3		
Watson, Alkana.....	1		6		
Greenwell, Robert..	1	2	3		
Bardey, Elijah.....	2		3		3
Steel, Arthur......	2	2	5		
McIntosh, William..	1		2		
Jefferson, Joshua..	1	1	5		
Hickman, Henry....	1	1	2		2
Ashin, William.....	1	1	1		1
Jewell, Basil......	1		2		
Walter, John......	2	1	2		8
Tracey, Osburn....	1		2		8
Broadhead, Thomas.	1		1		10
Bowie, Peter......	3				
Galloway, Samuel...	1	3	3		
Atwood, James.....	2	1	4		5
Norriss, Mary.....		1	2	2	5
Dennis, William...	1		1	3	
Steele, William...	1		2		
Jarboe, Ralph.....	1		2		5
Jarboe, Joseph....	1	2	4		3
Poore, Nicholas...	1		3		
Meloy, John......	1		2		13
Tucker, Elizabeth..		1	4		
Lovelace, Reazon...	1	2	2		
Hall, Aquila......	1	3	3		1
Ellett, Mark......	1	1	3		
Elrbin, Elias.....	2	2			
Higgins, John.....	1		1		3
Ellett, Mark......	3		2		9
Houser, Lewis.....	1	1	3		1
Dawson, Robert D..	1	4	3		7
Steel, Samuel.....	1	2			
Douglass, George..	1		2		
Shekles, Richard..	1	2	3		11
Burttes, Andrew...	2	1	3		2
Bevely, Rhoda.....	1	1	1		
Mookbey, Zephaniah	1	1	2		37
Tucker, Richard...	1	1	2		29
Cross, Benjamin...	3	2	2		
Wimsatt, James....	2	2	3		
Mollehorn, James..	2	1	5		1
Koontz, Jacob.....	2	1	2		
Locker, Mary.....	2		2		
Fry, Godfrey.....	1	3			
Berttes, Benjamin..	1	2	8		
Leeke, John......	1				1
Sullivern, Cornelius.	1	4	4		
Leeke, Joseph, Junior.	2	1	5		2
Boswell, Nicholas..	2	2	4		1
Burgess, Edward...	2	1	1		
Thompson, Moses...	2	2	3		
Darby, Ann.......	1		2		11
Anderson, Stephen.	1	1	1		1
Anderson, James...	1	1	1		
Grafton, Thomas...	3	2	1		
Brown, John A....	3	2	1		
Leeke, Joseph....	1	1	5	1	1
Leeke, Elizabeth..	1		1		1
Brown, James.....	1	1	1		
Mullikin, Basil...	1		1		4
Anchor, Snowden..	1	3	4		
Dryer, James.....	3		1		
Hawse, Michael...	2	2	5		
Buxton, John.....	2	2	4		1
Buxton, William..	2	2	1		1
Buxton, Thomas...	3	3	3		
Ducker, Nathaniel.	2	3	3		10
Hocker, Philip....	2	3	6		4
Candler, Daniel...	2		2		3
Dorsey, Nicholas W.	2	3	2		14
Cattero, Joseph....	1		2		
Green, Hugh.......	3	1	3		
Griffeth, Charles G.	1		1		23
Griffeth, Howard..	1	2	3		5
Barrett, Mary.....	2		2		
Riggs, Amon......	5	3	3		4
Johnson, Richard..	5	1	3		
Griffeth, Greenbury Sr.	2		2		4
Purdom, James....	1	2	2		
Carrico, Peter....	1	2	4		
Greene, Peter.....	2	1	1		
Newhouse, John...	3		1		
Newhouse, Benjamin.	2				
Newhouse, Thomas..	1	1	4		
Newhouse, William.	1	1	4		
Griffeth, Hezekiah.	1	4	4		5
Holmes, John.....	1	1	7		15
Almett, John.....	1	1	1	2	
Hathman, John....	1	4	7		2
Holland, Joel.....	1	3	3		
Freeman, Samuel...	2		2		1
Talbott, John.....	1		1		
Litchfield, John..	2		2	1	1
Purdom, John.....	2	2	6		
Fitzgerald, William.	2	1	9		
Purdom, Walter...	1	1	1		
Johnson, Benjamin.	2	5	3		1
Cahoe, William...	3		5		
Johnson, Benjamin.	2	1	2		7
Walker, Elizabeth.		1	4		
Nicholson, John...	1	4	6		
Loyd, Jeremiah....			2		
Wellins, John.....	2	4	4		
Bennett, Joshua...	4		3		
Summers, John....	1	2	4		
Wathan, John.....	3	1	6		
Judy, George J....	1	1	3		
Judy, Winebark...	1	1	3		
McAtee, Francis...	1	1	2		2
Burnes, William...	1	2	3		2
Howard, Greenbury.	1	2	2		2
Howard, Susanna..	1		2		2
Johnson, John....	2	5	4		3
McAtee, William..	1		3		
Ennis, Mary......	1		4		
Hoggins, Richard..	1	1	1		
Ray, Thomas.....	1	1	3		
Price, William...	2	2	3		5
Clary, Ashford...	1		2		2
Mills, Thomas....	1	1	5		
Wathan, Barton...	2	4	4		
Watson, Eley.....	2	3	2		1
Knott, William...	4		3		8
Knott, Zachariah..	2	6	4		4
Hoggins, Richard..	2		5		7
Sprigg, Frederick.	3	1	4		8
Simmons, Samuel, Junr.	1		1		
Wayman, Thomas..	1	5	3		1
Perry, Joshua....	1		3		6
Campdon, Joseph..	2	3	3		2
Sprigg, Samuel...	3	3	5		3
Wathan, John W...	1		3		
Wathan, Nacy....	1	2	2		
Wathan, Joseph...	1	2	3		
Miller, Thomas...	1		2		
Howard, Ann.....	1	2	3		6
Chiswell, Stephen N.	1		1		10
Hickman, Benjamin.	3		1	1	
Howard, Charles..	1		1		1
Whitter, William.	1		1		
Whitter, Henry...	1		1		
Judy, Henry.....	1	3	3		
White, Nathan...	1	1	1		9
Rittenhouse, Nicholas.	1	1	3		
Hardgrave, John..	2	2	4		
Douglass, Goodshall.	1		1		8
Higdon, John.....	1	1	2		
Cawood, Stephen..	1		2		
Lowe, Catharine..	2	3	3		
Joseph, Joseph...	3	1	6		5
Northcraft, Volinder.	1	1	5		9
Northcraft, Edward.	2	2	4		
McVey, Ninian...	2	2	7		
Davis, Lodowick..	2	1	3		3
Gittings, Thomas..	2		3		1
Redman, James...	1	3	2		
Appleby, Sarah...	2	2	5		
Reed, John......	1	2	2		7
Leech, Leonard...	2	2	3		
Callihorn, John...	5	1	2		
Penn, Charles....	5	2	3		
Burgess, John....	2	3	3		7
Parker, Fielder..	1	3	6		
Hopp, John......	1	2	5		
Dulany, Michael..	1	1	2		
Willett, Benjamin.	1	2	7		1
Johnson, Richard..	1		3		
Darbey, John.....	1		1		
Grendell, Thomas..	1		4		
Warfield, Levin..	2	1	4		3
Davis, Forrest...	1	1	5		
Rittenhouse, Samuel.	1				
Merryman, John...	1	2	3		1
Pigman, Ignatius..	3	1	5		1
Davis, Jeremiah..	2		2		1
Wilcoxen, William.	2	1	2		1
Wilcoxen, Josiah..	1	1	3		
Legg, Charles....	1	1	3		
Stewart, William.	2	3	5		
Lanham, William.	2	3	5		
Cox, Abraham....	2	3	5		
Palmore, Mary....	1	1	4		
Sheets, Henry....	1	1	2		
Davis, Charles...	1	4	3		
Duvall, Lewis....	2	4	5		6
Plummer, Joshua..	1		3		1
Bryan, Edward...	1	1			
Penn, Benjamin...	2	1	9		
Duvall, Levi.....	1	4	2		
Owen, John......	1	2	3		
Owen, Hezekiah..	1	2	2		
Hines, Ann......			2		
Story, Henry....	1				1
Moxley, William.	2		4		2
White, Samuel...	2	2	4		
Shively, Michael..	3		3		1
Penn, Shadrach..	3		2		
Summers, Hezekiah.	2	3	4		10
Mansfield, George.	3	1	3		10
Holland, William.	1	2	3		4
Poole, John.....	1		2		
Todd, Basil.....	1	2			
Norwood, James..	3		2		1
Poole, Samuel...	1	1	2		
Barnes, Mrs.....	1	1			
Roberts, Basil...	1		1		8
Hinton, John....	1	1	2		
Hinton, Mishok..	1	1	2		
Anderson, Charles.	4		2		
Hinton, Shadrach.	1		2		
McClain, William.	2		3		9
Clarey, John.....	2				
Ward, Edward...	4	3	5		1
Free, Alexander..	1	3	4		
King, John......	2	1	4		1
Coffee, John D...	1	3	3		3
Clarke, John....	4	3	5		2
Waters, Godfrey..	1				1
Waters, Joseph...	3	2	4		4
Hinton, Thomas..	2		2		
Cash, John......	5		2		
Cash, William...	2	3	2		
Nicholls, Archibald.	2	2	2		2
Cecill, Kinsey...	1		1		
Boyer, Peter....	1	1	2		
Price, William..	2	1	2		5
Cash, Richard...	3	4	2		
Cecill, Archibald.	1	1	3		
Dayly, John.....	1	1	5		
Anderson, Charles.	1	1	2		
Henley, Teale...	1	1	1		
Arnold, ———....	1				
Wilson, John....	3	2	5		17
Wilson, Jonathan.	1				10
Lashley, George..	2		6		
Harriss, Joseph..	1	1	2		2
Norriss, William.	2	1	3		2
Hardesty, Samuel.	1	1	5		14
Smith, Mary....	1		5		
Knewstab, Thompson.	1	1	5		8
Newton, John....	1		2		
Moore, Mary....	1		2		13
Briscoe, Roberts.	1		1		9
Ricketts, Anthony, Junr.	1	6	3		2
Wilson, Alexander.	1	2	6		
Brooks, Henry...	2	1	5		20
Burgess, Edward..	2	1	5		19
Boyd, William...	1	1	1	1	
Pope, Edward...	2	1	1		
Culver, William..	1	1	1		4
Trail, Archibald..	1	3	2	1	2
Trail, James....	1	1	1		5
Burgess, Ephraim.	1		5		2
Fulks, William..	2	1	3		
Fulks, Baltus....	1		1		
Lingenfilder, Valentine.	1		4		
Ricketts, Joseph..	1	2	3		
Robey, Zadok...	1		1		
Murphey, Darbey.	1	1	4		
Selbey, Richard..	2	1	4		
Peake, Hezekiah..	2	1	5		
Ricketts, Richard.	1	2	5		6

MONTGOMERY COUNTY—Continued.

NAME OF HEAD OF FAMILY.	Free white males of 16 years and upward, including heads of families.	Free white males under 16 years.	Free white females, including heads of families.	All other free persons.	Slaves.
Holland, Benjamin, Junr	2	3	6	..	1
Holland, Benjamin, Senr	2	..	1	..	..
Hackett, Philip	3	..	..	..	..
Lowe, David	2	1	2	..	3
Needham, William	1	..	4	..	..
Downes, William	1	..	4	..	..
Pendell, Thomas	1	1	2	..	..
Williams, Benjamin	1	2	6	..	4
Maccubbin, Zachariah	2	4	4	..	14
Gaither, Greenbury	1	2	3	..	8
Crocar, James	1	..	3	..	..
Durham, Patrick	2	1	4	..	..
Carlisle, Bas.l	1	1	4	..	..
Jones, Henry	1	..	1	..	5
Pope, John	1	1	2	..	5
Wheat, Hezekiah	1	4	5	..	..
Pack, Zepheniah	1	1	1	..	..
Benson, Mary	..	2	2	..	5
Ricketts, Benjamin	1	1	1	..	..
Chapple, Henry	2	..	3	..	..
Lowman, Jacob	1	..	1	..	..
Elliott, Samuel	1	2	1	..	5
Williams, Thomas	1	2	4	..	..
Randolph, Elizabeth	..	..	1	..	..
Shehan, Dennis	1	..	..	..	..
Simmons, Abraham	1	..	2	..	..
Simmons, Samuel	1	2	5	..	11
Gorden, John	1	1	2	..	..
Hodge, Benjamin	1	1	2	..	3
Moore, John	1	2	2	..	..
Leach, Josiah	2	4	8	..	..
Austin, Thomas	1	..	1	..	6
Pelly, Calvert	2	2	2	..	7
Rawlings, Priscilla	1	2	3	..	9
Moore, Barton	1	..	2	..	1
H.liad, Thomas	1	4	2	..	..
Worthington, William	2	1	1	..	16
Wilson, Sarah	..	..	1	..	11
Barney, Pearson	1	1	2	..	..
Williams, Charles	..	..	4	..	7
Williams, Amos	2	4	2	..	2
House, Edward	2	1	2	..	1
Sedgewick, Benjamin	4	1	5	..	..
Saffell, William	2	4	4	..	..
Stewart, James	2	..	3	..	..
Williams, William	2	2	3	..	5
Oden, David J.	3	1	3	..	..
Saffell, Charles	1	2	3	..	..
Anderson, Richard	1	1	2	..	10
Hill, Zachariah	1	1	4	..	..
Lee, Thomas S.	..	..	..	..	16
Thompson, William	..	4	3	..	2
Allison, Elisha	1	..	3	1	..
Ricketts, Robert	1	6	1	..	..
Allison, David	1	1	5	..	..
Claxson, Notley	1	5	2	..	4
Callihorn, Richard	2	..	3	..	..
Willett, Grace	1	..	2	..	8
Allison, Richard	2	..	4	..	6
Fish, Robert	4	3	7	..	2
Crabb, Jeremiah	2	2	4	..	20
Clarke, Thomas	2	4	4	..	..
Wilson, George	..	..	..	..	9
Greenwell, Philip	1	1	1	..	7
Griffeth, Greenbury, Junr	2	2	1	..	2
Crow, Edward	1	2	2	..	1

PRINCE GEORGES COUNTY.

NAME OF HEAD OF FAMILY.	Free white males of 16 years and upward, including heads of families.	Free white males under 16 years.	Free white females, including heads of families.	All other free persons.	Slaves.
Adam, George	..	..	3	1	..
Adams, George, Jr	1	3	2	..	..
Auston, Jonas	3	1	2	..	..
Addison, John Cole	2	4	2	..	24
Arnold, Christopher	3	5	..	..	..
Adams, Richard	1	4	5	..	12
Athey, Henry	..	2	1	..	..
Addison, Th' Grafton	1	..	..	..	25
Athey, Hezekiah	4	..	3	..	..
Addison, Anthony	4	4	2	..	68
Auston, William	1	2	5	..	..
Allen, Joseph	3	..	3	..	9
Adams, Margaret	..	..	1	1	7
Aldridge, Jacob	3	1	2	..	20
Atkins, Thomas	1	..	1	..	2
Allen, Auston	1	2	3	..	21
Albee, John	1	..	4	..	..
Allen, Ignatious	..	..	..	7	..
Arnt, George (Barber)	1	1	..	..	..
Allen, White	1	1	4	..	..
Arnold, William	1	1	2	..	..
Addison, Walter	1	..	..	..	20
Addison, John	1	..	..	..	20
Nichols, Ann	..	..	5	..	..
Atwell, Samuel	1	1	3	..	..
Ashton, John	3	..	..	..	82
Additon, Richard	1	2	1	..	..
Allen, John	1	3	2	..	..
Athey, Zepheniah	1	..	1	..	..
Arnold, William	1	..	2	..	..
Anderson, Samuel	1	1	2	..	..
Th', Abbigell	1	2	1	..	..
Moore, Ace	3	3	4	..	..
Atcherson, William	2	..	2	..	..
Adams, William	1	4	3	..	..
Adams, James	1	2	5	..	..
Athey, Zepheniah	1	..	..	..	1
Alden, Elisabeth	1	4	3	..	..
Alden, John	1	..	3	..	..
Alden, James	1	1	1	..	..
Adams, John	..	..	..	..	5
Arnold, William	..	1	2	..	..
Athey, Walter	1	1	5	..	..
Athey, Lucey	2	..	2	..	1
Anderson, William	1	2	2	..	1
Bowie, Feilder	2	2	3	..	60
Bowie, Robert	1	2	6	1	42
Brown, John, Jr	2	3	2	..	..
Boone, Priscilla	3	..	3	..	17
Botler, Edward	1	3	3	..	12
Bowie, Allen	1	..	3	..	30
Botler, Joseph	1	2	1	..	19
Brookes, John Smith	2	2	2	..	40
Beck, Samuel	2	1	1	..	8
Brooke, Thomas	2	1	3	..	10
Ball, John	1	..	2	1	3
Bryan, Simpkin	3	2	1	..	..
Booman, G. Ignatious	2	..	1	..	16
Beans, William, Junr	2	1	3	..	45
Beanes, Colmon	2	2	4	..	32
Burgess, Dr Richard	2	2	3	..	29
Berry, Sarah	1	2	3	..	6
Berry, Elisha	1	1	1	..	35
Brooke, Mary (Mill)	1	..	1	..	11
Brooke, Elisabeth (of Len)	2	2	..	3	11
Bowie, William, Jur	1	..	4	..	43
Brookes, Mary (of Henry)	1	..	2	..	24
Botler, Thomas	1	1	3	..	1
Brookes, Benjamin	2	..	..	..	17
Bird, John	3	2	2	..	4
Brightwell, Rich'd L.	1	1	3	..	..
Bean, John	1	1	2	..	1
Bowie, Dor F. John	1	..	2	..	50
Baden, John (of Th')	2	4	5	..	4
Brashears, Barten	2	..	2	..	1
Brookes, Ellsabeth (U.M.)	..	..	3	2	9
Brookes, Sarah (of Ben)	1	1	4	..	13
Botler, Walter	1	1	3	..	..
Beaven, William	1	..	2	..	1
Botler, Henry	2	2	4	1	1
Brookes, Walter	..	..	..	..	..
Brooke, Clement	..	..	..	..	..
Beddow, James	1	2	5	..	..
Bowie, William, 3rd	1	5	1	..	24
Baden, John, Jr	2	..	2	..	7
Bowie, Wm Sprigg	1	1	2	1	23
Bruce, Dr William	..	..	..	..	10
Brightwell, John L.	2	1	5	..	12
Beddow, Richard	1	4	4	..	1
Baden, Robert	1	..	2	..	11
Boswell, William	1	2	3	..	..
Bryan, Lucey	..	..	3	..	..
Branham, Laurance	1	..	3	..	..
Bonefant, James	2	1	5	..	10
Burch, Jonathan	2	1	2	..	14
Brooke, Oswell	1	..	1	..	15
Blacklock, Ann	..	..	1	..	17
Beall, Josias	5	1	2	..	47
Bryan, Richard	1	1	1	..	9
Boswell, John B.	4	1	6	..	..
Bond, Samuel	1	..	3	..	35
Beanes, John Collo	3	..	3	..	15
Bruse, William	5	..	..	..	2
Beall, Sarah	..	..	2	..	8
Boone, Ign' (of Henry)	1	..	..	..	..
Boone, Heneretta	1	..	4	..	7
Boone, Henry, Jr	1	..	1	..	7
Boone, Alextious	2	3	4	..	13
Boone, Francis	1	1	2	..	6
Boone, Henry, Senr	4	..	3	..	24
Botler, Lengham	2	1	5	..	12
Brooke, Margarett	1	..	1	..	16
Ball, Bennett	1	..	2	..	..
Beall, James, Senr	2	1	3	..	..
Beall, Partrick	2	2	3	..	15
Bean, William, Senr	4	..	2	..	19
Brashears, I. Pollenger	..	5	3	..	..
Barnes, John	1	..	3	..	..
Barnes, Henry, Senr	3	1	1	..	5
Baden, William	1	7	2	..	..
Burgess, William	1	6	3	..	..
Burch, Thomas	1	2	4	..	5
Burch, Benjamin, Senr	2	2	3	..	8
Beddow, Jonathan	2	1	4	..	2
Baker, Dr William	1	1	2	..	31
Blackburn, Elisabeth	1	2	3	..	2
Beggs, John	1	1	3	..	..
Berry, Benjamin	2	1	9	..	50
Boyd, Archibald	2	2	2	..	10
Bean, Christopher	2	1	2	..	..
Beall, John (of Nin)	1	1	6	..	..
Beck, Rebecca	1	3	3	..	11
Beall, Cap. Richard	5	..	5	..	14
Brashears, Joshua	1	1	2	..	4
Beck, Anthony	1	..	2	..	..
Berry, William	1	3	4	..	..
Bean, Thomas	1	..	4	..	1
Bayne George, Senr	2	..	4	..	9
Bayley, William	2	3	8	..	34
Brashears, Thomas	3	..	2	..	5
Bartley, Henry	1	1	3	..	..
Beall, Joshua	2	..	4	..	10
Beall, George, 3rd	1	1	5	..	17
Brown John (Shoemaker)	1	1	4	..	..
Blanford, James	..	..	1	..	..
Boyd, John	1	2	1	..	1
Boyd, Joseph	6	3	4	..	..
Belt, Osborn	3	4	4	..	5
Bowie, Walter	1	3	5	..	47
Belt, Thomas	1	..	..	..	7
Belt, Mary	1	1	3	..	27
Belt, Th' (of Mar)	2	3	4	..	3
Barber, John	2	2	4	..	..
Belt, Benjamin, Snr	2	1	6	..	22
Brashears, Zachy.	1	1	1	..	..
Belt, Cap. James	1	..	..	..	1
Brashears, Dr John.	2	..	2	3	..
Brown, John (Patuxent)	2	..	5	..	33
Bird, James	..	..	..	..	5
Boyd, Thomas, Snr	1	3	3	..	22
Brashears, John W.	2	..	3	..	16
Brashears, Th'	3	..	2	..	5
Beall, Basil	1	2	3	1	15
Brashears, Zadock	1	..	..	..	1
Boyd, Th', Jr	2	..	2	2	3
Buchan, John	4	1	3	..	6
Belt, Benje, Jr	3	..	..	..	8
Belt, Middleton	1	3	1	..	4
Bulger, Richard	1	..	2	..	..
Beall, James	1	..	..	..	..
Beall, Shadrick	2	3	6	..	1
Beall, William Dent	1	3	4	1	17
Benson, Thomas	1	..	3	..	..
Beall, John (Sheriff)	2	..	3	..	11
Brown, Peter	..	..	6	..	13
Bradford, Eleanor	..	..	3	..	20
Blanford, James	1	1	3	..	6
Boyd, Cole, Abraham	2	2	5	..	9
Burgess Joseph, Jr	2	2	4	..	..
Boswell, Jessey	1	3	4	..	..
Brown, Thomas	1	1	4	..	2
Burns, David	2	..	2	..	12
Bowcher, John Tho'	1	2	2	..	21
Burns, James	1	..	2	..	5
Berry, Mary	..	2	..	..	32
Beckett, John	4	1	4	..	..
Burgess, John Magruder	2	3	3	..	16
Burch, Benjamin	2	2	4	..	..
Berry, Zachauoh	2	4	3	..	46
Belt, Humphry	3	1	2	3	52
Bowie, Allen	1	..	..	..	12
Brown, Thomas (Shoe Mr)	1	..	4	..	..

PRINCE GEORGES COUNTY—Continued.

NAME OF HEAD OF FAMILY.	Free white males of 16 years and upward, including heads of families.	Free white males under 16 years.	Free white females, including heads of families.	All other free persons.	Slaves.
Baldwin, Thomas (Forrest)	1	1	1		9
Beall, David	2	2	6		3
Blacklock, Nicholas	2	3	3		23
Burgess, Charles	2	1	4	5	23
Berry, William	2		1		13
Bean, Quenton	2		1		
Bruce, John	1	1	3		
Brown, George	1	1	3		
Burgess, Joseph	1	3	4		
Burk, Partrick	1	1	2		
Beck, Richard	1	1	1		
Banks, Webb	1	1	3		
Barns, Greenberry	1	1	1		
Burgess, Edward	1	1	2		5
Boone, Walter	1	1	2		
Beaven, Charles	1	1	2		1
Barber, John	1		2		
Baldwin, Samuel	3	1	2		
Berry, William (B. smith)	1	3	4		
Beall, John Fendell	1	1	1		3
Backer, Thomas	1	1	2		
Burgess, Edward	3	2			8
Berry, William	2		1		
Butterworth, William	1	1	1		
Brian, Sempkin	1		1		
Butt, Edward	2	1	2		
Bigger, Mary			4		7
Brightwell, Allen	1	2	4		
Beaven, Charles	2	1	2		1
Beaven, John (Taylor)	1	3	4		
Brightwell, John, of Peter	3	1	3		
Buldon, Allen	1	2	2		
Beaven, Charles, Senr	1	1	2		1
Botler, Edward, of Charles	1	2	2		
Brown, George	1		1		
Botler, Mary		4	3		
Brightwell, Cage	1		3		
Burgess, Elisabeth		2			10
Beddow, Mary			2		
Barber, John	2	1	4		
Brashears, Samuel	2	1	1		10
Brian, Simpkin	4	1	1		
Bayne, Josias	3	5	5		
Boswell, John	2	1	4		
Brown, Ann		2	2	1	
Brown, Zachariah	2	2	2		
Butt, Aron	1	1	8		
Baynes, Noble	1	2	3		88
Brown, William	2		4		
Barron, Daniel	1	2	3		
Beall, Basil	1	1	1		1
Belt, Loyd	1		3		13
Blanford, Joseph	1	1	2		4
Blanford, Ignatious	1		3		
Bowling, William Lang	2	3	2		8
Burrows, Edward	2		2		7
Bowling, John	4	2	6		17
Burch, Richard	2	1	3		
Boarman, Joseph	5	1	1		30
Boone, Priscilla		1	3		20
Bryan, Richard, Jr	1	1	6		3
Ball, Hillery	1		3		
Bryan, George	1	5	5		
Burgess, Arnold	1		2		
Ball, Richard	3	3	2		2
Burch, Thomas	2	4	4		
Benson, John	1	4	4		7
Bean, Jane	1	1			
Bean, Charty	1		3		
Burch, Thorn	1	3	1		
Bean, Josiah	1	1	4		
Brian, Thomas	1	5			5
Ball, Stephen	4		2		5
Barns, Henry	1	1	2		
Barns, Basil	1		2		
Burch, Zachariah	1	1	2		1
Beall, Sarah		3	9		
Boswell, John Baptist	2	3	4		5
Burrell, John	1		1		
Brian, Peter	2		1		
Barrott, Joseph	2	1	2		
Baldwin, Thomas, Jr	1	2	2		
Beck, James, of Saml	1	2			5
Barnes James	1	1			
Baldwin, John	1	2	6		1
Beck, James, of Jams	1	2	2		5
Brashears, Sarah	2	4	3		2
Bowling, Thomas	1	2	4		2
Beall, Andrew, of Nin	1		3		2
Beall, Sarah, of Ben		3	4		
Benson, Thomas	2		2		
Barrett, Alexander	2	5	4		
Clark, Dr David	2	2	1	1	26

NAME OF HEAD OF FAMILY.	Free white males of 16 years and upward, including heads of families.	Free white males under 16 years.	Free white females, including heads of families.	All other free persons.	Slaves.
Clagett, Thomas, parson	1				8
Clagett, Thomas, Jr	1		2		4
Clagett, Thomas, Senr	1		2		13
Clagett, Sarah	1		3	1	2
Cranford, David	3	1	3		50
Cranford, Mary	1		1		17
Clarke, Thomas	3	2	2		28
Contee, Rich'd Alex	2		2		25
Clagett, Saml. White					7
Campbell, John	1	1	2		3
Coverton, Sarah	1	1	3		50
Clarke, Bailey	2				1
Cage, William	1	2	3		
Cole, George	1	1	4		
Contee, Thomas	2		4		25
Cox, Walter Brooke	3		3	2	14
Collings, James, Jr	1		2		4
Cracklan, William	1		5		
Cator, William	3	1	4		
Coe, Beckard	3	4	3		1
Clagett, Thomas, Mercht	3	2	3		40
Carnes, John	2		1		
Cunningham, John	1		1		
Cage, B. Peter	1		1	1	
Conner, Michael	1	1	4		
Cissell, Zachariah	2		2	4	4
Club, John	2		3		
Clarke, Abraham	1	2	1		
Clarkson, Edward	1	3	1		5
Clarkson, Sarah			2		10
Campbell, James	2	1			
Callis, Garland	2		1		21
Casey, John	1	2	1		17
Contee, John	1		1		17
Calvert, Elisabeth	2		1		228
Carr, Overton	2	2	4	2	27
Cotes, Dr Richard	2		1		25
Clarkson, Joseph	1	1	2		9
Cheney, Charles	1	3	2		
Craufurd, Jacob	1		3		
Clarke, Viney			3		
Cooke, Jeremiah	1	1	2		1
Craufurd, Elisabeth	2		2	1	
Craufurd, Thomas	3		2		3
Craufurd, Margarett	2	1	2		13
Craufurd, Alexander	2		3		10
Craycraft, John Sly	3		4		4
Craig, Adams	1	2	2		8
Cole, Richard	1		4		
Carroll, Elisabeth	1	1	4		
Craufurd, David	1	1	2		
Clarke, Daniel	1		2		12
Clarke, Ann	1		1		19
Clagett, Joseph White	2	1	1		26
Carrick, Henry, Senr	1	1	2	1	5
Club, Marthew	1		3		
Cross, Capt Joseph	3	1	1		19
Cross, Basil	1	3	4		3
Carrick, John, Junr	3	1	1	6	
Clarke, Abraham	2		4		4
Carrick, Mareen	2	3	5		3
Clarke, Caleb	1		6		2
Clarke, Henry	1				3
Crow, John	2	2	5		14
Carr, Benjamin	1	2	5		2
Cissell, Philip, Jur	1	3	5		3
Cheney, Samuel	1	2	2	2	
Cramphin, Richard	2				16
Carroll, Daniel, of Danl	1	1	2		13
Clagett, Charles	2	3	3		20
Craufurd, Nathl	2		4		30
Cooke, John (weaver)	1	3	5		
Coonce, Frederick	1	1	2		2
Carrick, Henry	1	1	2	2	
Clarke, John	1	1	1		
Carman, William	1		3		
Conner, Thomas	1	3	2		
Cunningham, Dr Cornelius			1	3	
Currants, William	1	1	3		
Callehan, John	3	1	5		
Clarkson, Thomas	3	3	6		13
Curtain, Edward	1	5	4		
Clements, Edward	1		4		1
Cossey, William	2		3		
Cave, Samuel	1		3		12
Collins, James	4		3	4	1
Currants, John	1		4		
Crooke, Charles	3	4	7		1
Cawood, Stephen	1	2	3		
Curtain, Denniss	1	2	6		
Cheney, Mordecai	2	2	2		
Cheney, Jessey	1		3		
Crook, William	1	1	3		
Crow, Samuel	1		1		
Cooms, Dorothy			6		
Crow, Joseph	1	2	1		

NAME OF HEAD OF FAMILY.	Free white males of 16 years and upward, including heads of families.	Free white males under 16 years.	Free white females, including heads of families.	All other free persons.	Slaves.
Conn, Jane	1	1	2		
Curry, William	1				
Clarke, Thomas	3	2	2		28
Coffery, Daniel	1	3	3		5
Cissell, Thomas	1				1
Cissell, James, Senr	2	2	2		
Clarke, Frederick	1	1	3		11
Cumpton, Henry Trueman	2				13
Curr, John			1	2	
Cox, Jacob			1	2	
Cawood, Thomas, Senr	1	3	3		
Clagett, Richard	1	1	3		18
Cawood, Thomas, Jr	1	1	3		
Club, Levin	1	1	3		
Clagett, Hanah	1	5	3		40
Chapman, John	1	2	1		
Clarkson, Henry	1				1
Clarvoe, John	3	2	1		7
Casteel, Catharine	1		2		
Cassell, John	2	2	5		
Cooke, Benjamin	4		3	1	1
Conner, Thomas	1	2			
Cooms, Dorothy			3		
Clagett, Jane			2		7
Club, Samuel	2	2	5		
Cooke, John			1		
Crooke, Richard	1	1	1		5
Carroll, Eleanor	2	1	4		
Carrico, Barton	2	4	7		
Conner, Cornelias	1		1		
Cox, Charles	1	3	1		1
Church, Thomas	1		1		
Church, Luke	1		1		1
Cooksey, Andrew	2		2		
Cooksey, James	2	1	3		2
Cissell, Sabret	1	1	2		
Cluney, Joseph	1	2	3		2
Craycroft, Joseph	1	1	6		
Chaney, James	2	4	3		
Conn, John	1	1	1		
Chaplain, William			2		
Clarke, Henry	1				3
Chaplain, John	1		1		
Cross, Joseph, Senr	1	1	1		2
Clagett, Mary			2		6
Cook, Samuel	1		2		
Cibley, James	2	4	3		
Carter, Edward	1		5		
Cissell, Barton	1	4	3		
Dorsett, Wm Newman					17
Digges, Mary	1		4		75
Digges, William					22
Davis, John	1	2	6		
Davis, Elisabeth					10
Dorsett, Thomas, Senr	1	1	2		10
Dorsett, Capt William	1	1	2		10
Dorsett, Thomas, Senr	2	1	6		12
Davis, Naylor	3	2	6		4
Dent, Walter	1		1		
Danford, William	1		6		
Dyer, Thomas	3	3	6		
Dyer, Francis Clement	1	4	4		9
Duckett, Samuel	1	4	4		
Darsey, John	1	5	5		2
Dyer, Giles	1	2	5		8
Dyer, George	1		2		5
Digges, George	2	2	2		105
Darnall, Robert	1	1	1		41
Dyer, William	1	4	1		
Dick, Robert			4	5	21
Duvall, Mareen Howard	4		4		5
Duckett, Thomas	1	3	4		35
Darnall, John	3	1	8		8
Duvall, Samuel	4	4	6		6
Duvall, Charles	2	3	6		5
Duvall, Benj., of Chappel	3	2	8		8
Duvall, Mareen	2		6		9
Duvall, Gabril, of Annpe	1	3	5		9
Duvall, Thomas, Jr	2	4	3		9
Duvall, Jessey	2	5	4		4
Duvall, Joseph	1	2	4		20
Duvall, Alexander	1	2	2		4
Drane, James, Jr	1	1	1		
Duvall, John, Senr	2		2		15
Duvall, John, Jur	1		3		6
Duvall, John, of Marsh	1	1	1		12
Duckett, Barrack	2		2		36
Deakins, Leonard	3	1	5		13
Duvall, John	3	5	5		
Duvall, Tho, of Ben	3	3	5		
Duvall, Benje, of Elie	2	5	4		6
Duvall, Allen	2		4	1	5
Darnall, Gerrard	1	1	4		6
Drane, Eleanor			4		2
Davis, George	2	3	1		4
Duckett, Isaac	2		3	1	31

PRINCE GEORGES COUNTY—Continued.

NAME OF HEAD OF FAMILY.	Free white males of 16 years and upward, including heads of families.	Free white males under 16 years.	Free white females, including heads of families.	All other free persons.	Slaves.
Davis, Jonathan	1	1	1		
Delahny, Joseph	3	1	3		
Dodson, John	1	5	3		1
Dent, Georg, Esqr					13
Deenure, Jacob		2	5		
Duckett, Dr Richd	1				1
Dyer, Annectious	1	2	5		5
Duckett, Richard	2		5		22
Deakins, William, Jr	2		1	2	4
Danfort, Joseph	1				
Domoneck, Thomas	3		2		
Domoneck, John	1	3	2		2
Duvall, Elisabeth			1		
Dove, Richard	1	5	5		
Duley, Jonathan	1		2		3
Ducker, William	1	2	3		
Duley, Henry	1	2	4		11
Davis, Jonathan	1	1	2		
Dent, Richard	2	2	3		15
Downey, Botler	1	3	2		1
Dunn, Mary			3		3
Downs, Eleanor	1		4		
Day, Luke	1		1		
Day, Ann		1	2		
Dove, Samuel	1		4		
Davis, Monecal		2	3		
Downs, John	1	1	1		
Daws, Josiah	2		1		
Duvall, Colmore	1		2		3
Duvall, Benja, of Marsh	1				1
Duvall, Daniel	1	1	4		
Drane, Anthony	1	4	2		4
Eversfield, Charles	1	1	2		27
Eversfield, Martha	2	3	8		78
Early, William	1		3		
Estep, Benjamin, Jur	1		2		
Ellis, Owen	1	4	2		2
Ellis, John	1				5
Ellis, Elisabeth			1		2
Eversfield, Eleanor	1	1	3		13
Edelen, Thos, flatman	2	1	4		
Evans, John	2				13
Evans, Philip	1	1		2	5
Edelen, Benedick	1		3		7
Edelen, Thomas, of Ths	1		2		8
Edelen, Richard, Jr	2		4		13
Edelen, Edward	1	2	2		30
Edelen, Saml	1		3		6
Edelen, Richd, of Ths	1	3	4		5
Evans, Robert	1	1	2		2
Edmonson, James	1	1	1		14
Edmonson, Niniam	2	4	1		2
Evans, Walter	2	2	1		8
Edelen, Botler	2	1	3		6
Elson, Archibald	2	1	3		5
Early, Thomas	2	2	3		4
Early, Benjamin	1	1	4		
Evans, Samuel	1	2	3		3
Estep, Joseph	1	3	1		2
Edmonson, Archibald	1	3	1		6
Edelen, P. Thomas	2	1	1		6
Estep, Benjamin, Senr	3	1	6		8
Ervin, Charles	1	1	2		
Eastwood, John	2	1	5		
Edelen, Christopher	1	1	4		2
Edelen, Joseph (of James)	2	1	2		26
Edelen, Clement	1	2	2		
Edelen, Mary	1		4		2
Emerson, John	3		2		
Emerson, James	1	1	4		1
Edelen, John	1	1	1		
Edelen, Richd, Senr	1				2
Edelen, Priscilla	3		2		2
Edelen, George	1		1		6
Edelen, Joseph (of Christr)	1	1	1		2
Edelen, Samuel (of Charles)	1	1	2		4
Ellis, Mary	1		4		2
Farrall, Benjamin	1	2	1		
Fetter, Sarah			1		2
Fowler, Joseph	1	2	2		7
Fowler, William, Jur	1	5	1		
Fields, Elisha	1	1	2		6
Fardser, Alexander	1	1	3		
Fakes, August John	1	1			
Fowler, Abraham	2	3	6		1
Fenwick, Ignatious	1	1	1		25
Farr, Nicholas	6	1	2		
Fraiser, James	1	4	2		
Farral, Ruth			3		
Fraser, Alexander	1	1	3		
Fogget, Richard	3		3		3
Furguson, Josiah	1	1	4		4
Farrall, William	1		3		
Furguson, William	1	6	4		6
Farrel, James	1	1	2		
Fields, Martain	3		1		
Farall, Benjamin	2	2	1		
Free, Nicholas	1		3		
Fowler, William, Jr	2		3		
Flanningham, Thomas	1		3		
Fraser, Henry	1	5	3		
Foster, Richard	2	1	2		
Ferrel, John	2	3	4	2	3
Fry, Elisabeth	1	1	4		3
Fields, Batholumy	1		2		
Fry, Leonard	1		1		
Francis, Alice	1		1		
Ford, William	3		2		1
Fraser, Daniel	1	2	5		
Finley, Patsey	2	2	4		15
Fraser, John	2	1	1		2
Frasier, Philip Lever	2	2	3		
Free, Charles	2	1	3		
Fowler, Samuel	1	3			
Fowler, Thomas	1	2	4		
Fuller, John	1	5	2		
Free, John	1		2		
Glascoe, Elisabeth	3		1		
Gibbons, Wales George	1		1		14
Gray, Leonard	2		2		
Gray, John	2	2	5		
Gates, Elisabeth	1				
Gover, William	1		4	1	2
Gardner, Clement	2	3	2		26
Gardner, Michael	3	5	3		
Greenfield, Gerrard	2	1	4		33
Gibbins, Thos (of Turner)	2	7	4		
Gibbins, John	3	3	5		2
Griffeth, Edward, Jr	3	2	1	1	
Grimes, John, Senr	2	2	5		
Gibbens, Walter	1	3	3		
Gant, James	1	1	1		11
Gant, George	1	1	3		8
Guyer, William Johnson	1	4	2		
Gray, Hezekiah	2	2	3		
Gates, James	2	1	1		
Green, Thos Edelen	2	1	6		6
Gray, Elisha	2	1	6		1
Griffeth, Matthew	1	1	2		
Grimes, John, Jur	1	2	2		1
Gibson, Thomas	1				33
Greenfield, Jarett	2	1	4		33
Godman, Humphry	3		3		2
Gloyd, Daniel	1		2		
Gaither, Benjamin	1	1			17
Green, Jacob	1	1	3		17
Gant, Fielder	1				13
Gant, Erasmas	1		2		12
Gant, Dr Edward	5	3	4		23
Gant, Thomas	4	1	2		46
Gist, Joshua	1				
Gwinn, Bennett	5				
Gorden, David(B.Smith)	1		3		
Gennings, Charles	1	5	3		
Groves, John	3				1
Gorden, Josiah	2	2	3		
Greenwell, Jesse	1		1		
Gordon, John, Jr	1	2	4		
Gray, Tobias				3	
Greenfield, William	1	2	2		29
Greyer, Benjamin	1	1	3		
Gloyd, Daniel	1		2		
Grayham, Nancey			3		
Gardner, John	2	1	1		
Guldean, James	1	3	2		
Glody, Samuel		4	3		
Gloyd, Daniel, Jur	1	2	3		
Green, Elisha	1	2			20
Grimes, John	1	1	2		
Gibbens, William	2	3	4		
Gibbens, Turner Thos	1	4	5		
Gibbens, Elisabeth	1		4		13
Gibbens, Arther	1	2	4		2
Gray, James	1	2	4		
German, John	1	1	2		
Galahan, John		2	3		
Gibbs, John Harris	1	5	2		3
Gray, Richard	1	1	4		1
Gant, Levy	2	5	6		32
Grimes, Mrs	1		3		
Goddart, John	1	1	3		
Gates, Joseph	2		2		
Gates, John	2		1		
Greggory, Violettee	1		3		
Gray, Thomas	1	2	4		
Galor, Thomas, Snr	1	1	2		
Gentle, Thomas	1	2	5		
Hellen, Capt Jersey	1		5		6
Hodgkin, Thomas	2		2		11
Humborstone, Richard	1	1	2		
Harvey, Eleanor	1		2		3
Hamilton, Thomas	2		4		3
Hamilton, Marian			3		10
Hutcherson, William, Jr	4	1	4		
Harvey, Newman	1	3	5		4
Hawkins, Ruben	1	1	5		
Hogan, Joseph	4	3	1		5
Halkerston, John	2		1	1	4
Hall, Henry	1		3		5
Hamilton, Francis	1	1	2		
Hoye, Thomas	2	4	4		14
Hamilton, Samuel	1		4		2
Hughs, John	2	1	4		
Harvey, GroomWilliam	2	1	6		8
Hanin, Elias	2		4		
Hugoo, William	2		2		3
Hegdon, Benjamin	2	1	3		
Hardy, F. John	1	1			
Hamilton, Alexander	3	2			5
Hardy, Dent George	1		2		2
Hardy, Mary			2	5	
Hurly, Salem	1	2	2		2
Hughs, William	2	1	1		26
Hawkins, James	1		5		16
Hardy, Anthony	1	2	5		
Haberna, Domoneck	1		2		
Harvey, Thomas, Snr	1		4		1
Harvey, Alexander	1	2	4		
Hardy, John	1	1	3		
Hellery, Walter	1	3			9
Hall, Alexander	1		2		5
Hurley, William J	1	1	3		
Hatten, Basil	1				2
Hatten, Henry	1	1	2		11
Hallen, George	1		3		4
Hallen, Joseph, Jr	2		3		16
Hill, Capt Henry	1	4	4		24
Hardy, George	1		4		2
Hurley, John	1		5		1
Henderson, Richard	1	1	8	2	25
Hewet, Thomas	1	3	4		4
Helbrogle, Belthazer	2	1	1		
Hopkins, Francis	2		3		
Hawkins, Cap. Henry	1		1		12
Hamilton, Alexr	1	1	2		5
Hamilton, Thomas	1		1	1	13
Hyde, Benjamin	1		3		
Hill, Clement	2	3	5		95
Henniss, Benjamin	1	2	1		1
Hays, Thomas	1		5		1
Hodkin, Rachael	2		2		5
Henniss, John	1	2	2		
Hillery, Capander	2	2	4		20
Hodges, Ths Ramsey	3	2	6		12
Hyat, Christopher	3	2	3		3
Hurley, William	1		5		
Hooper, John	1		5		
Hill, Joseph	1		1		
Hyde, George	1		1		
Hopper, Robert	2		4		
Hughs, James	1	3	4		
Harwood, Benjamin	3	1	3		24
Hodges, Chr Ramsey	2	2	6		17
Hillery, George	1		2		10
Harben, Elisha	1	2	6		
Hepburn, Saml	1	3	1	1	21
Hutcherson, Saml	1	2	2		
House, Henry	1		3		
Hall, William	3	6	3		10
Higgins, Joshua	2	3	7		1
Hardesty, Levy	1	2	5		
Hyat, William, Jr	1	3	6		
Hyat, Seth	1	3	1		
Hyat, James	1		3		
Hodkins, Philip	2		1		3
Hancock, John	2	3	4		
Halsey, John J	1		4		
Hurdle, Leonard	1	1	6		3
Hill, John	3		1		54
Hillery, Tilman	2	3	2		22
Hodges, Jos Ramsey	2	2	2		15
Holliday, Clement	1		3		
Hoofman, Mary			4		
Holliday, Dr Leonard	1		4	1	27
Holliday, Leonard, Jr	1		4		6
Hodges, John Ramsey	1		1	1	15
Hillery, Mary, of Benjs	1	1			3
Harris, F. Varnan	2		4		1
Hoye, Cephas	1	1	4		7
Hardy, Jessey			3		
Hall, Richd Bennett	3	1	3		57
Harriss, Edward	2		3		
Hall, Henry Lowe	2		1		16

PRINCE GEORGES COUNTY—Continued.

NAME OF HEAD OF FAMILY.	Free white males of 16 years and upward, including heads of families.	Free white males under 16 years.	Free white females, including heads of families.	All other free persons.	Slaves.
Hall, Benjamin	1		3		60
Harrison, John	1	1	1		
Hodges, James	1	1	1		12
Haden, Elias	1	1	3		
Hagan, Mary			3		
Heneriggle, Christopher	2	3	4		
Hunt, John	1		2		
Harbert, John, Jr	1		2		
Higdon, John	1	1	2	1	
Hodkins, Susanah	1	1	3		
Harbert, John, Snr	1		2		
Henry, Harper	1				
Hurley, Basil	1	1	1	1	
Harrison, Joseph	2	5	3		3
Hardy, George	2	2	5		
Hawkins, F. John	4	6	2		36
Hoxton, Susanah			2		42
Hodkins, Rachel		2	2		
Hays, Robert	1		1		
Hillery, John	1	2	4		
Hubly, William	1		1		
Hinton, Charles	1	1	4		
Hall, Rebecca	1		1		19
Hinton, Ann	1	1	5		
Hopkins, Mary			4		
Hooper, Thomas	1	3	2		
Harbeel, John	1		2		
Halsey, John	2		3		
Holmead, Anthony	3		3		6
Holmead, John	2				3
Holsey, John, Jur	1	2	4		
Howard, Peter	1	2	4		
Holland, Rebecca		1	2		
Hern, John	1		2		
Hill, Clement	1				11
Hyat, Abednego	1		1		6
Hagan, Thomas	2	4	3		2
Harris, Basil	1	1	4		1
Hegdon, Benjamin, Jr	5	1	3		
Holly, John	3	2	7		3
Harris, John	2	1	2		28
Hardy, Henry	2		5		22
Harrison, Joseph	2	5	3		3
Hatton, Nathaniel	1		1		35
Hatton, Joseph, Jur	1	1	3		3
Hardy, Ignatious	2		6		2
Holland, Rebecca		1	2		
Hart, Robert	1				
How, Elizabeth			2		
Harrison, Elisha	1	1	1		
Hagan, Electious	2				1
Harriss, Josias	1	2	2		3
Hilton, Elizabeth		1	4		4
Hall, Alexander	1	3	4		3
Hopper, Sarah	1	1	3		
Havis, James	3	7	4		
Hinton, Elsabeth	2		3		
Hurley, Mariah	1		3		6
Hadesty, Reason	3	1	2		
Hardesty, Levie	1	3	1		
Hern, Mary	2		2		
Hinton, John	1	4	2		
Hern, Peter	1	2	4		
Hooker, Robert	1	1	2		2
Hinton, William	1		4		
Harriss, Zadock	1	4	3		4
Harriss, Aron	1	5	5		4
Henry, John	1		4		
Jenkins, Wm (of John)	2		2		4
Jones, Charles	1				8
Jones, George	1	1	5		
Jones, Benjamin	2	1	2		
Jenkins, William (of Wm)	1		2		1
Jones, Lewis	2		11		
Jenkins, Thomas	1				1
Jenkins, Thos (of Francis)	1	1	2		2
Joye, Baptist	1	2	3		
Jones, Rorer	1	1	2		
Jenkins, Zadock	2	3	4		4
Jenkins, William	1	2	5		4
Jackson, William John	1	1	1		6
Isaac, Richard, Jr	1	1	3		2
Jacobs, Mordecai	1	1	2		11
Jacobs, Benjamin	2	2	4		8
Jones, Thomas	3	4	3		1
Jacobs, Ezekel	4	1	4		2
Jones, Thomas (snowdens)	1	4	3		
Jones, Thomas	2		2		
Jackson, Alexander	2	1	7		13
Jones, Josiah	2	4	6		7
Jones, Richard	3		2		3
Jones, Elizabeth			3		13

NAME OF HEAD OF FAMILY.	Free white males of 16 years and upward, including heads of families.	Free white males under 16 years.	Free white females, including heads of families.	All other free persons.	Slaves.
Jones, Henry	1	2	3		
Jenkins, Enoch	1		1		3
Jackson, William	2	3	5		7
Jacobs, Richard	1		2		
Jones, Zachariah	1	1	2		
Johnson, Renaldo	7		2		51
Jones, James	1	1	4		
Jones, Stephen	1	3	1		1
Jarvis, Jonathan	1	1	1		
Journey, Edward	1	2	1		
Jones, Joseph	1	1	3		1
Josshal, John	1		1		
Jones, Moses	2				
Jefferson, Alexander	3	1	1		3
Igleheart, John	3	1	1		3
Igleheart, William	1	3	3		1
Jacobs, Richard	1		2		2
Jemstone, Richard	2	2	5		1
Isaac, Joseph	1	1	1		
Jones, Charles	1	4	3		
Jenkins, Jason	1	2	3		
Johnson, Philip	2	3	2		
Jones, John	1	1	2		
Jones, Levin	1	3	3		5
Jones, Boller	1	1	1		3
Jerman, Sarah	1	1	4		
Jerman, Stephen	1	2	3		1
Jones, Edward	1	2	4		1
Jenkins, Zachariah	4	1	6		3
Jones, George	1	1	6		
Jones, Elisha	1	1	4		
Jones, William, Jr	1	4	3		2
Jenkins Pierce John	1		2		3
Jenkins, Edward	1		2		
Jenkins, Ann	1		3		5
Jones, Samuel	2		2		5
Jones, Notley	1	3	2		
Jones, Sarah		3	2		
Jones, Moses	2	1			
Jones, Elisabeth	1	1	2		
Johnson, Marthew	1		2		
Johnson, Thomas	2	1	4		
Ingleheart, Jacob	1		1		12
Isaac, Richard	1		4		9
Kelty, William	1		1		1
Keith, Ignatious	3	1	2		
King, Jonathan	1	3	2		
Key, Theophilas	1	3	5		1
King, John	3		4		
Kidwell, Benjamin	1	2	1		
Kidwell, William	1	1	4		
Kidwell, Nehemiah	1		3		
Kidwell, Marshall	2	5	1		
Kidwell, Jessey	1	1	4		
King, James	3	1	5		
King, Thomas (soldier)	2	1	2		
Kingsbury, Domillion	2		1		
Keadle, William	1	3	3		
Kellis, Garland	3	1	1		20
Kirby, Baptis John	1		1		16
King, Thomas, Senr	2	1	2		
King, William, Jur	1	4	4		1
Kirby, Francis	1	1	2		5
King, William (of Richd)	1	1	3		
King, Richard	2	5	4		
King, John (of Richd)	1	4	3		
Keadle, Wiseman	2	1	1		1
Keadle, Nancey	1		2		
Kidwell, Samuel	2	3	3		
Kahaly, David	1	2	3		
King, Elisha	1	3	3		
King, Ann			3		
King, Charles	2				4
Kidwell, William	1	2	3		
King, Thomas	1	1	2		
Keser, Notley	1	2	2		
Keough	1	2	2		
Kidwell, Benjamin, Jr	2	1	1		
King, Henry	2		6		
Keith, Garret	1	3	2		2
Keith, James	2	4	5		
Knott, John	1	3	4		
King, Eleanor		5	1		
Kee, Ignatious	3		3		
Knowland, John	1	1	2		
Kidwell, Thomas	2	1	1		
Kidwell, John, Jr	1	4	4		
Lansdale, Richard	1	2	2		11
Lanham, Jeremiah	2		4		6
Lovelace, Jacob	1	2	1		
Lowry, Gavin	1		1		1
Lowe, Zepheniah	4	2	1		3
Lucas, John	1	1	5		1
Lamar, Robert	4		3		8

NAME OF HEAD OF FAMILY.	Free white males of 16 years and upward, including heads of families.	Free white males under 16 years.	Free white females, including heads of families.	All other free persons.	Slaves.
Leach, John	2	3	5		
Lyles, Thomas	1		3		14
Lowe, Barbara	1	2	1		
Lang, Francis					
Lemon, John	1	2	2		2
Langham, James	1				4
Linsey, Charles	1		3		
Lehman, John	1	3	3		2
Lansdale, Henry	1		1		
Lemon, John	1				
Lovelace, Luke	2	1	5		
Lewis, Hugh	2		2		
Lewis, Thomas (soldier)	1		2		
Lusen, Elisabeth	2		3		
Lowe, William	1	1	3		
Lanham, Elisha	1		1		3
Leeper, George	2				10
Lanham, Stephen	1	2	3		
Lanham, Josias	1	2	2		
Luke, Mrs Ann	1	1	2		49
Lee, Ths Sim's (Quarter)					36
Lovejoy, John, Senr	2	3	5		
Leechworth, Marthew	1		2		8
Ladyman, Levin	1		2		
Leitch, Benjamin	3	1	5		2
Lovejoy, Alexander	3	4	3		
Lovejoy, Michael, Senr	3	2	2		2
Lyles, William	2	4	6		93
Lanham. Hezekiah	2	1	7		16
Lanham, Elisabeth	1				3
Lawson, William	1	4	2		
Lesby, Samuel	3	1	3		10
Lowe, John, Junr	1		3		16
Lowe, Nicholas	3		5		9
Lanham, Edward	2	1	2		26
Lanham, George (of Jo.)	1	2	4		1
Long, Thomas	1	2	2		
Lansdale, Charles	2		3		7
Lewis, Thomas	3	2	4		
Lovelace, Ignatious	1	3	2		
Lowe, Michael	3	1	4		17
Lowe, Mary	1	2	4		
Lanham, Quilla	2		2		
Lanham, Nathan, Snr	2		1		4
Lesner, John Jocum	1	2	1		
Linsey, Charles	1		1		
Lownds, Benjamin	1		2		7
Lownds, Richard	1		1		9
Lanham, Samuel	2	2	2		3
Lowe, William	2		3		
Lowe, Barten	1	3	1		1
Lowe, John, Jnr	2	2	5		11
Lansdale, Isaac	1		2		52
Lansdale, Thomas	1	1	4		10
Loveless, William	1		3		
Lambeth, H. John	1				3
Linsey, Samuel	1	1	2		1
Lanham, Soloman	1	3	4		5
Locker, Thomas	1		3		
Lovelace, Luke	3	1	8		
Lisby, John	1				
Locker, Philip	2	1	3		
Locker, Philip, Senr	2		3		
Lockwood, Stephen	1	1	2		
Linsey, John	1	1	3		2
Linsey, Charles	1		3		
Lucas, Adam	2	4	3		
Luke, Basil	1	2	3		
Lanham, Elie	1				4
Lanham, Elias	2	3	4		
Lovejoy, Michael, Jnr	1	1	1		
Lovejoy, John, Jnr	1	1	1		
Lanham, Nathan, Jnr	2		1		
Lowe, Elias	1	2	2		
Lanham, Stephen	1	2	3		
Lanham, Archabald	1	3	4		
Lehman, John	1		1		
Lanham, Hillery	1	2	3		
Lanham, Lewis	2	1	2		
Miles, John	1	3	3		
Moodie, John	1	2	2		
McMasters, Andrew	1	1	1		
Manley, William	1	2	2		
Marlow, James	3				
McDonald, William	1	1	1		
Mitchel, Ths (of Miles)	1	1	4		1
Magruder, John Read	4	3	3		39
Mollison, William	1	4	3		
Mahony, John	4	1	3		
Mitchell, Francis	1	2	2		
McDonold, Rubin	1	3	5		3
Morton, John	1	2	3		11
Magruder, Barbara			2		22

PRINCE GEORGES COUNTY—Continued.

NAME OF HEAD OF FAMILY.	Free white males of 16 years and upward, including heads of families.	Free white males under 16 years.	Free white females, including heads of families.	All other free persons.	Slaves.
Magruder, Leonard....	1	2	1		16
Makell, Benjamin, 5th..	2		1		26
Mobley, Edward, Jr....	1	5	3		
Mobley, Edward J....	2	3			
Mobly, Mary....		3	4		
Magruder, Margarett..	2		5		25
Magruder, Meek....		5	1		11
Morton, William....	1				8
Marlow, John....	1				3
Mahew, Basil....	3	3	4	1	2
Mahew, William....	1	1	5		
Magruder, Mary....	2		3		16
Magruder, George....	1		2		6
Magruder, Elisabeth....			9		29
Mattingly, Joseph....		1	2		
Mudd, Sarah....	1	2	2		5
Mudd, Thomas....	3	1	8		23
Mitchel, Richard....	1	5	5		
Marlow, Dr Samuel....	1		2		13
Mitchell, Elisabeth....	3	2	3		15
Miles, Nicholas....	1	2	5		8
Mud, Dr Joseph....	1				13
Mason, Philip....	1	3	3		
Mangton, John....	1	2	3		
Manley, William....	1	2	1		
McDonold, John....	1	4	4		8
Marshall, Thomas....	1		4		
Marshall, Dr Thomas..	2				20
Marshall, Dr William..	2	2	2		7
Mullekin, Samuel....	3	2	5		
Magruder, Denniss....	7	2	2		32
Maccatee, John....	1	3	6		
Maddok, Charles....	3	1	3		19
Mitchell, Sarah....	1	2	6		
Mockbee, Zadock....	1	5	1		
Messenger, Joseph....	1	3	2		10
Moore, James (of Ben)..	2	7	3		23
Morriss, The Barten....	1	2	2		8
Marbury, Luke....	2	3	5		25
Mangun, Mary....	1	1	2		
Mullekin, Thomas....		3			6
Mills, Easter....	1	1	3		
McMasters, Andrew....	1	2			1
Moodie, John....	1		3		
Manduct, Hannah....		3			11
Mitchell, John....	1	4	4		
Moore, Thomas....	1		4		2
McCauslen, Mary....	1		4	2	
McDonold, Walter....	1	6	2		
Mullekin, Richard....	1	2	5		1
Masters, Trephiniah....	1		3		
Masters, Ezekiel....	1		4	1	
Mahew, John....	2	2	5		
Morriss, Daniel....	2	1	1		2
Miller, John (Joiner)...	3				
Mockbee, James....	2	3	7		
Mead, William....	2	2	3		
Mangun, James....	1	4	3		
Mahew, Edward, Snr..	1	1	2		
Mahony, Edward, Jr...	1	3	3		
Milhard, William....	1	2			
Miles, John....	1		2		7
McGill, Robert....	1		2		16
Murdock, Margarett....			3		25
Magruder, Jeremiah....	1		1		36
Magruder, Henderson..	1				5
Marlow, Margarett....		1			11
Moore, Jonas....	2	2	6		1
Mullekin, James....	3	2	3		36
Mantle, John....	1		3		
Masters, John....	2	3	3		8
Masters, Philip....	1	1	3		
Morriss, William....	1	2	3		
Mahew, William....	1	2	5		
McCoy, John....	2	2	4		5
Mockbee, William J....	2	3	3		
Mitchell, Benjamin....	2	2	3		4
Mahew, Timothy....	2	2	4		
Moran, James....	1	3	3		
Magruder, Samuel....	1		1		14
Mahew, Robert....	1	1	6		
Magruder, Thos....	1		1		1
Magruder, Francis....	1		3		9
Murdock, Addison....	1				89
McCoy, Daniel....	1	2	2		
Miles, Frederick....	1	2	2		3
Moodie, William....	9	2	12		
Miles, Nathan....	1	3	7		12
Mitchell, Thos (of Mordecai)..	1	2	3		2
Miles, Edward....	1	1	1		
McDonold, John....	1	1	3		
Marten, Ann....		3	2		
Mangun, Zachariah....	1		2		
Mitchell, Miles....	1	3	2		
Mockbee, Mary....			6		
Mills, Zachariah....	1		1		
Marten, Hugh....	1				
Mitchell John, Jr....	1	1	2		
Mud, Henry Lowe....	1	2	5		6
Mud, Hezekiah....	1	1	5		8
Moland, Tebitha....	2	3	1		29
Murry, John....	1	3	1		
Mockbee, Joseph....	1		2		5
Marten, William....	1		3		
Mitchell, Ninian....	1	1	5		
Marten, Smith....	1	1	2		1
Marshall, John....	1		2		
Marthew, Findley....	1		4		14
Mattingly, Leonard....	2		3		3
Mattingly, Edward....	2	2	3		
Mahony, Edward....	1	3	4		
Moore, Zachariah....	1	1	1		4
McEldry, Partrick....	3	1	1		6
McClesh, Robert....	2	1	3		2
Morriss, William....	1	1	2		1
Mahew, Robert....	1		2		
Mishoe, John....	1		2		
McAtee, John....	1	1	4		2
McAtee, Walter....	1	2	3		6
McIntosh, John....	1				
Magruder, Haswell....	2	3	3		3
Moran, James....	1	2	2		1
Mahew, Brian....	1	2	3		
Moland, Tabitha....	2	3	1		18
Manning, John....	3	3	2		26
Marshall, Richard....	1	4	2		2
Marlow, Dorothy....	1		2		11
Mahew, Elisha....	1	3	4		
Marbrey, Patsey....	1		2		3
Mason, Philip....	1	2	2		
Marten, Henry....	2	3	3		1
Miles, James....	1	1	3		
Magruder, Alexr....	1	1	2		
Manley, John....	1	3	2		
Mockbee, John....	1	3	7		
Moore, Jeremiah....	1	2	2		
Mullikin, Sarah....		3	2		5
Mullikin, Thomas....	1	1	3		6
Nicholdson, Jeremiah....	1	3	5		
Nicholds, Edward....	1	2	2		12
Naylor, George (of Jas)..	4	1	4		2
Neagle, James....	1		2		
Naylor, George....	1	3	2		2
Naylor, Batson....	1				
Naylor, Lawson John..	1	4	3		14
Nevet, John, Jur....	1	3	4		5
Naylor, Joshua, Senr..	2	2	2		11
Naylor, Joshua, Jur....	1	1	1		
Nevet, Charles....	2	1	3		3
Nixson, John....	1		1		
Neven, John, Senr....	2		2		10
Neil, Fielder....	3		4		10
Newman, George....	1		4		10
Newman, Verlinda....	1	2	6		3
Nicholds, William, Jr..	2	4	3		8
Norwood, Edward....	1		2		12
Nyhten, Keser....	1	1	1		
Newton, Eleanor....	2		2		
Norriss, Philip....	1	1	1		
Neal, Sarah....	4	1	4		10
Nash, Mary....	2	2	2		
Nyhten, Samuel....	2	2			
Needham, John....	1	1	1		
Newton, Nathaniel....	2		4		46
Nevet, Richard, Jur....	1	2	2		1
Norton, Robert....	2	3	4		
Neal, Elisabeth....		2	7		
Ogden, Benjamin....	1				3
Osborn, Francis....	2	4	5		
Osborn, Denniss....	1	1	2		
Orme, Moses....	1	1	1		4
Orme, Samuel....	1	3	2		5
Oneal, William....	1	4	3		1
Oliver, Cornelias....	1	2	3		
Owens, John....	1	2	3		
Oneal, Anthony....	4	2	5		
Ogle, Benjamin....	1				26
Owens, Joseph....	1	3	2		
Owens, Zachariah....	1	6	2		5
Owens, William....	2	4	4		
Orme, Robert....	2	4	4		1
Oneal, Nathl....	1		3		
Oliver, Sarah....		1	5		
Osborn, Stephen....	1	1	2		
Owens, Benjamin....	3				15
Osborn, Joseph....	4		1		
Osborn, Archabel....	1		2		
Osborn, Oliver....	2				1
Owens, Samuel....	1	3	4		1
Peach, William....	2		2		
Poole, John....	3	1	5		
Pierce, James....	1	1	2		5
Pierce, Richard....	2	1	3		
Pierce, Caty....		4	2		
Perry, John....	4	3			42
Priggs, Jno F. Augustus..	1		2		17
Pagget, Henry, Jnr....	1		3		
Pagget, Benedic....	1		2		
Parker, John....	1	1	2		
Piles, Francis....	4	2	2		
Philbert, Joseph....	1	2	1		4
Phelps, Stephen....	2				1
Pumphry, William....	2	2	4		4
Perkins, Thomas....	1	3	3		
Ponsenby, Richard....	3	1	2		3
Pope, Joseph, Senr....	3		5		19
Pope, Nathaniel....	3		3		4
Peach, William J....	1		2		
Peach, Richard....	2	2	5		13
Plummer, John....	2	2	3		8
Plummer, Thomas....	4	6	5		3
Peters, Robert....	1				9
Peach, William....	1				12
Phelps, Robert....	4	1	2		1
Peter, Saml John....	1	1	5		
Pierce, Edward....	1	2	2		2
Pierce, Thomas....	1		4		1
Parker, Thomas....	1		4		2
Pierce, James....	1		2		5
Pumphry, Samuel....	2	2	2		4
Pollenger, Dr Robt....	4	3	6	2	74
Pratt, Eleanor....	2		3		12
Parrott, Christopher..	2	2	3		7
Page, Anthony....	2	3	4		5
Parks, Rogers....	1	3	4		
Plummer, Cupid....				6	
Phenix, Thomas....	2		1		
Parson, James....	1	2	2		
Poore, Thomas....	4	2	2		
Phelps, Jonathan....	1		1		1
Pope, Humphry....	1	2	2		
Phelps, Samuel....	1		1		1
Perry, Samuel....	1				
Powhorn, Henry....	1				
Pope, Joseph J....	1	1	1		1
Parnal, Thomas....	1	3	3		10
Prather, Ann....	2		4		7
Pope, Joseph, Jur....	1	1	2		3
Prather, Zepheniah....	3	2	6		7
Powell, Joseph....	2	2	3		
Parker, Smith Althea..	1		1		12
Payne, Francis....	2	1	3		
Perkins, Samuel....	1				
Prather, Joseph....	1	3	4		3
Prather, James....	1	1	3		
Piles, Dorothy....	2	2	5		
Parmer, William....	2	2	3		
Peacock, John....	1	1			1
Parker, Elisabeth....					5
Pumphry, James....	1	2	1		2
Pagget, Zachariah....	1		3		1
Prather, James, Jnr....	1		3		2
Perkins, William....	1	2	4		7
Phelps, Josias....	1	2	3		
Prather, Benjamin....	1	3	1		3
Phelps, Edward....	1	3	5		
Peters, John....	3		5		16
Prather, Nathan....	3		3		
Peach, Jo Elson....	1	1	1		
Queen, Francis....	2	1	1	1	11
Queen, Joseph....	3	1	3	1	7
Queen, Walter....	1	4	3		12
Queen, Richard....	1		4		21
Rawlings, Benjamin....	1		3		
Rogers, Margarett Lee..	1	4	2		25
Rawlings, Paulings....	2	2	2		1
Rawlings, Daniel....	1		3		
Richardson, Elisha....	1	1	1		1
Richards, Richard....	1	1	6		1
Roundell, Marthew....	1	3	4		24
Ryan, Darby....	1	2	5		2
Ryan, Sarah....			4		1
Ryan, John (of Nat.)..	1				
Rawlings, William....	1		2		3
Ranter, John....	2	3	2		6
Ryan, Clement....	1		1		
Rawlings, Thomas....	1		2		
Ryan, Joseph....	1				1
Robertson, Hezekiah..	1	3	2		
Robet, John....	1	3	2		
Ruglass, William....	1		1		1
Read, John....	1	1	1		2
Redman, Cap. Mathias..	1		2		5
Ryan, Sarah....	1		4		2
Ridgway, Benjamin, Senr..		2			
Ridgway, Richard, Senr..	2	1	4		
Rozer, Henry....	2		5		120
Ross, William....	3	1	6		
Ross, Arranna....	3	3	6		18

PRINCE GEORGES COUNTY—Continued.

NAME OF HEAD OF FAMILY.	Free white males of 16 years and upward, including heads of families.	Free white males under 16 years.	Free white females, including heads of families.	All other free persons.	Slaves.
Ross, Thomas	2				2
Riley, Mary		2	4		2
Riston, Rachel		1	3		
Ryan, Basil	2	1	3		1
Russell, Mary	2	1	3		
Riley, Johnson Michael	3	4	6		13
Ross, Richard	1	2	1		2
Riddle, Jacob	2		3		1
Ray, Benjamin	1	3	3		
Rawlings, James	1	3	2		16
Ray, John	2	1	3		6
Riston, Zadock	2	2	3		
Ryly, Margaret	2	1			
Russell, Benjamin	1	4	1		
Riston, Elisha	1		3		
Ridgway, John	1	3	1		14
Rob, Adam	1	1	1		3
Riston, Basil	1	1	1		
Ridgway, Benjamin, Jur	1		1		
Robertson, Cassander		3	2		
Rawlings, Moses			3		
Riley, Thomas	1	2	5		
Robertson, George	1	1	3		
Runnells, Thomas	1	3	4		3
Richardson, Capn Thos	4		1		2
Rawlings, Isaac	2	3	4		
Robertson, Benjamin	3	2	2		
Resin, Glascoe	2	3	4		3
Robertson, John	2	1	3		9
Robertson, Charles, Senr	1		1		3
Robertson, James	1	1	4		
Runnells, Thomas	1		3		3
Robertson, Charles	1	1	1		
Reed, James	1	6	2		6
Row, Anthony	3	4	2		
Richards, Cesor	2	2	6		4
Richards, William	1		4		8
Richardson, Jonas	1	1	2		
Roberts, Sarah	2	1	6		
Robertson, Stephen	1	2	4		
Robertson, Hezekiah	1	2	3		
Riddle, John, Senr	1	1	1		5
Ridgway, Richard, Jur	1	3	2		
Ray, Johanah	4	4	3	2	
Right, Robert	1	2	3		
Selby, Philip	1	2	6		6
Steal, Alexander	1	2	6		
Senkler			2		
Skinner, Priscilla	1	2	3		26
Smith, Joseph	2	4	6		3
Simmons, Robert	2	1	3		5
Sibbald, George	1	1	5		4
Strickland, Joseph	1	3	2		3
Scott, Judson	1	2	1		1
Summers, Levin	1	2	1		
Summervell, Cap. James	1	1	3		45
Smith, Thos (Constable)	1	1	3		3
Stamp, George	1	2	2		5
Sassor, William, Jur	2	4	4		
Screver, Richard	2	4	4		
Sassor, William, Senr	2		4		17
Sassor, Jonathan	1	2	3	1	
Swan, Henry	1	1	4		
Swan, Edward	1	2	3		
Scott, Charles	1	2	4		
Swan, James	2	3	4		15
Smith, Isaac	1	1	4		11
Strickland, William	1	1	3		
Shaw, Joseph	1		1		2
Smith, Dr Richard	2		4		18
Spalding, John	1	1	4		9
Spalding, James	2	2	3		3
Smallwood, John	1	1	1		1
Stephens, Thomas	1	4	3		6
Sansbury, Thomas	2	2	4		
Simms, Stephen	1		4		
Summers, Jonathan	1	2	1		5
Simpson, Thomas, Snr	1	1	4		
Simpson, Peter	2		2		
Saratt, Francis	2	6	2		
Savaree, Peter	1		2		18
Scott, Zachariah	3	1	5		
Stone, Joseph	4		3		
Stone, John	4		1		
Summers, George	1	2	1		4
Simmons, Robert	2	1	2		
Sesw, Nathan	1	2	6		
Summers, Josias	3	2	4		6
Soaper, Robert, Jr	1		2		
Soaper, Sarah	1		2		14
Soaper, Leonard	3	4	6		14
Soaper, John	2	1	3		9
Smith, Dr Clement	1		1		11
Short, James	1	1	2		
Scott, Watkins	1	1	1		

NAME OF HEAD OF FAMILY.	Free white males of 16 years and upward, including heads of families.	Free white males under 16 years.	Free white females, including heads of families.	All other free persons.	Slaves.
Swan, John	3		1		1
Soaper, Alexr	4		3		4
Sansbury, John	1	3	2		
Summers, Nathan	1	1	2		2
Simpson, Joseph	1		2		
Stewart, Dr John	2	2	4		13
Sydebottam, William	1	1			7
Shurlock, Robert	2	4	4		
Stamp, Joseph	2	2	2		
Sheriff, Thomas	1	2	6		
Standage, Eleanor		2	3		2
Stone, David	2	3	2		
Simmans, Jonathan	4	7	2		9
Suit, Smith John	1	2	2		1
Spalding, Philip	1		4		5
Smith, Henry	1	1	2		1
Skull, Fredk Constant			2		
Selby, Henry	3	2	5		
Scott, John (Taylor)	3		3		
Shreaves, John	1	2	4		
Smith, Edd Miles	2	4	1		
Sprigg, Richard	1		2		65
Sweaney, Darkey		1	3		
Sweaney, Loyd	1	1	5		
Soaper, Zadock	1	1	6		
Scott, Chs (B Smith)	3	3	2		3
Sute, Mary	1	2	3		1
Soper, Nathan	1	2	4		8
Selby, James	1	4	3		
Smith, Thomas	2	5	1		
Smith, H. James	2	3	6		11
Sheckells, Samuel	2	3	5		9
Senkler, George	3	1	1		1
Sparrow, Joseph	1	2	1		
Shaw, Charles	1	5	2		1
Snowden, Thomas	2	3	2	3	120
Snowden, Samuel	4	2	6	23	
Selby, Henry	2	3	4		
Slator, Jonathan	1		4		29
Sprigg, Osborn	1		2		43
Stallings, Thomas	3	1	2		8
Soaper, James	3		3		10
Sansbury, Francis	1	1	5		
Stephens, Edward	1	1	3		
Symmes, Alexr	1		3		10
Scott, Matthew	1		3		8
Sansbury, Elections	1		2		6
Sansbury, Eleanor		1	3		12
Stone, Zepheniah	1		3		
Sands, Robert	1	3	3		1
Seeburn, Zachariah	1		2		
Sparrow, Joseph	2	1	2		
Simms, Stephen	1		4		
Stone, John	1	5	3		
Sullivan, Patrick	1		2		
Sewell, Robert	1		2		17
Shreaves, Joshua	1	3	2		
Stephens, John, Senr	1		1		9
Simms, Edward	1	2	1	1	
Sutton, Thomas					
Simpson, John, Senr	1		4		
Smith, William	1	1	2		
Smith, John	1		3		
Summers, Elisabeth			4		4
Sutton, William	2	2	4		
Stephens, William	2	1	3		
Shaw, William	1	2	5		
Shearwood, Jacob	1	2	2		
Simpson, John (of Green)	2	1	7		16
Stonetheat, Richard	1	1	2		5
Simpson, John	1	2	1		
Simpson, James	1		2		
Shreaves, Joshua	1	2	2		
Schofield, Jasper	5	2	3		
Smith, James	1	2	3		
Riddle, Philip	1	1	2		
Simms, Darky		2	1		
Simms, William	1	2	1		2
Stewart, John	1	2	3		
Shade, Patsey		2	4		
Shearwood, Susanah		2	2		
Stephens, John, Jr.	1	1	3		1
Sansbery, Richard	1	2	1		
Sewell, Jamina			3		
Simpson, Joseph	1	2	3		
Summers, John	3	3	5		3
Selby, Nathan	1	1	5		1
Shipley, Resen	3	1	1		
Selby, William	3	1	6		3
Selby, Josiah	2	1	1		
Selby, Nathan	2		2		1
Turner, Elisha	1	1	7		
Tayman, Equilla	1	1	2		

NAME OF HEAD OF FAMILY.	Free white males of 16 years and upward, including heads of families.	Free white males under 16 years.	Free white females, including heads of families.	All other free persons.	Slaves.
Taylor, William	1	1	1		1
Tompson, Charles	1		3		
Taylor, John	1	1	4		
Townsend, Leonard	2		1		4
Taylor, Benjamin	2	4	3		5
Talbott, Thomas	2		3		
Tolson, Francis	1	3	5		24
Tompson, John	1	1	5		1
Talbott, Paul	2	2	4		
Talbott, Thomas, Jr	2	4	3		
Tennelly, William	2	4	3		
Talbott, Nathl	1	1	2		
Talbott, Zadock	1	2	3		2
Tilley, John	1		1		2
Tompson, James	3	3	4		
Talbott, Henry	1	2	4		
Talbott, Basil	2	3	4		
Talbott, Nathl, Senr	1	1	4		6
Tongue, William	2	5	5		1
Tarman, William	1	2	3		
Turner, Shadrick	2	1	4		6
Tyler, Samuel	2	2	5		15
Taylor, Gideon	1	1	3		
Thomas, Anthony	1	4	1		3
Thomas, William	1	5	4	2	
Tyler, William	1		6		10
Trueman, Monecai	2		5		
Tate, James	3	1	2		
Turner, Philip	4	3	6		22
Thursby, Edward	1		3		2
Talbott, Henry	1	2	3		1
Taylor, Priscilla	1	1	4		
Taylor, John	2	1	4		
Talbott, Tobias	1	4	5		
Tayman, Richard, Jr	1	1	4		6
Tylor, Bradley Robert	2	1	3		48
Tayman, Benjamin	2	1	4		3
Tucker, Sarah	2	2	4		
Thomas, Anthony	1	4	2		1
Turner, John	1	6	3		
Taylor, Soloman	1	1	4		
Tayman, Henry	1		4		
Tasker, Benjamin	1		3		
Tompson, James	1	3	2		
Truck, Partrick	1		2		
Taylor, John	1		3		
Tolbott, Tobias	1	5	4		
Thomas, Josias	1	1	1		2
Tilley, Mary	1		3		16
Tilley, Thomas	1	2	3		8
Turner, Bruce	3	1	3		8
Thrawls, Richard	1	1	2		
Townsend, Samuel, Senr	1	2	5		18
Townsend, Samuel, Jur	1	1	5		5
Thorn, Zachariah	2	2	2		1
Tompson, Clarke	2	2	2		
Taylor, Thomas	2		3		
Thorn, Burch	2		4		
Tuth, Timothy	1	2	1		
Thorn, Anthony	1		1		
Tippet, Charles	1	2	2		2
Tenley, Benjamin	3	3	3		
Turner, Benjamin				5	1
Thorn, Amelia	1	3	2		
Tasker, Richard	1		1		
Turvey, William	2	2	1		
Thomas, Thomas	2	4	6		
Thompson, F. John	1	2	1		1
Thorn, Thomas	1	1	3		2
Thomas, James	1	1	4		
Turner, Margarett	1		2		
Turner, Josiah	3	1	3		8
Turner, Catharine			3		3
Turner, Elisabeth			3		10
Turner, Samuel	2	2	2		3
Upton, George	2	4	6		
Upton, Thomas	1		4		
Underwood, Charity			4		
Underwood, Thomas	1	1	2		1
Underwood, George	1		2		
Vermillion, Giles	3	3	5		
Venables, William	1	4	2		1
Veitch, Mary		3	2		
Vermillion, Edward	2	2	8		
Vegal, Adam	1		2		
Vaughan, George	3	3	2		
Vermillion, Sarah	1		3		
Venables, Areeage			3		
Vincent, Cloye			3		
Veich, Mary	1	3	2		
Vermillion, John	3	5	5		
Vernan, Caleb	5		1		
Walker, Thomas	2	2	3		
Willett, Edward	4	2	5		11
Willson, James	3		3		27

PRINCE GEORGES COUNTY—Continued.

NAME OF HEAD OF FAMILY.	Free white males of 16 years and upward, including heads of families.	Free white males under 16 years.	Free white females, including heads of families.	All other free persons.	Slaves.
Williams, John Howard.	4				
Wales, Edward Loyd.	4		5		22
Watson, Thomas (of Jno).	2		4		1
Watson, James, Jur.	1	3	6		
Watson, William, Snr.	3		1		1
Watson, James.	1	3	2		3
Wills, Samuel.	1	3	2		
Wall, Thomas.	1	2	3		4
Wall, William.	1	1	3		2
Watson, William.	4	1	1		
Waugh, Singleton.	1	2	2		1
Watson, David.	1	4	4		
Watson, Walter.	3	1	5		
Warring, James.	1	4	3		2
Watson, Walter (of Jas).	1	1	3		2
Wall, George.	1	1	3	1	1
Warring, Leonard.	2	4	4		9
Wyfield, Mary.	1	1	2		
Watson, William, (of Wm).	1	2	2		
Watson, James (of Wm.)	1	3	6		
Watson, William, Jr.	2		2		3
Watson, John (of Isaac).	2	1	4		
Willson, Barnabee.	1			4	
Wright, Samuel.	2		4		10
Warring, Massam.	1				10
Warring, John.	1	2	3		68
Watson, James, Senr.	2		1		
Walker, John.	1		1		
Walker, Francis.	1	1	5		
Winkler, Christopher.	1	2	1		
Warters, Joseph.	1	2	1		
Wade, John.	1	2	2		
Watkins, Stephen.	1	3	4		1
Walker, Benjamin.	1		1		
Walker, John.	2	6	2		
Wade, George.	1	1	3		1
Wheat, Francis.	2	5	3		5
Wales, Levin.	1	1	6		14
Warthing, Leonard.	1		1		
Willson, William.	1	3	5		9
Willson, Elisabeth.					5
Willson, Joseph, Jur.	2		2		2
Willson, Nathaniel.	1	2	2		7
Willcoxen, Elizabeth.	2	3	4		12
Wright, Joseph.	1		1		5
Wood, Mary.	2		2		
Wood, Ignatious.	1	1	2		2
Wade, Cap. Robert.	2				16
White, Fielder.	1	3	4		
Williams, Owens Thos.	2	5	2		38
Willson, Joseph.	1	1	4		5
Willson, Elisabeth.	1		4		8
Washington, Nathl.	2				37
Willson, Joseph (of Lancelot).	1	1	2		5
Wegfield, Marthew.	3	2	4		3
Waugh, Mary.	2		4		
Waugh, John, Senr.	2		4		
Wise, Thomas, Senr.	2	3	2		
Warring, James, Snr.	2	1	2		8
Willson, James, Snr.	1				14
Wells, William.	1		1	1	3
Winsor, Ignatious.	2	4	1		
Willson, David.	1		4		
Warring, Elisabeth.	1		4		10
Willson, Thomas.	1	1	3		
Willson, Joseph.	1	1	1		
Williams, Richard.	1	2	4		8
Willett, Ninian.	1	1	1		4
Wallace, William.	2	1	4		
West, Jasper.	2		1		5
Webster, L. Philip.	3		1		
Walker, Isaac, Jr.	1			1	1
Warman, Berry Willm.	1		1		14
Wood, Peter.	1				10
Willson, Josias.	1	1	2		2
Williams, Verlinda.	3		2		42
Waters, William.	2		4		15
Waters, Jacob.	1		3		
Waters, Thomas.	1		2		11
Waters, Robert.	2	3	3		14
Welsh, Thomas.	1		3		4
Waters, Arnold.	1		2		36
Whitaker, Margery.		1	2		25
Wells, Jacob.	2	3	5		2
Wells, Elisabeth.		5	3		5
Woodward, Thos, Jur.	2	4	3		1
White, William.	1		3		6
Wells, Rachel.			3		1
Waters, Artridge.	1		3	3	1
Woodward, Thos, Senr.	1		2		8
Wells, Duckett John.	2	3	5		
Weems, Amelia.	2		4		38
Willson, Thomas.	2	2	4		
White, James, Senr.	1	1	2		9
White, John.	2	1	2		8
Willson, William.	2		5		
Woodward, Clement.	1	3	4		
Walker, Charles.	2	2	3		12
Walker, Joseph.	2	1	4		11
Willson, Willm (of James).	1	2	5		13
Wheatley, Richard.	1		2		10
Williams, John.	2	2	5		9
Wood, William.	1	1	2		
Wood, Leonard.	2	1	5		
Wooddart, Benedick.	1	2	4		
Wheeler, Clement.	1		4		2
Warring, Basil, Jr.	4	2	9		25
Wallingsford, George.	1	1	2		
Wood, John.	1	1	2		
Wallingsford, Joseph.	1	3	4		1
Weavor, Jacob.	1	2	6		
Warring, Basil, Senr.	1	1	2		62
Wheeler, Robert.	2	1	5		
Warring, John.	2	1	3		
Williams, Cave.	1		1		11
Wells, Nathan.	1		4		
Waugh, John.	2	2	4		
Whealor, Jacob.	1	3	2	1	
Watkins, Gassaway.	1		3		
Willson, Norando.	1	2	4		
Wheatley, Silvester.	1		4		
Walker, M. Duvall.	1	1	2		1
Weems, N. Chapman.					14
Willson, Clement.	1	1	2		
Williams, Richard.	2	1	4		6
Walls, Hannah.	2	3	3		7
West, Hannah.	3	1	7		147
Waters, Edward.	2	2	3		4
Waugh, Singleton.	1	1	2		
Wise, William.	1		1		
Weeden, Nathl.	1	1	4		1
Whitehead, Thomas.	1		3		
White, Benjamin.	1				5
White, Allen.	1	1	4		
White, Jonathan.	1		3		
Wells, Joseph.	1	2	5		11
Willson, Joseph.	2	2			7
Walter, Watson.	1	1	3		2
Wade, Lancelott.	2	1	2		6
White, Elisha.	1	1			3
White, John.	1		1		
White, James.	1			1	
Wise, Thomas.	1		1		
Wilburn, Margarett.			1	2	
Webster, William.	1				
White, Absolum.	1	2	4		
Willson, Joseph Sprgg.	1	1	4		8
Welsh, Thomas.	3		3		5
Williams, Elisabeth.			3		
Willson, Marianna.	1	2	3		
Wood, Zachariah.	1		1		
Willson, William.	1	1	8		
Wynn, Wm Smallwood.	1	1	4		
Wynn, Hesekiah.	1	2	4		2
Wade, Robert, Senr.	2		2		1
Wheeler, Hesekiah.	1		2		20
Walker, Henry.	2	2	5		
Wheat, John.	3	3	4		2
Wade, Ann.	3	1	2		
Wells, William.	2		3		
Wade, Lancelott.	2	1	3		5
Willson, Ann.	1	2	3		2
Wells, Martain.	1	2	3		
Willson, Nathaniel.	1	2	2		8
Willett, William.	2	4	4		2
Warum, William.	1	1	3		
Wootton, Turner.	1		1	1	53
Webster, James.	1	1	2		
Whitmore, Benjamin.	1	1	2		
Willing, Thomas.	1	1	1		3
Ward, Benjamin.	2	2	2		
Wade, Zachr (of Richd).	1	2	2		1
Warthing, Allias.	1		1		
White, Benjamin.	1	1	4		
White, Jonathan.	1	1	2		
Waters, Henry.	1	1	3		1
Waters, Richard.	1	2	2		1
Grimes, Partrick.	1				
Peters, William.	1				
Waters, Allen.		2	1		
Webb, Samuel.	2	3	2		
Winstead, Sarah.	2		4		
Walker, Isaac (of Isaac).	1	2	1		
Warring, Marcas.	1	2	2		10
Gleason, Thomas.	1	3	5		
Adkinson, Thomas.	1				
Bosswell, Edward.	2	3	5		
Young, William.	1	3	4		10
Young, Abraham.	1	2	3		12
Young, John.	1	1	1		
Young, Hezekiah.	1		2		3
Young, Robert.	2	4	4	2	19
Young, Thomas.	2	2	4		15
Young, Notley.	6	8			265
Young, Nicholas.	3	3	3		31
Bartley, William.	2	2	1		
McGill, Joseph.	2		1		
Burch, Edward.	2				
Lucas, Ignatious.	1	3	4		2
Selby, Joshua.	1		1	1	2
Burch, Thomas, Jr.	1	4	3		
Beall, John (of John).	2	3	3		1
Beall, Reason.	1		2		14
Brasheare, Samuel.	1	2	3		
Burger, Ezekel.	2	4	4		
Brown, John.	2	2	3		
Brown, Elisabeth.	1	1	2	1	1
Brown, William.	1	4	3		
Beall, Nathan.	1		1		
Beall, James, Jr.	1		2		
Brown, William, Jr.	1	2	2		10
Bowman, Jaret.	2		3		
Brashears, Samuel (Taylor).	1	2	3		2
Brasheare, Belt.	1	1	1		2
Cheney, Richard.	1	2			
Nan, Free.				5	
Henry, Froe.				5	
Nany, Froe.				4	
Jim, Free.				10	
Pegg, Free.				6	
White, Absolum.	1	2	4		
Benson, Thomas.					
Burge, Ezekel.					
Belt, Brashears.					

QUEEN ANNS COUNTY.

NAME OF HEAD OF FAMILY.	Free white males of 16 years and upward, including heads of families.	Free white males under 16 years.	Free white females, including heads of families.	All other free persons.	Slaves.
Paca, William.	2				92
Chew, Bennett.	2		2		39
Hemsley, William.	3	4	6		45
Tilghman, Richard.	4				85
Harris, Edward.	2	2	4		20
Wright, Robert.	1	4	4		30
Bordley, John Beall.	2		2		128
Botton, George.	2	1	2		
Nabb, John.	2	2	3		2
Hobb, Henry.	2		3		
Bayard, Pew F.	3			1	
Elliott, John.	2	1	3		2
Lesage, Thomas.	1	1	3		
Abbott, Thomas.	3		3		1
Butler, Robert.	2	2	3		11
Levick, Solomon.	1	3	2		
Scott, Henry.	1		2		15
Davis, Philip.	1	1	2		3
Camper, John.	1	1	3		
Emory, Gideon.	1		3	1	45
Emory, James.	1				6
Dawson, Robert.	1		3		
Thomas, Samuel.	4	2	2		22
Downes, John K.	3	1	2		20
Hall, Edward.	2	1	2		14
Hall, Francis.	3	1	3		60
Clayton, Solomon.	1	3	2		9
Earle, James.	2				24
Anderson, Rachel.			6		
Betton, Turbutt.	2		2		11
Betton, Dyer.	2	1	2		7
Betton, Samuel.	2	4	4		7
Tilghman, James.	3	3	5		50
Clayton, Mary.			3		11
Johnns, Kinsey.	3		1		2
Willson, Richard.	1	2	2		1
Barrack, Nicholas.	1		2		1
Read, Jacob.	1		3		1
Perkum, Elizabeth.			2		
Caradine, Thomas.	2		2		17
Barnes, Thomas.	1	1	4		19
Betton, Thomas.	2	4	4		20

QUEEN ANNS COUNTY—Continued.

NAME OF HEAD OF FAMILY.	Free white males of 16 years and upward, including heads of families.	Free white males under 16 years.	Free white females, including heads of families.	All other free persons.	Slaves.
Hanimon, John	2	2	4		16
Tilghman, William	2		4		37
Nevitt, William	3		2		4
Elitt, Mary			3	2	
Jackson, Elizabeth			2	14	27
Griffin, Edward	1	1	4		
Kent, John	1	1	2		3
Keys, Richard	1		1		
Pierce, Andrew	2	2	3		6
Glenn, Samuel	1	5	3		
Price, Mary			2		9
Rogers, Edward	1		5		13
Broun, Sarah		1	3		
Carey, Dennis	2		2		7
Seth, Rachel	1		3		
Mayson, William		3	6		3
Carmichael, Richard B	1	1	5		43
Harrington, Richard	1	1	4		1
Wrightson, Thomas	1		1	1	
Wrightson, Elizabeth		1	2		
Emory, William W	1		1		6
Chambers, Martha	1		2		
Wilson, Mary		4	3		27
Smyth, Nathan	1	1	1		
Coursey, Edward	1	1	1		45
Flamer, Solomon				9	
Dimond, William	1	1	3	4	
Wayman, Edward	3		2	1	3
Daphny, Free					2
Jennings, John	3		2	3	
Thomas, William	2	3	1		11
Thomas, Christopher	2	1	4		7
Sewell, Samuel	1	2	1		
Jeffries, Elias	1				11
Skeggs, Edward	2	2	2		3
Emory, Thomas L	1	1	7		28
Darden, Thomas	1	1	2		13
Emory, John	1				5
Caradine, William			1	1	9
Caradine, Christopher W	1		1	2	
Glinn, Charles	2	2	4		2
Broun, John	2	3	5		10
Wilkins, Mathew	1		1		1
Parsnett, David	1	1	1	1	9
Phillips, Sarah			2		4
Phillips, Christopher	1		2		4
Lanaway, Mary Ann			2	6	
Blake, Charles	3		6		58
Knotts, John	1	3	4		
Jump, Isaac	1	2	2		
Emory, Richard	2	2	1		1
Lowe, Thomas	3		2		
Garland, Thomas	5		2		1
Valiant, Robert		2	2		
Quinn, John	1	2	1		
Coursey, Henry	1	1	4		7
Valiant, James	1		2		
Pinder, James	4	2	2		3
Hargadine, Edward	2	2	3		
Bath, Elinder	1		1		
Cheese, Rebecca			1		
Caldwell, James	1		2		2
Noland, William	2	3	2		
McCallister, Patience	1	1	2		6
Barron, Jeremiah	1	1	3		
Robins, Mary	1		1		
Cheese, Hannah		2	1		1
Somervill, Henry	1		3		6
Jackson, Henry	2		1		12
Brown, Robert	3	3	2		47
Seth, Thomas J	1		4	14	18
Coursey, William	1		4		42
McDaniel, Andrew	1	2	1		
Dodd, Thomas	1	1	5		
Plummer, Phillip	2		3		
Chapman, Thomas	1	1			1
Hobbs, Joseph	2	2	3		
Holton, Solomon	1		1		6
Legar, Joseph	1	3	3		
Meridith, Thomas	1	3	3		
Coursey, Mary	1		4		13
Sarah, Free				4	
Willson, Eleanor		3	2		12
Gadd, Thomas			2		
Knotts, James B	1		3		1
Keys, Ann		1	3		
Emory, Arthur	2	1	5		12
Ratcliff, Robert	1	1	1		1
Downes, Edward	2	1	2		18
Wright, Samuel T	2		2	3	27
Emmerson, Vincent	1	1	3		
Wright, Rachel	1	1	3		31
Greenhalk, John	1	1	3		1
Downing, William	1		4	2	1
Read, Thomas	2	2	5	2	
Read, Jesse	2		2		6
Tane, Free				5	

NAME OF HEAD OF FAMILY.	Free white males of 16 years and upward, including heads of families.	Free white males under 16 years.	Free white females, including heads of families.	All other free persons.	Slaves.
Gordon, George	2	3	5		
Vin, Free				7	
Blake, Philomon C	1	3	1		19
Bolton, Sam¹, Stew⁴ of Poor House of Q. Anns County	6	9	15		4
Lowe, Aaron	4	2	4	1	3
Emmerson, Ephraim	1		3		20
Sedera, John	4	2	8		6
Yewell, Solomon	3	1	2		6
Tuite, Robert	1		2		30
Horne, William	1	1	1		1
Nicols, Sam¹	1		3		6
Clayton, Solomon, Jun	4	2	2		10
Cecil, Thomas	1	3	2		15
Willson, John	1	1	3	2	7
Colgan, Esau	1		2		
Jeffries, Benjaman	1		3		1
Nabb, Joseph	2	3	3		
Tresair, John	2	2	2		
Dames, John	2		3		9
Richardson, Daniel	6	3	5		8
Kent, Vachel	2		1		4
Harper, William	6		2		3
Bridle, Ann		3	5		46
Croney, Jane		2	5		
Brue, James	5	3	2	1	2
Scott, Mary	1		1		1
Fowler, Ann		2	1		
Dashield, Sarah		2	4		2
Vere, John	1	2	2		
Santee, Ann	1		1		3
Marchant, John	1		4		2
Kitwell, John	1		1		1
Craftin, Joseph	4		3		
Grant, William	2		7		8
Davidson, James	2	1	3		26
Lowe, Nicholas	2	4	1		4
Clements, Nathan	1		4		5
McHarner, Ann	2		4		
Clements, Rebecca			4		2
Emory, Elizabeth	1		4		
Murphy, Philemon	4	1	4		4
Tucker, Richard	2	5	9		6
Greenwood, William	1	1	4		
Harris, Solomon	2		3		
Jeffries, Peter	1	2	3		
Bryon, Solomon	2		4		1
Camper, Solomon	1				
Ward, John	1				6
Smyth, Emory	1				
Davis, Peter	2	1	8		12
St. Clair, Alexander	2	3	4		
Scott, John	1	1	3		
Collier, James	3	1	1	2	
Harrold, Daniel	1		2		
Green, Peter	1	2	2		6
Blake, John S	2	2	7		63
Lawrence, William	1		2		
Hindman, James	1		3		35
Tate, Robert, Jun'	1		2		17
Lesage, Robert	1		2		11
Fitzpatrick, David	1		3		
Clements, Lambert	3	1	3		3
Lowe, Edmund	2	2	2		2
Collier, Charles	2		3		
Harris, Robert	4	1	1		1
Harris, John	2		6		
Lee, John			6		
Bryon, William	1				
Green, Jacob	1				
Murphy, Philemon	2	1	3		6
Mansfield, Thomas	2	1	3		
Mansfield, William	1		1		
Tate, Robert	1		2		11
Braumin, Uriah	1	1	2		
Dickinson, Esther		1	2		
Tolson, Andrew	2	1	1		7
Olliver, William	2		1		
Chase, John	1	1	3		
Strull, Mary			1		
Ford, William	1	2	2		19
Hand, Mary		3	2	1	
Smyth, John	2	3	1		2
Tames, Eduard	1	1	3		
Collier, Diana	1		3		
Collier, John	2		4		
Imbert, John	2	5	4		11
Wrench, William	2	3	3		
Goodman, Richard	2	3	3		1
Blunt, John	1	2	1		3
Reynolds, James	1	2	1		
Davis, Mary			3		
Thorn, Mary Ann			3		
Walters, Joseph	1	3	1		
Meryday, Moses				5	
Boyd, Robert	1	4	2		23

NAME OF HEAD OF FAMILY.	Free white males of 16 years and upward, including heads of families.	Free white males under 16 years.	Free white females, including heads of families.	All other free persons.	Slaves.
Haycock, James, Jur				7	
Haycock, James				2	6
Haycock, Solomon				2	6
Haycock, William				2	
Allen, Ann			1		
Rimmer, Lambert	1	1	1		
Davis, William, Jur	1	1	3		6
Phillips, Nathaniel	3	1	3		3
Berryman, Chester			1	6	
Bryon, John	1		5		
Watkins, Joseph	1	2	2		2
Mayson, Dinah			2	6	
Hampton, Elizabeth		3	4		5
Jackson, Thomas	4		1		
Jackson, Elizabeth			1		
Downes, Elizabeth			2		
Caradino, Christopher					9
Grant, James	1	3	3	1	4
Wederstrandt, Conrad T	2	4	5		85
Wells, Tobias	2				17
Sudler, Clouds	1	2	5		14
Basnett, Charles	1		1	1	1
Basnett, Nathaniel	1		1		
Emory, Arthur					8
Fitzhugh, Peregrine	1	2	4		46
Goodman, Marmaduke	1	3	6		10
Rowles, Rezen	2		5		17
Walker, James	1	4	5		3
Tottson, Thomas	1	5	4		1
Davis, William	6	2	2		2
Elliott, William	1	5	2		21
Sudler, Benjamin	1		2		4
Weadon, Daniel	3	1	2		10
Weadon, Henry	1	2	4	1	4
Osborn, Samuel	3		4		
Osborn, William	1		5	2	1
Bishop, Joseph	1	1	2		
Saunders, Thomas	1	1	1		
Winchester, Thomas				2	20
Ringgold, Thomas	2	1	1	1	23
Rodenes, Joseph	2	3	4		
Knotts, James	2	1	2		
Ringgold, Thomas, Jun'	1	1	5		21
Cockey, John	2	2	7		17
Elliott, John	2		2		19
Earikson, Charles	1	1	4		8
Earikson, William	3	2	3		6
Earkson, Ann			3		
Aires, William		4	2		
Blunt, John W	3	2	1		2
Spalding, John	2		2		11
Faggett, Henry	2				
Connor, James					1
Blunt, James R	3	2	4		28
Hambleton, William			2	1	6
Barnes, Joseph	3	1	6		10
Sliney, John	3	1	5		12
Blunt, Samuel	2	1	5		11
Young, Benjamin	2		3		1
Winchester, Jacob	1	4	3		9
Hurst, William	2		4	2	4
Long, David	1	1	3	2	11
Weaver, John	1	3	3		
Jones, Abner	2	3	6		
Elliott, Thomas	2		1		
Bond, Charles	1	1	1		
Gardner, Robert	1	2	4		
Watters, Susannah			3		6
Bright, Ann			2		5
Meridith, John	1	1	3		
Conican, Elias	1	1	2		
Joiner, William	1	3	4		
Joiner, Samuel	1		4		
Courcey, William	1		4		
Hoxler, Ann			3		
Holt, Michael	1	1	1		
Bright, Francis	2	1	7	2	11
Hobb, Henry	2		3		
Sneed, Richard	1	2	4	1	10
Custor, Thomas	2		3		
Smyth, Jane	2		1		
Gray, Jane			1	2	
Mercy, William	1		2		
Davis, John	1	2	6	1	2
Derochbrune, James	1	1	3		
Sinners, Charles	1	1	2		
Goodhand, Jones	2		2		4
Ringgold, Jacob	2	3	3		20
Lewis, John	2	3	2		
Lewis, John, Jun'	2	1	1		
Baxter, William, Jun'	1	1	1		15
Hutchings, James	1	1	4	4	25
Brown, Aquila	1	3	4		12
Brown, Edward	1	3			5
Brown, William	1		3		5
Clayland, Sarah		1	1		2

QUEEN ANNS COUNTY—Continued.

NAME OF HEAD OF FAMILY.	Free white males of 16 years and upward, including heads of families.	Free white males under 16 years.	Free white females, including heads of families.	All other free persons.	Slaves.
Goodhand, Marmaduke.	3		3	2	18
Goodhand, John.	1	1	3		2
Watters, John.	2		2		13
Meridith, Mary.			1	3	
Savory, John.	1	1	1	1	
Baster, William.	1	1	2		18
Baster, Thomas.	2		4		5
Downey, William.	1		5		
Goodhan, Nathaniel.	2	4	3	1	8
Corrican, William.	1	1	3		
Earikson, Mary.	2		2	1	4
Richardson, Mary.	3		2	1	12
Chambers, William.	1	1	2		
Carter, Arthur.	2	1	5	1	9
Ellitt, Thomas.	2	2	2		11
Earlkson, James.	2	3	2		20
Chew, Elizabeth.			2		105
Wren, William.	1	2	1		1
Bryon, John.	1		1		
Bryon, William.	1	2	3		1
Huxter, Mary.			3	1	
Tottson, Jacob.	1		5		9
Finnin, Elizabeth.			3		
Stephens, Rachel.	1	1	4		15
Hand, John.	1	2	4		
Derochburn, Louis.	1		2		14
Watters, Robert.	1	2	5	1	9
Joiner, Daniel.	1		1		
Joiner, Absolom.	1				
Josples, Ruben.	1		3		1
Alloway, Thomas.	1	1	1		
Tottson, John.	1	1	2		2
Tanner, Benjamin.	1	1	2		
Osborn, Samuel, Junr.	1		2		
Grimes, John.	1	2	4		
Sliney, Elizabeth.		3	1		8
Gibson, Woolman.	1	1	1	1	2
Sercomb, Mary.			2	1	
Roberts, Jonathan.	1		2		22
Carter, Henry.	3		4		10
Carter, James.	1		2		8
Carter, Jacob.	1	1	1		12
Watters, Benjamin, Junr.	1				3
Hutchings, Elizabeth.			3		
Price, Thomas.	2	2	5		9
Dixon, Henry.	3	1	4		2
Gibbs, Abram.				3	
Gibbs, Absolom.				6	
Sweney, James.	1		2		7
Rolph, Thomas.	2	1	3		
Wright, Thomas.	1	2	5		
Strong, Abram.	1	2	5		
Rolph, John.	2	2	4		7
Price, Lettetia.			6		
Spry, John.	3	2	3	1	1
Keene, Young.	1	1	3		1
Gamble, Robert.	1	1	5		3
Burk, John L.	2		5		
Tharp, Thomas.	1	2	2		
Smyth, Abigail.			5		
Tharp, Augustine.	1		3		
Carson, Mary.		1	3		
Colbutt, Isaac.	3		3	1	
Alley, Bryon.	1		2		
Gilbert, James.	2	4	2		5
Little, Thomas.	3	4	6		7
Cook, Jacob.					10
Bramble, John.	1	1	3		
Caldwell, David.	2	1	2		
Turner, Joseph.	1	3	2		
Woodall, Edward.	1		3		1
Williams, Solomon.	2		4		35
Larwood, William.	4	2	4	1	26
Clark, Charles.	2		4		
Holding, Benjamin.	2		4		1
Vickers, Moses.	1	2	4		
Crosley, Isaac.	2	1	3	2	
Walls, Nathaniel.	1	1	2		
Clarkson, Levinus.	1	1	3		12
Linn, William.	1	1	4		
Steed, William.	1	1	2		
Clymer, James.	1		4		
Clark, Ebenezer.		2	4		
Cook, Joseph.					9
Crews, Eduard.	3	4	2		3
Clannahan, Samuel.	1	1	2		
Carmon, James.	2	1	2		5
Cox, Christopher, Junr.	1		5		10
Covington, James.	1		2		3
Covington, Elijah.	2	2	2		10
Costin, Henry.	1		2		
Carmon, John.	1		2		
Carmon, William.	1	4	3		
Clark, Lambert.	1	1	4		1
Clayton, Sarah.			4		1
Crisp, Benjamin.	1	2	4		

NAME OF HEAD OF FAMILY.	Free white males of 16 years and upward, including heads of families.	Free white males under 16 years.	Free white females, including heads of families.	All other free persons.	Slaves.
Chaires, Samuel S.	2		3		6
Covington, Wells.	1	2	3		5
Carson, Robert.	2	2	2		8
Clannahan, Thomas.	2		1	2	7
Conner, Elizabeth.			1	4	
Cartey, Thomas.	1	1	2		
Colgan, Richard.	1	2	4		5
Conneley, Patrick.	1	1	2		
Davis, Rebecca (W. of John).		1	3		2
Leg, Martha.			1		9
Leg, Samuel.	1	1	5		1
Leg, William.	2	3	3		
Leg, James.	2	1	1	1	
Leg, Samuel, Junr.	1	4	3		
Hunter, John.	2	1	3	1	
Chambers, Thomas.	1	3	4	2	
Knotts, Abner.	2	4	2		
Walters, Ben.	2	1	5		19
Prue, James.	1	2	2		26
Coger, Samuel.					7
Willson, Richard.					4
Grennage, Cusby.					5
Coger, Isaac.					3
Willson, James.					9
Foster, Dinah.					4
Greenwich, Thomas.					5
Willson, William.					10
Limas, Free.					1
O Bryon, James.	1		2		
Weadon, James.	1	3	2		2
Toltson, Sarah.		1	2		19
Carter, John.	1	1	5		18
Loller, David.	1	1	1		
Woolhand, Susannah.	2	1	3		
Faunt Le Roy, Sarah.			2	1	2
Blunt, Labin.	3	2	3		
Downey, Valentine.	2	2	1		
Harvey, Artridge.			1		16
Downey, Alexander.	1	3			
Anderson, William.	1	2	2		
Barnes, Thomas.	3	3			
Joiner, William.	2	1		6	
Wright, Samuel.	2		2	5	
Price, Mary.	2	2	2	1	4
Harper, Samuel.	1	1	2		
Collier, Thomas.	1		2		5
White, Samuel.	1	2	2		9
Ringgold, James.	1	1	2		2
Leg, Benjamin.	1	3	3	1	7
Sneed, Moses.	1	4	5		7
Stevens, John.	1		3		
Duhamiel, James.	1	3	2		6
Duhamiel, John.	1	3	2	1	
Duhamiel, James, Junr.	1	1	1		8
Deford, Thomas.	2		2		
Deford, Jesse.	2		3	4	
Deford, William, Junr.	1	1	3		
Deford, Joseph M.	1	1	1		
Devoux, Thomas.	3	1	3		
Daugherty, Robert.	1	2	1		
Deornish, John.	2		3		
Dailey, James.	1		2		
Dailey, John.	1	1	2		
Davis, Letitia.		1	1		
Davis, Rebecca.	1	1	1		
Dunn, David.					2
Durkery, Joseph.					5
Davis, Nathan.	2	4	3		
Dailey, John (B. D.).	2		3		
Elliott, George.	4		7		1
Emory, John R.	4		4		23
Emory, Robert.	1	2	3		13
Ewing, William.	2	3	3		8
Emory, James.	1	1	2		
Elbert, Jonathan.	4		2		1
Elegander, Esther.		2	4		
Eilers, Norris.	4	1	3		
Ervin, Henry.	1	1	3		12
Fade, Robert.	1	1	2		
Forman, Joseph, Jur.	1		2		
Forcum, Thomas.	1		2		
Forrester, Elias.	1		3		
Falconer, James.	1				
Forman, Joseph.			2		5
Finley, Margaret.	1		2		8
Finley, James, Jun.	1	2	2		
Forcum, John.	1	1	4		
Forcum, Robert.	1	1	2		4
Feddeman, Philip.	1	1	3		24
Finley, George.	3	2	2	1	17
Fowler, Juliana.	2		2		1
Godwin, Elizabeth.		2	2		
Green, Benjamin.	1				
Green, Esther.		1	2		
Glenn, Mary.			4		1

NAME OF HEAD OF FAMILY.	Free white males of 16 years and upward, including heads of families.	Free white males under 16 years.	Free white females, including heads of families.	All other free persons.	Slaves.
Godwin, James.	1		1		1
Grinnage, Benjamin (F. N.).			1	6	
Grinnage, Benjamin (F. M.).				6	
Goldsborough, Robert.	2	1	2		
Grinnage, Jacob (F. M.).				4	
Green, Sarah.		1	4		
Game, Stephen (F. M.).				2	
Glenn, Frederick.	1		2		
Gorman, Mary.		2	2		
Grinnage, Zachariah (F. M.).				8	
Godwin, Nathan.	3	3	2		7
Gould, James.	1	2	3		13
Godwin, John.	4	3	6		2
Gould, Benjamin.	2	1	3		9
Gibson, Rachel.			2		
Gould, Samuel.	3		2		6
Griffin, Thomas.	1	2	1		
Goldsborough, Willm.			2		7
Green, Philemon.	1	1	5		8
Hines, Margaret.	1		5		
Harrison, James.	1		2		
Highet, Isaac.	1		1		
Hopkins, Abram (F. M.).				1	1
Hollingsworth, William.	3	3	1		3
Harris, Edward.	7	2	3		
Hargadine, Mark, Junr.	2	2	2		
Hargadine, Mark.					
Hodgers, Samuel.	1	3	3		
Harris, Joseph.	1	1	3		
Hawkins, Matthew.	1		3		14
Honey, Valentine.	1	3	3	3	5
Hynson, Charles.	1	2	1		1
Hawkins, James.	1		3		11
Hollingsworth, Allen.	1		4		2
Holyday, James.	1		9		62
Harris, James.	2		5		
Harris, Thomas.	1	2	4		
Hewit, John.	2		4		
Hadley, James.	2	4	4		
Honey, James.	1	4	4		4
Harwood, David (F. M.).	2	1	4	7	2
Jackson, Nathan.					
Jones, Batt.	1				
Jeffers, William.	1	2	2		
Jones, John.	1			9	
Julis, John (free negro).					
Kent, James.	3	3	4		9
Kent, John.	1	3	4		1
Kersey, Rebecca.		1	1		
Kersey, Abram.	2	1	3		
Kersey, George.	2		3		
Kenton, Thomas.	2	2	2		
Lawrence, Peter.	2	2	3		
Lowman, James.	1	1	2		
Love, Robert.	1	2	2		
Lacey, Lawrence.	2		2		
Lang, James.	1				
Lane, Mary (F. N.).				4	
Morris, James.	1	1	2		
Merritt, Ezekiel.	1	1	1		
McDannel, Andrew.	1	1	1		
McPherson, Robert.	1		3		
Meredith, Sarah.			4		
McDanniel, Daniel (F. M).			2	4	4
Matthews, Peter.	4	1	2		1
Middlebrooks, Thomas.	2		3		
McCosh, William.	2		7		1
McCosh, Thomas.	1	3	6		1
Murphy, Philemon.	2		3		5
McLloyd, William N.	1	2	3		3
Meridith, Benjamin.	2	2	3		5
Meridith, Tristram.	2		3		3
Meridith, John.	1	2	3		5
Myers, Stephen.	4		3		3
Meridith, John, Junr.	4		3		1
Meridith, Willm (of M).	1	3	2		2
Meridith, William.	2	4	3		1
Meeds, Thomas.	2	1	1		2
Meridith, Job.	1	1	1		
Mayson, Matthew.	5		2		3
Meridith, James.	2	1	3		3
Nabb, Charles.	1	1	1		1
OBryon, James.	4	1	4		24
OBryon, Thomas Roe.	2	2	3		
Oidson, Salomon.	2		4		8
Potts, Thomas.	2	5	3		4
Price, John.	1	2	5		9
Porter, William.	1	3	6		12
Page, John.	1		2		
Pratt, John Roe.	4				7
Porter, George.	1	2	3		
Purse, Deborah.	2	2	1		

QUEEN ANNS COUNTY—Continued.

NAME OF HEAD OF FAMILY.	Free white males of 16 years and upward, including heads of families.	Free white males under 16 years.	Free white females, including heads of families.	All other free persons.	Slaves.
Price, Christopher	1				
Pickering, Ann	1	1	8		
Phillips, Nathan	1	1	4		
Pearce, William	1	1	3		8
Parish, John	1	1	3	1	
Roberts, James	1		3		
Rogers, William	1		3		
Reed, William	1	4	3		
Ratliff, Thomas	1	2	2		
Rice, Simon	1		2		
Reed, Richard	1	3	4		
Rigby, Lucretia	1		2		2
Rockins, Elizabeth		3	3		
Robinson, Alexander	1	1	2		
Redien, John	1		1		
Rage, Sarah	1	4	6		2
Robinson, Samuel S.	1	2	5	1	3
Roe, Benjamin	1		4		1
Rossiter, Margaret			2		2
Reed, James	1	1	2		3
Rigby, Benjamin	3	2	5		
Ringgold, Thomas, 3d	1	1	5		20
Rogers, Isaac	1	1	3	1	
Ringgold, John					23
Rippeth, James	1		2		5
Roe, Juliana		1	2		4
Reynolds, Robert	1	1	2	1	
Roe, Ann	1		2		1
Richardson, Anthony	3		4		
Rogers, Thomas	2	3	4		1
Robinson, John	1	1	2		
Smyth, James	1	3	2		
Stockwell, Thomas	1				
Savage, Elizabeth			2		
Sparks, Millington	1		3		
Sparks, Thomas	2	3	2		1
Sparks, Absolom	1	1	4		5
Sparks, Daniel	2				
Spry, John	2		1		6
Storey, Joseph	1		1		
Strong, Charles	1		1		
Summers, William	1				
Savage, James	2	5	2	1	
Scott, Wright	1		1		
Simmerter, Darkey (F. M.)				3	
Sparks, Noah	1	1	1		
Smith, Basil	1	2	3		
Scrivenor, James	2	1	2		1
Simmeter, Hannah (F N.)					
Robinson, John	1	4	5		6
Loper, Anthony					6
Morris, John					8
Jeffries, Rachel					4
Gooding, Henry					9
Dominick, Matthew					7
Trusty, Rebecca					6
Gibbs, Isaac					6
Boyer, William	2	1	1		
Barnes, James	1	4	2		5
Ward, Robert	2	1	1	5	5
Seegar, William	2		1	3	
Roberts, Benjamin	2		1	3	
Ewing, William	2		3		1
Peters, James	1	3	7	4	1
Taylor, Benjamin	1		3		
Leatherberry, Thomas	2	3	5		1
Johnson, Sophia	2		5		2
Taylor, Abram	2	2	5		1
Seney, James	2				
Rochester, Lambert	2		4		1
Seegar, Thomas	2	2	7	2	1
Jackson, Lambert	2	4	4		1
Downes, Vachel	2		2		11
Keene, Vachel	3	1	3		30
Phillips, Solomon	1	4	3		3
Hendrickson, Henry	4	3	3		2
Kelly, James	3	1	1		
Louman, Richard	2	3	3		2
Noland, Ann			2		
Morris, Thomas			4		
Fogwell, John	1		3		7
Nunam, Nathaniel	1	3	4		
Colbert, William	1		3		
Seegar, Benjamin	2	1	5	5	3
Falconer, Jerusha	2	4	4		18
Sartain, Sarah	1		4	2	11
Chase, William	3	1	3		
Sartain, Nathan	1		4		
Downey, Thomas	1	4	4		
Thompson, Wm	4	4	5		12
Herrin, William	1	2	3	1	1
Sudler, Arthur E.	1	2	1		14
Boyer, Jesse	2	1	1		
Seale, John	2	3	5		9
Gilbert, William	1		1		9

NAME OF HEAD OF FAMILY.	Free white males of 16 years and upward, including heads of families.	Free white males under 16 years.	Free white females, including heads of families.	All other free persons.	Slaves.
Peters, John	3		5		
Robinson, William	4	1	3		
Wallis, Sarah	2	2	3	2	4
Cary, John	1	4	2		7
Rage, Jane			1		1
Crosley, Sarah					6
Taylor, Crispin	3	2	2		
Clark, William B.	1	2	5	2	2
Barneciow, Charles	1	2	1		
Walls, James	1				
Burroughs, John	2		2		
Burroughs, Mary		1	3		
Rage, Mary		1	1	1	
Weathersby, Rachel			2		
Walls, Samuel	1	1	2		
Curry, John	1	2	2		
Burroughs, James	2	1	4		1
Burroughs, George	3		8		
Heathers, Edward	1	2	4		13
Conner, Thomas	1		1		
Start, Jonathan	1	1	3		
Ireland, Nelly	2		3		
Burroughs, Edward	2	3	1		
Attix, Stephen	2	4	2		1
Burris, Hannah			3		
Roberts, John	1	2	4		
Clark, Rebecca	1	2	2		
Swain, John	1	2	3		
Arscott, William	1	2	2		
Smyth, Robert	1	2	2		
Sands, John	1	2	1		2
Rage, William	2		2		
Nevil, David	1	2	3		
Newnam, Mary	1	3	3		
Burn, Elijah	1	1	2		
Sartain, Elijah	1	2	2		6
Matchler, John	1	2	4		
Holding, James	2		5		
Newnam, George	2		5		
Larry, Leonard	1	1	5		
Thomas, Samuel	3	2	4		11
Lamb, Francis	2		2		2
Greenwood, William	2	3	2		1
Varrant, Garrett	1	3	1		
Nicols, Thomas	1		3		
Park, Rachel	1	4	3		
Wilkinson, Joseph	4	2	5	1	
Course, Thomas	3	1	2		
Millan, Abram	1		3		
Bostick, Sarah			1	1	
Blackston, John					6
Vansant, Lamb	1	1	1	1	
Massey, Ame					2
Bartheson, Sibin	3		2		
Cary, Ann	1	3	4		3
Battin, Stanley	1	4	2		
Miers, William	3	1	3		
Stephens, William	3	4	1	3	6
Windle, George	3		5		
Satterfield, Nathaniel	1	2	3		
Simmons, Elizabeth			3		
Sollaway, Josiah, Jur.	1	1	1		
Bostick, James	1	2	1		
Sollaway, Josiah	2		2		1
Murphy, John	1		2		
Howard, James	1	1	2		
Sollaway, James	2		3		
Murett, Jacob			2	4	2
Chaddock, Richard	4	3	4		1
Williams, Joseph			3		
Green, John H.	1	2	7		
Kemp, William	1		7		
Ervine, Francis	1		3		
Clark, William	1		2		6
Meridith, Absolom	2		5	1	
Rosser, John	1	2	2		
Peters, William	2	3	6		8
Meredith, Thomas	2		3		
Simpson, William	3		3		
Rolph, William	2	4	1		
Deford, Joshua	1		1		
Clark, Charles	1	4	3		
Bramble, William	2	1	3		
Coleman, Richard	1		2		
Covington, Henry	4	4	1		
Taylor, John	2	3	2		7
Harris, Thomas	2	1	4		12
Murdock, Ezekiel	1	2	3		
McConnel, James	1	1	2		
Gilbert, Henry	3	2	1		
Mooth, James	2		1		5
Kelly, John	2	2	2		
Massey, James	1		2		
Massey, William	1	2	2		5
Rosier, Rebecca	2	1	2		
Newnam, John	1	1	2		
Smyth, Charles	2	2	3		

NAME OF HEAD OF FAMILY.	Free white males of 16 years and upward, including heads of families.	Free white males under 16 years.	Free white females, including heads of families.	All other free persons.	Slaves.
Fogwell, John, Jun.	2	1	5		3
Newnam, Nathaniel	1		2	1	1
Tharp, Vachel	1	3	3		
Tharp, Elizabeth	1	1	2		
Boot, Bartin			2		
Boots, Susannah	1		4		
Wicks, Charles		4	3		
Phillips, James	1	2	5		
Nicholson, Thomas	4	2	2		
Davis, John	1	2	2		
Clawson, John	2	2	3		
Kilpatrick, William	1	2	2		
Willcox, Samuel	2	2	1		3
High, John	2	1	2		
Lane, James	1				
Walker, William	3		3		
Lane, Samuel	1		1		2
Lane, Jonathan	1		2		3
Kelly, Sarah	1	1	1		
Kelly, William	1		3		
Kelly, Len	1	1	3		
Martain, James	1	2	3		
Pennington, James	2	3	1		1
Stanton, Sarah			3		
Taylor, William	2	3	6	1	1
Temple, George	1		1	1	1
Keene, Richard	2	3	4		13
Merchant, John	1		1		
Phillips, Nathan	1	2	2	1	
Keene, Andrew					11
Bush, William	1	2	2		30
Peacock, Nathan	2		4		
Strong, Edward	2	1	4		7
Carroll, John	1		3		
Wilson, William	1	3	1		
Lowman, James	1		1		6
McHay, James	4		1		7
Jackson, George	4		1		5
Tottson, Ruth			2	3	
Peters, John	1	3	5		
Dudley, James	1	1	2		2
Wicks, Benjamin	1		5		
Edmondson, Emanuel	1	1	7		
Boots, Mary			1		
Fowler, Robert	1	1	1		
Lavard, Ann			3		
Jackson, Stafford	2	3	3		
Anderson, James	1	1	4		
Arwood, John	3		5		
Amey. (Free Negro)				8	
Arsecott, Richard	1	1	6		
Austin, Thomas			1		
Banister, William	1		1		2
Banister, Sarah				7	
Benett, Samuel					
Blanchfield, George	2	1	1		
Blewott, Viney			2		
Bright, Samuel			5		
Bells, Mary	4	2	3		17
Benton, James	2	1	3		
Batman, James	2	1	1		4
Buchanan, Nathaniel	3	4	3		2
Baleman, Ann	2		1		
Baleman, Christopher	2		1		
Brown, John	2		3		56
Barber, Thomas	1		2		
Bishop, Richard	2	5	2		
Burgess, Samuel	3	1	6	3	11
Burgess, Charles	3		3		3
Brown, James	4	1	1		2
Benton, Vincent	4	1	1		
Buckly, Timothy	1	1	2		
Barnes, Thomas	1	2	3		
Byrns, James	1	2	3	2	4
Bostick, Robert	1		1		
Brown, William	1	2	1		23
Brown, Samuel	3		2		
Benton, John	3		2		11
Butler, John	2		3	2	1
Cornelius, John	2	1	2		
Chairs, James	2		1		
Carman, Thomas	3	2	2		6
Cornelius, Andrew	2		2		8
Colgan, Edward	2		3		
Comyges, Elizabeth	2	6	1		8
Cox, John	2	1	7		10
Cuff, Free				2	
Connelly, Lawrence	2	1	5		
Commigis, John	2		3		5
Coleman, William	2		3		
Condle, Henry	2		1		
Coppage, Benjamin	1	4	3		1
Comman, Joseph	1	1	1		
Cook, James	1	1	3		8
Crabbin, Alexander	1		5		
Cosdon, James	3	1	3		5
Cosdon, Samuel	1	3	4		5

QUEEN ANNS COUNTY—Continued.

NAME OF HEAD OF FAMILY.	Free white males of 16 years and upward, including heads of families.	Free white males under 16 years.	Free white females, including heads of families.	All other free persons.	Slaves.
Coppage, Ruth	2	2	2	2	1
Comyges, William	1		1		
Canady, Thomas					3
Clark, John	1	2	1		1
Campbell, James	1	1	4		1
Cosdon, William	1		4	2	
Cosdon, Sarah			4	1	
Comygis, Sarah		2	2	4	
Carman, Arnold	3		4		3
Cooper, John	2		4	4	
Cæsar, Free				6	
Dudley, William	1		2	1	1
Dempster, William	1	1	3		
Dunbrane, Nathan	1	1	3		
Deford, Isaac	1	2	4		
Darnell, James	1		4		
Deford, William	1	1	4		1
Deford, John	3	1	1		
Deford, Elisha	1		2		5
Deford, Ann		1	2		
Dice, George					8
Dunn, William	1	3	2		
Eagate, Valentine	1	1	4		
Elliott, Elizabeth			4	1	8
Elliott, Benjamin	1	2	5	1	7
Elbert, Henry	2	1	1	1	
Evans, Jonathan (Taylor)	1	2	6		
Bet, free negro				3	
Evans, Jonathan	1	2	4		
Eaton, Thomas	3		2		1
Erikson, James	1		3		2
Forman, Sweatman	1	1	4		11
Forman, Hambleton	1	2	4		5
Ferrel, Edmund	2		4		17
Ferrel, William	2	2	4		3
Ford, Isaac	1	2	2		5
Forman, Hannah		3	5		8
Forman, Joseph	1	2	4		32
Fray, William	2	4	5	1	5
Forman, Mary	1	3	4		6
Forman, John	1		2		3
Falconer, Abram	1	4	6	1	7
Ford, Mary	1		2	1	
Griffin, George	3	2	3	1	
Garnett, Benjamin	1	3	2		6
Gooding, Benjamin	1		2	1	3
Gould, Martha		2	3		3
Greenwood, William	2	2	2		
Gray, Ann			1		
Glanding, Nathan	1		4		
Gould, William	3	3	4		9
Gooding, William	2		2		5
Gafford, Mary	1	1	2		
Gafford, Jacob	1		2		1
Gafford, Valentine	1	2	4		
Gafford, William	1				
Gafford, Charles	3		3		1
Gafford, Abram		1	2		
George, Hannah	2	3	3		
Godwin, Thomas	1		2		
Gould, Benjamin, Jur	2		2		11
Gatoh, John	4	1	4		
Hart, John	1		2		
Hicks, Rebecca	1	2	2		
Hackett, Thomas	1	2	2		1
Harry, free				4	
Horsley, Thomas	1	3	1		
Harrison, Richard E	2	1	1		3
Haley, Richard	2		2		
Hollingsworth, James	1		2		1
Holding, Benjamin	4	2	4		2
Harrington, John	3		1		
Hackett, James	3		8		28
Hackett, Thomas	1		3		11
Hollingsworth, William	2	1	3		
Hamer, Catharine	1	2	4		
Hackett, James, Jun	1		6		
Hammond, James	1	1	3		15
Holding, William	1	3	3		6
Harris, Ann	1	3	3		
Harris, William	1	3	2		
Hall, Hannah			3		
Johnson, James	1	1	5	1	2
Johnson, Benjamin			4		
Jester, David	1		1		8
Johnson, William	1		6		
Jacob, Free Negro				4	
Jacobs, William	2	1	1		10
Johnson, Jonathan	2	2	2	1	
Johnson, George	2	1	2		1
Kerns, John	4	1			6
Knotts, James	1	1	2		
Kelly, Barbara	1		3		
Kent, William	1		4		25
Kemp, John	1	1			16

NAME OF HEAD OF FAMILY.	Free white males of 16 years and upward, including heads of families.	Free white males under 16 years.	Free white females, including heads of families.	All other free persons.	Slaves.
Latimore, Joseph	2	2	1		1
Lang, William	1		3		
Lacey, William	1	1	2		1
Loller, Francis	1	2	3	3	
Lewis, John	1		2		
Lee, William	1	1	2		1
Lamb, Eleanor			4		
Loffman, Benjamin	1	3	3		
Lee, William, Jun	1	2	1		
Lowman, James	1		3		
Laurence, William	1	2	1		
Latimore, Ann	1	1	2	1	
Lee, Amos	2		4		
Lee, Sarah		3	2		
Morris, Richard	1		1		
Mullin, William	1	1	4		
Maud, James	1	6	1		
Monsier, Ann		4	2		
McCay, William	2		1		
McGonnigill, Rachel			5		1
Mary, free				2	
Moreland, Henry	1	1			
Moss, William	3		4		
McCay, Revd James	1	1	2	1	
Meredith, John	2	3	2		2
McSkimming, Ervin	2		3		1
Morgan, Daniel	3	1	4		
Margaret, Free Negro				3	
Nuite, John	4	4	2		1
Nunam, Daniel	3	4	2		3
Neunam, Joseph	2	3	3		1
Nevill, James	1	3	3		4
Noland, Ann		2	3		
Osborn, Amos	1		3		
Osborn, John	1	1	3		2
Price, William	1	3	6		3
Pearce, John	2		4		
Primrose, George	1				4
Primrose, John	4	1	3		9
Porter, James	2	1	2		
Poe, Christopher	1	1	1		
Pinder, William	2		1		6
Perkins, Edward	2	1	2		
Powall, Thomas	1	2	2		
Prior, Susannah	1	2	2		2
Quinby, John	3	6	3	1	2
Richardson, Benjamin	1	5	5		13
Rogers, Hynson	1		4		
Roseberry, James	3		2		8
Rogers, James				5	
Read, Francis	1	2	3	1	1
Ruth, Thomas	1	2	4		2
Roberts, James	1	2	4		
Roberts, Thomas	1		3		5
Roberts, Hugh	1		3		
Richardson, John	2	1	2		1
Richardson, William	1		2		
Reynolds, Newnam	1	1	3		2
Read, Valentine	2		4		
Rowe, Thomas	2	3	1		
Rochester, William	3	3	5		
Rochester, Henry	3	1	5		4
Roberts, Henry	1	1	2		3
Rochester, Francis	3		3	1	11
Rochester, Daniel	1		2		
Rochester, Samuel	1	3	5		6
Rolingson, John	1	1	3		
Ruth, John	1	1	3		
Ruth, James	1		3		4
Ruth, James, Junr	1	1	2		
Roberts, Zachariah	1		2		3
Reed, James	1	1	4		11
Surrell, William	1	3	3		
Sparks, Levi	1	2	4		10
Sparks, John	2	4			
Smyth, Ann		1	2		
Stootly, Nimrod	1		3		
Stalcup, John	1	3	4		
Surry, John	3		1		17
Williams, Mary		1	4		
Woodall, Rachel		1	2		5
Walls, John	1	1	3		
Willson, George	1		1		
Willson, David					4
Willson, John	1		3		
Wallis, John	1	2	2		
Williamson, George	2	2	4		
Whittington, Thomas				6	5
Watts, Samuel	1		1		
Wheeling, Conrad	1	2	5		
Wicks, Simon	3	1	3		
Watters, Robert					38
Woods, Stephen	2		2	1	5
Young, Thomas	2	3	1	1	
Yardsley, John	1	3	4	2	1
Young, Benjamin, Junr	1	3	2		2

NAME OF HEAD OF FAMILY.	Free white males of 16 years and upward, including heads of families.	Free white males under 16 years.	Free white females, including heads of families.	All other free persons.	Slaves.
Young, Benjamin	1	2	2		1
Younger, Mary	1	2	4		
Young, Daniel	1	2	4		
Young, Robert	1	2	2		
Alls, John	1	2	4		18
Aylor, Thomas	1	2	3		
Andrew, Free				1	
Abram, Free				1	
Adam, Free				1	
Anthony, John	2		1		
Alloway, Mary	2		4		11
Arlet, George			1		
Buckley, Jonathan	2	1	4		1
Baynard, George	2		3		18
Burk, John	3	3	3		2
Bucker, John	1	2	2		
Brady, Jonathan	4		4	1	8
Ben, Sam				1	
Burnett, John	1		4		
Bartlett, John	1	1	2		7
Brown, John	1		4		
Burn, John	1		2		
Braly, Nathaniel	1	1	2		1
Baker, James	1	1	6		
Barnett, Thomas	1	1	3		13
Barniclow, Mary	2		3		
Brayly, Sarah	1		5		
Baggs, Thomas	1	1	2		
Burk, Henry				1	
Browne, John E	2		3		
Beall, John		2	5		4
Baker, Thomas	1	1	3		
Browne, Sarah		1	3		12
Boyd, Sarah			1		
Blunt, Thomas	1	1	7		
Bucklin, Rebecca		2	2		
Baker, Mary Ann	2		2		4
Bowen, John	1	2	2		
Bowser, Ruth				6	
Beacham, Joseph	1		1		
Bordley, James	1	3	1	1	15
Cannon, William	3	4	2		6
Council, John	3	4	4		8
Cook, Joseph	3		5		9
Carter, Solomon	3		3		
Crowick, William	5	1	3		1
Clark, William	2		5		
Cecil, John	1	4	4		3
Conway, Michael				1	
Cannon, Andrew			1	1	
Cooper, Richard	1		2		1
Connely, James	3	3	5		
Cox, Christopher	1	1	4		11
Cotner, Henry	1	1	4		
Chambers, Richard	1		3		22
Covington, Samuel	1	2	3		
Cohee, Vincent	1		3		
Copis, George	1	1	4		
Covington, Thomas	1	2	3		
Coglan, Elizabeth			3		
Caster, Henry	2		4		4
Cain, Mary		3	4		
Carey, Elizabeth	1		4		
Camper, William	1	4	4		6
Dodd, John	1	4	3		3
Downes, George	1	4	3		11
Downes, Charles, Junr	2	1	5		5
Davis, Thomas	3		4		5
Downes, Ann			4		6
Dodd, Mary		2	3		1
Dundy, Free				1	
Dodd, Mark	3	4	7		3
Davis, John	3	2	3		3
Davis, Catharine			2		2
Denny, Peter	3	3	6		
Dunn, John				1	
Davage, Elizabeth		2	1		11
Deford, Benjamin			1		
Denny, John	1	1	3		8
Downes, John	1	2	2		3
Downes, James	1	2	3		6
Downes, Hynson	2	4	2		2
Dodd, Ebenezer			2		
Downes, Lodman	1	2	2		
Downey, Thomas	1	3	5		
Emory, William	3	3	2		
Elliott, Joseph	1	3	5		4
Evans, William	3	3	3		10
Emory, John (B. S.)	2	2	5		2
Embert, James	1	1	7		
Elliott, Robert	1	1	2		
Evirett, Levi	1	4	1	1	2
Emmerson, John	1	1	3		
Emory, James	2	1	3		22
Earle, Henrietta Maria	1	1	3	2	29
Elliott, Benjamin	1	2	3		2

QUEEN ANNS COUNTY—Continued.

NAME OF HEAD OF FAMILY.	Free white males of 16 years and upward, including heads of families.	Free white males under 16 years.	Free white females, including heads of families.	All other free persons.	Slaves.
Emory, Thomas	1		1	1	11
Emory, John R	2				7
Emory, Arthur (of Thomas)	1	2	1		15
Emmerson, Vincent	1		2		
Furguson, George	4	2	9		1
Falconer, Jonathan	2	2	4		7
Falconer, Benjamin	2	2	2		5
Fisher, John	2	1	3		27
Frank, Free				3	
Pomp, Free				1	
Farbanks, John	3	3	3		1
Falconer, John	1		3		
Falconer, James	1		3	1	15
Frazier, Charles	1		3	1	8
Griffith, William	2	2	4		
Griffith, William E	1	4	4		8
Golt, William	2	2	4		4
Glanding, Vincent	2	3	3		2
Glanding, William	3	3	2		
Griffith, John	1	2	3		3
Gorge, Free				1	1
Green, Jacob	1		2	1	
Griffith, Thomas				1	
Galbert, John				1	
Golt, John	2		2	1	1
Grenage, Rachel			2	1	
Green, Henry			2	1	
George, Joseph	2		2	1	8
Glanding, John	1		1		
Gardner, William	1		2		
Glanding, Levi	1	1	4		2
Green, Joan			2		
Green, Jacob	1		2		
Griffith, Grenberry	2	1	3		2
Glanding, Susannah	2		1		
Green, Philemon	3		5		12
Golt, William	2	3	3		4
Harrington, Anthony	2	1	4		4
Hynson, Henry	1	1	4		3
Hall, Thomas	2	1	2		2
Hall, Sarah			2		2
Harrington, James	2	3	1		4
Harrington, Ann		2	2		3
Hinds, Moses	2	1	4		8
Hart, Augustine	2	1	4		4
Hall, Edward	2	1	4		4
Hollingsworth, John	2	1	3		4
Hadder, Thomas	1	2	5		5
Hackett, William	1	2	6		16
Hossin, Daniel				1	
Hall, Richard	2		3	1	3
Hinold, John				1	
Hinold, Charles				1	
Harris, Joseph				1	
Hollingsworth, Thomas	1		1		
Harris, Margaret		2	4		
Hughbanks, Thomas	1		4		
Huard, George	1	2	3		
Howell, Jonathan	2	2	3		
Harris, William	1	2	2		
Harris, Richard	2	6	7		7
Hall, John E	2	3	8		8
Hall, Lawrence	2	2	4		14
Harris, John	1	1	3		
Harrington, Abner	1	3	2		1
Hynson, Ann	1		3		
Hynson, William	3	3	3		
Howell, Jonathan	2	2	5		
Harris, Samuel	1	1	3		
Hughs, John	1	2	4		
Hall, John	2	1	1		1
Horn, William, Junr	1		2		
Hargadine, Joseph T	2	2	2		7
Hargadine, John	3		4		1
Jones, James	1		2		1
Jackson, Catharine	4	2	5		5
Jones, Isabel	1	2	3		5
Jones, David				1	
Joiner, Moses				1	
Jones, William	1	3	1		
Jeffries, George	3	3	4		5
Jeffries, Sarah	2	3	3		8
Irons, Francis	1	1	3		
Jeffries, John	1	2	4		
Jeffries, George	3		4		
Kerney, William	1	1	4		13
Keene, John Y	2	1	2		16
Knotts, Rebecca	2	1	5		
Kirby, Jesse	1		4		2
Kirsey, Rebecca			2		
Lee, William	2	1	4		
Leg, James	1	1	2		3
Livinston, Andrew	1	2	4		16
Lassell, John	4	2	4		1
Longfellow, James	2	3	4		3
Lowd, Robert	1	2	2		
Lynch, Thomas	2	5	4		1
Lloyd, James	3	3	3		
Lane, Elizabeth			1	4	
Leech, James	1	3	2		9
Longfellow, Elizabeth			1	1	
Mecomican, John	3		1	6	12
Morton, Thomas	3	1	7		13
Meads, Elkana	3	1	5		5
Mahuel, William					1
Mattox, William	1		3		
Meads, John	2	4	3		7
Meads, John H	2	3	3		8
Molly, Free			1	4	
Mosley, Henry	1	2	2		1
Morton, Elizabeth			2		
Morton, Jonathan	1	1	8		1
Meads, John (of E.)	2	4	5		3
Melony, James	3	1	4		
Moore, Mary			2		
Meconnican, John, Jur	1	3	3		4
Meloney, John	4		6		
Morton, John	2		2		3
Minta, Free				5	
Nicholson, Elizabeth	1	1	3		18
Noble, Nehemiah	3		2		13
Pinckfield, William		3	2		
Nabb, Susannah		1	1	1	
Oldson, Ann	3		5		2
OBryon, Joseph	1	2	3		4
Oldson, Abram	1	3	3		
Price, Thomas	2	2	4		1
Phillips, Richard	3	1	3		2
Phillips, John	1	2	1		
Pemberton, John	1		2		9
Patrick, John	1	1	2		3
Pratt, Thomas	4	3	3		4
Plummer, John, Jun	2	2	5		
Pratt, Elizabeth	1		1		
Price, William, 3d	1	1	1		
Price, Elizabeth			3		
Pain, Molly					1
Price, Henry	1	3	2		3
Price, William	1	1	3		
Phillips, John			2		
Price, William (of Thos.)	3		5		8
Pratt, William			2		3
Palmer, Jonathan	1	3	3		
Palmer, Betty					2
Price, Mary	1		3		13
Price, James			1	1	1
Phillips, Jonathan	2	1	4		
Plummer, William	1	3	4		
Plummer, Levi	3	1	5		1
Pratt, Elizabeth			1		
Pratt, James R	4		2		4
Price, Charles	3	1	5		9
Price, Prudence			3		2
Pratt, Henry	3	2	3		36
Ridgaway, Lettelia	2	2	3		15
Rakes, Fisher	2	4	4		9
Richardson, William	1	6	1		
Rook, William	3	6	2		3
Rook, Ann		3	3		
Rickets, Ruben	6	1	1		1
Rogers, Samuel			1		
Robinson, Thomas	2	1	2		1
Redman, John	1		2		
Rippith, James	2	1	4		
Ringgold, William	1	2	2		11
Rogers, Edward	1		1		18
Richmond, William	1		1		18
Rachel, Free				2	
Rouse, Elizabeth			3		
Ross, John	1	4	2		
Robinson, Elijah	3	2	3		
Ratcliff, George	2	2	3		1
Reed, John Allen	3		3		1
Rathett, Samuel	4	1	3		
Rakes, Easter		1	3		4
Rich, Violet	1		3		
Ross, John	2	3	4		1
Rouse, George	1	2	4		
Murphy, William	3		5		12
Scott, Solomon	3	2	5		8
Starkey, Thomas	1	1	3		8
Smyth, John Green	1	1	4		6
Smyth, John	2	1	3		4
Scrivoner, John			2	1	
Saturfield, William	2	3	3		1
Saturfield, Thomas	2	4	3		
Sylvester, Joshua	1		7		19
Smyth, Richard	2		3	1	
Stark, James	1	3	3		
Sudler, Emory	5		1		6
Sinnett, Solomon	2		5		7
Starkey, Miller	1	2	1		
Starkey, John	1		6		
Score, Joseph				1	
Sylvester, Samuel				1	
Storey, Henry	7	2	3		10
Sias, Fred				1	
Sneed, Moses	1		1		10
Sylvester, Jacob				1	
Stephens, William	1		1		
Seth, William	2	2	2		16
Sparks, George				5	
Studley, Major	1		2		
Straddle, Griffin	1		2		
Smyth, Jonathan	1		1		
Saxton, James	1	1	3		
Saturfield, Henry	1		3		
Starkey, Rebecca		2	2		
Speck, Molly			4		
Start, Molly		1	4		
Stewart, Charles				2	
Scott, William	1	1	1		
Saturfield, Thomas, Junr	1	3	4		1
Skinner, William	1	3	3		1
Sparks, John Butts	1	2	5		1
Thomas, James	3	1	2		4
Tarbutton, Solomon	2	2	3		5
Tarman, Hezekiah	1				
Tarbutton, William	2		2		
Thomas, Edward	2	2	4		21
Tapp, James	2	2	5		
Turner, Thomas	2		5		
Timms, John	1	4	7		
Welsh, William	1	3	1		5
Wright, Joseph	1		4		3
Waoters, Thomas	1		2		8
Waoters, James	1	1	1		
Williams, James	1		1		
Wright, Nathaniel	2		2		12
Wood, Samuel	1		3		
Whitby, Nathaniel	1	2	2		
Wheatley, James				2	
Willkins, James	1	1	5		
Wiggins, James	1	3	4		
Wicks, Richard			2	2	
Willkins, Elizabeth	2	1	3		1
Williams, James	2		7		7
Walker, Daniel	1	1	2		
Wright, Solomon	1	5	2		5
Wright, Coursey	1	2	3		
Williams, John, Jur	1	2	4		
Wiggins, Elijah	1	3	4		
Winchester, Thomas	1		5		22
Wilkinson, Sophia	1	5	4		
Weyat, John	2	1	4		2
Williams, George	3	1	6		
White, John	2	1	5		
Williams, Sarah	2	2	3		5
Walker, Christopher	2	2	5		16
Whely, Nathan	1	2	3		
Wooten, David	2	2	1		4
Young, William	1				
Yoe, John	1		2		
Young, James	1		4		
Yoe, Thomas	1	2	6		
Vanderford, John, Junr	1	2	1		1
Vanderford, William	3	1	4		7
Vanderford, John	1		4		2
Vinson, Emet	4	4	1		
Vinson, James	1	1	3	1	
Vinson, John, Junr	1		2		
Valiant, John	1		2		
Vinson, John	1	1	2		
Brown, Sarah			1		1
Brown, Edward	2		3		9
Bailey, Thomas	1	3	7		11
Bruff, William	1	2	3		10
Burahinal, Benjamin	1	1	3		4
Biscoe, Susannah	1	2	2		5
Biscoe, Jonathan	4	2	3		4
Brown, James	3	1	3		11
Braley, John		2	4		2
Blackstone, Michael	2	5	4		
Boon, Thomas	2	1	4		2
Bruff, James	3		3	1	5
Brenard, John	2		3		
Briggs, William	1	3	2		
Baker, Thomas	1		2		2
Brooks, Esau			5		
Bishop, William	2		2		1
Babey, Thomas (free)				6	
Bliss, George	1				
Barnett, Ann		1	4		
Baills, William		1	4		
Bright, Nathan	1	1	3		
Butcher, Robert (free)			1	4	
Botton, Mary Ann			1		

QUEEN ANNS COUNTY—Continued.

NAME OF HEAD OF FAMILY.	Free white males of 16 years and upward, including heads of families.	Free white males under 16 years.	Free white females, including heads of families.	All other free persons.	Slaves.
Bussells, John	1	1	1		
Butler, James	1	2	4		
Blunkall, William	1	1	2		
Biscoe, Basil	1	2	2		1
Clayton, Hannah			3		14
Clayland, James, Junr	2	1	15		
Cook, Easther	1	2	5		6
Clayton, William	1		2		15
Collins, Richard	2	1	3		2
Chaires, John	1		1	5	10
Chaires, Catharine	2		3		8
Cant, James	3		5		5
Carman, William B	2	2	5		2
Cain, John	1				1
Catline, Charles	1		1		3
Cohea, John	1	4	2		
Shoebrooks, Margaret		2	4		
Sylvester, David	1	1	2		
Stinson, James	1	1	5		3
Starkey, John	1	2	1	1	
Storey, Ephraim W	1	2	3	1	5
Sewall, Clement	2	2	5	1	23
Sparks, William	2				12
Sparks, Solomon	3	3	2		7
Smyth, Rachel		1	4		1
Stenson, John	1	1	3		
Sparks, Rachel	2	6	3		
Seth, Charles	2	1	3		2
Toltson, Alexander	1	2	3		1
Taylor, George	1	2	2		
Tucker, William	2		1		
Turner, William	1	2	3		
Tilghman, Susan					15
Tomkins, Abram	1	2	3	4	
Tippings, John	6	1	3	3	9
Thomas, Richard	1	1	3		
Toltson, Benjamin	2	5	2		
Thompson, Samuel	4	1	8		19
Thomas, Charles	1	2	4		10
Tarbutton, Edward	3	2	4		2
Taylor, Elizabeth	1	1	3		7
Sam, Free					
Thomas, Edmond	1	2	2		3
Willmot, William	1	2	1		
Whiticoe, William	1		4		
Willson, John	1				
Wyatt, John	1	1	4		1
Welsh, James	2	1			1
Watson, Esther			2		
Willson, Samuel (F.M.)					3
Walker, Daniel (F.M)			1	3	
Winters, Jonathan	1	2	4		
Wilcocks, Thomas	2	1	2		1
Wan, Daphney (F.N.)			1	3	
Wright, Robert					6
Watson, John	3	2	3		4
White, James	1	1	2		2
Warfield, Alexander	3	1	1		11
Wright, Nathan S. T.	2	3	4		5
Wright, Solomon	4				19
Willson, Robert (F.M.)				8	
Willson, Solomon (F.M.)				9	
Wilcocks, Henry (F.M.)	2	3	5		7
Willson, Thomas (F.M.)			3		7
Whittecoe, Joshua	2		2		
White, Margaret	1	1	3		
White, William	1	2	3		1
Wright, Robert, Jur	1	2			5
Watters, Robert	1				23
Seney, Horatio	1	1			4
Seney, Jonathan	1				
Sparks, James	1	2	3		
Seney, Mary		2	2		
Sparks, Nathan	2	3	3		
Sparks, Abner	1	5	5		4
Seward, William	1	4	3		
Sparks, Mordecai	1	5	4		3
Seward, George	4		1		2
Sam, Free				5	
Seney, Samuel	1	3	2		
Spry, Samuel	1	2	3	1	3
Spry, Thomas	2		4		19
Sudler, Richard	1	1	3		9
Sparks, Solomon	2	1	4		
Sutton, Margaret	1	1	3		
State, Margaret	2	1	5		
Sanders, Thomas					
Scott, Eduard	3	1	3		3
Smyth, Bartus	1	1	2		
Surrell, Archibald	1	2	4		
Smyth, William	1				5
Smyth, Daniel	2	2	3	1	3
Smyth, Bartholomew	1	1	1		
Shaw, John	1	1	1		
Seward, John	3	1	3		
Seward, Griffith	1	1	3		
Still, Thomas	1	1	1		2
Taylor, Richard	1	1	2		4
Thompson, Luke	1	1	1		
Tittle, John	2	2	4		1
Thompson, John	1		3		38
Thompson, Susannah		2	4		
Taylor, Thomas	1	2	4		1
Vanderford, Thomas	1	1	2		9
Vanderford, Sarah	1		4		9
Vansanst, Ann		2	3		
Willson, Isaac	1	1			
Whittington, Joseph					10
Whittington, John	1	1			10
Wright, Nathaniel, Jur	1	1			7
Willetts, Job	2	2	2		1
Sparks, Elizabeth		2	3		

ST. MARYS COUNTY.

NAME OF HEAD OF FAMILY.	Free white males of 16 years and upward, including heads of families.	Free white males under 16 years.	Free white females, including heads of families.	All other free persons.	Slaves.
Addams, Phoeby			3		
Addams, James			2		
Armsworthy, Aaron	1		3		
Armsworthy, John	1	1	4		
Addams, Solomon	1	6	3		1
Armsworthy, Aaron Senr	1		3		
Armsworthy, Bennet	2	1	1		
Armsworthy, Susanna		1	5		
Addams, John	2		3		4
Armstrong, John	3	1	3		8
Aud, John	1	1	2		
Armsworthy, Abraham	2	1	4		1
Asquith, Elizabeth	1	1	3		5
Alvey, John	1		2	1	
Aud, William	1	2	2		1
Aud, Thomas	1	5	3		1
Bradburn, Charles	1		1		
Budd, John	1	3	2		
Brown, James	2		1	1	
Barnes, Richard	2		1		209
Booth, Joseph	1	1	1		
Bowis, Monica	1		1		2
Bowis, John B	1	1	1		1
Bradburn, William	1		1		6
Bean, Thomas	2	2	2		3
Bean, John	2	2	3		5
Booth, John	3	2	3		4
Boult, Thomas	2	2	2	1	15
Baxter, Anthony	2		1		6
Bean, John	1	3	1		6
Burnet, Stephen	1	1	5		
Biscoe, Stephen	1				4
Bruce, John	1	1	3		
Booth, George	1		1		
Booth, Jesse	1				
Bean, Elizabeth	2		3		1
Baxter, Thomas	1		3		
Brian, Abigail			3		
Booth, James	1	2	2		
Bright, John B	1	2	2		
Biscoe, Littleton	1		2		5
Cole, Lidia			3		
Cole, Valentine	1		2		
Carbery, Peter	1	2	3		
Clark, Bennet	1	1	3		4
Clark, Zachariah	1				
Cissel, John	2			1	4
Combs, Ignatius	1		1	1	4
Combs, Raphael	1	1	4		9
Combs, William	3	1	4		5
Carter, John	1		1		
Cooke, Thomas	2	1	4		1
Con, George	2		4		
Cissel, William	1	2	4		
Combs, William	1	3	4		6
Chiveral, Jesse	2	2	3		
Cain, Barbara	1		2		
Cox, Elizabeth		3	5	1	
Curtis, Easter				7	
Cole, John	2	2	5		3
Cullison, John	2	3	3		
Cissel, Bennet	1	1	3		1
Carpenter, John	1	5	4		7
Combs, Bennet	2	1	4		19
Cole, John	2	1	4		12
Crawly, William	2				
Gaft, William	2	1	1	1	1
Dorsey, Walter	1				1
Daggins, John	2	5	1		
Dyer, Mary	1	2	2		
Doxy, William	1		1		6
Dunkerson, Robert	1		2		15
Downs, John	1	2	2		
Downs, Joseph	1	1	2		3
Howard, Eleanor	1	1	2		
Dillhay, Arther	3		2		4
Davis, Hizakiah	1	1	5		1
Downs, Ignatius	1	3	2		
Dabson, Hannah			2		
Drury, Jeremiah	1		2		
Dillion, Thomas	2		2		6
Crain, James A	1	2	6		6
Crawly, Benjamin				5	
Egan, Thomas	1			1	
Fowler, Eleanor			3		
Files, Thomas	1	3	5		1
Fenwick, Cuthbert	1	2	7		4
Ford, Joseph	1	4	2		8
Fletcher, John	1				
Files, William	1			2	
Fermiah, Jeremiah	1		2		2
Clark, Mathias	4	2	1		11
Ford, John G	1		3		10
Fletcher, Ann				3	
Fields, Catharine		1	1		
Ford, John	1		2		1
Greenwell, Ann	1	1	1		
Gough, James	2	3	5		8
Gough, Stephen	1	3	4		10
Greenwell, John	3	1	6		14
Greenwell, William	3	4	4		35
Greenwell, Elizabeth	2	1	3		1
Greenwell, Stephen	1	1	3		6
Goldsbury, John B	1		4		
Goldsbury, Stephen	1	6	4		
Greenwell, Bennet	2	4	1		
Greenwell, Joshua	1	3	3		
Greenwell, Barnaby	3	1	3		3
Gibbons, John	1		2		1
Greves, Catharine		3	2		1
Guyther, George	1				10
Gibbons, Hannah			3		3
Greenwell, Clemt	1	3	3		
Gornbaly, James	1	1	1		1
Greenwell, Eleanor		1	1		
Goldsbury, William	2	2	4		
Greenwell, Archabald	1		3		5
Goldsbury, Nicholas	1	1	3		
Guyther, William	2		2		8
Greenwell, Noah		3	2		
Hardy, Thomas	1	1	2		
Howard, Joseph	2	2	4		
Henning, Gilbert	2	3	1		
Hacate, Eleanor	1	2	6		
Halket, Mary			2		
Hopewell, Bennet	2		3		3
Haden, Ignatius	2		4		5
Howard, Eleanor			3		
Haden, Mary		1	2		
Herbert, Francis	2	1		2	6
Hopewell, Richard	1	3	4	1	2
Harper, John	1	3	4	1	4
Hammet, Joseph	8	17	27	1	3
Holton, William	1		2		3
Hammet, John	1		2		3
Horrel, Bennet	1		2		1
Hopewell, John	1		3		9
Hall, Joseph	1		2		
Hopewell, Frances			1		
Hening, Jeremiah	1	3	4		
Hebb, Joshua	1	6	6		
Hilton, Francis	3	1	1		4
Hening, Bennet	1	1	2		
Hammet, John	1	5	3		
Heard, Richard	2		3	1	7
Heard, William	1	6	3		3
Henry, Martin	1	1	3		
Hebb, Thomas	1	1	6		6
Hammet, James	2	1	4		1
Hill, William	1	4	2		
Hebb, William	1	4	1		16
Heath, James	1	3	2		2
Hammett, William	1	1	3		15
Jenkins, Suston	3		1		33
Jones, Soloman	2	1	1		13
Jarboe, Peter	2		2		
Jarboe, Ann			2		
Jarboe, Mary			2		
Johns, David	1	1	4		
Jones, Mathias	3	3	3		19

NAME OF HEAD OF FAMILY.	Free white males of 16 years and upward, including heads of families.	Free white males under 16 years.	Free white females, including heads of families.	All other free persons.	Slaves.
Jones, William	1	3	2		3
Jenkins, Edmund	2		2		13
Jones, Thomas	2		4		
Jordan, John	1	4	5		1
Jarboe, Bennet	1		2		
Joy, Thomas	1	2	2		
King, Elisabeth		1	3		
Kirby, Zachariah	3	1	3		
King, Henry	1	1	5	1	2
Keese, William			8		
Kerby, Hopewell	2	1		1	
Kerby, Charles	1	2	2		1
Leigh, George H	2		2		10
Lusty, James	2	2	5		
Lynch, Stephen	1	2	4		12
Lynch, John	1		3		3
Lowe, Bennet	1		3		
Leigh, William	2	2	1		8
Lenmore, Jarbena	1	3	2		
Lynch, Thomas	1		2		2
Lusty, John	1		1		1
Linch, John	1	1	4		
Lake, Barbara	3	1	4		1
McLeim, William	1	3	2		
Mangers, Ann	2	2	3		3
Mareman, Joshua	2	3	5		
Mareman, Joseph	2		5		7
Miles, Henry	1		1		14
Mugg, John	1		1		2
Mugg, Walter	2		2		
Medley, William	2		1		5
Medly, Philip	1	1	2		16
Medley, Joseph	2		2		2
Mills, Winifred	1		2		12
Martin, William	1	3	5		12
Martin, Thomas	2	2	1	3	1
MoKay, George	2		3	1	3
Mason, Henry				13	
Martin, George	1	3	2	1	3
McClelan, John	2	1	2		
Mitchel, Benjamin	1	1	3		
MoKay, Benjamin	2		2		3
McLeland, Robert	2	2	4	1	1
McLaland, John	1	1	2	1	2
MoKay, John	1	2	3		2
Medley, Henry	1	1	2		12
Mason, Elisabeth				4	
McLeland, John	5		2		13
Medly, Enoch	1	1	3		
Neale, Charles	1	1	1		2
Nevett, Joseph	4	2	3		1
Norris, Vincent	1	2	4		
Norris, Gerard	1		4		
Nottingham, Philip	1	2	2		3
Norris, Ann			2		
Norris, John	2	2	2		
Norris, Edmund	2	2	1		
Norvell, John B			3		
Norvell, Jeremiah	2		4		
Norvell, Henry	1	2	3		
Norris, John	1	1	3		1
Norris, Mathew	1		1		
Norris, Bennet	1	2	6		1
Norris, Susanna			6		
Norris, Philip	2	2	5		
Nottingham, Bennet	2		2		2
Norris, Clement	2	3	2		
Norris, Thomas	1		3		5
Newton, Zachariah	1	2	4		
Norris, Ignatius	3	2	4		
Newton, Barnaba	1	1	5		
Nugent, Bennet	1	1	2		2
Owings, John	1	1	4		
Price, Robert	2	1	4	4	6
Payn, Ralph	1		3		
Payn, Vincent	2		2		
Patterson, James	2		3		1
Pike, Henry	2	2	3		9
Peake, Heneretta	1	2	5		
Pembrooke, George	2	2	5		9
Payne, Leonard	2	1	1		
Perie, Susanna			2		
Powell, Mary		5	4		
Peake, Peter	2	1	4		4
Pompy				3	4
Parsons, James	2	2	3		
Riswick, Thomas	2	3	4		
Riswick, Joseph	1	1	2		2
Rally, John					
Redman, Benjamin	2	3	4		1
Ridgill, Staisa		3			
Ridgill, Charles	1		2		
Richardson, William	1		3		8
Ross, John	1	3	5		1
Redman, William	1	4	3		

NAME OF HEAD OF FAMILY.	Free white males of 16 years and upward, including heads of families.	Free white males under 16 years.	Free white females, including heads of families.	All other free persons.	Slaves.
Tarlton, Philip	1		2		4
Thomas, William	1		2		
Thompson, Joseph	1	1	2		5
Thompson, Robert	2		1		2
Thompson, Charles	1		2		
Thompson, John B	2	4	3		2
Thompson, John B	1	1	5		7
Thompson, John A	3		2		20
Thomas, Robert	1		2		2
Tarlton, Joshua	1	2	3		4
Taylor, John	1	1	4		4
Tarlton, Susanna		2	2		3
Thompson, Peter	2	2	2		13
Thompson, Arther	1		3	3	3
Tarlton, Thomas	1	4	3		3
Thompson, James	3	3	4		4
Thompson, John	2		4		14
Tarlton, John	1	3	4		6
Tarlton, John, Jr	1	3	3		
Tarlton, Moses	3	4	3		
Tarlton, Frederick	1		2		4
Tarlton, James	1	4	2		
Taylor, John (B stone)	2	1	1		7
Taylor, James	1		2		
Taylor, John	4	1	1		12
Thompson, Joseph	1	1	1		1
Wimsatt, John B	1	1	1		
Wood, Gabaral	3				1
Wheatly, John	1	2	3		1
Williams, Ann	1	1	3		13
Williams, Francis	1		2		8
Wise, Donas					
Waring, Edward	2		2		
Wootton, John	1	3	3		
Wherritt, John	2	2	2		2
Wheritt, Thomas	3	1	2		6
Wootton, Thomas	1	1	3		
Wheatly, William	1		3		
Wheritt, Abner	1		6		
Wheritt, Will H	1				
Watts, Henry					19
Watts, Willoughby	1	2	4	2	
Woodland, Luke					7
Wheritt, Rebecca	2	1	4		
Wanghop, Elisabeth			4		29
Wood, Henrietta				2	
Watts, Kenelin	1	2	3	1	5
Watts, Joshua	1		3		
Wise, Mathew	1		3		
Wise, Adam	2	3	3	1	2
Yates, James	1	2	4		2
Sewall, Clement	1	3	5	12	
Smith, Jane	1		3	12	
Strickling, Johana			3		
Shaw, William	2		3		
Someville, Will	1	2	3		108
Silener, William	1		3		
Somervill, Geo	1		2	2	55
Sanner, John	2		1		
Sanner, Josias	2		4		
Stone, Edward	1	6	2		
Spink, William	1		3		9
Sewall, Mary	1		2		3
Sewall, Charles	1		2		1
Smoot, William B	1		4		16
Shadrick, John	1		2		9
Shadrick, Thomas	1		2		3
Simpson, Joseph	1		2		18
Banner, Joseph	1	5	2		4
Sanner, Vincent	1		2		
Sanner, Jeremiah	1		2		
Sanner, Thomas	2		2		
Russellon, Silvester					9
Silence, Thomas	1	1	2		
Smith, Ann	2		1		
Aisquith, Celia	1	1	2		11
Aisquith, John	1	3	2		11
Atwood, Sarah		1	1		
Abell, John H	2	1	1		8
Artist, Joseph	1	1	4		
Armstrong, Robert	1		2		8
Alison, William	1		2		
Allison, Henry	1	2	2		
Adkerson, James	1	4	3		
Adams, Abraham	1	1	2	2	
Adams, Thee			2		
Barnhouse, George	1	2	1		6
Beverly, Adam	1		2		
Bryan, William	1		3	1	
Bullock, Ann			3		
Breeden, Sarah			3		
Bohannan, George	3	2	3		
Baker, William	1		2		2
Booth, Richard	1	1	1		1
Bellwood, Rebecca	1	1	3		10

NAME OF HEAD OF FAMILY.	Free white males of 16 years and upward, including heads of families.	Free white males under 16 years.	Free white females, including heads of families.	All other free persons.	Slaves.
Batson, Eleanor	1		2		
Bennett, William		2	6		13
Barnhouse, Rodolph	1		2		3
Biscoe, Bennet	1	1	1		3
Beale, John	1		2		13
Biscoe, James, Sen	2	2	6		25
Booth, Basil	1	1	4		1
Bryan, Jane	1		3		
Beale, William	1	3	4		
Bean, Jacob		1	2	2	
Biscoe, James	1		2		1
Biscoe, Josias	1	4	4		7
Bennett, Joseph	1	5	5		19
Biscoe, Mikay	2	1	4		4
Biscoe, Elisabeth		2	4		8
Biscoe, Thomas	1		1		8
Biscoe, Bennet	1		1		8
Biscoe, Sarah	1	1	3		12
Barnhouse, Richard	1	1	3		9
Bennett, Richard	1	1	3		9
Bennett, Susanna	1	3	5		3
Biscoe, James	1		2		3
Bean, Benjamin	1	3	2	1	13
Bally, John	1	3	2		
Bunn, John	1		2		
Bean, Alexander	2	4	5		
Bean, Joshua			3		
Bright, Basil	1		2	1	1
Clark, Cuthbert	3	1	4		
Combs, Enoch	1		5		13
Chilton, Charles	1		1		6
Chilton, Mary			3		
Chilton, William	1	1	2		6
Clark, William	1	1	2		2
Combs, Mary		5	3		31
Cambell, Enoch	1	2	4		
Clocker, Benjamin	1	1	2		
Chisely, Robert	1	1	7	4	14
Curtis, Mary				2	2
Cole, Ann			2		
Coram, James	1		2		2
Clark, Ally		1	2		
Craighill, George	2		1	5	6
Connaly, Joshua	2	3	2		
Corbin, Jacob	1		2		
Chisholm, Martha			3		
Coe, William	1	1	2		3
Clark, John	1		1		5
Cullison, Joseph	1		2		
Clark, Charles	1	2	3		13
Cissell, Francis	1		3		2
Coode, Joseph, Snr	1	1	1		8
Cissell, John	1		4		8
Cole, Valentine	1	1	2		
Cadwell, William					2
Cissell, Francis	1	2	2		
Cissell, Jeremiah	2	2	2		8
Cullison, Joseph	1	2	2		
Cole, George	1		2		10
Cole, Mary			1		
Coode, James	2	1	1		3
Dant, Charles	1	1	2	1	2
Daffin, Robert	1	1	2	1	4
Duke, Jonathan	2	1	2		
Diment, Mathew	1	2	1		2
Diment, George	2	2	1		
Daffin, James	1		3		4
Drury, Joseph	1	1	1		
Drury, Chrysostum	1		2		
Drury, John	3	1	3		
Dixon, William R	1	1	3		15
Dixey, William	1	1	3		
Dorsey, Auston S	1		4		10
Durbar, John	1	3	5		13
Doxey, James	3		2		
Doran, Ann			3		
Cullison, John	2	1	2		1
Clark, Richard	2	4	2		8
Cissell, Francis	1	3	2		
Carbery, Mary		4			8
Carbery, Thomas	1		2		9
Evans, Philip	2		1		
Evans, Jeremiah	1	1	1		2
Evans, Ignatius	1		2		3
Evans, John	3	1	4		3
Egerton, John	2		3		
Enge, Vincent	2				1
Fish, Joseph	1	6	2		
Flowers, John	2	1	2		
Fardwell, Francis	1	1	1		
Fenwick, Richard	1		2		7
Ford, Robert	1	4	2		
Fenwick, Richard	2	1	6		10
Fenwick, John	2	1	7		18
Flowers, Moses	1	2		1	3

ST. MARYS COUNTY—Continued.

NAME OF HEAD OF FAMILY.	Free white males of 16 years and upward, including heads of families.	Free white males under 16 years.	Free white females, including heads of families.	All other free persons.	Slaves.
Fenwick, James	1		1		25
Fielder, Mary			3		
Ford, Charles A	1	3	3		
Fenwick, Ann	1	3	8		20
Ford, Philip	2	2	6		18
French, Barton	1		8		
Greenwell, Stephen	1	2	4		
Goodrum, John	3	1	2		4
Green, Jeremiah	3	2			1
Griffin, Thomas	2		2		19
Greigs, George	1	1	2		
Gough, George	6		3		7
Greenwell, Bennet	1	1	2		1
Gill, Mary	3	1	6		
Griffin, Ann	1				10
Grant, Elisabeth			3		1
Greenwell, James	2	3	4		
Greenwell, Robert	1	1	1		
Hebb, Susanna	1	2	2		9
Holton, William	2	1	3		14
Horn, John	4	1	2		
Howard, John B	1	5	3		
Hammett, McKelvie	3	1	3		3
Hening, Gilbert					
Hayes, Eleanor	2		1		
Hopewell, John	1		2		10
Haw, Amy				3	
Holly, Joseph				8	
Wilton, William	1		6		
Hall, Elisabeth					
Herbert, William	2	1	4	1	7
Herbert, Barbara	2		4		3
Herbert, Mary	2		3		11
Hagan, Mathew	2		2		
Harkerson, Elisabeth	1				1
Hopkins, Basil	2	3	3		3
Henry, Elias	1	2	2		
Hendly, Robert	1		4		
Heckman, Nathaniel	1	2	3		
Hebb, Caleb	1	3	5		
Hammet, John	1		2		3
Haywood, Thomas	1	3	2		12
Hebb, Joseph	1	2	5		11
Hebb, Ann	1	1	2		9
Hendly, John	1		4		3
Hebb, Vernon	2	1	6		67
Hopewell, Pollard	2		1		34
Hammett, Richard	2	2	3		6
Hickman, Daniel	1	1	3		
Hopewell, George	3	1	9		15
Jarboe, Robert	3	1	6		18
Jenkins, Jeremiah	1	1	1		
Jenkins, Mary	2	1	2		11
Jenkins, Mary			2		16
Jarboe, Clement	1	1	1		1
Jenkins, George	1		2		
Jarboe, Henry	2	1	2		10
Jarboe, Joseph	1	2	3		
Jarboe, Rodolph	1	1	3		2
Jones, Ann			3		2
Jefferis, Michael	1		2		
Jefferis, Sarah		1	4		2
Jefferis, Whitton	2	2	4		
Jones, Mordeca	2	3	4		21
Jefferis, Henerietta			1		
Jordan, Jeremiah	2		1		4
Kirby, William	2	1	2		4
King, James	2	1	3		6
Kiemer, Thomas	1	2	4		9
Kirks, Joseph	2	4	2		6
Kemb, Samuel	1		1		1
Leigh, John	2		5		
Linch, John	1	2	2		
Lyons, Cornelius	1		3		2
Loker, William		2	6		11
Leigh, Richard	1		2		
Leigh, Charles	1	2	3		5
Leigh, Joseph	1	3	1		13
Lynch, Isabella			3		
Loker, George			3		2
Loker, Thomas	2		6		7
Langly, William	2	1	6		21
Langly, James	2	3	2		5
Leigh, Walter	2		2		13
Laurance, William	1	2	4		2
Leigh, Marcus	1	1	6		2
Lilburn, William	1	2	4		10
McCaul, John, Jur	2		2		22
Moore, Ignatius	2		2		
Milbm, Stephen	3	2	2		
McCaul, John, Sr	1	1	2		5
Milburn, Richard, Jr	1		2		4
Milburn, Rich'd, Sr	1	1	2		10
McWherton, Andrew	1	1	2		
McLain, Richard	1	1	3		
Milbm, William	2	1	3		
Mason, Joseph			6		

NAME OF HEAD OF FAMILY.	Free white males of 16 years and upward, including heads of families.	Free white males under 16 years.	Free white females, including heads of families.	All other free persons.	Slaves.
Milburn, Joseph	1	4	2		
Mann, Richard	2	2	2		
Milburn, Will	2	1	1		4
Mitchel, David	1		1		
Milburn, Edward	1		2		9
Milburn, Auston	2	1	3		7
McClain, Elisabeth	2	1	2		4
Moore, Bennett	1		2		1
Mandly, Mathew	2	5	2		
Milburn, Joseph, Jr	1	1	3		1
Morgan, Benjamin	2		2		2
Mandly, Basel	3				
McCaulley, John	2	2	2		
Morris, John	2		4		
Moore, Bennett	1	1	4		
Morgan, Susanna				2	
Morgan, James				2	
Morgan, Jane				5	
McKenny, Soloman	1		2		
Moore, Will	1	1	2		1
Moore, Mary			2		
Mattingly, Elisabeth	2		2		4
Murry, Edward		4	1	1	
Newton, John	2		5		
Norris, Stephen	3	4	1		
Owings, Robert	1		4		
Pain, William	3	2	5		
Price, William	1		2		
Price, John	1	3	1		
Price, Joseph	2		4		
Pooly, Richard	4	3	4		4
Price, John	5	2	2		1
Price, Sarah	2	2	3		6
Price, Archibald	1	1	7		1
Richardson, Willough	2		2		
Redman, Joshua	2		6		
Rice, George	1		1		1
Rice, John	2	2	1		1
Rally, Bennet	2	3	2		
Roads, Barnaby	2	1	3		3
Risner, George				5	
Richardson, Thomas	2		2		9
Richardson, James	2	1	8		10
Ramsey, Joseph	1	1	3		
Reed, Samuel	1		3		3
Ralley, Bennet	2	1	3		6
Stone, Joseph	2	1	3		20
Silence, Enoch	1	3	1		
Smith, John	1		5		
Smoot, Thomas	2				12
Smith, Ann			1		
Smith, John	1	2	2		2
Smith, Will W	2		5		
Sherbintine, Abehton	1	3	2		
Smith, Thomas	3	1	2	1	4
Shirley, Bennet	1		7	1	4
Shirley, Joshua	1	1	2		1
Sewall, Nicholas L	2		2		39
Sewall, Nicholas	4		1		57
Smith, Mary	1		2		
Simmons, Mathew	1				1
Smoot, William	1	5	2		3
Smoot, Alexander	1		2		
Smoot, Hezekiah	1		4		3
Smoot, Elisabeth	2	1	3		
Smith, Caleb	1		4		2
Smith, James	1	6	2		
Smith, Samuel	2	1	5		1
Smoot, Thomas	2				1
Smith, Elevely	4	2	4		15
Smith, James	1	1	7		5
Smoot, James	1		6		5
Smoot, Willoughby	2		1		1
Banner, Isaac	3	1	2		2
Banner, John	1	2	7		
Shirly, Ignatius	1	4	4		
Swann, Edward	2	5			
Shirbindine, James	1		6		
Sword, Ignatius	1	3	3		1
Swall, Ann			4		
Thorp, Mary		1	4		
Thomas, Herbert	2	5	2		2
Tabbs, Barton	1	2	4		17
Tariton, William	1	1	6		4
Thorp, Mary	1		2		
Taylor, Joseph	1		3		2
Thomas, Levin	1				5
Thomas, William	2		5		9
Taylor, Ann			5		2
Thomas, Philip	2	2	5		
Thompson, James	1	1	4	1	
Thomas, Taylor	1	3	4		1
Taylor, Richard	1		3		
Tarlton, Bennet	2	1	3		18
Timmus, Elisabeth		2	4		
Taylor, James	1	1	3		
Taylor, Henry	1	3	1		

NAME OF HEAD OF FAMILY.	Free white males of 16 years and upward, including heads of families.	Free white males under 16 years.	Free white females, including heads of families.	All other free persons.	Slaves.
Tarlton, Ignatius	1	2	3		
Taylor, William	1	1	2		21
Vaughan, Thomas	1	3	2		1
Underwood, Charles	1	1	4		2
Vessels, Charles	1	2	4		
Wooton, Joseph, Jr	2	2	1		1
Wilkerson, James	2	1	4		
Watt, Mary			5		2
Wilkerson, Mark	1	2	5		
Wooton, Joseph, Sr	1		2		
Wooton, Elisabeth			1		
Wise, William	1	2	3		8
Williter, Thomas	1	1	3		9
White, James	3	4	2		28
Walton, James	2				
Wheatly, Bennett	2		2		
White, Christian			2		2
Witherington, Monica			4		
Williams, Benjamin	1	1	3		11
Williams, Ann			3		7
Williams, Ann	1		2		16
Watt, Thomas	2	2	6		7
Waughop, Thomas P	2		4		34
Wilson, Elisabeth			1	1	
Watts, Richard	2		2		15
Walker, Francis			2		
Wilsonholme, Daniel	1	1	3		25
Williter, Maryan			2		
Wise, Jeremiah	1		3		
Williams, James	1	2	4		21
Howard, George	2	1	4		2
Wimset, William	1	2	2		
Howard, Ignatius	1	1	2	1	
Bradburn, Eleanor		2	1		
Griffin, Ignatius	1		2		1
Stell, Ann	1		2		5
Pecke, Susanna			2	1	
Cissil, John	2	1	2		
Howard, Leonard	1	3	2		2
Howard, Mary			2		
Thompson, Ignatius	1		1		
Booth, Leonard	1	3	3	1	2
Booth, James	1	3	2		
Wimmset, Robert	1	2	2		
Hoskins, Elizabeth			2		
Morgan, James	1		6	3	3
Greenwell, Robert	1	1	2		5
Campbell, Edward	1	4	4		
Long, James	1	1	6		
Curtis, Mary			2		5
Smith, Peter	1				
Silburn, Robert	3		1		
Alvey, Jeremiah	2	3	9		6
Allen, Zachariah	1		2		1
Alexander, Samuel	1	1	2		
Alvey, John B	4		1		1
Adams, Jenny			3	3	
Ashcom, Samuel	1	2	3		
Anderson, Cloe	1	2	3		
Ashcom, Nathaniel	1	4	3		5
Anderson, Ignatius	2	1	1		
Alvey, Basil	2		1		3
Allstone, Thomas, Ser	1	2	3		1
Abell, Joseph Abner	1		3		
Allstone, Thomas, Jur	2	5	4	1	7
Anderson, Alexander	1		5		
Alvey, Clement	1	2	2		1
Abell, Clark	1	3	3	8	
Abell, Philip	1		3		
Abell, John Boothe	1	2	3		7
Abell, Cuthbert	1	2	2		7
Abell, Francis	1	1	3		4
Abell, John Standfield	2		4		6
Abell, Edward					12
Abell, Benjamin				1	
Abell, John, Ser	2				4
Abell, John (J. P.)	2	1	4		21
Abell, Ignatius	1	3	4		8
Abell, Samuel	1		2		11
Abell, Henry	2		3		7
Adams, Joseph				8	
Abell, Burton	1	2	3		3
Alvey, Jesse	2	4		4	
Adams, James			1		1
Burroughs, Hezekiah	1	2	1		1
Burroughs, Mathew	2		1		
Branson, Michael	1	1	2		
Burroughs, Normand	1	2	3		3
Barnes, James	1	2	3		
Branson, Luke	2		3		3
Blethen, Samuel	1	2	4		
Brown, Bennett	1	2	4	1	1
Bradburn, John, Ser	3	2	3	1	
Bailey, John	3	2	2		10
Barber, John M	2	1	5		10
Bond, Peregrine	1	1	2		13
Bridgett, Thomas, Jur	1	2	4		

ST. MARYS COUNTY—Continued.

NAME OF HEAD OF FAMILY.	Free white males of 16 years and upward, including heads of families.	Free white males under 16 years.	Free white females, including heads of families.	All other free persons.	Slaves.
Briscoe, Hanson	5	2	7		33
Briscoe, Doctor John H.	1	3	2	1	26
Buckman, Francis	3		2		
Brookbank, James	3		4		3
Barber, Luke, Ser	2		1		6
Barber, Luke, Jur	1	1	1		1
Barber, Elias	1	4	3		5
Billingsley, Allen	1	1	2		7
Branson, Briscoe D	1	1	5		
Bateman, George	1	2	4		
Barber, Cornelius	3		1		39
Bond, John (of Thos)	2		2	1	35
Barber, Barnet W	2	1	5		34
Brady, Henry	2	1	3		
Barber, Hezekiah	1		1		7
Briscoe, Clement	1		6		27
Bryan, Philip	1	1	4		
Barber, Ann		1	4	1	27
Brooke, Revd Clement	1	2	3		12
Brookbank, John	2	2	4		
Bond, Thomas	1	3	3		12
Bryan, William	1	3	6		
Brewer, Mark	1	3	3		1
Branson, Baptist	1	2	2		
Broday, James	1	2	2		
Burroughs, Wilson	1	2	6		
Barber, Edward	2	2	6		3
Buckman, Charles	1	3	1		1
Buckman, John B	4		1		10
Bond, Cecilia	1	1	2		13
Bramhall, Jonathan	1	4	4		
Burroughs, Hezekiah, Ser	3	3			
Burroughs, John, Ser	2				4
Burroughs, Eleanor	1				8
Burroughs, Henry	1	1			1
Bruce, Elizabeth	2				10
Briscoe, Henry	1	1			
Burroughs, Samuel, Jur	1	1			2
Burroughs, John, Jur	2	2	3		
Burroughs, Samuel, Ser	3	1	2		
Broom, John H	3	1	5		16
Bennett, Susanna	4	1	6		
Bowles, John	2	2	3		
Briscoe, Margaret			1		1
Bradburn, Benjamin	1	1	4		
Bond, Richard	1	1	7	4	55
Bridgett, Charles	1	1	3		1
Boothe, George, Jur	1	1	2		
Buckler, Benjamin	3		4		
Brown, Doctor Gustavus			3		31
Booker, James	1		2		
Buckler, Bennett	1		1		
Buckler, George	1		1		
Brodrick, John	1	2	2		
Brewer Mark, Ser	3	3	4		4
Boothe, Rodolpus	3	1	2		
Brown, Ignatius, Ser	1	1	3		1
Brooke, Francis	2	1	8		24
Brown, Joseph	2	2	4		
Brown, James	2		4		
Bowie, William	1	1	2		5
Boarman, Ignatius	1	1	2		
Bowling, William	1		3		5
Bullock, George	2	2	3		
Bond, Jeremiah	1	2	2		4
Bright, James	3	1	6		
Buckler, Stephen	1	1	1		
Buckler, Robert	3	3	1		8
Bailie, John, Ser	2		2		
Bond, John, Ser	2	1	7		16
Bull, Deborah			3		
Blackistone, Herbert	2	4	6		22
Blackistone, John	1		2		15
Bowen, Mark	1	1	8		4
Bullock, Jesse	1		1		1
Brown, Nehimiah	1	1			
Brown, Ignatius, Jur	2		3		
Boothe, George, Ser	1	2	3		11
Bright, John	1	2	3		
Breeding, Rachel	1		2		
Bright, Joseph	1	1	2	1	3
Brown, Raphael	1		2		1
Bright, William	1		2		
Biscoe, George	6	1	5		50
Bohannon, John	2	1	2		
Bohannon, Moses	1		2		
Bohannon, Hannah		2	1		
Cooke, James		1	1		
Cooke, John M	2	1	1		3
Cawood, Benjamin	1	2	5		
Cooke, Alexander	1		1		7
Cheshire, Alsey					
Cusick, Bennett	2	3	5		
Cusick, James	1	3	2		
Chappelear, Henry	1		4		1

NAME OF HEAD OF FAMILY.	Free white males of 16 years and upward, including heads of families.	Free white males under 16 years.	Free white females, including heads of families.	All other free persons.	Slaves.
Cartwright, Dyson I	2		2		
Craig, Peter	1	3	3		1
Cartwright, Jesse	1	3	1	7	7
Cusick, Michael	1	2	2	7	2
Curtis, Joseph			2	7	7
Cawood, Stephen	3	2	4		7
Clark, Henry	1	3	4		
Cartwright, John, Jur	2		2		2
Cawood, Anna	1		2		6
Callis, James A	2				10
Cheshire, Benjamin B	2	4	4		2
Cheshire, Tennison	2		6		3
Cooper, Thomas	1		2		11
Carroll, Susanna			6		
Cartwright, Samuel	1	4	1		5
Cartwright, William	1	1	2		9
Cartwright, John	1	4	2		21
Copsey, Thomas	1		2		
Craycroft, Edward	2		3		6
Coal, Mary			4		
Copsey, Charles	1	1	3		
Copsey, Patty	1	1	1		
Chesley, John	1	1	1		7
Clark, Isaac	1		4		
Carpenter, George	3	2	3		10
Craig, Reuben	3	1	4		37
Cheseldine, William	1	2	2		7
Clark, Ignatius	1	1	2		
Clark, Thomas	1	4	4		
Cox, Mary	2	2	3		
Clark, Mary			2	2	
Cheseldine, Kenelm	3	2			
Coode, John	2		4		14
Carter, Philip	3		4	4	
Carberry, Patrick	2	3	1		2
Clayton, Thomas	1	1	4		
Carter, Anthony					3
Courts, George	1		2		
Clark, John	1		4		
Clark, Lydia	3		4		1
Clark, Philip	3	1	3		14
Clark, George M	2		5		19
Clark, Rodger	2	2	5		1
Clark, Kenelm	2		5		5
Carpenter, William	2	4	3		8
Coale, Milla					8
Coram, John	1	2	2		2
Clark, Cloe	1		5		2
Campbell, John	1		3		
Currey, John	1		2		
Campbell, Ignatius	2		3		
Curtis, Sarah					5
Crahall, William			2		1
Clark, William	1	3	5		1
Dent, Mary Ann	2		5		1
Dent, George	1	1	2		1
Davis, Perigrine	1		3		
Dean, John	1	4	5		
Dean, James	1	2	5		
Dunbar, Milla	1	2	4		
Dixon, Susanna	2		3		
Drury, Peter	2	3	7		
Drury, William	1	2	2		
Davis, Anthony	1	1	2	2	
Dunbar, Joseph	2		4	2	8
Dixon, Susanna (widow of Jnos)		1	4		1
Dick, Henry	1		4		1
Dick, John W	1		2		
Davis, George	3	3	4		7
Davis, Susanna	1	2	1		
Debutts, John	3	1	4		34
Davis, Philip	2	2	4		3
Dixon, Susanna (widow of George)	2		1		
Dart, Thomas	2		1		
Davis, Philip, Jur	1	2	2		6
Dixon, Sarah	1		3		
Deserena, Peter	1	1	2		
Davis, Margaret	1	3	4		4
Dixon, Absolem	3	4	5		
Davis, Enos	2		2		1
Dixon, Thomas	1		5	2	
Davis, Elizabeth		1	4		
Drury, Philip	3	3	4		
Dunn, John	1		1		
Dean, John B	1		1		
Davarax, Mary			3		
Davis, Stephen	3	2	4		3
Davis, John B	2		4		
Drury, Enoch	2	1	7	1	5
Drury, Baptist	1	1	4		
Davis, Joseph	2		6		1
Dorsey, Winnefred	2	2	5		
Drury, Eleanor	2	1	3		
Drury, Michael	2	1	3		1

NAME OF HEAD OF FAMILY.	Free white males of 16 years and upward, including heads of families.	Free white males under 16 years.	Free white females, including heads of families.	All other free persons.	Slaves.
Daft, John	1	1	5		2
Dorsey, Joseph	1	1	1		
Davis, Walter	1		1		2
Drury, Monica			3		
Daft, Mathew	1		2		
Drudge, Ann		2	3		
Duggins, Henna		2	1		
Edwards, Sarah	1	1	4	1	
Edwards, Ignatius	3		3		
Edwards, Stourton (of Jno)	1	2	4		2
Edwards, Thomas	1	4	2		2
Edwards, Stourton (of Igns)	2		3		1
Edwards, Benjamin	2	1	4		2
Edwards, Joseph	2	3	1		4
Estep, Joshua	2		3		3
Estep, Philemon	2		1		11
Edwards, Mary		1	5		2
Edwards, Jesse	2				
Edwards, Johanna		1	4		
Ewing, Nathaniel	1	1	2		12
Edley, John	1	1	4		2
Evans, Ann	1		4		
Ellis, James	2		2	1	
Eden, Betty	1		3		17
Ellis, Elizabeth (Wd. of Jno)	1	1	6	1	1
Eden, Margarett	1	1	6	1	22
Ellis, Elizabeth Wde of Thos	1	3	2		
Evans, Richard	2	2	5		
Ellis, Thomas	1		5		
Eden, Betty Ann					13
Forrest, Zachariah	3	1	7		15
French, Rodolphus	1	2	3		
Farr, John	2		4		
Fowler, William	2	3	4		7
Fryar, Thomas	1	1	3		
Fowler, Eleanor	2	1	4		2
Yarmouth, Free				3	1
Felid, Joseph	2		5		
Ford, John (of Peter)	3		6		
Ford, Philip (of John)	1	3	4		2
Fenwick, John	1	3	2		3
Forrest, Zephaniah	1	3	3		5
Forrest, Thomas	1		2		
Forrest, Henrietta					8
Fenwick, Francis	1		3		7
Fenwick, Michael	1		3		6
Fenwick, Monica		2	4		1
Fenwick, Elizabeth			1		6
Floyd, Jesse	3	3	4		13
Ford, Peter	1	5	2		1
Fenwick, Jane	3	1	2		5
Fenwick, James	1	4	2	1	14
Ford, John, Jur	1		1	1	
French, John	3	3	5		
Ford, Margarett			1		
Ferroll, William	1	2	2		
Foster, William	1		1		
Fowler, Charles	1		3		
Fenwick, Benjamin	2		1		1
Fenwick, George	2	4	5		12
Fenwick, William	2	1	3		7
French, Ignatius	2		3		
Ford, Raphael	1		1		9
French, Martin	2		2		
Felid, Ann		1	2		
Ford, Henry	2	2	3		2
Ferroll, William, Jur	3		4		
Ford, Joseph	2	2	4		3
Felid, Ambrose	2		1		
Ford, Robert	1	1	2		10
Ford, John (weaver)	1		1		8
Gardiner, John	1		1		3
Gibbons, Thomas	2	2	2	2	3
Greenfeld, Thomas	2	2	2		4
Greaves, John, Jur	4	4	2		9
Grindall, Josiah B	4		2		
Gunn, John					
Gardiner, Edward	2	1	3		9
Gardiner, Bullett	1				12
Goddard, Edward B	1	2	2		3
Greaves, Joshua	2		1		12
Greasty, Richard	1		2		
Graham, Alexander	2				3
Greenfeld, Susanna			4	4	18
Goddard, Ignatius	1		1		
Goldsmith, Mary			1		
Grey, Randolph	1	1	4		1
Gadden, Nicholas	3		1		
Goldsmith, Thomas	2		1		
Goldie, Revd George	1		1		26
Goldsmith, John	1	3	5		8
Gardiner, Thomas	1	4	4		1

FIRST CENSUS OF THE UNITED STATES.

ST. MARYS COUNTY—Continued.

NAME OF HEAD OF FAMILY.	Free white males of 16 years and upward, including heads of families.	Free white males under 16 years.	Free white females, including heads of families.	All other free persons.	Slaves.
Gardiner, William	1		2		
Gardiner, Clement	4		1	3	22
Gardiner, Henry	1		1		10
Gibson, Robert	1	1	1		
Goldsmith, John M	1	1	4		13
Gibson, Jeremiah, Ser	2		4	5	
Gibson, Joshua, Jur	1	3	2	6	
Goodwin, Mathew	2	3	1		
Gibson, Rodolphus	1		2		1
Goldsmith, Notley	1		2		2
Gibson, William	3	1	3		13
Goodrum, Mary	2		4		
Godard, John B	1	4	3		2
Greenwell, Mary	1	1	2		
Greenwell, William	2		5		
Greenwell, Joseph	1	1	3		
Greenwell, Thomas (of Philip)	3		5		
Greenwell, Ostend	1	1	3		
Greenwell, Thomas	1	5	3		9
Goddard, John	2	4	2		1
Greenwell, Henry	2		2		
Greenwell, Edmund B	4		2		1
Greenwell, Ignatius	1	3	4		
Greaves, John, Ser	4		2		
Goldsmith, Judith		2	2		
Gibson, Joshua	1		1		12
Greenwell, Peter	1		4		
Greenwell, Ignatius, Jur	2		5		
Greaves, Joshua, Jur	1	1	3		
Green, Nicholas D	3		6		
Greaves, Jeremiah	1	2	4		
Greaves, Ann	1		2		1
Hunt, Gladden	1	1	5		5
Hayden, James (Chapten)	1		3		5
Harrison, Joseph	2	3	8		3
Hopkins, Jacob	1	1	1		
Hill, Henry	1		1		16
Hall, Joseph	1	2	3		
Hutchinges, Thomas	2		2		
Herbert, Jane	2	3	6		
Hendley, John	3	3	4		
Hilton, Mary		1	4		
Highfield, Leonard	3	2	6		
Harrison, Benjamin	2		2		4
Harris, Samuel	2	3	2		
Howe, Elizabeth	2	4	3		
Hayes, Ruth H	1		2		1
Howe, John	1	2	2		1
Hazle, Bennett	1	2	3		7
Hazle, Edwards	1	3	3		
Hayden, Gerrard	1	4	3		
Hayden, George	4	2	5		9
Hayden, William	2		3		1
Howard, William	1	1	1		
Hackett, Ann			3		
Hardesty, John	1	4	4	1	1
Hammett, Zachariah	1		1		1
Hill, Ignatius	2	2	7		
Hill, Thomas	2	2	2		
Hill, Richard	2	1	4		
Harrison, Nathaniel	3	3	3	2	
Harrison, Robert	1	4	3		11
Harrison, John	1	4	3		
Hunt, Shadrack	1	4	2		
Hazle, Henry	1	1	1		
Howe, Ann			3		19
Howard, Joseph	1	5	3		3
Horrell, John	1	4	1		28
Hardesty, Thomas	1	1	2		
Hill, George	1	1	1		
Hazle, Ann	1	1	2		
Hutchings, Robert	1	1	4		6
Heard, William	1		3		1
Heard, James	1		3		2
Hughs, George				2	
Harrison, Elizabeth	1	1	2		
Howard, James	1	1	3		
Harding, Baptist	3		4		
Howard, Basil	2		3		8
Hoskins, Benjamin	1	1	3		
Hoskins, Mary		1	3		
Hayden, James (of James)	1				5
Hayden, Jonathan	2	3	5	1	
Heard, John	2	3	3		13
Hayden, Thomas	1	1	3		
Hamilton, James	1	2	3		
Hall, Eleanor	1	2	3		
Hutchings, John	2	1	2		1
Hazle, Jeremiah	1	5	4		7
Hutchings, Bennett	1	3	3		2
Hall, Basil	2	3	4		
Hopewell, James	5				25
Hackett, Mary			3		
Hammett, McKelvie	2		5		14
Heard, Edmund	1	1	2		9
Heard, Ignatius	1		2		8
Hayden, Richard (of Rich'd)	1		4		2
Horrell, Henry	1	2	2		6
Heard, Mathew	2	3	8		7
Hopewell, Eleanor	2		4		4
Higgins, Bryan	2	1	2		1
Hayden, Clement	1	3	3		
Hayden, Francis	2	3	4		
Howard, Gabrel	1	3	2		3
Hamersly, Francis	4	4	2	1	54
Joseph, Fanny			2		
Joseph, John	3	1	6		10
Johnson, Charles	1	2	2		
Johnson, James, Jur	1	3	1		1
Johnson, Zachariah	1		2		1
Jarboe, Raphael	1		2		5
Johnson, James, Ser	2	1	2		
Johnson, Leonard	1	4	5		4
Johnson, David	2	4	4		
Joy, Arthur	3		6		2
Joy, Robert	1	2	3		5
Jordan, Jeremiah	5	1	3		52
Joy, William	1	1	4		
Joy, Peter	1		5		
Jarboe, Margaret	2	2	2		
Joy, Tecla			2		2
Joy, Thomas	1	3	5		
Johnson, Elisha	1	1	5		2
Jarboe, Joshua	4	3	4		2
Joy, Ignatius, Ser	1	4	5		4
Joy, Rebecca		2	4		
Joy, Ignatius, Jur	1	4	3		7
Jarboe, Robert	1	2	4		
Jarboe, Mathew	3	2	3		
Johnson, Francis	4		2		
Killgour, William	2	1	6		13
Killgour, James	1	1	2		6
Kendrick, William	1	1	4		
Knott, Francis	1	1	5	1	5
Knott, William	1	1	3		10
King, Benjamin	1		2		
Keech, James	1	5	2		
Kendrick, Jasper	2	2	3		
Keech, John	4	2	2		16
King, Cornelius	1	1	3		4
Knott, James (of John)	1	3	2		
Knott, Elias	1	2	2		
Knott, John	4		3		
Knott, James (Chaptico)	2	2	2		7
Key, Philip	4	3	3	1	23
King, Charles	3	1	2		1
Lyon, Richard	1	2	4		9
Little, Peter	1		4		1
Lucas, James	1		3		10
Lock, Jesse	1		4		21
Langley, Ignatius	1	1	1		
Lattimer, James	2	2	4		11
Leach, Nehemiah	1		5		
Lyon, John, Ser	1	2	2	1	4
Lyon, Michael		2	7	1	
Lock, Thomas	1		2		7
Lyon, John, Jur	1	3	2		2
Lyon, Henry, Jur	1	2	1		6
Long, Peregrine	1	3			1
Lyon, Walter	1	2	4		12
Long, Charles	2		5		
Lathcom, Susanna	1		5		
Leach, Elizabeth		1	5		
Lyon, Walter, Jur	1	1	2		2
Long, John, Ser	1	1	2		
Lee, John H	1		4		
Long, Jenny			2		
Lock, George	1	1	5	1	10
Long, Jeremiah	1	2	2		2
Lee, Jane			2		6
Llewellin, Charles	1	1	2		27
Lee, Richard	1		2		20
Long, Thomas	1	3	2		1
Llewellin, Richard	1	2	2		18
Lancaster, Jeremiah	2	2	4	1	3
Mills, John	2		2		2
Mattingly, William	1	3	3		
Mort, Eleanor		2	5	1	
Mills, Charles N	1	5	5		7
Mattingley, Luke	1	2	2		1
Mattingley, Ignatius, Jur	2	1	5	3	
Mattingley, John B	5	5	3	1	3
Mills, James A	2	3	3		1
Morgan, Joseph	1	2	2		2
Mattingley, John	3		6		
Mills, James	2	1	2		33
Melton, Richard	3	2	3		11
Morgan, James	1	2	2		
McIver, William	2	4	4		3
Moran, Hezekiah	1	3	4		1
Moore, William	2	1	5		2
Monruk, John	2		4		2
Miller, Francis	2		4		9
Morgan, Ignatius	2	1	1	4	
Morton, Samuel	2	1	1		10
Moore, George	2		5		
Moran, Jonathan	1	1	4		1
Moran, John	1		6		1
McGee, William	1	1	1		
Murphy, Zephaniah	1		3		
Miles, John	2	1	4	1	3
Mills, Joshua	1		3		14
Miller, Joseph	2	4	6		35
Mattingley, Ignatius, Ser	1	1	2	2	5
Monarch, Edward	1		2		
McGee, Hanson	1		3		
McGee, John	1		3		
Martin, Samuel	1		2		1
McGee, Raphael	1	2	4	1	1
McGill, Arthur		3	3		
McGill, Mary			1		
Mattingley, Edward	1	1	3		8
Mattingley, James	1	1	1		4
Martin, John	1	1	3		3
Maddox, Samuel	1		3		8
Maddox, John	1		3		3
Mason, John	2		4	2	
Medcalf, Kenelm	1	1	2		4
Mattingley, Zachariah	4		3		15
Mattingley, Bennett	1		3		12
Morgan, Cherry	1	1	3		2
Melton, James	1		3		6
Muir, William	1	2	2		14
Murray, James	1		2	1	
Moore, Mary			5		
Mills, Justinian	3	1	1		8
Mills, Joseph	2	1	1		
Millar, Joshua	2		2		16
Moore, John	1		1		
McWilliams, Mary	2	4	4		22
McWilliams, Elizabeth	2		6		14
McLeland, Mary Ann			4		2
Moore, James	2		5		
Mattingley, Barton	2	2	2		1
Milburn, Jeremiah	1		2		13
Mattingley, Eleanor		2	4		
Monarch, Thomas	1	5	4		
Mattingley, Samuel	1	1	1		
Neale, Henry	2		6		60
Noe, Joseph	2		6		
Nicholls, Jane			4		3
Nettle, James	2	1	3		6
Nugent, Jeremiah	1	1	5		27
Newton, Ignatius	1	1	2		
Newton, Thomas	1	1	2		6
Newton, Clement	1		2		1
Newton, William	1	2	2		1
Norris, Baptist	2	3	4		
Neale, Wilfred	4	3	3		51
Neale, Mary			4		24
Neale, James (of Bennett)	2				
Neale, James (Clements Boy)	2	4	4		9
Neale, Jeremiah	5	5	2		23
Neale, Raphael	1		5		22
Norris, Mathew, Jur	1		4		
Norris, Deaden		1	1		
Norris, Mark	1	1	5		1
Newton, Delbet	3	1	4		
Nugent, Bennett	1	1	2		
Newton, Zachariah	1	2	2		2
Norris, Mary			3		3
Nelson, Seneca	2	2	3		5
Neverson, Abraham	1		2		1
Owings, Joseph	4	2	2		
Pantory, Jeremiah	1		5		
Power, Jane	1		4		10
Power, Joshua (Manager for John Forbes of Charles County)	1		2		29
Parsons, Clement	3		1		7
Power, Thomas	1	3	5		9
Price, Benedict	2		4		12
Price, Mary			3		1
Payne, Basil	2	5	3		
Power, Philip	1	3			
Philips, Henry	1	2	4		
Philips, Ann			4		
Power, Edward	1	3	4		
Power, Joseph	2	2	4		2
Pilkington, Richard	1		2		
Pearsall, Richard	2	2	4		
Plowden, Edmund	2	2	4		64
Peacock, Ignatius	4		1		
Plowden, Henrietta			1		20
Payne, John B	1		3		

ST. MARYS COUNTY—Continued.

NAME OF HEAD OF FAMILY.	Free white males of 16 years and upward, including heads of families.	Free white males under 16 years.	Free white females, including heads of families.	All other free persons.	Slaves.
Peacock, Paul					
Peak, John	2	1	6	7	
Payne, James	1		6	3	
Plater, George	7	1	2	3	1
Quiggins, John	1	2	3	3	93
Riney, John	1	1	4	5	
Reeder, Thomas A	1	1	1	5	21
Reeder, Thomas, Jr	2	8	3	3	
Riney, Thomas	2	1		5	8
Rock William	1	1	2		
Read, Sarah					5
Robinson, Elizabeth			2		
Richardson, Forrest	1		3	1	
Roach, William H.	1		1		1
Reynolds, John	1	1	4	4	
Reintzel, Anthony	1			3	
Rapour, William	1		2		
Reynolds, Mary			2	1	6
Read, Philip	2		1		13
Railey, John B.	1	1	1	4	
Rodgers, George	3		4		2
Rhodes, Abraham	2	1	4		13
Redmond, William	3		2	6	
Russell, William	1	1	1	4	
Railey, Henry	2	1	1	4	
Railey, Ignatius	1	1	2	2	
Rock, John	2	3	2		
Railey, John (of John)	1	2	2	2	
Railey, John, Sr	2		3	2	
Railey, John M	1	2	3		
Reeder, Elizabeth		2	3	5	23
Rose, William	1				
Railey, Bennett	1		1		16
Railey, Ann	2		2		5
Russell, James	1	3	2	1	1
Smith, John	1	1	4		32
Suit, Dent	3	5	4		
Saxton, Robert	3	1	3		5
Shamwell, Joseph	1	6	2		
Somerhill, William	1		2		8
Sothoron, Samuel	1		2		12
Smith, Joseph	1		2		1
Swann, John	1	1			
Saint Clair, Vernon	1				8
Smith, Basil (Birds Crook)		4	2		1
Suit, Benjamin	1		2		2
Suit, Thomas	1	2	3		1
Segar, James	1	1	2		1
Spalding, Thomas, Sr	3		1		3
Spalding, Philip	1		1		6
Suttle, Judith	1	2	4		1
Suit, James	2	1	2		4
Scott, Edward	2	1	1	2	
Scott, Charles	2	1	3		
Sothoron, Richard, Jr	2	1	4	1	8
Sothoron, Jane			4	1	6
Sothoron, Richard, Sr	2	1	5	1	2
Sothoron, John Johnson	1	1	5		10
Segar, Nathaniel	2		3		
Sothoron, Henry Greenfield	3	3	4		46
u t John	1	1	3		1
Simpson, Edward	1	2	1		1
Swann, Samuel, Sr	1	2	3		
Swann, Zachariah	1	5	3		9
Swann, Zephaniah	1	1	1		
Seale, Elizabeth					
Smith, Basil, (Patuxent)					6
Spalding, Michael, Sr	1		1		4
Spalding, John (of Peter)	1		4		2
Spalding, Michael, Jr	1	2	4		
Spalding, Henry, Sr	2		3		11
Spalding, Barnard	1		1		4
Spalding, Thomas, Jr	3	2	4		8
Smith, Richard	1		3		5
Spalding, Aaron	1	1	3	2	1
Spalding, Henry (of Peter)	2		1	1	2

NAME OF HEAD OF FAMILY.	Free white males of 16 years and upward, including heads of families.	Free white males under 16 years.	Free white females, including heads of families.	All other free persons.	Slaves.
Spalding, Henry (of Wm)	3	1	2		7
Stone, William H.	3		3		8
Spalding, Bennett	3	3	6		
Stone, Ignatius	2	1	2		3
Swann, Samuel, Jr	2		2		
Smith, Elias	1		3		12
Sherrad, Francis	2	1	6		
Shanks, John	2	2	2	1	20
Seale, Leonard	2	6	2	5	
Strabo, Betty					2
Strabo, Sally					6
Spalding, Statia		3	4		1
Spalding, Edward	1	3	4		
Simpson, Josias	1	1	3		
Smith, James	2		3		
Swainey, William	1		3		
Simms, Anthony	3	3	4		8
Stone, Joseph	1	3	2		
Swails, Eleanor	2	1	5		3
Stone, Enoch	1	1	3		
Sciel, Barton	1	1	3		
Stone, Joseph (Constable)	1	3	2		1
Stone, William, Jr	1	1	3		1
Spalding, Benedict	1	5	6		10
Spalding, George	1	3	2		
Spalding, Ann	1		3		4
Spalding, Francis	1	1	1		4
Schirloeff, Francis E	1		3		
Simpson, Mary		2	3		
Strabo, Drady				3	
Sciel, Susanna	2	1	5		
Tippett, Nelson	2	1	5	2	1
Tippett, John, Sr	3		2		
Tippett, Thomas	1	2	4		3
Tuel, Joseph	1	3	4		
Tippett, Cartwright	1	2	3		
Tennison, Jesse	1	1	5		
Turner, Joshua	1	2	2		
Tippett, Zachariah	1	2	2	1	6
Turner, Joseph	4	4	4		
Tippett, Notley	3	2	4	1	12
Tippett, Josias	1		2		6
Tippett, Eleanor	1	2	2		
Thomas, Elizabeth					4
Thompson, Joseph (of James)	1	5	4		8
True, John	1	5	4		
Thompson, William, Sr	1	1	3		
Thompson, William, Jr	1	1	1		3
Thompson, Bennett	1		5		1
Thomas, William, Sr	1		2	1	
Tubman, Henry	2		3		30
Tippett, Jonathan	2	2	2	1	29
Tippett, Jane			4		2
Tippett, John (of William)	1		2		2
Ticer, William	1	2	4		
Thompson, Wilfred	1	1	2		
Thorn, Benjamin	1	2	2		
Thompson, Joseph, Jr	1	2	3		1
Thomas, William, Jr	1	2	2	3	61
Thompson, John B	2		4		
Taney, Eleanor	2	4	4		13
Taney, Raphael	1		2		
Thompson, Thomas E.	1	1	2		4
Turner, Charles	1		2		
Tennison, Ann	1	5	3	2	8
Thompson, Joseph, Sr	1	1	2	1	
Thompson, Aaron	1	1	4		
Tarlton, Stephen	1	5	6		14
Thompson, Jesse	1		4		
Thompson, Richard	1		4		
Tennison, John		2	4		
Thompson, Elizabeth	1		2		7
Taylor, Ignatius	1	3	4		1
Taylor, Ann	1	2	3		
Thomas, Thomas	1	2	3		
Thompson, James	2	2	5		
Thornton, Vincent	2	2	2		8

NAME OF HEAD OF FAMILY.	Free white males of 16 years and upward, including heads of families.	Free white males under 16 years.	Free white females, including heads of families.	All other free persons.	Slaves.
Tippett, Nancy		3	3		3
Tippett, Ann		3	1		3
Thompson, Raphael		1	1		
Vessels, Ephraim	1		1	6	
Valentine, Thomas			1	1	
Vymear, Sarah			1		4
Vowles, Mathew	2		2	4	
Williams, Henry	2		2	2	8
Wingate, Henry	1	1	2	3	
Woodward, John	1		2	5	
Williams, James	1		3	5	
Watson, John, Sr	1		4	5	8
Watson, John, Jr	1			5	
Wainwright, Richard	1	1	1	4	9
Wainwright, Tamar			1	3	
Ward, Ann			1	3	
Watson, James	3		3	5	9
Walter, Lawrence (Commander of Sloop Hope)	4	4	4		1
Wathan, Elizabeth	2	4	5		
Wathan, Thomas	2	3	5		
Wheeler, Francis		1	4		
Wakelin, Ann	2	3	3		
Wood, Charles				7	
Wheatly, Elias	1				12
Wood, Leonard	1		3		4
Wood, John	1		3		2
Waters, Joseph	1	1	2		5
Woodburn, Jonathan	2	1	2		
Witherton, James	2	2	2		3
Warren, Doctor Basil	2		1		9
Watson, Daniel	2		2		
Woodburn, Daniel	1		2		1
Wood, Nathan	1		4		
Wood, Jeremiah	1		2		
Wood, Sarah			4		
Walter, William	1	6	4	1	5
Walker, James, Sr	3	2	3		
Walker, Joseph, Jr	2	5	2		
Wildman, Cornelius	2		6		10
Wheeler, Ignatius	2	1	1		40
Woodward, William	2	2	1	1	7
West, Thomas	1		3		
West, Jeremiah	1	1	2		
Wharton, Jesse	2	1	2		24
Williams, George	2	2	3		3
Walker, James, Jr	2		3		12
Wise, Nehemiah	1		3		1
Williams, Hugh	1	2	2		
Wise, Richard	1		4		
Walker, John	1		1		
Wathan, Francis H	3		1		11
Wathan, James H.	3	1	3		
Wimsatt, Robert	1	2	6		9
Wimsatt, John	1	2	2		1
Wheatley, Francis	2		4		
Wheatley, Henrietta			4		
Willinghame, John B	2	4	8		
Woodward, Joseph	1	4	1		
Walker, Joseph, Sr	4	4	8		11
Bean, Robert	1	1	2		5
Batts, John	1		1		1
Brown, Henrietta			4		
Bowes, Timothy	3		2		
Brown, Nicholas	4		2		7
Brewer, John	1	2	3		
Brewer, Thomas	1	5	2		4
Blair, William	1		3		
Blair, Joseph	3	3	4		
Brown, Richard	1		2		
Brown, Statia			3		
Bradburn, William	1	1	3		
Brown, John	1	2	4		24
Yates, John	2	1	2		
Young, Robert	1		4		5
Yates, Martin	4		3		1
Yates, Edward	2	2	4		

SOMERSETT COUNTY.

[Schedules destroyed.]

TALBOT COUNTY.

NAME OF HEAD OF FAMILY.	M16+	M-16	F	Other	Slaves
Allen, Moses	1		1	18	10
Abbot, John	3				
Aldridge, John				5	
Anderson, Thomas	1			3	
Armstrong, Francis	2	2	4		6
Anthony, Negroe				7	
Anderson, Alexander				5	7
Austin, James	2		6	2	
Austin, Thomas	2	3	2	2	
Austin, John	2	2	2		7
Adkinson, Aaron	2	2	4	4	

NAME OF HEAD OF FAMILY.	M16+	M-16	F	Other	Slaves
Austin, Cloudberry	2	2	1	1	5
All, Robert	3		1	1	1
Allen, Nathan	1		3		
Anderson, Isaac	1	1	3		
Allen, Henry	3	1	3		
Allen, Emanuel			3	5	
Blake, John	6		3		
Bristol, Negroe			1	6	
Bowers, Thomas	2		3		
Ball, Lydia			3		
Bosman, John	1		1	3	

NAME OF HEAD OF FAMILY.	M16+	M-16	F	Other	Slaves
Bullen, James	1	1	4		1
Banckes, Solomer					
Bowie, John	5	9	3		25
Benney, Walker	1	2	3		
Bell, Margaret			2		
Byles, William	2	1	5		2
Bullet, Thomas	2		5		10
Barwick, John	1	2	3		
Burgess, William	2		4		
Benney, William	1		2		
Barwick, William	1	5	4		10

TALBOT COUNTY—Continued.

NAME OF HEAD OF FAMILY.	Free white males of 16 years and upward, including heads of families.	Free white males under 16 years.	Free white females, including heads of families.	All other free persons.	Slaves.
Blakes, John	1				
Benny, Mary Ann			2		
Burn, James				5	
Bordley, Mary	2		2		20
Blake, William	3	4	3	8	1
Banny, Benjamin	1	3	3		4
Berry, James	1		4	2	2
Botton, John	2		3		11
Barrister, William	1	2	3		2
Berwick, George	1		4		4
Berwick, Richard	1		4		4
Bewley, Ann	1		7		18
Butter, Moses	2	5	3		
Barrow, Samuel	3				4
Betty, Negroe				4	
Bruscutt, Jonathan	2		2		
Bramble, Andrew	1	3	1		
Barnett, Thomas	1	2	1		
Brin, Mary		3	4		
Bell, Ann		2	4		
Boothe, Richard	1		1		
Boothe, Anthony	1		3		
Boothe, Anthony	2	1	3		
Barnwell, James	3	1	5		5
Barnwell, Mary	2		3		8
Bent, William			3		
Burgess, John	3	2	4		2
Blades, Isaiah	1	2	2		
Bender, William	1		2		
Christian, Quayle			1		
Cooper, Sarah	1		2		
Crowney, James	8	1	2		1
Chambers, William	2				1
Carnan, Daniel	1	3		1	
Crisp, John	1	1	2		
Covey, Allen	1	1	2		
Chester, William				4	
Catrip, John	1		2		6
Corkian, John	1		2		15
Cocken, Carter	2		1	2	2
Castrop, Lemon				2	
Crouch, James	1	2	2		
Catrip, William	1		5		15
Chapman, Uriah	1		2		
Chambers, John	3				7
Cooper, Christopher	1		1		1
Cummins, Norris			4		
Covey, Henry	1		3		
Cheesely, Robert	2	1	3	2	
Cheesely, James	2	3	2		5
Crueson, Jacob	2		2	1	
Cooper, Thomas	2	2	2	1	4
Chambers, Hymon	1		3		
Crumpton, John	1	3	3		
Cotner, Thomas	2	2	2		3
Corkrel, John	2	2	2		6
Cole, Sarah	1		1		
Corkrel, Bradberry	1	1	2		1
Callihan, Joseph	5		4	1	1
Chapman, Woolmer	1	1			
Clark, Arthur	1		1		11
Cain, Daniel	1	1	1		80
Corrie, John	2				5
Collins, Patrick	1		3		
Cheves, Susannah			2		
Chambers, Elizabeth	2	1	1		
Cœcil, Williams	2	4	2		1
Clog, Elizabeth		2	2		
Caldwell, Edward	1		3		
Christian, Catharine	1		3		
Corner, Noah	1	2	3		2
Chambers, Isaac	2	2	7		
Cooper, Thomas					3
Costa, John		2	4		
Clark, John	3	3	2		2
Clark, Edward	2	2	2		
Clark, Elizah	1	1	3	4	
Duling, Nelly		2	5	2	
Dudley, James	2	2	2	5	2
Dougherty, John	4		3		13
Dawson, Sarah	1		2		7
Dorrit, Rebeccah		3	2		
Dobson, William	2		4		
Davis, Henry	1	2	3		
Davis, Benjamin	2	2	5		1
Dick, Negroe				6	
Dawson, James	1		5		
Diggins, William	1		4		
Dobson, Catharine	1	2	4		
Dawson, William	1	2	1		1
Dawson, John	1		3		
Dudley, Richard	5	3	7	1	
Dawson, Mary			2		4
Dudley, George	3		2		3
Dudley, Mary			3		4
Dudley, Rebeccah	1		4		8

NAME OF HEAD OF FAMILY.	Free white males of 16 years and upward, including heads of families.	Free white males under 16 years.	Free white females, including heads of families.	All other free persons.	Slaves.
Earle, James	5				2
Ewen, James	3	2	1		19
Ewen, Robert	4	1	3		9
Edmondson, William	3		3	2	
Edgell, Susanah			2	1	
Eubanks, Thomas	1		2		
Eubanks, Adam	1		2		
Elbert, Joshua	1	1	2		9
Elbert, John	1	2	1		16
Essino, Henry	2				1
Eaton, John	2	2	5		2
Frost, George	1	1	2		
Flemming, David	1		1		
Faulkner, James	4				1
Faulkner, Isaac	1		1		
Freeman, Matthius	1		4		17
Feams, John	1	1	3		
Fairbanks, Jere	2	1	3		
Fish, James	1	2	1	4	
Follin, Aquilla	1	2	3		13
Ferguson, James	1	1	2	3	
Ferguson, William					19
Faulkner, Jonathan	1		3		
Faulkner, Sophia		1	3		1
Frampton, Mary			3		
Faukner, Joseph	1	1	2		8
Frampton, Thomas	4	3	3		2
Fountain, Massey	3	3	2		6
Frampton, Thomas	2	2	4		1
Frampton, Robert	2	1	3		
Faulkner, James	1		2		
Faulkner, William	1	1	3		
Frampton, Joseph	2	2	3		
Grant, Jonothan	2	2	3		
Gregory, Elizabeth			4		
Grace, Rebecca	1	3	8	1	2
Garland, Jeremiah	4	2	2		
Gregory, Ann		2	2	1	9
Gibson, John	3	1	2		13
Gibson, Elizabeth			2		16
Grace, Negroe				2	
Grant, Thomas	1	3	1		11
Gadd, Thomas	1	1	3		
Gollehon, James	1		2		1
Gibson, Woolman	2		3		18
Greenhauk, Richard		5	3		1
Greenhauk, Jonathan		1	1		
Gordon, William	1	2	2		
Gore, Samuel	1		4		
Gore, John	1	3	4		2
Gill, Whittonton	2	2	3		
George, Negroe				4	
Garey, Henry	2	3	4		2
Gardner, Mary		1	3		
Hunter, James	2				5
Hunter, William	2				5
Hagar, Negroe					3
Henry, Negroe					3
Hopkins, Lambert	1	4	3		
Hains, John	2	2	3		2
Hooper, John A	3		2		
Horney, William	1		1	1	
Hook, Mary		1	2	2	
Hussey, Robert	2	1	1		
Haskins, Joseph	2		3		10
Hindman, William	2				61
Hasset, John	1				
Hart, Mary		1	8		
Hindman, John	2	1	2		16
Hall, John	1	3	2		
Hall, George	1	2	3		4
Hardcastle, John	1	2	2		22
Harris, Perry	1	2	2		
Harwood, Robert	3	1	3		1
James, Negroe				6	
Jack, Negroe				6	
Jackson, James	1		4		
James, Solomon				7	
Jessup, Thomas	1	2	2		
Johnson, Henry	2		4		17
Joseph, Negroe				6	
Jeffers, Jonathan	1	1	2		3
Jones, McMurdy	1	1	2		1
Jackon, Rachel			3		
Judah, Negroe				4	10
Jones, Robert	2	2	3		10
Jones, James	2	1	4		
Job, Thomas	1		3		
Jacob, Negroe				5	
Joseph, Negroe				2	
Jadwin, Robert	3	2	3		4
Johns, Richard	2	1	2		19
Kerr, David	2	3	2		10
King, James	2		2	5	2
Kirby, Lambert	1		1		1
King, Solomon				4	

NAME OF HEAD OF FAMILY.	Free white males of 16 years and upward, including heads of families.	Free white males under 16 years.	Free white females, including heads of families.	All other free persons.	Slaves.
Kirby, Rachel	2		3		
Kernon, Thomas	1	2	2		6
Keets, Thomas	3		2		4
Kennard, Joshua	1	2	2	2	1
Kennard, Nathaniel	1				7
Keets, John	2	2	6		
Keets, William	2		4	1	
Kemp, William	1		4	1	4
Kemp, Alice					17
Kemp, John	2	3	3		
Kirby, William	3	2	3		2
Kirby, William	2	3	3		
Kirby, Daniel	1		3		
Kirby, Michal	2	4	3		
Kirby, Michal	3	1	3	1	
Kirby, Elizabeth	1	2	3		
Kinnamont, Hopkins	1	3	2		
Kinnamont, Mary	1	1	5		
Kindard, James	2	1	2		
Kirby, Robert	2	1	2		
Kirby, John	2		3		
Kirby, Abner	1	1	4		1
Kirby, Richard	1	1	2		
Kirby, Lambert	1	1	1		
Keys, Joseph				2	
Lamb, John	1	1	3	2	1
Logan, John	2				1
Lamb, Margaret			4		
Loveday, Thomas	1	1	4		8
Lucas, Morgan	2	3	2		
Louther, Sarah	1		5		3
Londagin, Ann	1	1	3		6
Loveday, William	1	3	4		6
Jackson, Rachel			3		
Littleton, John	3	1	3		
Leverton, Isaac	1	1	5		3
Leverton, Thomas	1	2	4	1	
Larrimore, Richard	2		3		
Lucas, North	2	1	3		1
Lowe, William	1	1	3		
Martin, Ennalls	4		3		5
Martin, William	4	3	3		3
M'Keel, Thomas	1	1	1	1	1
M'Keel, James	1	1	1		
Meeley, William	2	1	2		
M'Carty, James				3	
Mackery, James				3	
Merchant, James	1		4		5
Merchant, Rachel	3				3
Memory, Negroe				3	
M'Namarra, Thomas	2		4		
M'Cormic, Dennis	1				8
Millington, George	1		1		1
Murphy, John	1		2	1	
Matthews, William	1	2	4		1
Matthews, Thomas	3		4		
M'Daniel, Pearce	1		2		
Morgan, Thomas			3		8
M'Bride, Joseph	2		2		
Millington, Richard	1	2	2		2
Matthews, Ann			2		
M'Keebler, Jacob	2	1	3		
Matthews, Ann			4		
Morgan, Hannah	1	1	2		
Manning, Hugh	1	1	2		
M'Quay, Jere	1	1	2		
M'Namarra, Thomas	1		2		
Millington, Sarah			2		3
Milless, James	2	2	1		
Martiner, James	1		2	1	2
Murphy, William	2		2		
Milless, James	1	1	3		
Maday, James	1	1	3		
Middleton, Major	1	1	5		6
Loveday, Nicholas	2	1	4		
Morgan, Reese	1	1	4		
Nice, David	1		1		
Nanny, Negroe				2	
Nicolls, Henry	1	1	3	1	30
North, Jacob	1	1	6		
Norton, Richard		1	2		1
Newnham, Skinner	2	2	2		
Newnham, Daniel	3	2	4		14
Nabb, Charles	3	2	4		
Norris, Richard	1	1	2		3
Needles, Edward	1	2	4	2	7
Ozment, Jonathan	2		3	2	3
Ozment, Thomas	2	2	2		5
Orem, Andrew	2	2	5		
Preice, James	2				
Peter, Negroe				4	3
Parratt, James	2	1	2		
Parratt, Perry	2	1	4	2	12
Price, Jacob	1	1	2		
Porter, Nathan	1		4		
Porter, Perry	1	1	3		

TALBOT COUNTY—Continued.

NAME OF HEAD OF FAMILY.	Free white males of 16 years and upward, including heads of families.	Free white males under 16 years.	Free white females, including heads of families.	All other free persons.	Slaves.
Plumsole, Abel					
Pearson, William	1	1	3		
Price, Gilbert	1	3	3	3	
Porter, Philemon	2	1	1		
Peck, Frank			1	5	34
Pearce, Negroe				7	
Plummer, Philemon	3	6	4	3	1
Price, William	3	6	1	2	
Palmer, Isaac	2	2	2		8
Pinkind, Michal	2	2	4		
Plummer, John	1	1	1		1
Plummer, James	6		8		2
Porter, Joseph	1	2	2		
Porter, Thomas	1	3	2		
Porter, William	2	2	4		
Perkins, Francis				5	
Price, Vincent	1	2	2		
Plummer, Solomon	1	1	2		
Price, Samuel	1	2	3		
Pennington, James			2		2
Powell, Howel	1	1	2		7
Peter, Negroe			2	1	
Rutter, Moses	2	1	1		
Register, David	1	3	2		
Register, John	4	6	5		1
Register, Samuel	3		5		18
Rose, William	4	1	5		8
Robinson, Lambert	1	1	2		
Roberts, Thomas	2	1	2		
Russan, Thomas	2	1	4		
Roberts, Thomas	1	3	1		5
Roberts, Edward	3	1	1	9	8
Ridgeway, William	3	2	1		2
Roberts, John	3	1	3		20
Rathel, Joseph	2	1	2		8
Rathel, William	2	1	2		
Rose, Sarah			4		
Register, Francis		2	1		
Roe, Parratt	1		1		7
Rose, Negroe	2	4	6		9
Sharp, Samuel	2				1
Skinner, William	1		2		
Stewart, Thomas	1	2	5		
Suitor, Alexander	2	2	2		6
Sambo, Negroe	2	2	3		1
Short, Samuel	1	2	4		
Scott, John	1		3		
Scott, Jonathan	1	1	2		
Strahan, George	1	4	2	1	1
Summers, Solomon	1	2	2		
Seth, Thomas M	1	2	2		
Stewart, Elisha	1				12
Sanders, Elizabeth		3	3		5
Severe, Vachel	2	3	2		
Stewart, Charles	2	5	1		9
Sherwin, Abram	2	3	3		
Summers, Mary		1	1	3	
Smart, Stephen	3		4		
Smith, John	1	4	1		
Scipio, Negroe				7	
Samuel, Negroe				7	
Shields, Mary		3	3	4	
Samuel, Negroe				6	
Shannahan, Jane		2	6		
Sherwood, Elizabeth	1	2	5	1	
Sewel, William	2	5	1		4
Sylvester, Herrington	1		3		
Simon, Negroe				6	
Sharp, James				4	
Sherwood, Mary	1	1	1	1	8
Sarah, Negroe				3	
Troup, Sarah				3	
Troup, Charles	3		2		6
Tyler, Thomas	6	1	1	2	
Tony, Mary			1	2	
Tyler, Elijah	1	2	4		
Tom				5	
Tibbats, John	2	5	5	2	
Torrard, William	1		2		2
Turner, Austin	3	3	2		
Turner, Edward	3	1	6	1	11
Turner, James	1		3		
Thomas, John	1	2	3		16
Turner, Joseph	3	3	4		17
Turner, Edward	2	1	2	2	
Thorton, Brooks	1	2	2		
Taylor, Cornelius		2	3	1	
Troth, William	1		3	1	
Turner, John	4	1	2		29
Toby, Negroe				6	
Tomlinson, William	1	2	1	1	
Violer, Edward	1		4	1	1
Vickers, Sarah	1		2		15
Vincent, John	1		6		
Vincent, David	1	2	3		
Wainwright, James	1	4	1		

NAME OF HEAD OF FAMILY.	Free white males of 16 years and upward, including heads of families.	Free white males under 16 years.	Free white females, including heads of families.	All other free persons.	Slaves.
Willson, Christopher	3		5		
Walker, Richard	1		3		
Wilson, George	1	1	5		6
Works, Hugh	3	2	4		2
Warner, John	1		3		
Warner, Robert	2		4		
Warner, John	1	1	2		1
Williams, Ann	1	1	2		1
Wales, William	1		4		
Williams, Robert	2	2	2	4	2
Weyman, Edmond	3		3		3
Willson, James	3		2	2	16
Wooters, John	2	3	4		
Wooters, Benjamin	2	5	2	7	
Wertin, Thomas	1	2	6		
Warren, William	3	3	2	1	
Wyatt, Daniel	3		4		
Whitly, Thomas	2	2	4		
Willam, Hannah			1		
Yates, Thomas	1			2	1
Yarnell, Martha			2	1	1
Young, Frank				2	1
Meriah, Negro				9	
Memory, Negro				7	
Madery, William	2	4	4		2
Minnor, William	1	2	3	1	
Airs, Ann			2	4	
Adly, Richard					4
Arrington, Richard	1	2	2		
Arrington, Lodmon	2	1			
Adams, Samuel				5	
Arrindle, William	1				3
Adams, Moses	1		4	8	3
Adkinson, Aaron	3		1	1	
Applegarth, William	4	1	1		
Alexander, William	4		1		
Allen, William	1		1		
Acres, William	4		2		
Edmondson, James	2		1		6
Arrington, Ann			1		
Arrington, William	1	1	3		5
Anderson, William	1	3	4		
Berry, William	2	2	2		
Barnaby, Richard			4	5	
Beaver, Mary		4	1	7	
Bromwell, Edward, Jun	3	1	1		17
Baldwin, Samuel	3		5	1	
Boxer, James				3	
Bromford, William	1	1	1		
Brittington, Abram	1	4	1		4
Banning, Henry	2		1		
Brooks, Grace				3	
Bennett, John				3	
Boston, William	2		1		4
Benney, James		1	2		
Bowdle, Loftis	1	2			
Buckley, James	2	2	3		1
Bromwell, Jacob	1		2		5
Bowdle, Stephen	1		2		6
Bromwell, Edward	1		5		7
Bewley, John	1	3	7		13
Benson, James	4		2		
Blamer, Charles				2	
Barnet, Thomas					7
Bowdle, William	1	4	5		
Bush, John	3	3	2		1
Browning, Elizabeth	2		4		
Bowdle, Harry				14	
Bridge, Harry				3	
Brinsfield, Moses	2	1	5		
Barnett, Peter				1	
Brown, Thomas				4	
Brown, Dark				7	
Barnett, Noble	2		4		
Bell, Lucy				6	
Bull, Adam				4	
Brinsfield, Mary	2		5		1
Brinsfield, Moses	2	5	1		
Brown, William	1	2	2		
Brown, Adam	2		7	2	
Buckley, Thomas	1	3	4		3
Berridge, William	2	1	5		
Buckley, Bennett	2	3	5		1
Birckhead, Henrietta	2	1	2		21
Brown, John	2	2	2		
Bowdle, Tristram	(*)	(*)	(*)	(*)	(*)
Buckley, Margaret				5	
Brown, George	1	1	4		
Catrip, Solomon	1		3		
Clash, Jonathan	1		1		
Clash, James				1	3
Craddock, Isabel	2		5		
Coward, Richard	1	2	5	1	9
Cornish, Charles				3	
Clash, Elizabeth	1		3		
Callender, Andrew	3	2			10

NAME OF HEAD OF FAMILY.	Free white males of 16 years and upward, including heads of families.	Free white males under 16 years.	Free white females, including heads of families.	All other free persons.	Slaves.
Carse, James					
Carus, William				13	
Comer, Solomon	1	3	3		
Coleman, Nicholas	2	1	3		5
Carny, William	6		1		
Cowan, James	4		1		1
Cox, Edward					5
Cronch, Ammon				4	
Chamberlain, Henrietta	3	2	7		60
Cox, Daniel P	1	2	2		22
Cain, John	1		2		
Clift, Henry	1		1		
Coward, Bridget			2		
Cray, James		3	4	1	4
Cocky, John	1	4	3		5
Coward, Thomas	2	4	4		
Chamberlain, Samuel	3	3	8	1	76
Colson, Jeremiah	1	3	3		6
Collins, William	1	1	4		2
Colbourn, Lambert	1		5		
Cox, Jane	1		3		1
Carey, Joseph	1	2	4		
Conney, John	1	3	4		3
Clark, William				1	
Currell, Lucy				1	
Clark, William	2		1		11
Chaplain, Margaret		2	3		1
Chaplain, William	2		3		4
Cox, Isaac	2	3	3		
Clemency, Mary		1			
Clash, John			3	1	
Cooper, Dick				8	1
Clements, Samuel	1		2	4	
Corner, William	1		4		
Cooper, Jack				5	
Clements, John	1	2	3		
Dickinson, Samuel	1	2	2		28
Darden, Joseph	2	2	3		
Blanch, Thomas			2	6	
Bantum, George				3	7
Bowdle, Henry	1	1	4		7
Cannon, Sales	2	1	2		
Consodant, James	2	1	1		
Cooper, Ben				9	
Clark, George	3	2	5		2
Clark, Jere				5	
Cook, George		1	2		
Dickinson, John		2	4	2	
Darden, Stephen	1	2	3	1	4
Denney, Peter	1	2	5	1	
Denney, Joseph				1	
Dawson, Joseph	2	1	2	1	
Dorrell, Joseph				5	
Dawson, James	2		2		
Dickinson, Susan			2	2	
Delahay, Henry	2	2	4		2
Dogan, Catharine			5		
Delahay, James	1	2	3	1	
Davis, John M	1		3		7
Doll, Matthew	3	2	4		
Delahay, Mark	1	1	3		10
Duling, John	1	1	4		
Duncan, John	3	3	4		
Delahay, Thomas	2	1	3		
Erskine, John	2	1	1		4
Eason, Samuel	1		3		1
Elsby, Samuel			3		2
Elsby, John	1	2	3		7
Elsby, William	2	2	3		2
Eason, Sarah	1		3		5
Erkins, Tom				4	
Edmondson, Pollard	2	2	3	3	40
Buckley, Samuel	2		6		1
Buckley, Henry	1	2	7		
Berry, Daniel	1	2	7		
Bullen, Thomas	1	1	4		
Burgess, Allen	1	1	4		5
Brinsfield, Perry	1	4	4		
Brooks, Isaac	2		4	1	7
Flemming, Thomas	1	1	4		
Fonerdon, John	2	2	1	2	
Farron, Samuel	2		4		
Foster, Joseph	1		3		
Flemming, James	2	3	3	1	3
Goldsborough, James	1		2		17
Gooby, Ben				5	
Goldsborough, Rachel	1		2		3
Gibson, Ben				4	
Gore, John				1	
Gordon, Thomas	1	2	1		2
Gannon, Abner					
Hughs, James					
Higgens, John	3	4	3		1
Hunt, George	1		1		
Harrison, John W	1	1	3		17
Higby, John	1	1	3		

* Illegible.

TALBOT COUNTY—Continued.

NAME OF HEAD OF FAMILY.	Free white males of 16 years and upward, including heads of families	Free white males under 16 years	Free white females, including heads of families	All other free persons	Slaves
Hopkins, John			5		
Hall, Thomas	1		4	1	
Hopkins, Dennis	3	2	6		1
Higgins, David	1		2		
Hindman, William	1	1	1		
Hason, John	1	2	1		
Hunter, William				5	
Holt, Horatio			2		
Hutton, Samuel	1	1	2		
Hicks, John	1	2	2		
Horney, Philemon	1			10	
Holmes, Solomon	2	2	6		4
Holmes, Francis	2	2	4		2
Harrison, George	1		1		
Holmes, John	2	3	2		1
Hopkins, James	2	2	3		1
Higgins, John	4	2	3		5
Hull, John	4	6	3		1
Higgins, Thomas	1	1	2		
Harris, Margaret			4	3	
Hudson, John	1		1		
Hardin, James	1	1	5		3
Higgins, Elenor	1		2		
Hunt, George	1	1	3		
Hardagin, Matthew	1	2	2		
Higby, John	1	1	2		1
Hopkins, Moses	1	2	2		
Hopkins, Sarah			4		2
Hayward, William	4		3		62
Johns, Judah				1	2
Hunt, George	1	1	3		
Jenkins, Rachel			2		
Jones, Thomas	2	1	1		1
Jones, John	2	3	2		15
Jenkinson, John	4	3	2	1	6
Insley, Abram	1	1	2		
Iden, Jacob	1		1		
James, Alexander	2	1	4		2
Jiles, Andrew	1	2	1	1	
Jenkins, Thomas	1	1	2	2	13
Jones, David	1	3			
Jenkins, Walter	2	1	1		18
Johnson, Randolph	3	4			10
Jenkins, Mary			2		
Jenkins, George	1	4	2		7
Jenkins, Lewis	1	4	3		5
Jones, Leah			3		2
Jones, Elizabeth	1		3		1
Kemp, James	2	4	2		
Kirby, Cloudsberry	1	2	3		
Kennard, Owen	1	1	1		3
Kersey, John	1			1	
Kimbro, Edward			1	1	
Kirby, Cloudsberry	1	3	2	1	
Keys, Thomas	3	1	5		
Kemp, Elizabeth		2	3		
Kemp, Solomon	1	2	3		
Kemp, Benjamin	1	4	3		
Kerr, Mary Ann	1	4	5		2
Kutley, Jacob	2	2	2		
Killum, Nicholas	1				7
Lloyd, James	3	3	2		18
Love, Christopher	1				
Leddenham, Edward	1	5	2	1	
Lowe, Peter					
Lurty, Elizabeth			2		17
Lee, John	1	1	3		1
Lion, John	2	1	3		
Lee, Oliver	1	3	2		
Love, Thomas	3	2	6		
Murry, Daniel	1	1	1		
Marr, Thomas	1		1		
Murphy, Mary		1	3		
Maynadier, William	2	1	4		23
Haskins's, Joseph, Quarter					8
McEnhammor, Nicholas			2		
Mehan, Michal	1		2		
McCallum, William	4	1	4	1	6
McCallum, Alexander	3	1	4	7	10
McGinney, Sally	1				
Marshall, Molly		1	1		2
McGinney, Daniel	1	2	3		2
Marckland, John	2	2	5		6
Sani, Negroe				2	
Priss, Negroe				1	
Mullican, Patrick	2	2	9		13
Martin, Robert	1	1	4		14
Martin, Henry	2		4		14
Martin, Nicholas	3	2	3		8
Martin, Mary	3	1	5	1	27
Martin, Tristian	3		5		13
Martin, Henry	3	1	4		
Martin, Solomon	2	2	6	1	
Moore, Robert	1	3	5	1	
Mullican, Elizabeth	1	2	5		5
Mullican, Jesse	1	2	2		7
Merrick, Matthias	1	3	3		
Miller, Jacob	2	1	1	1	3
Mackey, Philemon	4	1	2	3	1
Mullican, Adam				8	
Meers, John	2		3		
McClayland, Alexander	2	1	3		
McKey, Thomas				5	
McKenney, Alexander	1	1	4		
Meers, Alipha	1	1	1		
McClayland, Thomas	1	1	5	1	
Mullican, Samuel	1	1	2		
Miller, Jacob	1	1	4		
McNaham, Richard	2	2	3		
McNaham, John	1	1	3		
Moore, Richard	1		3		
Marshall, Margaret		1	2		
McClayland, Elizabeth	1	2	4		
McMahan, James	2	3	2		
McClayland, Margaret			2		
Marshall, Samuel	1	2	2		
Merrick, Matthias	1	3	3		
Martin, Robert	1	4	4		
Mullican, William	6		3		5
Merrick, James	1	1	3		
Murphy, John	1	3	3	2	2
Nicolls, John	2	1	4		
Hercules, Negroe				5	
Bett, Negroe				3	
Peg, Negroe				6	
Nielle, Robert	2	2	2		4
Nielle, Joseph	4		1		
Lin, Negroe				3	
Nesmith, John	2		2		
Needles, Tristiam	4	2	4	1	
Needles, John	3	3	2	1	
Noah, Negroe				4	
Nielle, Solomon	3	1	5		2
Henney, Negroe				2	
Noles, John	2		6		1
Sidney, Negroe				2	
Rose, Negroe				1	
Phillis, Negroe				4	
Hannah, Negroe				6	
Dick, Negroe				6	
Nash, Page	1		2	9	
Isaac, Negroe				9	
Norwood, John	2	1	1		
Caesar, Negroe				5	
Newnham, John	2	3	3		1
Nielle, James	1	1	2		
Robin, Negroe				3	
Lucy, Negroe				5	
George, Negroe				3	
Anthony, Negroe				3	
Macky, Dick, Negroe				1	4
Sinah, Negroe				6	
Ben, Negroe				7	
Tom, Negroe				4	1
Maria, Negroe				4	1
Alice, Negroe				1	
Negroe				1	
Anthony, Negroe				4	
Hannah, Negroe				4	
Mable, Negroe				3	
Nox, William				3	2
Ogden, Thomas	2	1	5		
Ozment, John	1	2	2	1	1
Oldham, Ann			3		11
Poor House	4	8	20	1	
Parvin, Benjamin	2	6	11		
Price, Foster	2		3		6
Price, Joseph	2	2	2		10
Parsons, Benjamin	1	1	1		2
Price, Nicholas	1		3		2
Pone, Judah			2	2	
Price, Thomas	2	1	3		2
Priestly, Perrigrine	2	1	4		1
Parratt, John	1	1	3		1
Pearson, John	1	1	3		
Price, Thomas	2	3	3		1
Parratt, Slighter	1	2	3		
Parsons, Joseph	4	1	4		3
Powell, Howell	2		4		5
Peacock, Elizabeth		1	4		
Perry, Henry	1	1	2		3
Pickering, Charles	4	1	4		
Pritchard, John	1	2	3		
Parratt, James	1	2	3		1
Price, Nathan	1	1	2		1
Price, John	3	2	2		1
Pritchard, Rachel	1	2	5		
Pritchard, Walter	1	2	2		2
Parratt, Abner	2	2	5		
Parratt, Abner	2	2	3		5
Pritchard, Samuel	1	1	3		
Price, Andrew	1		2		2
Prichard, Molly		1	2		3
Porter, John	1		1		9
Parratt, James	2		3		18
Pickering, Charles	2	1	4		8
Parratt, Henry	5	3	2		4
Proctor, Daniel				2	
Perrys, William, Quarter					14
Robinson, David	2	1	4		8
Robinson, Sarah			3		1
Ridgeway, Ben				4	
Robinson, Thomas	1		3		1
Rogers, Michal	1		2		
Rakes, Henry			2		
Roberts, Rebecca		1	1		
Rakes, Mary			5		
Rakes, William	1	2	4		
Roach, Thomas	1		2		
Ridgeway, Joseph	1	4	8		4
Roper, James	2	1	1		
Robinson, Daniel	2	1	1		7
Sherwood, Philemon	1		1		12
Stableford, Rachel		2	4		
Stevens, William	2	2	3		7
Stoker, Benjamin	2	1	3		
Sherwood, Samuel	1		1		12
Slow, Mathew				8	
Spence, Richard	1		3		2
Stevens, Benjamin	4				
Snider, Peter	3		1		
Spenning, Luen	2		2		2
Sanguine, Mary			1		
Sherwood, Robert	2	1	2		2
Smith, Poll				1	4
Steward, Ann		1	2		
Stevens, Edward	1	3	2		6
Shepherd, John	1	1	2		
Spence, Rachel			2		
Scoudric, William	1	2	1		
Stevens, John	1	2	1		8
Summers, Joseph	1		1	1	
Small, Samuel	2	2	4		
Street, William	2	1	3		2
Summers, Thomas	2		2		
Stevens, Samuel	2	1	3	1	10
Smith, Moses			7		
Stevens, Peter	1		1		8
Small, Prudence		2	4		
Seamer, Joseph	2	5	4		
Skinner, John	2	1	5		
Sewel, Nathan	2	1	3		
Standley, James	1	2	2		
Singleton, John	2		2		30
Sherwood, James	2	1	4		8
Sherwood, Elizabeth	1		2		15
Tibballs, Rebecca			1		
Thomas, James	2	1	6		22
Troth, Samuel	2	3	1	1	4
Troth, William	1	1	1		4
Tusies, Rachel			2	1	
Trippe, William	6	1	4		9
Troth, James	7	1	4		7
Thomas, Rachel			5		30
Tomlinson, William				5	
Thornberry, Robert	2		3		
Turbutt, Samuel	1	1	3		9
Thomas, Margaret			5		7
Tucker, John	1	2	2		
Toby, James	2	1	4		
Thomas, William	2		3	1	14
Tarr, James	1		2		
Thompson, George	1	2	2		1
Trippe, Richard	1		1		30
Vansandt, James	4	2	5	2	
Vickers, Charles	1	1	2		
Varnum, William	1	1	1		
Walker, James			2		
Walker, John	2		2		
Warfield, Elizabeth			2		
Willson, John	3		3		
Wickersham, Thomas	3		3		
Whitlocks, William			4		
Weaver, William	3		4		7
Willson, Lydia			1		
Wheetly, Nancy			2		
Wilkins, Richard	2		1		
Waulds, Alice			4		
Walker, Williams				6	1
Willis, John	1		5		
Walker, Francis	2	5	3		4
Walters, William			7	7	
Wash, Thomas	6	1	4		1
Ward, Benjamin	2	1	1		2
White, Samuel	2		5		2
Webb, Peter	1	3	5	2	10
West, Henry			3		2
Wardlow, Hannah			2		
Walker, Daniel	1		3		2

TALBOT COUNTY—Continued.

NAME OF HEAD OF FAMILY.	Free white males of 16 years and upward, including heads of families.	Free white males under 16 years.	Free white females, including heads of families.	All other free persons.	Slaves.
Yarnell, Samuel	4	2	3		
Goldsborough, Sarah	2	1	6		14
Radish, Joseph	2	2	2		
Baker, Thomas	1	2	3		
Bratcher, John	3	4	4		
Hickson, Richard	4	1	3		1
Hopkins, Joshua	2	2	4		
Holmes, James	1		2		4
Holmes, John	3	1	4		1
Harris, John	1	4	3		6
Harris, Sarah		2	3		1
Sherwood, Sarah			2		2
Sharp, Margaret	1	2	7		11
Smith, Mable	2	1	3		4
Stevens, John	1		5		15
Nicolls, Robert D	1	1	3		24
Price, William	1	1	3		2
Sears, William	2	6	6		28
Hughs, Ja°	1	4	3		
Larimer, Dolly		2	3	1	
Adkinson, Sarah	2		4		
Applegarth, Thomas	1	2	1		1
Auld, Hugh		4	4		5
Auld, John		2	1		2
Auld, James	1		3		
Arrington, Joseph	1	3	8	2	
Auld, Samuel	1	3	2	3	1
Applegarth, George	2	4	2		1
Alicock, Samuel	1		2		
Auld, Daniel	3		2		4
Auld, Philemon	2	2	4		2
Aldridge, Thomas				3	
Ashcroft, Thomas	2	3	4		
Arrington, John	1	2	3		
Arrington, Joseph	1	3	3		2
Arrington, Nathan	1	3	2		
Aulding, Rebecca		2	3		11
Benson, Perry	3		3	18	
Benson, James	1	1	1		
Bruff, Christopher	2	1	1	6	
Barrow, James	1	1	10		
Barrow, Thomas	5		2		5
Bolfield, Abednigo	1		2		7
Barrow, Margaret			2		
Bracco, Ann	1	1	2		5
Bracco, John	2		3		25
Blades, James	1	1	4		1
Blake, William	1		1		6
Bryon, Thomas	1		1		
Bob, Roc				1	
Bullen, Henry	1	5	2		5
Blades, James	1	1	3		
Bromwell, Abram	1	4	3		
Bordley, William				1	
Bonman, John					1
Bridges, William	1	2	7		1
Ball, James	4	1	3		5
Barnes, James	2	1	2		5
Barnes, William	2	2	3		
Ball, Thomas	3	1	1		1
Ball, William	2		2		
Bridges, Daniel	1	1	6		
Bridges, Joseph	1	4	4		
Bryon, Richard	2	4	5		1
Bruff, John	2	4	5		
Brown, Peter	1		2		
Blades, John	2	3	5		6
Blades, Edmund	2	2	4		
Barney, William	3	3	4		
Benson, Perry	2	3	4		4
Benson, Thomas	3	5	2		
Benson, Nicholas	1	1	1	2	2
Bullen, Thomas	1	1	1	2	2
Banning, Henry	2	2	3	8	
Bartlet, Richard	2	3	4		
Bartlet, Elizabeth	2	1	4		
Banning, Jere	1				29
Catrip, Stephen	2		2		
Blades, Edmund	2	2	2		
Catrip, William M	1	3	4		15
Conden, Lambert	1	3	3		
Conden, James	3	3	4		2
Carter, Cocken	1		1	2	
Countess, William	1	1	3	1	2
Calvert, John	3	4	4		13
Camper, Charles	1	3	2		
Crowder, John	3	3	2		
Couden, Rachel			3		
Collins, Henry	2	1	2		1
Camper, William	3	1	2		3
Caulk, Peter	1	1	2		
Cooper, Thomas	1		2		
Cooper, Hadaway	1		3		
Caulk, Mary			3		
Collison, Francis			2		8
Cummins, James	2	1	2		
Cummins, Thomas	1	1	5		
Cummins, Nicholas	1	3	5		

NAME OF HEAD OF FAMILY.	Free white males of 16 years and upward, including heads of families.	Free white males under 16 years.	Free white females, including heads of families.	All other free persons.	Slaves.
Cummins, William	2	2	2		
Cummins, Elizabeth			3		
Caldwell, Martha				2	
Colbourn, Jonathan		2	6		
Camper, Thomas	2	3	3		1
Camper, William	4		1		
Caulk, Daniel	1		2		2
Caulk, John	1	1	2		14
Cardiff, William	1		2		
Carroll, James	3	1	4		
Cooper, Thomas	1	2	3		
Cooper, John			1		
Connely, Henry	1	3	3		
Chaplain, James	1		3		1
Caulk, John	1	2	2		1
Colbourn, Catharine		1	2		
Colson, James	2	2	8		6
Colson, Henry	2	4	5		2
Colson, Alice	3		2		1
Chamberlain, Thomas				28	1
Carrol, John	1	1	2		
Cornish, Beck				2	
Cooper, Charles			1		
Chapman, Thomas	1		2		1
Colbourn, Sophia			2		
Dixon, William	2	3	7	1	1
Denney, James E	1	3	4		6
Dawson, William	2	1	4	4	16
Davis, Sarah	1	3	2		
Dawson, Impey	3		2		26
Dawson, Nicholas	1	3	4		5
Denney, Joseph	2	3	6		1
Dawson, Robert	1	3	3		1
Dawson, Robert	1	1	1		1
Dawson, William	1		1		
Dawson, Hugh	1		6		
Dodson, Robert	2	1	2	6	
Dodson, Thomas	2	1	2		
Diragin, John	3	2	4		
Denney, Richard	2	3	5		4
Denney, Joseph	1	1	4		2
Eubanks, Mary			4		
Erven, Esther			3		
Evident, William	1	1	2		
Edgar, Catharine		1	3		
Elliot, Sarah	2		3		3
Edgar, Robert	1	1	1		1
Eaton, Richard	1	2	2		
Eagst, Thomas	3	2	5		2
Eubanks, James	1	2	2		7
Flemming, John	2	1	3		
Faulkner, Isaac	1		3		
Faulkner, Levi	1	2	2		4
Fergerson, Robert	1	4	1		1
Fairbank, John	1	1	1		
Fairbank, Joseph	2	2	5		1
Fairbank, David	4	2	5		
Fairbank, Elizabeth	1	2	5		1
Fairbank, Daniel	1	2	6		
Fiddeman, Ann			2		11
Fairbank, Thomas	1	1	5		
Floyd, Robert	1	2	3		
Garland, Traverse	2	2	3	1	3
Grace, Mary			3		
Grace, Elizabeth		2	4		1
Gordon, Mary			2		37
Gibson, John	1	2	3		2
Gardiner, Charles	2	2	8		13
Grason, Richard	1	4	4		
Garey, Obediah	4	2	2		7
Greentree, Matthew	2	2	3	18	1
Gibson, Jacob	2	4	1		12
Grace, James	2	4	1		
Grant, John					1
Grace, Jane	2	1	2		
Greenfield, Nancy			2		
Grace, William	5		2		
Graham, Margaret	2	2	8		1
Greenfield, Elizabeth	1	1	3		
Gossage, Charles	2	1	2		
Gossage, Robert	1	4	4		
Goldsborough, Tho°	1	1	5		13
Grace, Nathaniel	1	1	3		
Goldsborough, Howes	2	4	6		37
Gannon, Absalem				5	
Goldsborough, Mary Ann	1		2		22
Goldsborough, Robert	2	1	2		41
Granger, Richard	1		2		
Goldsborough, William, Quarter					22
Grason, George	1		1		1
Gossage, Daniel	1	2	1		
Gossage, John	2		3		
Gossage, Greenberry	2		4		
Hussey, Woolman	1		1		

NAME OF HEAD OF FAMILY.	Free white males of 16 years and upward, including heads of families.	Free white males under 16 years.	Free white females, including heads of families.	All other free persons.	Slaves.
Hollyday, Ann	2		7	1	78
Henrix, Edward	6	4	6	2	25
Harwood, Elizabeth			4		1
Harwood, Richard	1		5		2
Harwood, John	3		2		12
Hambleton, William			5		
Gossage, Samuel	1	1	5		
Harwood, Peter	2	1	1		
Hickason, Jane			3		
Hussey, Robert	1		3		
Hunt, John	1	2	5		3
Harwood, Thomas	2	2	3		
Hobbs, Sarah	1	1	3		
Hennesy, Andrew	1	1	3		
Hazletine, James	1	3	2		1
Hughley, Woolman	2	1	2		12
Holland, James	2		2		4
Hopkins, Jonathan	1	1	2		1
Harrison, William	2	4	4	1	3
Hopkins, William	1	2	3		12
Hambleton, William	2	1	3		
Hull, Patty			1		
Harrison, James	3	2	5		
Harrison, Edward	2	1	1		1
Horney, John	2		3		
Hadaway, Oakley	2	2	2		2
Hadaway, William W	2	2	8		10
Harris, William	2	2	4		
Harris, Joseph	1	2	4		13
Harrison, Joseph	4	3	4		9
Hughs, John	1	1	4		
Horney, Thomas	1	2	3		
Horney, John	1	1	3		
Hadaway, William	1	2	5		5
Hall, John	1	2	4		
Hadaway, John	1	1	3	1	
Horney, Thomas	1	1	2		
Hadaway, Daniel	1		2		4
Harris, Benjamin	1	1	3		
Hopkins, Joseph	1	1	3		1
Hunt, Peter	1		2		
Hadaway, Thomas	3		3		2
Harris, Robert	1	2	7		
Hunt, James	1	1	2		1
Hadaway, James	1	2	5		
Hunt, Peter	1	1	1		
Hunt, Samuel	2	1	1		1
Harrison, Joseph	1	1	6		
Hambleton, William	2	4	4		16
Hadaway, Robert	1	4	4		2
Hambleton, Phill	1	5	2		
Harris, William	1	2	3		
Harris, James	1	2	3		
Harris, James	1	1	1		
Hadaway, Thomas	1	2	1		3
Harris, Thomas	2	1	2	1	10
Harris, Thomas	3	1	3		
Harris, Thomas	2	2	2		
Hay, Robert	1				1
Hopkins, Joseph	2		4		
Hubbard, William	1		4		
Harris, John	4	1	3		2
Hopkins, Mary			3		
Hopkins, William	1	1	4		
Hayward, William	1	1	3		28
Hughy, Mary	1	1	2		2
Holland, William	1	1	5		
Hopkins, Robert	2	2	3		2
Hopkins, James	2		3		
Hopkins, Francia	3	1	7		1
Hopkins, Richard	1	3	3		
Jones, Robert	1	1	2		
Jackson, Elijah	1	3	2		
Jones, Reubes	1	2	1		
Jefferson, Thomas	1	2	1		
Jones, William	1	2	1		
Jones, James	1	2	2		
Jefferson, George	4	2	6		2
Kinaman, John	2	2	6		
Kirby, Emory	3	1	6		1
King, Alexander	1		1		8
Kerr, Davids, Quarter					18
Kersey, John	1	2	4	17	14
Kemp, Benjamin	1	2	6		
Kemp, John	1	1	4	2	1
Kemp, Magdalee			2		
Kersey, George				3	1
Kilman, Thomas	1		6		
Keetley, Nancy			5		
Kemp, Thomas	2	2	5		2
Kirby, William	1	2	4	1	3
Kirby, Benjamin	1	4	6		4
Kirby, Cloudsberry	1		5		
Kirby, James	1	4	4		
Kirby, Anthony	2	4	3	2	
Kirby, Mary	1	1	5		
Lavill, William	1	3	4		10
Love, John	1		2		1

TALBOT COUNTY—Continued.

NAME OF HEAD OF FAMILY.	Free white males of 16 years and upward, including heads of families.	Free white males under 16 years.	Free white females, including heads of families.	All other free persons.	Slaves.
Lamdin, Wrightson	1		2		11
Lamdin, Robert	1		1		14
Lowe, James	4	1	4		11
Lamdin, Francis	1	1	4		
Lamdin, Thomas	1		2		
Lamdin, Francis	1	1	4		
Lowry, Richard	1		2		1
Larrimore, James	1		4		
Lamdin, Daniel	1	3	4		5
Lamdin, Robert	1	2	4		4
Lamdin, William	1	4	3		16
Lamdin, Daniel	1	1	2	2	
Lancashire, Mary			2		
Larrimore, Massey	2	1	2		
Leddenham, Nathaniel	2		7		
Lowry, John	3	2	5		2
Leddenham, Shardric	1	2	3		
Larrimore, Robert	1	4	2		
Lowry, Robert	1		2		2
Lowry, Elizabeth	1	2	6		4
Larrimore, Alexander	2		2		2
Larrimore, Jonathan	1	2	6		
Larrimore, Richard	2		2		2
Larrimore, Catharine	1	1	2		
Leddenham, Daniel	1		4		
Leonard, Sarah	2	1	2		
Lloyd, Edward	3	1	7		305
Leonard, William	1		2		
Leonard Jonathan	1	2	5		1
Leonard, Esther	1	2	3		
Leonard, James	1	1	2		1
Leonard, James	3		1		1
Leonard, Eliza	3		2		
Leonard, Thomas	1	3	1		
Leonard, Jonathan	1	1	3		
Miller, George	1	1	5		4
Marshall, Arthur	1	1	8		
McNicolls, John	1				
McQuay, John	1	3	2		
McQuay, Ephraim	1	2	4		
Mansfield, Sarah		1	2		
Moore, Thomas	2		2		
Matthews, Ann	1	1	2		
McDaniel, John	3	3	5		1
Marshall, Sarah	2	1	7		
Morsell, James	1	3	2		11
Mason, William	1		4		
McQuay, John	2	1	5		
Mansfield, Richard	3	2	4		1
Merchant, John	2	1	3		
Mansfield, Levin	2				3
Marshall, Elijah	1		2		
Miller, Richard	1	3	2		
Marshall, Joseph	3	2	2		
McNeal, Archibald	3	2	5		
Marshall, Merideth	1	4	3		3
Maynard, Foster	2	2	2		6
Matthews, William	2		6		1
Marshall, James	2	4	3		
Matthews, Daniel	2	2	4		
Morling, Francis	1	1	3	2	6
Peg, Negroe				1	
James, Negroe				8	
Dianna, Negroe				7	
Ben, Negroe				4	
John, Negroe				7	
Peter, Negroe				5	
Rachel, Negroe				5	
Neighbours, Samuel	1	2	5		1
Nuttle, John	1	1	5		
Ambrose, Negroe				5	
Dianna, Negroe				2	
Lydia, Negroe				1	
Loudos, Negroe				1	
James, Negroe				2	
Patt, Negroe				5	
McQuay, Patrick	2	2	4		5
Sam, Negroe				3	
James, Negroe				2	
Nuttle, Solomon	3		2		
Phillis, Negroe				5	
Ibby, Negroe				4	
Rose, Negroe				2	
Lougo, Negroe				6	
Norwood, William	4		2		
Oxford, Negroe				2	
Hannah, Negroe				2	
Phillis, Negroe				4	
Bett, Negroe				5	
Nanny, Negroe				7	
Phill, Negroe				3	4
Frank, Negroe				4	
Dick, Negroe				5	
Norris, Lambert	1	1		2	8
Phill, Negroe				4	
Bett, Negroe				7	
Frank, Negroe				4	
Jem, Negroe				7	
Elizabeth, Negroe				6	1
Daniel, Negroe				4	
Newcome, Robert	3	2			16
Sidney, Negroe				3	
Ozment, John	1	6	9	1	1
Oram, Hugh	2		1		7
Oram, Spedding	1		3		1
Oram, Nicholas	1	1	4		4
Parish, William	1		2		
Pearson, William	2	2	4	3	
Pickering, Robert	1		2	1	15
Porter, Nathan	1	1	2		
Porter, John	2	3	3		9
Porter, Joseph	2	1			4
Porter, Joseph	1	2	1		2
Pocum, Iby				11	
Porter, John H	1	3	3		
Plummer, Solomon	1		1		
Plummer, John	1	4	1		
Perry, William	1	1	4	1	35
Pone, James				7	
Porter, Jonathan	1	1	4		4
Perry, Parthenia		1	2		
Rigby, Philip	1		3		10
Robinson, Lucy		1	2		
Ray, Thomas	3	3	3		9
Rightson, Elizabeth		1	1	1	
Roberts, Perry	1	2	6		
Roberts, Benjamin	1	2	4		2
Robinson, Thomas	1	4	3		1
Richardson, Daniel	3	1	4		
Rightson, Joshua	2	1	4		
Radish, Robert	1				4
Roll, Robert	1	2	5		11
Richardson, Nathan	2	3	2		
Rightson, Sarah	2	1	3	1	3
Ringrose, Mable	1	2	4		3
Richardson, Joshua	1	2	4		1
Richardson, Peter	7	1	3		
Radish, Joseph	1		3		
Roll, John	1	2	5		18
Richardson, Robert	1	3	3		9
Rigby, Moses	2		4		5
Robinson, John	5	1	3		5
Robinson, Thomas	1	3	4		
Rigby, Thomas	2	1	2		3
Richardson, Daniel	1	1	2		
Robinson, Elizabeth		3	4		
Ridgway, James	1	3	4		3
Robinson, John	1	1	4		2
Roach, Moses				4	
Ringrose, Moses	1		1		
Rigby, Jonathan	2	5	3		5
Robinson, John	1	1	2		
Robinson, Thomas	1	3	3		
Robinson, Andrew	2	3	6		3
Swan, James	1		4		
Seth, James	1	1	3		9
Stud, Elizabeth			1		
Shaw, Matthew	2		2		
Sewel, John	1	1	2		
Sidney, Francis	1	1	2		
Sherwood, John	2	2	3		
Sherwood, Thomas	1	1	3		
Smith, Lucy				5	
Skinner, Andrew	1		2		12
Sherwood, Jonathan	1	1	5		3
Sparks, Moses	1	2	2		
Skinner, Christian		1	2		2
Stanfield, Richard	2	3	3		11
Stains, Moses	2	4	2		
S[t] Clair, John	1	3	2		
Spencer, Philemon	5		3		8
S[t] Clair, William	1		3		
Smith, Thomas	2	2	3		9
Sherwood, Nicholas	2	1	3		5
Sewel, Bazill	4	2	2		14
Smith, Charles	3		4		
Sands, Benjamin	3		3		1
Shields, William	2	2	3		3
Sewel, Mark	1	4	4		
Sherwood, Thomas	2		2		15
Spencer, Richard	5	3	2		2
Spencer, Perrigrine	2	2	5		1
Swan, John	1		2		
Skinner, Zebulon	2	2	2		1
Skinner, John	3	1	6		2
S[t] Clair, Jonathan	1	2	1		
Shannahan, John	2	1	5		19
Stoker, John	1	5	3		
Stoker, Elijah	2	3	4		
Stitchberry, Philip	1	2	2		
Spencer, Mary	1		1		
Seamer, John	1	1	3		
Skinner, Mordecai	1	1	2		6
Seamer, Henry	2	5	2		
Sewel, John	1	1	2		
Slaughter, James	1	2	2		
Tibballs, Thomas	2		3		8
Tibballs, Henry	1	2	3		1
Tilghman, James	1		3		6
Tarry, Richard				3	2
Tarr, Jonathan	1	1	2		
Turner, John	1	2	4		
Tibbals, Thomas	3	2	3		9
Tilghman, Lloyd, Quarters					66
Tilghman, Ann	1		11	1	59
Tilghmans, Ann, Jun[r], Quarter					10
Tenant, Samuel	3	1	1		1
Thompson, John	1	2	3		1
Townsend, Thomas	1	1	3		1
Townsend, Thomas	3	5	3		
Townsend, John	2	2	2		
Townsend, Benjamin	1	1	1		
Tilghman, Richard	2	3	3		51
Tilghman, Perrigrine	1	3	3		73
Townsend, Benjamin	1	1	1		
Townsend, George	1		3		1
Vinton, Solomon	2	2	5		
Vinton, Samuel	1	2	6		
Valient, John	2	4	5		2
Valient, Richard	1	1	2		
Valient, Thomas	1	1	2		
Valient, Jonathan	1	2	2		
Wott, Margaret			1		
Watts, William	2				6
Wallace, Richard				4	1
Weedon, Robert	2	2	3		3
Windstandley, William	1	3	4		4
Wells, Elizabeth	1	2	5		
Winterbottom, Thomas	1		2		
Weyman, Thomas	1	1	3		10
Williams, Griffin	1	1	2		
Wharton, Sarah	2		2		
West, William	2		5		
Williams, David	1				
West, Benjamin	1	2	2		
Watts, William	1	2	4		6
Watts, Hugh	1		2		6
Wilson, Robert	1	1			
Warring, Thomas	1	1	4		
Sears, William	2	6	6		28
James, Hughs	1	4	3		
Larrimore, Dorothy		2	3		1
Tydings, Richard	1	2	2		11
Weyman, Francis	1		3		1
Winterbottom, Robert	2	1	6		

WASHINGTON COUNTY.

NAME OF HEAD OF FAMILY.	Free white males of 16 years and upward, including heads of families.	Free white males under 16 years.	Free white females, including heads of families.	All other free persons.	Slaves.
Baker, Abraham	2	3	3		
Roberts, William	2	2	7		
Glass, Peter	2		4		
Cretzer, Leonard	3	4	2		
Hawn, Peter	3	2	3		
Clagett, Postumous	1		1		12
Clagett, Zacariah	3	1	3		4
Carnau, Leonard	2	2	3		
Maghamee, Hugh	2	2	4		
Brown, Rudolph	4	4	7		
Norris, Precilla	2		6		3
Roderock, John	1	1	3		
Butler, Henry	2	3	3		5
Stall, Jesse	1	6	1		
Hart, Christopher	1	3	3		
Hog, Thomas	1		2		8
Gardner, Yost	2		5		
Grimm, Abraham	1		2		
Ludwick, George	1	1	1		
Wals, John	1		3		
Frush, George	2	2	4		
Hofmaster, Francis	1	3	1		
Havermill, John	1	2	3		
Deaver, John	3		3		
Snyder, John	1	4	3		
Rodrock, John	1	1	3		
Cyders, Frederick	2	3	4		

WASHINGTON COUNTY—Continued.

NAME OF HEAD OF FAMILY.	Free white males of 16 years and upward, including heads of families.	Free white males under 16 years.	Free white females, including heads of families.	All other free persons.	Slaves.
Cyders, Solomon	1	4	2		
Curpman, Philip	1	5	2		
Curpman, Jacob	1	2	5		
Grimm, Alexander	5		2		
Rhiner, Jacob	1	2	4		
Houser, John	1	3	2		
Warfield, Alexander	1	1	1		6
Fraiser, John	1	4	1		3
Trentor, Joseph	1	1	1		
Kirk, Dan'l	1		3		
Jarvis, William	1	4	3		
Lishe, Henry	1	4	1		
Ainker, Mary	1		1		
Trentor, Sam'l	1	2	4		
Allen, James	1	1	3		9
Butler, Edward	1				
Butler, William	2		2		1
Furguson, Daniel	1		6		
Yates, William	2	1	1		2
Merryarthur, Jacob	2	3	2		
Jasson, Bennet	1		1		
Austin, James	1		2		
Cheshire, John	1	3	4		
Thomas, William	1		2		
Hicks, Nathaniel	1				
Waters, George	1	1	2		
Framer, John	1		2		
Smith, John	1		1		
Crutohly, Benjamin		1	1	1	
Demora, John	1	1	1		
Obrian, Bridget			1		
Waller, William	1	3	2		
Thomas, Jeremiah	1	3	2		
Buts, Christian	2	1	5		
Fraliey, John	2				
Herren, Thomas	3				
Roderock, Ludwick	2		3		
Roderock, Dan'l	1	2	2		
Armstrong, William	1	3	1		2
Roberts, Geshan	1	1	2		
Buts, William	2	3	2		
Brillmine, Henry	1	1	3		
Perkins, Mary		1	3		
Yates, Elizabeth	1		2		3
Shuble, Henry	1	2	2		
Reel, Joseph	3	2	2		2
Baker, Tillman	1		1		
Grimm, Jacob	1	4	3		
Harman, Mich'l	1	1	1		
Barnett, Thomas	1	1	4		
Crampton, Thomas	5	1	4		7
Kimball, William	1		3		
Roderock, Jacob	1	1	3		
Frush, Jacob	2	1	3		
Hill, Mary			3		
Gerdy, Peter	1		2		3
Huffer, John	3	2	4		
Eastern, William	1	4	4		
Lambert, Henry	1	1	3		
Connor, William	1	3	2		
Taylor, John	1		2		
Willcox, James	2		3		
Lewis, William	1	3	3		
Murphy, Michael	2	1	3		
Gladdie, William	2	2	3		
Farling, Benjamin	1	2	2		
Dean, James				5	
Lewis, Ezabell		1	6		
Grimes, John				7	
Hamilton, Archibald	1				
Buzzard, Thomas	1				
Evanier, John	1	1	2		
Doud, Charles	1				4
Branan, Patrick	1		5		
Jourdan, William	1	1	2		
Farling, John	1	1	2		
White, Timothy	1	1	5		
Luckett, John	1	1	1		
Cahill, Catharine			1		
Owing, Hugh	1		1		
Evans, Thomas	1		4		
Shepherd, John	10	5	4		
Ritohie, John	1		2		48
Gregory, William		2	4		
James, Easter			2		5
Baker, Philip	1	4	4		
Bartlet, James	1	2	4		
Keepers, Joseph	2	2	5		
Kingery, Christian	1	2	2		
Barton, John	1		2		
Fox, John	1	1	2		
Tomar, Christian		1	2		
Dedis, Solomon	1		1		
Grim, Daniel	1	2	5		
Ainsberger, Christian	2	5	3		
Huffman, Robert	1	4	4		
Showman, John, Junr	1		1		
Schnabely, Casper	2	2	1		
Houser, Jacob	2		1		
Peck, Jacob	2		1		
Showman, George	3	3	3		
Roberts, Conrad	2		5		
Benskin, John	1	2	3		
Grimm, Andrew	1	2	5		
Thomas, George	2		1		
Nicholls, Michael	1	3	5		
Smutz, Abraham	1	3	4		
Houser, Abraham	2	1	3		
Roderock, Andrew	1	1	3		
Hyatt, Christopher	1	2	4		
Moore, Daniel	1	1	3	1	
Hyatt, John	1	1	3		
Moore, Richard	2		4		
Keedy, Daniel	2		3		
Rulett, Elizabeth	2	1	3		
Igantor, John	1	3	4		
Feter, Philip	1	4	2		
Troxill, George I	1	2	3		
Abry, John	1		2		
Myer, Peter	1	4	5		
Ensworth, Thomas	1		1		
Keedy, John	1		1		
Dash, Lewis	1		1		
Beard, John	1	1	1		
Fisher, John	1	2	4		
Painter, George	2		5		
Conn, Michael	1	3	3		
Russell, Jacob	1		1		
Keedy, George	3	3	6		
Hess, Jacob	3	2	5		
Magnamee, Joab	1		1		
Baker, Andrew	3		3		
Thumb, Michael	2		6		
Bunell, Peter	2	4	2		
Zimmermon, Rachel			2		
Poole, Basil					2
Bunell, Benjamin	2	1	1		2
Shephert, Michael	1	3	4		
Thomas, Jacob	1		4		
Tener, Yost	2	2	5		
Shott, Margaret	1		4		
Sybert, Isaac	1	3	1		
Grove, Jacob	3	2	2		
Walker, James	1	3	3		
Ringer, John	2	1	2		
Ringer, Jacob	1		3		
Hardman, John	1	1	3		
Smelser, Leonard	1		3		
Ringer, Conrad		2	4		
Taylor, Michael	3		3		
Taylor, John	1	2	2		
Walker, James	1	3	3		
Morgan, Moses	1	2	2		
Slusher, Henry	1	4	2		
Clunk, Andrew	1		1		
Welty, Frederick	1		7		
Wolfe, Frederick	4		1		
Stot, John	1		4		
Sine, Martin	1		4		
Nichodemus, Conrad	2	2	5		
Tulty, John	1		1		
Spealman, Conrad	2	4	1		
Crossly, William	2	2	1		
Shroyer, David	1	2	2		
Fresler, Peter	1	3	5		
Fitzpatrick, Daniel	1	5	2		
Boone, William	1	3	3		
Boyer, Philip	1	6	3		
Claughbagh, Martin	1	3	3		
Fasnaught, Henry	1	2	3		
Fasnaught, John	1		1		
Etterhouse, Conrad	1	1	4		
Rood, Jacob	1	1	4		
Newcomer, Peter	2	4	2		
Hoover, Jacob	2	1	2		
Nunamauker, Samuel	1		2		
Houser, Abraham	2	6	4		
Dorsey, William	2		4		
Bumberger, John	2		4		
Bowman, Benjamin	1	3	5		
Rice, Daniel	1		4		
Houser, Isaac, Jur	2	3	2		
Houser, Isaac, Senr	1		1		
Spilky, Codlip	1	2	1		
Heckaberger, John	1	1	3		
Knuple, Christopher	1	4	3		
Hartsock, Conrad	1		3		
Dick, Henry	2	3	1		
Lauber, Frederick	2	2	1		
Bear, David	3	3	1		
Martin, Jacob	3	1	5		
Sydersticker, Abram	1		1		
Whitmire, George	1	2	7		
Bowman, Joseph	2	2	5		
Adams, Geo	1		1		
Horine, Adam	1	5	2		
Totton, Joseph	1		1		
Schnavely, John	1	2	1		
Newcomer, Henry	4	5	5		
M'Kindy, Robert				3	
Switzer, Samuel	1	1	1		
Wise, Peter	1	2	2		
Harvey, David	3	3	5		4
Shootz, Conrad	3	2	4		
Fowlass, John	1		3		
Craytor, Frederick	1		3		
Deetz, Adam	1		1		
Keedy, Ludwick	2	2	2		
Coonce, Frederick	2	3	4		
Furguson, Abigal			2		
Good, William	4	2	3		5
Harper, Robert	2	5	3		
Boner, George	1	2	6		
Hinceman, Henry	1	1	3		
Stone, John	2	2	3		
Armstrong, James			1		
Thompson, Mary			4		
Breckly, Philip	1		1		
Petterman, John	1	1	2		
Kadigh, Ludwick	1	3	2		
Light, Peter	1		2		
Hedrick, Vernet	2	3	2		
Sandman, Jacob	2		3		
Long, Christian	1		4		
Highberger, John	1	1	2		
Thomson, Alexander	1	2	3		
Walker, William	3	2	3		
Aumen, John	3		4		
Shop, Joseph	1	1	4		
Fox, Christina			3		
Hamm, Peter	3	4	1		
Chapline, Joseph	4		3		10
Swearingen, Benona	2	2	3		
Chapline, Jeremiah	1		3		10
Smith, George	1	5	3		
Yonkah, Daniel	1		2		
M'Coy, John	3	5	3		
Hays, Nathan	1		3		
Wolfe, Catharine			2		
Bealer, Christian	3	1	2		
Smith, George	1	2	1		
Hine, Jacob	1	1	1		
Rhiner, Michael	1		4		
Wichart, Melchor	1		1		
Long, Martin	1		1		
Himes, Andrew	1	3	1		
Myers, Adam	2		2		
Stryder, Gillian	2	1	2		
M'Mim, Robert	3	1	2		
Beckly, Jacob	1	4	2		
Kniester, Frederick	1		2		
Bower, Henry	1	1	1		
Halverstay, Honicle	1	1	1		
Stone, John	2	2	1		
Coonce, Mathias	2	2	6		
Curtis, John	1	2	2		
Grove, John	1	5	2		
Cretzinger, Solomon	1		3		
Gelvin, Jeremiah	1		4		
Benner, John	1	2	2		
Diver, Christopher	1	1	4		
Swedier, Peter	1	1	1		
Baker, Frederick	1	3	4		
Sandman, William	1		4		
Burdone, Jacob	1	1	2		
Whitmire, William	1	2	4		
Little, Henry	1		3		
Cretzminger, George	1		4	1	
Normon, George			1		
Huffman, John	1		3	2	
M'Nitt, Hannah		3	4		
Piper, Margaret			5		
Smith, Ludwick	1	1	2		
Smith, Jacob	1	1	3		
Dunahom, John	2		3		
Spong, Leonard	2		4		
Loar, Christopher	1		2		
Eckart, Henry	1	6	5	1	1
Orendorff, Christopher	5	6	4		7
Orendorff, Christian			1		4
Long, Jacob	1		1		7
Shryock, Henry	3	3	5		5
Young, Samuel	3	3	5		5
Neff, George	1	2	2		
Bumberger, John	3	1	4		
Strong, James	3	1	2		
Davis, Albinus	1	4	1		3
Nigh, George	2	4	1		1
Frank, Michael	2		5		
Funk, Henry	2	1	5		
Shultz, Adam	2	1	2		

WASHINGTON COUNTY—Continued.

NAME OF HEAD OF FAMILY.	Free white males of 16 years and upward, including heads of families.	Free white males under 16 years.	Free white females, including heads of families.	All other free persons.	Slaves.
Lee, John	3	1	6		2
Elliott, Robert	3	7	5		2
Lackland, Elisha	1	1	2		4
Waggoner, John	2	1	2		
Orendorff, Henry	1	1	3		
Hager, Johnathan	1	1	4		
Struble, Christopher	1	3	4		
Bane, Jacob	1	2	2		
Kershner, John	3		3		
Hoffar, Jacob	3	4	2		1
Steffy, Andrew	4	2	2		
Van Swearingen, Thomas	2	2	7		4
Spoon, Philip	3	4	4		
Swailes, Francis	4	1	3		2
Willson, William	1		2		
Baker, Morris	2	4	5		
Chapline, James	2	2	4		
McGlaughlin, John	2	4	4		
Shively, Jacob	2	1	4		
Hoover, John	2	4	2		
Worieg, Thomas	2	4	4		1
Kershner, Johnathan	1	1	4		
Ciliers, John	1	1	5		
Clarke, John	1		2		6
Whiteman, Jacob	1	3	6		
Winters, Elizabeth			4		
Fysher, John	3		4		
Harkins, Dan'l	2	2	4		
Lighter, Christian	3		3		
Lighter, John	1	1	3		
Hayner, Joseph	2		3		
Taylor, Michael	2		3		
Barnet, Jacob	1	3	4		2
Funk, Henry	3	2	5		
Miller, David	2	2	2		
Piper, Jacob	3	2	7		
Flick, Andrew	4	2	2		
Shainaberger, Peter	3	1	2		
Koofer, Frederick	4	2	2		
Good, Christian	1	2	6		
Lambert, George	2	4	4		
Dinkle, Daniel	2	1	1		
Monday, Balser	5	1	6		
Wolfe, Jacob	1	5	6		
Rohrer, Jacob	2	1	4		
Posteller, Andrew	2		4		
Morris, John	2		4		
McKee, Robert	1		4		1
Kershner, Philip	1	5	3		
Smith, Joseph	8		4		
Bragonier, George	1		3		
Stemple, Godfrit	1	2	3		
Shively, John	1		2		
Painter, George	1	1	2		
Funk, David	10		2		2
Huffman, John	1	2	2		
Shank, Christian	3	3	3		
Schnabely, John	3		6		
Winter, George	1	2	2		
Pillmone, John	1		3		
Brentier, Henry	2	1	4		
Ward, Philip	1		5		
Fener, Martin	1	2	5		
Miller, Michael	1		3		
Cropinger, George	1	2	3		
Boovy, Jacob	2	4	6		
Hoffly, Michael	3	5	2		
Minich, Philip	4	1	4		
Fackler, Michael	4	5	4		2
Campbell, Benjamin	2	2	3		1
Young, George	1		3		
Wise, George	2	1	2		
Copp, Micheal	2	4	3		1
Reser, Peter	1	1	3		
Bishop, George	2	1	6		5
Prutzman, John	1	3	4		1
Harry, David	5		4		
Pinkly, Jacob	2		3		
Alter, Henry	2	3	1		
Doyle, George	1	1	1		
Hafely, Peter	2	3	3		8
Davis, Resin	2		3		5
Beltzhoober, Melchor	2	6	1		5
Hieskell, Frederick	2	6	1		
Gordon, Andrew	2		4		
Cook, David	1		5		
Iglebergor, Davalt	2		3		
Rison, John	2	2	4		
Hose, Frederick	1		2		
Watson, James	2		5		
Owing, Rebecca	6	2	4		
Winghart, Henry	2		3		
Tropp, Christopher	2	3	2		
Walgly, John	1		3		
Walter, Philip	2	1	5		
Selsar, Charles	1	2	5		
House, Michael	2	2	2		
Emmerick, John	1	2	1		
Bower, George	2		5		
Bower, Moritz	1		3		
Miller, Peter	1	1	1		
Yakle, Michael	1		3		
Nave, Abraham	2		1		
Prather, Jennet			2		3
Kalaufer, Devalt		2	3		
Lee, William			1		
Alter, Frederick	2	1	6		
Kirby, Thomas	1		2		
Hose, Jacob	2	2	2		
Alter, Christopher	2		6		4
Conn, Gerrard	2	4	2		2
Shryock, Mary			4		
Shryock, Henry	1	1	3		
Dusinger, Philip	2		2		
Lochman, Casper	4		2		
Duce, Christian	2	1	5		
Divile, Michael	2	1	2		
Cashady, James	2	1	1		
Miller, Adam			2		
Strum, Michael	1		1		
Boward, Henry	2		2		
Harry, Susannah	2	3	4		2
Gigher, John	5		2		1
Harry, Jacob	5	3	5		1
Nud, Daniel	3	2	3		
McKintosh, William	2	2	3		
Harshbaugh, Frederick	1	3	4		
Baker, Bostian	11	2	3		2
Bringman, Martin	3		1		
Startzman, Henry	4	3	5		22
Clagett, Alexander	1	1	2		9
Boroff, Adam	1	5	4		
Clagett, John	1	1	4		18
Hart, Thomas	1	2	2		11
Rochester, Nathaniel	2		2		16
Pindell, Richard	2	3	2		1
Runnels, William	2	2	2		
Lewis, William		3	1		
Ragan, John	4	1	4		2
Harry, John	3	3	5		
Prutzman, Laurence	1	1	2		
Riddle, John	1	2	3		
Schnabely, Jacob	1		3		4
Stidinger, Frederick	2	1	2		
Hanser, Jacob	2		2		
Kifer, George	3	1	2		
Chapline, William	3		1		
Deck, Peter	2	1	1		
Young, Jacob	1	3	2		
Filton, Martin	2		3		
Ridenour, David	1	2	5		
Miller, John	2	1	2		
Craver, Jacob	5	1	4		
Byer, John	1	3	1		
Friener, John	1	2	3		
Levy, Andrew	1	1	3		1
Hess, Nicholas	1	1	2		
Harry, Johnathan	2	1	3		
Goel, Balser	6	2	1		
Bower, Abraham	1		1		
Snyder Henry	1		2		
Felter, Ann			2		
Crabb, Thomas	5	3	2		
Davis, John	1		3		
Conrad, Catharine	1		3		
Brentlinger, Frederick	1	3	2		
Ott, Jacob	2	2	6		
Fangler, Ann Mary			1		
Rinehart, George	1	1	1		
Hager, Johnathan	3	4	3		1
Fruit, Samuel	3		4		
Hamm, George	1	1	1		
Onawert, John	1		1		
Hufner, George	1	1	1		
Shaver, Devalt	2	1	4		
Hornage, Philip	1		6		
Wiegle, Henry	1	1	3		
Gyer, Jacob	1		1		
Miller, Henry	1	1	2		
Sailor, Modelena			2		
Doyle, Adam	1	2	1		
Kerns, Abram	1	1	1		
Waggoner, Peter	2	1	2		
Bailey, Nicholas	1		2		
Flinn, Alexander	1		1		
Miller, Andrew		1	1		
Douglas, Robert	2		5		
Grove, Henry	2	1	2		
Bower, Michael	1	2	3		
Miller, Andrew	1	1	2		
Conn, Edward	2	2	2		
Berghon, Catharine			2		
Benner, Melchor	1	1	3		
Fogler Ann			2		
Galewix, Charles	1	3	6		
Kitsmiller, Casper	3		1		
Zimmerman, Henry	1				
Baker, Jacob	1	2	1		
Kifer, Henry	1		4		
Hess, William	2		3		
Doyle, Theodius	2	2	2		
Rawlings, Solomon	2	2	3		
Ott, Adam	5		3		5
Cofrod, Conrad	2		4		
Shryock, John	2		4		1
McCardill, William	2		4		
Moore, John	1	2	4		
Beard, William	1		4		5
Bradshaw, George	4	3	6		
McCardill, James	4		3		
Kreps, Martin	2		1		
McCardill, Margaret			2		
Criner, John	1	2	4		
Shall, George	2		4		
Hocky, Christian	2	3	2		
Whip, Dan'l	4	1	4		
Whatt, John	2	3	3		
Nicholl, Jacob	2		2		
Tootwiler, Johnathan	2		1		
Ervin, John	2		1		
Borse, John	2	1	1		
Heddinger, John	1		4		
Clagett, Hezekiah	1	2	4		3
Young, Ludwick	1		1		
Brown, John	2	4	4		1
Clapsaddle, Daniel	1	2	3		
Gordon, William	2	2	1		
Downey, William	2		2		1
Oster, John	2	1	1		
Downey, David	1		1		
Needy, Isaac	1		6		
Needy, Henry	1		2		
Snell, Mathias	1		3		
Creager, Philip	1	3	5		
Hose, Peter	1	4	1		
Pygly, Peter	1		3		
Miller, Henry	1	1	3		
Hout, Peter	1		3		
Cox, Conrad	1	1	2		
Croft, Jacob	1		1		
Shade, John	1				
Bomgardner, William	1		1		3
Bomgardner, John	1	1	1		
Trompour, Leonard	1		4		
Welck, Andrew	1		1		
Criley, Francis	1	1	4		
Rinehart, Titus	1		2		
Woltz, Peter	1		4		
Woltz, George	5	5	4		
Thompson, William	2	1	3		6
Barnes, Francis	1	1	1		
Art, Mathias	1		1		
McGlasky, Stephen	1		1		
Beltzhoober, Jacob	1	1	3		
Cotts, Jacob	1		5		
Oldvine, Charles	1		2		
Lotterbarger, George	1	2	1		
Winebruner, Christoper	1		1		
Shank, Christian	1		1		
Hocky, Nicholas	1	4	2		
Ebber, Elizabeth	2		2		
Fregar, Peter	2	3	3		3
Rohrer, Jacob	3	1	5		
Hinceman, Joseph	1		1		
Stropp, Joseph	2	3	2		
Engelston, Juda			1		
Bailey, Mathias	1	2	3		
Shupe, Jacob	1	2	3		
Depan, Joseph	1		2		
Humbert, Michael	1	2	6		
Snell, Henry	1		2		
Werley, Henry	3	1	2		
Lisinger, Devalt	1	1	1		
Perry, Thomas	1		2		
Lisinger, Henry	1		2		
Wymer, Sellama		3	2		
Herr, John	2		1		
Snyder, John	1		1		
Barkman, Henry	1		4		
Longanacre, Christian	1	2	3		
Stamm, Jacob	1		3		
Rinehart, Thomas	1	2	3		
Dailey, William	1		2		
Shupe, Frederick	1	1	2		
Downey, Joseph	2	1	2		
Kenny, James	2		2		
Lowery, Michael	2	3	2		
Lowery, Jacob	2		3		
Gracen, Thomas	1	1	2		3
Bridenbaugh, John	1		3		

WASHINGTON COUNTY—Continued.

NAME OF HEAD OF FAMILY.	Free white males of 16 years and upward, including heads of families.	Free white males under 16 years.	Free white females, including heads of families.	All other free persons.	Slaves.
Cline, Henry	1	1	1		
Faigh, Barbara			2		
Sydle, Cotlape	1	3	4		
Richardson, Samuel	1	1	2		
Dowdle, Alexander	1	1	1		
Temple, Conrad	1	1	1		
Werking, Peter	1	2	1		
Boyer, John	2	3	5		
McCartney, John	2	1			
McDonald, Alexander	1		5		
Haines, Charles	1	1	4		
River, Peter	1	2	5		
Kreps, George	1	1	2		
Kooter, Engiehart	1	1	1		
George, Joseph	1	1	1		
Stoneslfer, John	1	1	7		
Hyser, William	1	1	1		
Hyser, Ann		2	3	1	
Kalinger, Casper	1	1	1		
Lorsebaugh, Harman	3	2	3		
Souder, Felix	1	1	1		
Gonter, John	2	1			
Stake, Martin	1		2		
Michael, Everhart	2		2		
Konser, John	2	1	6		
Righter, Peter	2		2		
Louderberger, George	2	2	3		
Snyder, Jacob	1	1	1		
Fichte, John	1	1	3		
Streight, Leonard	1		2		
Belch, Catharine			1		
Ply, Rudolph	1	3	4		
Studs, Ernst	2	1	2		
Crumbaugh, Conrad	2	2	1		
Crumbaugh, John	2		1		
Crumbaugh, John, Senr	1		2		
Lighter, Abram	1	1	3		
Shank, George	2		3		
Herbert, Steward	1	1	2		
Rape, John	1		6		
Rohrer, Frederick	2	2	3		
Hoover, Henry	1		2		
Conly, Elizabeth			1		
Morgan, Nathaniel	1	1	1		1
Tootwiler, Henry	1	1	2		
Klien, Henry	1		2		
Grayham, Edmond	1		2		2
Coke, Henry	1	1	3		
McCalley, Charles	1	3	2		2
Teter, Jacob	1	2	4		
Lower, George	1	2	2		
Crech, Philip	4		4		
Price, Josiah	2				14
Bently, John	1	1	2		
Metz, Christian	1	3	4		
Leaf, Henry	4	2	4		
Pry, John	1	2	1		
Knable, Jacob	1	1	5		
Row, Peter	5	1	1		1
Noggle, Elizabeth			2		
Mann, John	1		3		
Stults, Henry	1	3	3		
Stutzman, David	2	3	4		
Haden, William	1		2		
Blair, John	2	2	3		4
Blair, James	1	2	4		2
Lear, Philip	1	3	5		
Tyler, Jacob	1	4	3		1
Stucky, Barbara	3	1	3		
Painter, George	3	3	2		
Helser, George	1		2		
Peck, John	1		1		
Bowles, Thomas	1		2		3
Tyler, Catharine			1		
Henricks, Peter	1	1	2		
Troup, Catharine	2	1	4		
Millhouse, John	2		1		
Picket, Martin	1				
Householder, George Adam	3	4	5		6
Ridgwood, Peter	2	2	2		
Dines, Mary	1	2	2		
Utsler, Martin	1	3	1		
Steward, Rachel	1		2		
Naigly, Peter	1	1	1		
Kelly, William	1		2		
McCoy, John	1	4	2		
Scott, George	2			2	18
Dalley, Cornelius	3	1	2		
John, Peter, Junr	1		2		
Carlisle, James	4	5	3		
Checter, Ventle	1	2	3		
Calor, Margaret			2		
Stoneslfer, Daniel	2		2		
Skile, Jacob	1		2		
John, Peter, Senr	5		3		

NAME OF HEAD OF FAMILY.	Free white males of 16 years and upward, including heads of families.	Free white males under 16 years.	Free white females, including heads of families.	All other free persons.	Slaves.
Dagan, Jacob	1		2		
Wolond, Barnet	1		3		
Shower, George	1	2	3		
Thomas, Michael	2		3		
Cost, Frederick	2		5		
Barker, William	1		5		
Line, Jacob	1	1	5		
Miller, Michael	4	1	3		
Nichodemus, Frederick	2		4		
Hiester, Abraham	1	2	5		
Grayham, William	2	1	1		
Bilimire, Martin	3	2	2		
Miller, Christian	1		2		
Baker, Samuel	2	3	5		
Schnavely, Henry	3	1	4		
Keedy, Henry	1	2	2		
Tresler, Michael	2	2	5		
Thomb, Peter	2	2	5		
Banack, John	2	2	4		
Beard, John	1		2		
Ainsworth, Thomas	1	1	2		
Hostler, Jacob	1		2		
Iier, Philip	1	2	2		
James, Griffith	1	2	2		
James, Joseph	1	3	2		
Calbert, John	1		5		
Homer, Peter	1	4	1		
Agner, George	1	1	3		
Bruce, Frederick	1		4		
Aigner, Ludwick	2	1	4		
House, George	1		4		2
Kale, Christian	1	3	4		
Macomen, John	1	2	6		
Flood, Henry	1	1	3		
Conrad, Robert	1		3		
Flood, Michael	1	1	1		
Beard, Adam	1	2	1		
Raytor, John	1		4		
Reynalds, William	1	4	2		
Harvey, John	1	2	2		
Ingram, Francis	1	3	6	1	
Johnson, Thomas	1		3		
Harper, Robert	1	1	2		
Harper, John	1	2	2		
Waters, James	1	1	5		
Neice, William	1		5		
Sulaman, Thomas	1	1	5		
Hall, William	1	1	6		
Alt, Jacob	1	1	5		
Bond, Patrick	1	2	2		
Harper, Josiah	1		2		
Osborn, Thomas	1		2		
Johnson, William	1		3		
Meck, James	1		4		
Smith, James	31	2	7		
Forth, Robert	1	2	3		
Gaver, Samuel	2		2		
Roland, James	1		2		
Arnold, George	2	3	3		
Hughs, William	1		3		
Westerberger, David	1		3		
Hoover, Martin	1		8		
Frank, Philip	2	2	5		
Coplar, Barnabas	1		7		
Stone, Joseph	1	2	5		
Roby, Owen	2	2	6	3	
Crytz, George	2	2	9		
Melone, John	1	2	3		
Armstrong, John	1		3		
Reader, John	1		3		
Powell, Peter	1				
Worland, William		2	4		
Williams, John	1	2	4		
Cross, William	2		2		
Powell, George	1	3	3		
Powell, Joseph	1	3	3		1
Cross, John	1	2	5		
Shaver, John	2	1	2		
Kill, Benjamin	2		4		
Mughler, Christian	1	1	3		
Pence, Philip	1		2		
Lancaster, Joseph	1		2		
Cheney, Robert	1	1	2		
Lape, Henry	1		4		
Cheney, Susannah	1	1	4		
Robinson, John	1	1	2		
Cheny, Joseph	2		4		2
Chetister, Eliphalet	2	3	4		
Kindle, William	1	2	4		
Helmer, William	1	1	2		
Petery, Jacob	2	3	6		
South, Benjamen	1	3	5		
Roland, David	3	4	3		
Naigly, Peter	1	1	1		
Snyder, John	1		2		
Grayham, Joseph	1	1	2		

NAME OF HEAD OF FAMILY.	Free white males of 16 years and upward, including heads of families.	Free white males under 16 years.	Free white females, including heads of families.	All other free persons.	Slaves.
James, Hezekiah	1	1	1		
Hamston, Susannah		1	2		
Rawlings, Moses	2		2		12
Oat, Elizabeth	2		7		2
Carlisle, David	2		3		5
Jaques, Lancelot	3			1	12
Mills, William	1		4		
Mills, Robert	1		1		
Day, John	1	3	4		
Thomas, John	1	3	4		
King, Samuel	1	4			1
Westlake, George	1	4	2		
Dolar, Richard	2		2		
Burnett, Peter	1	2	1		
Brindle, Jacob	1	2	1		
Cashady, John	1		1		
Hart, Edward	1		3		
Stout, George	1		2		
Cox, Abraham	2	4	2		
Cox, Sarah	3		1		
Dart, John	1	4	3		
Snyder, Henry	1	2	1		
Beard, Christopher	1	1	1		
Alabagh, Jacob	1	1	5		1
Cummings, Joseph	1	5	4		
Myers, Elias	1	2	2		
Conner, Thomas	1	2	3		
Paner, George	1		2		
Yates, Sarah	2		3		
Rose, Ann			3		3
Palmer, Thomas	1		3		2
Waggoner, John	1	1	3		
Hammeson, Cammel	1		2		1
Yates, Joseph	2		1		
Worman, Henry	3		2		
Claton, Elisha	1	1	2		
Bolton, John	1	1	1		
Grimes, Thomas	1	1	3		
Sloop, Joseph	1	1	1		
Cummings, Margaret			2		
Berry, William	1	1	2		
Gibson, William	1	1	2		
Smith, John	1	2	2		
McPherson, Samuel	1	2	5		2
Parret, Nicholas	1	2	2		
Cheston, Susannah			1		
Hunter, John	1	1	2		
Thrall, Joseph	1	1	2		
Prutzman, Daniel	2	2	3		1
Donavan, John	2	1	2		
Martin, Ralph	1	2	2		
Reed, John	1	1	5		9
Swope, Christopher	1	2	2		
Weller, Peter	1	2	1		
Shaver, Andrew	1	3	3		
Botts, Andrew	3	5	3		
Wolfelsberger, John	3	1	1		
Zuke, Michael	1	2	1		
Prgh, Philip	1	1	2		
Garehart, John	1	2	2		
Repp, Peter	1		1		
McClure, John	1	2	3		
Wlond, Yost	1	4	2		
Gaither, Henry	1	2	5		1
Linen, Jeremiah	1		1		
Yakely, Peter	1	2	1		
Rohrer, Jacob	3	1	5		
Gardner, Francis	1	1	2		
Immell, Joseph	1		1		
Myer, Peter	1	1			
Repp, Christian	1		4		
Fulk, David	1		2		
Bower, Frederick	1	3	4		
Snyder, Sarah			1		
Gallaway, Summerset				1	1
Bolton, Henry	2	1	2	1	
Zuke, Henry	2	3	2		
Longman, John	1	3	2		
Longenake, Barbara			1		
Montle, George	1	4	5		
Myers, John	1	4	5		
Zimmer, Peter	1	3	3		
Fasnagh, Adam	1	3	3		
Wolfe, Christian	1		5		
Miller, Philip	1	2	4		
Swigert, Philip	1		1		
Stockman, Christian	4		1		
Funk, John	2	3	6		
Swingly, Nicholas	2	3	1		1
Beard, Zacariah	2	3	5		
Melott, Elias	1	5	1		
Amos, Nicholas	2	5	5		2
Roland, Jacob	5		3		
Roland, Abraham	1	4	3		
Melott, Benjamin	1	4	3		2
Melott, Thomas	2	1	3		

WASHINGTON COUNTY—Continued.

NAME OF HEAD OF FAMILY.	Free white males of 16 years and upward, including heads of families	Free white males under 16 years	Free white females, including heads of families	All other free persons	Slaves
Melott, John	1	3	2		
Melott, Peter	4	1	2		3
Roland, Henry	1	3	4		
Wetstone, Daniel	2	5	1		
Howard, James	5	2	5		16
Adams, William	2	1	3		
Hause, John	1		2		
Hause, Leonard	2	3	3		
Creigh, Jacob	1	2	4		
Adams, John	1	3	2		
Younker, Jacob	1	4	6		
Perrin, Rachel		2	5		
Kitsmiller, Jacob	2	6	2		
Sergeant, William	2	1	1		
Ferrin, James	1	3	3		
Ostman, John	1	4	2		
Polmer, Peter	4	6	4		
Polmer, John	1		1		
Noodle, John	1	5	5		
King, Joseph	1	1	3		
Pronk, Ann		3	3		
Pronk, John	2	1	4		
Clarke, Ann	1	4	4		
Stock, Elizabeth			1		
Bettz, Mary	1	2	3		
Raytor, Elizabeth			1		
Swearingen, Charles	5	2	5		11
Hadler, Samuel	3		1		
Klien, Philip, Senr	3		3		
Ray, Joseph	1		2		
Klien, Philip	1	2	2		
Faig, George	2	3	1		
Bolton, Conrad	1		1		
Garland, Gracy		2	4		
Davis, Rachel	1				6
Powlas, Christian	1		5		
McDill, Catharine	1	1	4		
Sailor, Ullerick	3	4	4		
Coss, John	1	2	4		
Bayhan, Patrick	2	1	1		
Darkiss, Henry	2	1	3		
Clarke, Joseph	1	1	3		
Preur, Burchart		1	3		1
Darkins, John	1				
Shusser, George	1	3	2		
Sellars, George		6	3		
Miller, Abraham	1	1	2		
Fronaberger, Lewis	1	1	3		
Cramer, Jacob	1		1		
Miller, Jacob	1		5		
Weaver, Jacob	3	4	4		
Smith, Nicholas	1	1	5		
Klesecker, Philip	1	1	4		
Gonter, Martin	1	3	2		
Sockman, Henry	2	2	5		
Snell, Adam	1	1	3		
Rohrer, John	2	1	2		1
Raup, Michael	2	2	5		
Carnicomb, Ludwick	1	3	6		
Wright, Thomas	1	1	5		
Hawn, Christian		1	1		
Asher, Gabriel			2		
Ervine, Jacob	2				
Jacobs, George	1		2		
Yost, Charles	1	1	4		
Fackler, Adam	1		1		
McKewan, William	1	2	7		
Oharro, John	2	6	3		
Zimmerman, Yost	1	2	7		
Balt, Geo	1		2		
Kennedy, William	2	2	7		
Burchart, Jacob	1		2		
Heiten, Jacob	1		1		
Garehart, Jacob	1	1	1		
Null, Conrad	1	3	2		
Tracy, Martha	1	2	3		
Rud, Thomas	1	2	5		
Roof, Rudolph	1	3	3		
Ridenour, John	1	2	4		
Creager, Peter	1		2		
Garman, Adam		4	5		
Brumbach, Jacob	3	4	4		
Rentch, Andrew	3	1	5		15
Carter, Bennet			3		
Reader, John	1	4	3		9
Darby, Benjamin					
Waggoner, Martin	1	4	1	1	
Roderock, Philip				2	
Fulliton, Galep				1	
Rager, Conrad	2	1	3		
Rentch, John	2	1	3		1
Carroll, Charles	1		2		33
Steward, Hugh	3	3	3		
Carrico, Basil	1		2		
Scott, John	2		6		
Woodhouse, Mary			1		
Rodes, Frederick	2	2	4		

NAME OF HEAD OF FAMILY.	Free white males of 16 years and upward, including heads of families	Free white males under 16 years	Free white females, including heads of families	All other free persons	Slaves
Shock, Adam	2	2	4		
Truelock, Isaac	2	1	4		
Deal, John	1	2	3		
Inglehart, John	1		2		
Heckrode, Henry	1	2	2		
Loy, Adam	3	2	5		
Sanders, John	1		1		
Jupen, John	1	3	6		1
Wright, Elijah	1		1		
Brinick, Daniel	1	1	1		
Currer, Thomas	1	1	5		
Frederick, Augustian	1	4	2		
Eakle, Johnathan					
Cline, Joseph	2	8	5		
Cline, William	1	2	1		
Clarke, Robert	1	3	3		2
Schnabely, Henry	6	1	1		11
Hulder, Isaiah	1		1		
Page, Nathaniel	1	3	4		
Witaker, John	1	3	5		1
Amos, Mordical	1	1	1		
Brand, Richard	1	2	2		2
Duvall, Benjamin	1		4		
South, William	2	2	4		1
Adams, John	2	2	2		
Melott, John	1	3	2		
Allison, Andrew	1	4	4		
Zook, Henry	1	3	3		
Barnes, Joshua	1	1	2		
Barnes, John	2	2	5		
Darkis, Frederick	2	1	3		
Null, Christina				2	3
Crytz, George	2	3	6		
McGonagale, Philip	2	3	1		
Daugherty, John	1	1	1		
Donovan, Peter	1	2	2		
Shellars, William	1	1	6		
Cothers, David	1		3		
Rockhole, Thomas	1	4	3		
McGlaughlin, Charles	1		3		
Clarke, Joseph	2		1		
Muckiowany, Mary	1		2		
McNallan, Patrick	1	1			
Linkswiler, George	2	1	1		
Bowser, Henry	3	1	6		
Hymes, Susannah			1		
Clutz, Isaac		2	4		
Dugan, John	2	4	4		5
Sanderson, Thomas	1	1	3		
Wells, Resin	1		2		
Reed, William		3	5		
Ammerman, John	1	2	7		
Mark, William	1		2		3
Ammerman, Philip	1	4	3		
Carrack, Walter	2	4	3		
Householder, John	2	2	4		
Doney, William	2	3	5		
Caraline, John	1		3		
Farr, John	1		2		
Lemaster, Hugh	2	1	2		
Wells, Jeremiah	1	1	5		
Craig, Samuel	1	1	2		
Owens, Edward	1	1	2		
McGlaughlin, Charles	1		1		
Taylor, Michael	1	1	5		
Pyrod, Michael	1		2		
Teler, Petor	1	4	6		
Miller, George	1	2	3		
Thompson, Bennet	1	3	4		
Owens, George	1	3	2		
Madcap, William	3	2	5		
Farmer, Catharine	1	2	4		
Seller, Hardman	4		1		
Lefavor, David	3	1			1
Fogle, George	4	1	2		
Robinson, John	1	2	3		
Walker, Jacob	2	1	2		
Darnall, Susannah	1	2	3		1
Frey, George	3		3		
Roberts, William	2	3	4		
Fysher, Peter	1		2		
Plummer, Samuel	1		2		
Lower, John	1	4	3		
Spicer, Jeremiah	2	3	4		4
Beckly, Mathias	3	3	3		1
Miller, John	1	4	5		
Miller, John	3	1	2		
Cooghle, John	1	1	2		
Spicer, James	1	1	2		
Spicer, Zepheniah	1	5	5		
Walker, Barnet	1		3		1
Maxfield, George	2	1	4		
Spicer, Solomon	1	5	3		
Hammond, James	1	1	3		2
Simmonds, Richard	2	4	5		2
Simmons, Johnathan	3		4		
Simmons, Allender	1	1	3		3

NAME OF HEAD OF FAMILY.	Free white males of 16 years and upward, including heads of families	Free white males under 16 years	Free white females, including heads of families	All other free persons	Slaves
Cross, Jeremiah	1		2		
Robey, Laurence	1	3	2		
Forster, Ephraim	1	1	2		
Steward, Charles	1	2	5		
Byard, Jacob	2		4		
Waters, Lucy			2		
Sailor, George	1		4		
Barnes, James	1	2	1		
Waters, Solomon	2				
Farmer, Jane	2	2	3		1
Hudgel, Catharine	1	2	5		
Rodes, Basil	1		2		
Rodes, Nicholas	1	1	4		
Rodes, Ezekiel	1		4		
Fry, Barnabas	1	3	1		
Hays, Jeremiah	2	3	6		
Farmer, Charles	1	1	1		
Haines, Joseph	1	1	2		
English, Elizabeth			2		
McClain, Thomas	2	2	3		1
Dial, Simon	4	1	3		
Myers, Joseph	1	1	2		
Williams, Benjamin	1		4		
Dial, James	1	3	3		
Barnes, John	2	2	1		
Ridgley, Isaac	1		1		1
Edmondson, Archbald	1	2	2		1
Edmondson, Blanchiana	1	4			2
Runnalds, Lucy		3	3		
Lewis, William	1	1	3		
Alvey, Michael	1		4		
Garehart, Catrout	2	2	4		
Fox, Elizabeth		1	5		
Knode, John	1	1	5		2
Barnes, Robert, Jr	4	1	2		
Farmer, Samuel	1	1	4		
Thompson, William	1	1	5		
Lucket, James	1	3	1		1
Lucket, Samuel	1	1	3		
Lynch, Samuel	1	1	5		6
Prather, Rignald	2	2	3		
Barnes, Robert	1	4	3		4
Abright, William	2	1	2		
Smide, John	2	2	2		
Hobier, William	2	2	4		
Wyand, Jacob	2	2	2		
Carter, John	1	2	2		3
Sensley, Peter	1	2	2		
Ludwick, Jacob	2	2	3		
Nave, Francis	1		3		
Klien, John	1	4	4		
Shofestall, John	4	3	4		
Smith, John	1	2	2		
Thomas, David	1	2	2		
Stonebraker, Henry	1	2	5		
Coplar, Barnet	1	2	5		
Sennuff, Philip	1		2		
Peck, Edward	3		6		
Deal, Moreta	3		2		
Berton, Joshua	1	2	2		
Ross, James	1		5		
Swan, Edward	2	3	5		
Myers, John	1	1	3		
Craig, John	1	1	3		
Wood, Thomas	1		2		
Coonce, Catharine			1		
Johnson, Barnet	5	2	5	2	5
Thomas, John	2	1	5		
Price, Benjamin	1	1	3		
Matony, Abram	1		2		
Garman, Abraham	1	1	2		
Reader, Isaac	1		4		
Frees, John	2				
Magacha, William	2		3		
Berry, Thomas	1		4		
Barton, John	1	2	4		
Goucher, Henry	1	3	1		
Martin, John	1		1		
Fuller, Ephaim	1		2		
Bennington, Mary			2		
Fuller, Daniel			5		
Burk, Michael	2	2	5		
Storm, Elizabeth		3	2		
Jamison, Sam'l	1	2	3		
Dean, Charles	1	1	3		
Bennet, Thomas	2		2		
Garlock, John	2	2	4		
Wemmer, Isaac	1	1	4		
Maskimmings, David	5	2	2		
Bisley, Dan'l	2	3	4		
Marton, William	1				
Martins, Charity			2		
Berry, James		2	3		
Haines, Jacob	2	3	6		
Willson, John	1	3	1		
Bennington, Joab	1		3		
Murphy, John	1	3	3		

WASHINGTON COUNTY—Continued.

NAME OF HEAD OF FAMILY.	Free white males of 16 years and upward, including heads of families.	Free white males under 16 years.	Free white females, including heads of families.	All other free persons.	Slaves.
Potts, Johnathan	1	3	2		
Martin, Joseph	1	2	8		
Fauver, Henry	2	2	2		
Barnhard, George	1	1	2		
Brand, Abram	1	1	2	1	3
Ferrel, Catharine	1	2	1		
Bidinger, George	2		4		6
Donathan, Joseph	1	1	2		
Carroll, Charles	1	1	2		
Fuller, Thomas	2	3	4		
Rose, James	2	1	1		
Griffy, Evan	1	1	2		
Rose, John	1		2		
Stomb, Jacob	3	2	2		
Ox, John	2		3		
Shafer, Barbara			2		
Shepherd, Christian	1	4	1		
Ridenour, Conrad	1		1		
Singleton, Amos	1		4		
Flint, John	1	4	4		
Hiler, Peter	1	2	4		
Schnavely, John	3		6		
Schnavely, Jacob	1		2		
Schnavely, Michael	2	2	4		
Barnes, James	1	3	2		
Golding, John	1	2	2		
Thrall, Richard	2	1	3		
Powell, John	2	3	3		
Nott, Ignatius	1	3	3		
Thomas, John	3	4	1		9
Jennings, Henry	1	3	4		
Chapline, Thomas					
Stillwell, Jeremiah	2	4	5		
Hofmer, Samuel					
Lewis, Ezekiel	1	3	5		
Davis, Thomas	1	4	3		
Waters, Gideon	1		3		
McAlister, James	2	1	1		
Roberts, Johnathan	1	2	2		
Roberts, Margaret	3		2		
Hancock, Edward	1	1	2		
Durram, Jeremiah	1		2		
Flint, Charity	1		3		5
Grome, Abraham	1	2	2		
Martin, Ralph	1	2	2		
Prutzman, Henry					
Berry, James	1		2		
Johnson, Thomas	1	2	1		
Van Buskirk, John	3	2	1		
Lynn, Levy	1	2	1		
Reynalds, James	1	1	4		
Adams, Jacob				10	
Rodes, Zacaniah	1	1	3		
Sewall, Jacob	1	2	3		
Alabagh, John	2	1	4		
Becktle, Isaac	1	2	3		
Long, Christian	1	2	5		
Seyburn, John	1	1	7		
Lukehart, Conrad	1	2	7		
Beevans, Daniel	1	4		2	
Noyer, Thomas	2		3		
Fry, John	1	2	2		
Branan, John	1	1	2		
Gain, Lewis	1	2	2		
Mouse, Jacob	2	2	2		
Maines, Mary	3		2		
Dixon, Nathaniel	1	3	4		
Conly, Michael	1	3	4		
Forsythe, John					
Brieon, Archibald	2	3	4		
Hurst, Joseph	3	2	3		1
Starttipper, Anthony	2	6	3		
Mills, Michael	2	2	3		
Mills, Jacob	3	1	1		
Jaques, Thomas	1		1		2
Cummings, Jaba	1		1		
Morrison, William	1	3	6		
Dunn, George	1	4	1		
Kelvelan, Thomas	1		4		
Chatswell, Thomas	2	3	3		
Welch, James	1	3	2		
Mills, Robert	4		3		
McMachin, Barnabas	2		1		
Mills, Samuel	1	2			
Rook, Richard	2		2		
Nesbit, Nathaniel	3	2	4		2
Nesbit, John	1		2		
Noggle, George	1	4	2		
Prather, Lydda			3		2
Miller, George	1	2	3		
Rankin, John	1	1	3		
Rodey, Henry	1	2	1		
Bergeant, John	1	2	3		
Downey, James	1	1	4		
Pool, William	3		4	5	
Bowins, Thomas	3		3		
Biddle, Simon	1		3		
Hartle, William	1		1		
Kelly, Mary			2		
Morrison, James	1		3		
Goodin, George	2		3		
Dryden, Rebecca		1	3		
Bailey, Thomas	1	2	5		
Dowler, Joseph	1	2	7		
Wooldbridge, Stephen	1	1	4		
Roseberry, John	1		4		
Jaques, Denton	21	2	4	1	19
Crayton, Richard	1		4		
Lyn, John	3	1	3		4
Miller, Valentine	1	2	1		
Dialena, William	1	1			
Claycomb, Frederick	1		3		
Wilkison, John	1	1	3		
Carpenter, John	1	5	4		
Bair, John	1		2		
Ford, James	1	4	6		9
Cain, Patrick	1		2		
Praither, James	2	1	3		2
Easter, John	3	2	2		
Bruner, Peter	3	1	2		
France, Emanuel	3	3	2		
Showman, Thomas	1	3	2		
Bowman, Simon	1	1	4		
Sturr, William	1	1	2		
Heller, John	1	1	7		
Smith, Nicholas	1	2	4		5
Lessly, John	1		2		
Barnet, Philip	1	1	6		
Night, Jacob	1	1	2		
Kepera, Jacob	1	1	1		
McCullum, Alexander	2	3	3		3
Burns, Patrick	2	1	5		
Airs, James		2	5		
Ewin, John	2		1		
Umstead, Abraham	2		1		
Sparling, Andrew	1	2	4		1
Pore, Christian	1	2	1		
Queen, James	2		1		
Cooper, William	1		1		
Dotson, William	1		3		
Kerick, Benjamin	2	1	1		
Dagner, Patrick	1		3		
Snyder, Casper	1	5	4		
Barkman, Jacob	2	3	3		
Fisher, John	1	1	2		
Flick, George	1		2		
Fry, John	1		3		
Peck, Devalt	2		2		
Miller, George	2		7		
Barton, William	1	6	3		
Myer, Peter	1	4	1		
Kisinger, George	1	2	2		
Wallis, John	1	2	5		
Piper, Emanuel	2	3	5		
Friend, Jacob	4		3		4
Williams, John		3	4		
Shock, John	1	1	3		
James, John	1	2	3		
Pain, Ambrosiah	1	2	3		
Ash, Henry	2	2	3		1
Hainley, Christopher	2	2	4		
Crowl, Conrad	1		2		
Grenen, John	1		4		1
Haines, John	1	3	4		2
Edwards, John	1	1	3		
Conner, Joseph	1	2	3		
Moudy, John	1		1		
Myers, Johnathan	1	5	4		
McClain, James	2	1	4		1
Smith, Joseph	1	4	4		
Fisher, George	1	5	3		
Jones, William	1	3	3		
Minsen, William	3		6		
Brewer, Peter	2	4	1		
Brewer, Joseph	3		4		2
Brewer, Mary			2		
Brewer, John	1		2		
Brewer, Henry	1	2	1		
Houke, Michael	1	7	3		
Tanner, Abram					
Wooden, Beal	1	2	2		
Miller, Jacob	1	1	1		
Raymond, Jacob	1		2		
Macky, George	1		1		
Claycomb, George	1				
Snell, Daniel	1				
Snell, George	1				
Snell, David	1				
Lighter, John	1	1	5		
Burkett, Margaret		2	2		
Miser, Adam	2	1	3		
Storm, George	2	1	2		
Slusser, Peter	2	1	3		
Yontz, Cornelius	1	2	3		
Danielson, Samuel	1	4	5		
Melone, James	1	5	5		1
Loisebaugh, Philip	1		3		
Eckle, Henry	1	3	3		
Hufman, Jacob	1	4	2		1
Hufman, Catharine			3		
Ebert, John	1		4		
Hufman, John	1	1	2		
Grove, David	1	2	5		
Wilhelm, John	2	2	4		
Griffith, Elisha	1	3	4		
Young, Nathaniel	2	3	5		
Grove, Abram	2		2		
Kepler, John	1				
Cretzer, Henry	1				
Werble, John	2	2	2		
Clayton, Daniel	2	1	2		
Hayberger, Conrad	2		3		
Fox, Michael	1	2	2		
Benner, Christian	5		2		
Patrick, William	1	4	4		
Brown, John	1	5	3		
Clumm, Jacob	1	3	5		
Walter, Jacob	1	3	6		
Catahour, Jacob	2	3	1		
Moyer, Jacob	2		4		
Moyer, Michael	1	1	2		
Becher, Peter	1	1	2		
Domar, Christian	1	3	3		
Brown, Edward	1		1		
Domar, John	1		3		
Willson, Maryan		4	4		
Bowers, Conrad	1	1	2		
Shepherd, Thomas	2	3	2		
White, Mathew	1	1	2		
Loher, Peter	2	1	1		1
McNitt, Alexander	3		1		1
Carrico, Basil	1	2	2		
Steward, James	1	2	2		
Steward, William	1	2	1		
Warland, John	1	1	2		
Darkin, Henry	1	1	1		
Bower, Jacob	1	1	4		
Bower, Adam	1	2	4		
Thompson, William	1	2	2		
Condron, James	1	1	2		
Strom, Abraham	1				
Bechtell, Martin	5	2	4		
Fonk, Joseph	3		3		
Webb, John	4	1	3		
Pecktill, Samuel	4				
Rocker, Casper	1				
Webb, William	1	3	1		
Webb, John	1	3	1		
Young, Ludwick	2		4		
Young, Jacob	2	1	4		
Huckle, John	1		3		
Wotring, Abraham	2		5		
Miller, Jacob	2		5		
Eversole, Abraham	5	5	3		
Rohrer, Christopher	2		4		
Rohrer, Christian	2	3	4		
Wolferd, Adam	2	3	4		
Shaw, Mathew	1	4	6		
Reed, John	1	3	6		
McDill, James	1	3	6		
Shepler, George	2	3	8		
Beard, Michael	2				
Nicomer, Christian	3	3	2		
Petterson, William	2	1	6		
Shaw, Jacob	2				
Shaver, Christian	1				
Welty, Jacob	1	2	4		
Acle, Magnus	1				
Hammer, Philip	4	1	6		
Rohrer, Frederick	1		4		
Shaw, John	2	2	4		
Bowman, Jacob	2				
Shalnafelt, William	2	1	3		
Bane, Philip	1	1	3		
McCormac, William	1	1	3		
Lutz, Andrew	1		3		
Tomm, George	1	3	2		
Worland, Mary	3	3	4	1	1
McNabb, John	18	3	6	2	6
Hughs, Daniel	5	2	6	6	6
Toby, John	1	1	3		
Light, Ludwick	1	1	3		
Hartle, Michael	1	1	6		
Ave, Jacob	1	1	3		
Lyda, Adam	1		3		
Hoover, Ludwick	2		3		
Hoover, Peter	2	1	2		
Prutzman, Francis	1	2	2		
Logan, Thomas	1	2	3		

WASHINGTON COUNTY—Continued.

NAME OF HEAD OF FAMILY.	Free white males of 16 years and upward, including heads of families.	Free white males under 16 years.	Free white females, including heads of families.	All other free persons.	Slaves.
Murphy, Susannah	4	1	2		
McKleseck, James	3		3		
Kyser, Michael	1	2	5		
Miller, Jacob	1		3		
Morghandoll, Frederick	2	1	2		
Eckart, Frederick	1	2	4		
Brewbaker, Jacob	1	3	2		
Bane, Martin	4	3	7		
Hoover, Jacob	1	2	3		
Myers, Ludwick	1	2	5		
Eckart, Frederick	1	2	4		
Hardline, Sam'l	1	3	2		
Oigher, Abramham	1	5	3		
Hogman, Henry	1		2		
Byerly, Michael	2	2	6		
Shainaberger, Peter	3	1	6		
Cryder, Martin	2		11		
Branstettler, Andrew	1	3	4		
Kifer, Henry	1	3	3		
Shank, Jacob	2	1	8		
Augustian, Abram	1				
Lyser, William	1		2		
Barkdoll Peter	2		3		
Coaler, George	1	1	3		
Coaler, John	1	2	4		
Kyser, Catharine	2		2		
Beard, John	2		2		
Walter, Henry	2		7		
Mung, Devalt	1	3	4		
Kiles, Markes			2		
Funk, Martin, Senr	2		2		
Funk, Martin, Jur	1		2		
Igher, Abraham	1	5	3		
Shank, Jacob	1	4	3		
Stern, Philip	1	2	3		
Haws, Adam	4	1	5		
Shank, John	1	6	3		
Niswonger, Abraham	1	4	2		
Anderson, Richard	4	3	5		
Allendel, Richard	2	3	2		
Charlton, Pointing	1	5	2		
Webb, Margaret			2		
Draper, John	1		4		
Shank, John	2	1	4		
Marshal, Rachel		2	1		
Tomm, Adam	1	3	2		
Tomm, Henry	1	3	2		
Adams, John	2	2	2		
Austin, John	2	2	2		
Shaver, Jacob	1		2		
Barger, Barbara		2	2		
Coaler, George, Jr	1	2	3		
Simms, Ignatius	1	2	3		8
Carrico, Thos. Igns	2	5	1		6
Bricker, Ludwick	1	4	4		
Conrod, Daniel	4		3		
Rensh, Peter	3	3	1		1
Weaver, Daniel	1	3	3		
Miller, John Hen	2		2		
Lance, Christian	1	3	2		
Essington, John	1	1			
Ford, Henry	3		4		
Lowderbergs, John	1	3	2		
Bell, Anthony	3	4	3		
Werner, George	1	1	4		
Dowler, John	3	4	4		
Parker, Alexander	1		2		
Coon, Henry			2		
Augustian, George	5	2	4		
Backten, Peter	1	5	4		
Coaler, John	1	2	3		
Huffman, Elias	1		1		
Hoover, Henry	1		1		
Hoover, John	2	1	3		
Fuget, Peter	1	2	2		1
Fulton, James	1	2	7		
Augustian, George	1	5	6		
Fuget, John	1	5			
Shaver, Jacob	1		2		
Shaver, John	2	1	4		
Stoner, John	1	2	2		
Floney, John	3	2	4		
Darby, Henry	2		3		
Stonaker, Catharine		2	2		
Smith, Henry	1		3		
Hoover, Adam	1		2		
Ridenour, George	1	3	4		
Ridenour, Henry	1		2		
Young, George	1	1	3		
Ridenour, Martin	1	2	3		
Shaver, Nicholas	1	1	3		
Ridenour, Jacob	1	1	3		
Baringer, Adam	1	2	2		
Prince, Henry	1	1	1		
Walleck, George	1	3	5		
Bowman, Benedict	1	3	9		
Baringer, Catharine		3	3		

NAME OF HEAD OF FAMILY.	Free white males of 16 years and upward, including heads of families.	Free white males under 16 years.	Free white females, including heads of families.	All other free persons.	Slaves.
Trestler, Goodhart	1	3	4		
Widdus, Isaac	2	2	7		
Coon, Jacob	1	2	4		
Lanehart, Peter	1	2	4		
Steffy, Leonard	1	4	3		
Piper, John	1		3		
Wolfe, Jacob	3	3	5		
Wolfe, Michael	1	1	1		
Crow, Jacob	1	4	1		
Weaver, John	1	1	3		
Callaflower, Michael	1	2	2		
Callaflower, George	1	2	2		
Hewet, Ludwick	3	2	4		
Snyder, Henry	2	1	3		4
Callaflower, George	1	2	4		
Reynull, Daniel	1		4		
Reynull, Peter	1	2	3		
Cassing, Richard	9	3	4		
Hopkins, Catharine			1		
Holt, Thomas	1	2	2		
Bailey, Thomas	1	1	1		
McClasking, John	1		2		
Mason, William	1	4	2		
Rook, John	1	4	3		
Field, Jacob	1	2	1		
Rankin, Alexander	1	1	1		
Miller, Charles	1	5	3		
Gray, Peter	1	2	5		
Hays, John	2	3	5		
Rankin, Leonard	1	1	1		
James, George	1	1	1		
Morrison, Alexander	2	5	3		
Sabert, Jacob	1	1	1		
Corbert, John	1	1	1		
Steece, Zachariah	2	1	6		
Shultz, Martin	3		5		
Funk, Samuel	1	2	4		
Gray, Samuel	2		2		
Mung, George Nich^s	1		2		
Mung, Adam	1	3	1		
Mung, Jacob	1	2	1		
Renner, Peter	1	3	4		
Walter, Abraham	1	1	1		
Williams, James	2	3	3		
Grover, Christian			7		
Jaxson, John	2	5	5		7
Knode, Conrad	2	2	4		
Nikesk, Michael	1	1	1		
Piper, John	1	1	2		
Cheney, Daniel	1	1	2		
Hullinger, Jacob	1	3	2		
Carlisle, James	1	5	3		
Bare, Jacob	1	3	2		
Shaver, Conrad	2	1	2		
Lape, John	1	1	3		
Pinkley, John	1	1	1		
Woodenberger, Jacob	2	1	6		
Shaver, Jacob	2		4		
Thompson, John	2	2	3		2
Middleton, Hugh	1	5	3		
Henning, Thomas	1				
Danielson, Rachel		2	2		
Hannah, William	2	2	5		
Hannah, Samuel	1		2		
Gallaba, John	1	2	2		
McCoy, James	1	2	3		
Stover, Jacob	2	2	3		
Tomm, George	1	4	3		
Young, Adam	1				
Rutter, Edward	2	6	2		
Lonanacre, Peter	2	1	2		
Daislow, Paul	2	1	2		
Statler, Peter	2	2	2		
Statler, Henry	1	1	1		
Lackey, Benson	1	3	2		
Lane, John	1	1	4		
Logan, Patrick	1	1	2		
Mucklewsser, David	1	1	3		
Shanon, Peter	1	1	1		
Chaney, William	1	1	1		1
Lewis, Robert	1	1	2		
Chaney, Jeremiah	3	2	3		4
Shifler, Nicholas	2	2	5		
Bare, Isaac	3		2		
Betser, Anthony	1	1	4		
Sidener, Christopher	1	4	2		
Shauns, Nicholas	1		2		
Price, John	3	4	3		
Gallaher, John	1	1	1		
Lockerman, Paul	1		1		
McCoy, Archibald	1	2	2		2
Roland, Jacob	1		4		
Myer, Henry	2	1	4		
Winder, Thomas	2	2	4		
Van Pool, Henry	2	1	5		
Frish, Michael	1	5	2		
Stover, Michael	1	1	5		

NAME OF HEAD OF FAMILY.	Free white males of 16 years and upward, including heads of families.	Free white males under 16 years.	Free white females, including heads of families.	All other free persons.	Slaves.
Klinger, Henry	3		1		
Edelen, George	1	1	3		5
Cramer, Ebbert	1		1		
Shillar, William	1	1	6		
Lackland, Aaron	1	1	5		1
Hammond, Nolly	1		1		
Jams, Richard	1	5	2		
Stambagh, Philip	1	1	2		
Miller, Joseph	3	1	4		
Burn, Henry	1	1	2		
Burn, Ernst	1	2	1		
Bizler, Abram	1		3		
Fry, George	2		2		
Smurr, John	2	1	2		
Heck, Peter	1	2	2		
Melott, Thedoros	1	1	2		1
Legget, George	3	2	2		
Gregory, James	1	3	6		
Nave, Jacob	3		4		
Kershner, George	3	1	4		
Sybot, John	1		4		
Garehart, Idle	1	1	3		
George, John	1		5		
Eads, James	2	3			
Eads, Johnathan	2		3		
Fenel, James	2		3		
Eads, Henry	1	1	5		
Bugher, Ann			1		
Wolfe, John	2	4	1		
Hoover, Adam	3	4	3		
Stare, Frederick	2		7		
Magraw, William	2		1		
Wile, William	2	3	2		
Kesler, Mathias	2	2	2		
Wile, Jacob	1		2		
Stull, John	1	2	3		10
Hunter, George	1		1		
Stonebraker, Adam	1	4	3		
Fell, George	2		3		
Bowler, Susannah	2	3	4		6
Quantrill, Prettyman	2	1			
Baker, Douglass	1		1		
Alley, Isaac			3		
Yakely, Henry	1		1		
Heeslberger, John	2	2	4		
Odefler, John	1		1		
Henry, Peter	3	2	2		
Angle, Henry	2		2		
Myer, Jacob	1	1	1		
Klien, Henry	1	3			
Mullwitz, Henry	1	1	3		
Baringer, Laurenue	2		4		
Full, Peter	2	1	1		
Full, John	1				
Sybert, Jacob	3	3	4		
Crechner, Devalt			1		
Knabeler, George	2	2	2		
Cushwan, John	3		4		
Pottorff, Simon	1	2	2		
Swigart, Peter	2	4			
Fierl, Henry	1				
Lower, George	2	2	1		
Shaver, George	2		1	1	5
Bovey, Christian	1		1		
Kingry, John	1	4	3		
Crouse, John	2	2	2		
Morris, John	1		1		
Long, John	1	1	4	1	
Long, John	1	2	5		
Willson, William	1	2	5		
Wetsley, John	1	3	5		
Fice, Henry	2	4	4		
Schnavely, John	2		9		
Hershbagh, Martin	1	5	1		
Baker, Margaret			2		
Clagett, Mary	1	1	2		
Welty, Jacob	1	1	3		
Hause, Peter	1	1	7		
Ridenour, Henry	1	4	1		
Snell, Henry	1	1			
Eckabeger, Valentine	2	1			
Darr, Jacob	2	2	3		1
Hogmine, Conrad	2	3	4		
Ridenour, George	1	3	3		
Smith, David	2	3	2		
Alley, Abraham	1				
Calor, Jacob	1				
Nikerk, John	1		1		
Boyer, Abraham	3	1	4		
Pence, Henry	2		1		
Bowman, Henry	2		4		
Arehart, Philip	1				
Adams, George	2	2	4		
Bowslow, Peter	2	1	4		
Klien, Peter	2		3		
Werterbeger, John	1		2		
McCoy, Joseph	1		2		

WASHINGTON COUNTY—Continued.

NAME OF HEAD OF FAMILY.	Free white males of 16 years and upward, including heads of families.	Free white males under 16 years.	Free white females, including heads of families.	All other free persons.	Slaves.
Harding, Michael	1				
McCoy, Martha			2		
Beord, William	2	2	1		
McCoy, John	2	2	2		
Ford, William	2	2	1		
Eller, Joseph	2	1	7		
Eller, Henry	1	1	4		
McCoy, Patrick	2	2	2		
Clarke, Jacob	2		1		
Walling, James	1	1	1		9
Forker, Robert	2	2	5		
Simkins, William	1	2	3		
Bostetter, Jacob	2	1	2		
Coltgiesser, Henry	1	1	2		
Myer, George	3	3	5		
Pronk, Christian	2	1	3		
Bowslow, Peter	1	1	4		
Shank, Christian	1		4		
Boyd, Walter	1	2	2		
Price, Benjamin	1		4		
Miller, Daniel	2	1	3		
Babel, Christian	2		3		
Flummer, Jacob	1	2	4		
Gabriel, Jacob	2	3	4		
Miller, Peter	2	2	2		1
Miller, John	1		1		
Darby, Benjamin		1	2		1
Light, Benjamin	1	1	2		
Miller, Jacob	1		3		
Smith, Christian	2	4	3		
Layburn, John	1	1	2		
Kessler, John	1	2	3		
Barnet, John	1	3	4		2
Kempler, Michael	1	1	1		
Teach, Mathias	1	1	3		
Piper, Leonard	1	1	1		
Egleberger, Conrad	3		4		
Mower, Nicholas	2	4	5		
King, Elenor	3		5		
Bennet, Caleb		2	1		
Shank, Christian	2	3	1		
Burchart, John	1		4		
Tice, Andrew	1	2	1		
Linkswiler, Nicholas	2	2	3		
Holland, Jacob	1	3	2		
Hoy, Paul	2	1	3		18
Kershman, George	2	1	8		
Bowman, John	1		2		
Bowman, Daniel	2	1	3		
Bowlanch, John	1		1		
Steward, John	2	1	3		
McClarey, Patrick	1	1	3		
Dill, Henry	2	3	5		
Kindell, Casper	2	3	3		
Ridenour, Nicholas	1	2	4		
Anderson, Thomas	1		2		
Ridenour, Henry	1	2	2		
Rutter, William	1	2	2		
Hoover, Peter	1	2	2		
McCalep, Henry	1	3	4		
Carr, Sarah	1	2	2		
Bower, Peter	1	1	1		
Dugan, Jeremiah	1	1	4		
Miller, John	1	2	4		
Medler, Bostian	2		1		
Ash, Abram	1	1	3		
Shults, Jacob	1	2	2		
Garlock, Adam	1	2	2		1
Garlock, Henry	1		1		
Rutter, Elizabeth			1		
Rodes, John	2		3		6
Cramer, Codfry	2		3		
Rush, John	1		4		
Householder, Jacob	1	3	2		
Swingly, Barbara	1		2		
Widener, Michael	1	1	1		
Young, Mary			1		
Snyder, John	4	2	7		11
Dorsett, John	1		2		
Bugh, George	1	3	2		
Dorsett, John	1	1	2		1
Sprigg, Thomas	5	2	3		44
Saloier, Peter	1	1	3		
Muckleroy, Thomas	3		1		
Carr, John	1	2	5		9
Tenny, Patrick	1	1	1		
Ablehart, Conrad	1	1	2		
Belt, Thomas	1		1		17
Connelly, Joseph	1	1	4		
Deamot, John	1	2	4		
Clapper, Henry	4	1	2		
Sprigg, Joseph	1		1		3
King, Henry	1	2	3		9
Parker, Archibald	4		8		
Brice, Robert	1		1		
Jicha, William	2	1	3		
Bower, John Adam	2	1	4		

NAME OF HEAD OF FAMILY.	Free white males of 16 years and upward, including heads of families.	Free white males under 16 years.	Free white females, including heads of families.	All other free persons.	Slaves.
Ridonour, Mathias	1	2	4		
Startzman, Peter	1	2	4		
Miller, Henry	1		4		
Moringer, Henry	3	3	4		
Hedrick, John	3	2	4		
Hedrick, Henry	1	1	1		
Nash, Joseph	1	1	1		
Startzman, Henry	4	2	5		
Colestock, Christian	1	1	2		
Walling, Delasmet	2		6		
Gates, John	2		2		
James, Thomas	1	2	4		
Fennessig, Joseph	1		2		
Musgrove, John	1		1		
Williams, Richard	1	2	1		
Dunwoody, David	1	1	2		2
Downey, Jane			2		
Tarr, Jacob	1	3	3		
Brumbagh, John	1		4		
Brumbagh, Jacob	1	4	2		
Hufman, John	1				
Wolfe, John	1				
Needler, Conrad	1				
Dillion, William	1	1	2		
Cammercer, Ludwick	3		2		
McNicil, Samuel	1				
Schnavely, John	2	5	2		4
Beel, Frederick	1	1	2		
Summer, Henry	1		2		
Harter, Conrad	1	1	2		
Ritter, Jacob	2		2		
Ritter, Tobias	1	1	3		
Ripple, Philip	2	2	3		
Harter, Christian	1	4	6		
Ziegler, Jacob	1	3	5		
Smith, George	4	2	4		
Legrone, Jacob	3	2	6		
Harter, George	1		1		
Harter, Jacob	1	1	1		
Cow, Frederick	1		4		
Copiar, Abram	1	1	4		
Albright, Peter	1	2	4		
Hurly, Moses	1	1	2		
Downey, John	2	2	1		8
Gordon, Sarah	1		4		
Rogers, John	2	3	2		
Baghtill, Samuel	6	2	4		
McMullun, John	1				
Fumbauk, John	1				
Strum, Michael	2		2		
Young, Adam	1	1	3		
Smith, Adam	1	4	2		
Arnold, Conrad	1				
Travinger, Christian	1	4	4		
Craft, Peter	1	4	3		
Marker, Michael	1	6	4		
Middlecalf, John	2	3	1		
Highberger, John	1		2		
Dolphit, Elsy			2		
Myers, John	2	1	3		
Bean, Joshia	1	2	4		
Wade, John	1	2	5		
Hufman, Philip	1		4		
Leary, Edward	1		1		
Needler, Conrad	1				
Werner, Paul	2	4	4		
Wiseman, Robert	1	2	4		6
Curtis, Garret	1		2		
Bean, George	1	2	2		
Fisher, Fendell	1				
Wicks, John	2	2	6		
Baker, Henry	2	2	5		
Hager, John	1	2	2		
Trosile, Mottiena	1		2		
Roudebush, Mary			2		
Gull, John	1	1	3		
Hufman, Henry	1	2	2		
Schnablely, Leonard	1	1	1		
Long, John	1	1	4		
Klien, Peter	2		2		
Stonehill, Conrad	1		3		
Whiteman, Christian	1	1	2		
Swartz, Samuel					
Fenwick, Richard	2		2		1
Becktill, Martin	2	4	4		
Pine, James	1	3	3		
Peller, John	1	1	2		
Grill, John	1	2	5		
Adams, John, Senr	1		3		
Adams, John, Jur	1	4	3		
Winebruner, Christian	1	1	3		
Flenner, Rudolp	2	2	6		
Miller, John, Jur	2	5	2		
Miller, Daniel	1		1		
Fisher, John	2	3	1		
Chapline, Joseph	1				
Cillars, Jacob, Senr	1		2		1

NAME OF HEAD OF FAMILY.	Free white males of 16 years and upward, including heads of families.	Free white males under 16 years.	Free white females, including heads of families.	All other free persons.	Slaves.
Cillars, Jacob, Jur	1		2		1
Wolgamot, Mary	1	1	3		6
Long, David	1		1		
Tice, Peter	2		1		
Willson, Elenor	1		1		
Cramor, Ernest	1		1		
Lonabagh, Elizabeth	1	1	2		
Hetler, Bostian	1	2	3		
Flemming, Margaret				1	
Winders, Isaac	1		1		
Winders, John	1	1	3		4
Hunter, George	1		2		
Sybet, Nentle	1	4	2		
Conrad, Catharine			3		
Worley, William	2	2	3		1
Rinehart, Frederick	1	1	2		
Kissinger, George	2	4	2		
Worner, Jacob	1	2	5		
Carey, Ann	2	3	3		
Lighter, Peter	1	2	3		
Waisamon, John	1	2	4		
Steer, Nicholas	1	2	4		
Lighter, Jacob	3	4	4		
Spader, Jacob	1	1	3		
Fink, William	1	1	4		
Snell, Henry	1	1	3		
Crist, George	2		4		
Keeper, Martin	1	3	4		
Lowman, Martin	1	3	6		
Fogler, Simon	2		3		
Gabby, John	4		3		
Jacob, George	1		3		
Spitsnoggie, Leonard	1	4	3		
Peter, Henry	1	1	3		
Orenbaum, Ludwick	1	3	1		
Lance, George	4	1	3		
Lance, Christian	1				
Lance, Elizabeth			2		
Rice, John	1	2	2		
Cooncie, John	1	3	2		
Long, Joseph	3	1	2		
Nimond, David	1	5	4		
Bean, Benjamin	1	2	2		
Miller, Maunus	1	2	2		
Thompson, James	1				
Beel, Elizabeth		2			
Look, Peter	1	3	3		
Murphy, John	1	3			
Middlecalf, Leonard	1		2		
Grove, Philip	1	1	2		
Lesler, Thomas	3	2	6		
Edmonson, Nathan	2	1	1		1
Middlecalf, Jacob	2	1	2		
Shuff, Johnathan	1		2		
Shuff, Jacob	1	3	4		
Baker, Morris	3	1	2		
Thompson, William	1	3	5		
Eversole, Christian	2	1	5		4
Baker, Henry	1		2		
Clovus, John	1	3	4		
Acle, Peter	4		3		
Aivey, Joseph	3		4		
Cary, George	3		1		1
Smith, Adam	1	1	2		
Langly, John	1	1	2		
Carter, Francis	3	1	2		6
Sigh, Jacob	1	1	2		
Scoffie, John	1		2		
Geogohagen, Abrose	1	3	2		7
Roland, John	1	3	6		
Cunningham, Henry	2	1	5		
Haines, John	2	3	5		
Smith, Robert	2		1		8
Aicle, Henry	1	1	3		
Aicle, Henry, Jur	1	1	2		
Baker, Parker	1	3	3		
Yunters, Daniel	2	1	2		
Motes, Margaret	1		2		
Gaaff, John	1	2	2		
Hammore, Peter	1	1	2		
Panfenberger, John	1		1		
Panfenberger, Christian	1		1		
Runnalds, Elizabeth			1		
Pence, Jacob	1	2	8		
Runnalds, Joseph	1	5	2		3
Shepler, John	1	2	3		
Knode, John	4	1	1		
Clefford, Ernst	1		2		
Mound, William	1		2		
Harper, Moses	1	3	3		
Clarke, William	3	5	3		
McCoy, James	1	2	2		
Wade, Augustine	1	2	2		
McCoy, Thomas	1	3	2		
Davis, Joseph	3	4	3		2
Davis, Dennis	1	1	2		1
Dalley, Catharine			1		

WASHINGTON COUNTY—Continued.

NAME OF HEAD OF FAMILY.	Free white males of 16 years and upward, including heads of families.	Free white males under 16 years.	Free white females, including heads of families.	All other free persons.	Slaves.
Demude, Abraham	1	1	3		
Ground, Philip	1	3	2		
Panfenberger, John	1	2	1		
Bowers, Moddiena			2		
Magraw, Martin	1	4	3		
Biagis, Richard	1	3	2	4	
Clarke, Ralph	1	2	4		
Shull, George	1		1		
Hymer, John	5		3		
Dorsey, Elie	2	1	4	1	
Panfenberger Samuel	1	1	4		
Lefter, Jacob	2	1	7		
Barnes, John	5				75
Prather, Samuel	4	1	4		6
Miller, Philip	1	2	3		
Fible, Frederick	5	2	4		
Depanee, Jacob	1	3	3		
Swartz, Christian	1	2	4		
Tanner, Abraham	2	4	4		
Myer, John	1	1	3		
Creps, Ludwick	1	2	5		
Smith, William	1	1	4		
Kreps, John	1		2		
Sword, George	2	7	3		
Swope, Peter	1		6	1	
Brown, Susannah			1		
Flancher, Adam	1	6	4		
Snyder, Jacob	2	4	4		
Pottorf, Andrew	2	1	1		
Bean, William	2	1	5		
Hilton, Thomas	3	5	4		
McKernen, Michael	3		1	1	
Anconi, John	1	1	5		
Begold, William	1	6	5		
Fien, Joseph	3	1	4		
Spech, Martin	1	2	4		
Anconi, Henry	4	2	3		
Jams, William	1	4	4	7	
Tallman, John	1	4	3		
Shaver, John	1	2	5		
Snyder, Johnathan	4	2	2		
James, Johnathan	1	3	3		
Smelser, Albrech	1	1	2		
Shaver, Peter	1	3	2		
Fry, John	1		3		
Tropp, Jacob	2	2	3		
Ayten, Henry	2	1	4		13
Fayler, Frederick	1	1	1		
Clarke, Robin	1	1	4	2	
Young, George	1	3	1		
Halter, Ludwick	1		4		
Carrol, Peter	3	5	6		
Prufslen, Henry	1	1	5		
Vanpool, Jacob	1	1	3		
Ecker, Christian	1	2	3		
Ond, John	1	2	4		
Hoover, Adam	1	6	4		
Rafesnyder, Andrew	1	1	6		
Hoover, David	1	2	2		
Rohrer, Martin	2		6		
Kern, Nicholas	1	1	2		
Holland, John	1		2		
Sailor, Peter	1	1	7		
Erech, Jacob	1	3	3		
Wile, John	1	2	3		
Yost, George	1		2		
Shainafelt, Jacob	1		6		
Wile, George	2	2	2		
Yost, Arnold	1	1	1		
Myers, John	1		2		
Bond, Charles	1				
Hammell, John	1	4	3		
Hiesone, Adam	5	1	5		
Coonce, Daniel	1	5	4		
Smith, John	1	3	4		
Slice, Peter	1		3		
Hiesen, Peter	1	2	1		
Bard, Nicholas	4		4		
Orewalt, Philip	1	3	3		
Wattson, Mary	1	2	1		
Row, John	1		2		
Helserode, Francis	1	1	2		
Domar, Ludwick	2		2		
Zimmermon, Henry	1	1	2		
Loudumon, Peter	1	2	6		
Martin, Jacob	1		1		
Creager, John	1				
M°Coy, John	1		1		
Young, Philip	1				
Shryver, John	1	4	5		
Lower, Mathias	1	1	2		
Artle, Frederick	1	2	9		
Metz, Jacob	1	3	4		
Cow, Devalt	1	3	1		
Hartle, Margaret			1		
Lutz, Jacob	1		2		
Motz, Jacob	5	2	6		
Shank, Catharine			2		
Kyder, Martin	2		1		
Handy, Samuel	1	3	2		
Byorly, Michael	2	2	5		
Sullum, Henry	1		3		
Bennerd, Peter	1	3	4		
Carver, Christopher	1	5	7		
Bennerd, Henry	2	4	1		
Frederick, Adam	1	4	2		
Fox, Michael	1		2		
Tipp, Henry	2		1		
Burchart, John	1		3		
Burchart, Christian	1	1	1		1
Snyder, John	1	1	1		
Burchart, Christian, Ser	1		2		2
Bell, Frederick	1		1		
Burchart, George	1	2	4		
Sheeze, Peter	1	1	6		
Wolfe, John	1				
Hardway, George	1	3	4		
Hufmer, John	2	3	5		
Shiwer, Henry	1		2		
Witeseli, Peter	1	4	5		
Keefer, Frederick	1	1	2		
Shiwer, Henry	1	1	3		
Ridenour, Mathias	4	1	4		
Oster, Conrad	1	2	1		
Ridenour, Henry	3	1	3		
Fasnach, John	1		2		
Baker, Peter	4	1	4		
Hartsock, Daniel	1		1		
Etenine, Daniel	2	1	2		
Barkman, Frederick	2	2	3		
Wise, Valentine	1	1	7		
Bugh, Michael	1		2		
Brentner, John	1	1	2		
Aulabaugh, John	1	1	2		
Wrist, Leonard	1		2		
Wentlinger, Peter	3	2	5		
Summer, John	1	2	3		
Bennet, Quili	1		2		
Ailabaugh, Ann		2	3		
Domar, Michael	2	3	4		
Bash, Andrew	2	2	7		
Kessinger, Jacob	1	1	4		
Worner, George	1		1		
Garman, Abraham	1		2		
Crutz, Christopher	2		4		
Hogg, John	1		3		
Henderson, Patrick	1	1	1		
Morgan, William	1		6		
Re, Jesse					
Coymets, William	1		4		
Boyer, Philip	1	1	3		
Deneas, William	1	1	2		
Deneas, Valentine	1	1	1		1
Culp, Michael	1		2		
Frum, David	2		4		
Brentner, George	2	1	1		
Lantz, Jacob	2	4	3		
Mineck, Mary	1		2		
Frummer, Barnet	2		1		
Thumb, Conrad	1	2	2		
Shower, George	1	4	2		
Stockman, Martin	1	1	2		
Swope, Nicholas	1				
Worner, John	1				
Lose, William			2		
Grim, Andrew, Ser	3		1		
Grim, Daniel	1	2	5		
Bower, George	1	1	2		
Grim, Andrew, Jr	1	3	4		
Clapper, John	2	3	4		
Kepler, Adam	2	3	4		
Grim, Martin	1	3	1		
Houser, Jacob	1		2		
Rechter, Jacob	1	2	4		
Keefer, Philip	2	4	1		
Rohrer, Frederick	2	4	4		
Rohrer, Jacob	1	1	4		
Long, John	1	1	3		
Miller, John	1		3		
Bower, Francis	1				
Reel, Michael	1				
Pecker, Michael	1		2		
Lyders, George	1				
Rohrer, John	1	1	3		
Bower, Conrad	2		7		
Bower, Barnet	1		1		
Wiand, Christian	1	2	3		
Smith, Yost	1	2	7		
Mikesell, John	1	4	3		
Tobey, Catrout	2	1	5		
Baker, Tillman	1		2		
Shilt, Mathias	1	2	2		
Funy, David	1	1	6		
Higgins, Robert	1	2	3		
Schnavely, Casper	2	2	3		
Bane, Christopher	2		1		
Snyder, Peter	2	4	6		
Rice, John	2	2	1		
Panfenberger, Jacob	1	1			
Ziegier, Jacob	5		2		
Brener, Joseph	2	1	4		
Vanlear, Mathew	3		3	1	4
Boyd, William	1	2	6		
Shymer, John	2	2	3	1	1
Rentch, Jacob	1		3	1	2
Beall, William	3	3	3		
Brewan, Henry	3	1	1		
Binkley, Christian	3	1	1		
Tootwiler, Isaac	1				1
Maciefish, Thomas	2	3	3		2
Faig, George	2		4	2	
Hogmire, Jonas	1	2	2		2
Steffy, Andrew	4	2	3		
Cromwell, Richard	3	5	2		13
Petticoat, Hannah	3		2		
Westerberger, Francis	2	1	3		
Shaver, Abraham	1	2	2		
McCollum, Thomas	1		2		
Kitsminger, Adam	1	7	2		
Clutt, Isaac	1	1	3		
Beard, Andrew	1		2		
Kershner, Jacob	2	2	3		
Cassell, Peter	2	1	2		
Gray, Peter	1	2	5		
Stout, George	1		1		
Baker, Peter	3	2	4		
Bovey, Michael	2	2	4		
Calor, John	1		2		
Fyher, John	2		2		
Niswanger, Catharine	2	3	5		
Flenner, John	2	3	3		
Householder, George	2	4	5		
Sheetz, Jacob	2	1	3		
Ruie, George	1	4	2		
Frentch, Peter	1	2	2	1	1
Hughs, Kinsey	1		2		
Bond, John	1	6	1		
Goodwin, William	1	1	4		
M°Donald, Angus	2		4		
Gwinn, Donald	1	1	2		
Glasier, David	1				
Oar, George			1		
Shipten, John	1	2	3		
Sweney, Mary		2	1		
Funk, Martin	1		4		
Funk, Margaret	1		1		
Funk, Henry	1	3	2		
M°Coy, Poregrime	2	2	2		
Igieberger, Philip, Jr	1	2	1		
Igieberger, Philip, Snr	1		3		
Seaber, Jacob	1			1	
Myer, Samuel	2		4		
Dereling, John	2	3	3		
Crestian, Daniel	1	1			
Conrad, Daniel	4	2	5		
Lape, John	1		1		
Rinehart	1		1		
Anderson, Alexander	1				
White, Margaret	3		4		4
Holt, Sampson	1				
Resly, George	2	2	3		
Froxill, David	1		1		
Crenk, Jacob	1		2		
Howard, Anthony	1	2	2		
Keishner, Martin	2	2	6		2
Highland, Hugh	2	3	2		3
Johnson, Amelia			2		
Vanlear, John	1		2		
Beckwith, William	2	1	1		1
Steuet, James	2	2			
Banon, Joseph	1				
Runtchy, Eddy	1		2		
Beall, Samuel	1				
Tucker, Mary			5		
Porter, Samuel	2	2	2		2
Hogg, John	3	1	5		1
Davis, Amos	1	1	2		
Rator, Marten	2		7		
Steck, George	1				
Moier, Jacob	2		3		
Syster, Henry	2		3		
Clinger, Henry	1				
Vanlear, William	3	2	3		1
Wysel, Daniel	1	1			
Dillinger, Frederick	1	4	2		
Garvin, Hugh	1				
Snyder, Andrew	2	3	2		
Stark, Lawrence	1	1	2		

WASHINGTON COUNTY—Continued.

NAME OF HEAD OF FAMILY.	Free white males of 16 years and upward, including heads of families.	Free white males under 16 years.	Free white females, including heads of families.	All other free persons.	Slaves.
Funesser, Henry	1	1	1		
Seelars, David	2		2		
McCartney, Robert	2		5		
Steck, John	3	4	3		
Steffy, Philip	1	2	4		
Hain, Burchart	2				
Perrin, Robert	1				
Martin, James	1	3	4		
Orbison, John	1	5	2		1
Ainsminger, Christian	1	3	4		
Brookes, Charles	1	1	1		
Harrisen, Samuel	2	1	2		2
Roubush, John	1	1	3		
Crotzer, Abraham	1		2		
Peter, Jacob	2		1		
Steel, Timothy	1		1		
Davis, Richard	1	2	7		
Dull, Henry	1	3			
Hess, Peter	1	3	1		
Protius, Jacob	1	4	1		
Henry, James	1	1	2		
Hardman, Conrad	1	1	2		
Keeding, Adam	1	3	3		
Brown, Conrad	1	5	2		
Ridenour, Martin	2	3	6		
Morgan, William	1	3			
Sneckaberger, John	1		2		
Sneckaberger, Christian	1		1		
Rhodes, John	1	3	4		
Kershner, George	4	3	4		
Santers, John	1		3		
Aledridge, Joseph	1		2		
Chambers, Fobert	2	4	2		
Fouts, Peter	1		2		
Stemple, Godfrit	1	2	8		
Fisher, Essell	1		1		
Householder, Michael	1	4	1		
Swiler, Peter	1	1	4		
Baker, Nicholas	1				
Rigginbaugh, Martin	1		1		
Hughen, Daniel	1				
Kieth, George	4		4		9
Winebruner, Jacob	1	2	3		
Ridenour, Jacob	2	4	4		
Hawn, John	1	4	3		
Buckler, Edward	1		2		
Calor, Andrew	1	2	2		
Buckly, William	2	2	2		
Waggoner, Fredinand	1		1		
Zimmermon, Abraham	1		2		
Heskins, Richard	1	1	4		
Buttonsbell, John	1		2		
Thompson, William	2	1	2		
Condron, James	1	1	2		
Fisher, Thomas	1	1	2		
Howard, John	2		3		
Homer, Jacob	1	1	2		
Homer, Conrad	1	2	2		
Roby, John	1	1	4		
Hornbaker, John	2	1	4		
Barnes, Abel	2	1	4		1
Howard, John	2		3		
Mahony, Henry	2	1	5		
Hucle, John	1	2	2		
Nucen, John	2	2	4		
Beck, Daniel	2	3	2		
Berry, Basil	2	1	5		
Hoss, Christian	1	2	1		
Nave, Leonard	1	1	4		
Silver, Steffy	1		2		
Brett, Henry	1		1	2	
Tomm, Adam	1	3	4		
Mock, Rinehart	1				
Perry, William	1	1	2	1	
Young, Adam	1	1			
Maclefish, Richard	2	1	1		
Gyer, Henry	1	4	3		
Nave, Jacob	2				
Thompson, Jacob	1		3		
Robinson, Charles	1		3		1
Flinn, Alexander	1		4		
Oneal, John	1		1		
Shupe, Adam	4				
Aivey, Christian	1	2	3		
Stover, Mathias	1	4	4		
Aivey, Henry	2	2	3		
Widener, John	1				
Hoover, John	1	1	2		
Fasnach, Jacob	1	2	2		
Price, Amond	1	1	2		
Aivey, Elizabeth			2		
Ingram, John	1				4
Barnhard, John	3	2	3		
Henning, John	1		2		
Stover, Jacob	1	1	1		
Ockamon, Paul	1		2		
Obrian, Daniel	1		1		
McKinseg, Alexander	1				
Stonebraker, Garrest	3	4	3		
Wait, Samuel	1		1		
Streck, John	1	1	5		
Taylor, Ignatius	2	1	7		54
Clapper, Henry	2	2	2		
Hays, Lovin	1	2	4		4
Williams, Elie	2	3	4		7
Snyder, Jacob	2	3	5		
Server, Michael	1	1	6		

WORCESTER COUNTY.

NAME OF HEAD OF FAMILY.	Free white males of 16 years and upward, including heads of families.	Free white males under 16 years.	Free white females, including heads of families.	All other free persons.	Slaves.
Aydolet, Benjamin	1	1	1		8
Aydolet, William	1	2	3		6
Adams, Ann				2	
Ball, Levi	2	3	4		4
Boston, Isaac	2	2	2	2	4
Boston, Esaw	2	4	4		9
Brittingham, John	2		5		3
Benson, Billy	1	3	1		3
Buntin, E.	1	1	2		1
Buchanan, John	1	4	5		11
Burnitt, Elijah	1		5		3
Dreadon, Noble	2		5		
Drummond, L.				2	
Davis, Major	1	3	1		
Dickerson, James	2		1		
Dickerson, Elizabeth	2	1	3		
Davis, Wm	1	3	3		
Ellis, Wm	1	3	4		
Gillett, Ayers	1	2	1	1	8
Henderson, Daniel	1	1	6		
Hill, Babel	1	5	3		
Houston, Joseph	3	2	4		7
Henderson, Samuel	1	1	2	1	
Harris, Thomas	1				5
Handy, Col Samuel	2	2	10		35
Handy, Wm					55
Johnson, John	1		2		
Jones, Elisha	2	1	5	5	1
Long, Jesse	1	1	3		3
Lane, Wm	1		2	9	
Layfield, Isaac	2	1	5		14
Mills, Wm	2		8		9
Mills, Hugh	1		5		6
McMasters, The Revd Saml	2	3	2		8
Merrill, Thomas	1		4	1	7
Mills, Samuel	2	2	4		1
Marshall, John	2		4	12	
Mills, John	1	3	2	1	3
Nelson, Hugh	1				
Pallison, Andrew	1	2	1		4
Powell, Samuel	2		3		
Pallison, Sarah	2	1	3		13
Stevenson, Jonathan	3	4	5	2	3
Selby, James, Esqr	1	1	4		16
Smith, James	2	2	3		
Schoolfield, Joseph	3	2	2		3
Schoolfield, Joseph, Junr	2		3		
Smith, Samuel	1	1	6		
Stevenson, Joseph	1		2		
Taylor, Littleton	1	2	6		
Tull, James	1	2	6		
Townsend, Elijah	1	3	5		1
Benson, Elijah	1	2	3		3
Long, Littleton	1	2	4		7
Vardin, James	2	1	4		
Wheeler, Zadok	2	1	4		7
White, Stephen	2	1	2	1	
Whittington, Esther	1		5		10
Young, Daniel, Junr	1	1			
Bradshaw, Morgan	1	2	2		4
Aydolet, Benjn, of Wm	2		4		1
Aydolet, James	1	1	2		1
Allen, Stephen	2	3	4		4
Burnitt, James, Senr	2	3	4		5
Burch, George	1		3		
Ball, Samuel	1		2		
Broadwater, Joshua	2	1	2		
Conner, James	2		1		
Tarr, Jno	1		2		
Challie, John	2	2	2		2
Duse, Joshua	2	2	2		1
Dorman, Nehemiah	2	4	3		2
Dukes, Parker	2	2	4		
Delistatius, Joseph	1	2	2		5
Fountain, Samuel	1	5	3		2
Gutthny, Wm, Junr	1	2	2		3
Gunby, Cole John	1	2	3	1	13
Graves, Sarah	1	1	3		
Hudson, Sabin	1	2	4		
Hammond, Wm	1	2	3		1
Hill, Levin	3	1	3		8
Hopkins, Samuel	1	1	3		1
Hopkins, James	1		4		2
Harper, Samuel Adams	1	4	2		2
Holland, Maj William	2		5	10	
Johnson, John, of Leond	1	5	3		2
Johnson, McCajah	1		3		1
Lindsey, James	2		4		6
Melson, Jonathan	1	3	4		
Marrett, John	2	1	4		
Merrill, Levi	1		2		
Mifflin, Jonathan				4	
Merrill, Elijah	1	1	2		6
Milbourn, Wm	1	1	2		2
Milbourn, John	1		2		4
Milbourn, Thomas	1	3	2		
Nelson, Moses	4		4		
Newton, Levin	1		5	1	6
Newton, Selby	1		4		6
America, George				6	
Porter, Solomon Claywell	1	3	5		
Purnell, Robert	3		4		
Price, Wm	3		2		
Patrick, John	1	1	2		
Poynter, Marshall	1		4		
Poor of Worcester County	1	7	19	3	
Pruitt, Walter	1		5		
Pruitt, John	2	1	3		
Pruitt, Selby	1		5		
Coston, Ezekiel	1	2	5		10
Johnson, Eleakin	2	2	4		8
Richardson, Robert M.	2	2	4	3	7
Richardson, George	2	1	3		10
Reed, Watter	1	1	1		
Reed, James	1	1	2		
Rowley, Arthur	1	3	2	1	1
Reggin, Joshua	1	3	2	1	
Sturgis, John O	3		3		3
Schoolfield, Robert	1	2	3		5
Selby, Parker, of Mathw	2		3		5
Stevenson, James (Mercht)	3	1	8	1	32
Selby, Capt John	2	1	3	2	
Sturgis, Levin	3	2	2		
Sturgis, John, of Thomas	2		2		
Sturgis, Outten, of Thomas	1	2	4		
Sturgis, John O, Junr	1		3		
Stevenson, Hugh	2	1	3		
Slocomb, Robert				3	
Sturgis, Stephen, Senr	3		4		
Sturgis, Richd	2	2	4		
Sturgis, Joshua, Junr	1	2	4		
Sturgis, Joshua, Senr	2		4		
Selby, Daniel, of Capt	1	3	1		6
Selby, Zadok, Senr	3	1	4		14
Sturgis, Abraham	1	2	2		6
Selby, James, of Capt Jno	1		4		13
Sturgis, Capt Outton	1		4		
Tull, Benjamin	1	6	1		
Taylor, Joshua	1		1		
Truitt, George, Senr	1	2	2		9
Taylor, John, BS	2	5	3		7
Taylor, Thomas	1	1	5		2
Tarr, Joshua	3	1	2		
Tarr, Michl, Senr	1		4		1
Tarr, Michal, Junr	2	1	6		
Townsend, Joshua, of Major	1		2		4
Vezey, Southy	3		2		
Williams, Dani	1			5	
Walton, Major	1		4	3	
Waters, Jesse	1		2		1
Walton, Wm	1	1	5		8
Jones, Major	1	1	3		4

WORCESTER COUNTY—Continued.

NAME OF HEAD OF FAMILY.	Free white males of 16 years and upward, including heads of families.	Free white males under 16 years.	Free white females, including heads of families.	All other free persons.	Slaves.
Armstrong, Bayham				5	
Bishop, Joseph	3	2	2		1
Brittingham, Joshua	2	1	1		8
Dure, James	1		4		2
Dennis, Ann		1	2		5
Cottingham, Isaac	5	2	3	1	2
Cottingham, Wm	3	2	2		3
Dennis, Littleton, Esqr	2		1	2	2
Evans, Joshua	2	1	4		1
Evans, John	1		4		6
Givans, James	1	1	4		1
Gruar, Moses	1		4		
Graham, Wm	5		3		6
Gunn, Samuel	3	1	2		2
Gunn, John	6		2		4
Gunby, Isaac	1		2		
Handy, James	1		2		9
Haynie, Doct. E	2		2		5
Hudson, John	3	5	2		
Hudson, Sterling	1	1	2		1
Hudson, Elizabeth	2	2	2		1
Hutchinson, Jonathan	2	3	4		5
Johnson, Daniel	1	2	4		
Kellam, Joseph	3		5		10
Kollock, Mary			5		
Long, Levin	2	2	2		2
Martin, Cole James	1		3		33
Martin, Thomas, Esqr	3	1	3		6
Murphey, Philip	1		2		1
McMullin, John	1	2	3		
McFadden, James	1	1	2		
McFadden, Tabitha			2		1
Nicholds, Samuel	2		4		
Porter, McKemmey	4	1	4		2
Quinton, Major Philip	3	4	5	1	16
Rosse, Mrs. Elizr	2	1	3		4
Rock, John	1	1	4		
Randall, Francis	1	1	4		4
Smith, Walter	5	3	5		6
Selby, Zadoc, Junr	3		1		1
Stering, Elenor			1	4	
Selby, William (S. H.)		2	2		5
Sturgis, Zadok	2	2	3		3
Spence, Margret			3		19
Stanford, Jonathan	2	2	3		
Tarr, John	1	3	3		
Tarr, Eli	2	2	4		
Truitt, Betty			3		
Tarr, Comfal			2		
Wise, John	2	2	2		11
Ware, James	3	2	1		1
White, Peter	2	1	3		1
Webb, Hannah			2		
Willett, Henry	1		2	3	1
Townsend, Joshua, Senr	1	2	3		10
Ayres, John	1		1		5
Bratten, James	2		2		
Bradford, Samuel	1	2	6		
Burch, Danl	2	1	4		
Bennitt, Jesse	1		2		8
Bishop, Benjl	2		4		3
Bratten, Nathl		4	4	4	
Bishop, Benjn, of Josh	1	1	2		
Bishop, John	2	1	5		5
Burch, Amey			3		
Bowdin, Jesse	1	1	2		
Bowdin, Wm	1	4	2		
Bowdin, Uriah	1	1	1		
Bishop, Wm Senr	6	2	2		2
Blair, John	1	3	2		
Brittingham, Thos	1	2	4		
Bishop, Wm, Junr	1	1	2		
Bishop, Ann	1	1	3		
Bishop, Betty	1	2	3		4
Bennitt, Charles (Seaside)	2	1	4		
Bennitt, McCajah	1	1	2		2
Selby, James, of McCajah	1	1	2		
Selby, Levin	1	1	2		3
Selby, Wm, of McCajah	1		3		
Nicholds, Isaac	1		3		3
Bennitt, Wm, of Wm	1	2	5		2
Johnson, Lovern	1	2	2		
Parrimore, Mary	1		2		15
Conner, Abner			2		
Atkinson, Henry	1	1	2		
Brittingham, Bolitha	2	3	4		4
Brittingham, Wm, Senr	1	1	2		
Brittingham, Wm., of Wm	1	2	3		1
Bowen, John, Senr	2	2	3		
Sullivan, Wm	1	1	2		
Campbell, Wm	3	2	2		
Claywell, Moses	2	2	5		
Cottingham, Thomas	1	1	4		1
Conner, Fredrick	1	3	4	1	
Clogg, Walter	1	2	3		

NAME OF HEAD OF FAMILY.	Free white males of 16 years and upward, including heads of families.	Free white males under 16 years.	Free white females, including heads of families.	All other free persons.	Slaves.
Jones, Elisha, of Giles	1	2	3		
Johnson, Hezekiah	2	2	4		5
Cowley, Hindman	1	1	2		
Claywell, Thomas	1	1	2		
Cox, Samuel	1		4		
Cowles, John	1	2	3		
Dreadon, Wm	1	2	5		
Dreadon, David	1	2	3		
Dreadon, Samuel, of Jno	1	2	3	1	
Dreadon, Moses	1	2	2		
Davis, Nathaniel	2	3	2		
Dreadon, Samuel, BS	2		2	1	
Dennis, George	1	2	3		
Devorix, John	2	1	2		
Devorix, Wm	1	1	2		
Deavorix, Samuel	1		2		2
Ennis, Joseph	1	1	2		10
Ennis, Cornelius, Senr	1	3	2		9
Freeman, John			2	3	
Gornwell, Major & mothers family	1	1	3		
Gutthny, Capt Wm	1	2	3		
Houlston, John	2	2	1		
Hopkins, Matthew	2	2	2		4
Houston, Ralph	2		5		
Hudson, Levi	1		2		5
Henderson, Jesse	1	2	3		2
Harman, Nimrod				5	
Harman, Lazarin				6	
Henderson, Bishop	1	2	3		
Harman, Jeremiah				2	
Hughs, Jesse	2	3	2		
Hudson, John, of Major	1	2	3		
Selby, Tabitha wd of Dan	1	2	3		10
Johnson, Zerobable	2		1	1	1
Johnson, George	2		1		
Johnson, Samuel	1		2		
Johnson, John, of Thos	2	2	4		
Jones, James	2	2	3	1	3
Johnson, Thomas	1		1		
Long, Wm	2	1	1		
Long, Samuel Joiner	1	1	1		
Latchem, McCajah	1	1	1		
Martin, George, of Thos	1	1	6		12
Morris, James R	3	3	2	1	5
Martin, Levin	1	2	2		20
Mitchell, Thomas	2	2	9		9
Marchment, Riley	1	1	2		
McCalley, John	2	1	3		
Marsh, Philip	1	2	3		6
Marritt, Samuel	1	1	4		
Neighembur, Thomas	1	1	2		
Nicholdson, John (Matt)	1	1	3		
Purnell, Major Wm	2	1	3	1	16
Pepper, Eli	2	1	3		
Purnell, John S	2	1	4		20
Purnell, George	3	1	1		14
Porter, Wm	1		3		10
Purnell, Elisha, of Wm	1		3	10	
Porter, Betty			1	1	2
Robins, Ann	1	1	3		15
Richardson, Shadrick	1	1	2		2
Riggen, Levin	2	1	4		
Robins, Thomas	1	1	2		
Richardson, Whittington	1	3	5		
Richardson, Levi	1	2	3		1
Richardson, Robt, Junr	1	2	3		
Robins, Littleton	1		1		13
Richardson, Charles Ditch	2		1		
Richardson, Charles, of Robt	1	2	3		
Richardson, Robt, Senr	2	2	4		3
Richardson, Mary, wd of Thos		2	2		2
Stevenson, John	4	1	4		2
Scarborough, Samuel	3	1	4		13
Scarborough, John	3	2	3		1
Slocomb, Thomas	1	2	3		1
Scarborough, Kendall	1	2	4		
Spence, George	2	4	3		27
Scott, James	1	1	4		
Smith, John	1	2	4		1
Sturgis, John, Senr	1	1	3		5
Sawyer, Charles	2		4		
Sturgis, Elijah	1		2		
Slocomb, Linah		2	3		
Stevenson, James (Mill)	3	1	2		
Stevenson, Adam	2	2	3		
Sned, Wm	1		1		
Sned, John	1		2		
Truitt, Benjamin	2	2	2		1
Teague, George	2	1	3		
Truitt, Rownd	1	1	3		5

NAME OF HEAD OF FAMILY.	Free white males of 16 years and upward, including heads of families.	Free white males under 16 years.	Free white females, including heads of families.	All other free persons.	Slaves.
Truitt, Wm, Junr	1	3	2		2
Truitt, Eli	1		1		7
Truitt, Wm, Senr	1		3		1
Taylor, Teackle	1	2	1		8
Townsend, Major	2	3	3		
Townsend, Lazarus	2		3		
Truitt, Edward	1		4		
Townsend, Levin, of Lazr	1		1		
Parker, Rebecca	1	2	3		1
Waters, Patrick	2	2	5		4
Wise, Mitchell	1		4		3
Wise, Ezekiel	1		1		2
Allen, Sarah		1	3		
Bowen, Joshua	3	2	1	1	1
Bowen, Jesse	2		9		3
Beavins, Benjn	1		3	1	
Bowen, Elijah	1		2		
Bradford, Zedekiah	2	1	3		
Bowen, Jethro	2	1	2	6	
Brown, Wm	1	1	3		
Bowen, Nathl	1	1	3		1
Bowen, Rachel	3	5	2		
Baker, Levin	2		6		
Bowen, John, Joiner	1	2	3		7
Bradford, Solomon	1		3		
Bradford, Avery	1		4		
Bowen, David	1	2	3		
Burbage, Elias	3	1	5		
Crapper, Edmond, Junr	2	1	3	3	
Crapper, Edmond, Senr	2		2		5
Collins, Chambers	2		4		
Challfee, Moses	1	2	4	5	
Crapper, Levi	1		1		14
Christice, Wm	1		1	5	
Crapper, Wm, of Wm	1		3		1
Dunear, Isaac	2		2		
Davis, Shadrik	2	4	2		3
Davis, Edmond	2	2	2		
Davis, Benjn	3	1	3		
Davis, Thomas, of Benjn	1	1	2		
Duncan, Josiah	1	1	2		1
Davis, Charles	1	3	2		
Davis, Nehemiah	1	4	4		
Davis, John (Mill)	1	2	5		9
Dunbarr, John	1	2	1		4
Ennis, Nathaniel	3		1		1
Ennis, George	1		6		
Franklin, Wm, of Wm	1	4	1		6
Griffin, Milby	1		5		
Hammond, Edward	2	1	5		8
Hook, Bolitha	2	2	3		
Hudson, Dennis	3	1	5		
Henderson, Jesse, Junr	2		2		
Henderson, Mary (wd of Levin)		1	4	1	
Henderson, Benjamin	1		4	1	
Hammond, William, of Edwd	3	1	3		5
Hammond, Wm, of Wm	1	2	4		
Hudson, Robert	1	1	2		2
Hudson, James H	1	1	2		2
Jones, John (of Joshua)	1	1	5		3
Hosler, Henry	1	1	1		
Jones, Jesse	1	3	5		3
Jones, Bridget		2	2		
Jones, Thomas	2	2	4		3
Jones, James	2	1	2		
Jackson, Wm	2	1	3		
Jerman, Isaac	1	3	3		
Knox, Ezekiel	1	1	2		5
Lister, William, Junr	1	2	4		2
Lister, Wm, Senr	1	1	2		
Morris, Wm, Esq	2	2	5		33
Morris, Philip	2	1	1		
Morris, Edward	2		2		
Morris, Isaac	1		4		
Morris, John (Mink)	1	4	1	1	
Macklin, Wm	1	1	1		
Morris, Luke	1		2		
Marshall, Isaac, Esqr	1	2	2		10
Morris, James (Swamp)	2		2		
McGee, Edward					5
Marshall, Zadok	2		3		23
Marshall, John	1	2	4		
Priddeaux, Thomas, Junr	1		4		6
Purnell, Elisha, Senr	1		8		7
Purnell, Matthew	2		2		8
Parker, James	2		2		2
Purnell, Zadok, Junr	1	2	1		
Poynter, Eleas	1	2	1		
Porter, Saml	3		1		1
Purnell, Catherine (wd of Peter)		1	2	4	
Perkins, John	1	2	1		9
Powell, Elias	2	2	1		
Porter, B. Purnell	2	2	1		
Priddeaux, John	1	3	4		5

WORCESTER COUNTY—Continued.

NAME OF HEAD OF FAMILY.	Free white males of 16 years and upward, including heads of families.	Free white males under 16 years.	Free white females, including heads of families.	All other free persons.	Slaves.
Priddeaux, Whittington	1	3	3		3
Purnell, Sarah Wm	2	1	2		26
Purnell, Eliza		2	2		
Purnell, Delila	1	2	3		10
Richards, Isaac, Senr	2	1	3		
Richards, John	1	1	2		5
Rackliffe, Charles	2	1	3		15
Rownd, Hampton	2		3		8
Rigby, Thomas	1		2		
Rownd, Saml, Doctr	1	3	3		7
Rownd, John, Senr	1	2	2		9
Richards, William	1	2	2		
Ridley, Wm	1		2		
Richards, Isaac, Junr	3		3		
Smock, Levi	1		2		
Selby, Parker, Senr	1		2		4
Smasshe, Wm	1	1	1		
Smasshe, Leah		2			
Smith, Daniel	2		4		
Smock, Rhoda	1	1	3		
Stevenson, James (S.W.)	1				
Townsend, Jeremiah	3	2	5		8
Truitt, Sampson	1	2	1		
Teeling, Luke			4		
Undrill, Capt Wm	1		3	1	7
Wilson, David	1		3		19
Victor, John	1	2	3		
Walker, John	2	2	3		1
Wilson, Docr James	2	1	3		12
Wright, John	2	2	4		2
Quinton, James	1		4		6
Purnell, Capt Thomas	2	1	7		31
Bradford, John	2		3		2
Baker, Levin	2		2		
Bowen, Wm	1		2		
Burbage, Hampton			1		7
Bowen, Whittington	2	2	5		7
Baker, Handcook	1	2	1		
Bowen, James	1		2		4
Brittingham, Eliza	3	1	1		1
Brittingham, James	1		1		
Brittingham, Isaac	3	1	1		1
Baynam, Wm	4	2	2		
Curtis, Joseph	2	2	2		
Crapper, Noble	1		2		
Caudry, Mary		1	4		5
Caudry, Abraham	1	1	2		
Crapper, Nathl	1		2		3
Carey, Sole	1	1	1		
Collier, Thabitha			2		
Collier, Peter	1	2	3		10
Cord, Wm	1	1	5		2
Custis, Aden	1		1		
Crapper, Issabella		1	3		1
Collins, Sarah	3	2	2		
Crapper, Ruben	2	2	6		1
Campbell, Wm	1		7		
Catlin, Benjamin	1	1	6		
Dennis, Annanias	1	1	2		
Dennis, John	1	3	1		12
Deal, Josiah	3		2		4
Deal, Ebenizer	1	1	1		
Davis, Matthias	3	3	2		8
Dunbarr, John	1	1	1		
Davis, Abijah	2	3	3		4
Evans, Powell	1		3		
Evans, Nathl	1				
Evans, Peter	1		2		3
Evans, Annanias	1	1	3		
Franklin, Wm, of Edw	1	3	3		5
Franklin, John, Senr	3	3	2		9
Franklin, John, Junr	1	1	2		5
Freeman, Michael	2	3	3		
Fassitt, Margret	1	2	3		7
Franklin, Samuel	1	2	3		1
Franklin, Peal	2	1	4		
Fassitt, John	1		2		3
Fassitt, Rouse	2		3		17
Fassitt, Wm	2		1		4
Fisher, John	1		3		
Farewell, Ann			5		
Fassitt, James M.	1		3		1
Fassitt, Mary, Wd of Jno		1	3		10
Williams, Nancy		1,	3		3
Green, Joseph	1		4		10
Gault, Wm	1	2	5		1
Gray, Jesse	3	2	4		6
Guthery, James	1	1	3		4
Horsey, Lambert	1	2	4		13
Hill, Isaac (of Rob)	4	2	1		1
Henry, Edward	1	3	1		16
Hudson, Annanias	2		2		12
Hosier, Wm	1	1	7		
Hill, Elizabeth	2	1	1		9
Hudson, John	2	1	3		12
Hudson, Esther	1		2		16
Hudson, McKenney	1	4	2		5

NAME OF HEAD OF FAMILY.	Free white males of 16 years and upward, including heads of families.	Free white males under 16 years.	Free white females, including heads of families.	All other free persons.	Slaves.
Harmanson, Edward	1	1	3		1
Henderson, Purnell	1	1	2		
Holloway, Ann		1	3		
Hickman, Wm	1		3		1
Hopkins, Hampton	1		3		6
Henry, Francis J.	1		2		50
German, Annalias	1	1	3		2
Jones, Mary	2	2	4		5
Jones, Joshua	1				
Jones, Wm	2	3	3		
German, John, Senr	2	1	4		
German, John, Junr	2		2		
Jones, Ebez	1	1	2		
Ironshier, Esther			2		1
Johnson, Saben	1	2	3		11
Franklin, Henry	4	2	5		30
Jones, Morgan	1		2		
Kerby, John	1	2	2		10
Kennitt, Wm	3	1	3		3
Kennitt, Susanna	1	1	4		7
Long, Solomon	1	2	2		
Lockwood, Samuel	1	2	3		7
Long, Colbourn	1		2		1
Long, Samuel, Senr	4		2		
Leatherberry, Arthur	1		2		6
Lewis, Mary		1	3		
Merrill, Wm, B.S.	2	3	3		
Murray, Dancan	2	2	2		1
Mitchell, Cole Joshua	2		1		17
McCormick, Benjamin	1	1	2		1
Marsh, Martha	1		2		
Mills, Samuel	1	3	4		
Mitchell, Robt	1	1			
Mumford, Major	1		2		9
Mills, Levi	1	4	5		14
Marshall, John, junr	2		1	1	4
Mumford, John	1		2		
Mitchell, Josiah	4	1	3		27
Parker, Henry (Trap)	3	1	4		5
Powell, Thomas	1	1	3		3
Powell, Bolitha	1		2		
Pellett, Absolum	1	1	2		
Davis, Wm, B S	2	2	3		
Postly, John, Esq.	1		4		14
Friddeaux, Thomas, Senr	2	1	2		
Justice, Stephen	2	2	4		24
Justice, Wm	1	2	2		
Johnson, Joseph	1	1	1		1
Johnson, Patieence			6		1
Johnson, David	1	1	4		2
King, James	1	1	2		5
Lunch, Jacob	3	1	1		
Latchem, John Kendall	2	2	1		
Lynch, Baker	1	4	1		
Laws, Obed	1		2		
Landall, John	2	4	5	1	
Lynch, Elisha	1		2		
Laws, James	1	2	2		
Lynch, David	1		2		6
Lynch, Caleb	2	1	2		
Lawrance, Mary			3		
McGee, Barney	2		1		12
Mumford, James	1	1	2		4
Mumford, Rebecca	1	1	3		
Miller, John	3	1	5		5
McGreeger, Wm	1	1	1		
Perkins, Sole	1		4		
Selby, Thomas	1	5	2		
Selby, Nelly		2			
Sampson, Richd	1	1	1		
Schoolfield, John	1	3	2		
Stewart, Rachel			1		
Tull, Jacob	2	2	5		
Briddwell, David	3		4		
Owens, Peter	1		3		
Dashiell, Cole Go	5	3	3		11
Smullin, Randall	2	2	2		
Hearn, John	2		2		
Hearn, Isaac	1	2	4		
Reggen, Joseph	1	1	5		
Culver, Jesse	1	3	2		
Kersey, Patrick	1	2	5		
Philips, Isaac	3	4	2		
Atkins, Stanton	1		3		
Penewell, Richard	1	3	4		
Calhoon, Benjn	2	2	4		
Baker, Zadok	3	2	5		
Gray, John	3		2		
Gray, Bolitha	1	1	3		
Scott, Thomas	1	1	4		
Givans, George	1	3	2		
Atkins, Nimrod	1	3	4		
Parker, Ayres	1	1	1		2
Atkins, Middleton	1		6		
Davis, John	2	1	6		
Brown, Levi	2	3	2		
Perdue, Jas, Junr	1	1	2		

NAME OF HEAD OF FAMILY.	Free white males of 16 years and upward, including heads of families.	Free white males under 16 years.	Free white females, including heads of families.	All other free persons.	Slaves.
McGee, Saml	3	1	5		
Kirkwell, Henry	1	1	2		
Roach, Charles	1	1	4		
Parsons, John			4		1
Layfield, Wm	1		4		
Watson, Boaz	3	2	4		
Levingston, Tod.	1		3		2
Levingston, George	1		2		2
Stevens, Levi	1		1		1
Levingston, James	1	3	1		
Smith, George, B.S.	1		1		
Smith, George (of Andw)		1	1		1
Mills, Richard	2	1	7		1
Dashiell, Susanna			2		6
Bluitt, Mrs			1		10
Taylor, Thos, of Jno	1		5		1
Harrison, John		5	4		
Cathell, Jane, wd of Danl	1	5	4		
Driskell, Wm	1		2		
Stengis, John. of Jos	1	2	3		3
Toadvine, Stephen	1	2	4		4
Christopher, Matthias	2	1	4		
Purnell, James	1		3		4
Parris, John	1	1	1		
Bainum, Elijah	2		4		
Parsons, Zefeniah	2	1	4		
Porter, James	1	1	4		
Atkins, Milby	1		1		
Glass, Christopher	1		1		
Beatherds, Wm	1	2			
Hosier, Levinah	1	2	2		
Kelly, Henry, Jur	1	2	2		
Powder, Richard	1		2		
Parsons, John, Jur	1	2	2		
Parsons, Matthew	1	1	3		
McLych, Tho	1	2	3		
Turner, Zadok	1		2		
Fox, Jonathan	2	1	5		10
Fosque, Thos	2	4	3		
Fox, Elijah	2	1	3		2
Le Count, Anthony	3		3		
Coal, John	1	3	2		
Downes, Barnett	3		1		
Parker, Philip	3		1	1	
Speer, Henry	1		5		
Givan, Alexander	1		4		
Walley, Isaac	2		5		
Mitchell, Thomas W	1	2	4		
Truitt, Bolitha	1		2		
Penewell, Luke	1	2	4		
Baker, Sole	3		3		7
Webb, Jeptha	3	1	2		
Williams, Mary	2		3		
Williams, Price	1		2		
Brittingham, Sole	1	1	1		
Dreadon, Mary			1		
Dale, Matthew	1	1	2		4
Timmonds, Whittington	1	1	2		1
Hogshier, Wm	1		1		
Johnson, Wm	1		2	7	
Brittingham, Purnell	1	2	3		4
Blizzard, John	2	2	2		
Blizzard, Thomas	1	2	2		
Bratten, Bolitha	2		2		
Baker, Solomon	2	2	4		
Colbourn, John	3	2	2		
Kollock, Samuel	2	1	3		
Cutler, Rachel		2	1		
Claywell, Ezekiel	1		2		
Davis, Hezekiah	1		1		
Davis, Truitt	1	3	4		
Davis, Nixon	1	2	1		1
Davis, Benjn	1		4		
Davis, Shadrik	1	2	1		
Henderson, Curtis	1		2		17
Houston, Capt Isaac	3	2	8		25
Holland, Levi	2	1	3		4
Maddux, Hambleton	2		2		
Houston, Capt James	2	1	4		19
Hayward, Sarah			4		20
Johnson, Henry	1		1		2
Jones, Wm, of Jno	1	4	2		
Jones, Obed	1		2		
Jones, Elisha, of Jno	1	2	3		1
Jones, John, Jno Town	3	3	2		
Jones, Jiles	3	1	2		
Johnson, Smith	1	2			
Johnson, Purnell	2	1	6		
Johnson, Benjn	2	1	5		2
Kelley, Henry	1	1	4		
Kelley, Robt	1		4		
Kelley, Charles	2	3	4		
Kellam, Jno	2	3	6		7
Mumford, Shadrick	1		4		
Morris, Jethro	2	3	4		
Morris, Wm (Ferred)	2	3	3		1
Morris, Cornelius	2	3	3		

WORCESTER COUNTY—Continued.

NAME OF HEAD OF FAMILY.	Free white males of 16 years and upward, including heads of families.	Free white males under 16 years.	Free white females, including heads of families.	All other free persons.	Slaves.
Mitchell, Jno Pope	2	3	2		21
McAllen, Alexander	2	2	4		6
Mumford, Turvell	1	1	3		
Morris, Jno, of Thos	2	1	5		
Mumford, James	1	2	4		
Mumford, Jno	2	2	4		
Hosier, Wm			2		
Mungar, Martha			2		
Martin, Thomas, Senr	2	3	3		28
Martin, George, Senr	3	3	3		15
Mumford, Jno	1	2	4		
Nearn, James	2		6		13
Nicholds, Joseph	1	2	3		
Nicholds, Isaac	1		2		3
Noble, Wm	1	1	1		
Davis, Zedekiah	1	1	9		7
Outlew, Levi	1	1	3		
Davis, Jno, of Geo	1	3	6		3
Parker, Thomas	1		3		
Parker, Selby	2	1	4		7
Parker, Wm	1	2	5		5
Parker, Henry, Senr	2	1	4		1
Purnell, Benjn Senr	1	3	6		17
Parker, Schoolfield	1				5
Parsons, Wm, of Jno	1	2	1		
Powell, Gaberal, Jr	1		2		
Powell, Wm	1		3		
Parker, John	1	2	3		
Powell, Zadok	1	2	2		
Powell, Gaberal, Junr	1	2	5		
Richardson, Samuel	1	2	1		
Ruark, Daniel	2	1	4		
Rian, John	2	2	4		
Reed, John	2	1	4		
Davis, Robt	2	1	1		
Evans, Jacob	1	2	4		
Selby, Major	1	3			1
Shockly, Richd, Senr	1				6
Shockly, Benjamin, Senr	3		3		
Sturgis, Jacob	2	1	3		
Smith, James	1	4	3		
Shockly, Jno, of Benjn	1		3		1
Shockly, Nobl	1	2	3		
Shockly, Jno, of Richd	1	2	3		
Smith, Geo, of Richd	1	2	3		
Shockly, Benjn, of Jono	1	4	1		
Shockley, Solomon	1	2	4		3
Shockley, Wm	1	1	2		
Farlow, Wm	1	3	2		
Fooks, Jonathan	2		3		
Townsend, Zadok	1	1	3		
Townsend, Sole, Junr	1	3	5		3
Townsend, Charles	1	5	4		1
Turner, George	2	2	3		
Truitt, George, of Job	1	1	2		
Townsend, Joshua, Junr	1		2		2
Townsend, Levin	1	1	4		2
Turner, Jackson	1		2		11
Townsend, Bartly	2	1	4		8
Twilly, Wm	2	2	6		
Truitt, George (of Jno)	2	1	2		
Truitt, James	1	3	2		
Townsend, Jno	1		8		5
Victor, Thomas, Junr	1		1	1	2
Victor, Thomas, Senr	1	2	3		1
Victor, James	1		2		
White, Wm, BB	2		4		
Wimbrow, Thomas P	2	1	2		
White, Joshua	1		2		8
Wright, Abel	3		2		
Kellam, Mary		2	3		
Lewis, Wm	1	2	2		
Lewis, George	1	2	2		
Lewis, Thomas	2	2	4		
Lewis, Jas	1	1	1		
Parker, Jno, of Chas	1	2	4		
Atkinson, Thomas	2	1	3	3	11
Atkinson, James, Senr	4		3		4
Adams, Jacob	1	1	3		5
Atkinson, James, Junr	1	3	3		
Allen, Wm, Esqr	3		1	1	50
Atkinson, Comfort		3	4		8
Atkinson, Sarah	2	4	4		6
Atkinson, Angelia			2		
Payne, Moses	2		2		
Richardson, Matthew	2	1	2		
Butler, Wm	2		1	1	
Beavins, Thomas	2		3	1	4
Bennitt, Capt Charles	1	4	6		16
Bacon, James	2	1	3		14
Brown, Andrew, Senr	2	1	3		
Butler, Sol	1	3	3		5
Barns, Thomas	1	3	3		
Beavins, Roland, Senr	2	3	3		4
Beavins, Wm, Senr	4	2	4		
Broadwater, James	1	2	2		
Brown, Andrew, Junr	1	2	3		2

NAME OF HEAD OF FAMILY.	Free white males of 16 years and upward, including heads of families.	Free white males under 16 years.	Free white females, including heads of families.	All other free persons.	Slaves.
Batts, Henry	1		1		
Brown, Wm	1		2		1
Battle, Joshua	1	2	2		
Shockley, Leah		2	2		
Rownd, Wm	2	2	4		4
Corbin, Wm	2	2	4	1	8
Cottingham, Betty	3		2		
Cottingham, Jno, Senr	1	2	3		5
Crappe, Edmond	1	2	2		
Clark, Roads	1		3		
Cottingham, Joshua	2	1	2		
Timmonds, Wm	1	1	2		
Dorman, Mathew	2		4		
Dukes, Jno	2		2		
Drummond, Burrell	2	2	5		
Dickerson, Corneilus	1		1		16
Dorman, James	1		2		
Dennison, James	1	2	1		
Dickson, Thomas	1		4		6
Dickerson, Josiah	1	2	1		
Dorman, Elias	1		2		1
Dougal, James H	1	4	3		
Dukes, Robert	1	3	3		
Eashon, Daniel		4	2		1
Eashon, Sole, Senr	1	2	2		
Eashon, Sole, Junr	1		1		
Eshon, Jona, Junr	1		1		
Flemmin, Jno	1	2			6
Flemmin, Wm	3		2		6
Gibbs, John	1		2		3
Gibbs, Abr	1	2	2		6
Hudson, Jonathan	2	1	2		25
Handy, Wm, of Thos	3		2		
Harris, Wm	1	2	2		
Timmonds, Nehemiah	1	1	1		
Johnson, Shepherd	2	1	2		7
Timmonds, Joseph	1	2	1		
Lankford, Stephen	1	1			2
Lokey, Jno	2	2	4		
Maddux, Marcey	1	1	4		8
McDaniel, Sarah	1	3	1		2
Melburn, Thomas	1	1	1		
Truitt, Ell	1	1	2		
Newton, Job	1	1	2		
Truitt, Joseph	1		2		
Otwell, James	1		1		
Otwell, Wm	1		2		
Truitt, Arcada		2	2		
Puzey, George	2	2			
Powell, Elijah	1	3	3		
Powell, Wm	1	1	2		
Pellett, Widdow (of Edwd)			2		
Puzey, Isaac	1	2	3		
Richards, Joseph	2	1	3		9
Ruark, Elgel	1	1	4		
Roach, James				4	
Reggen, Eliza	1	1	1		
Reggen, Jno	1	3	3		
Roach, Charles				5	
Selby, Wm, Senr	2		2		3
Selby, Ezekiel	1	1	2		7
Scott, John	1	2	5	2	2
Scott, Joseph	1		2		6
Stevenson, Samuel	1	1	2		
Selby, Joshua	2	1	3		
Selby, Danl	1				
Selby, Jno, Senr	1		1		1
Selby, Jno (of Jno)	1		3		4
Schoolfield, Rachel			3		
Smith, Henry	1	3	2		
Smullin, Wm	2		1		
Smullin, Ephriam	1	1	1		
Townsend, Wm, of Hy	1	1	2		
Truitt, Zedediah	1		1		
Truitt, Jno, Junr	1	1	3		
Tilghman, Ephriam	1	1	1		2
Taylor, Elias	1	3	6		4
Townsend, Elias	1	3	3		
Townsend, Ephriam	2	1	2		
Tilghman, Wm	2			1	
Tilghman, Joseph	1	1	4		
Tilghman, Saml	1	2	2		1
Townsend, Stephen	4	1	1		
Townsend, Jemima	1		2		12
Townsend, Jamea	2		1		
Townsend, Absolom	1		1		
Tracey, Jamea	1	1	2		
Tunnell, James	1	1	3		
Taylor, Saml	1	2	2		
Turner, Henry	1	2	3		
Ayers, Isaac	1	2	5		7
Baker, Wm	1	2	2		
White, Henry	1	3	1		1
White, Major	1		3		18
Wells, Mary		1	3		
White, Wm	2	3	3		

NAME OF HEAD OF FAMILY.	Free white males of 16 years and upward, including heads of families.	Free white males under 16 years.	Free white females, including heads of families.	All other free persons.	Slaves.
Williams, Jno	2		7		8
Briddle, Elihu	1	2	3		2
Richardson, John	2	3	6		5
Driskill, Elget	2	2	3		
Johnson, Joshua	2	1	2		1
Flint, John	1	2	4		
Brulington, Wm	1	1	4		11
Gordy, Wm	1	1	6		2
Parker, Elisha	1	1	2		
Parker, John, of Elisha	1	2	5		4
Parsons, Jonathan	2	1	2		2
Dykes, Ephraim	1	2	2		
Shockley, Capt Elijah	1	3	1	1	1
Dennis, Atkins	2		4		
Briddell, John	1	2	3		6
Morris, Joshua	2	2	3		
Sturgis, Joshua, Senr	2		3		8
Fooks, Jesse	2	3			
Toadvine, Henry	2		3		7
Hammond, Edward	1	1	2		
Powell, John	1		3		
Powell, Wm	1	1	2		
Dashiell, John	1	2	5		3
Shockley, Saul	1		5		
Gurly, Francis				9	
Perdue, James	2	4	5		5
Taylor, Elias	1	1	2		
Penewell, Elisha	3		4		
Hammond, Leah	1		4		4
Selms, Edward N	1	2	2		9
Parsons, Wm, Senr	2		3		11
Messen, George	1	2	3		6
Cathell, John	1		2		20
Willis, Wm	1	1	2		
Garder, Nathan	1		3		1
Parsons, Samuel	1	2	2		
Dixon, Nathl	1	2	4		12
Driskell, Moses	1		2		
Fooks, Wm of Wm	1	1	4		1
Perdue, John	1	2	2		
Perdue, Eli	3		3		
Harris, Charles	1	3	6		2
Davis, Samuel	1		2		1
Parsons, George	1	6	3		2
Smith, Elijah	1		3		7
Parr, Samuel	1		3		1
Flint, John, Senr	1	2	2		
Pollitt, Wm	1		2		8
Owens, Jonathan	2	1	3		2
Christopher, Adam	2	1	2		
Ennis, Corneilus	2	2	5		3
Parsons, Levin	2	1	2		
James, Wm	3		4		
Jailey, Wm	2	4	2	1	2
Philips, Samuel	2	1	3		
Wright, Wm	1		3		
Brulington, John	3		3		
Davis, James	1	1	4		
Bruington, James	1	3	4		1
Davis, Claria, wd of Jno		3	6		5
Parker, Jacob	2		3		1
Parker, George	1	2	4		
Perdue, Jno, Junr	1	2	1		
Perdue, George	1	2	3		
Parsons, Wm, Junr	1	2	1		
McGoo, John	2	1	1		
Shockley, Jno (of Elijah)	1		2		
Savage, Zerobable	1	2	2		
Dennis, Benjn (of Atkins)	1		3		
Savage, Benjn	1		3		1
Auston, John	2	3	3		1
Richardson, Wm	1		1		9
Handy's, Robt (Heirs)	1		3		
Durkey, Shadrick	1	1	3		2
Fooks, Thomas	1		3		
Mitchell, Stephen	1	3	4		
Purnell, Colo Zadok	1		4		14
Purnell, Eliza (wd of Wm)	1	2	4		17
Purnell, Isaac, Esqr	1		4		3
Purnell, Catherine			2		19
Purnell, Thomas, of Walt	1	3	4		15
Parker, Peter	1		4		
Purnell, Zadok, Junr, Esqr	1		3		17
Pitt, Hillery	1	3	4		15
Quillen, Benjamin	1	3	3		
Reed, Wm	1	3	6		
Riley, Levin	1		3		10
Ridley, Kesiah	1	1	1		
Riley, Thomas	1	2	2		3
Riley, Ann		1	4		
Rackliffe, Mary, of Nathl	1	2	3		16
Rackliffe, John					40
Rankin, The Revd John	1	2	3		9
Smith, Purnell	1		1		1
Stevenson, Wm	1	3	5		8
Smith, John	1	1	7		

WORCESTER COUNTY—Continued.

NAME OF HEAD OF FAMILY.	Free white males of 16 years and upward, including heads of families.	Free white males under 16 years.	Free white females, including heads of families.	All other free persons.	Slaves.	NAME OF HEAD OF FAMILY.	Free white males of 16 years and upward, including heads of families.	Free white males under 16 years.	Free white females, including heads of families.	All other free persons.	Slaves.	NAME OF HEAD OF FAMILY	Free white males of 16 years and upward, including heads of families.	Free white males under 16 years.	Free white females, including heads of families.	All other free persons.	Slaves.
Smith, Thomas, of Jno	2		1		3	Wilson, Aaron	1	1	3			Patey, Kendale	1	2	2		
Smith, John, of Jno	1		2			Walley, Seth	1	2	2		2	Quillin, Samuel	1	1	2		
Stevens, Joshua	1	2				Webb, Wm	3	2	2			Smith, Levi	1	2	2		
Smith, Thomas, Senr	2	3	4			Walter, Comfort	1		3			Showell, Samuel	1	1	1		
Shaw, Thomas	2			1		White, Philip	1		2			Taylor, Charles	1	2	2		10
Selby, James	2	1			2	Webb, Scarborough	3	2	3		9	Townsend, Luke	2	2	5		
Scott, Benjamin	1	4	1		11	Webb, Thomas	3	2	3			Tingle, James	2	1	4	1	
Savage, Isaac	1	1	2	1		Atkins, John	1		2			Timmonds, Elijah	1				4
Smith, Melby	1		4	2	4	Atkins, Wm	2	3	4			Timmonds, Joseph	1	1			
Steel, Alexander	1		1			Beavins, Wm	6	5	4			Timmonds, Thomas	1		1		
Slattery, Barthom	1	1	4	1		Bridwell, Benja	2	2	1		3	Timmonds, Stephen	1		4		
Truitt, George, of Paty	1		3	1		Bratten, James	2	1	3			Tillitt, Thomas	1	1			
Taylor, John	1	2	5		7	Blake, Thomas	1		2			Timmonds, James	1	2	2		
Tubba, Samuel	1		2			Bussell, James	1		2			Taylor, Laben	1		1		
Truitt, Wm	1		4			Barrott, John	1	1	2			Taylor, Alexander	1	2	3		
Tubba, John	1	5	2			Bratten, Jesse	1	2	3			Williams, Ishmeal	1	2	1		
Truitt, Mary	1		2		3	Beavans, Thomas, Senr	2		3		2	Williams, Esaw	2	1	4		
Timmonds, Benjamin	1	3	2			Ball, Wm	2	4	3			Williams, Ruben	1				
Tingle, Caleb, Jur	3		3			Bishop, Hannah			4		7	Williams, Nathl	1	2	1		
Truitt, Nehemiah	2	3	6		23	Candry, John	3	1	4		5	Williams, David	1	2	1		
Taylor, Nevit	2		2			Cottingham, Thos, Senr	2		3	1		Watts, Wm	1	2	3		
Tubbs, Joseph	1	2	2			Cottingham, Elijah	1	1	5	1		Wright, Obed	1	2	2		
Taylor, David	2		1			Cottingham, John, Junr	1		2			Williams, Risdon	1	2	3		
Vandom, Edward	1		4		10	Carmine, Lowder	1		2			Wyatt, Caleb	2	2	4		3
Williams, Isaac	1	1	2			Culver, John	1	2	3			Warren, Pharoh	1	2	1		
Warren, Richard	2	2	1		9	Chaille, Cole Peter	1	1	1			Warrington, Alexander	2		3		
Waters, James	1		3			Davis, Philip	2		6		22	Warren, Isaac	2		2		
Warren, John	1		1			Dreadon, Saml, Senr	2	2	2			Wainwright, John	1	2	4	2	
Waters, Mary, of Wm	3	1	5		2	Dennis, Johnson	3		2		4	Baynum, Elisha	1		2		1
Townsend, Rives	1	2	2			Dennis, John	1	2	2			Bassitt, John	1				
Walter, John	1		6			Dorman, Samuel	2	3	4			Bassitt, Wm	1	1	1	2	
White, John	2	1	2			Dreadon, Isaac	1		2		3	Brumble, Fassitt	1		1		
White, Wm	1		4		6	Dennis, Valintine	1	3	4	2		Bowen, Luke	1	2	2		
Warren, Thomas	2	2	3		15	Dreadon, Thomas	3		2		4	Burbage, Thomas	1	2	2		
Waytt, Comfort			2			Davis, James	1		2	1		Crapper, Wm	1				
Welden, Anthony	1		6			Davis, Samuel	1	4	2	1		Duncan, Levin	1	1	1		
Williams, Isaac	2	2	2		6	Duncan, Charles	1		2		1	Hill, Johnson	1	1	2		
Aydolet, Hayward	1	2	6			Dennis, Benja	1	1	5		1	Mumford, Matthias	1	2	3		2
Buckley, John	1	2	1			Davis, Joshua	2	2	5		7	Mumford, Charles	1		2		2
Bratten, Samuel	3	1	6			Driskill, Adam	1	2	2			Porter, Joseph	1		3		
Brevard, John	2	3	4		8	Davis, Thomas	2	2	2			Purnell, Isaac, of Mas	1	1	2		2
Blades, Benja	1		1			Eashon, Jonathan	2	1	1	7		Rowds, John Whittington	1				6
Baker, George	3		2			Dickerson, Wm	2	2	3			Smith, Jesse	1	1	2		
Baker, Selathel	3	4	2			Fooks, Daniel	3	3	5		4	Smock, John	1				
Baker, Archibald	1		6			Farlow, John	3	1	4			Selby, Sarah	2		3	4	
Bratten, Jesse	1	1	3			Farlow, Benja	1		2			Coston, Abel				4	
Clark, Edward	1					Givan, Robt	1		5		2	Coston, Wm				1	
Crapper, John	1		2		1	Givan, John	1	2	3			Kollok, Simon				6	
Cobb, Elias	1	1	2			Godfree, Charles	1		3		12	Hindman, James	1	2	2		
Coe, Avery	2	5	1			Godfree, James	1	1	3			Halls, John	2	2	4		
Collins, Eli	2		1			German, James	1		3			Steel, James	2		4		
Coe, Hannah	1	1	5			German, Wm (of Geo)	1		3			Winants, John	1		3		6
Crapper, George	1		3		1	German, George (of Wm)	2		2			Ayers, Rachel	1	1	2		2
Dale, Thomas	2	4	7		13	German, Wm, Senr	1	2	2			Alen, John	1	2	4		
Davis, Joshua	4	1	1			German, George, Senr	1		2			Brittingham, John	1	2	2		
Duncan, Wm	1		3			Bratten, Adam	1	1	2			Beeby, James	1		2		
Davis, Rosannah	1	2	1			Benson, John	1	1	2			Blake, George				4	
Deal, Jesse	1		6		2	Beatherds, Danl C	2	1	3			Casey, Soles, Senr	1	2	2		
Davis, Jesse	2	4	4		3	Baker, Sole	1	1	1			Casey, Smith	2	2	4		
Deal, James	1	1	1		2	Bratten, Wm	1		2		2	Casy, Jeremiah	2	2	4		
Deal, Ebe	1		3			Collier, Wm	1		2			Casey, Soles, Junr	2	2	4		
Dymock, Wm	2	2	3			Collier, Sarah			3			Collins, Eliza	2	2	2		2
Evans, Zeno	2		1		1	Crapper, Joseph	1	1	2			Davis, Wm	1	2	3		
Evans, Martha		1	4			Carey, Jonathan	1		3		5	Dickerson, Jesse	1	2	3		
Evans, Deal	1		3			Deal, Jno	1	1	3			Davis, Alexr	1	2	3		
Evans, Joseph	4	1	2		1	Deal, Jas (forrist)	1		2			Dixon, David	1	2	3		8
Evans, Isaac	2	2	5			Deal, Annanias	1		3			Dukes, John	1	1	2		
Fassitt, Elijah	1	2	3		7	Duncan, John	1		2		1	Ffloyd, Wm	1	1	2		
Fassitt, James	1	2	2		8	Davis, Edwd	2	2	4			Ffloyd, John	1	1	1		
Gray, Jedediah	1	1	2		4	Franklin, Ebenezr	1	2	2		4	Handcock, John, Junr	1	1	1		
Gray, Benjamin	1	2	1			Freeman, Moses	1	2	2			Handcock, John, Senr	2	2	3		
Gray, Thomas	2	1	4		11	Farewell, Gidion	1	2	2			Henderson, Brittingham	1	2	2		
Gault, Archibald	1	2	6		2	Gray, Joseph	1	2	4		11	Henderson, Jenkins	2	1	4		
Holloway, Levi	3	4	2		7	Gray, Johnson	1		3			Handcock, Danl, Senr	2	1	3		
Hamblin, Solomon	1		6			Griffen, Bolitha	1	2	2			Handcock, Wm, Senr	2	1	2		
Howard, John	1		5			Gray, Bolitha	1		1			Handcock, Wm, of Danl	2	2	3		4
Hudson, Richd	1			1	1	Hook, Wm	1	2	2			Jester, Southy	2	2	3		
Hamblin, Benja	1		1			Harrison, Erasmus, Jur	1		2			Jones, Wm, of Jno	2	2	2		
Holloway, Elijah	1	4	1			Hadder, John	1	2	3			Jones, Elisha	1		2		
Holloway, Thomas, Senr	2	4	3			Holloway, Ebezr	1	2	2			Jones, John, Senr	3	2	2		10
Holloway, Joseph	1	2	4		2	Holloway, Moses	1	2	4		7	Jones, John, Junr	2	2	2		
Purnell, Benja (Waltr)	1		2	1	10	Hickman, Joshua	2		3			Johnson, James	1	2	2		2
Holland, Saml	1	1	2			Hudson, Thomas	1	2	2		8	Maddux, Thomas	1	2	2		4
Hickman, Navel	1	2	2			Hudson, Henry	1	1	2			Price, Arthur	1		3		
Hudson, Henry	4	1	3		2	Hudson, Job	1	2	1			Price, Rebecca	1		3		
Holloway, Jesse	1	2	2			Handcock, Henry	1		3			Pilchard, Elijah	1	1	2		3
Holloway, Thomas, Junr	1		3			Holloway, Jacob	1	1	3			Purnell John Scott	1	2	3		
Holloway, John	1	1	3			Hadder, Shadrick	1	2	1			Pilchard, Jabez	2	2	3		
Townsend, Izeral, Senr	1		3			Jones, Joseph	1		3			Pepper, Solomon	1	2	2		
Townsend, Izeral, Junr	1		3			German, Truitt	1	1	3			Payne, Wrixum	1		2		
Townsend, Bolitha	1	1	3			German, Isaac	2	2	4			Reed, Levin	1	2	2		
Taylor, George	2	2	4		6	Latchem, Nehemiah	2	1	2			Robins, Capt Daniel	1	2	4		15
Taylor, Rachl			4			Massey, John	1	1	2			Turpin, William	1	1	2	2	6
Townsend, Wm	3	2	3		10	Massey, Elias	1		3			Taylor, Ayers	1		2		
Taylor, Levin	1		4			Powell, Thomas, Junr	2	2	4			Taylor, Oled	1	1	2		
Tull, John	1	5	1		10	Powell, Zadok	1	2	2								
Wayatt, Sarah		2	4		3	Pepper, Levi	1	2	3								

WORCESTER COUNTY—Continued.

NAME OF HEAD OF FAMILY.	Free white males of 16 years and upward, including heads of families.	Free white males under 16 years.	Free white females, including heads of families.	All other free persons.	Slaves.	NAME OF HEAD OF FAMILY.	Free white males of 16 years and upward, including heads of families.	Free white males under 16 years.	Free white females, including heads of families.	All other free persons.	Slaves.	NAME OF HEAD OF FAMILY.	Free white males of 16 years and upward, including heads of families.	Free white males under 16 years.	Free white females, including heads of families.	All other free persons.	Slaves.
Trayder, Statten	1	2	3		4	Melvin, Wᵐ	1	2	3			McGee, Ruben	1	2	1		
Tarr, Izeral	1	1	3			Melvin, Robⁱ	1	2	2		3	Noble, Jonᵃ	2	1	3		
Tarr, Eli (of Eli)	1	1	2			Merrill, Wᵐ	2	2	3		9	Allivant, Matthew	2	2	2		
Walston, Major	1	2	2			Milton, Ayres Smith	1	2	1			Pollett, George	1	3	2		
Watson, John, of West	1	3	2			Carey, Levin	1	1	1			Riggs, Joseph	1	2	2		
Watson, Levin	1	2	2			Kinsey, Saul	1	2	3			Rigg n, Joseph	1	3	3		
Blades, Samuel	1	2	2			Carey, Levin, of Thomas	1	2	4			Shockley, Jonᵃ	2	1	3		
Blades, John	2	2	4			Payne, Levin	1	2	2			Showell, Eli	1	2	1		
Boston, Elijah	1	2	3			Pilchard, Levi	2	1	3			Slocomb, Capⁱ ——	2	3	2		4
Benson, Zepheniah	2	2	4		1	Powell, Levin	1	2	4		6	Smith, Moses Claywell	1	1	2		2
Boston, Jacob	1	2	2			Roach, Stephen	2	2	3		4	Wilson, Wᵐ	2	2	2		
Burnett, James	1	1	1			Sharply, Thomas	1	2	2			Taylor, Jn⁰	1	1	3		
Dickerson, Jos⁰	1	2	2			Tull, John	2	3	2		6	Tull, Jacob	1	1	2		
Davis, Benjᵃ	1	1	1			Watson, John West	1	1	2			Townsend, Jaˢ	1	2	3		
Dickerson, Thomas	1	2	2			Webb, Sol⁰, Senʳ	2	2	4		9	Tilghman, Jn⁰	1	2	1		
Ellis, Levi	1	2	1			Webb, Sol⁰, Junʳ	1	2	2			Alexander, Jn⁰ S	1	2	3		
Henderson, John, of B	1	2	2		1	Watson, John	2	2	3			Dreadon, Jn⁰, B. S	2	2	4		
Hudson, Aaron	2	2	4		1	Young, Ezek.el	1	1	1			Denston, Isaac	1	2	3		
Henderson, Jacob	1	2	2		2	Young, Bayly	1	2	1		1	Denston, Levin	1	2	2		
Henderson, Jn⁰ T	1	3	2			Dr skill, Moses, Junʳ	1	2	2			Maddux, Zerobable	2	1	2		
Henderson, Wᵐ, Senʳ	2	2	4		10	Dykes, Danˡ	2	2	3			Noble, Jaˢ	1	3	2		
Henderson, Joseph	1	1	2		1	Dixon, Ambros	1	2	4			Owens, Only	1	2	2		
Houston, Jn⁰	1					Dixon, Outter Bridge	1	1	2			Taytor Joseph Gray	1	3	2		
Houston, Wᵐ		2	2			Dykes, Wᵐ	2	2	2			Townsend, Charles	1	2	3		
Houston, Levi	1	3	2			Flnt, Jn⁰	1	2	3			Townsend, Danwood	2	2	2		3
Henderson, Benjᵃ, Senʳ	1	1	1			Freeney, Jos⁰	1	2	1			White, Stephen	2	2	4		
Henderson, Wᵐ M	1	2	2		1	Freeney, Wᵐ	2	1	2			Newton, Selby, Junʳ	2	2	4		
Henderson, Thomas	1	2	3			Hall, Jn⁰	1	1	2			Cotlom, Tho⁰	1	2	2		
Jones, Danˡ	1	2	4		1	Hayman, Charles, Jur	1	2	2			Holland, John	3	2	2		10
Jones, James	1	1	2		3	Holloway, Joshⁿ	2	2	3			Johnson, Elisha	1	2	2		
Johnson, John	1	2	2		1	Hayman, Charles, Senʳ	2	3	3			Gutthery, Nelly	1	1	1		
Jones, Major	1	2	3		4	Hayman, Jn⁰ of Jaˢ	1	2	1			Selby, Wᵐ A	1	2	3		
Lambertson, Samuel	1	2	2			Hayman, Nicholas	1	3	1			Davis, Spencer	2	2	4		
Lambertson, Abraham	1					Hayman, Jn⁰	2	3	2			Henderson, Wᵐ, Maᵗ⁰	1	1	2		
Landon, Thomas	2					Hayman, Johnson	1	4	2			Haws, Charles			4		
Long, David	2	2	4		7	Lank, Cawmon	1	2	1			Siers, John	1		1		
Melson, John	1	2	3			Lambertson, Jn⁰	1	1	4			Batts, Wᵐ	1	1	1		
Mason, Daniel	1	1	3			Maddux, Hezea	1	3	2			Merrille, Levi	1		3		7
Mills, Gillitt	1	2	2		4	Melson, Danˡ	2	2	3			Henderson, Bishop	1		3		
Melvin, Jonᵃ	1	2	3			Messix, George	2	2	3			Handy, Levin	1		5		7

INDEX.[1]

Aaron, 45.
Aaron, negro, 78.
Abbot, Jesse, 35.
Abbot, John, 109.
Abbott, Jacob F., 47.
Abbott, Thomas, 98.
Abbott, William, 47.
Abell, Benjamin, 106.
Abell, Burton, 106.
Abell, Clark, 106.
Abell, Cuthbert, 106.
Abell, Edward, 106.
Abell, Francis, 106.
Abell, Henry, 106.
Abell, Ignatius, 106.
Abell, John (J. P.), 106.
Abell, John, Ser, 106.
Abell, John Boothe, 106.
Abell, John H., 105.
Abell, John Standfield, 106.
Abell, Joseph Abner, 106.
Abell, Philip, 106.
Abell, Samuel, 106.
Abit, W^m, 26.
Ablehart, Conrad, 121.
Abraham, 45.
Abraham, negro, 38.
Abrahams, Richard, 46.
Abram, Free, 102.
Abrams, Jacob, 29.
Abright, Flora, 65.
Abright, William, 118.
Abry, John, 115.
Ackerman, George, 20.
Ackerman, George, 58.
Acle, Maunus, 119.
Acle, Peter, 121.
Acres, William, 111.
Alcorn, Henry, of Jn°, 47.
Acton, James, 47.
Acton, John, 47.
Acton, John, Junr, 47.
Acton, Osborne R., 47.
Adair, John, 41.
Adair, Joseph, 40.
Adair, William, 13.
Adam, 20.
Adam, Free, 102.
Adam, George, 92.
Adam, negro, 78.
Adamousky, Thadeus, 22.
Adams, Abraham, 105.
Adams, Adam, Free Negro, 47.
Adams, Alexander, 20.
Adams, Alex^r, 88.
Adams, Andrew, 58.
Adams, Ann (Mulatto), 47.
Adams, Ann (Mulatto), 47.
Adams, Ann, 63.
Adams, Ann, 123.
Adams, Benj^a, 47.
Adams, Captain, 17.
Adams, Charles, 47.
Adams, Charles, 57.
Adams, Edward, 57.
Adams, Edward, 86.
Adams, George, 25.
Adams, George, 47.
Adams, George, 47.
Adams, George, 57.
Adams, George, 57.
Adams, George, 72.
Adams, George, Jr., 92.
Adams, Geo., 115.
Adams, George, 120.
Adams, Henrietta, 47.
Adams, Ignatius, 47.
Adams, Jacob, 119.
Adams, Jacob, 126.
Adams, James, 22.
Adams, Ja^s (Over^r for Saml Edelen), 47.
Adams, James, 92.
Adams, James, 106.
Adams, Jenny, 106.
Adams, Jeremiah, 67.
Adams, John, 47.

Adams, John, Junr, 47.
Adams, John, 73.
Adams, John, 76
Adams, John, 90.
Adams, John, 92.
Adams, John, 118.
Adams, John, 118.
Adams, John, 120.
Adams, John, Senr, 121.
Adams, John, Ju^r, 121.
Adams, John R., 47.
Adams, Joseph (Nanjemoy), 47.
Adams Joseph, 60.
Adams, Joseph, 67.
Adams, Joseph, 106.
Adams, Joshua, 16.
Adams, Leonard, 47.
Adams, Margaret, 92.
Adams, Martin, 62.
Adams, Mary, 46.
Adams, Moses, 111.
Adams, Rhody, 47.
Adams, Rich^d, Senr, 47.
Adams, Richard, 47.
Adams, Richard, 92.
Adams, Samuel, 17.
Adams, Samuel, 47.
Adams, Samuel, 111.
Adams, Sarah, 16.
Adams, Stephen, 88.
Adams, Stophel, 68.
Adams, Thee, 105.
Adams, Thomas, 62.
Adams, Valentine, 67.
Adams, William, 17.
Adams, W^m, 26.
Adams, W^m, 29.
Adams, W^m, 32.
Adams, William, 47.
Adams, William, 92.
Adams, William, 118.
Adams, Zeph^a, 47.
Adamson, John, 21.
Adamson, John, 89.
Addams, James, 104.
Addams, John, 104.
Addams, Phoeby, 104.
Addams, Solomon, 104.
Addelspurgor, Thomas, 60.
Addelspurgor, Anthony, 92.
Addison, John, 92.
Addison, John Cole, 92.
Addison, Robert, 61.
Addison, Th° Grafton, 92.
Addison, Walter, 92.
Additon, Richard, 92.
Adkerson, James, 105.
Adketson, Joseph, 29.
Adkin, Greenb^y, 77.
Adkins, Charles, 70.
Adkins, William, 62.
Adkinson, Aaron, 109.
Adkinson, Aaron, 111.
Adkinson, Sarah, 113.
Adkinson, Thomas, 98.
Adlum, John, 67.
Adly Richard, 111.
Adricks, John, 19.
Ady, W^m, 74.
Agan, Rich^d, 74.
Agey, Jonathan, 62.
Agie, Peter, 63.
Agner, George, 117.
Aicle, Henry, 121.
Aicle, Henry, Ju^r, 121.
Aigner, Ludwick, 117.
Aiken, George, 18.
Aiken, Robt, 44.
Ailabaugh, Ann, 122.
Ailey, Abraham, 120.
Ailey, Isaac, 120.
Ainker, Mary, 115.
Ainsberger, Christian, 115.
Ainsminger, Christian, 123.
Ainsworth, Thomas, 117.
Aires, William, 99.
Airey, Nancy, 56.
Airey, Thos Hill, 56.

Airs, Ann, 111.
Airs, James, 119.
Aisquith, Celia, 105.
Aisquith, John, 105.
Aisquith, Lester, 22.
Aisquith, William, 20.
Aitkin, Andrew, 17.
Aivey, Christian, 123.
Aivey, Elizabeth, 123.
Aivey, Henry, 123.
Aivey, Joseph, 121.
Aivey, Michael, 118.
Ake, Jacob, 70.
Ake, John, 25.
Alabagh, Jacob, 117.
Alabagh, John, 119.
Albagh, Christian, 58.
Albaugh, Daniel, 61.
Albaugh, Daniel, 71.
Albaugh, David, 58.
Albaugh, John, 58.
Albaugh, Peter, 58.
Albaugh, Philip, 58.
Albaugh, William, 58.
Albaugh, William, Junr, 58.
Albaugh, Zachariah, 58.
Albaugh, Zacheriah, 29.
Albee, John, 92.
Albert, Jn., 74.
Albert, Phillip, 75.
Albright, Henry, 65.
Albright, Peter, 121.
Alburt, Zacheriah, 29.
Alby, Joseph, 86.
Alcock, James, 20.
Alcock, Joseph, 20.
Alcock, Mansel, 20.
Alcock, William, 20.
Alcorn, William, 42.
Alden, Elisabeth, 92.
Alden, James, 92.
Alder, Mary, 29.
Alderidge, Joseph, 15.
Alderidge, Zachariah, 12.
Aldergate, John, 22.
Aldridge, Fredus, 42.
Aldridge, Jacob, 92.
Aldridge, John, 86.
Aldridge, John, 109.
Aldridge, Sally, 73.
Aldridge, Samuel, 42.
Aldridge, Thomas, 90.
Aldridge, Thomas, 113.
Aldrige, John, 35.
Aledridge, Joseph, 123.
Aleoke, Samuel, 57.
Alexander, Amos, 34.
Alexander, Andrew, 76.
Alexander, Arthur, 44.
Alexander, Arthur, 46.
Alexander, George, 43.
Alexander, Henry, 69.
Alexander, Isaac, 40.
Alexander, Isabella, 43.
Alexander, Jacob, 65.
Alexander, James, 21.
Alexander, James, 40.
Alexander, James, 43.
Alexander, James, 46.
Alexander, James, 47.
Alexander, Jno, 75.
Alexander, Jamison, 40.
Alexander, Jane, 76.
Alexander, John, 43.
Alexander, John, 46.
Alexander, John, 70.
Alexander, Jn°, 76.
Alexander, Jn° S., 128.
Alexander, Josiah, 43.
Alexander, Justis, 42.
Alexander, Justis, 46.
Alexander, Mary, 40.
Alexander, Samuel, 106.
Alexander, Sarah, 43.
Alexander, Thomas, 62.
Alexander, Valentine, 65.
Alexander, William, 111.
Alford, Aaron, 35.

Alford, Aron, 81.
Alford, Maccabus, 35.
Alford, Matthias, 35.
Alford, Moses, 81.
Alford, Rachael, 84.
Alford, William, 35.
Algier, Rachel, 72.
Algular, Jacob, 29.
Algular, John, 29.
Alhorn, John, 90.
Alice, Negroe, 112.
Alies, John, 43.
Alison, William, 105.
Ali, Edword, 28.
All, Robert, 109.
Aliander, Nicholas, 77.
Alibough, Simeon, 69.
Alibrite, John, 35.
Alibrite, Peter, 35.
Alibrittain, Charles, 47.
Alibrittain, William, 47.
Alicock, Samuel, 113.
Alicock, Thos., 35.
Allein, ——, 10.
Allein, Adam, 10.
Allein, Ann, 11.
Allein, John, 13.
Allein, John, 14.
Allein, John, 16.
Allein, Johnathan, 13.
Allein, Mary, 16.
Allein, Richard, 11.
Allein, William, 12.
Allen, Alex^r, 87.
Allen, Ann, 35.
Allen, Ann, 99.
Allen, Auston, 92.
Allen, Avarilla, 79.
Allen, Emanuel, 109.
Allen, Francis, 47.
Allen, George, 47.
Allen, Henry, 109.
Allen, Hugh, 26.
Allen, Ignatious, 92.
Allen, James, 19.
Allen, Jam^s, 26.
Allen, James, 46.
Allen, James, 47.
Allen, Jm^s, 74.
Allen, Jm^s, 76.
Allen, James, 115.
Allen, John, 26.
Allen, John, 26.
Allen, John, 28.
Allen, John, 28.
Allen, John, 34.
Allen, John, 47.
Allen, Jn., 74.
Allen, John, 92.
Allen, John, 127.
Allen, Joseph, 47.
Allen, Joseph, 92.
Allen, Mary, 35.
Allen, Michael, 35.
Allen, Mordecai, 47.
Allen, Mrs., 20.
Allen, Moses, 109.
Allen, Nathan, 109.
Allen, Nich^l, 79.
Allen, Patrick, 34.
Allen, Patrick, 34.
Allen, Patrick, 29.
Allen, Rebecca, 76.
Allen, Reubin, 35.
Allen, Rich^d, 29.
Allen, Sarah, 124.
Allen, Solomond, 29.
Allen, Stephen, 123.
Allen, White, 92.
Allen, William, 21.
Allen, W^m, 28.
Allen, W^m, 28.
Allen, W^m, 35.
Allen, William, 35.
Allen, William, 46.
Allen, William, 47.
Allen, William, 47.
Allen, William (of Ja^s, 47).

Allen, William, 111.
Allen, Wm Esqr, 126.
Allen, Zachariah, 106.
Allen, Zecheariah, 47.
Allendel, Richard, 120.
Allender, Frederick, 26.
Allender, Jane, 79.
Allender, John, 79.
Allender, Joshua, 34.
Allender, M^r, 21.
Allender, W^m, 26.
Allender, W^m, 34.
Allender, W^m, 74.
Alley, 10.
Alley, Bryon, 100.
Alley, John, 82.
Alley, M^rs, 21.
Algeriar, Jacob, 29.
Algeriar, John Junr, 29.
Allibone, Benjamin, 14.
Allin, Thomas, 89.
Allison, Andrew, 118.
Allison, Charles, 87.
Allison, David, 92.
Allison, Elenor, 85.
Allison, Elisha, 92.
Allison, Hendry, 89.
Allison, Henry, 105.
Allison, James, 64.
Allison, James, 88.
Allison, John, 61.
Allison, John Senr, 88.
Allison, John Junr, 88.
Allison, M^rs, 89.
Allison, Patrick, 19.
Allison, Posey, 89.
Allison, Richard, 92.
Allison, Samuel, 88.
Allivant, Matthew, 128.
Allmen, John, 76.
Alloway, Mary, 102.
Alloway, Thomas, 100.
Alls, John, 102.
Allsock, John, 68.
Allstone, Thomas Ser, 106.
Allstone, Thomas Ju^r, 106.
Allworth, Benj^a, 73.
Almack, W^m, 29.
Alman, Isaac, 40.
Almany, John, 24.
Almett, John, 91.
Alnutt, James, 88.
Alnutt, James, 88.
Alnutt, Jesse, 88.
Alnutt, Lawrence, 88.
Alphin, Edward, 87.
Alricks, Joseph, 44.
Alt, Jacob, 117.
Alter, Charles, 26.
Alter, Christopher, 35.
Alter, Christopher, 116.
Alter, Frederick, 116.
Alter, Henry, 116.
Alter, John, 17.
Altham, Spencer, 41.
Altony, Thos, 26.
Altow, Priscilla, 70.
Alven, Rafe, 29.
Alvey, Basil, 106.
Alvey, Clement, 106.
Alvey, Jeremiah, 106.
Alvey, Jesse, 106.
Alvey, John, 104.
Alvey, John B., 106.
Alwell, Sarah, 15.
Alwell, William, 16.
Alwood, William, 23.
Alwood, W^m, 29.
Amas, Thos, 28.
Ambers, W^m, 29.
Ambis, W^m, Jur, 29.
Ambours, Stevins, 26.
Ambrose, Catharine, 63.
Ambrose, Christopher, 65.
Ambrose, Henry, 64.
Ambrose, James, 23.
Ambrose, Matthew, 83.

[1] No attempt has been made in this publication to correct mistakes in spelling made by the deputy marshals, but the names have been reproduced as they appear upon the census schedules.

(129)